Mastering™
Integrated HTML and CSS

Mastering™
Integrated HTML and CSS

Virginia DeBolt

1807 WILEY 2007
BICENTENNIAL

Wiley Publishing, Inc.

Acquisitions Editor: Pete Gaughan
Development Editor: Jim Compton
Technical Editor: Zoe Gillenwater
Production Editor: Sarah Groff-Palermo
Copy Editor: Sally Engelfried
Production Manager: Tim Tate
Vice President and Executive Group Publisher: Richard Swadley
Vice President and Executive Publisher: Joseph B. Wikert
Vice President and Publisher: Neil Edde
Media Project Supervisor: Laura Atkinson
Media Development Specialist: Kit Malone
Book Designers: Maureen Forys and Judy Fung
Compositor: Laurie Stewart, Happenstance Type-O-Rama
Proofreader: Nancy Riddiough
Indexer: Ted Laux
Anniversary Logo Design: Richard Pacifico
Cover Designer: Ryan Sneed
Cover Image: © Peter Gardner/Digital Vision/Getty Images

Published simultaneously in Canada

ISBN: 978-0-4700-9754-0

Library of Congress Cataloging-in-Publication Data is available from the publisher.

10 9 8 7 6 5 4 3 2 1

Dear Reader,

Thank you for choosing *Mastering Integrated HTML and CSS*. This book is part of a family of premium quality Sybex graphics books, all written by outstanding authors who combine practical experience with a gift for teaching.

Sybex was founded in 1976. More than thirty years later, we're still committed to producing consistently exceptional books. With each of our graphics titles we're working hard to set a new standard for the industry. From the writers and artists we work with to the paper we print on, our goal is to bring you the best graphics books available.

I hope you see all that reflected in these pages. I'd be very interested to hear your comments and get your feedback on how we're doing. Feel free to let me know what you think about this or any other Sybex book by sending me an email at nedde@wiley.com, or if you think you've found an error in this book, please visit `http://wiley.custhelp.com`. Customer feedback is critical to our efforts at Sybex.

Best regards,

Neil Edde
Vice President and Publisher
Sybex, an Imprint of Wiley

To Will and Phoenix, who remain the center of my lif

Acknowledgments

I am grateful to Pete Gaughan, acquisitions editor at John Wiley & Sons, Inc., for believing in me and convincing me to write this book. He felt the book belonged in Wiley's Mastering series, and he helped me enormously with preparing a proposal and getting it approved.

Jim Compton, the development editor for the book, deserves my gratitude as well. He backed me up and helped me with knotty problems of organization, structure, and grammar.

Sarah Groff-Palermo came though with cheerful pick-me-ups and laughs and did a very fine job as the book's production editor in the process.

Others at Wiley toiled away at copy editing, illustration, and composition. I didn't interact directly with these unseen helpers, but I'm grateful for their work on my behalf.

I was allowed to suggest the person I wanted as my technical editor. There was no doubt in my mind that Zoe Gillenwater was the perfect choice. She demonstrates a brilliant grasp of CSS, and her ability to keep the details of hacks, accessibility, and DOCTYPES straight at the same time is astonishing. Thanks for agreeing to help make this book its technical best, Zoe.

Thanks to all those who entered designs in the Style Me Challenge, and congratulations to the four winners. The winning designs are featured in the color section in the center of this book.

A big thank you goes to Dori Smith for maintaining the wise-women.org listserv and to all the wise women (and men) who participate in this online group for their help and support. They responded to all my requests for help in testing the practice exercises for the book and offered helpful advice about many topics.

A number of companies allowed us to provide software, browsers, and color pop-ups for the accompanying CD: Bare Bones Software's Text Wrangler, Visi-Bone color charts, Bradbury's Top Style Pro, Westciv's StyleMaster, EditPlus, Coffee Cup's HTML Editor, Panic's Transmit FTP, Ipswitch's WS_FTP, and Adobe Acrobat Reader. Microsoft, Mozilla, Apple Computer, Opera, and Netscape provided the latest browser versions (Internet Explorer, Mozilla Firefox, Safari, Opera, and Netscape, respectively) for the CD.

About the Author

Virginia DeBolt grew up in southern Colorado, where her father often took her fishing and hunti She can still walk off with a teddy bear from the shooting gallery at the fair. After receiving her lege degrees, she taught in public schools in Colorado and New Mexico. Her first computer w a Commodore 64. The schools were using Apple IIe computers and Virginia quickly became t "computer person" in the school.

Her first four books were written to teach writing using cooperative learning and are still i print and selling well. She graduated to a blazingly fast 8 MHz Mac Classic to celebrate her sta as a working writer.

In the mid-1990s, she moved to Texas and took some classes with the notion of finding work a technical writer. One class was in HTML, and Virginia's life was never the same after that. HT took over her thoughts, dreams, conversation, time, and energy. Soon she had a contract tech w ing job by day, and a part time gig teaching HTML at the community college by night. The dini room of her home was filled with office tables and a web of wires between two Macs, two Windo boxes, assorted scanners, printers, and Zip drives. In the free time between her two jobs, she w making web sites for fun.

The HTML teaching job sent her searching in places like SXSW Interactive conferences for answers and ideas. But what she heard in the conference halls and what she saw in the books t were available to teach HTML and Dreamweaver were 180 degrees apart. In 2001, she started w ing reviews of these books on her blog at `www.webteacher.ws`. The Web Teacher blog brought to the attention of computer book publishers. After contributing to books written by other peo she decided to write her own book to promote her theory that HTML and CSS should be taught integrated skills, not as two distinct and separate ideas. The first book was *Integrated HTML an CSS: A Smarter, Faster Way to Learn* (Wiley, 2004). The second is the one you hold in your hand n

Oh, her latest computer? There's just one. A Mac laptop that needs almost no wires strung ab and does Windows on demand.

Contents at a Glance

Contents

Introduction

This book combines the teaching of Extensible Hypertext Markup Language (XHTML) and of Cascading Style Sheets (CSS) into an integrated and unified experience.

Many HTML books teach you all about HTML first and all about CSS later. I believe that the two go hand-in-hand and should be learned at the same time. With an integrated approach, you learn how to structure XHTML properly from the beginning of your design process so that your content will work well with CSS when you are ready to style it. With an integrated approach, you don't have to use practices that are out-of-date or non-standards-compliant while waiting to learn CSS, because you learn CSS as you learn XHTML.

This book also emphasizes techniques for creating web pages that are accessible to the widest possible range of visitors as an integrated part of the site building process, not as something that gets added later.

Who Should Read This Book

Mastering Integrated HTML and CSS takes readers from the beginning stages of learning XHTML and CSS to mastery-level development and advanced techniques. If you already know some of the basics, you can still profit from the advanced material and exercises in the book.

If you learned HTML several years ago and want to improve your out-of-date skills by learning more about CSS and how to use CSS layouts in your web pages, this book will help you advance to a new level.

The book is chock-full of hands-on exercises that will help the independent learner or be valuable activities for a college or university classroom. For educational settings, there are also available materials such as chapter tests and chapter presentations that benefit instructors.

Chapters that explain some of the basics of blog customization and making the most of Dreamweaver 8 when writing CSS will help readers who are interested in blogging or want to improve their Dreamweaver skills.

What You Will Learn

This book will teach you to write standards-based, accessible web pages and style them with CSS.

You will learn the latest version of Hypertext Markup Language (HTML), which is called XHTML. There were several versions of HTML prior to XHTML. The version known as HTML 4.01 is still in widespread use and creates web pages that work quite well. The differences between XHTML and HTML 4.01 are small, and you will be capable of writing either one after reading this book.

XHTML was chosen for this book because it is the current specification. Using current specifications (also called *standards*) allows you to design web pages with a more consistent display across browsers and devices.

There are also several versions of CSS. You will learn CSS 2, again because it is the latest standard or specification.

The emphasis here is on learning to write XHTML and CSS according to standard specifications. Learning standards-compliant XHTML and CSS will help you write web pages that will work more reliably in all browsers and devices. I will touch very lightly on techniques that are not part of the standards. Such nonstandard techniques are called hacks, filters, or workarounds. Only those hacks or workarounds that are absolutely essential will be mentioned. You will be prepared to make your website accessible after reading this book. *Accessibility* can be defined as a lack of barriers to the accessing of your content. You will learn to write web pages that are accessible to all platforms, browsers, and devices.

What Is Covered in This Book

Mastering Integrated HTML and CSS is organized in a sensible progression that matches the process of web-page design and construction. Each chapter adds to your knowledge so that by the book's end you'll be adept with web page building and styling. As you learn each new XHTML element, you'll learn to style your efforts with CSS. You'll create actual pages in most chapters for hands-on experience to develop and extend your skills.

Chapters 1 and 2 give you some background and basics about the Web and the tools used to build web pages. Chapter 1 covers basics like how to write XHTML and CSS using correct syntax conventions. In Chapter 2 you learn about the cascade that governs how CSS style rules are applied and how the location of styles affects the cascade.

By Chapter 3 you'll create a simple web page and styles to control its presentation.

Chapters 4 through 11 each walk you through a new aspect of web page design and construction, building new XHTML and CSS skills in an incremental manner. In Chapter 4 you create headings and learn how to use image replacement for headings. You'll work with fixed and fluid two- and three-column CSS layouts in Chapter 5. Chapter 6 covers many XHTML elements that are used to create text. Advanced CSS selectors such as child selectors, attribute selectors, and generated content are applied to the text you work with in Chapter 6, and you'll make a print media style sheet.

Chapter 7 is about links and link styles. You'll learn how to make a CSS pop-up for a link. Chapter 8 deals with images and multimedia objects. You'll learn basic image optimization techniques, make a simple image gallery, and discover how to add Flash or QuickTime to a web page. Chapter 9 ties everything you learned about links, backgrounds, and pop-ups together with the coding and styling of the various lists. You'll make a horizontal and a vertical list into navigation elements.

Although every chapter stresses accessibility, Chapters 10 and 11 help you with two of most difficult aspects of accessibility. Chapter 10 deals with accessible tables and table styles. Chapter 11 teaches you how to make and style an accessible form.

Chapters 1–11 are written as a sequential progression. Chapters 12–16, however, can be read whenever the information is needed or relevant. Chapter 12 describes the steps in getting your web pages onto the World Wide Web using FTP. You'll learn about finding web hosting and getting a domain name. You'll also examine some of the ways you can test your pages for validity and accessibility. Chapter 13 teaches how to create and style a weblog (or "blog"). Chapter 14 presents fundamental principles of designing web pages, using diagrams to help you understand design concepts such as visual hierarchy, alignment, repetition, and contrast. In Chapter 15 you'll create style sheets for handheld devices. Handheld CSS is more and more important as the number of people using handheld devices continues to grow rapidly.

Knowing how to hand code XHTML and CSS makes it easy to become a power user of visual tools such as Dreamweaver. In light of that, Chapter 16 explains how to write CSS effectively using Dreamweaver 8.

At the end of each chapter you'll find Real-World Scenarios with examples of actual websites that illustrate ideas from the chapter. Each chapter has assignments and exercises that are designed to help you reinforce and extend what you learned in the chapter. Answers to these exercises can be found in the Appendix, but you should always try to work them out yourself first.

The Mastering Series

The *Mastering* series from Sybex provides outstanding instruction for readers with intermediate and advanced skills, in the form of top-notch training and development for those already working in their field and clear, serious education for those aspiring to become pros. Every *Mastering* book includes:

- Real-World Scenarios, ranging from case studies to interviews, that show how the tool, technique, or knowledge presented is applied in actual practice.
- Skill-based instruction, with chapters organized around real tasks rather than abstract concepts or subjects.
- Self-review test questions, so you can be certain you're equipped to do the job right.

Resources on the CD

Files that you need to work along with each chapter are included on the CD. You will use these files to do the real work of learning the XHTML and CSS, because you will actually work through the material as each chapter progresses. You immediately see the effect of what you have done in a browser.

The CD contains a Style Me Challenge Page. After you have completed the book, you can create style sheets to control the presentation of this simple HTML page. Getting successful style sheets written for the Style Me page will prove to you that you are ready for a real-world website of your own design. (There are examples of designs for the Style Me Challenge in the book's color insert.)

Trial versions of several HTML and CSS text editing software tools for both Windows and Mac are also provided on the CD. These sample software tools are not required to write HTML or CSS—any basic text editor will do—but they have handy features such as color coding and indenting that make writing HTML easier. This collection includes:

- TopStyle® Pro 3.12
- TextWrangler™ 2.1.3
- Coffeecup HTML Editor 2007
- Style Master 4.6
- EditPlus 2.30
- Transmit® 3.5.3
- WS_FTP Pro
- Coffeecup Free FTP

EditPlus 2.30 is a 30-day evaluation version and requires a registration fee to keep using it beyond the evaluation period.

VisiBone (`www.visibone.com`) allowed us to include their color pop-ups on the CD. These are color palettes you can keep open on your computer desktop in order to choose colors and color names while you write your HTML.

Contacting the Author

Comments from readers are always welcome. You can reach me by e-mail at `virginia@vdebolt.com` or by visiting my Web Teacher blog at `www.webteacher.ws`.

Mastering™

Integrated HTML and CSS

Chapter 1

How to Write XHTML and CSS

XHTML and CSS are two different specifications used to create web pages. Each has a distinct look and purpose. When used together, the combination can produce a useful, information-rich, and highly attractive web page. That's what this book is all about—learning how to use the two specifications seamlessly to build effective web pages.

In the exercises throughout this book you're going to work with examples of XHTML and CSS code. Studying and incorporating code that others have written to solve the same problems you're facing is one of the best ways to learn any web development language. You'll need to type these code examples into your pages exactly as they appear in the book for them to work. The various keywords and symbols are all significant. The rules defining how a language is put together are its *syntax*. In this chapter, you will learn the syntax of XHTML and CSS. You will learn what each of these specifications does and how to write code in its syntax. Basic rules for typing both XHTML and CSS, such as when to use the spacebar, when to type a semicolon, or when to type a bracket, will also be explained in this chapter.

This book assumes that most people starting out with CSS have probably written some HTML. If that's the case, you can treat this chapter as a refresher and an introduction to CSS. If you are already familiar with the basics of both HTML and CSS syntax, you can skip ahead to Chapter 2 without damage to your mental health or your social life.

In this chapter, you will learn to:

- Identify what constitutes a website.
- Identify what XHTML and HTML are.
- Explain similarities and differences in XHTML and HTML.
- Describe what CSS is.
- Write XHTML syntax.
- Write CSS syntax.

Anatomy of a Website

A summary of what goes into a website may help you understand what HTML/XHTML and CSS do and how they can work together to implement your vision. If you've already worked with one of the "visual tools" like Dreamweaver or FrontPage, you're a little further along the learning curve, but this recap will still help to put what you're about to learn into perspective. Understanding the underlying basics can give you better control over your visual tools as well.

A web page may contain text, images, links, sounds, and movies or moving images. You may also be aware that some pages use scripts written in various languages such as JavaScript, PHP, or ASP to create interactivity, to connect the page to a database, or to collect information submitted in a form.

HTML or XHTML is the glue that holds all those pieces and parts together and displays them in a readable or usable manner in a browser such as Internet Explorer, Firefox, Safari, or Netscape Navigator. The browser is your window on the World Wide Web; XHTML is the language used to tell the browser how to format the pieces and parts of a web page.

You'll use XHTML to structure the headings, paragraphs, tables, images, and lists that logically organize your information so that you can convey your message with words, images, and information. XHTML pages without any CSS attached might look plain and simple, but all your information and content still displays in an organized and clearly meaningful way. Without the correctly marked up and semantically organized underpinnings built in XHTML, no amount of CSS can save your web page from mistaken interpretation, inaccessibility, and poor performance.

CSS enters the scene by adding style to the elements on a web page. Whereas XHTML markup identifies each element in the page logically, defining its function within the overall structure, CSS styles tell the browser how each element should look. The style might involve color, placement, images, fonts, or spacing, but it does not change the underlying pieces and parts formatted by the XHTML. CSS is about presentation. CSS determines whether something is blue or green, aligned on the left or on the right, large or small, visible or hidden, has bullets or doesn't have bullets. However, these styles, grouped into style sheets, have to be applied to some kind of content, such as XHTML pages, to have any effect.

Web content is displayed in more ways than on a computer monitor. It appears in various handheld devices such as PDAs and cell phones. It is read aloud by aural screen readers. It is printed. A single page of XHTML content can be styled in various ways by different CSS rules for the most effective presentation in all of the devices mentioned.

The driving force behind the creation of CSS several years ago was to enable the separation of content from appearance (Figure 1.1). One page can be used in many devices with the proper styling. Your XHTML pages become universally usable, accessible on any device.

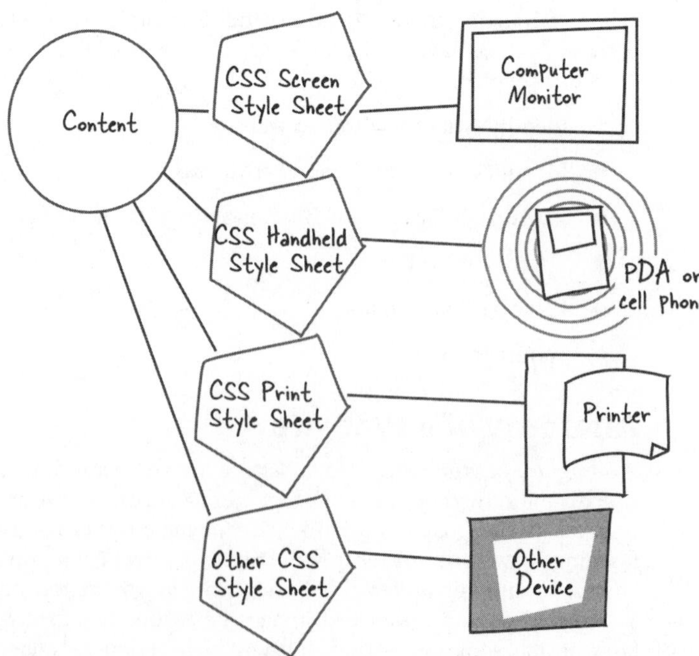

FIGURE 1.1 Create one semantically sensible XHTML page and style it for many different devices using CSS.

What Are XHTML and HTML?

Hypertext Markup Language (HTML) is the programming specification for how web pages can be written so they can be understood and properly displayed by computers or other Internet-capable devices. XHTML is an acronym for Extensible Hypertext Markup Language, a specification that grew out of HTML. You'll see what "extensible" means in a moment, but to understand the role of HTML and XHTML, you need to understand the three terms in HTML.

Hypertext is simply text as it exists in what is called "hyperspace"—the Internet. It is plain text that carries the content of your web page and the programming information needed to display that page and link it to other pages. Hypertext is formatted via a *markup language*—a standardized set of symbols and codes that all browsers can interpret.

WHO MAKES THE RULES?

Oh, yeah? Sez who! In the world of Internet technology, the guys with the "say" are in the W3C. The organization devoted to creating and publishing the standardized rules for various web technologies, including XHTML, is the World Wide Web Consortium, or W3C, at `www.w3.org`. See also the Web Standards Project, a grassroots coalition fighting for the adoption of web standards, at `www.webstandards.org`.

Markup is used to convey two kinds of information about text or other content on a web page: first, it identifies what kind of *structure* the content requires. If you think of a web page as simply a whole lot of words, the HTML is the markup, or framework, that specifies that certain words are headings or lists or paragraphs. The way you mark up the text on the page structures the page into chunks of meaningful information such as headings, subheads, and quotes. I often refer to such chunks of meaningful information as *semantic* structures.

Markup may also define the *presentation* of those elements; for example, the different fonts to be used for headings and subheadings. When it was first developed, HTML was the only tool for defining visual presentation on screen. When the World Wide Web began, the only information transmitted using the *Hypertext Transfer Protocol (HTTP)* was text. As the capability to transfer images, sounds, and other information was added, presentational markup was added to HTML to help format the new information. After a few years of amazing growth, the HTML that was being used to mark up individual elements reached burdensome proportions. It became apparent that markup for presentation was an inefficient way to define what every item of text or graphics on a website should look like, and the web community developed Cascading Style Sheets (CSS) as a better way to handle presentation.

What's the Difference between XHTML and HTML?

The title of this book refers to HTML, because XHTML actually *is* HTML. You'll quickly notice that an XHTML document is saved with a filename ending in `.html`, for example `mypage.html`. XHTML was chosen for the basis of all the code used in this book, but HTML 4.01 is still a perfectly good choice for writing web pages. You will be learning HTML when you learn XHTML. It is a two-for-the-price-of-one bargain. There are a few basic differences in writing XHTML versus writing HTML, and these will be pointed out to you at appropriate times in the book.

Many writers choose to emphasize that XHTML is HTML by using the term (X)HTML to indicate that what they are saying applies to both. Good XHTML is also good HTML. Don't be misled by the book's title into thinking that you won't learn XHTML.

But how are XHTML and HTML different? XHTML is more than HTML, because it is extensible XHTML uses the syntax rules of the *Extensible Markup Language (XML)*. Those syntax rules will b explained later in this chapter. An extensible markup language can be extended with modules tha do things such as make math calculations, draw graphical images, or use microformats such as XFN (XHTML Friends Network). Web pages written in XHTML interact with XML easily.

What Is CSS?

CSS is an acronym for Cascading Style Sheets, another programming specification. CSS uses rule called *styles* to determine visual presentation. The style rules are integrated with the content of th web page in several ways. In this book, we will deal with style rules that are embedded in the we page itself, as well as with sets of style rules, known as style sheets, that are linked to or importe into a web page. You will learn to write the style rules and how to import, link, or embed them i the web pages you make.

In HTML, styles can be written into the flow of the HTML, or *inline*, as well. You'll learn mor abut linked, embedded and inline styles in Chapter 2.

CSS can also be integrated into web pages in other ways. Sometimes you have no control ove these rules. Browsers allow users to set up certain CSS style rules, or user styles, according to thei own preferences. The user preferences can override style rules you write. Further, all browsers come with built-in style rules. Generally these built-in styles can be overridden by your CSS styl rules. Built-in browser display rules are referred to as *default* presentation rules. Part of what yo will learn is what to expect from a browser by default, in order to develop any new CSS rules to override those default display values. You can accept the browser default display, too. If you are happy with what the browser does to style the content, then there's no need to create a rule to ove ride it. It's common for designers to start a style sheet by setting the paddings and margins to 0p to override the browser's default padding and margin settings. Yet other default browser styles, such as the blank line separating one paragraph from another, may be left alone.

Getting Started with XHTML Syntax

The building blocks of XHTML syntax are *tags*, which are used to mark up *elements*. A tag is a cod that gives an element its name. For example, the tag used to mark up a paragraph is a `p` tag, whic is called either a "paragraph tag" or "a p tag." When text is marked up with a `p` tag, it is an instru tion to the browser to display the element as a paragraph.

Elements in XHTML, such as paragraphs, can also have attributes and values assigned to them But before you find out about attributes and values, let's dig into tags just a bit more.

Opening and Closing Tags

Opening and closing tags are used to specify elements. Here is a marked up paragraph element:

```
<p>This is the text of the paragraph.</p>
```

The paragraph is opened with a `p` tag. Tags are delineated with angle brackets (< and >). So th markup `<p>` instructs the browser that a paragraph starts now.

A closing tag `</p>` indicates the end of the paragraph. Notice that the closing tag is the same a the opening tag, with the addition of a forward slash (/) inside the opening bracket of the tag. Tag are like on and off switches: turn on a paragraph here and turn it off there. With a few more sentences added to make the paragraph show up, and a second identical paragraph added, this element would appear in a browser something like Figure 1.2.

FIGURE 1.2
Two paragraph elements

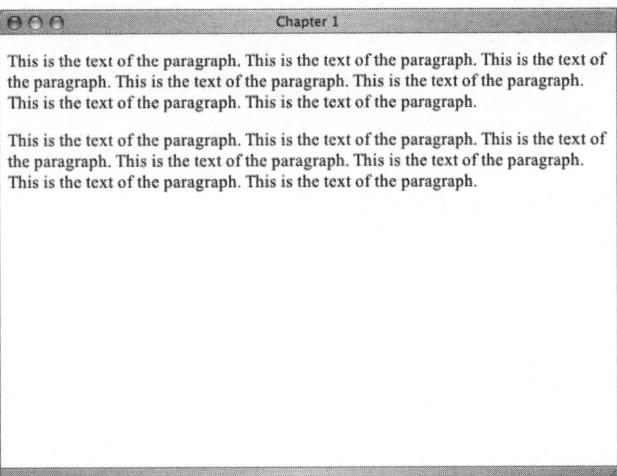

Notice that the browser left a blank line between the two paragraphs and that there is no indenting. This is an example of a *default* paragraph. A default display is the browser's built-in interpretation of how the element should be presented. One way to change the browser's default interpretation of an element is to include additional instructions in the form of *attributes* and *values* that further define the element.

DOCTYPEs AND PRESENTATIONAL ATTRIBUTES

In Chapter 3 you will learn about DOCTYPEs, which identify the specific version of XHTML a web document conforms to, and therefore which syntax elements will be allowed.

Keep in mind that while a Transitional HTML or XHTML DOCTYPE allows attribute and value instructions in the element, a Strict DOCTYPE does not allow presentational attributes and values. That's because presentational attributes and values determine *appearance*, an activity better left to the CSS. Separation of content from appearance is one thing a Strict DOCTYPE enforces, well, strictly.

The concept of attributes and values is a widely used way of organizing information. In general, an attribute identifies a category of information about a given type of element, and the value identifies how the attribute is implemented in a specific instance of that element. In XHTML, an example of an attribute that might define a paragraph is alignment. All paragraphs have this characteristic; all are aligned in some way. Text in paragraphs can be left-aligned, right-aligned, centered, or justified. As you can see in Figure 1.2, the browser default for text alignment is left-aligned. In XHTML, the type of alignment you choose is the value. The exact attribute is `align`. The value of this attribute could be `left`, `right`, `center`, or `justify`.

An attribute is written as part of the opening tag. The attribute name is followed by an equal sign (=) and the value in quotation marks (").

Here is a marked up paragraph element with an attribute and value.

```
<p align="right">This is the text of the paragraph.</p>
```

By adding `align="right"` to the first paragraph element in the XHTML that generated Figure 1.2, you can see the alignment change to an appearance similar to Figure 1.3.

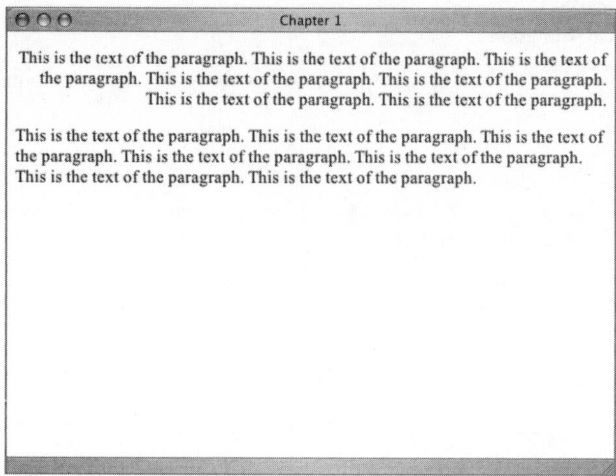

FIGURE 1.3
The first paragraph with align="right"

There are two important things to take note of in this example. First, there is a space between the tag name and the attribute name, `align`. The attribute is followed by an equal sign and the attribute value `"right"` is enclosed in quotation marks with no surrounding spaces. Attribute/value pairs in HTML/XHTML always follow this syntax. Also notice the closing tag. It does the job of ending the paragraph and the effect of the paragraph's attributes merely by using the forward slash (/) and the `p` again. When the paragraph ends, all of its attributes and values terminate with it.

One of the distinctions between XHTML and HTML is that closing tags are *required* by XHTML. In HTML, closing tags are not always required.

Empty Elements

An element with text in it, such as the paragraph examples we've seen, is considered nonempty. Some elements you put on a web page do not contain text. Such elements don't need closing tags and are referred to as *empty elements*. An example would be an image or a line break. Empty elements have specific requirements in XHTML, but let's start with an example in HTML:

```
<p>Jingle bells, jingle bells,<br>
Jingle all the way...</p>
```

The HTML tag `br` (for break) is used for a line break in formatting this paragraph. The line break doesn't have to open and close, it merely has to *be*. A line break moves whatever comes next down to a new line, without any intervening white space, which you would get by default if you put the second line in a new paragraph element.

Formatted with a break in the first line, this paragraph would display like Figure 1.4 in a browser. Look again at Figure 1.2 to note the difference between a line break and a new paragraph.

However, XHTML uses syntax based on the rules of Extensible Markup Language (XML) to write HTML. One of the requirements of XML is that every element must be terminated even if it's empty. That means every opening tag must have a corresponding closing tag. This concept is known as *well-formedness*. A well-formed document has no unclosed tags. You may be asking how an element such as `br` can be "terminated" if there is no closing tag. The solution in XML and XHTML is to add the closing forward slash to the empty tag itself. Empty tags in XHTML look like this example.

```
<p>Jingle bells, jingle bells,<br />
Jingle all the way...</p>
```

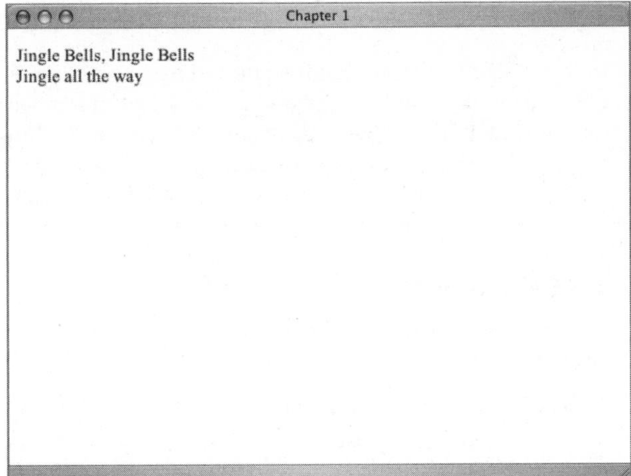

FIGURE 1.4
The line break moves the text down to the next line.

Even empty tags with attributes and values can be closed in this way. Notice the space between the `br` and the forward slash (/). That's the way it will be shown in the examples in this book, but the space doesn't *have to* be there.

The `img` (for image) tag is another empty element. Look at this example:

```
<img src="photo.gif" />
```

This empty element places an image on the page, and the source (`src`) of the image is given as an attribute of the `img` tag. The space and forward slash at the end give the empty element the required XHTML closing.

There are not many empty elements in XHTML. Others include horizontal rules (`hr`), the `link` element, and `meta` elements. Most of the time you will mark up text with both opening and closing tags. Even if you are writing HTML, where closing tags are not always required, it is considered good practice to include closing tags whenever possible.

SAY, HONEY, JUST HOW OLD IS YOUR BROWSER, ANYWAY?

The space before the closing forward slash is not required by XHTML. In other words, `<br/>` with no space before the forward slash, is correct. However, inserting a space enables older browsers to correctly display the document, so I will use the space here. (Older browsers are those venerable antiques earlier than version 5, such as Netscape 4.7.) As of this writing Microsoft Corp. is very close to releasing version 7 of Internet Explorer, which most web designers fervently hope will quickly send all older versions of Internet Explorer to the land of the Model T and the Studebaker along with creaky veterans like Netscape 4.*x*.

When Internet Explorer 7 is released, it will join the ranks of other modern browsers such as Firefox, Opera, and Safari in rendering web pages using standards developed by the W3C. If examples used in this book do not render according to current standards in older browsers, I will explain how to work around that problem.

REQUIRED VS. PRESENTATIONAL ATTRIBUTES

Isn't `src="photo.gif"` an attribute and value set? Earlier I said that XHTML had a DOCTYPE that didn't allow attributes and values, and now your alarm bells are all clanging. Yes, I did say that, you catch on fast. But `src` is *required*, even when using an XHTML Strict DOCTYPE. Without it, the browser doesn't know which image to display. Only attributes and values that have to do with how an element *looks* are not allowed in HTML and XHTML Strict.

XHTML: Specific Requirements

As mentioned previously, XHTML uses XML syntax rules. There are several specifics about writing XHTML syntax:

- Every element must be terminated. (In HTML you can sometimes get away with only using an opening tag, although it isn't a good practice.)
- Specific DOCTYPE declarations are required, which you will learn about in Chapter 3. (In HTML you can just have `<html>` with no DOCTYPE at the beginning of the document. Not a good practice, but possible.)
- All elements, attributes, and values must be in lowercase. (In HTML you can put them in caps if you want.)
- All values must be enclosed in quotation marks. Values can be quoted with single or double quotation marks, but you must be consistent about using the same type each time. The examples in this book will consistently be in double quotation marks ("). (In HTML you can leave out the quotes on the values. Again, not a good practice.)
- Every attribute must be given an explicit value. (In HTML, some attributes don't need explicit values.)
- Comments are not valid within a tag.
- Comments may not contain two hyphens in a row, other than at the beginning and end of the comment.

LEAVE A COMMENT

An XHTML comment is not displayed on a web page. It's used to leave notes to yourself. The syntax is `<!--put the comment here-->`. Anything enclosed in the `<!-- -->` comment marks will be ignored by the browser. They're human readable. You, being human, can read comments any time you look at the code. Just be aware of how many hyphens you type in a row.

As you proceed through the book you'll see examples of comments used to provide information about what certain bits of code are about. The syntax for writing comments in CSS is different. You will learn about CSS comments later in the book.

Although the preceding rules are not required when writing HTML, they all work just fine in HTML. The only XHTML syntax rule that does not produce valid HTML is using the forward slash to terminate an empty element. Should you decide to use valid HTML instead of XHTML, you will need to make only the minor adjustment to your coding habits to leave out the terminal forward slash in an empty element. I just mentioned it, but it bears repeating: there is nothing wrong with using valid HTML 4.01 to write your web pages. A choice had to be made for the examples in the book, and XHTML was selected. That choice does not diminish the value of value HTML 4.01. One of the reasons XHTML was selected for this book is that learning the rules of XHTML provides you with a set of good habits (for example, including a closing tag for elements like paragraphs and list items) that are good practices when writing HTML.

I threw the word *valid* around a couple of times in the last paragraph. You'll find out what that is in Chapter 3 when you learn about DOCTYPEs.

KEEP IT SIMPLE: SWITCHING FROM XHTML TO HTML

Q: I don't want to write XHTML, I want to write HTML this time. What do I have to remember?

A: Not much. Change the DOCTYPE and don't use a forward slash in empty elements.

SO MANY TAGS, SO LITTLE TIME

Throughout this book you'll learn the most important XHTML elements and attributes, but as you begin working on your own you'll find it valuable to have a complete reference to the language. You can find that reference in *HTML Complete* (Sybex, 2003), a compilation of useful information that also contains a command reference for CSS.

You can learn everything about every single element in HTML or XHTML from the W3C. For example, the specification for XHTML 1 is at `www.w3.org/TR/xhtml1`.

Getting Started with CSS Syntax

Cascading Style Sheets (CSS) are used to add presentational features to elements within your markup. CSS can set colors, fonts, backgrounds, borders, margins, and even the placement of elements on the page.

A style sheet is simply a text document containing one or more style rules. Style rules can be either placed directly in an XHTML document or linked to it as a completely separate file. In Chapter 2 you'll explore both these approaches, but most of the time CSS is linked to the XHTML page. In one document, you'll have your XHTML page, which you will learn to plan in a clean, logical structure of the headings, paragraphs, links, and images needed to present your ideas. In another file, you'll have your style sheet, which gives color, layout, emphasis, and pizzazz to your display. This way, you can change the way your web page looks simply by changing the styles in your style sheet or attaching a different style sheet, without changing the content at all.

The power to change a site's complete appearance by changing the style rules gives you great flexibility in its appearance. It also saves enormous amounts of time on maintenance and upkeep, since style rules are in a file that is apart from the content. Any number of web pages can be linked to a single style sheet, so it becomes merely a matter of minutes to make sweeping changes to the appearance of all those pages. When the style sheet is downloaded by a browser, it is saved in a special folder called *cache*. The next time the browser downloads a page using that style sheet, there is no wait for the user while it downloads because the browser already has it in cache. So every page that uses that style sheet will download very quickly, saving waiting time and bandwidth charges.

A further benefit of the separation of content from presentation is that your web pages are more accessible to all sorts of devices. That clean and logical structure in your XHTML that I mentioned makes your pages easier to index by search engines, too.

Styles and style sheets look very different from XHTML, and a different set of syntax rules is used for writing styles.

CSS TIPPING POINT

Visit `www.csszengarden.com` to see inspirational examples of the same content styled in many different ways using CSS. This website created the tipping point in the wide adoption of CSS for styling web pages by visibly proving that a well-structured page of HTML could have literally thousands of different presentations with CSS. Seeing is believing.

Selectors and Declarations

Style rules are written with *selectors* and *declarations*. Selectors identify which elements of an XHTML page the style will apply to. The most basic selector is the *element selector*, sometimes called the *type selector* because it selects a particular type of element. For example, the selector `p` selects all the paragraph elements on a page and is therefore an element or type selector.

For each selector, you write a set of declarations that govern how the selected element will display. Together the selector and declarations make up a style rule or, more simply, a style. Here is a style rule for the selector `p`:

```
p {
font-family: Arial, Helvetica, sans-serif;
font-size: small;
color: blue;
}
```

Let's examine that bit by bit. You already know that the `p` is the selector. Everything that comes between the two curly braces (`{}`) is the declaration block, which contains three different declarations in this example.

A declaration consists of a *property* followed by a colon, a space, and then the *value*. A semicolon follows the value. As you can see in this example, a property in CSS is similar to an attribute in XHTML. They both identify a characteristic of the element you are formatting. The first property declared in this example is the font family to be used for text in the paragraphs. Arial is the first choice, if the user's computer has it. If not, Helvetica will do, and if neither is available, the system's default sans-serif font will have to do.

FONT FAMILIES AND TYPEFACES

Font family is the slightly fussy typographical term for what we usually call a *typeface* or just a *font*. Strictly speaking, every variation in size and weight within a typeface is considered a separate font, and the whole set of these variations is considered the font family.

You'll learn more about fonts and font families in Chapter 4. Typography and fonts are the topic of many books, including *The Non-Designer's Design Book* by Robin Williams (Peachpit Press, 2003). The Web Style Guide at `www.webstyleguide.com/type/index.html` provides a good introduction to the topic.

It is considered good practice to include more than one font family in a declaration because not all computer systems come equipped with the same set of fonts. As in this example, the fonts are normally listed in the order of preference.

Generally, if no font family is specified, a browser will use Times as the default. Times is a serif font.

The second declaration in the preceding rule is `font-size: small`. You will learn more about the various options in font sizes in Chapters 4 and 5, but I'm sure you can guess that this declaration sets the font for all the `p` elements to a small size. The final declaration sets the color to `blue`. Color values are most often expressed with a code, but there are few colors that can be given by name. You'll learn more about the way to code color choices in Chapter 3. The CSS property `color` refers to elements in the foreground, in this example color of the paragraph text. To set a background color for a paragraph (or any other selector being styled), use the property `background-color`.

BROWSER DEFAULT FONT SIZES

Unless a user has changed the browser default settings, the default `font-size` setting in most browsers is `medium`. There are several keywords used for `font-size: xx-small, x-small, small, medium, large, x-large, xx-large, smaller, larger`. These keywords are considered relative measures, since font sizes specified by the designer will be sized in relation to whatever default font size is set. You'll find out more about this in Chapter 2.

The style rule example above has the effect of making every paragraph on that page appear in a font that is slightly smaller than normal, blue, and Arial.

In the examples in this book, each style declaration is written on a separate line, and the closing curly brace is on its own line as well. This makes the style easier for humans to read. However, style rules don't have to be typed in exactly that form for browsers to read them. For example, you could write the rule like this:

```
p {font-family: Arial, Helvetica, sans-serif; font-size: small; color: blue;}
```

If you do put more than one declaration on a line, be sure to leave a space after the semicolon separating one property declaration from the next.

Some style properties can be written in shorthand form. For example, `font` can be used as shorthand for all the font properties including `font-style`, `font-variant`, `font-weight`, `font-size`, `line-height`, and `font-family`. That allows you to combine the two previous declarations about fonts into one shorthand declaration like this:

```
p {
font: small Arial, Helvetica, sans-serif;
color: blue;
}
```

To expand the paragraph example a bit with more shorthand, here's another example:

```
p {
font: bold small/150% Arial, Helvetica, sans-serif;
color: blue;
}
```

This shorthand rule sets the `font-weight` to `bold`. The `small/150%` represents `font-size` and `line-height` in shorthand. The rest of the rule is already familiar to you.

Selectors Get Specific

Often you'll need to be more explicit in styling elements in the XHTML than the first example shows. CSS does allow for more specific selectors than the general element selector already described. Since the selector distinguishes what element in the document will be affected by the style rule, an element selector such as the p selector in the example above will affect all the p elements. There are times when you want particular (or what CSS terms *specific*) instances of paragraphs to follow different rules from those assigned to all p elements in general. Two of those types of selectors are the *ID selector* and the *class selector*. These two selectors allow you to write style rules for elements in a particular context. For example, instead of styling all the paragraphs on a page, you can style only the paragraphs of a certain class or ID.

> **Selectors in This Book**
>
> You'll learn to use the following selectors in this book: adjacent-sibling selectors, attribute selectors, child selectors, element selectors, class selectors, ID selectors, descendant selectors, pseudo class selectors, pseudo-element selectors, the universal selector, and group selectors.

ID Selectors

IDs can only be used once per XHTML page. They are usually used to identify content that you style as a structural unit, such as a header, footer, content block, or menu. You will be working with this concept in almost every chapter of this book, but for now, you will simply see how ID selectors look in a style sheet.

ID selectors are preceded by this symbol: #. The correct term for this symbol is "octothorpe," but most people in the United States call it a pound sign or hash sign. In this book, we will use the term hash sign for this symbol. An `id` rule in a style sheet looks like this:

```
#footer {
font-size: x-small;
}
```

This rule makes everything in the section (or division) of the page identified as `footer` extra small. Notice that there is no space between the hash sign and the `id` name. Other page elements in addition to the `div` (or division) can be identified with an `id`. You'll see examples of various ways to use ID selectors throughout the book.

But a footer division may contain other elements, such as an `address`, that you don't want to style as `x-small`. Or suppose you want only the `address` in the footer to be extra small?

You could accomplish this using a *descendant selector* that applies to only an `address` in the page division identified as `footer`:

```
#footer address {
font-size: small;
}
```

Notice the space between the `#footer` and the `address`. This `font-size` value won't apply to other elements on the page, only to `address` elements placed within the context of the `footer` division. This use of the ID selector followed by the element selector is very specific to only particular elements in particular parts of the page.

The selector `#footer address` is a contextual (or descendant) selector. You can build contextual selectors into your XHTML with named IDs that allow for finely drawn CSS selectors, but contextual selectors are not just used with IDs. In the upcoming chapters, you will use descendant selectors to create many CSS styles. Chapter 2 explains more about the hierarchical relationship of HTML elements that creates a descendant element.

You create the names for the `id` selectors yourself. They don't have to relate to any XHTML tag. It is good practice to create a simple and meaningful name that reflects the structural purpose of the content of the section identified with an `id`. The `id` selector `#footer` is a good example of a name that reflects some meaningful purpose on the page. If you worked on a style sheet and went back to it after several months, the id selector `#footer` would still make sense to you as you reviewed and changed the style sheet.

Class Selectors

Class selectors can be used as many times as you want per XHTML page. Class selectors are preceded by a period (`.`). As with `id` selectors, you create the `class` name yourself. If you want a style that will highlight certain terms on your page, you can create a `class` and name it `term`.

```
.term {
background-color: silver;
}
```

This style rule would put a silver background behind any words or phrases that were identified as being in the class `term`. Notice that there is no space between the preceding period and the name of the class. In Chapter 2, you'll learn how to apply both class and id attributes to your XHTML elements.

THERE'S AN ART TO NAMING CLASSES AND IDS

One of the reasons CSS is popular is because a page's whole look can change almost instantly. It is good practice to choose class names that express purpose rather than some momentary choice such as a color, which might be changed later. So a class named `.term` is a better choice here than a class named `.silver` because the name `term` will continue to make sense no matter what color is used.

Supposed you were creating divs and IDs for a layout with navigation in a column on the left side. You would need to think up an ID name for the navigation column. An ID named `#nav` would be a better choice than `#leftcol` because the navigation will always be navigation, but the left column might be positioned somewhere else in a later redesign.

So use functional or semantic terms when dreaming up class and ID names. It will help you keep your CSS selectors meaningful over time.

You can use complex combinations of selectors, IDs, and classes to style specific sections of your pages. The following selector would apply only to paragraphs of a class called `term` in a division of the page called `footer`.

```
#footer p.term {
background-color: gray;
}
```

Notice that when writing a style declaration for an XHTML element that is assigned to a particular class, such as the `p` element, there is no space between the element and the period and class name: `p.term`.

GET YOUR SELECTORS TRANSLATED INTO ENGLISH

It's often useful to study and adapt the code behind websites that use features you want to try, but CSS selectors can look dauntingly complex. SelectORacle is a free tool at `gallery.theopalgroup.com/selectoracle/` that will translate complex CSS selectors into plain English to help you understand exactly what elements CSS rules are selecting. For example, SelectORacle helpfully explains that the selector `#content .feature a` selects any `a` element that is a descendant of any element with a class attribute that contains the word `feature` that is a descendant of any element with an `id` attribute that equals `content`.

GROUPING SELECTORS

You may want to use the same style for several elements on your page. Perhaps you want all the paragraphs, lists, and block quotes on the page to have the same font size. To achieve this effect, lis the selectors, separated by commas, and give the `font-size` declaration:

```
p, li, blockquote {
font-size: medium;
}
```

This rule makes the text in any paragraph, list, or block quote have the font size `medium`. Notic that there is a space between each item in the comma-separated list of selectors.

DESCENDANT SELECTORS

In the previous example, the comma sets up a rule for every element in the comma-separated list Here is a similar rule with no comma:

```
blockquote em {
font-size: medium;
}
```

Without the comma, it looks a whole lot like the preceding comma-free `#footer p` rule, doesn' it? The selector `blockquote em`, with no comma, styles only an `em` (emphasized) element that's par of a `blockquote`, not every `em` element.

The comma (or the lack of a comma) is an important distinction between grouped selectors an descendant selectors. Grouped selectors use commas. Descendant selectors do not.

SPACES, COMMAS, SEMI-COLONS, BRACKETS: IT ALL MATTERS

XHTML and CSS are highly detail-oriented pursuits. You have to pay attention to the details such as whether you see a comma, a colon, a semicolon, a space, quotation marks, a bracket or brace. Type carefully. Do this and you will have greater success with both the XHTML and the CSS examples in the book. If you do an exercise and it doesn't seem to work as I say it should, check carefully for typos. The syntax is exacting, and a missing semicolon or quotation mark can cause a whole page to render as gibberish. And I don't mean the kind of gibberish you get when you use one of those "lorem ipsum" generators to fill a page with a lot of meaningless text so you can see how a layout works.

Quotation Marks

The last difference between the syntax rules for writing XHTML and writing CSS that you'll look at before moving on to Chapter 2 involves quotation marks.

You recall that in XHTML, all attribute values in a tag must be enclosed in quotation marks. In CSS style declarations, however, property values do not appear in quotes. Most of the time, you don't see quotation marks in style sheets except when listing a font whose name contains two or three words.

For example, you looked at this style rule earlier, in which no quotes were used:

```
p {
font-family: Arial, Helvetica, sans-serif;
font-size: small;
color: blue;
}
```

The fonts listed here are one-word font names. Sans-serif is hyphenated and doesn't have a space, so it is considered one word. However, if you want to list a font name such as Times New Roman, which is more than one word and includes spaces, you wrap the name in quotation marks, like this:

```
p {
font-family: "Times New Roman", Times, Georgia, serif;
}
```

Notice that the comma separating Times New Roman from Times is *after* the ending quotation mark. Also note that although specific font-family names such as Times are capitalized, generic font names such as serif are not.

You may see quotation marks in the URL to an image in a style sheet. Quotation marks are optional, not required, in URLs. Here's an example, written three different ways, all correct, with various examples of quotation mark use (or no quotation marks).

```
p {
background-image: url(bg.gif);
}
p {
background-image: url('bg.gif');
}
p {
background-image: url("bg.gif");
}
```

Although the W3C considers single quotation marks legal, they aren't supported by Mac versions of Internet Explorer, so it's wise to stick with either no quotation marks or double quotation marks in the style sheet.

In Chapter 2, you will build XHTML documents and CSS style sheets. While you're doing that, you'll learn where to write styles and how to link to styles. Chapter 2 will explain the meaning of the *cascade* in Cascading Style Sheets.

Real-World Scenario

A strong thread emphasized throughout this book is that the use of the standard specification recommended by the W3C by both web professionals and browser manufacturers makes writin XHTML and CSS easier, faster, and more universal.

There is a grassroots group working hard for the implementation of web standards called Th Web Standards Project (WaSP) at `www.webstandards.org` (Figure 1.5).

The Web Standards Project site provides opportunities for you to take action in favor of web standards and offers information to help you learn to use those standards.

Exemplary attention to standards, valid code using a strict DOCTYPE, progressive examples c CSS and other web technologies are to be expected from this website. It delivers. Use the browser' View Source option to look at this site's clearly structured and valid XHTML.

It will be helpful when viewing the real-world examples in this book, and in testing your own wor as you progress through the book, if you download the Mozilla Firefox browser at `www.mozilla.con firefox`. After you have installed the Firefox browser, download and install the Firefox Web Deve oper Add-on, from `https://addons.mozilla.org/firefox/60`. Using the Web Developer add-o toolbar gives you easy-to-reach tools to view HTML and CSS code for any web page.

Be aware that any site given as a "Real-World Scenario"—in fact, any site referred to in this book—is protected by copyright law from being copied. Copyright law protects both the images and the text in a website. I encourage you to look and learn but not to take. There may be a few exceptions—for example, some CSS layout sites say in very clear terms that you have permissio to take the material for your own use—but in general, it is best to assume that you do not have pe mission to "borrow" material from any website.

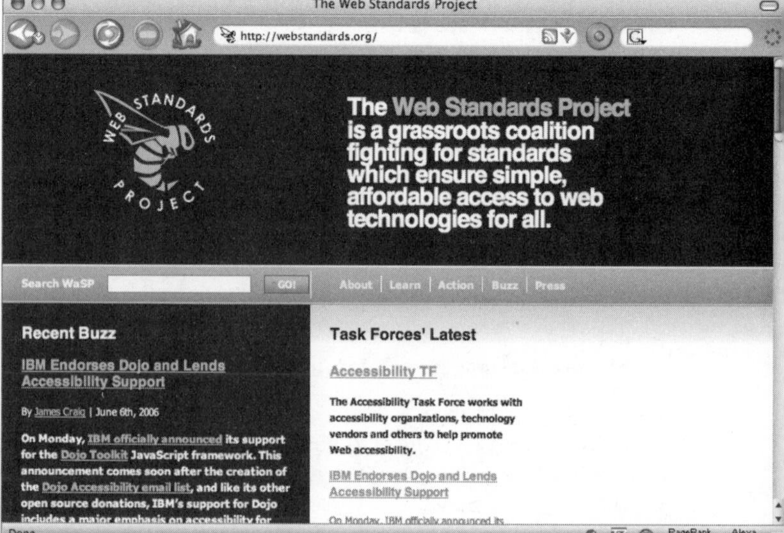

FIGURE 1.5 The Web Standards Project home page contains news in a section called Recent Buzz—listen to that WaSP buzz!

The Bottom Line

Identify what constitutes a website Websites are built with many interconnected technologies and applications. You should be familiar with how XHTML and CSS fit into that puzzle.

Master It Describe the purpose of XHTML and CSS in building a web page.

Identify what XHTML and HTML are XHTML and HTML are markup languages. XHTML is an extension of HTML based on XML, itself a markup language.

Master It What do the acronyms HTML and XHTML mean?

Explain similarities and differences in XHTML and HTML Since XHTML is based on HTML, there are many similarities between the two. The important differences arise from the distinction that XHTML uses XML syntax, while HTML is not required to follow XML syntax rules.

Master It List XML syntax rules that XHTML must follow. Make note of any that do not apply to HTML.

Describe what CSS is CSS stands for Cascading Style Sheets, a specification that sets out properties and values that may be applied to the presentation of HTML or XHTML elements.

Master It Explain how CSS rules are applied to a web page.

Write XHTML Syntax Meaningful elements in the content of a web page are marked up with XHTML tags, which may or may not have attributes and values giving more information about the element.

Master It To demonstrate XHTML syntax, write two complete XHTML elements demonstrating the difference between an element with attributes and values and one without.

Write CSS Syntax Style rules are written with *selectors* and *declarations*. The most basic selector is the element selector. Other types of selectors include adjacent-sibling selectors, attribute selectors, child selectors, class selectors, ID selectors, descendant selectors, pseudo class selectors, pseudo-element selectors, the universal selector, and group selectors.

For each selector, the declarations of properties and values for that selector govern how the element will display. Together the selector and declarations make up a style rule or, more simply, a style.

Master It Write a style rule for the selector `h1` that sets the `font-family` to `Arial, Helvetica, sans-serif` and sets the `font-size` to `1.5em`. Write the rule in full and then write it again in shorthand.

Chapter 2

Location, Location: Where to Put a Style

There are some foundation concepts about the way Cascading Style Sheets work to discuss before starting with the specific details of building XHTML pages and style sheets. This chapter explores how the placement of CSS style rules within the XHTML code for a page affects the way those rules will be applied in building the page. There are several possible places where style rules can be located in a page, and more than one set of style rules might be implemented in a particular XHTML page. This means that for a given page element, there might be conflicting rules for styling it. The way these possible conflicts in style rules are resolved is referred to as the *cascade*.

This chapter is all about conflict resolution: you will learn the basics of how the location of a style sheet places style rules in the cascade and the rules for resolving conflicting styles.

Other basic concepts that are important to the way style rules are implemented in instances of conflict involve the factors of *inheritance* and *specificity*. Inheritance refers to the fact that elements in an XHTML document are nested within one another in a relationship that is referred to as parent and child, or ancestor and descendant. Specificity allows style rules to have *weight*, or importance. A more specific rule has more weight than a less specific rule and would therefore be used in preference to a less specific rule.

Taking the time to grasp the basic concepts of the cascade, inheritance, and specificity will help you understand how, where, and when to add style rules in order to make your XHTML pages display as you want.

In this chapter you will learn to:

- Understand and use the cascade to resolve style conflicts.
- Understand where styles can be located and how that affects the cascade.
- Use `link` or `@import` to attach an external style sheet.
- Understand inheritance and know when it applies to a style.
- Understand specificity and use it to your advantage when creating selectors.

The Cascade

There are a number of complex rules regarding the cascade, but for the purpose of getting started, I can boil them down to two simplified statements:

1. The closest rule wins.
2. The most specific rule wins.

A Resource

A handy reference book about CSS is *HTML, XHTML, and CSS Bible, 3rd Edition*, by Bryan Pfafffenberger, et al. (Wiley, 2004).

We'll walk through the cascade using a paragraph on a very simple XHTML page as an example. We'll take this paragraph through the various levels of the cascade. See Figure 2.1.

The Cascade
cascade begins
Default Browser Style
p {font: 14px Times; color: #000;}
User Style
p {font: 2em Verdana; color: #000;} /* If declared !important, overrides any of the following rules*/
Result: p {font: 2em Verdana; color: #000;}
Web Author External Style
p {font: 0.9em Arial; color: #333;}
Result: p {font: 0.9em Arial; color: #333;}
Web Author Embedded Style
p {font-family: Georgia;}
Result: p {font: 0.9em Georgia; color: #333;}
element styled
Web Author Inline Style
p {color: #00F;}
Result: p {font: 0.9em Georgia; color: #00F;}
Other things being equal, the rule closer to the element being styled Prevails

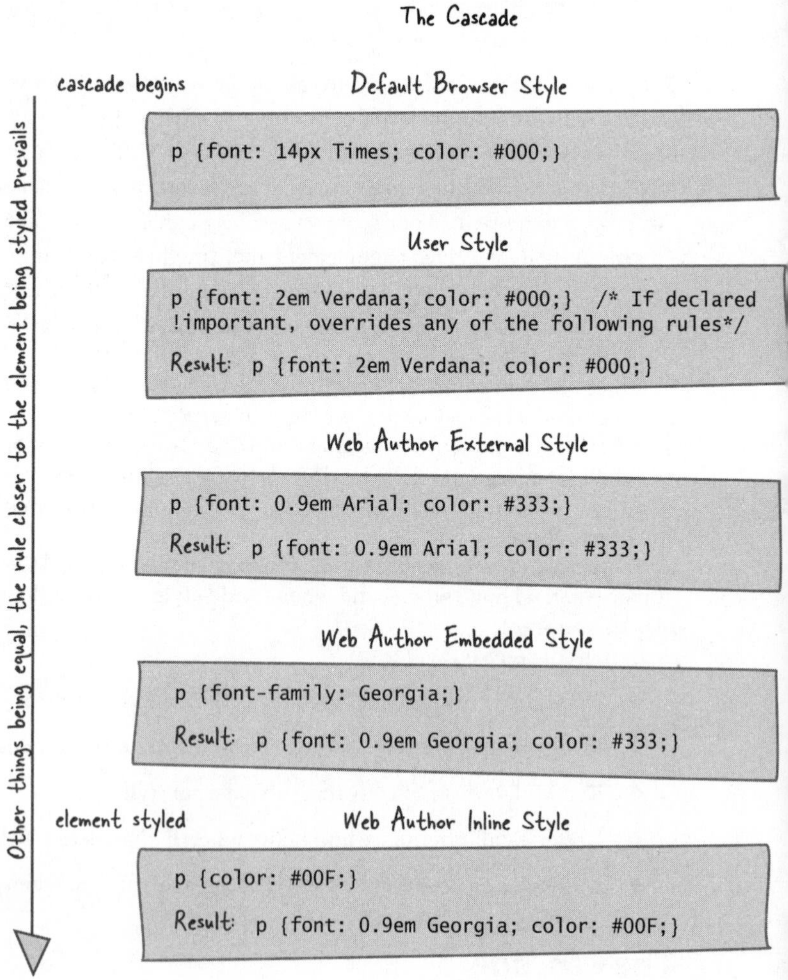

Figure 2.1
The cascade's effect on a paragraph style. Everything else being equal, the rule closest to the element being styled prevails.

Begin with the Browser

Each browser has a set of style rules that it will apply to display any page in the absence of closer or more specific rules. These rules commonly set up basic display properties such as black text and font sizes for various elements.

The browser style rules are at the beginning of the cascade. The browser style is the farthest away from any element, and the browser style rules are less specific than any rules placed subsequently in the cascade. Or, to put it another way, if no rules are written in user style sheets, external style sheets, or embedded style sheets to change the styles set up by the browser, then the browser rules govern the appearance of a web page.

Figure 2.2 illustrates a paragraph displayed using a set of styles inherent in the browser with no additional style rules.

FIGURE 2.2
A paragraph displayed with the browser's styles

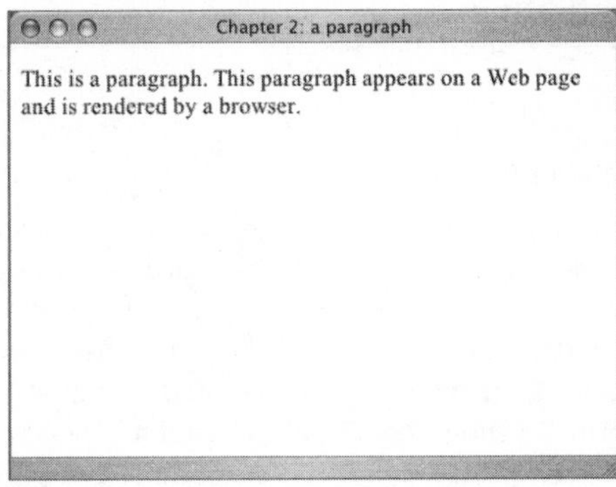

This page is available on the accompanying CD in the folder for Chapter 2. If you copy it from the CD and save it on your computer, you can work along with the following examples. The file you want is `ch2_paragraph.html`. There are many XHTML, CSS, and image files in this book that you will want to save to your computer from the accompanying CD. Create a new folder on your computer named `Mastering Integrated HTML and CSS`. Inside this folder, you can add a subfolder for each chapter of the book. When you work on exercises for each chapter, save them to your computer in the appropriate folder.

If you work on the page as you go along, you will need to open it in a basic text editor such as Notepad or Text Edit in plain text mode. There are text editors on the accompanying CD that are specifically for writing code. Try one of them if you prefer. If you work in code view, you can do these exercises in software such as Dreamweaver or GoLive.

You can see the page rendered in a browser by opening a browser, using File ➤ Open File and browsing to the `ch2_paragraph.html` file on your computer. The page text is shown in Listing 2.1.

There are several mysterious and as yet unexplained codes and symbols on this basic page. For the moment, you can ignore all of it except the particular sections I point out in discussing the location of style rules and the cascade. In later chapters, you will learn everything there is to know about the other mysteries of this basic page.

LISTING 2.1: A Basic XHTML Page

```
<!DOCTYPE html PUBLIC "-//W3C//DTD XHTML 1.0 Transitional//EN"
   "http://www.w3.org/TR/xhtml1/DTD/xhtml1-transitional.dtd">
<html xmlns="http://www.w3.org/1999/xhtml">
<head>
<title>Chapter 2: a paragraph</title>
</head>
<body>
   <p>This is a paragraph. This paragraph appears on a Web page
      and is rendered by a browser.</p>
</body>
</html>
```

User Styles

At the cascade's next step, all browsers allow users the option of setting up style rules of their own—*user styles*. These options are primarily used by people who have barriers to accessing the Web, such as poor eyesight, and most other users are not even aware that they exist. By includin an `!important` directive as discussed in the next section, users can set their own rules to be mor important than any style rules created by the web page designer.

Figure 2.3 shows one browser's preferences for web content. Notice the unselected option calle Use My Style Sheet. Below it is a Select Style Sheet button that, when Use My Style Sheet is selectec allows a user to locate on their computer a style sheet written for their particular needs. Because thi user has not selected Use My Style Sheet, web content will be determined by the browser's defaul styles and the web designer's style sheet on top of those.

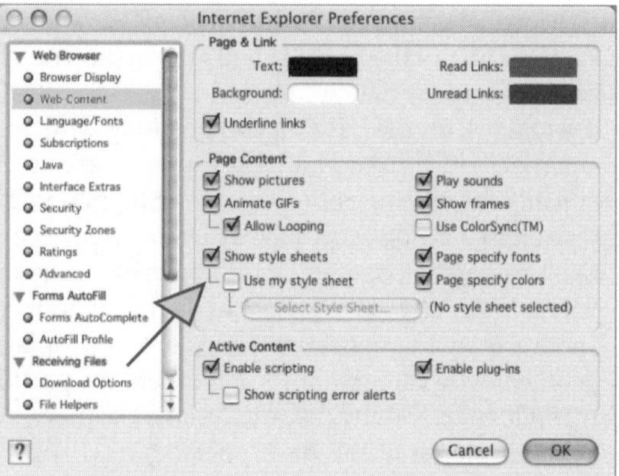

FIGURE 2.3
Internet Explorer (Mac) preferences for web content

THE IMPORTANCE OF BEING *!IMPORTANT*

Although normally a web designer's style sheet overrides a user's personal style sheet, CSS provides the `!important` rule so that users (and web designers) can specify that a preference is so important that it overrules any other rule anywhere in the cascade. A user could specify a personal style sheet containing a rule like this:

```
body {
font-size: 48px !important;
}
```

Note the `!important` before the closing semicolon in the font-size declaration. If you have more than one value in a declaration, be sure the `!important` is at the end of the declaration but before the semicolon, as in the following example.

```
body {
font: 48px Arial, Helvetica, sans-serif !important;
}
```

Now you have another rule to add to the two simple cascade rules I listed previously: `!important` always prevails.

As I mentioned, both the web designer (also called the author) and user style sheets may contain `!important` declarations, and user `!important` rules override author `!important` rules.

USER LANGUAGE/FONTS PREFERENCES

In Figure 2.4 you see the Languages/Fonts category in the IE (Macintosh) browser preferences, which are typical of most browsers. Here the user may set a particular font size and font family for their default display. Setting personal browser preferences for font-size will affect how the designer's styles are rendered if the designer uses relative font measures such as percentages or ems. A designer's style sheet may overrule default choices such as a proportional font. These preferences may also be affected by any `!important` rule in a user's personal style sheet.

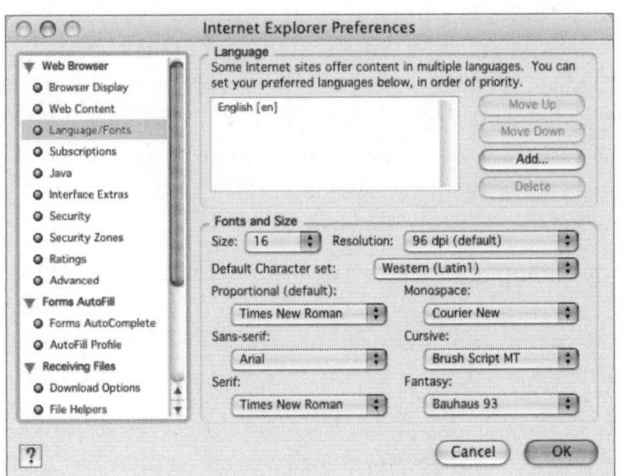

FIGURE 2.4
Internet Explorer (Mac) preferences for language/fonts

RELATIVELY SPEAKING

Notice that the user in Figure 2.4 has the preference for font size set to 16. In this book, you will deal extensively with style sheets that use font sizes of 100 percent or 1 em or a keyword such as small. Ems, percents, and keyword sizes are font size measurements relative to the user's preference. In the Figure 2.4 user's case, 100 percent or 1 em is equal to 16 as the font size. In every case, measurements in percents, ems, or keywords are relative to the user's font size preference, whatever it may be.

The complete list of keyword values for `font-size` is: `xx-small`, `x-small`, `small`, `medium`, `large`, `x-large`, `xx-large`, `smaller`, `larger`.

The value of using relative `font-size` measures is that it gives control over size decisions to the user, who can quickly increase or decrease text size using browser controls such as those under the View menu or, in some browsers, the Ctrl + or Ctrl– (Macintosh Command + or Command –) keyboard combination. If you use an absolute value for `font-size`, for example, pixels, the user may be stuck with your idea of what a readable size for text is, Sadly, your favorite size is often not the best choice for every user. An individual user's setup may vary from yours, as well. Computer monitors vary in size and resolution, causing text to appear to be a different size in different situations.

If you have the `ch2_paragraph.html` file open in your browser, you can experiment with your browser preferences for font size to see what difference it makes in the way the paragraph displays. After you change and save a preference, reload (refresh) your browser to see the change. When you finish experimenting, revert back to your normal settings.

External Styles

The browser and user style sheets are out of your control. The first opportunity you as a designer have to enter the cascade is with an external style sheet.

CONTROL FREAKS: PERIL LIES AHEAD

The fact that some things about the way a web page renders are out of your control is a hard concept for some beginners to grasp. Designers often want to achieve an exact appearance under all circumstances. Although XHTML and CSS provide a very high degree of control, they don't allow absolute control. You can create pages that work well and look wonderful in different browsers on different platforms or Internet-capable devices with various styles. But because of the rules of the cascade, user preferences, and differences in browsers and platforms, not to mention other devices such as screen readers, PDAs, and mobile phones, your page will not always have exactly the same appearance in every situation.

If you can maintain an attitude of flexibility and design with the idea in mind that user devices and user preferences may cause changes to your design vision, your daily siesta will be more peaceful. That's what web standards are all about—device independence, or content that works everywhere for everyone.

What I'll try to help you master is control over the *possibilities*. What about the possibility that one user has an 800×600 screen resolution and another has 1368×768? What about the possibility that a user bumps up the text size four or five sizes? What about the possibility that some business traveler is viewing your site on a BlackBerry? As you continue through the book, free your mind to the possibilities.

An external style sheet is a text document created in Notepad or some similar text editor and saved with the file extension `.css`. There is one on the CD named `ch2external.css`; it is shown in Listing 2.2. Save it to your computer and have it open along with `ch2_paragraph.html`.

LISTING 2.2: A Simple Style Sheet

```
p {
font: 0.9em Arial;
color: #000;
}
```

This style sheet has a rule for the `p` element. It uses 0.9em as the font size, which makes the paragraph slightly smaller than the size the user has as their preference, since 0.9em is slightly smaller than 1em. Remember, 1em is equal to whatever font size the user set in Preferences, for example, 16px. The rule also changes the font to Arial and sets a color code (`#000`) that represents black, which is the same as the browser's default choice, so you won't notice a color change yet. (Later in this exercise you'll change it to blue.)

You integrate that external style rule with your XHTML page by adding a `link` element to the page. Assuming you saved the CSS in the same folder on your computer as `ch2_paragraph.html`, here's how to link to the style sheet in the `ch2_paragraph.html` page.

The `link` element is inserted into the XTHML document head. I prefer to place it following the `title` element and preceding the closing `head` tag, like this:

```
<title>Chapter 2: a paragraph</title>
<link href="ch2external.css" rel="stylesheet" type="text/css" />
</head>
```

The `link` element links the XHTML page to a document whose relation (`rel`) to it is that of `stylesheet`. The style sheet `type` is `text/css`. At the present, `text/css` is the only style `type` in use, but there may be others in the future. If other style languages are developed in the future, this link element will still work as intended with no modification.

The `href` attribute is the URL of the style sheet.

With the link to the external style sheet in place, save the XHTML page and refresh (reload) the browser page to render the paragraph with a new style rule. Figure 2.5 shows the original page with no attached style rules behind a rendering of the page after the `ch2external.css` file was linked. You can clearly see the difference made by linking to the external style sheet. The rule in the external style sheet overrides the rule in the browser's default style sheet, and the font displayed is now a slightly smaller-sized Arial.

COMING ATTRACTIONS: *@IMPORT*

Later in the chapter you'll see the second method of integrating an external style sheet with an XHTML page, using an `@import` directive. This method affects the cascade, so we'll complete our exploration of the cascade and the related concepts of inheritance and specificity before discussing it.

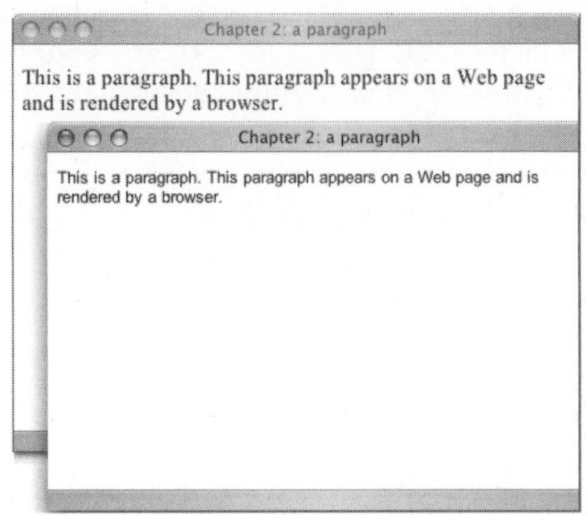

FIGURE 2.5
An external style sheet is linked to the page. The back browser page is the default style. The front browser page is the one with the external style sheet link. Note the change in font family and font size.

To review what you've just done with the cascade, the linked external style sheet, `ch2external.css` is closer to the styled element than the browser style sheet, and the closest style rules in deciding how the paragraph will be rendered. The two `p` rules were in conflict about `font-family` and `font-size`: the rules of the cascade solved the conflict. You just put the cascade in action!

The style sheet `ch2external.css` could be linked to an unlimited number of XHTML pages. If the rule for `p` in `ch2external.css` later changed in any way, the rendering of every page linked to the style sheet would instantly reflect that change. Talk about easy! Talk about powerful! One external style sheet can change dozens, hundreds, or thousands of XHTML pages in a few seconds. You can redesign your entire website by doing no more than changing the rules in your style sheet.

Embedded Styles

We continue to dig deeper down into the cascade. Style rules may be located in the head of a XHTML document. Such styles are referred to as *internal styles* or *embedded styles*. Embedded styles apply only to the document in which they are placed. If you are making a web page that will stand alone as a one-page document, embedded styles make sense.

Embedded styles also make sense when you have an external style sheet linked to a page but you want to change something slightly on just one page.

IF IT'S EARLY, EMBED

Embedded styles are sometimes used in the first stages of designing and building a new website. This helps with testing and approving a page design because everything needed to test or critique the page is in one file. When partners or clients have had their say and the first page is completed in the desired manner, the styles are moved to an external style sheet so they can be used with other pages in the site.

Besides making professional collaboration easier, this approach also helps web designers continue their self-education. Many people join online web communities where members exchange tips, ideas, helpful code checks, site inspections, and other help. It is much easier for someone in such an online group to take a quick look at a page in question if both the XHTML and the CSS are in one file.

The embedded style rules go in the XHTML document head. Once again place it following the title but before the closing head tag. Although the head element must contain a title element, the title element isn't required to be the first element in the head, as in these examples. Here's how it looks in your document now:

```
<title>Chapter 2: a paragraph</title>
<![CDATA[
p {
font-family: Georgia;
}
]]>
</style>
</head>
```

You will notice that the syntax for this style rule is similar to that used on the external style sheet, except it is enclosed in a style element. The style element must have type="text/css" as an attribute for the browser to render the styles properly.

In XHTML, style elements are declared as having #PCDATA content. Wrapping the content of the style element within a CDATA marked section ensures that < and & will be treated as the start of markup, and entities such as < and & will be recognized as entity references.

With the external style sheet attached and this embedded style rule, there are two rules for font-family now in conflict.

The embedded style example changes the font-family to Georgia. Two declarations from the external style sheet, font-size and color, are not mentioned in the embedded style. Therefore, the font-size remains 0.9em, and the color remains #000 (black).

The link to the external style sheet is listed before the style element in the document head. This preserves the flow of the cascade from external to embedded as well, because the embedded styles are listed after the external styles.

In cascade terms, that means the embedded style is closer than the external style. Order matters here. With both the linked style sheet and the embedded style sheet, the code looks like this:

```
<title>Chapter 2: a paragraph</title>
<link href="ch2external.css" rel="stylesheet" type="text/css" />
<style type="text/css">
<![CDATA[
p {
font-family: Georgia;
}
]]>
</style>
</head>
```

With this new embedded rule added to the cascade, you'll see a result similar to the browser display at the top of the stack in Figure 2.6. Note that the rule setting the font to Georgia in the embedded style overrides the rule setting the font to Arial in the external style. There are now three rules—default, external, and internal—clamoring to control the font-family of our lovely paragraph. Once again, the closest style rules. Once again you have used the rules of the cascade to achieve the desired result.

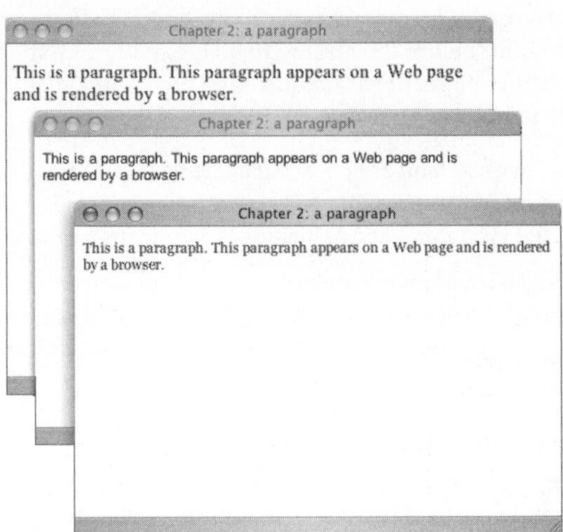

FIGURE 2.6
The embedded styles override the external styles. The topmost browser window shows the page with embedded style changing the font-family to Georgia.

COMMENTS, EMBEDDED STYLES, AND MORE COMMENTS

In older browsers, embedded styles were enclosed in HTML comment marks, like this:

```
<style type="text/css">
<!--
p {
font: 0.9em Georgia;
color: #000;
}
-->
</style>
```

Notice the symbols `<!--` and `-->` surrounding the whole set of style declarations in the `style` element; these are comment markers. As I explained in Chapter 1, *comments* are a way of telling the browser "don't display this." XHTML comments begin with an opening angle bracket, followed by an exclamation mark and two hyphens. The comment ends with two hyphens and a closing angle bracket:

```
<!-- the comment goes here -->
```

Commenting is a time-honored programming convention for including annotations about what a program is doing at each stage. Most languages include symbols that tell a compiler (the software interpreting the program), "Whatever appears between these two marks is not an instruction for you to execute." A secondary purpose is to temporarily disable part of a program by enclosing it in comment markers ("commenting it out," in programmer slang), which can later be removed.

But assuming you want the style rules to have effect, why would you comment a style block? Some old browsers do not know what styles are, and the comments prevent them from adding the style rules to the displayed page as if they were part of your text. Modern browsers, which do know what styles are, simply ignore the comment markers and read and follow the style rules as you intend. The need for comment marks in embedded styles has lessened since more and more users have modern browsers, so I do not include them here. If you know that you have visitors to your site who use one of the very old browsers, then you may need to include the comment marks in embedded style elements.

In general, comments are extremely useful when mixed with the XHTML making up the body of the document. They are a way for you as the page designer to leave notes and pertinent information for future reference. The comments are not rendered visually in the browser, but they are visible to anyone reading the code.

CSS USES COMMENTS, TOO

Comments are used within CSS style definitions. Of course, they are different from XHTML comments—stay on your toes where comments are concerned. You can't put XHTML comments in a page of CSS. And you can't put CSS comments in XHTML elements.

CSS comments begin with /* and end with */. As with XHTML comments, CSS comments tell the browser to ignore the material enclosed in the comment markers. You will see this in action in practice exercises later in the book.

An example of a CSS comment:

```
p {
font: 0.9em Georgia;
/*color: #000;*/
}
```

Because of the comment marks around the color declaration, the browser ignores that particular instruction.

Inline Styles

Inline (in the flow of the text) styles are a one-time-use affair. They are technically an embedded style, but people usually make a distinction between styles embedded in the document head and those embedded inline by calling the latter inline styles.

Inline styles are right in the XHTML as an attribute of the element you are styling. In terms of the cascade, they are the closest any style rule can possibly get to the element they are meant to style.

Making extensive use of inline styles defeats the purpose of controlling document display with one (or only a few) external documents. It also adds code to the page, which means extensive use of inline styles starts bumping up your document size, bandwidth demands, and download time. And inline styles commit the sin of inserting presentational instructions into the XHTML code. Exactly what you are trying to avoid, right? So, using inline styles extensively is not the best practice. In fact, inline styles are *deprecated* in XHTML 1.1. Nevertheless, you may find them useful from time to time, so I'll explain them. And inline styles do figure into the cascade, so you need to know about them just for the sake of completeness.

Although I've included an explanation of inline styles here, that is not the same as recommending their use. Inline styles violate the basic tenet of separating content from presentation.

DEPRECATED ELEMENTS ARE LAST WEEK'S MEAT LOAF

An element that's been dropped from the current DTD (or DOCTYPE) but was available in previous DTDs is considered *deprecated*. Deprecated elements can be used with transitional DOCTYPEs but not with strict DOCTYPEs.

Each time you want to use an inline style, you have to type it right into the specific element, similar to an attribute and value in the opening tag. The only element on the `ch2_paragraph.html` page is a `p` element. With an inline style added, the `p` element would look like this:

```
<p style="color: #00F;">This is a paragraph. This paragraph appears on a Web page
and is rendered by a browser.</p>
```

This style rule changes the `color` to `#00F` (blue) for this single paragraph element. It's not obvious from Figure 2.7, but the final example browser window displays blue text.

Notice one more thing about Figure 2.7. The font in the front-most example browser window is still Georgia. Because nothing in the inline style changed the rule for the `font-family` style embedded in the document head, the value `Georgia` was retained for the font family of this `p` element.

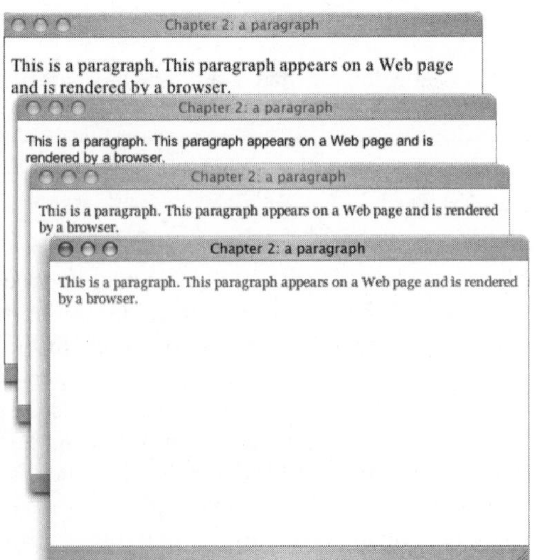

FIGURE 2.7
The inline style makes the color blue. In this grayscale figure, you can only tell that the color is slightly lighter. Try it in your own browser to see the brilliant blue color.

KEEP IT SIMPLE: THE CASCADE

Q: Can't you make the cascade simple?

A: Yes!

- The closest rule wins.
- The most specific rule wins.
- `!important` always wins.

Inheritance

Inheritance isn't part of the cascade, but it affects the rendering of styles. Styles are inherited from antecedent (or parent) elements. XHTML documents are rendered using a hierarchical system. Elements are nested one inside another in an ever-descending hierarchy. In Listing 2.1, or `ch2_paragrah.html`, you see examples of this. The document hierarchy begins with the `html` element:

```
<html xmlns="http://www.w3.org/1999/xhtml">
```

and terminates with `</html>`.

Everything in the document is a *descendant* of the `html` element. The next level in the hierarchy (or *document tree*) is the `body` element. The `p` element is a descendant of the `body` element. A stripped down view of these elements and their hierarchical relationship is

```
<html>
   <body>
      <p></p>
   </body>
</html>
```

Let's examine the interaction the cascade and inheritance have in the way a particular element might render. Suppose you have an external style sheet that sets a `font-family: Arial` rule for the `body` selector, like this:

```
body {
font-family: Arial;
}
```

If there were no other style rules for the `p` element anywhere in the cascade, the value `Arial` would be inherited by the `p` element as a descendant of the `body` element.

Not all CSS properties can be inherited; `font-family` is a good one to know about because it's a time-saver to set the `font-family` in a `body` rule and let it inherit throughout the entire document tree. Otherwise, you'll write `font-family` rules for every element on the page and end up with a huge CSS file and tired typing muscles. If you don't want absolutely everything in the same font, merely change the few elements you don't want to inherit a style from the body rule.

Specificity

The W3C has a set of mathematical formulas to determine the weight of any particular style rule. Selectors with higher specificity, or more weight, override styles with less weight.

Let's look at a much more complex XHTML page than what you've seen so far, shown in Listing 2.3.

LISTING 2.3: A More Complex XHTML Page with Numerous Elements

```
<!DOCTYPE html PUBLIC "-//W3C//DTD XHTML 1.0 Transitional//EN"
  "http://www.w3.org/TR/xhtml1/DTD/xhtml1-transitional.dtd">
<html xmlns="http://www.w3.org/1999/xhtml">
<head>
<meta http-equiv="Content-Type" content="text/html; charset=iso-8859-1"/>
<title>Chapter 2 Example</title>
<link rel="stylesheet" href="mystyles.css" type="text/css" />
</head>
<body>
<div id="masthead">
   <h1 id="siteName">My Daily Rant</h1>
   <div id="globalNav">
      <a href="home.html"> home </a> | <a href="archives.html"> archives </a> |
      <a href="about.html"> about </a> | <a href="contact.html"> contact </a>
   </div>
</div>

<div id="content">
   <h2 id="pageName">Recently...</h2>
   <div class="feature">
      <img src="specificity.gif" alt="library mural" width="280" height="200" />
      <h3>Art in Public Places </h3>
      <p>The Art in Public Places project has installed ...</p>
      <p>This mural has provoked ...</p>
   </div>
</div>

<div id="sidebar">
   <div id="hotnews">
      <h3>Today's News Quote</h3>
      <p class="newsbite">&#8220;This new bill will bring immediate relief
         to overburdened taxpayers.&#8221;<br />
         <span class="source">&ndash;The President </span></p>
      <p class="comment">To which I say, this doesn't help anyone in my tax
         bracket. How about a raise in the minimum wage instead?</p>
   </div>
</div>
</body>
</html>
```

There is a good bit of code in this listing that you haven't learned anything about yet. Once again, I encourage you to ignore the unexplained parts for now and focus on the bits and pieces needed to understand specificity as I point them out in the next few paragraphs.

In the browser, with a linked external style sheet, Listing 2.3 renders something like Figure 2.8. There are several `p` elements in Listing 2.3, for example:

```
<p>The Art in Public Places project has installed a mural, a photo of which you
see on the left, on the library courtyard wall.</p>
```

A closer look at the document reveals that this particular paragraph is a descendant of an element identified with a class attribute, namely `<div class="feature">`. In terms of specificity or weight, a class selector has more weight than a general selector. I can create a selector that targets only `p` elements descended from an element in the `.feature` class: `.feature p`.

SMART NAMES

The class name `feature` is a good example of conceiving good names for the classes you create. The `div` with this class name is intended to display the feature story or featured information on the page. The class name will retain its meaning over time.

Suppose the style sheet for Listing 2.3 contained the following rules:

```
p {
font-family: Georgia;
}
```

and

```
.feature p {
font-family: Arial;
}
```

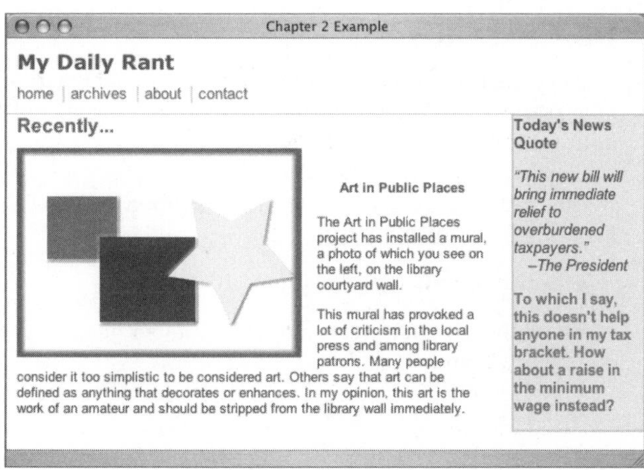

FIGURE 2.8
A styled rendering of the code in Listing 2.3

The paragraphs on the page cannot be both Georgia and Arial. One of the rules is more specific than the other, however. It's the rule with the selector `.feature p`. This selector targets `p` elements that are descendants of any element with a class attribute that contains the word `feature`. The second rule has a higher specificity and will be used for the paragraph in question. As you will see when you learn to do the actual math to calculate specificity, the selector `.feature p` earns points for its class selector and for its element selector.

DO YOU WANT THAT *DIV* WITH A *CLASS* OR WITH AN *ID*?

A `div` (for division) is a generic container element in XHTML. It can literally contain anything on a web page. By assigning a `class` or `id` selector to a `div`, you can structure the page to take advantage of the rules of specificity and write very specific descendant selectors for every purpose.

ID selectors have greater specificity than element selectors. Look at this section of Listing 2.3:

```
<div id="globalNav">
```

I can create a selector that targets only a elements descended from an element with the id `globalNav`:. The selector is `#globalNav a`. In a conflict between these two rules,

```
a {
font-size: 1.6em;
}
```

and

```
#globalNav a {
font-size: 1.4em;
}
```

the second rule has a higher specificity and would be used to style the particular `a` element in question. (The `a`, or anchor, element creates the clickable link used in navigation.)

Do the Math

To calculate specificity, selectors are given a mathematical value. Leaving out the possibility of inline styles in HTML for the moment, I'll concentrate only on the three-number system needed to figure specificity in strict XHTML.

Start with this number: 0, 0, 0.

The first number from the left is the number of ID selectors. If the selector had one ID selector, the number would be: 1, 0, 0.

`#footer` specificity = 1, 0, 0

The second number represents the number of class, pseudo-class and attribute selectors. Each one earns a point.

`.term` specificity = 0, 1, 0

`#footer .term` specificity = 1, 1, 0

The third number represents the number of element and pseudo-element selectors. Each earns one point.

`p` specificity = 0, 0, 1

`div p` specificity = 0, 0, 2

`div#footer` specificity = 1, 0, 1

This is not a base 10 numbering system, however. A specificity of 1, 0, 0 is not the same thing as the number 100 in base 10. If the total to count goes above 9, things get tricky. The W3C recommends instead that it be thought of as values of *a*, *b*, and *c*. Using this method, *b* outweighs any number of *c*, and that *a* outweighs any number of *b*.

A selector's specificity is calculated as follows:

- Count the number of ID attributes in the selector (= a).
- Count the number of other attributes and pseudo-classes in the selector (= b).
- Count the number of element names in the selector (= c).
- Ignore pseudo-elements.

The bigger the number, the more specific the rule. The more specific rule prevails. Using the *a*, *b*, *c*, method, the selector with the most ids wins. If there's a tie, the selector with the most classes wins. If there is still a tie, the selector with the most elements wins. If two selectors have the same specificity, then the conflict falls back into being resolved by the cascade rules.

Keep in mind that the ID earns the most points in the specificity game. If you are having trouble getting a rule to apply where you want it, consider increasing the specificity of your selector by adding an `id` to the element and including the `id` in your selector.

Now Add Inline Styles to the Math

There's a fourth possibility in HTML—the inline style. It takes four places to calculate this, as in 0, 0, 0, 0.

The first place, which was missing from the preceding discussion, is for inline styles—one point for each inline style. The next three places represent id selectors, class selectors, and element selectors exactly as described previously.

In this four-digit mathematical scheme, the selector `#footer` would have a specificity of 0, 1, 0, 0. The selector `.term` would have a specificity of 0, 0, 1, 0; `#footer .term` would be 0, 1, 1, 0, and so on.

An inline style would have a specific value of 1, 0, 0, 0. Here's an example for an inline style applied to a paragraph in a footer.

The CSS rule:

```
#footer {color: blue;}
```

The HTML:

```
<div id="footer">
    <p style="color: red;">The paragraph here</p>
</div>
```

The calculated value for the `p` element with the inline style is 1, 0, 0, 1. That's 1, 0, 0, 0 for the inline style, plus 0,0,0,1 for the `p` element it's placed on, making the total 1, 0, 0, 1.

What about Multiple Classes?

I'll bet your mother didn't tell you there'd be days like this: you have an element in your XHTML with multiple classes, all of the same specificity. Look at an example bit of CSS:

```
.blogtitle { border: 3px solid red }
.blogitem { border: 2px solid red }
.blogdate { border: 1px solid red }
```

And an example bit of XHTML:

```
<h2 class="blogtitle blogdate blogitem ">Multiple classes assigned to a single
element: will specificity reign?</h2>
```

Will the border of the H2 element be 3, 2, or 1 pixel wide? The rules of specificity and the rules of the cascade work together here. The last highest-weighted rule wins, so the border will be 1px. It's the order of the rules in the style sheet that controls which takes precedence, not the order of the class names in the class attribute.

Internet Explorer 6 and below have a problem with multiple class attributes applied to a single element, but modern browsers properly render elements with multiple classes.

There's no real need to become a whiz at calculating specificity. But you do need to understand that ID and class selectors carry more weight than element selectors. A good selector gives you power, control and design options. The rules of specificity are a part of what make selectors work. ID selectors, in particular, make themselves useful by being very high on the specificity charts. A selector like

```
#navBar ul a:link
```

is a bull's-eye hit for an `a:link` that is descended from a `ul` element that is descended from a navBar element. When you can reach down into the guts of a page of XHTML, pick out a single element you want to style, and use a selector specifically weighted to target just that element, you have control over appearance down to the most minute detail.

Using *@import*

Earlier in the chapter you saw how to use the `link` element to link your XHTML page to an external style sheet. The second way to do this is with an `@import` directive. Both `link` and `@import` can be used more than once, which means it is possible to have several style sheets affecting your document in various ways simultaneously. The cascade, the rules of inheritance, and the rules of specificity will resolve any conflicts that arise when using more than one set of style rules.

A LINK BY ANY OTHER NAME IS STILL A LINK

Whether you use the `link` element or the `@import` directive to link to an external style sheet, the style sheet is referred to as being "linked" to your document. In casual conversation, people may refer to imported styles as distinct from linked styles, but the correct term for either is linked.

While both the `link` element and the `@import` directive do the same job, namely linking your XHTML page to a set of style rules, the `link` element is generally used unless there is a particular need for the unique attributes of `@import`.

The `@import` directive looks like this in the document head:

```
<style type="text/css">
@import url(myotherstyles.css);
</style>
```

As you can see, the directive is contained in a `style` element, like embedded styles. The statement gives the URL of the style sheet to be imported. In this example, the `myotherstyles.css` is stored in the same folder or directory as the XHTML document. Style sheets can be stored anywhere in the directory structure of a site. You'll learn about links to files outside the current directory in Chapter 7.

The `@import` directive is popular among web designers who know that their target audience may still be using that venerable old antique, Netscape Navigator 4.*x*. Netscape 4 does not know very many of the style specifications implemented in modern browsers. More importantly, it does not know what an `@import` directive is. To accommodate Netscape 4 in addition to the more current browsers, designers put styles Netscape 4 and other older browsers don't understand in an imported style sheet because those browsers skip right over the `@import` directive while the more modern browsers obey the commands. If we didn't isolate the styles that older browsers don't understand, their users wouldn't see the page at all, or they would see a garbled mess. This way, they at least see the page with browser-default formatting, while most users see it in all its formatted glory. This reason for using `@import` becomes less and less important as time goes by and fewer and fewer people cling to the old warhorse Netscape 4.*x*.

There are other reasons `@import` can be useful. An external style sheet can be linked to *another style sheet* using an `@import` directive such as

```
@import url(http://www.example.com/styles.css)
```

As you can see from the URL value in the example, the imported style sheet does not need to be part of your site, it can be on another site.

To import one style sheet into another style sheet, `@import` must come before any other rules in the style sheet. Using an `@import` directive in `ch2external.css` would result in this:

```
@import url(myotherstyles.css)
p {
font: 0.9em Arial;
color: #000;
}
```

Once again the rules in the `@import` style sheet would be hidden from Netscape 4, but the rules in `ch2external.css` would be visible. In the XHTML, there is only the `link` element for `ch2external.css`, which in turn imports the rules from `myotherstyles.css`.

There is a unique drawback to using `@import`, however. If there is no `link` or `script` element referenced in the `head` of a document, the presence of an `@import` directive will create an effect in Internet Explorer 6 known as a *flash of unstyled content (FOUC)*. The effect of FOUC is for the page to display completely unstyled for a brief moment the first time the page is loaded and then redraw itself using the imported style rules. Once the page is in the user's cache, they will not see the FOUC again. This is why the `link` element is the standard choice, with `@import` being used only in cases of specific need, or when a `link` or `script` element is also present.

Embedded styles, such as those you worked on previously, can be added to the `style` element tha includes the `@import` directive. If you include some embedded style rules on an XHTML page that also contains an `@import` directive, the `@import` must come first. For example,

```
<style type="text/css">
@import url(myotherstyles.css);
p {font-size: medium;}
</style>
```

Here, you are importing a style sheet called `myotherstyles.css`, and you are also adding an embedded style for the `p` element. Remember that the imported style sheet can be linked to unlin ited documents, but the embedded style will only affect this particular document.

You can combine `link` elements, `@import` directives, and embedded styles to create a connectio between your XHTML page and any number of style sheets, like this:

```
<link rel="stylesheet" type="text/css" href="mystyles.css" media="screen" />
<link rel="stylesheet" type="text/css" href="printstyle.css" media="print" />
<style type="text/css">
@import url(myotherstyles.css);
p {font-size: medium;}
</style>
```

MEDIA ATTRIBUTES

The `link` element or `@import` rule may contain a `media` attribute. CSS allows you to write styles intended for specific devices, such as screen, print, or handheld devices. Using a `media` attribute allows you to link to one style sheet for screen display and a slightly different one for printers. For example:

```
<link rel="stylesheet" type="text/css" href="mystyles.css" media="screen" />
<link rel="stylesheet" type="text/css" href="printstyle.css" media="print" />
```

All media types are not supported by web browsers yet. The complete list of media types includes `all`, `aural`, `Braille`, `embossed`, `handheld`, `print`, `projection`, `screen`, TTY, TV. Most modern browsers support `all`, `screen`, and `print` at this time. `Projection`, `handheld`, and other media support is growing among all the browser versions, including browsers designed for handhelds and other Internet-capable devices.

You will write a print style sheet in Chapter 6.

In Chapter 3 you will write your own XHTML pages and your own style sheets.

Real-World Scenario

Kineda Magazine: Asian American Entertainment, Pop Culture and Lifestyle at `www.kineda.com` is a con mercial site. It meets all XHTML, CSS, and accessibility standards. This site is an example of a pra tice that is becoming more and more common: using a blog as a main commercial site, rather than as an adjunct to a commercial site. In this case the blog software is Wordpress. The blog provides an RSS feed to allow readers to subscribe to keep alerted to new articles. Blogs will be discussed in more detail in Chapter 13.

The site probably has visitors from all over the world, including users from Asia with Asian character sets on their computers. It provides an example of `UTF-8` character encoding in a `meta` element. There are also `@import` and `link` style sheet links and style sheets for both screen and print.

Here's a code snippet from the Kineda home page `head` element.

```
<meta http-equiv="Content-Type" content="text/html; charset=utf-8" />
<style type="text/css" media="screen">
   @import url( http://www.kineda.com/wp-content/themes/chocolate/style.css );
</style>
<link rel="stylesheet" href="/wp-content/themes/chocolate/css/sIFR-screen.css"
type="text/css" media="screen" />
<link rel="stylesheet" href="/wp-content/themes/chocolate/css/sIFR-print.css"
type="text/css" media="print" />
```

A further advantage gained from the blog interface for this site is that readers can leave comments on the articles. Readers are invited to submit articles, an example of another fast growing trend in the web world: user created content (see Figure 2.9).

The main page has a gallery style layout, with small images and brief descriptions leading the user to articles of interest. When the user selects an article and moves to an inner page on the site, the left column displays a large image, while the right column continues to promote other choices (see Figure 2.10). The layout is created with a header area, a `div` for the main content, and a `div` for the featured content in the smaller side column. A footer sits under it. This easy to use and flexible layout adapts to display the smaller items on the main page or the wider feature articles on the inner pages.

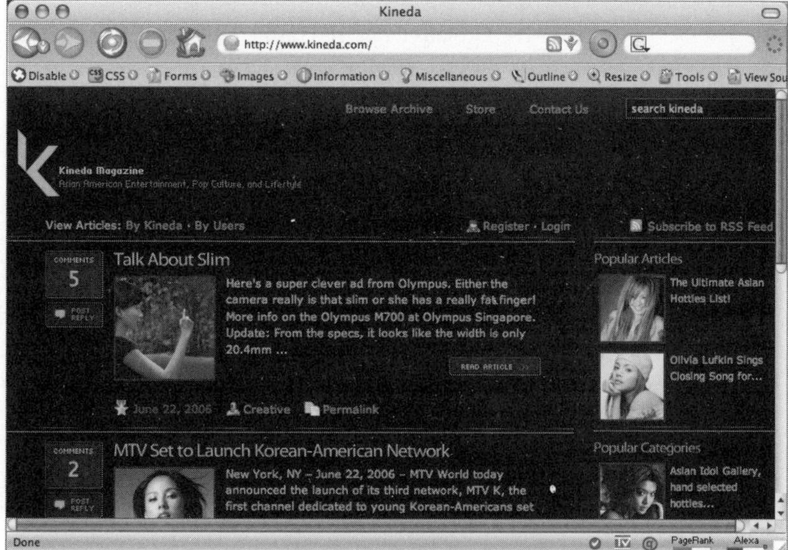

FIGURE 2.9
Kineda Magazine is modern in every sense. This is the home page.

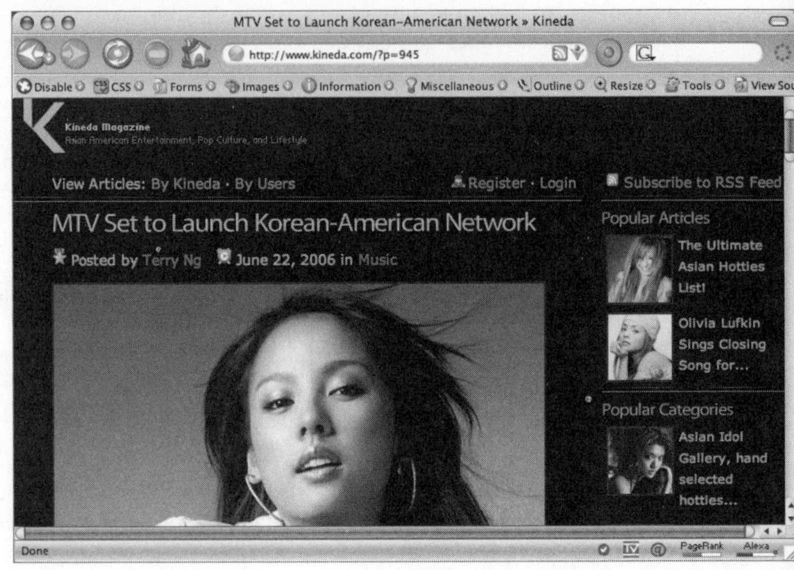

FIGURE 2.10
An inner page from *Kineda Magazine* features a single article and invites reader comment and feedback.

The Bottom Line

Understand and use the cascade to resolve style conflicts. When the browser reads your XHTML page, it reads (or cascades) from top to bottom and external to internal. Assuming there is no user style sheet to consider, the browser first reads the style rules in linked external files. Next, it reads the rules in the embedded `style` element in the document head. Finally, it reads any inline style rules.

Master It Explain what the conflict is in these two styles and describe how the rules of the cascade would resolve the conflict.

```
body {
    font: 1em Verdana, Arial, Helvetica;
}
h1 {
    font-size: 1.8em;
}
```

Understand where styles can be located and how that affects the cascade. Styles cascade from the user agent (such as a browser), the user, and a web author. CSS can be integrated with `link` elements, by `@import` directives, and by styles embedded in the XHTML page itself. If the same element can be selected by two or more rules, then the cascade determines which style will be displayed.

Master It Explain how an external style sheet would be affected by the presence of an embedded style.

Use `link` or `@import` to link to an external style sheet. Style sheets are linked to XHTML documents by either (or both) the `link` element and/or the `@import` directive.

Master It Write XHTML links to one style sheet called `main.css` and to a style sheet called `forms.css`. Use `link` for one and `@import` for the other.

Understand inheritance and know when it applies to a style. XHTML documents are constructed in a hierarchical relationship where elements are descended from antecedent elements. Many properties of the parent element are inherited by the child elements.

Master It Create an outline of a document tree demonstrating the hierarchical relationship of the following elements. An `html` element, containing a `body` element, containing a `div` element, containing an `h1` element.

Understand specificity and use it to your advantage when creating selectors. The W3C has a set of mathematical formulas to determine the weight (or importance) of any particular style rule. Selectors with higher specificity or more weight override styles with less weight.

Master It Calculate the specificity of the following selectors:

```
h1
h2.feature
div h2
#content
```

Chapter 3

Page Basics: DOCTYPE, Head, Body, and Body Styles

When you look at a page on the Web, what you see is everything that's within the body element. But when you create a web page, there are some things you must do, even before you begin writing the content that will appear in the body. Yes, a web page is more than just a beautiful body.

In this chapter, you will learn about DOCTYPE declarations, which are placed on the page before the document head. You will also learn about the document head itself, which must contain the document title and may contain other useful elements, such as links to style sheets.

These, then, are the basics of every page: the DOCTYPE declaration, the `head` element, and the `body` element. In every activity or exercise you do in the remainder of this book, you will begin and end every web page you make with the basic elements we discuss in this chapter.

In this chapter you will:

- Understand the DOCTYPE or DTD.
- Use an appropriate DOCTYPE on your page.
- Write elements in the document head.
- Write CSS for the body of your document.

XHTML: What Every Page Requires

You must take several steps before you write anything that actually appears in the browser window. You can decide on the color, background, and margins for your page even before you put content on it. You saw this in the HTML page on the accompanying CD for Chapter 2, but most of it went unexplained. Now you will be the full details.

The Goal

Listing 3.1 shows the complete first page you will make as it will appear when you are finished. You will build it step-by-step in this chapter, and I will explain each part of the page as we move along. The code in Listing 3.1 is available on the accompanying CD as `listing3-1.html`. When you have completed the following activity, compare your results with Listing 3.1.

LISTING 3.1: A Complete, Valid XHTML Page

```
<!DOCTYPE html PUBLIC "-//W3C//DTD XHTML 1.0 Transitional//EN"
        "http://www.w3.org/TR/2000/REC-xhtml1-20000126/DTD/xhtml1-
transitional.dtd">
<html xmlns="http://www.w3.org/1999/xhtml">
<head>
<title>Chapter 3 Exercises</title>
</head>
<body>
<h1>This is a level one heading</h1>
<p>This is a paragraph element. My English teacher told me a paragraph needed to
have at least three sentences. I think that is optional, not required.</p>
</body>
</html>
```

Every page you create for the exercises in this book will include these elements. You will chang the page title and the contents in the body, of course, but every page will begin and end in this way The highlighted sections of Listing 3.1 could be considered a page template, if you want to save jus that part for reuse later. Notice that the exercises in the book will be using an XHTML 1.0 Transitional DOCTYPE. This chapter is where you finally get the full story on DOCTYPEs.

Let's build a page like Listing 3.1 bit by bit.

DOCTYPEs

The rules for different versions of HTML have been organized into *Document Type Definitions (DTDs* and are declared using a declaration known as the *DOCTYPE declaration.* The DTD sets out the variou elements and attributes that are considered legal for the particular DOCTYPE you are using. You nee to be aware of the different versions of HTML and XHTML, because a Document Type Definition dete mines whether the markup you've written for a page is valid for the document type you've chosen.

If you'd like to download and look at a DTD, there are links at `www.w3.org/TR/xhtml1/#a_dtd_XHTML-1.0-Transitional`. DTDs are not particularly reader friendly. In each chapter of thi book, as you master the XHTML section of the chapter, you are learning the DTD specification.

READING A DTD

In Chapter 1, you learned that the `img` element is an empty element and that an attribute (or `attrs`) and value giving the URL (or URI) of the `src` of the image is required. Another required attribute and value in an `img` element is `alt` text, which is used to describe the image as an alternative source of information for users whose browsers do not display images. In the XHTML Transitional DTD, there are other attributes that are legal (the W3C calls them implied) but not required. Here's how the same information looks in a DTD:

```
<!ELEMENT img EMPTY>
<!ATTLIST img
  %attrs;
```

```
src        %URI;          #REQUIRED
alt        %Text;         #REQUIRED
name       NMTOKEN        #IMPLIED
longdesc   %URI;          #IMPLIED
height     %Length;       #IMPLIED
width      %Length;       #IMPLIED
usemap     %URI;          #IMPLIED
ismap      (ismap)        #IMPLIED
align      %ImgAlign;     #IMPLIED
border     %Length;       #IMPLIED
hspace     %Pixels;       #IMPLIED
vspace     %Pixels;       #IMPLIED
>
```

Again, the XHTML sections in each chapter translate a relevant portion of the DTD into plain English.

Valid simply means that you picked a DTD and wrote your XHTML according to the rules in that DTD. You can write XHTML without declaring a DTD, but in order to claim that your code is valid, there must be a DTD somewhere to check it against.

The theory behind writing valid code is that browsers know the same rules. If you use the standard rules and the browsers use the standard rules, then everything should work the way you intend when you design a page. Reality doesn't match this theory perfectly yet, but the latest versions of the browsers are much closer to a dependable use of standards than they were during the nightmare years of web design when the browser makers were striving for leadership by creating techniques that only worked in their particular brand of browser. (When Internet Explorer 7 is released, many of the buggy behaviors of previous versions of that browser will be gone, bringing the most common browser in use closer to standards-compliance.)

Many repositories of DTDs exist, but the World Wide Web Consortium (W3C), found at `www.w3.org`, holds the one you are most interested in. In addition to creating and keeping track of the various versions of HTML and XHTML, the W3C provides a service that lets you check your code with a validator at `http://validator.w3.org`. If you downloaded the Mozilla Firefox browser with the Web Developer add-on, as I suggested in Chapter 1, you have handy tools to check the validity of your code, based on the DTD you are using.

There are three possible DOCTYPE declarations for both HTML and XHTML: *strict*, *transitional*, and *frameset*.

These are the three DOCTYPE declarations for XHTML:

◆ Strict

```
<!DOCTYPE html PUBLIC "-//W3C//DTD XHTML 1.0 Strict//EN"
   "http://www.w3.org/TR/xhtml1/DTD/ xhtml1-strict.dtd">
```

◆ Transitional

```
<!DOCTYPE html PUBLIC "-//W3C//DTD XHTML 1.0 Transitional//EN"
   "http://www.w3.org/TR/xhtml1/DTD/xhtml1-transitional.dtd">
```

◆ Frameset

```
<!DOCTYPE html PUBLIC "-//W3C//DTD XHTML 1.0 Frameset//EN"
   "http://www.w3.org/TR/xhtml1/DTD/xhtml1-frameset.dtd">
```

The three possible DOCTYPE declarations for HTML are

◆ Strict

```
<!DOCTYPE html PUBLIC "-//W3C//DTD HTML 4.01//EN"
   "http://www.w3.org/TR/html4/strict.dtd">
```

◆ Transitional

```
<!DOCTYPE html PUBLIC "-//W3C//DTD HTML 4.01 Transitional//EN"
   "http://www.w3.org/TR/html4/loose.dtd">
```

◆ Frameset

```
<!DOCTYPE html PUBLIC "-//W3C//DTD HTML 4.01 Frameset//EN"
   "http://www.w3.org/TR/html4/frameset.dtd">
```

To write valid HTML or XHTML, you pick one of these DTDs and declare it at the beginning o your page. Then make sure you follow the rules for that DOCTYPE by running your page throug a validator after you finish writing it. The validator reports errors line by line so you can find an correct them.

Let's dissect an XHTML DOCTYPE piece by piece to see what it is saying. The first part simpl means that you are declaring the DTD for your document, which is going to be written in XHTMI and this DTD is available to the public. Next you state that the DTD you are declaring is locate at the W3C, is a particular DTD for XHTML, and is written in English. Finally, you give the URI for the particular DTD you picked.

Using a strict DTD means that the only elements and attributes available are those for structur not presentation. With a transitional DTD, some presentation elements and attributes that are n longer part of the XHTML specification can be used. A frameset DTD is used for the frameset do ument when using frames.

There won't be any framesets used in this book. CSS renders it unnecessary, and framed doc ments are not easily accessible.

Nor will any of the exercises in the book use HTML 4.01, although it's a good choice for creatin web pages and should not be ruled out as a valuable specification merely because the exercises he are in XHTML.

I've mentioned that in a transitional DTD, some elements and attributes that are no longer pa of the specifications can be used successfully. Such elements are described as *deprecated*. The W3 states that deprecated elements or attributes are those that have been replaced by newer construct Deprecated elements may become obsolete in future versions of XHTML. Using a transitional DT gives you the option of using presentational elements and attributes, since they do come in hand in certain situations. Many web designers who have achieved mastery level use a strict DOCTYP they do not depend on any presentational attributes in their XHTML. All the presentation rules a in the CSS.

Although the examples in this book use a transitional DTD, they generally would validate as strict, except for an occasional example that I include for complete coverage of a topic. I chose to us a transitional DTD on the example pages for that reason.

The attribute `align="right"` that was used with a `p` element in Chapter 1 is an example of a deprecated attribute. The recommended method of achieving text alignment now is with CSS (for example, `text-align: right;`). With a transitional DTD, presentational attributes such as `align="right"` can still be used in the XHTML. In a strict DTD, the attribute would not validate.

If you're striving for the clearest separation of content from presentation, a strict DOCTYPE is the best choice. When a page validates as either strict HTML or XHTML, the web author can be assured that the code is reliable, accessible, usable, and transferable. A validated transitional document meets standards but may be less reliable when rendered on devices other than a computer monitor.

All disclaimers aside, the DTD in Listing 3.1, and the one we will use for all remaining examples, is

```
<!DOCTYPE html PUBLIC "-//W3C//DTD XHTML 1.0 Transitional//EN"
   "http://www.w3.org/TR/xhtml1/DTD/xhtml1-transitional.dtd">
```

QUIRKS

Older web pages may have no DOCTYPE. Some content management tools in use today do not generate a DOCTYPE. It's possible to construct an HTML page with nothing more than this skeleton:

```
<html>
<head></head>
<body></body>
</html>
```

If you use View Source in your browser to see how other people put web pages together, you will see examples of this practice. It is not good practice, however, because of something known as *quirks mode*.

Using any DOCTYPE declaration ensures that a browser will render the page in a rendering mode that follows the W3C specifications as closely as possible. This is referred to as *standards mode*. If an incomplete DOCTYPE declaration is used, or if no DOCTYPE declaration is present at all, the browser uses a rendering mode referred to as quirks mode. The fact that a browser might switch from one rendering mode to another depending on the document's DOCTYPE declaration is known as *DOCTYPE switching*. In quirks mode, a browser uses whatever out-of-date, incorrect, or proprietary features it knows to render your page. This means that appearance may vary widely from one browser to another if your page is rendered in quirks mode.

Craig Saila has more information about DOCTYPES and quirks mode at `www.saila.com/usage/tips/defn.shtml?doctype`.

The XML Declaration

If you're using XHTML, the W3C suggests that you include an XML declaration before your DOCTYPE declaration. An XML declaration looks like this:

```
<?xml version="1.0" encoding="utf-8"?>
```

It tells the browser that a version of XML follows, and that the character encoding is UTF-8. (UTF-8 is Unicode, a universal character set that includes character sets for every language plus math characters and other symbols that might appear on a web page.)

Further, the W3C suggests that you combine the opening `html` element with the XML namespace (`xmlns`) after your DOCTYPE declaration. (A *namespace* is rather like an address; it tells where something is located.) The XML namespace gives the URL of the specifications on the W3C site and looks like this:

```
xmlns="http://www.w3.org/1999/xhtml"
```

The complete lines as recommended by the W3C look like this:

```
<?xml version="1.0" encoding="utf-8"?>
<!DOCTYPE html PUBLIC "-//W3C//DTD XHTML 1.0 Transitional//EN"
   "http://www.w3.org/TR/xhtml1/DTD/xhtml1-transitional.dtd">
<html xmlns="http://www.w3.org/1999/xhtml">
```

However, this is one of those situations where theory and reality bump heads. In this book, you are going to do only part of what the W3C suggests because the XML declaration causes an unexpected problem in Internet Explorer 6 and earlier on Windows: IE 6 goes into quirks mode when the XML prolog is present. IE 5 is always in quirks mode. To ensure that IE 6 follows the standard rules set up in the W3C specifications—standards mode—simply leave out the XML declaration. According to XML specifications, the XML declaration is optional, so I don't use it in the examples in this book. The next Internet Explorer, version 7, will render in standards mode even with the XML declaration as part of the DOCTYPE. Using the XML declaration may eventually become standard practice for XHTML DTDs.

You do need to include the opening `html` tag and XML namespace, however; that is, include this line

```
<html xmlns="http://www.w3.org/1999/xhtml">
```

HTML is not a version of XML, so there is never a question of an XML declaration in any HTML DTD.

CONTENT TYPES

There are four possible content types (also called media type or mime type) an XHTML documents can be labeled:

```
'text/html'
'application/xhtml+xml'
'application/xml'
'text/xml'
```

The mime type may be set on the server, or it may be inserted in an XML declaration. In this book, we are not including an XML declaration, for the reasons I explained. If desired, a web author can use a `meta http-equiv` statement, like this:

```
<meta http-equiv="Content-Type" content="text/html; charset=ISO-8859-1" />
```

in the document head. This would only be needed in situations where the server was not set up to do this automatically, or where you needed a different character set than the one used by the server.

If you use `content="text/html"` your document will be compatible with HTML 4.01, but this is not suitable for any XHTML that adds elements and attributes from foreign namespaces, such as XHTML+MathML.

The `'application/xhtml+xml'` media type is used to serve XHTML to XHTML user agents when certain XML functions are required.

Any XHTML document may be served as 'application/xml'. However, such a document may not always be processed as XHTML.

The 'text/xml' media type is a generic media type for XML documents. This would not be compatible with HTML rendering devices.

The XHTML you are learning in this book is compatible with HTML and can be served as text/html so that it can be displayed by all current browsers, even ones like Internet Explorer 6 and lower, which cannot display XHTML when it is served properly as application/xhtml+xml.

Let's Get Started

Now that you know what DOCTYPE declaration you will be using, you are ready to start typing. Open a text editor such as Notepad, Simple Text, Text Edit, or any other plain text editor. Type the DOCTYPE declaration and the opening html tag:

```
<!DOCTYPE html PUBLIC "-//W3C//DTD XHTML 1.0 Transitional//EN"
   "http://www.w3.org/TR/xhtml1/DTD/xhtml1-transitional.dtd">
<html xmlns="http://www.w3.org/1999/xhtml">
```

There are some free or very inexpensive text editors designed to help you write XHTML easily. They use color coding and indenting to help make your HTML more readable. Several are provided on the CD. You can also find many at www.tucows.com, including such popular choices as the Coffee Cup HTML Editor, Edit PLUS, Text Wrangler, and Ultra Edit.

DECLARING A LANGUAGE FOR THE CONTENT OF THE PAGE

The primary language for a web page can be set in several places. If you need to, you can add it to the opening html tag. With XHTML being served as the content type text/html, you redundantly declare the language twice. The first (lang="en") serves when the page is treated as HTML. The second (xml:lang="en") serves when the page is treated as XML. Here's how it looks:

```
<html lang="en" xml:lang="en" xmlns="http://www.w3.org/1999/xhtml">
```

Often the language is declared on the server. The method just described is the best choice for XHTML, if a language declaration is needed.

Sometimes you see documents that declare a language in a meta element in the document head. My recommendation is to declare the page's primary language in the html tag, as just described.

For identifying phrases in languages that differ from the main language declared in the html element, you can add an inline language attribute, like this:

```
<p>The French for <em>hat</em> is <em lang="fr">chapeau</em>.</p>
```

For a quick summary of Best Practices for Declaring Languages in HTML and XHTML see this article at www.webstandards.org/2005/09/04/best-practices-for-declaring-languages-in-html-and-xhtml.

The Head

Immediately after the DOCTYPE declaration and the opening `html` tag is the document `head`. Th `head` may contain many things including JavaScript, links to style sheets, and information about th document itself such as the document title. The only thing *required* in the head is the `title`.

Type **<head>**, leave a couple of blank lines and type **</head>** to open and close the `head` elemen With these additions, you should have:

```
<!DOCTYPE html PUBLIC "-//W3C//DTD XHTML 1.0 Transitional//EN"
   "http://www.w3.org/TR/xhtml1/DTD/xhtml1-transitional.dtd">
<html xmlns="http://www.w3.org/1999/xhtml">
<head>

</head>
```

The Title

The `title` element goes inside the head. After the opening `head` tag, but before the closing `head` tag, type **`<title>Chapter 3 Exercises</title>`**. The head now looks like this:

```
<head>
<title>Chapter 3 Exercises</title>
</head>
```

The title must contain only text and character entities. (I will explain character entities in Cha ter 6.) You may not use any XHTML in the title; for example, you cannot specify italics or color.

So far you haven't typed anything that will appear in the browser window when you look at your page. The content of the head does not appear in the browser window, although the title doe appear in the title bar at the top of the browser.

Even though the title does not appear on the browser page, a good title is incredibly importa to your page's success. There are three reasons why titles are so important.

1. The title is what is saved when a person adds your page to their Favorites or Bookmarks lis
2. Search engines use the titles when they are indexing and cataloging the millions of web page they search. Assume you have a craft site called Homemade Crafts and one of your pages tel how to make homemade play dough. Also assume there is a mom out there frantically searc ing for a recipe for homemade play dough for her three kids who have been inside all day o a rainy day. If your page has a title like Homemade Crafts: How to Make Play Dough, that frantic mom will probably find it at the top of her search results. A good title results in succes for you and for the mom in a hurry.
3. A good title helps the user know exactly where they are when the page opens. A page titl such as Homemade Crafts: How to Make Play Dough tells the user the name of the site an the name of the specific page within the site, two helpful orientation facts.

SEARCH ENGINE RESOURCES

For more information about search engines and how to place well in search engine rankings, see Search Engine Watch at `searchenginewatch.com`, High Rankings at `www.highrankings.com` or Google's Webmaster Help Center at `www.google.com/support/webmasters`.

Saving

This is a good time to save your work. If you haven't already, make a new folder on your hard drive called `Mastering Integrated HTML and CSS`. Save everything you do in this book to that folder. When you save XHTML (or CSS) pages, the filenames you use should not have any spaces. Using all lowercase letters for filenames is preferred but not required. Save your document with an explanatory name like `ch3practice.html`. If you are not in the habit of typing the file extension (the `.html` in this case), you need to remember to type it when you save XHTML pages.

If your computer automatically adds a `.txt` file extension to your XHTML pages, you need to remove it so it will display properly in a browser.

Even though this is XHTML, the file extension when saving pages is `.html`. The root element in any XHTML page is actually `html` and it is saved as such. (There is an `.xhtml` file extension, but it is not used yet because of lack of browser support.)

You may have noticed web pages with the file extension `.htm`. This works too, and you can use it if you want. Just be consistent about whether you use `.htm` or `.html` so you don't end up with mistakes and broken links due to inconsistent filename extensions.

As you travel the Internet, you may see web pages that have other filename extensions such as `.asp` and `.php`. This generally means that a scripting language, such as ASP (Active Server Pages), has been used to generate an HTML document.

SHOW FILE EXTENSIONS

If your computer is set not to show file extensions in Windows Explorer or Finder views, change the setting to show file extensions. Often in this book, the CSS and HTML files have similar names. For example, an exercise might use a document named `exercise.html` with a document named `exercise.css`. It is easier to distinguish the one you want when the file extensions are shown.

The Body

The content of the body is what appears in the browser window. After the closing `head` tag, type **<body>**. Skip a line and type **</body>**. When the body ends, the page ends, so you also need to add a closing `html` tag.

```
</head>
<body>

</body>
</html>
```

Are you wondering where the opening `html` tag was? The `html` began at the very top of the page as part of your opening element. It was

```
<html xmlns="http://www.w3.org/1999/xhtml">
```

This element contained the opening `html` tag and the XML namespace. Everything on the page is contained within that opening `html` tag and the closing `html` tag at the end of the page. Thus, as I mentioned, `html` is the root element of any XHTML page.

Now it's time to put a bit of text in the body so there will be something to see on the page when you do the following exercises. Type this or something similar of your own choosing following after the opening body tag.

```
<body>
<h1>This is a level one heading</h1>
<p>This is a paragraph element. My English teacher told me a paragraph needed to
have at least three sentences. I think that is optional, not required.</p>
</body>
```

Take a Look in a Browser

It is time for the magical moment known as a "browser check." Make sure the latest version of `ch3practice.html` has been saved. Open your browser of choice. Under the File menu there will be a command such as Open File that will allow you to browse through your hard drive to the `Mastering Integrated HTML and CSS` folder and open the page `ch3practice.html`.

You should see something similar to Figure 3.1 in the browser.

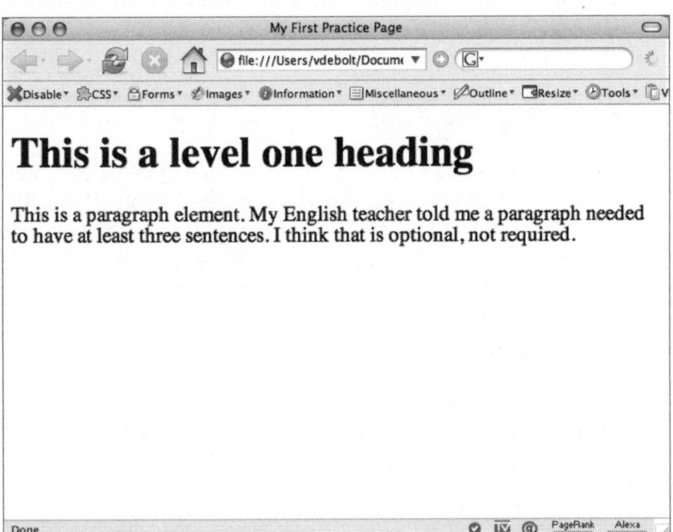

FIGURE 3.1
The XHTML page before any CSS is added

CSS: A Stylish Body

You have a real web page finished. Granted, it isn't very impressive yet, but it does have an element that must be styled for every page you write in the future. That element is the body. Every page has a body, every body needs a style. It seems a fitting element to use to begin working with CSS.

As with every element in HTML, there are an array of choices with CSS for the body element. In this chapter, you will learn about background color and background image options for the body

You will also learn about setting margins for the body. What you learn about backgrounds and margins will serve you throughout the rest of this book, because CSS can determine background colors, background images, and margins for any XHTML element!

As you proceed through the book, you can build on what you learn about margins, background colors, and background images by applying such styles to other elements in addition to the `body` element.

Create the Style Sheet

Start with an external style sheet. This gives you the flexibility to link the style sheet to more than one XHTML page.

Open a new blank document in your text editor. Leave your `ch3practice.html` page open, too, because you need to work on both pages. Type **body** on the first line. Type the opening and closing curly braces now, as well.

```
body {
}
```

That is all you need to begin a style sheet—nothing but the beginnings of a style rule. You don't need DOCTYPEs or opening and closing tags: just the style rule. Save the page. Give it the filename `ch3practice.css` and save it in the folder you made called `Mastering Integrated HTML and CSS`. Each time you make a change to the style sheet, save it again.

The Background

First, you will add a background color to the page. On a new line after the opening curly brace, type **`background-color: #9CC;`**. This is a light blue color (the next section explains the notation). Feel free to use some other color if you don't want to use light blue. Pick a light color because your text is going to be the default black and you want to be able to read it.

```
body {
background-color: #9CC;
}
```

You made a change, so save the CSS page. Before you do any more with the CSS for the `body`, let's make a brief tour through color codes.

Specifying Colors for Web Pages

Devices displaying web pages create colors by mixing various combinations of red, green, and blue, or *RGB colors*. There are three ways to indicate exactly how much of each component is in a color. With 8 bits per RGB channel, there are 256 possible levels of each color, and in HTML this value can be expressed as a hexadecimal or decimal number, or as a percentage. The most commonly used format is hexadecimal (base-16) notation, which expresses color values with numerals (0–9) and letters (A–F) such as #FF3366 (a shade of pink) or #A1A1A1 (a shade of gray). The opening hash mark is required with hexadecimal color notation. The first two characters (FF) represent the red, the middle two (33) the green, and the last two (66) the blue. If all three components are the same, the color is black (#000000), white (#FFFFFF), or a shade of gray (as in #A1A1A1).

When a hexadecimal number has three pairs of matched letters or numbers for the RGB values the color can be expressed in shorthand by using just one character each; #FF3366 is the same as #F36. However, in #A1A1A1, where there are no matching pairs, the value cannot be expressed in shorthand.

What About Web-Safe Color?

A color value created with any combination of pairs of 00, 33, 66, 99, CC, or FF is considered a *web-safe color*. Some examples are #003399 (a dark purple), #CCFF99 (a light green), and #FF0000 (red). Most computer monitors can display millions of colors, but only 216 colors are labeled web safe, which means that they should display in a similar shade on any device, platform, or operating system. Because the color #A1A1A1 is not any combination of the pairs I just mentioned, it is not considered a web-safe color. At one time it was considered important to stick with web-safe colors, but that is no longer necessary. Most computer monitors display millions of colors and designers no longer feel bound by the limitations of the web-safe color palette.

The second method of expressing RGB values is with percentages. In this method, instead of giving a code for the amount of red, green, or blue, you give a percentage for how much red, green or blue is needed in a color. In a style rule it would look like this: `color: rgb(100%,100%,100%);` (the value for white). As you would expect with percentages, values can range between 0 percent and 100 percent.

The third way to express color values is the numeric form using numbers between 0 and 255. A rule in a style sheet would look like this:

```
color: rgb(255,255,255);
```

(the value for white).

Whether you use any of the following CSS rules:

```
color: #FFF;
color: #FFFFFF;
color: rgb(100%,100%,100%);
color: rgb(255,255,255);
```

you end up with white.

You may recall some examples in Chapters 1 and 2 that expressed colors by name. There are 16 color names that are considered *predefined colors* and can be declared by name. These include colors such as white, black, red, blue, green, gray, purple, teal, and aqua. In a style rule they would be used like this:

```
color: white;
```

Most of the time this book will use hexadecimal notation, but don't be afraid to try out the other types of color notation on your own.

Helpful color resources include the following websites:

- Colors on the Web:

  `www.colorsontheweb.com/`

- Developer Zone's Color Chooser:

  `http://archive.devx.com/projectcool/developer/reference/color-chart.html`

- Lynda.com:

  `www.lynda.com/hex.html`

- Color Schemer Online:

  `www.colorschemer.com/online.html`

These websites have various resources including the web-safe color charts, many additional colors that are not considered web safe, color scheme choosers for sets of several colors, and other helpful information about color.

On the accompanying CD, the Visibone company (`www.visibone.com`) has provided pop-up color charts that you can keep handy on your desktop. These pop-ups provide codes for the web-safe colors.

Link to the Style Sheet

On the page of XHTML, `ch3practice.html`, add a link to connect your new style sheet to the XHTML page. The link to the style sheet goes in the head. Type this:

```
<link href="ch3practice.css" rel="stylesheet" type="text/css" />
```

anywhere after the opening `head` tag but before the closing `head` tag, like this:

```
<head>
<title>My First Practice Page</title>
<link href="ch3practice.css" rel="stylesheet" type="text/css" />
</head>
```

Take a closer look at that `link` element. The `link` element links the style sheet to this XHTML page. You can use the same `link` element on other XHTML pages and they will be linked to the same style sheet. A change in the style sheet will be instantly reflected on any page that contains a link to it.

The `href` attribute gives the hypertext reference (`href`) to the filename and location of the style sheet you linked. The `rel` stands for relation: in this case, the linked document is a style sheet for the linking document. The `type` expresses the type of data to be loaded, which is a text file of CSS rules.

Take a Look

Time for another browser check. Make sure the latest version of both the `ch3practice.html` and the `ch3practice.css` are saved. In the browser, click Refresh (Reload) and the changed page will be displayed by the browser. You should see something similar to Figure 3.2. Your display will be in color, of course, not grayscale.

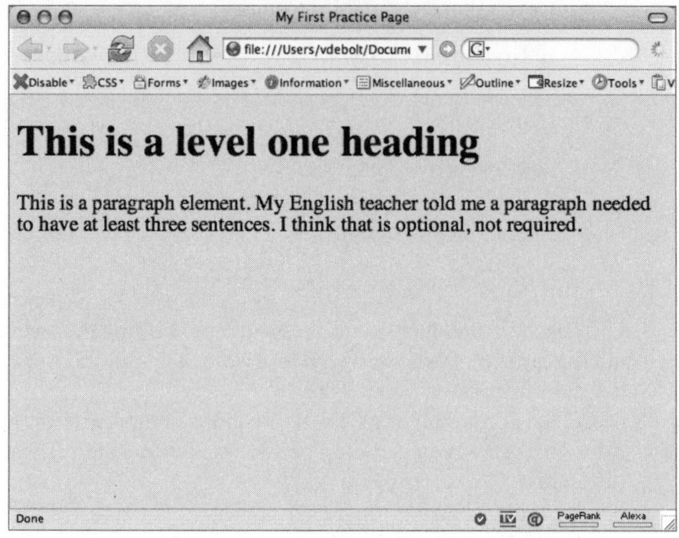

FIGURE 3.2
Reloading the page in the browser shows changes you have saved.

The Margins

Notice that the text in the body of your document is offset a few pixels from the top and the left of th browser window. That is because there is a default browser margin for the body element. You can increase or decrease that margin on the top, right, bottom, or left sides of the body with a style rul

Leave this page open in the browser. Switch back to your text editor and open the `ch3practice.css` page.

A couple of experiments and exercises with margins will get you moving on body styles. First, se the top and the left margin to 0. On the page `ch3practice.css`, type **`margin-top: 0;`** within the curly braces of the body rule. Press Return (Enter) and type **`margin-left: 0;`**. With these change this is the body rule.

```
body {
background-color: #9CC;
margin-top: 0;
margin-left: 0;
}
```

Save the style sheet. Switch back to the browser. Your page has not changed, but the style rul for how it will be displayed has changed. To see that change, click Refresh (Reload) and you wil see the effect of the 0 margin rule, as in Figure 3.3. (To fully see the effect of `margin-top: 0;` in al browsers, it would be a good exercise for you to set the padding for the body element to 0 as wel You can clearly see the influence of some default `padding-top` above the heading in Figure 3.3.)

At this point, that text looks pretty crowded where it is. Maybe leaving margins wasn't such bad idea after all.

MARGIN, PADDING, AND BORDER SYNTAX

When listing `margin` values in a style sheet, begin at the top, then give the right, bottom, and left sides in clockwise order. If you don't specifically mention a `margin` value, it remains at its default setting. CSS rules for giving values for `padding` and `border` also follow this practice of listing values for top, right, bottom, and left sides of an element in clockwise order.

You can list all four margins explicitly as in:

```
body {
margin-top: 0px;
margin-right: 0px;
margin-bottom: 0px;
margin-left: 0px;
}
```

The same rule in shorthand is

```
body {
margin: 0px;
}
```

This shorthand sets all four margins at 0px. You may not want all the margins to have the same value. You can set each individually. You can also use a mixture of measurement types. For example:

```
body {
margin-top: 0px;
margin-right: 15%;
margin-bottom; 1em;
margin-left: 0px;
}
```

In shorthand, if you want the top and bottom margin to be the same, you can express it with one value, and the same left and right margins can be set with a second value:

```
body {
margin: 5px 10px;
}
```

Using shorthand makes your CSS documents smaller in size, saving download time and bandwidth charges.

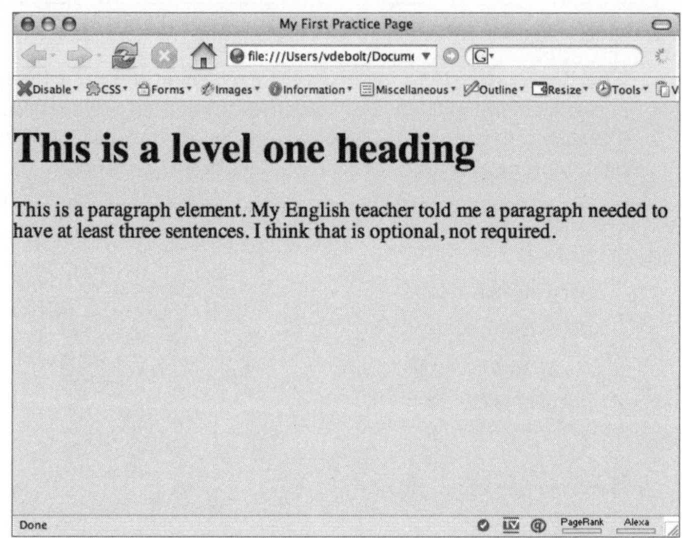

FIGURE 3.3
Your page with top and left margins set to 0. The default margin and line height on the heading element is preventing it from hugging the top of the browser viewport in the same manner that the text is hugging the left edge of the browser. You will learn more about working with headings in Chapter 4.

HOW FAR IS THAT?

A computer screen displays tiny dots of colored light arranged in a grid. Dots in this grid are called *pixels (px)*. Any spot on the screen can be mapped by figuring out how many pixels that spot is from the left and from the top. The measurements stating distance from the left and the top are referred to, respectively, as the *x-* and *y-coordinates*, a concept you may recall from math class. The x-coordinates run from left to right horizontally across the screen; the y-coordinates run from top to bottom vertically down the screen.

You just set the body exactly 0 pixels from the left and 0 pixels from the top margin. At the common screen resolution, 800600, an inch is about 72 pixels. Normally, inches are not used at all in web measurement, but that familiar measurement does give you some idea of the space that an element measuring 72 pixels in width might occupy.

Margins can be set with percentages, ems, pixels, the keyword `auto`, or various combinations of these values used together. When you set a value other than zero, you always have to specify the unit after the value so the browser knows which measurement you are trying to use.

Move Your Body

Give the scrunched up text some surrounding whitespace by changing the margin rule in your style sheet. Change the `margin-top` to 10% and the `margin-left` to 15%. Save the style sheet and refresh the browser page to see the change.

```
body {
background-color: #9CC;
margin-top: 10%;
margin-left: 15%;
}
```

Your body content should now be placed something like Figure 3.4. The background color covers the entire viewport, not just the body.

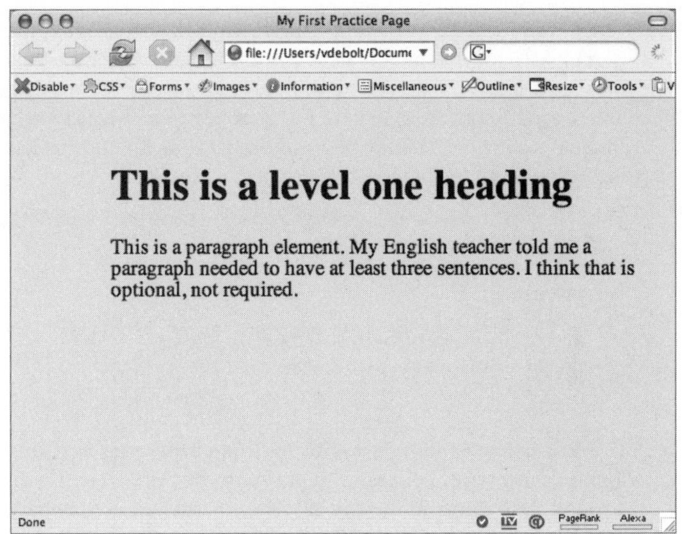

FIGURE 3.4
The body is now 10 percent from the top and 15 percent from the left. Notice that the background color covers the entire viewport.

Color Isn't Everything

In addition to solid colors, images can also be used as backgrounds. Background images can be used with any element, including body, paragraphs, headings, divisions, and tables. Background images can be fixed in place, repeated on one or both axes, given a set horizontal or vertical position, and even changed to something different when the element is in the hover state. Many of the exciting and beautiful designs you see based on CSS take excellent advantage of the ability to use background images to achieve stunning visual effects.

Before CSS, the only elements that could have background images were the `body` and the `table` elements. With CSS, anything can have a background color and/or background image.

To see how this works, you'll add a background image to your practice page. In the Chapter 3 folder on the CD accompanying this book, find the file `ch3bg_sm.gif`. The GIF is a small stylized star (or snowflake) image that you can place in various ways to learn about background rules. Copy it to the same folder on your computer in which you are saving the `ch3practice.html` file.

Even with a background image in the `body`, it is a good practice to give the background a color as well. So keep the blue background color and add this graphic to the page as a background image. The image is a GIF with a transparent background, which allows the blue background of the body to shine through.

GRAPHICS AND THE PNG DILEMMA

Graphics on the Web are generally in GIF, JPEG, or PNG format. JPEG is often used for images and photographs with thousands of colors. The GIF format is often used for buttons and other images with fewer colors.

Only GIF and PNG files can have transparent backgrounds. Using certain types of transparency in PNG files is not supported in Internet Explorer 6 and older for Windows, so PNG files were not widely used until recently. PNG transparency is supported in IE 7, however. Both backgrounds and images should begin to appear in PNG format more often. PNG has more versatile options for transparency than GIF. Many people consider PNG the better choice, so the problems with implementation in IE have been a source of frustration for several years.

There are all sorts of workarounds and scripts that have been created to try to deal with the lack of support for PNG transparency in IE 6/Win and older. Two methods using a proprietary Microsoft preloader or a JavaScript are described in "Cross-Browser Variable Opacity with PNG: A Real Solution" at `www.alistapart.com/articles/pngopacity`. Others have come up with workarounds using conditional comments, another Microsoft-specific technique that lets you serve up various styles for different browsers.

The solution I find cleanest uses the `!important` hack and both a transparent GIF and a transparent PNG. Here's some example CSS:

```
body {
background: url(myimage.png) no-repeat right top !important;
background: url(myimage.gif) no-repeat right top;
}
```

IE 6 and below cannot deal with multiple properties in a single rule. It ignores the first rule and applies the last one, disregarding the `!important` effect on the cascade. Other browsers honor the `!important` rule and display the PNG. There is the drawback of having to prepare two different image formats of a similar image, but, to my mind, the lack of any other needed workaround or script is a big plus for this method.

The syntax for the location of the background image is given as `url(`*`filename`*`);`. Instructions for the `background-repeat` property are set to `repeat` to make the image repeat over and over both across and down the page (the default behavior if you don't set the background-repeat property at all). Type the following for the complete background-image rule:

```
background-image: url(ch3bg_sm.gif);
background-repeat: repeat;
```

Your CSS document should look like this:

```
body {
background-color: #9CC;
background-image: url(ch3bg_sm.gif);
background-repeat: repeat;
margin-top: 10px;
margin-left: 15px;
}
```

Save the style sheet and then switch to the browser and Refresh (Reload) the page to see what happens. You should see something similar to Figure 3.5.

The preceding background declarations can be combined using CSS shorthand to just

```
background: #9CC url(ch3bg_sm.gif) repeat;.
```

When using CSS shorthand, the `background` property can have the following values, in any order: `background-color`, `background-image`, `background-repeat`, `background-attachment`, `background-position`. You will have an opportunity to try out each of these background properties as you proceed through the book.

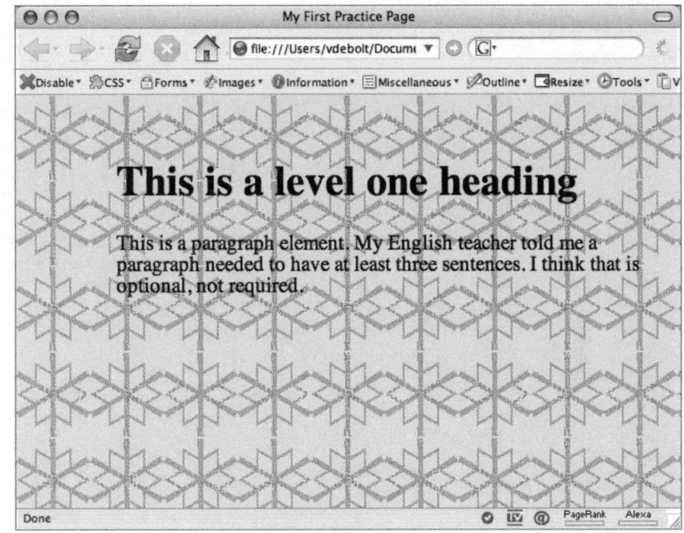

FIGURE 3.5
The page with a repeating background image. Notice that the image repeats across the entire viewport, not just the area occupied by the body.

Using the same image, change the style so that the background image repeats only on the x-axis (or across).

```
body {
background-color: #9CC;
background-image: url(ch3bg_sm.gif);
background-repeat: repeat-x;
margin-top: 10%;
margin-left: 15%;
}
```

As you can see in Figure 3.6, the background image repeats across the x-axis for only one row.

With keywords such as `left`, `center`, `right` or values such as percentages, pixels, or ems, you can use background images in even more ways. For example, to make the background image appear in the center of the page, add `background-position: center;` to your rule. This will cause the background image to repeat on the x-axis with the center of the image aligned with the center of the originating position (in this case, the body). See Figure 3.7.

```
body {
background-color: #9CC;
background-image: url(ch3bg_sm.gif);
background-repeat: repeat-x;
background-position: center;
margin-top: 10%;
margin-left: 15%;
}
```

Test carefully in a number of different browsers when setting the background image to a center position to make sure you like the results. Browsers differ on their interpretation of whether the body stretches to the bottom of the viewport or only fills the space occupied by the content of the body element.

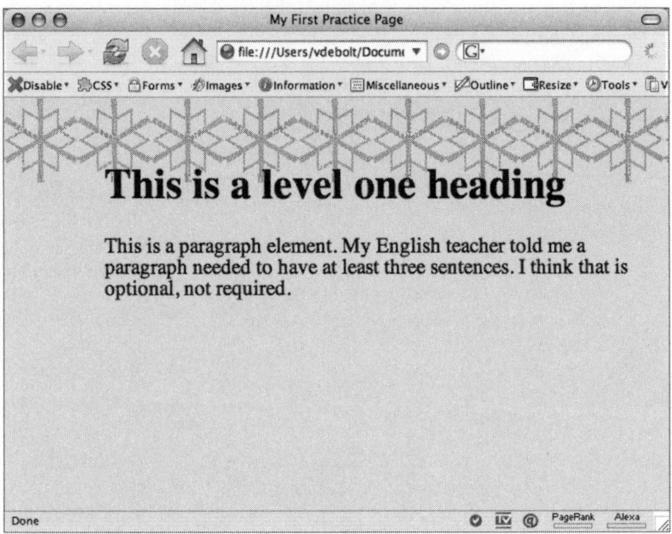

FIGURE 3.6
The background image set to `repeat-x`

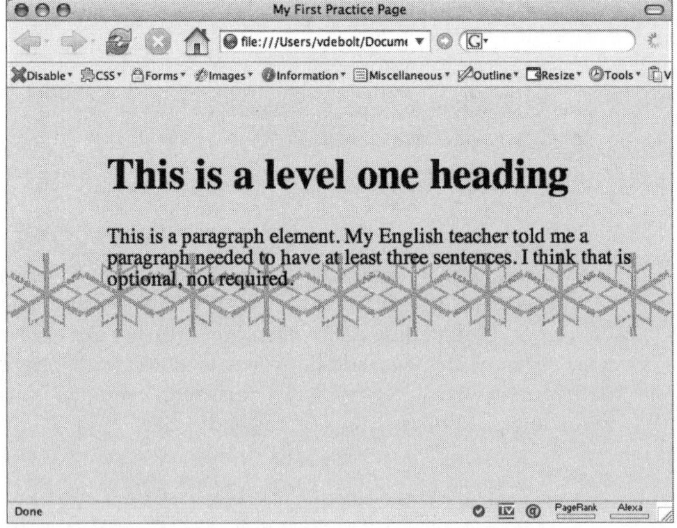

FIGURE 3.7
The Firefox browser's interpretation of background-image repeated on the x-axis, with the position set to center. The background image may appear in a different "center" in IE or Safari.

Keywords for background-position are `top`, `bottom`, `left`, `right`, and `center`. You can positio a background image on both the x- and y-axes with two values such as `background-position: top left;`. The first value is the x-axis location, the second is the y-axis location. You cannot mi keywords and values; for example, you cannot use `background-position: top 30%;`.

Pixels, ems, and percentage measurement can be used for `background-position`. If you use one percentage value it will apply to both the x- and y-axes. If you use two percentage values, the first will apply to the x-axis position, and the second will apply to the y-axis position. In the following example, the background position is set to 100 percent of the x-axis (which is the same as using the keyword `right`) and 50 percent of the y-axis (which is the same as using the keyword `center`). To distinguish this from the example in Figure 3.7, change the `background-repeat` to `no-repeat`.

```
body {
background-color: #9CC;
background-image: url(ch3bg_sm.gif);
background-repeat: no-repeat;
background-position: 100% 50%;
margin-top: 10%;
margin-left: 15%;
}
```

This style would look like Figure 3.8 in the browser. Of course, you can use any percent value you need, such as 21% or 83%, to achieve a particular appearance when placing background images. The only percentage values that correlate with keywords are 0%, 50%, and 100%. Once again there is a difference of opinion among browsers as to whether 100% represents 100% of the viewport or 100% of the space occupied by the element's content block. Test this placement in numerous browsers before you use it to be sure the results are satisfactory.

If you express length in pixels or ems, one value applies to both x- and y-axes, and two values apply to first the x-axis and then the y-axis.

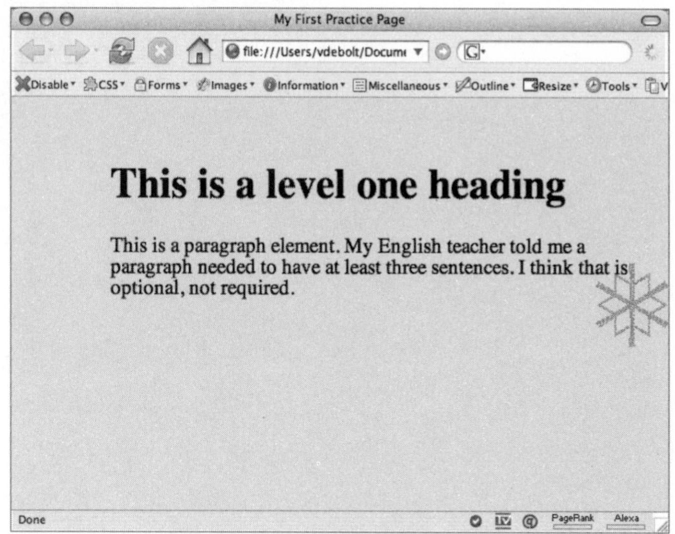

FIGURE 3.8 The Firefox browser's interpretation of `background-position: 100% 50%;` with no-repeat creates this effect.

One more example with the `ch3bg_sm.gif` should cement your understanding of placement of background images. Change the background position to 0% (which is the same as the keyword `left`) and 100% (which is the same as the keyword `bottom`). The result should look like Figure 3.9. Again, you are dealing with the issue of browser interpretation of `botto` or 100%, so your browser may not show the image placed in exactly the same position as Figure 3.9 shows it.

```
body {
background-color: #9CC;
background-image: url(ch3bg_sm.gif);
background-repeat: no-repeat;
background-position: 0% 100%;
margin-top: 10%;
margin-left: 15%;
}
```

Figure 3.10 summarizes the various `background-image` rules we've used .

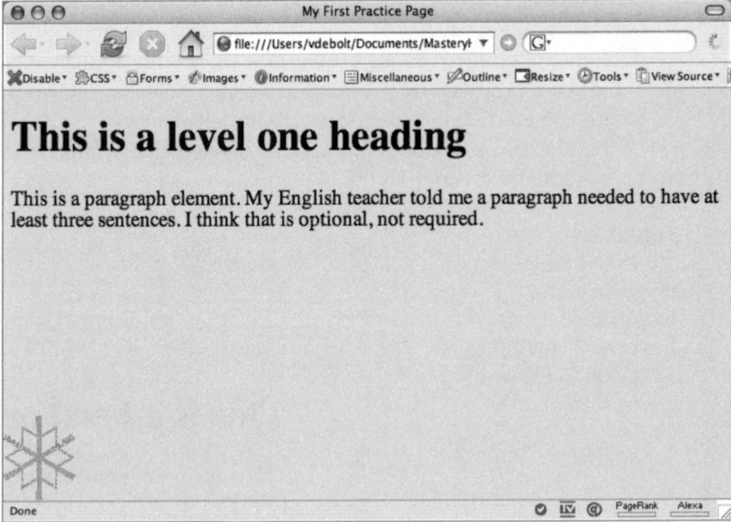

FIGURE 3.9
The background-position is 0% on the x-axis and 100% on the y-axis.

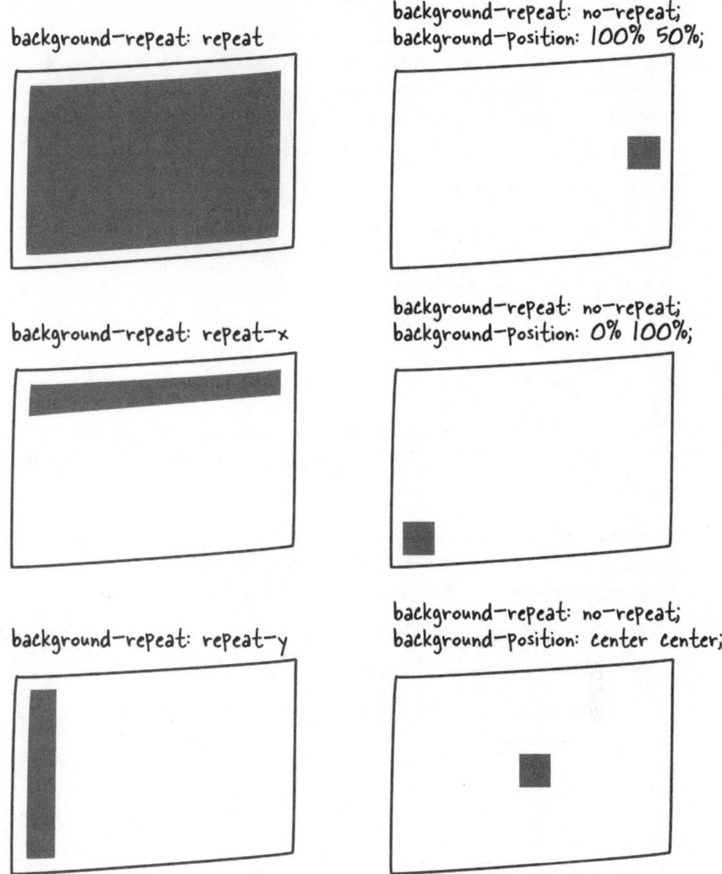

FIGURE 3.10 Various repeat and position settings are represented by the gray rectangle enclosed in a browser window.

Attached Background Images

There are two options for `background-attachment`: `fixed` or `scroll`. `Scroll` is the default; the image stays in the same relative position as the user scrolls through the document. A fixed background attachment stays fixed in one spot and does not scroll with the document.

In IE 6/Win and below, `background-attachment: fixed` only works properly on the `body` element. In more modern browsers, `background-attachment: fixed` can be used on other elements as well.

CONDITIONAL COMMENTS

Earlier in the chapter I mentioned conditional comments with regard to PNG transparency. Conditional comments are a Microsoft proprietary construct that must be placed in the XHTML document, not in the CSS. Conditional comments can be used to insert or import alternate styles when there is a problem with an older Internet Explorer browser.

The syntax that will help you filter out versions of Internet Explorer that are less than (`lt`) version 7 is this:

```
<!--[if  lt IE 7]>
<style type="text/css">
@import ("ieonly.css");
</style>
<![endif]-->
```

This conditional comment allows you to import a style sheet meant only for versions of IE less than 7. In that style sheet, you could adjust any element (other than body) that had `background-attachment: fixed` as a rule.

When using conditional comments, the links for the conditional comments must come later than the main CSS file link in the XHTML source. Rules imported with conditional comments must have the same or higher specificity than any similar rules in the main sheet.

Another example of a time when a conditional comment would be useful is if you center a body element using this rule:

```
body {
margin-right: auto;
margin-left: auto;
}
```

This is the correct way to center the body (or any) element, but IE 5 and below does not support the method, and neither does IE 6 when it's in quirks mode. There's a thorough explanation in Chapter 8 showing one way to work around this problem. Using a conditional comment linking to styles only for IE would be another good solution.

To really see the fixed background in action, a longer page of body text is required. One is on the accompanying CD. Save `ch3_longpage.html` to your computer and open the page in a text editor to add a link to the CSS.

Link the same style sheet that you have been using throughout this chapter to `ch3_longpage.html`. Then change the `ch3practice.css` file to the following:

```
body {
background-color: #9CC;
background-image: url(ch3bg_sm.gif);
background-repeat: no-repeat;
background-position: center;
background-attachment: fixed;

}
```

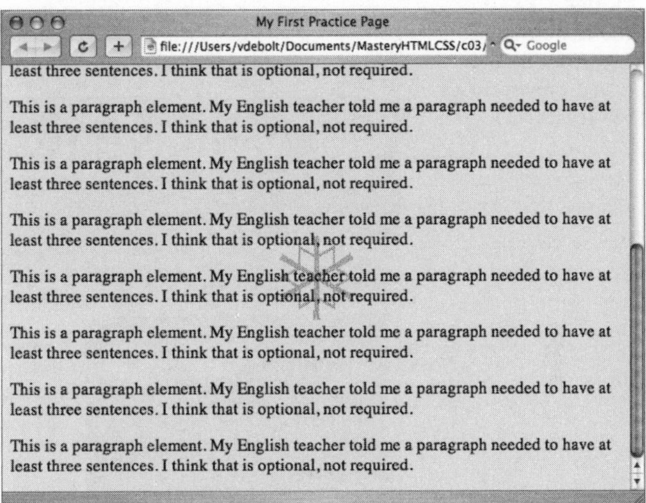

FIGURE 3.11
Although I have scrolled all the way to the bottom of the page, the background image is still attached in the center.

Look at `ch3_longpage.html` in a browser and scroll down the page. The background image will stay in the center of the page in a modern browser, even as you scroll down the page. See Figure 3.11.

Assign a Class or ID to the Body Element

Assigning a `class` or `id` to the `body` element is an innovative idea that is used more and more often. As currently implemented, this technique is often used to create a shared set of styles that are used for both a two-column or three-column layout.

Place either a `class` or `id` attribute in the `body` element, then create descendant selectors based on that `class` or `id` to control the desired layout. Common elements used in either layout such as font choices or footer information are also included in the style sheet. In this simple but effective manner, one style sheet can create numerous arrangements of common page elements. This is a helpful technique on a site that sometimes needs to vary positioning or layout but must retain a consistent look and feel. The Real-World Scenario in this chapter shows how one site took this idea and developed it even further.

This is a purely CSS solution that accomplishes in a small way almost what a JavaScript or PHP script style switcher accomplishes, but with no scripting. In Chapter 5, as you look at different ways of creating page layouts, keep this idea in mind.

Real-World Scenario

The Vitamin site is a resource for web designers, developers, and entrepreneurs at `www.thinkvitamin.com`. It is packed with high quality, useful articles, and features for web professionals.

This is another example of a site relying on Wordpress blog software to manage content and provide some of the structure. But the designers of this site have gone Wordpress one better, by using an `id` in the body element of every page that allows one style sheet to contain styles for multiple page layouts. It's all based on descendant selectors.

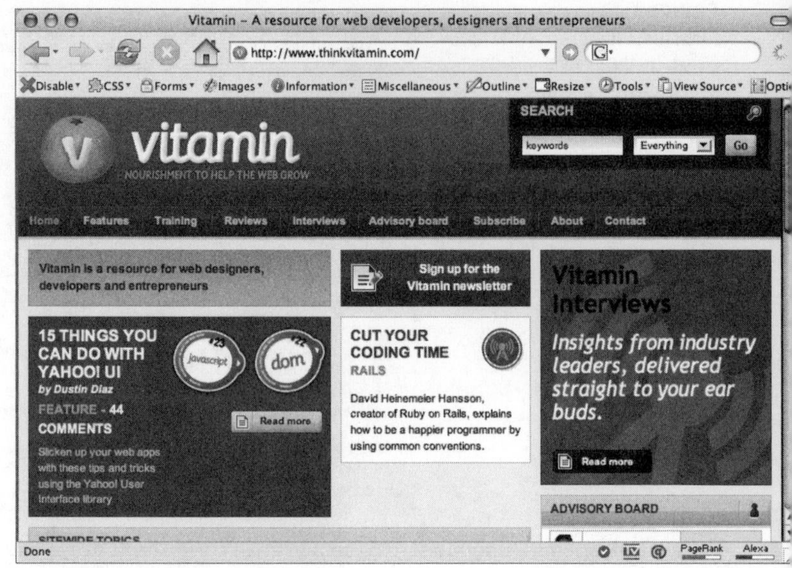

FIGURE 3.12
The Vitamin home page. View the page on your browser to see how it uses color.

Use View Source to examine how the home page is assembled and you notice this: `<body id="homepage">`. Take a peek at the CSS for the home page and you find a section with numerous selectors based on an `id` in the `body` element:

```
body#homepage
body#featurepage
body#trainingpage
body#interviewpage
body#reviewpage
body#advboardpage
body#subscribepage
body#contactpage
```

Click one of the feature articles, such as one from the biz section as shown in Figure 3.13. On the feature page, a look at View Source reveals not just an `id` for the `body` element, but also a class:

```
<body id="featurepage" class="searchcatresults">
```

The preceding list of selectors includes the `#featurepage` selector, providing a second set of rules for the body based on the look wanted for a feature page. A glance at the CSS reveals the existence of this selector: `body.searchcatresults`. The choice to identify various pages with an ID or class in the body element provides the designers with a powerful array of descendant rules that can be applied to specific pages. And by putting multiple page designs in a single style sheet, it also cuts down the number of different linked style sheets that require maintenance.

In Chapter 4 you will work with headings and learn how to style them.

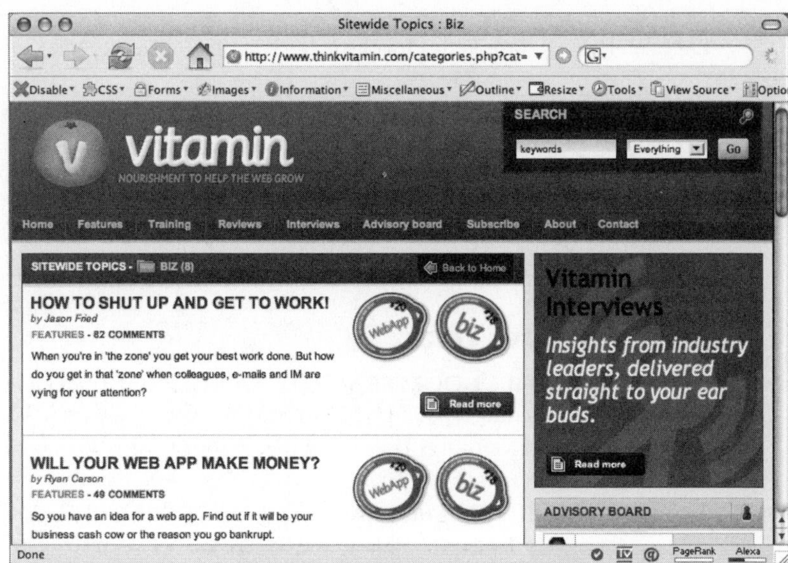

FIGURE 3.13
A biz section page from the Vitamin site

CSS Properties for the *body* Element

Table 3.1 lists the CSS properties discussed in this chapter that apply to the body element. Remember that other elements, in addition to body, can have styled backgrounds and margins. The body element can also have other styles not listed here that you will learn about in future chapters.

TABLE 3.1: Properties for the *body* Selector

PROPERTY	POSSIBLE VALUES
background-color	#*<hex RGB code>*, *<color name>*, rgb(*<red>*, *<green>*, *<blue>*)
background-image	url(imagename.gif)
background-repeat	repeat, no-repeat, repeat-x, repeat-y
background-position	top, center, bottom, left, right, *<percentage>*, *<length>*
background-attachment	scroll, fixed
margin	*<percentage>*, *<length>*
margin-top	*<percentage>*, *<length>*

TABLE 3.1: Properties for the *body* Selector *(CONTINUED)*

PROPERTY	POSSIBLE VALUES
margin-right	*<percentage>*, *<length>*
margin-bottom	*<percentage>*, *<length>*
margin-left	*<percentage>*, *<length>*

The Bottom Line

Understand the DOCTYPE or DTD. A Document Type Definition (DTD) is the set of rules for the particular type of HTML or XHTML your page uses. It's inserted in the XHTML as th DOCTYPE declaration. It's placed first in the document, before the opening `html` tag and `hea` element.

Master It Write the three XHTML DOCTYPEs and the three HTML 4.01 DOCTYPEs. The write a brief explanation of the difference between strict, transitional, and frameset.

Use an appropriate DOCTYPE on your page. Either a strict HTML 4.01 or XHTML DOCTYP that is validated will produce good results if the goal is pure separation of content from present tion. Transitional DOCTYPES allow for the use of *some* presentational material mixed into the co tent or XHTML. Valid transitional documents are also a good choice.

Master It Explain what DOCTYPE you would use for a new business site for the neighbo hood bowling lanes.

Write elements in the document head. The `head` contains the page title, links to style sheet and `meta` elements and can also contain other material such as JavaScripts. Information in th document head does not appear on the browser page; therefore `head` elements cannot be style for presentation. The `head` must include a `title` element.

Master It Here is a small section from the head of the home page of the Real-World Scenari example site Vitamin. Explain what each element is.

```
<head>
<meta http-equiv="Content-type" content="text/html; charset=utf-8" />
<title>Vitamin - A resource for web developers, designers and entrepreneurs</
title>
<link type="text/css" media="all" rel="stylesheet" href="/css/main.css" />
<link type="text/css" media="all" rel="stylesheet" href="/css/home.css" />
<script src="/scripts/global20060504.js" type="text/javascript"></script>
</head>
```

Write CSS for the body of your document. The body element contains everything that appea in the browser window. The body is the basic container for everything on your page and can be styled with CSS presentation rules.

The style for the body of your document can determine (among other things) background colo background image, and margins.

Master It Do at least three of the following exercises using the CSS style sheet you created in Chapter 3. Demonstrate your results in a browser.

Change the background color to #93C or to #0D520F.

In an image editing program, resize `ch3bg_sm.gif` so that it is 100×100 pixels in size and save it with the filename `ch3bg100.gif`. Then change the name of the image in the `url` value to the new name.

Use the new 100×100 pixel gif with the `background-repeat` set to `repeat-y`. Then try it set to `no-repeat`.

Make or find a different background image and use it instead of `ch3bg_sm.gif`. Try it with at least three repeat or position rules.

Change the `margin-top` and `margin-left` measurements to 5 percent.

Change every `margin` to `0` in one shorthand declaration.

Chapter 4

Headings and Heading Styles

In Chapter 4 you will explore the structural role that headings play on an XHTML page, and you will learn how CSS style rules can determine the appearance of headings.

Headings organize information into meaningful chunks, thereby adding structure and clarity to your content. A well-written heading at the beginning of a web page serves you in two ways: it helps your visitor quickly grasp the topic of your page, and it provides meaningful keywords to the search engines.

In this chapter you will:

- Use CSS rules for color, font, background, and border to create distinctive headings.
- Use a `class` selector to style headings.
- Use image replacement to create headings.
- Understand and use the visual formatting model (or box model) that determines how XHTML elements respond to CSS rules.

XHTML: The Heading Tags

If this book were a web page, the chapter title would be an `h1` and the subtitle of this section ("XHTML: The Heading Tags") would be an `h2`. There are six levels of headings in XHTML, represented by the `h` tag followed by a number: `h1`, `h2`, `h3`, `h4`, `h5`, `h6`.

On a web page, the title of this chapter would be marked up like this:

```
<h1>Chapter 4: Headings and Heading Styles</h1>
```

The subtitle of this section, as you can probably guess, would be

```
<h2>XHTML: The Heading Tags</h2>
```

Even before you apply any CSS rules to headings, they have certain default features. They are *block-level* elements. A block-level element is displayed on its own line, and any element following it is automatically placed on the next line. Headings are bold by default. The `h1` is the most important heading on the page, so it's the largest by default. An `h2`, like the second level of an outline, is meant to be a subheading related to the main heading on the page, and its default appearance is slightly smaller than that of an `h1`. A level three heading, or `h3`, is slightly smaller, and so on down to `h6`, as shown in Figure 4.1.

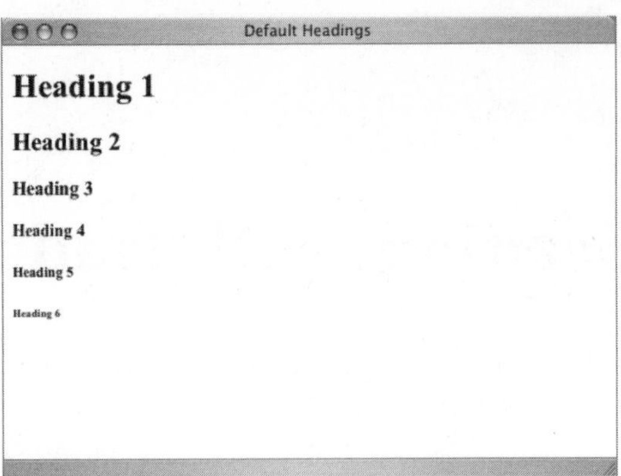

FIGURE 4.1
Default heading display

Building Structure with Headings

XHTML headings are simple but important. Headings are used to identify page names and t title subsections of a page. Heading elements by themselves *do* give structure to a page, but i order to take full advantage of the CSS rules of specificity, it's often good practice to augmen the structure of the heading elements. (You can review the concept of specificity in Chapter 2 Here's how:

- Place the heading element in a `div` element identified with an `id` attribute. For example, yo can create two `h1` elements of different appearance with selectors such as `#sitename h1` an `#content h1`.
- Use `class` or `id` attributes to distinguish heading elements. For example, if a `content` di contained three `h2` elements, each could be assigned to a different `class` to create three di ferent presentations for the `h2` elements based on the `class` attributes.

We will explore using *divisions* (divs) on the page in depth in Chapter 5, but you'll get a preview of them in this chapter, where several `div` elements give structural names to page components.

In essence, XHTML gives your content semantic structure. Creating an `h1` element conveys th semantic logic that this is the main heading on the page. Any device that can access the Internet whether it's a computer, a cell phone, a screen reader, or a personal digital assistant, understand an `h1` element as the main heading on the page and displays it accordingly. There are six levels c headings in XHTML: `h1`, `h2`, `h3`, `h4`, `h5`, `h6`. You've seen the default display of these headings in pr vious pages of this book. But you are by no means limited to the default display of headings. Wit CSS, headings can take any appearance you want and will continue to fulfill their semantic role a headings identifying blocks of information.

To maintain this semantic function and accessibility, use heading elements only for text tha is, in fact, a heading. Don't use heading elements to make text look large or bold if the text is nc actually a heading. Conversely, text that has been made to look large and bold but is not marke up as a heading element should not be placed at the top of a page or page section *as if* it were heading.

INSERT KEYWORD HERE

Heading elements are indexed by some of the search engines. They look for `h1` elements to decide what the page is about. Having important keywords describing the contents of the page in the headings can help your placement in search results. The Far and Wee Balloon site, an entirely fictional page for the exercises for this chapter, sports a heading that says "Floating on Air." In a real site that would actually be on the Web, a more keyword-rich heading such as "Ride in a Hot Air Balloon" would be more informative to a search engine index.

You'll learn more about coding for search engine placement in Chapter 12.

Following the semantic rules of XHTML helps ensure that any Internet-capable device can access your content.

How to Work through the Chapter

There are some images, partially completed XHTML pages, and partially completed CSS pages in the Chapter 4 folder on the companion CD. Copy these files to the `Mastering Integrated HTML and CSS` folder on your computer. The files you need are

```
ch4_start.css
ch4_start.html
ch4_stretchy.css
ch4_ir.css
ch4_ir.html
star.gif
yellowgradient.gif
multi_bg_700.jpg
multi_bg_1000.jpg
multi_ir_bg.jpg
threeballoon.jpg
```

Open the `ch4_start.html` file in your text editor of choice. Look at the page in the browser; you should see something like Figure 4.2.

As you can see, the page includes a few headings, a `nav` element (that doesn't go anywhere), a couple of paragraphs, and an image. The style sheet already linked to the page, `ch4_start.css`, provides some simple color and structure to the page. Open it in your text editor of choice.

In your text editor, you should see the XHTML markup for the page, as shown in Listing 4.1.

A NAVIGATION NOTE

In Chapter 3 and again in this chapter's page example, you see the site navigation links as a string of words separated by vertical bars, for example: home | about us | contact.

Chapter 7 will show you a more semantically correct way to create navigation using lists. Stay tuned until then before you draw any conclusions about the best way to code nav bars.

FIGURE 4.2 The original headings page

LISTING 4.1: The XHTML *ch4_start.html* Page

```
<!DOCTYPE html PUBLIC "-//W3C//DTD XHTML 1.0 Transitional//EN" "http://www.w3.org/
TR/xhtml1/DTD/xhtml1-transitional.dtd">
<html xmlns="http://www.w3.org/1999/xhtml">
<head>
<title>Chapter 4: Headings</title>
<link href="ch4_start.css" rel="stylesheet" type="text/css" media="all" />
</head>
<body>
<div id="container">
  <div id="sitename">
    <h1>Far and Wee Balloons</h1>
  </div>
  <div id="nav">Home | About Us | Balloon Facts | Balloon Fiesta | Balloon
Museum</div>
  <div id="content">
    <h2>Floating on Air </h2>
    <p><img src="threeballoon.jpg" alt="Three Balloons" width="400" height="300"
>Welcome to Far and Wee Balloons, where your dreams of floating on air can come
true. We design and make hot air balloons for every use. Our balloons will give
you a magical ride over country, mountains, and ocean.</p>
    <p>Come to our famous build-a-balloon design shop and you can enjoy a test
flight in one of our many pre-made balloons. We organized birthday, anniversary,
```

```
wedding, honeymoon and many other special occasion balloon flights for up to 100
people!</p>
    <p>Inside these pages you can examine some of the many example balloon photos
as seen at balloon races,  fiestas and rallies all around the world. </p>
    <p>It's all  fun at Far and Wee Balloons. Don't wait another minute to begin
your fun by coming by our Balloon Museum or our famous build-a-balloon design
shop. Both are located in Timbuktu on the Avon right off US Interstate Highway
165.</p>
    <h3>The Balloon Museum</h3>
    <p>See balloons from history and do experiments with the science of air. Stand
in the same gondola that went around the world in 90 days and never made history.
Thrill to the roar of the gas burners and the silence of the wind in our balloon
flight simulator with surround sound and rock-a-billy motion enhancers. </p>
    <p>Our Balloon Museum computers will let you design your own patterns and
shapes for the balloon in your future. So get here now! </p>
  </div>
  <div id="footer">&copy; Far and Wee Balloons, 2007, with thanks to e.e. cummings
for his phrase <q>the little lame balloon man whistles far and wee</q>. </div>
</div>
</body>
</html>
```

The structure of the start page has some `div` elements already in place to allow for a simple one-column layout. They include a container `div`, which holds all the content. Nested in the container `div` is a `div` called `sitename`, where you see an `h1` element. There is also a `div` called `nav`, which has text that could become links. Next you see a `div` called `content`, which contains the main content of the page, including a couple of heading elements, an image, and some paragraphs.

The first heading on the page, `<h1>Far and Wee Balloons</h1>`, sits in a `div` with the `id="sitename"`. The page uses only one `h1` element: this is structurally very specific.

In the `content` area, there is one `h2` and one `h3` element, also a structurally specific arrangement. The semantic development of the page implies that the `h1` heading is the most important, the `h2` is next in importance, and the `h3` is next in importance. Heading elements identify areas of a page in almost the same way as the main topic headings in an outline, because they organize content into topics and put those topics and subtopics in a hierarchy of importance.

CSS: Style a Heading

Take a look at the CSS page (Listing 4.2) in your text editor and examine the style rules prepared in advance. Notice that the `body` background color and the fonts have been set and that the container `div`, which contains everything in the body, has a background color of white (`#FFFFFF`). The `body` element has a background color (`#CCD7FF`), which completely surrounds the white background of the `container` element.

Note that the `container` element is a fixed 700 pixels in width and is centered using right and left auto margins. (This method of centering is not supported in some older browsers. I explain a workaround in Chapter 8 in the sidebar called "Centering Issues.") As you work through the exercises, you'll change that width to percentages for a nonfixed or stretchy `container` element.

Note that the style sheet has some selectors with empty rule declarations, for example,

```
#content h2 {
}
```

These will be used in the exercises that follow.

Finally, notice the CSS comments, such as `/*basic structure and organization*/` used in the style sheet. The comments help organize the rules and help you understand the purpose of the rules.

In such a simple page with a one-column layout, you could use the simplest type selectors (`h1`, `h2`, and `h3`) to style the headings. I've set it up for you with contextual selectors to give you additional work with that concept. You'll use `#sitename h1`, `#content h2`, and `#content h3` as your selectors. If the page grew more complicated—perhaps with two columns, sidebars, callouts, or other additions that required additional heading elements—such descendant selectors would still target the headings in the appropriate context.

LISTING 4.2: The *ch4_start.css* Page

```
/*basic structure and organization*/
body {
   font: 100% Arial, Helvetica, sans-serif;
   background: #CCD7FF;
   color: #333333;
}
#container {
   width: 700px;
   margin-right: auto;
   margin-left: auto;
   background: #FFFFFF;
}
#sitename {
}
#nav {
   text-align: center;
}
#content {
}
#footer {
   font-size: 80%;
   clear: both;
   }
/*heading styles*/
#sitename h1 {
   font: italic 300% Georgia, "Times New Roman", Times, serif;
```

```
}
#content h2 {
}
#content h3 {
}

/*other styles*/
#content img {
   float: left;
   padding-right: 5px;
   padding-bottom: 5px;
}
```

A page width of about 800 pixels is considered by some to be the maximum size for a design. If you subtract space to use for the browser's borders and scroll bars, you are limited to about 768 pixels in width. Many monitors cannot display pages that are wider than this without horizontal scrolling. As monitor sizes and screen resolutions continue to increase, that number may change. In Chapter 12 you'll learn how to get statistics about who uses your website and what screen resolution they have.

At the same time that devices grow larger, they also grow smaller. For example the popularity of handheld devices with very small screens is booming. While a fixed width design would not survive a trip to the small screen, there is a `handheld media` attribute, which allows style sheets for handheld devices to be added to the cascade of linked style sheets for any page.

Start with a Background Image

The first example of a heading style uses a background image behind the `h1` element.

The container `div` was preset for 700px in width, because the `multi_bg_700.jpg` image will become the background of the `h1` element. It measures 113×700px, and you want to show it all. On `ch4_start.css`, the existing `#sitename h1` rule already has a `font` rule in place. Add the line highlighted here:

```
#sitename h1 {
   font: italic 300% Georgia, "Times New Roman", Times, serif;
   background: url(multi_bg_700.jpg) no-repeat;
}
```

This style rule puts the image behind the `h1` element, but not all of the image is visible. See Figure 4.3.

FIGURE 4.3 The `multi_bg_700.jpg` in its entirety

Note that the `h1 font-size` is set for 300%. The visible background behind the `h1` represent the space occupied by the text and its line-height with the font Georgia rendered at 300 percen See Figure 4.4.

You can attempt to reveal the entire background image with a `min-height` and `width` setting fo the `h1` element.

Set the `min-height` and `width` for the `h1` element to match the size of the image in order to show the entire image. Add the following to the rule:

```
#sitename h1 {
   font: italic 300% Georgia, "Times New Roman", Times, serif;
   background: url(multi_bg_700.jpg) no-repeat;
   min-height: 113px;
   width: 700px;
}
```

With values that match the `min-height` and `width` of the `h1` element to that of the backgroun image, a browser renders the page something like Figure 4.5.

Internet Explorer does not support `min-height`, although it would treat a height declaration a `min-height`.

Using an image behind a text element in this manner demonstrates an important concept, but i actual practice, a user might enlarge the text and the `h1` would quickly outgrow the image and th space allotted to it. Give the `h1` a `background-color` that comes close to the blue sky in the imag (perhaps #719FC3) to lessen the possible unpleasant impact of the `h1` overflowing its container.

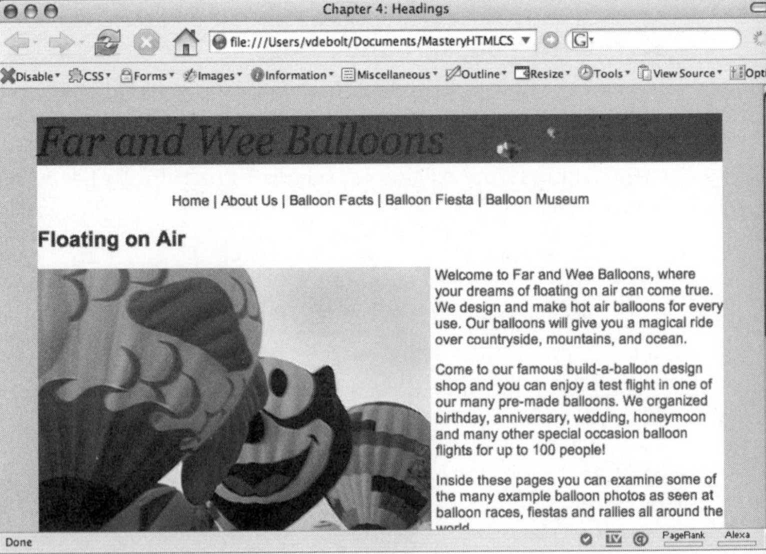

FIGURE 4.4
A background image appears behind the `h1` text. The amount of background image visible matches the space required for the text.

FIGURE 4.5
With a specific `min-height` and `width` set for the `h1`, the entire background image is revealed.

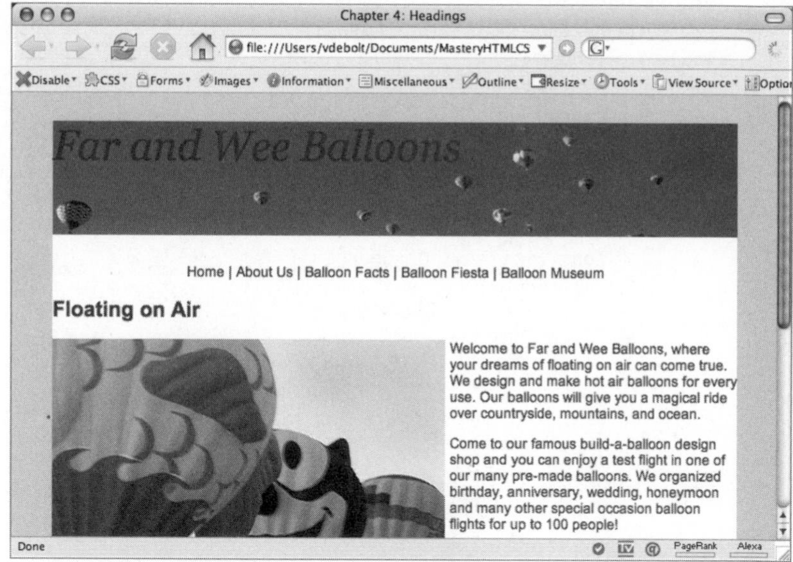

The fact that a background image is not completely revealed behind an element except under certain conditions is very important. I will come back to that idea later in the chapter.

First, add a bit more style to the `h1` element by centering the text, increasing the letter spacing, and changing the font color to white. See Figure 4.6. The rule becomes

```
#sitename h1 {
    color: #FFFFFF;
    text-align: center;
    letter-spacing: 0.3em;
    font: italic 300% Georgia, "Times New Roman", Times, serif;
    background: #719FC3 url(multi_bg_700.jpg) no-repeat;
    height: 113px;
    width: 700px;
}
```

Feel free to adjust the value of the `font-size` and `letter-spacing`, deepending on your computer monitor resolution and settings. Actually, adjusting values and experimenting with the styles as you move along will help you get a grip on exactly what the changes you are making really do. What would happen if you changed the `font-size` to 500% or the `letter-spacing` to `1em`? Take the time to experiment with such questions as you go along to deepen your comprehension of what you are learning. Changes to `font-size` and `letter-spacing` may have different effects at different browser sizes or screen resolutions, so your individual results may not be exactly like those in Figure 4.6.

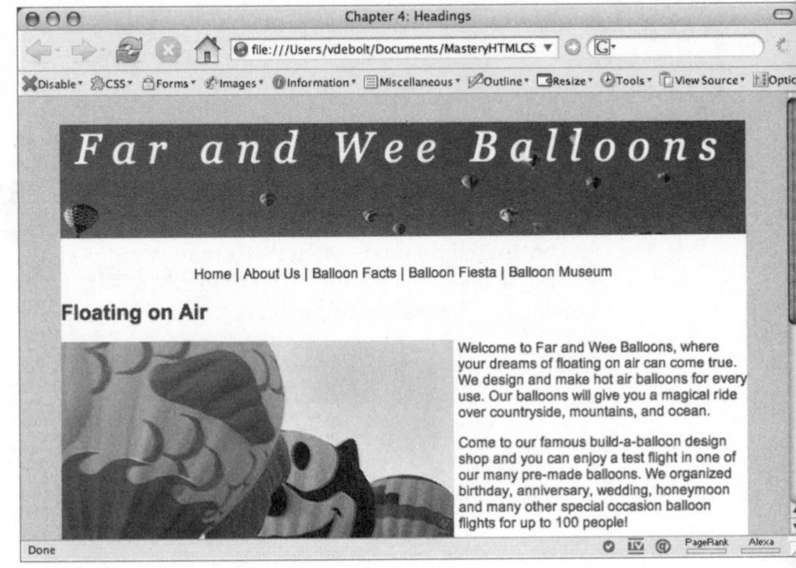

FIGURE 4.6 Changes to the color and letter spacing of the `h1` element result in this appearance.

A Fluid Design

In the preceding exercise, you learned that background images display partially or completely, depending on the size of the element they are behind. Creative use of the ability to hide and reve bits and pieces of background images can create what appear to be image rollovers, translucency and other interesting visual effects. You'll use this to create a fluid or stretchy-looking `sitename` heading.

> **IT DOESN'T STRETCH, IT SLIDES**
>
> One advanced technique, known as "sliding doors," creates a tab-like menu with interesting effects from background image placement. Read about it in an article in the online magazine A List Apart at `www.alistapart.com/articles/slidingdoors`. This technique involves the `a:hover` pseudo-element and selectively revealing different parts of a background image when a link is hovered over.

On the accompanying CD, find `ch4_stretchy.css`, save it to your computer, and open it. Notic that it's almost exactly like the `ch_start.css` document, except that the `container` element now a percentage width, centered by using percentage values on the right and left margins. Here is th new `#container` rule:

```
#container {
   width: 80%;
   margin-right: 10%;
   margin-left: 10%;
   background: #FFFFFF;

}
```

Using the same `ch4_start.html` document as before, change the link to the stretchy style sheet, thus:

```
<link href="ch4_stretchy.css" rel="stylesheet" type="text/css" media="all" />
```

Save everything and load it in the browser. It looks almost exactly like what you started with before, except that if you resize your browser window using the pull handle in the lower right corner, the size of the container expands or contracts to maintain the 80 percent width of the browser window. See Figure 4.7.

You can control the point at which the container stops contracting or expanding with the `min-width` and `max-width` properties. Note that `min-width` and `max-width` are not supported by older versions of IE/Windows. On compliant browsers, when the value set for `min-` or `max-width` is reached, the container width stops its fluid behavior. Let's add a `min-width` property to the `#container` rule:

```
#container {
   width: 80%;
   margin-right: 10%;
   margin-left: 10%;
   background: #FFFFFF;
   padding: 0;
   min-width: 650px;
}
```

If you narrow the browser window in a compliant browser now, the container will stop contracting when you reach the 650px point, and the contents will not all be visible. See Figure 4.8. This fact about `min-width` and `max-width` isn't all that earth shaking when dealing with a one-column layout, but it comes in very handy when you design a layout with two or three columns, so store it away in the memory vaults for future explorations into the topic of layouts.

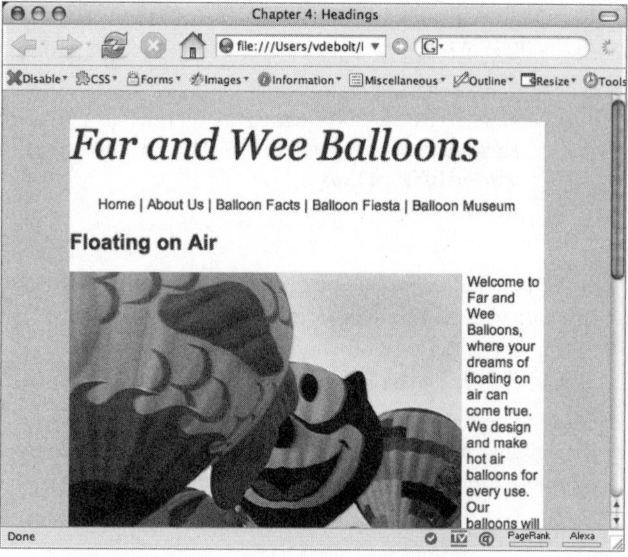

FIGURE 4.7
When the container size is a percentage value, the contents contract or expand to fit the browser window size.

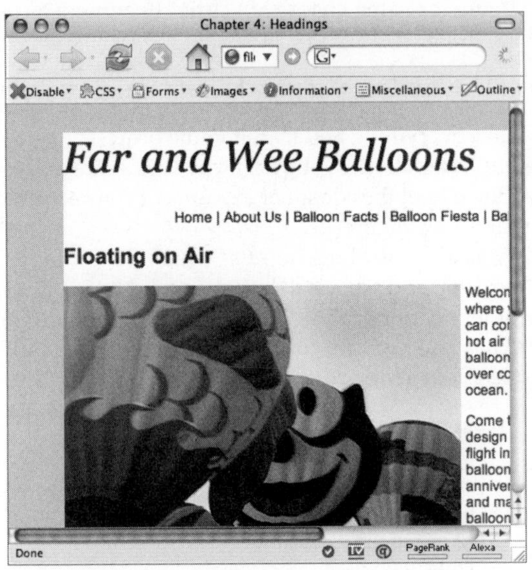

FIGURE 4.8 The container will not contract beyond the `min-width` set for 650 pixels. This puts some of the content outside the browser viewport. A horizontal scrollbar appears so that the user can scroll to the side to see the remaining content.

With the `container` set for fluid behavior, go back to the background for `#sitename h1`. Thi time use `multi_bg_1000.jpg` for the background image. This version of the image is 1000 pixel in width.

For some large monitors, 1000 pixels might not be enough width. It doesn't hurt to make a image you want to have show over a possibly very wide area as much as 1600 pixels or large in width.

To keep the background image in place, position it horizontally at the left and vertically at th top. Once again set the `min-height` to 113 pixels. The `width` must be variable so it will expand an contract with the `container` size. Set the width to 100%. This width is 100 percent of the `#sitename h1`, which is in turn 100 percent of the container. The container, as you recall, occupies 80 percen of the body width.

```
#sitename h1 {
   font: italic 300% Georgia, "Times New Roman", Times, serif;
   background: #719FC3 url(multi_bg_1000.jpg) no-repeat left top;
   min-height: 113px;
   width: 100%;
}
```

Whether a user has a narrow or wide browser window, the image in the `sitename h1` elemen appears to expand or contract to fit the browser width. See Figure 4.9.

Style the *h2* and *h3*

Moving on to the `h2` and `h3` elements, begin with rules to determine `font-size`. The `h1` element was given a size using a percentage. To gain some experience with ems, add rules using ems to th `h2` and `h3` selectors.

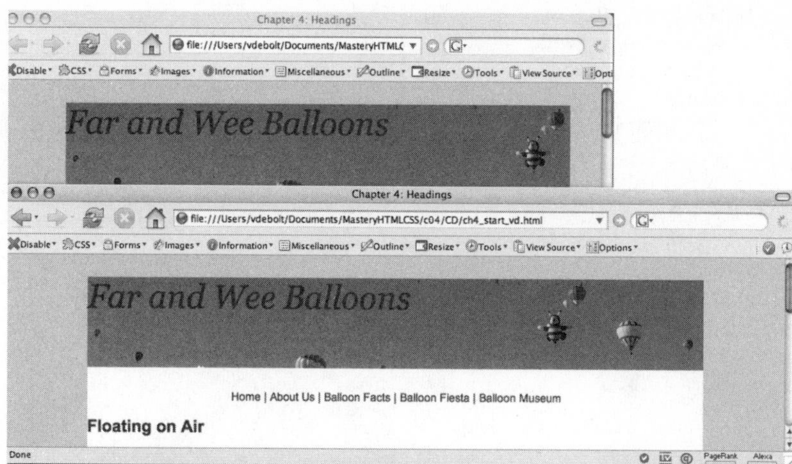

FIGURE 4.9
The same page open in two browser windows. The wider browser window reveals more of sitename `h1` element's background image.

There is a relationship between the relative measures `em` and %. Here are some mathematically expressed relationships: 1em = 100 percent, 1.25em = 125 percent, 2.2em = 220 percent. In this book I've switched between them simply to give you more experience; but in the real world there's no reason to do that, and there's no reason to prefer one over the other as a design choice.

```
#content h2 {
  font-size: 1.7em;
}
#content h3 {
   font-size: 1.5em;
}
```

Here's a new CSS property: `font-variant`. The values for `font-variant` are either `normal` or `small-caps`. Add to the `#content h2` rule to create small caps for that heading.

```
#content h2 {
   font-size: 1.7em;
   font-variant: small-caps;
}
```

You can see the effect of that rule in Figure 4.10. The `h2` could use a bit of white space on the left and a few additional features. Create the white space with a bit of margin. Add 3 pixels to both the left and right margin.

```
#content h2 {
   font-size: 1.7em;
   font-variant: small-caps;
   margin-right: 3px;
   margin-left: 3px;
}
```

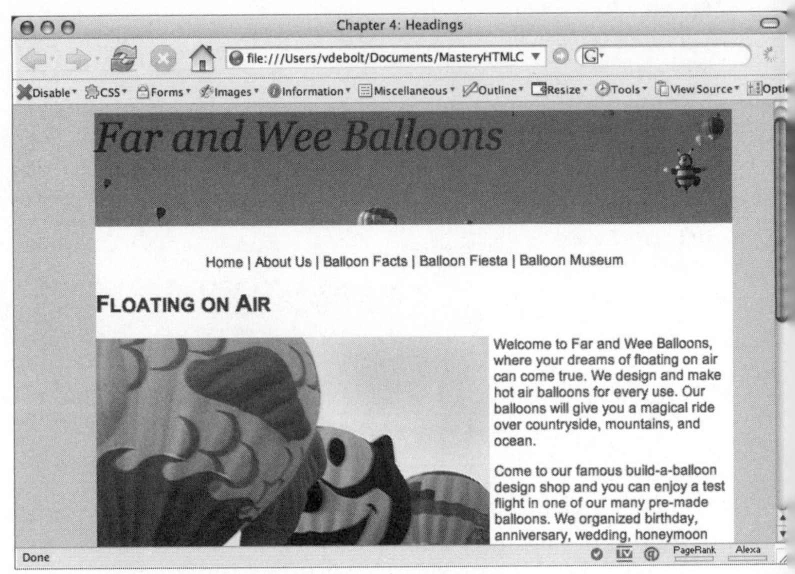

FIGURE 4.10
The h2 heading with a bit of margin and the `small caps` `font-variant`

At this stage, you can't visually distinguish the `margin-right`, but if you add borders to the h element, you'll see the margin on the right as well. Like `margin` and `padding`, `border` can be adde to elements on the top, right, bottom, or left. There are a number of `border` styles including `dotte` `solid`, `groove`, `ridge`, and `inset`. Border widths can be expressed in pixels, ems, percentages, o with the keywords `thin`, `medium`, and `thick`. The width, style, and color of each border can be se independently. To see all this in action, add borders to three sides of the `content h2` element:

```
#content h2 {
   font-size: 1.7em;
   font-variant: small-caps;
   margin-right: 3px;
   margin-left: 3px;
   border-left: 1px solid #666666;
   border-top: 2px dotted #999999;
   border-right: 1px solid #666666;
}
```

Figure 4.11 shows the results in a browser.

In creating this style, you've learned a couple of new concepts. First, you can alter text to displa as small caps with `font-variant`. Even more useful, elements can have `border` properties with varying values. Borders go around the outer edge of the `padding`.

Not all border styles are rendered properly by all the browsers yet. Figure 4.12 shows exampl of several of the border styles as interpreted by the Safari browser; notice that the groove, inset, an outset styles appear to be the same as the solid border.

You used a background image with the `h1` element, but background images can do much mo than fill a large space. They can be used as accents. In a list (see Chapter 7), a background image ca be used as a bullet character. As you continue the example here, you will incorporate a yellow accent image (`yellowgradient.gif`) in the `h2`.

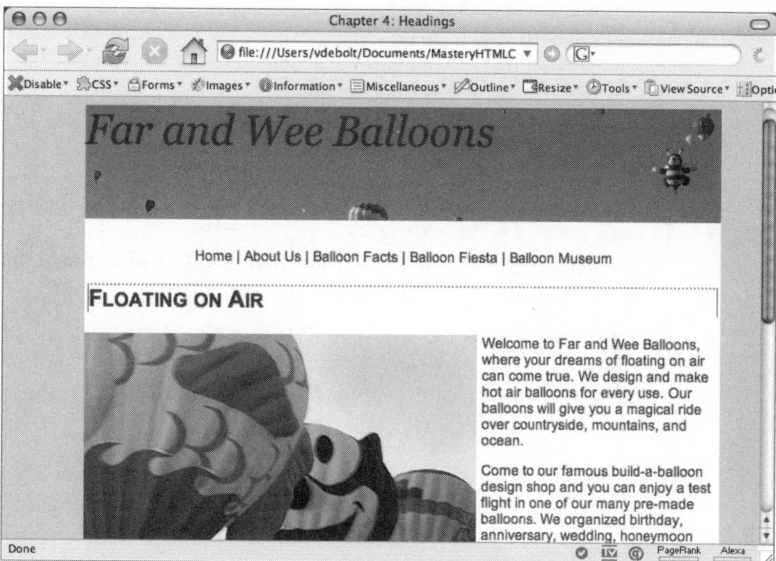

FIGURE 4.11
The small left and right margin becomes visible when a border is added to the h2 element. Note that borders can be of varying width, styles, and colors for any (or none) of the four sides of the element.

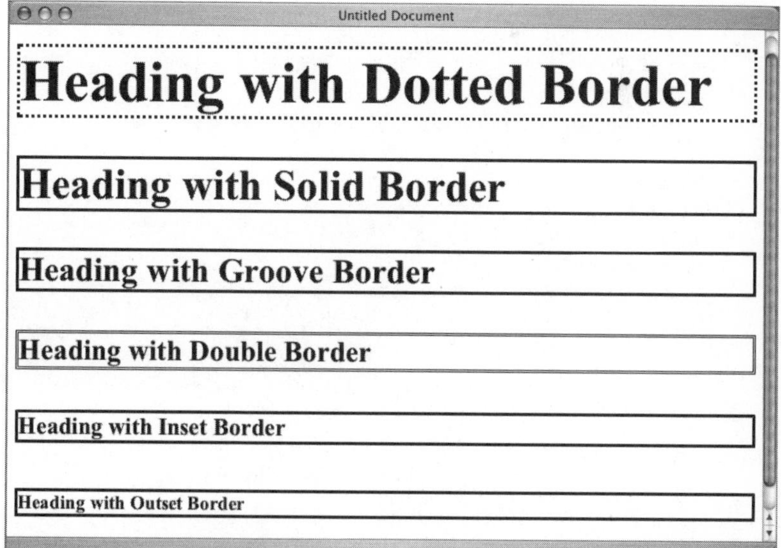

FIGURE 4.12
Not all border styles are rendered correctly by the Safari browser.

The yellow background accent is designed to repeat on the *y*-axis (vertically) and be completely over to the right side of the h2 box. The image is a mere 10 pixels in height, so having it repeat on the y-axis allows it to fill whatever space is available. See Figure 4.13. Here is the complete rule:

```
#content h2 {
   font-size: 1.7em;
   background: url(yellowgradient.gif) repeat-y right;
   font-variant: small-caps;
```

```
    margin-right: 3px;
    margin-left: 3px;
    border-left: 1px solid #666666;
    border-top: 2px dotted #999999;
    border-right: 1px solid #666666;
}
```

Turn your attention to the content `h3` element now. We'll use a `background-image` (`star.gif` to learn more about padding.

The background for the `h3` will be on the `left`. You do not want it to repeat. Add this to the exis ing `#content h3` selector rule:

```
#content h3 {
    font-size: 1.5em;
    background: url(star.gif) no-repeat left;
}
```

Look at the `h3` element in the browser (Figure 4.14). You notice that the heading text sits atop th star graphic. You can shift the heading over to the right a bit with 20px of padding on the left. Her is the additional rule:

```
#content h3 {
    font-size: 1.5em;
    background: url(star.gif) no-repeat left;
    padding-left: 20px;
}
```

The results should look similar to Figure 4.15.

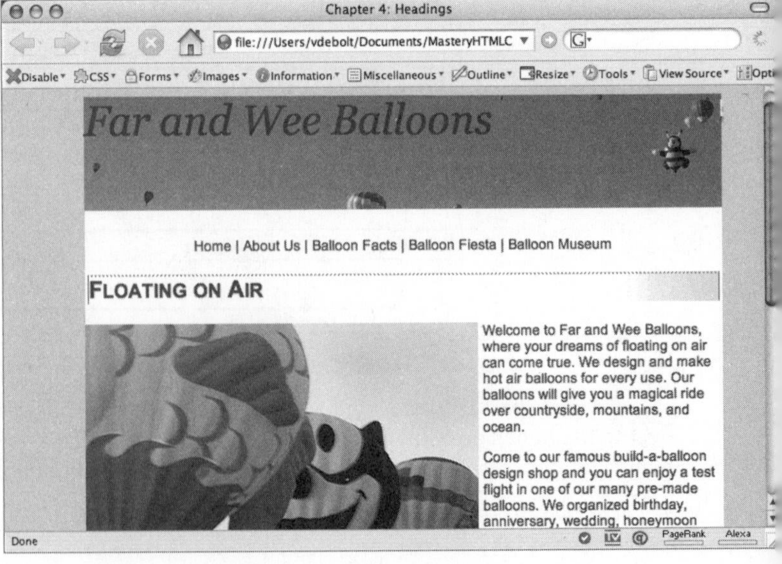

FIGURE 4.13
A small background image at the right of the h2 box creates a graphic accent for the heading.

FIGURE 4.14 With no padding, the h3 heading partly obscures the star graphic.

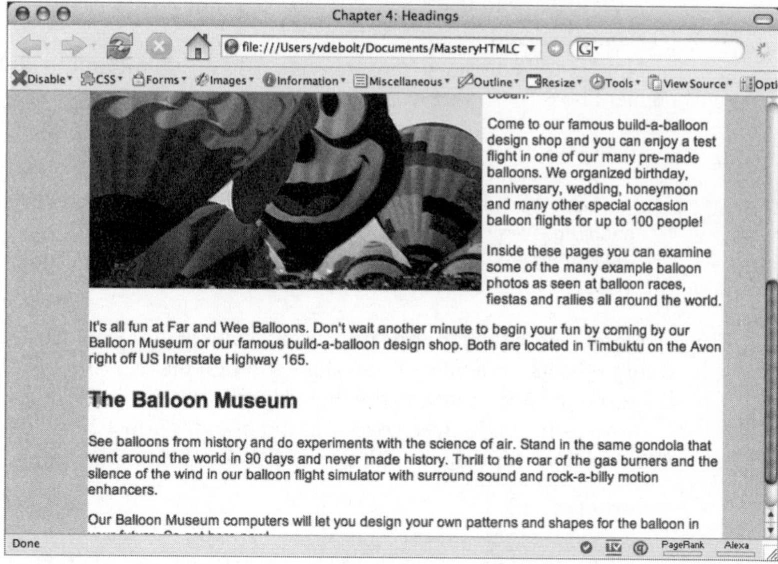

FIGURE 4.15 Using padding moves the heading away from the left margin to allow the star in the background to be more prominent.

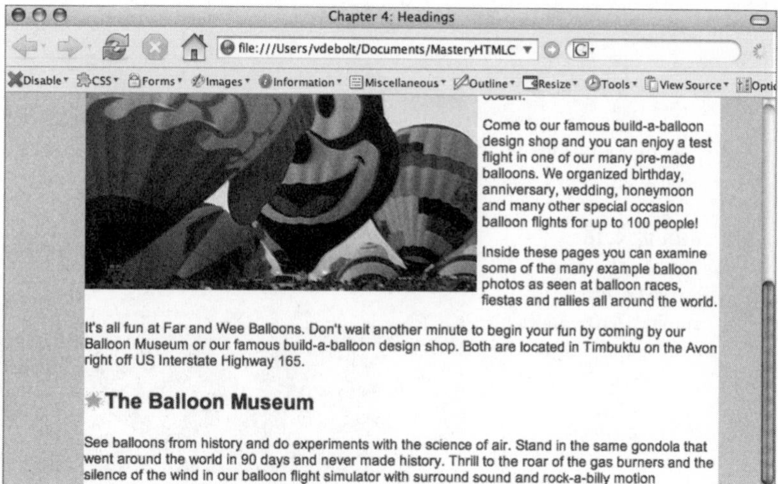

We haven't yet looked at the relationship between padding, margin, border, and background color. The discussion of the box model later in this chapter will help clarify these relationships. To give you a concrete example, you will add a background color to the h3 element and do more hands-on work with the box model.

Add a very light blue (#CDE8FC) `background-color` to the existing shorthand background rule:

```
#content h3 {
   font-size: 1.5em;
   background: #CDE8FC url(star.gif) no-repeat left;
   padding-left: 20px;
}
```

In Figure 4.16, notice that the new background color fills the entire box occupied by the `content h3` element, including the padding.

Now you'll add `margin` to the mix. Add a 1em margin to all four sides of the `content h1` element box.

```
#content h3 {
   font-size: 1.5em;
   background: #CDE8FC url(star.gif) no-repeat left;
padding-left: 20px;
margin: 1em;
}
```

Observe that `margin` appears on a four sides of the element (see Figure 4.17), but the background color of the `h3` element does not shine through the margin. (Instead, you see the color set for the background of the `content` div, in this particular design.) The margin is outside the padding.

Any border sits between padding and margin. Add a 2px wide, double style border in the color #848BA5 to all four sides, with this addition:

```
#content h3 {
   font-size: 1.5em;
   background: #CDE8FC url(star.gif) no-repeat left;
   padding-left: 20px;
   border: 2px double #848BA5;
   margin: 1em;
}
```

As you can see from Figure 4.18, the border goes around the padding, but not the margin. This behavior is an example of the CSS box model for formatting, which we'll explore later in the chapter.

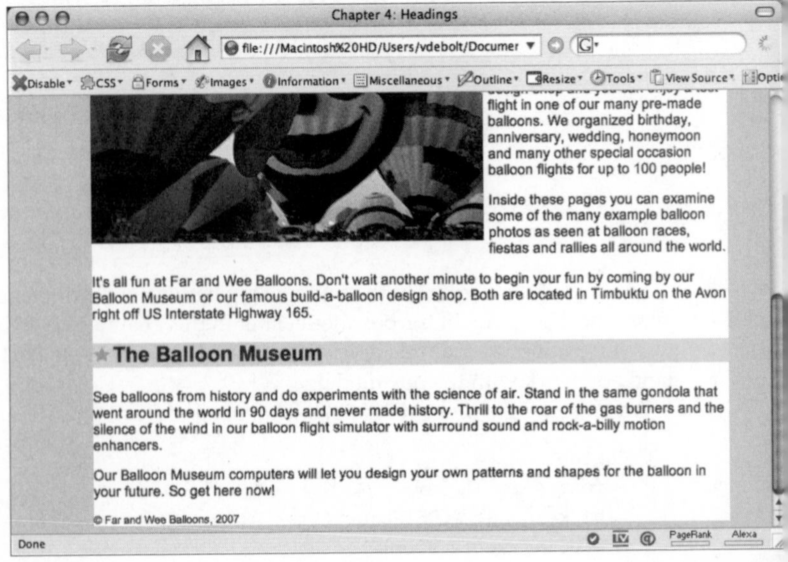

FIGURE 4.16
The box occupied by the heading is emphasized by adding a background color.

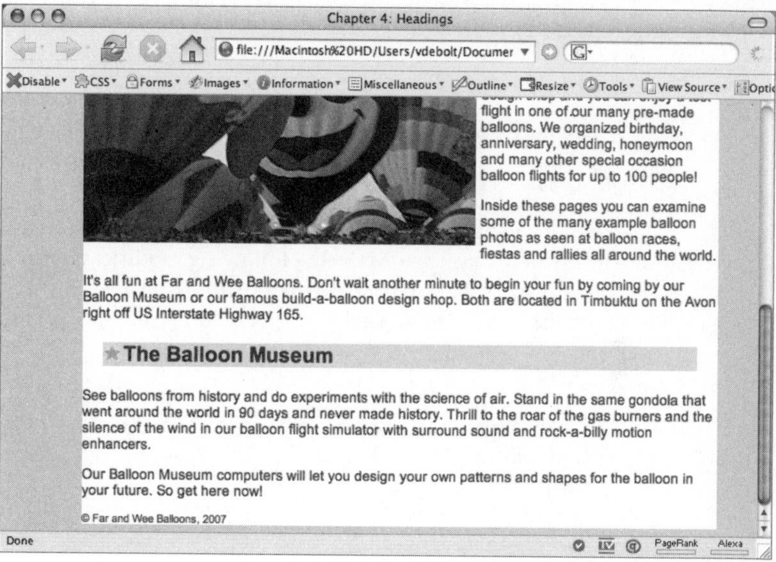

FIGURE 4.17
The margin, which is outside the padding, does not show the background color of the element.

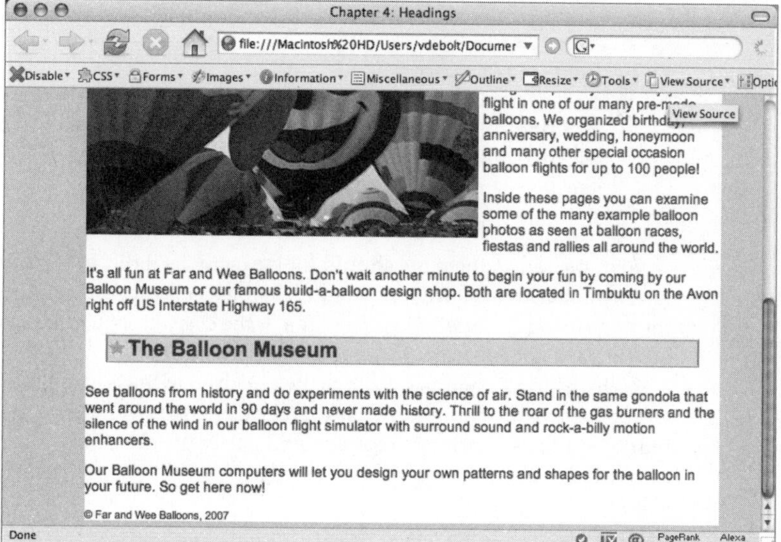

FIGURE 4.18
The h3 element has padding (only on the left), border, and margin, showing the box model in action.

A Class Alternative

The example page has one h2 and one h3 element. Suppose you are convinced that the two headings are of equal importance and therefore both of the headings in the content area deserve to be h2 elements? How could you make them look similar to what you last achieved with the yellow accent and the star?

The answer is a CSS class. Make a couple of changes in the XHTML page. First assign a class to the existing h2:

```
<h2 class="feature">Floating on Air </h2>
```

Change the h3 to an h2 and give it a class assignment as well.

```
<h2 class="item">The Balloon Museum</h2>
```

Now that you have class attributes in the XHTML, you need to change the CSS selectors to target those h2 elements by class. Make the following modifications to the style rules. Change the selector #content h2 to h2.feature. Keep the same rule, just change the selector. Change the selector #content h3 to h2.item. Again, keep the same rule, just change the selector. The new CSS:

```
h2.feature {
    font-size: 1.7em;
    background: url(yellowgradient.gif) repeat-y right;
    font-variant: small-caps;
    margin-right: 3px;
    margin-left: 3px;
    border-left: 1px solid #666666;
    border-top: 2px dotted #999999;
    border-right: 1px solid #666666;
    }
h2.item {
    font-size: 1.5em;
    background: #CDE8FC url(star.gif) no-repeat left;
    padding-left: 1em;
    margin: 20px;
    border: 2px double #848BA5;
}
```

In appearance, the page should look exactly as it did in Figure 4.15 or Figure 4.18. The two different appearing headings are created using a class attribute. Other h2 elements could be added to the page using either the class feature or the class item. Unlike id elements, which must be unique on the page, a class can be used more than once.

Note that on a page as simple as the one used in these exercises, the selectors .feature or .item would be specific enough. A class can be assigned to any element, for example a table or a paragraph, but the selector h2.feature will apply the class only to an h2 element that has the class attribute feature.

Image Replacement for Headings

Designers often want special effects for headings—special fonts or highly stylized text—such designed text can only be created in an image-editing program like Photoshop or perhaps Flash and then inserted.

Many designers simply insert an image into the XHTML marked up as a heading. With some `alt` text (see Chapter 3) to describe the image, the designer is done. The XHTML looks something like this:

```
<div id="sitename">
    <h1><img src="multi_ir_bg.jpg" alt="Far and Wee Balloons" width="800"
height="113" /></h1>
</div>
```

If the user viewing the page cannot see the image, they see the `alt` text, so the information is available. This also works for users with screen readers that read text aloud; the page is accessible. The limitation with this method involves the fact that there is no actual text in the heading element, therefore there is no opportunity to get important text in the most important heading (or any heading displayed as an image) on the page passed over to the search engines when they index the page.

Web designers conceived the idea of *image replacement* to deal with this problem. Basically, an image is created with beautifully designed text. That image is used as a replacement, often a background image, for an element. (The element does not have to be a heading.) The text in the element is hidden with CSS but is still there (theoretically, at least) for search engines or screen readers to read.

The first image replacement technique, called Fahrner Image Replacement (FIR) for its creator Todd Fahrner, lead to the development of several other techniques for image replacement. The image replacement craze, combined with the explosive success of the CSS Zen Garden (`www.csszengarden.com`) site, which works principally by using image replacement to achieve its fabulous design results, has contributed mightily to the beautification of the Web.

Perfection is hard to achieve, however, and that applies to the various image replacement techniques I'll describe. Some image replacement techniques don't work if the user does not have CSS capability. Some don't work if the user doesn't have JavaScript enabled. Some don't work if the user can't view images. Some aren't accessible to screen readers. Some don't work cross-browser.

The FIR method was adopted widely, but its flaws quickly became apparent. It uses the CSS property and value `display: none` to hide the text. This succeeds in hiding the text from many viewers, but it also hides it from a screen reader or anyone viewing the page with images set not to display.

The Rundle Method

This method, by Mike Rundle, is also known as the Phark method, because Rundle's site is `www.phark.net`. It uses negative `text-indent` to move text off the screen and out of the viewport. It isn't reliable in IE/Win 5, however.

Work along and try out each technique as I describe it using files from the accompanying CD. They are `ch4_ir.html`, `ch4_ir.css` and `multi_ir_bg.jpg`. Open the two text files from your hard drive. The `ch4_ir.css` style sheet is very like the `ch4_start.css` one you used earlier, except there's a fixed width for the `container` (800 pixels). The `multi_ir_bg.jpg` image contains the site name as part of the graphic.

Here's how the Rundle method works. The XHTML:

```
<div id="sitename">
    <h1>Far and Wee Balloons</h1>
  </div>
```

The CSS:

```
#sitename h1 {
text-indent: -5000px;
background: url(multi_ir_bg.jpg) no-repeat;
height: 113px;
}
```

Although screen readers and search engines can "see" the text indented far to the left, a user with images turned off cannot. A user with CSS off, however, would see the h1 text. See Figure 4.1

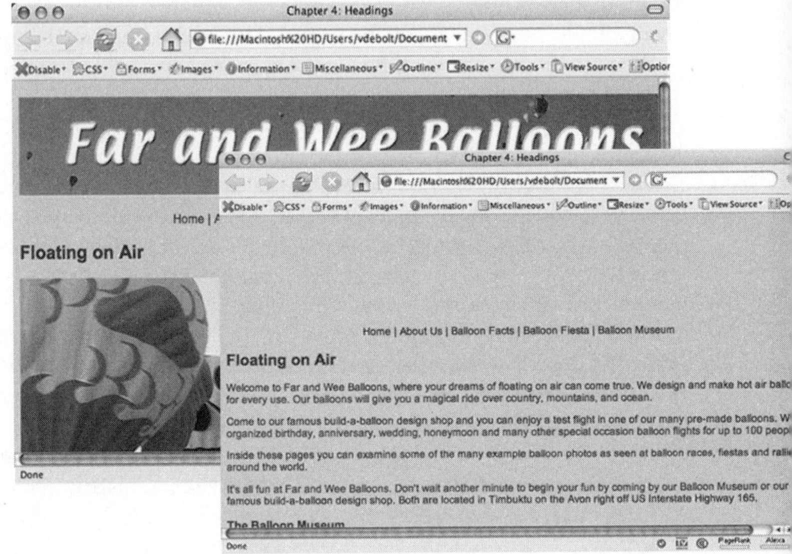

FIGURE 4.19
The Rundle method in two views: one with images on, one with images off

The Gilder/Levin Method

Tom Gilder and Levin Alexander get credit for this version. It hides the text by putting the imag *over it*. The text shows even when images are off. It's accessible to screen readers. Since the imag itself hides the text, the image cannot be transparent, or the text will show through. If the user enlarges the text, the hidden element may outgrow the image covering it and show around the edges. The final caveat is that the technique requires the addition of a nonsemantic empty span i the element to be replaced.

The XHTML:

```
<div id="sitename">
    <h1><span></span>Far and Wee Balloons</h1>
  </div>
```

The CSS:

```
#sitename h1 {
   width: 800px;
   height: 113px;
   position: relative;
}
#sitename h1 span {
   background: url(multi_ir_bg.jpg) no-repeat;
   position: absolute;
   width: 100%;
   height: 100%;
}
```

In Chapter 5, you'll find out more about `position: relative;` and `position: absolute;`. For now just use the rules as shown. Figure 4.20 shows three examples of how different browser settings interpret the Gilder/Levin method. The browser in back shows the intended result: images and CSS on, the text hidden. In the center view, you see images off and a clearly visible `h1` heading announcing the site name. Again, excellent results. Only in the third view, where the text has been greatly enlarged by the user, do you see part of the `h1` text poking out below the image. The `h1` text in the example was left at the default `font-size` for an `h1` element. If you reduce the `font-size` of the `h1` element, it takes a lot more enlargement of the text for the smaller `font-size` element to outgrow the covering image. Don't reduce the `font-size` to the point where it's not readable with images off. Reduce it enough, however, to maintain the excellent results you get with the Gilder/Levin method for a longer period when the user ups the browser text size.

Each of these techniques has issues. You have to make the judgment call yourself as to whether to use them, and select the one will work best for your users and your situation.

FIGURE 4.20 Three possible browser interpretations of the Gilder/Levin technique

BONUS IMAGE REPLACEMENT SOLUTIONS

There are two other image replacement solutions worth mentioning. I'm not going to explain them here because they involve Flash and JavaScript, both beyond the scope of this book. The first is the Inman Flash Replacement (IFR), which you can learn about at Shaun Inman's site. He wrote several articles about it, but this one seems to be conclusive: `www.shauninman.com/plete/2004/04/ifr-revisited-and-revised`.

The second is the Scalable Inman Flash Replacement (sIFR), which you can learn about on Mike Davidson's site at `www.mikeindustries.com/blog/archive/2004/08/sifr` and from the Adobe Developer Center at `www.adobe.com/devnet/dreamweaver/articles/sifr_demo.html`.

Then there's IE5/Mac. Internet Explorer 5 for Macintosh has its own set of image replacement issues. An article here describes some Gilder/Levin adaptations for IE/Mac: `www.ryznardesign.com/web_coding/image_replacement`. This article also provides a glimpse into image replacement techniques on the horizon with future browser changes and future CSS changes.

The CSS Box Model

In this chapter and the previous one, I've touched on `margin`, `padding`, and `border` properties. Let's take a look at the way these properties work together visually.

The W3C specification for how elements in a document display is referred to as a *visual formatting model*. Using this CSS model, every element on the page generates a rectangular box. This box, called *the box model*, is represented in the diagram of Figure 4.21.

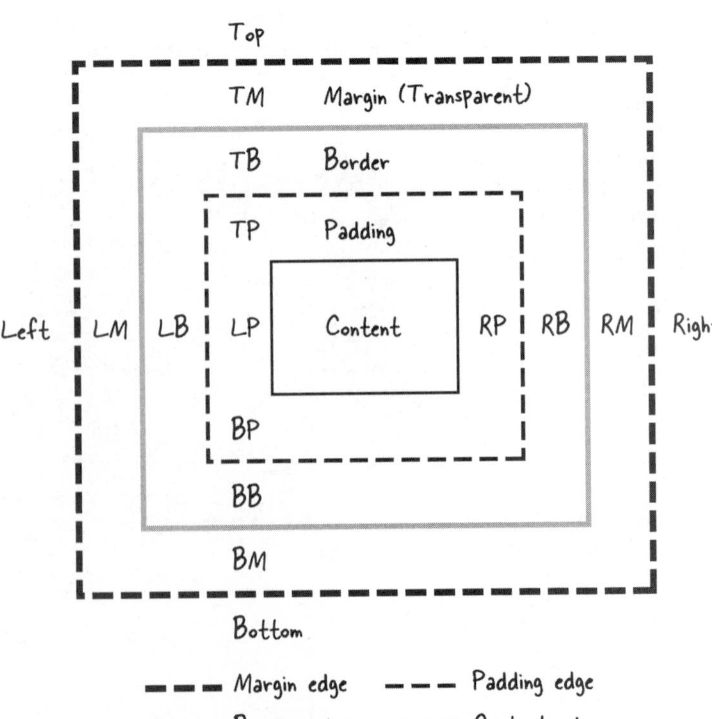

FIGURE 4.21
The box model

Each box has a content area (for example, text, an image, and so on) and optional surrounding padding, border, and margin areas. Padding and margin are transparent, allowing the background or background image of the element (or parent elements) to show through. Values for each of these properties can be defined collectively or individually for top, right, bottom, and left. These visual formatting properties apply to every element on a page, not just headings. Everything from the entire body down to the individual letter exists in its own box, and that content box can be formatted with individual padding, border, and margin values on all four sides.

According to the W3C specifications, "The box width is given by the sum of the left and right margins, border, padding, and the content width. The height is given by the sum of the top and bottom margins, border, padding, and the content height." Understanding the box model will help you calculate how much space the various elements in your page design will fill.

Suppose, for example, you have a rule like this:

```
div {
   width: 100px;
   padding: 10px;
   border: 5px;
   margin: 10px;
}
```

How much width does the W3C specification say that box occupies? Add it up: (margin-left) 10px + (border-left) 5px + (padding-left) 10px + (content) 100px + (padding-right) 10px + (border-right) 5px + (margin-right) 10px = 150px.

Hacking the Box Model

Internet Explorer for Windows before version 6 did not correctly implement the box model. This broken interpretation of the box model was the impetus for one the very first CSS hacks (or filters) ever put to wide use. The IE box model bug affects CSS-aware versions of IE/Win up to version six. Internet Explorer 6 is not affected in standards-compliant mode, only in quirks mode. The W3C says that the width of a block level element is the width of its content. However, the box model bug in IE causes that browser to interpret the width of a block level element to be content + padding + border.

A good reference page on CSS filters to bookmark is at `http://centricle.com/ref/css/filters`, where you see the box model hack created by Tantek Çelik listed as the first filter in the table. There are many other filters listed in this table and information about which specific browsers the filters target.

CSS filters allow you to write rules that set one value for standards-compliant browsers and one for a characteristic of another browser that does not meet that standard. Tantek's box model hack has given way to other box model hacks that are less complicated.

A couple of filters can be combined to create the *modified simplified box model hack*. How's that for a name? It's also known as the Tan hack, much less of a mouthful. The first filter uses the *escaped property hack*. It adds an escape character (\) within a property. An escape character is legal in CSS and should be ignored by the browser. But IE5.*x*/Win doesn't ignore it. An example looks like this:

```
#nav {
   width: 120px; /* a widened width for browsers who have a broken box model */
   w\idth: 100px; /* hidden from IE 5.x Win but read by most modern browsers */
   }
```

Visual Space in More Depth

An in-depth discussion of the box model is available at `www.w3.org/TR/REC-CSS2/box.html`.

An interesting and enlightening 3-D version that demonstrates the box model is at `www.hicksdesign.co.uk/boxmodel`.

All modern browsers except IE 5.*x* for Windows ignore the escape character and implement th second rule. IE 5.*x* Win thinks it is part of the property name. Since it doesn't recognize the propert name, it ignores the rule and implements the first rule.

The *star HTML hack* targets IE6/Win and earlier versions. Internet Explorer 7 will not recognize th star HTML hack. In Chapter 2, I explained that the root element for all XHTML documents was th `html` element. However, IE 6 and earlier wrap that in another unnamed element. The star HTML hac uses the universal selector (*) to target the HTML element, and thereby apply rules to only those I versions, like this:

```
* html h1{
border: 1px dotted red; /*recognized only by IE6 and below*/
}
```

Put the star HTML hack and the escaped property hack together and you get the modified sir plified box model hack:

```
* html #nav {
   width: 120px; /* width for IE5.x Win*/
   w\idth: 100px; /* width for IE6+ Win*/
   }
#nav {
   width: 100px; /*width for all modern browsers*/
   }
```

Many web authors prefer to isolate hacks or filters in a separate style sheet for easier maintenanc That style sheet is attached in the normal way.

It's also possible to use conditional comments to good effect with hacks or filters. If the style meant to hack the box model are isolated in a separate style sheet and a conditional comment in th XHTML is used to link to those styles under the appropriate conditions, then the hacks are isolate from a site's main styles. Here's an example of a conditional comment that links to a style sheet co taining hacks meant for IE5.*x*/Win.

```
<!--[if IE 5]>
<link rel="stylesheet" type="text/css" href="ie5hacks.css" />
<![endif]-->
```

More Help for Broken Boxes

For more information and other filters and hacks aimed at the IE box model bug, check the free article "The Box Model Problem" by John Gallant, and Holly Bergevin at Community MX: `www.communitymx.com/abstract.cfm?cid=20B41`.

In Chapter 5 you will learn more about using the `div` element and how it creates structure and allows you powerful options with contextual selectors.

Real-World Scenario

Evans Jones is a company located in the U.K. providing access consulting in building, town planning, and architecture. See Figure 4.22 for a look at the home page, `www.evansjones.co.uk`.

The heading elements on the page are used to good effect, organizing the content in an easy to understand informational groupings. The headings are not obvious at first glance, however, because the page uses image replacement for the `h1` heading at the upper left where the logo appears.

A CSS class hides the text far off to the left of the viewport:

```
.hide {
    position:absolute;
    left:-9999px;
    text-align:left;
}
```

With CSS off, the hidden text becomes visible, although it isn't visible if images are off.

The four images in the right column identifying the various aspects of the consultancy are background images in a list, a very interesting use of background image. The list text is fully accessible as links to the relevant inner pages.

Inner pages use a more obvious heading structure. See Figure 4.23. There's a heading serving as a page title: Access. The previous Location heading is used again. Farther down the page (beyond the screen capture view) there's another heading: Useful Access Links. Again the page uses the semantic concept of the heading element to make the content clear and organized.

Evans Jones is not in the business of making accessible websites. But their business *is* accessibility, and they are a good example of carrying the philosophy of accessibility into everything they do with this accessible website.

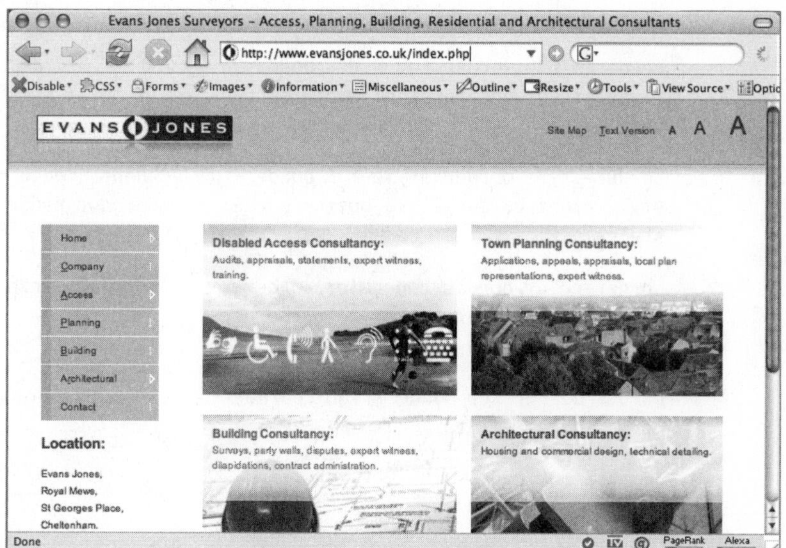

FIGURE 4.22 The main page of the Evans Jones site uses heading elements for the logo at the upper left and the Location text on the left.

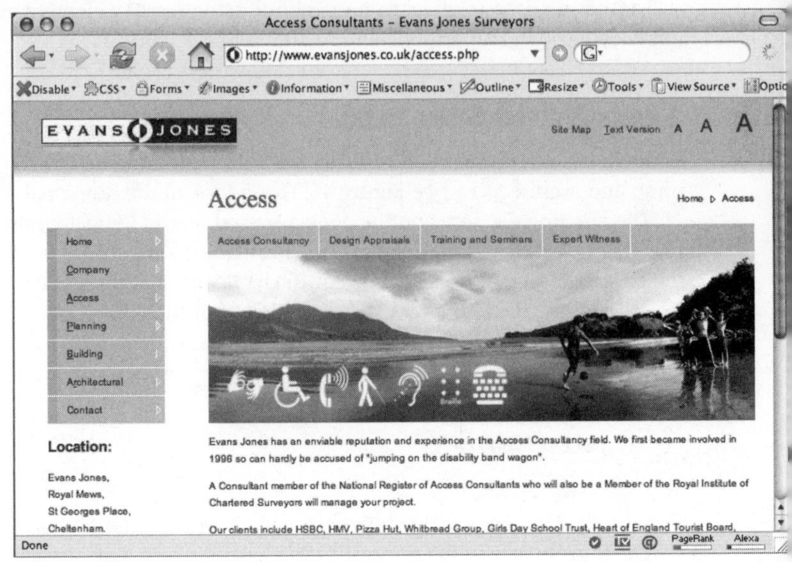

FIGURE 4.23
An inner page of the Evans Jones site contains more text, therefore more heading elements.

CSS Properties for Headings

Table 4.1 summarizes the properties described in this chapter. Keep in mind that `border` and `padding` and `margin` can be applied to all elements, not only to heading elements. Similarly, `font-style`, `font-variant`, and `text-align` values can be applied to any text, not only to heading elements.

TABLE 4.1: Some Properties for the Heading Selectors: *h1, h2, h3, h4, h5, h6*

PROPERTIES	POSSIBLE VALUES
`border-width`, `border-top-width`, `border-right-width`, `border-bottom-width`, `border-left-width`	`thin`, `medium`, `thick`, *<percentage>*, *<length>*, `inherit`
`border-style`, `border-style-top`, `border-style-right`, `border-style-bottom`, `border-style-left`	`none`, `hidden`, `dotted`, `dashed`, `solid`, `double`, `groove`, `ridge`, `inset`, `outset`, `inherit`
`border-color`, `border-top-color`, `border-right-color`, `border-bottom-color`, `border-left-color`	*<color>*, `transparent`, `inherit`
`border`, `border-top`, `border-right`, `border-bottom`, `border-left`	Accepts shorthand declarations of width, style, and color

TABLE 4.1: Some Properties for the Heading Selectors: *h1, h2, h3, h4, h5, h6* (CONTINUED)

PROPERTIES	POSSIBLE VALUES
`padding`, `padding-top`, `padding-right`, `padding-bottom`, `padding-left`	*<percentage>*, *<length>*, *inherit*
`font-style`	`italic`, `oblique`, `normal`, `inherit`
`font-variant`	`small-caps`, `normal`, `inherit`
`text-align`	`left`, `right`, `center`, `justify`, `inherit`
`display`	`none, inline, block, inline-block, inherit` Other display properties apply to lists and tables. These will be mentioned in subsequent chapters.

The Bottom Line

Use CSS rules for color, font, background, and border to create distinctive headings. It is an effective visual help to give headings a distinctive look. It makes a page easier to scan for a particular block of information or content.

Master It Add an `h4` element to the `ch4_stretchy.html` page and write a style rule for it. Change the `h1` in `ch4_stretchy.css` to be centered and a different color. Demonstrate the results in a browser.

Use a `class` selector to style headings. Unlike `id` elements, which must be unique on the page, a `class` can be used more than once.

Master It Assign the class `feature` to the exercise page with `h2` headings. Use the same class for both headings. Then rewrite the rule for the class to completely change the appearance of the headings to a style of your own design. Demonstrate the results in a browser.

Use image replacement to create headings. Many more fonts are available as graphics than can be displayed as text. When decorative fonts are required, designers replace or hide the text in various ways and use images instead.

Master It Use the file `floatingonair.jpg` from the accompanying CD and one of the image replacement techniques described in the chapter to replace the heading *Floating on Air* in the XHMTL page. Be ready to explain the pros and cons of the method you selected and to demonstrate the results in a browser.

Understand and use the visual formatting model (or box model) that determines how XHTML elements respond to CSS rules. The box model determines the interaction of content, padding, border, and margin in all its various combinations. A box should have content. Padding, border, and margin are optional and can be used in numerous ways.

Master It Create a page of example headings that demonstrate the following box model uses:

1. Content with no padding, border, or margin
2. Content with padding and a border
3. Content with a margin but no border and no padding
4. Content with a lot of top and bottom padding
5. Content with borders and a lot of left and right margin

Chapter 5

Page Divisions: *div* for Structure and Layout

When you look at a web page, you may react to the way it "looks." But before you begin to think about designing the presentation of the page, you need to think about structuring the markup with logical use of XHTML elements so that the CSS will be easy to apply later.

In terms of this book, structure is what you implement in XHTML and presentation is CSS. The distinction between structure and presentation is basic to the successful integration of XHTML and CSS. Structure defines how the site is organized, and presentation defines how it looks. If you take the raw text and images that will become the content of your website and mark it up with XHTML elements such as headings, paragraphs, lists, and block quotes, you are structuring your document. The XHTML elements carry structural or semantic logic with them. Well-structured pages can be displayed (or presented) in various ways in various Internet-capable devices and still be structurally sensible as headings, lists, or other content.

One element in particular, the `div` (for division), provides what the W3C calls a generic mechanism for adding structure. A `div`, with a `class` or unique `id` attribute assigned to it, assumes a structural role on the page according to your particular needs. If you need a banner, a content area, a sidebar, and a footer, you can create that structure with `div` elements. Using `id` labels like `"banner"`, `"content"`, `"sidebar"`, and `"footer"` with the `div` element gives you the ability to create page components that build in structural CSS hooks.

Cleanly structured XHTML with well-planned structural elements generates the power of CSS contextual selectors to create a multitude of presentation styles. First, write well-structured XHTML. Later, you can do anything you want to your page with CSS because the structural elements you need for your CSS selectors are built into the markup.

In this chapter you will:

- Use `div` and `id` to create structure for styling.
- Create layouts with `absolute` and `relative` positioning.
- Create layouts based on `float`, `margin`, and `z-index`.
- Understand `float` for images and other elements.
- Use `clear` with floated elements.

Learn the XHTML

XHTML represents the successful result of the drive to separate presentational elements from the structure of a web page. You probably noticed in previous chapters that XHTML by itself provides only a simple roster of headings, paragraphs, lists, and other very elemental building blocks. That simplicity of structure makes content flow without stumbling blocks between devices such as we browsers, cell phones, and personal digital assistants.

You must first build your page with logical, structural XHTML markup. To make CSS really capable of meeting the demand for beautiful presentation, certain elements and attributes are needed in XHTML to allow the specificity of selectors and the inheritance of the cascade to shine all its glory. You will use four of these markup elements and attributes to pry structure and pre sentation apart: `div`, `span`, `id`, and `class`. (You saw evidence of these in previous chapters.) Fir you will learn to use these elements and attributes to structure a page into CSS-readiness. Then you'll learn to position and lay out these elements using CSS.

div The content of a page falls into logical divisions (divs), such as banners, navigation, sul navigation, search boxes, ads, content, and footers. By enclosing each of these page divisions a generic container with a named `id`, for example,

```
<div id="search">search content here</div>
```

you create a unique structural element on the page that can be presented to the viewer using sp cific CSS rules. The `div` is a block-level element.

id The `id` attribute, which *identifies* the element it's assigned to, does more than merely serv as a style sheet selector, although that is certainly an important job. The `id` attribute can also b a target for a hypertext link or a referenced object in a script. An `id` attribute can be assigned any element, either block or inline.

Remember that any `id` can only be used one time on a page; it must be unique. An `id` attribu must begin with a letter or an underscore (although IE will not apply rules from a selector th starts with an underscore). It can contain letters and numbers, plus underscores and hyphen but cannot contain blank spaces.

class For elements that are not unique on the page—that is, styles you plan to use more tha one time per page—there is the `class` attribute. Just like an `id`, a `class` attribute can be assigne to any element.

The `class` attribute follows the same restrictions on naming as the `id` attribute, just describe

`Class` and `id` names are case sensitive, meaning there is a difference between "siteName" an "sitename" as a class or id name. Using "siteName" is neither better nor worse than using "si name." Make the choice and be consistent about whether you intend to use all lowercase or mix of lower- and uppercase. More important than a decision about case is the name itself. Th name should describe purpose rather than appearance. For example, "mainNav" or "mainna is a better choice than "redBar" or "redbar".

CLASS TRASH

While the ability to create classes is indeed a wonderful tool in CSS, don't get carried away with the notion and apply `class` attributes to every element. Remember, part of what you are hoping to accomplish is lean and clean XHTML. If you structure the page with appropriate and logical markup and use well-named `div` elements, you generally have sufficient context for most CSS descendant selectors you will need.

For example, if you wanted a particular set of list items to be in a certain class, it's a better practice to apply the class attribute to the opening list element (or possibly to the div containing the list) than to litter up your XHTML with a class attribute applied to each individual list item.

Heavy use of class attributes ("class trash") on a page should be a clue to you to examine your structure to see if you can find elements higher up in the document hierarchy to base descendant selectors on, thus applying the class in fewer but more effective ways.

Organizing Content Structurally

With some revisions, we'll use the Far and Wee Balloons example from Chapter 4 for the following exercises. The page contains some prebuilt structure in the form of `div` elements. We'll look at each `div` to see what structural need it fills. Listing 5.1 is similar to the page you saw in Chapter 4, with some added comments to note where `div` elements are closed. Also notice that the `nav` element has changed from a string of words separated by vertical bars to a list. You'll work with this list in depth in Chapters 7 and 9. For now, it's enough to know that the `nav` is easier to move around in the layout exercises as a list; and it's more structurally logical, too. (I'm calling it `nav` as if it actually contained navigation hyperlinks. In Chapters 7 and 9, you will use a list like this one to create a functioning `nav` element with hyperlinks.) Another change to the XHTML is in `footer`. The reference to the poem by e.e. cummings is gone. It was there to give you the origin of the whimsical "Far and Wee Balloons" page title. The footer looks better without it, however, so it's missing in this chapter.

LISTING 5.1: The Far and Wee Balloon Page with Some Changes and Comments Added

```
<!DOCTYPE html PUBLIC "-//W3C//DTD XHTML 1.0 Transitional//EN" "http://www.w3.org/
TR/xhtml1/DTD/xhtml1-transitional.dtd">
<html xmlns="http://www.w3.org/1999/xhtml">
<head>
<title>Chapter 5: Page Divisions</title>
<link href="ch5_start.css" rel="style sheet" type="text/css" />
</head>
<body>
<div id="container">
  <div id="sitename">
    <h1>Far and Wee Balloons </h1>
  <!-- end of the sitename div -->
  </div>
  <div id="nav">
  <ul>
  <li>Home</li>
  <li>About Us</li>
  <li>Balloon Facts</li>
  <li>Balloon Fiesta</li>
  <li>Balloon Museum</li>
  </ul>
```

```
    <!-- end of the nav div -->
    </div>
    <div id="content">
      <h2>Floating on Air </h2>
      <p><img src="threeballoon.jpg" alt="Three Balloons" width="400" height="300"
  >Welcome to Far and Wee Balloons, where your dreams of floating on air can come
  true. We design and make hot air balloons for every use. Our balloons will give
  you a magical ride over country, mountains, and ocean.</p>
      <p>Come to our famous build-a-balloon design shop and you can enjoy a test
  flight in one of our many pre-made balloons. We organized birthday, anniversary,
  wedding, honeymoon and many other special occasion balloon flights for up to 100
  people!</p>
      <p>Inside these pages you can examine some of the many example balloon photos
  as seen at balloon races,  fiestas and rallies all around the world. </p>
      <p>It's all  fun at Far and Wee Balloons. Don't wait another minute to begin
  your fun by coming by our Balloon Museum or our famous build-a-balloon design
  shop. Both are located in Timbuktu on the Avon right off US Interstate Highway
  165.</p>
      <h3>The Balloon Museum</h3>
      <p>See balloons from history and do experiments with the science of air. Stand
  in the same gondola that went around the world in 90 days and never made history.
  Thrill to the roar of the gas burners and the silence of the wind in our balloon
  flight simulator with surround sound and rock-a-billy motion enhancers. </p>
      <p>Our Balloon Museum computers will let you design your own patterns and
  shapes for the balloon in your future. So get here now! </p>
    <!-- end of the content div -->
    </div>
    <div id="footer">&copy; Far and Wee Balloons, 2007
    <!-- end of the footer div -->
    </div>
  <!-- end of the container div -->
  </div>
  </body>
  </html>
```

The first div you see, <div id="container">, encloses everything on the page. This div was styled with a white background color. If the page had a different body background color—say, white instead of light blue—or if the text on the page was a different color, this structural device might not be needed. The container also provides a way to constrain the elements on the page t a certain size.

Notice that the value given to the id attribute for this div reflects its purpose in the overall stru ture of the page, not its appearance.

You often see a div called "wrapper." This serves the same purpose as a container division. Co tainers or wrappers are used to group elements for various purposes: semantic groupings, present tional groupings, layout groupings, special effect groupings, or to give elements a common ancesto Later in the chapter you'll use a container div enclosing a second container with the id main-body Containers may be nested.

WHAT'S IN A NAME?

Naming elements with descriptive `id` and `class` attribute values that reflect structural purpose or type of content contained is a good practice. Pick names that will hold up over time or as your site changes. If you come back to a site weeks or months after designing it and want to update or change the style rules, well-named `id` and `class` attributes can be very helpful. Names such as `banner`, `header`, `sitename`, `mainnav`, `subnav`, `search`, `contact`, `footer`, `ad`, `content`, and `blogdate` are examples of IDs that would be meaningful later.

Next you see `<div id="sitename">`. In Chapter 4, you wrote several style rules for the `h1` element in the `div sitename`. In addition to the `h1` element in the `sitename div`, such an area on a page might also contain other relevant information such as contact information, search boxes, or various links. If you put additional site-wide features such as global links, search or sign-in boxes in the `div` intended to sit atop the page, a name such as "masthead" or "pagehead" might be more appropriate than the "sitename" example here.

Moving on through Listing 5.1, you see `<div id="nav">`. This `div` encloses a list of future links—they aren't real links at this point—for navigating the site. By creating an element on the page called `nav`, you can take advantage of the CSS rules of specificity to write style rules especially for this unique element. Some sites have several types of navigation lists with `div ids` like "mainnav," "subnav," or "sectionnav," to identify and create individual style hooks for each area of navigation. Remember, the `div` is a generic mechanism to add structure. Some pages have more complex structural needs than others, but the handy-dandy `div` element is up to the challenge.

The next `div` on the page, `<div id="content">`, is well named because it holds the page's main content. There could be further `div` elements in the content area, perhaps as hooks for CSS selectors styling particular types of content or images. You don't need that much detail to move the content about in the layout exercises.

Finally, notice the `<div id="footer">`. This is normally a less prominent spot where bits of information such as copyright notices, legal notices, and webmaster contacts are placed.

When to Use *div*

The `div` elements should not replace other, more specific logically structured XHTML elements.

For example, look at the complete `<div id="content">` again:

```
<div id="content">
    <h2>Floating on Air </h2>
    <p><img src="threeballoon.jpg" alt="Three Balloons" width="400" height="300"
/>Welcome to Far and Wee Balloons, where your dreams of floating on air can come
true. We design and make hot air balloons for every use. Our balloons will give
you a magical ride over country, mountains, and ocean.</p>
    <p>Come to our famous build-a-balloon design shop and you can enjoy a test
flight in one of our many pre-made balloons. We organized birthday, anniversary,
wedding, honeymoon and many other special occasion balloon flights for up to 100
people!</p>
    <p>Inside these pages you can examine some of the many example balloon photos
as seen at balloon races,  fiestas and rallies all around the world.</p>
    <p>It's all  fun at Far and Wee Balloons. Don't wait another minute to begin
your fun by coming by our Balloon Museum or our famous build-a-balloon design
```

```
shop. Both are located in Timbuktu on the Avon right off US Interstate Highway
165.</p>
    <h3>The Balloon Museum</h3>
    <p>See balloons from history and do experiments with the science of air.
Stand in the same gondola that went around the world in 90 days and never made
history.  Thrill to the roar of the gas burners and the silence of the wind in
our balloon flight simulator with surround sound and rock-a-billy motion
enhancers. </p>
    <p>Our Balloon Museum computers will let you design your own patterns and
shapes for the balloon in your future. So get here now! </p>
  <!-- end of the content div -->
  </div>
```

There are h2, h3, and p elements in content that structure the information. The information i organized sensibly, even without any attached CSS to give the div elements layout. If you look a the page before any CSS is added, you still have content with structure that can be understood. Th XHTML structure is apparent in Figure 5.1.

As you see in Figure 5.1, the generic div that groups elements in a container called "content does not appear as an element in the browser. You may be wondering why it is needed if it isn't visible part of the document structure. It's part of the markup that makes the page *ready for CSS*. Th structure created by the div elements waits for the CSS magic to come.

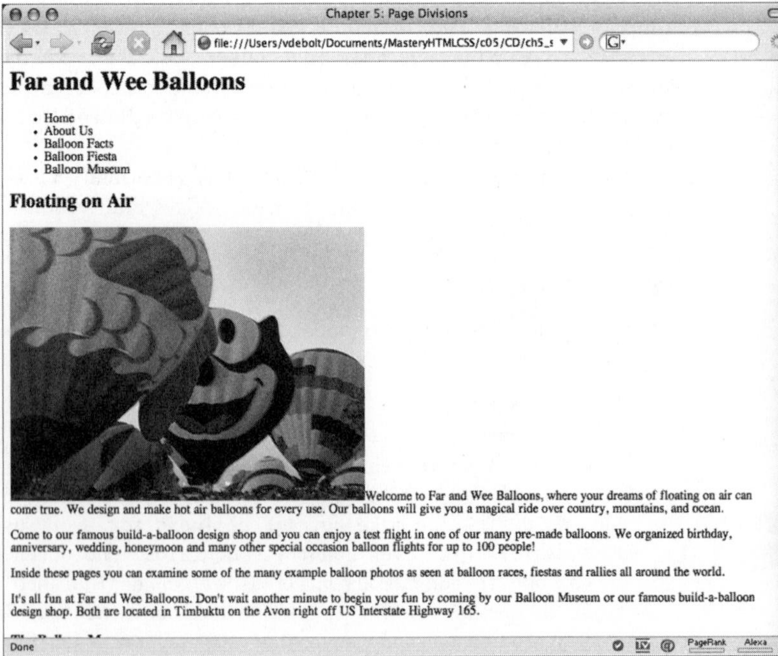

FIGURE 5.1
The page from Listing 5.1, prior to adding any CSS, reveals content organized only by the XHTML elements.

Building pages with div, id, and class involves finding related elements that serve a "structura purpose" on your page (such as a list of links) and wrapping them into a unit with a div element. Th adds a level of context to the possible CSS selectors that might be used to style this page. For exampl while you could write a CSS rule for the selector `p`, you can use the element "`content`" to write a different CSS rule for the selector `#content p`. While the first selector, `p`, would style every paragraph on the page, the second selector, `#content p`, would style only the paragraphs that were descendants of `content`. While the Far and Wee Balloon site doesn't have `p` elements anywhere but in the `content`, a more fully developed site might have `p` elements in `sidebars`, `footers`, `pullquotes`, and various other structural divs. The ability to target selectors that appear only in a specific context is the benefit of using carefully planned `div`, `id`, and `class` elements and attributes.

The main use you have seen for `span` up to this point is to add a structural element for image replacement. It's possible to assign a CSS `class` or `id` to an element by wrapping it in a `span`. In Chapter 6, you'll put this in action to use `span` to style inline text. `Span` is an inline element. It does add a structural hook for CSS but is not normally used to create layout.

CSS-READINESS

An example of a CSS-ready page can be found in the XHTML file for the CSS Zen Garden at `www.csszengarden.com`. CSS Zen Garden invites users to submit style sheets that may be used to present the page in various designs. Look for the Download the Sample html File link. After you have the XHTML page open in the browser, use the browser's View menu to view the source of the page. You will see the "Swiss army knife" of XHTML pages, ready for multiple uses by many different style sheets and allowing for rules of many degrees of specificity. People who submit to CSS Zen Garden are not allowed to change the XHTML file in any way; they can only submit a style sheet. Therefore, CSS Zen Garden creator Dave Shea created markup that allows for maximum flexibility. In doing that, he had to make some concessions to lean and clean structural markup.

For your own designs, you don't need to add redundancy like that at CSS Zen Garden. Plan your design, determine the needed elements to structure your page, and build your XHTML for that. Keep in mind that one of the reasons for using CSS is to keep XHTML files lean and mean so they download quickly.

THE STYLE ME CHALLENGE

Based on the resounding success of CSS Zen Garden in proving that CSS can create beautiful design, I was inspired to create a similar (but less complex) type of page for readers of this book. It's an excellent exercise of your burgeoning CSS skills to create a style sheet for someone else's XHTML. It's on the accompanying CD in a folder called `styleme`. When you finish the book, be sure to give yourself the challenge and fun of designing a style sheet for the `styleme.html` page. The Style Me Challenge includes a table element, which is not something you have the opportunity to practice styling on CSS Zen Garden.

Learn the CSS

One of the ways CSS is used for layout involves positioning. There are not many position values in CSS. Even though the choices are few, they are a bit tricky. Move the following files from the Chapter 5 folder on the CD to the `Mastering Integrated HTML and CSS` folder on your computer to get ready to do some work with layout:

```
ch5_start.css
ch5_start.html
ch5_threecol.css
ch5_threecol.html
ch5_z-index.css
```

```
ch5_z-index.html
threeballoon.jpg
multi_bg_1000.jpg
ballloonglow.jpg
header.jpg
content.jpg
right1.jpg
right2.jpg
right3.jpg
fixed800.gif
```

You should recognize `ch5_start.html` and `ch5_start.css` as similar to Chapter 4, but ther are some differences. The CSS file has several significant points to notice. See Listing 5.2, where tl significant changes are highlighted. The reason for these rules will be explained in the next sectio "Absolute Positioning."

LISTING 5.2: The *ch5_start.css* Page

```
/*basic structure and organization*/
body {
   font: 100% Arial, Helvetica, sans-serif;
   background: #CCD7FF;
   color: #333333;
}
#container {
   width: 700px;
   background: #FFFFFF;
   position: relative;
   margin: 0px auto;
}
#sitename {
   background: url(multi_bg_1000.jpg) no-repeat left top;
   letter-spacing: .2em;
   text-align: center;
   height: 113px;
   word-spacing: .3em;
}
#nav {
   width: 175px;
   position: absolute;
   left: 10px;
   top: 165px;
}
#content {
   margin-left: 200px;
}
```

```
#footer {
   font-size: 80%;
   clear: both;
}
/*heading styles*/
#sitename h1 {
   font: italic 300% Georgia, "Times New Roman", Times, serif;
   color: #FFFFFF;
   padding-top: .6em;
}
#content h2 {
}
#content h3 {
}
/*other styles*/
#content img {
   float: left;
   padding-right: 5px;
   padding-bottom: 5px;
}
```

In a browser, the ch5_start.html page, with ch5_start.css attached, looks something like Figure 5.2.

Open ch5_start.css in your text editor and let the positioning begin! You will use absolute positioning, relative positioning, and layouts based on float, margin, and z-index in the following pages.

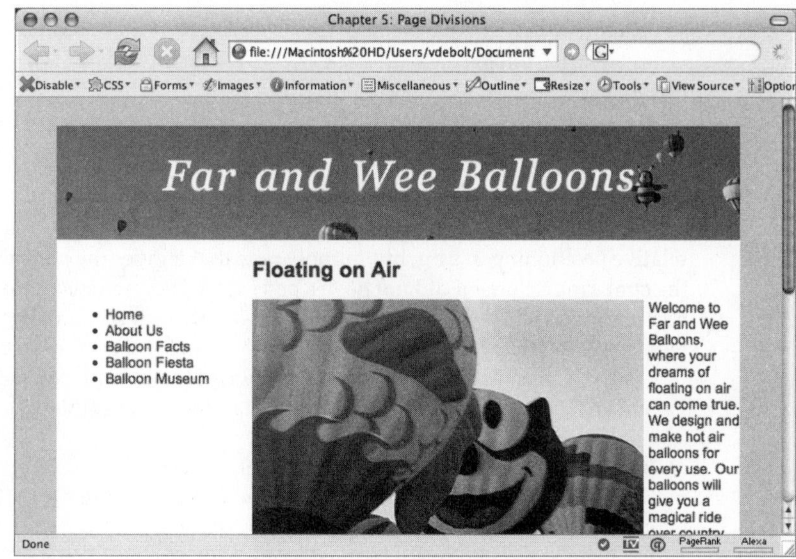

FIGURE 5.2 The Chapter 5 start page with ch5_start.css attached shows an absolutely positioned nav element.

Absolute Positioning

The normal behavior of the browser (for English) is to read the document from left to right and to to bottom. This is referred to as *document flow*. In the normal flow, each block element sits on a new line beneath the previous block element, and each inline element sits beside each previous inlin element. In other words, the normal flow of a page is one long document with items stacked dow the page. An element can be removed from that normal flow with the CSS properties `position` o `float` to create layouts with columns.

There are several concepts to understand regarding *absolute positioning*. An absolutely positione element is removed from the document flow and positioned with regard to its nearest positioned ancestor.

The only element with absolute positioning in your document is `<div id="nav">`. The CSS rul positioning this element reads:

```
#nav {
   width: 175px;
   position: absolute;
   left: 10px;
   top: 165px;
}
```

In this rule, the `position` property has the value `absolute`. That means that no matter what els happens on the page, this element goes in the exact position within its nearest positioned ancest or containing block (in this case, the `container div`). You specify the position with a measureme from the top and left of the containing block. In this rule, the `nav` element is placed exactly 165 pixe from the top and 10 pixels from the left. The measurement of distance from the top and left coul also be expressed in ems or percentages.

The phrase "position within its nearest positioned ancestor" is important. The `container` has position assigned as well:

```
#container {
   width: 700px;
   background: #FFFFFF;
   position: relative;
   margin: 0px auto;
}
```

Relative positioning does not remove an element from the normal document flow. We'll get int relative positioning in a bit, but for now note that it gives the `container` the `position` property. the `container` element did not have a `position` value set, the `nav` element would be positioned i relation to the *initial containing block* (in most browsers the initial containing block is the `html` el ment), which would require very different values for the offset from the `top` and `left`.

This is the reason the Gilder/Levin method of image replacement in Chapter 4 used `position` `relative`. That positioned the element containing the absolutely positioned image hiding the te in the heading element.

By positioning the `nav` element absolutely, you have removed it for presentation from the no mal document flow, or the order the elements appear in the XHTML. To get a true understandin of the fact that absolute positioning removes the element from the document flow, move the enti `nav` element somewhere else in the document source and see what happens.

RELATIVELY POSITIONED ANCESTORS IN IE5.5 AND IE6 ON WINDOWS

For an absolutely positioned element inside a relatively positioned element in IE6/Win and earlier, you need to make sure the relatively positioned element has some dimension set. Setting dimensions for the relatively positioned ancestor can be as easy as setting a width or height for the element. This creates an effect in Internet Explorer called *hasLayout*. If IE doesn't think an element hasLayout, the child element gets positioned in relation to the viewport, not the nearest positioned ancestor.

Open `ch5_start.html` in your text editor. A snippet of the `container` element is shown in Listing 5.3. You see the nav element in the document source *before* the `content` element.

LISTING 5.3: The *ch5_start.html* Page *container* Element

```
<div id="container">
  <div id="sitename">
    <h1>Far and Wee Balloons </h1>
  <!-- end of the sitename div -->
  </div>
  <div id="nav">
  <ul>
  <li>Home</li>
  <li>About Us</li>
  <li>Balloon Facts</li>
  <li>Balloon Fiesta</li>
  <li>Balloon Museum</li>
  </ul>
  <!-- end of the nav div -->
  </div>
  <div id="content">
    <h2>Floating on Air </h2>
    <p><img src="threeballoon.jpg" alt="Three Balloons" width="400" height="300" /
>Welcome to Far and Wee Balloons, where your dreams of floating on air can come
true. We design and make hot air balloons for every use. Our balloons will give
you a magical ride over country, mountains, and ocean.</p>
...snip...
    <p>Our Balloon Museum computers will let you design your own patterns and
shapes for the balloon in your future. So get here now! </p>
  <!-- end of the content div -->
  </div>
  <div id="footer">&copy; Far and Wee Balloons, 2007
  <!-- end of the footer div -->
  </div>
<!-- end of the container div -->
</div>
```

Cut the entire nav element and cut and paste it *after* the close of the <div id="content"> elemen
Now the last part of the page should look like this snippet:

```
...snip...
<p>Our Balloon Museum computers will let you design your own patterns and shapes
for the balloon in your future. So get here now! </p>
  <!-- end of the content div -->
  </div>
<div id="nav">
  <ul>
  <li>Home</li>
  <li>About Us</li>
  <li>Balloon Facts</li>
  <li>Balloon Fiesta</li>
  <li>Balloon Museum</li>
  </ul>
  <!-- end of the nav div -->
  </div>
  <div id="footer">&copy; Far and Wee Balloons, 2007
  <!-- end of the footer div -->
  </div>
<!-- end of the container div -->
</div>
```

Save the page and look at it in the browser. Since the absolute positioning of the nav element placed it 165px from the top and 10px from the left of the container, you should see no differenc whatever from its appearance in Figure 5.2. It doesn't matter whether the nav element falls near th top or the bottom in the document source, as long as it stays inside the container, because position absolute; removed this element from the document flow. See Figure 5.3.

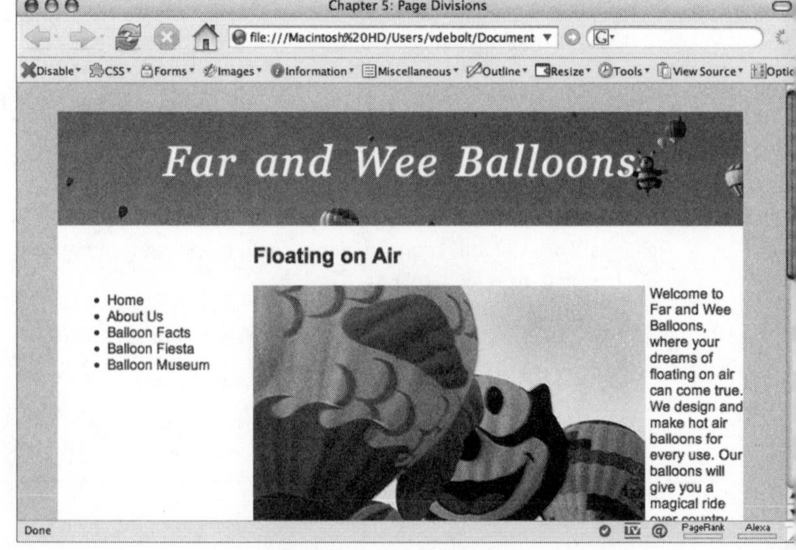

FIGURE 5.3
The effect of moving the nav element in the document source is imperceptible in the browser because absolute positioning has placed the nav in a set position.

However, if you remove the link to the style sheet and look at this document without any style rules attached, the `nav` element appears at the end of the document, just as it is now in the document flow, as shown in Figure 5.4

There are situations where presenting the links at the end of the content is desirable in terms of usability and accessibility. Users with screen readers especially appreciate not having to wade through link after link at the beginning of a document before getting to the main content. When content appears at the beginning, it is read first by search engines, too, giving a truer picture of what the site is about than a list of links provides. Absolute positioning is not the only way to achieve the "content first" goal. It is possible with `float` as well.

> **CAN'T USE ABSOLUTE POSITIONING? TRY SKIPPING**
>
> Many designers use "skip" navigation links to give users of screen readers a quick way to bypass long lists of links at the beginning of a document. It's a viable option if the design does not put the content div at the beginning of the document flow. You'll find out more about skip navigation in Chapter 7, "Links and Link Styles."

With absolute positioning, elements can appear visually anywhere you want no matter where they are in the document flow. That sounds like a really wonderful proposition, but absolute positioning is fraught with drawbacks. One never knows what monitor size or screen resolution a user will have, or if the user's default text size will immediately outgrow the space your absolutely positioned element is allotted. Other elements on the page render as if the absolutely positioned element doesn't exist, so overlaps are a frequent problem.

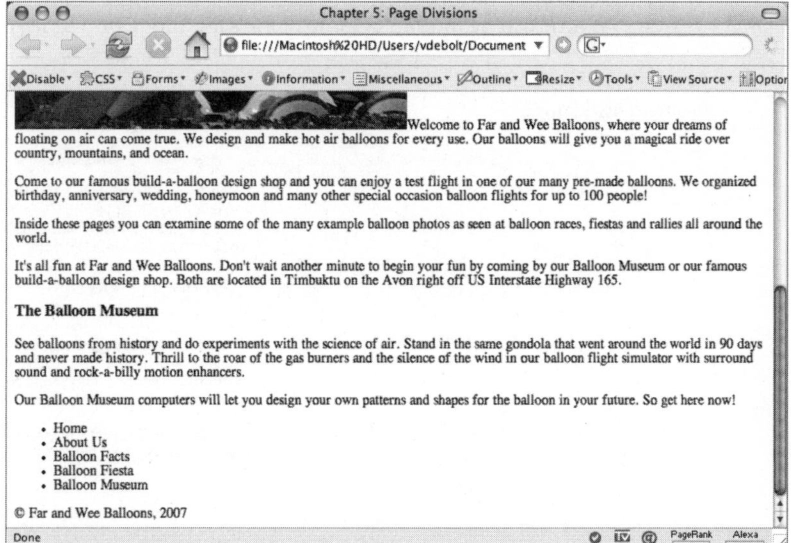

FIGURE 5.4 The document with no style rules attached clearly shows the `nav` element near the end of the document flow.

Relative Positioning

The chief distinction between absolute and relative position is that an element with `position: relative` is first positioned as if it were in the normal document flow, so that the other element around it can make room for it, and then offset by whatever value is specified from that normal po tion. It stays where it is in the document, but it can be shifted around, or offset, by a pixel, em, or pe centage value. It's important to note that it's shifted relative to its normal flow position, not from th position of its ancestor, as absolute elements are. If a relatively positioned element is offset by larg amounts, it can overlap other elements. Other elements do not move in response to the shifting abo of the relatively positioned element, even though its place in the document flow is still there.

Merely assigning `position: relative` to an element does not change its position. It appears i the normal place. When you add an offset from the `left` or `top`, it shifts position according to thos values.

Change the CSS rule for `#nav` to this:

```
#nav {
    width: 175px;
    position: relative;
    left: 10px;
    top: 35px;
}
```

With the `nav` element in the document flow after the `content` element, `nav` is now 35 pixels down from its normal position after `content`, and it's 10 pixels to the left of its normal position. It covering the footer! See Figure 5.5, which zooms in on the position of the `nav` element.

If you increased the offset to `top: 100px;` for the `#nav` rule, the element would likely be outsic of the normal viewing area, although it would still be in the document itself. This is obviously n a good idea for the page navigation, but it does illustrate the fact that elements that are not remove from the flow can be hidden outside of viewing range or overlapped in this way.

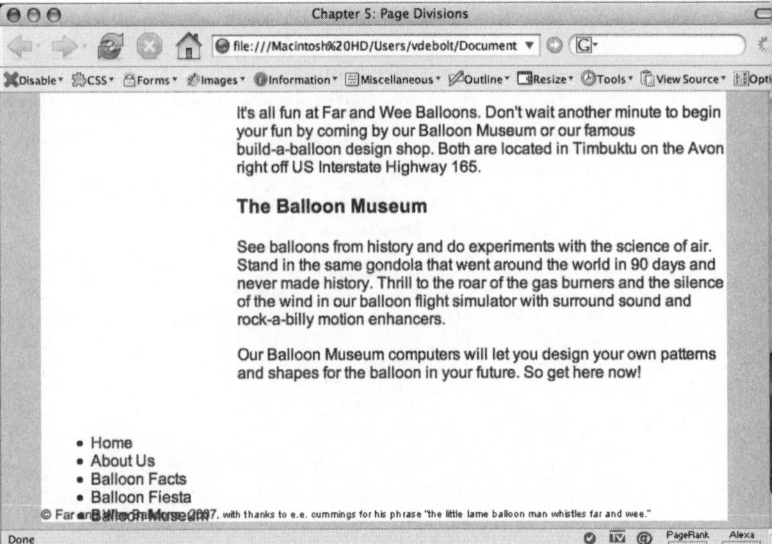

FIGURE 5.5 Relative positioning of the nav element

A more useful purpose for `position: relative` is to offset something slightly relative to where it is expected to be in the document. Keep in mind that a relatively positioned element initially appears to stay in the document flow where it is expected to be and is then offset from that position by pixels, ems, or percent values.

Fixed Positioning

With `position: fixed;` the element stays fixed in place, even if you scroll down the page. It is fixed in relation to the user's *viewport*, or the view in the browser window. To see how this works, you must abuse the poor `nav` element again. Several rules in the CSS also need adaptations. While we're at it, let's also work with a fluid, percentage-based layout. Give the `container` a percentage width:

```
#container {
   width: 90%;
   background: #FFFFFF;
   position: relative;
   margin: 0px auto;
}
```

Change the `margin-left` on the content to a percentage:

```
#content {
   margin-left: 30%;
}
```

Finally, change the `nav` rule to use `position:fixed`, like this:

```
#nav {
   width: 25%;
   position: fixed;
   left: 5%;
   top: 135px;
}
```

Save that and move to the browser.

When the page is reloaded in a browser (other than IE6 and below) you must scroll down the page to see the effect. The `nav` element stays fixed in position in relation to the viewport window, no matter how far you scroll down the page. See Figure 5.6.

FIXING FIXED POSITION

IE6 and below do not support fixed positioning. A solution, if you really want to use fixed positioning, is to add a JavaScript to make IE6 and below behave more like IE7. Most people use a script by Dean Edwards, found at `http://dean.edwards.name/ie7`. When this script is implemented on the server, a user browsing with IE5/6 will see a fixed positioned element behaving as it would in other more standards-compliant browsers.

Conditional comments for IE can also be used, a solution requiring no JavaScript. Simon Jessey explains how in this article: `http://jessey.net/simon/articles/007.html`.

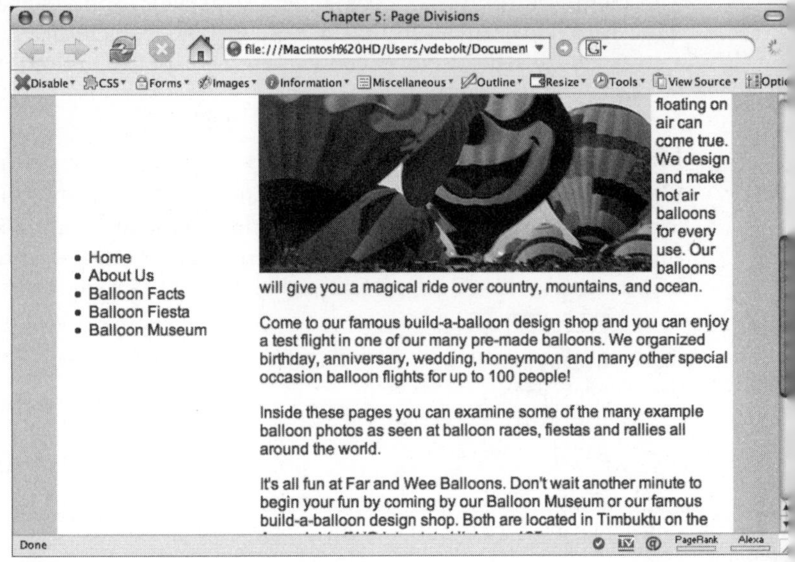

FIGURE 5.6
The nav in `position: fixed` stays where it is set to be, even as the user scrolls down the page

Page and element background images can also be given `position: fixed` so that the view scrol over an unmoving `background-image`. (IE *does* support fixed background images when they are applied to the body element.) As you saw in Chapter 3 when trying to position a background imag at the right and bottom of the browser window, there are browser variations in interpretation of what that means. Using `position: fixed` at the right and bottom for any element is a problem. B cautious if you want to use `position: fixed` for a footer or other element meant to stay at the bo tom of the viewport: test it in all browsers before implementing it.

> **WHAT ONCE WAS FRAMED**
>
> Sites using frames, which aren't included in this book in any detail because they are not accessible in most implementations, may appear to have a nav bar or footer in a fixed position. Framed sites actually display more than one page of XHTML at a time in windows, or frames, within the viewport. You may scroll down one of the windows in the framed site, while the others remain untouched, creating a stationary effect for part of the viewport. `Position: fixed` is meant to replace the less accessible framed way of keeping certain elements always in view. The long wait for Internet Explorer to catch up with more modern browsers has made the use of `position: fixed` slow to be adopted.

STATIC POSITIONING

There is also a `position` value called `static`. Since `static` amounts to the normal positioning i the normal document flow, you aren't going to spend any time working with it in this book.

You might have need for `position: static` if a style sheet further up in the cascade set a di ferent positioning value on an element. The value `static` allows you to explicitly set the `positic` attribute back to the default `static` value.

Using Margins to Arrange Content

You are already working with an element that uses margin for layout. Do you know which one it is? If you said `content`, you are right. Look at the `#content` selector. Here's the rule:

```
#content {
  margin-left: 30%;
}
```

This rule puts a 30 percent margin on the left side of the content. This explains the expanse of unused whitespace in which to place the `nav` element and why the page appears to have two columns.

Let's change it around so that 30 percent is on the right, like this:

```
#content {
  margin-right: 30%;
}
```

Save that and look in the browser. Oops, you have a problem. The page now looks like Figure 5.7, with the `nav` and the `content` sitting in the same place.

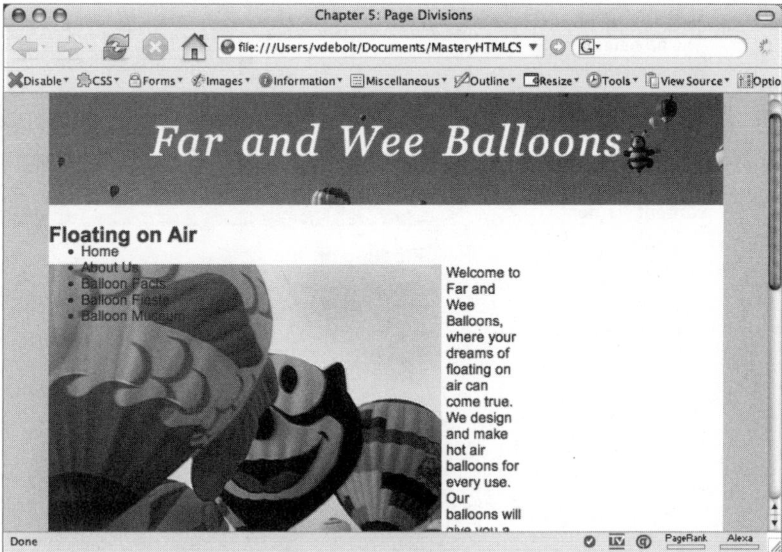

FIGURE 5.7
The `content` and `nav` collide because the position of the `nav` sets it in the same space as the `content`

Once again, you need to go back to your `#nav` selector. The rule currently there puts the `nav` in a specific position, even with other text there, too. There are very good design reasons to sometimes stack the contents of one element right on top of the contents of another element (see the upcoming section on `z-index`) but not in this case. In this case, you need to move the two elements apart. The content element does not have an explicit width. Technically you have 70 percent of the page available because the margin-right is 30 percent. However, long lines of text might run together in a two-column arrangement like this—you have no borders or padding to create a visual separation—if

you fill the entire 70 percent with textual elements. So add a width of 65 percent to the content, thu
allowing a little whitespace to form naturally between the two columns.

```
#content {
   width: 65%;
   margin-right: 30%;
}
```

If it isn't already, the `container` should be set to `position: relative`. You'll move the nav el ment to the right side of the page, using absolute positioning once again. To move the nav elemen change the rule to this:

```
#nav {
   width: 25%;
   position: absolute;
   left: 70%;
   top: 15%;}
}
```

The layout becomes readable once again. You should see something like Figure 5.8 in your browse

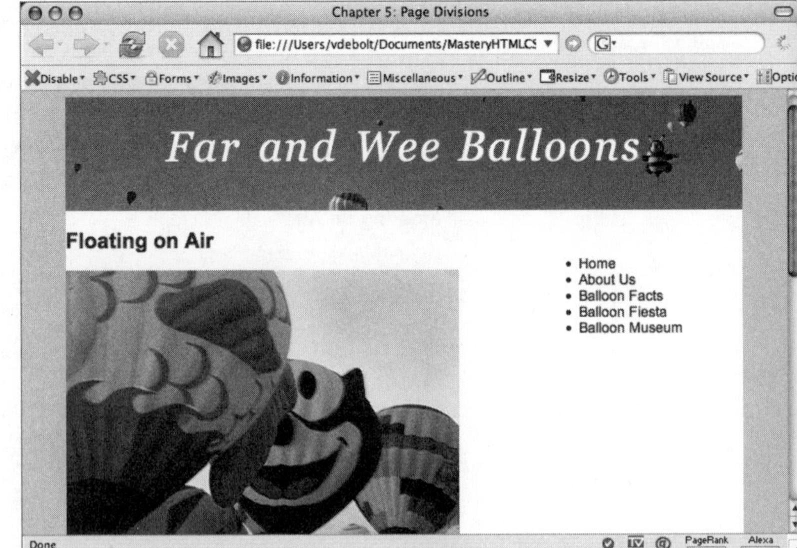

FIGURE 5.8 The nav element moves to the right based on absolute positioning, filling an area created by a wide `margin-right` on the content element

Using *float* to Arrange Content

The true purpose of the `float` property is to move an element to either the right or left side of its container. The `float` property is not a positioning scheme. Elements such as images, callouts, pull quotes, and other page layout features are often used with `float`. The text next to the floated elemer wraps around it. Although `float` often creates layouts, using `float` to create the illusion of a colum is actually a workaround for the problems associated with creating columns in CSS using `positio` Layouts based on `float` are often more stable and less problematic than layouts based on `positio`

You may have noticed that the example CSS file has been using `float` since Chapter 4. Here's the relevant selector with the `float` property:

```
#content img {
  float: left;
  margin-right: 5px;
  margin-bottom: 5px;
}
```

You've seen the three balloon image floated to the left each time you've viewed the balloon site up to now. The rule makes *any* image in the `content` element float to the left. What does that mean? Well, when an element floats, other content flows or wraps around it. If an element floats to the left, then it moves to the left and other content flows around it on the right. In order to fully understand that statement, let's examine how the image and text display without floating.

The values for `float` are `left` and `right`.There is no up, down, top, or bottom value for `float`.

FLOAT RESOURCES

There are many online resources to help you understand floats. Two excellent resources are "Containing Floats" by Eric Meyer at `www.complexspiral.com/publications/containing-floats` and "Floatutorial" at `http://css.maxdesign.com.au/floatutorial/`.

You can use CSS comments to disable the `float` attribute briefly, like this:

```
#content img {
  /*float: left;*/
  margin-right: 5px;
  margin-bottom: 5px;
}
```

By enclosing the `float` attribute and value in CSS comments, you instruct the browser to ignore that rule, and the image will not be floated. If you look at the page in the browser, you should see the arrangement shown in Figure 5.9.

Notice that the image element appears at the beginning of a paragraph element. The image is *in* the paragraph, like this:

```
<p><img src="threeballoon.jpg" alt="Three Balloons" width="400" height="300" />
```

Essentially, in Figure 5.9, the image and the text in the paragraph are sitting on the same baseline. (If you comment out the `margin-bottom: 5px;` rule, you can see this relationship even more clearly.) The browser is doing as instructed, since the image is inline content *in* the paragraph, but it looks like some sort of mistake.

EVERYTHING ABOUT IMAGES

The attributes associated with images will be discussed in detail later. The exercises are using many images without any explaining in depth what you're doing, but it's coming in Chapter 8.

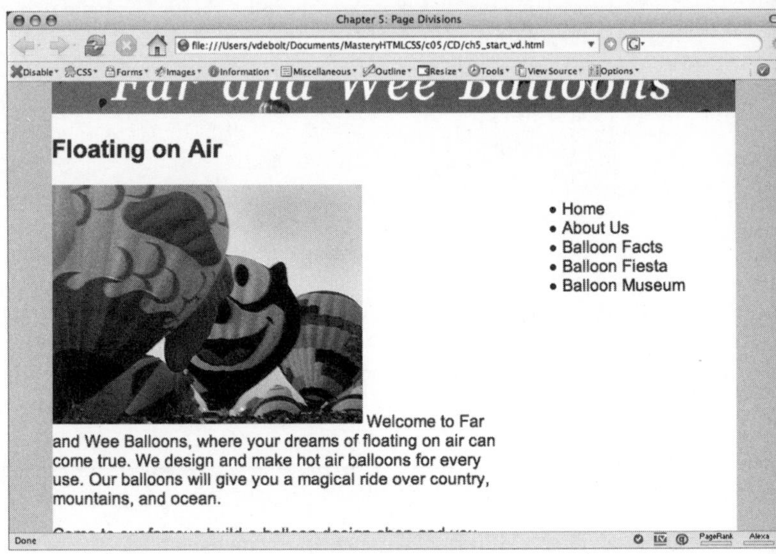

FIGURE 5.9 When the image is not set to `float:left`, the text does not wrap around it.

For comparison purposes and to further clarify how the image would look without any floa move the image element out of the paragraph like this:

```
<h2>Floating on Air </h2>
   <img src="threeballoon.jpg" alt="Three Balloons" width="400" height="300" />

<p>Welcome to Far and Wee Balloons...
```

Your results should look similar to Figure 5.10.

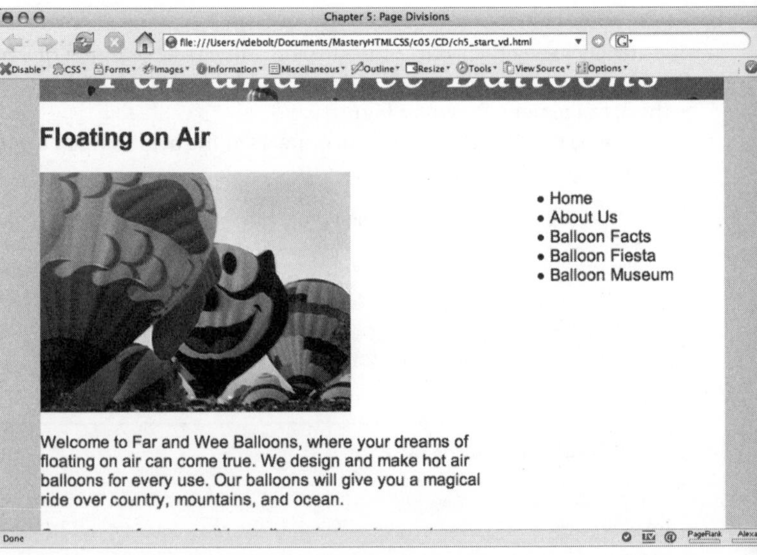

FIGURE 5.10 The nonfloated image removed from the paragraph element—the paragraph no longer begins on the same baseline as the image.

Since a paragraph is a block-level element, it automatically begins on a new line under the image element. While this layout no longer looks like a mistake, the text doesn't flow around the image. Depending on your design needs, then, you may or may not want to float images so that the text wraps around them.

Leave the image element where it is in the XHTML (outside the paragraph), and go back to the style sheet. You will make some changes to the `#content img` selector. Try `float: right;`. Change the space around the image created with the padding to bottom and left, so the text isn't bumping into the image. The new rule reads:

```
#content img {
   float: right;
   padding-bottom: 5px;
   padding-left: 5px;
}
```

Now the image should be on the right, with the text flowing all around it on the left, as shown in Figure 5.11. When an element floats—an image, a div, a table, or anything else—it moves to the right or left inside the containing element. Or it may move to the right or the left of another floated element.

Floated elements can also extend beyond the bounding box of their containing element. Move the image one more time, in order to see what happens when you float it near the end of the `content`. Cut and paste to place the `img` element between the last to paragraphs, like this:

```
<p>See balloons from history and do experiments with the science of air. Stand in
the same gondola that went around the world in 90 days and never made history.
Thrill to the roar of the gas burners and the silence of the wind in our balloon
flight simulator with surround sound and rock-a-billy motion enhancers.</p>
<img src="threeballoon.jpg" alt="Three Balloons" width="400" height="300" />
    <p>Our Balloon Museum computers will let you design your own patterns and
shapes for the balloon in your future. So get here now!</p>
```

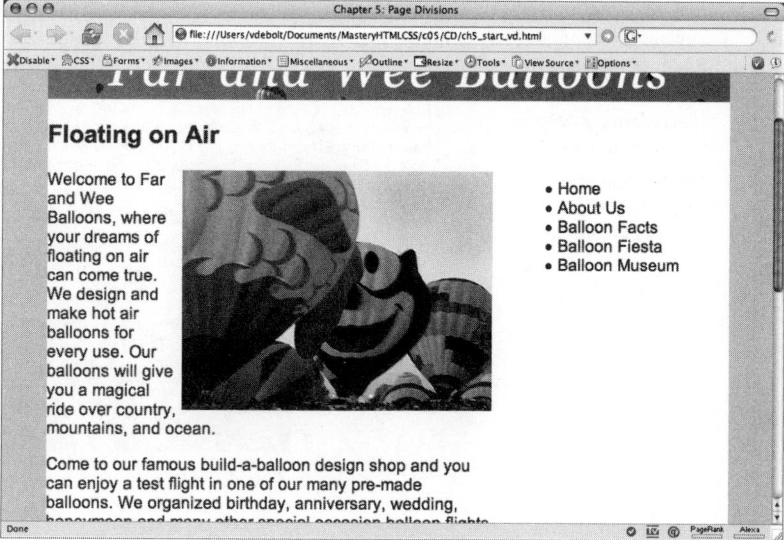

FIGURE 5.11
Using `float: right` to move the image to the right side of the content element, with the text wrapping around it on the left

You can see how the floated element extends beyond its container if you make a temporary change to the CSS rule for content. Add a 2-pixel wide, solid black (#000000) border to the conten rule, like this:

```
#content {
   width: 65%;
   margin-right: 30%;
   border: 2px solid #000000;
}
```

Your browser view should look something like Figure 5.12. As you can see from the way the image extends beyond the black borders of the `content` element, a floated element may cause unexpected changes in other parts of a layout because floats, like positioned elements, are remove from the normal document flow.

The floated image is *not* overlapping the `footer` element. Look at the rule for the footer:

```
#footer {
   font-size: 80%;
   clear: both;
   }
```

The `clear: both` rule has been in the `footer` all along. Now you'll find out why. The `float` an `clear attributes` go hand in hand: floats often need to be cleared.

More Floating, with *Clear* to the Rescue

To understand `float` and `clear`, you are going to change from the current layout to a two-colum layout created with `float`. Floating is probably the most reliable and popular way to create two and three-column layouts, but you have to know what you're doing to make it work.

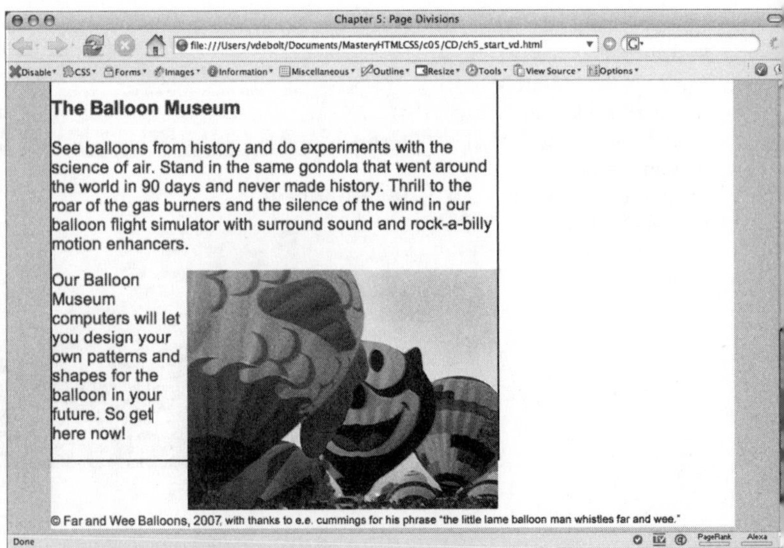

FIGURE 5.12 Because the image is floated, it may extend beyond the bounds of its containing box in some situations. Here the containing element is bordered in black, and you can see that the image pokes out of its parent element.

Start with some changes in the XHTML. First add another image (`balloonglow.jpg`) to the page, at the beginning of the first paragraph, like this:

```
<h2>Floating on Air </h2>
   <p><img src="balloonglow.jpg" alt="Balloon Glow" width="300" height="225" /
>Welcome to Far and Wee Balloons . . .
```

This new image is meant simply to help you with the concept of floating an image; it doesn't have any bearing on creating a two-column layout with float.

Next, change the placement of the three balloon image to *inside* the last paragraph on the page, like this:

```
<p><img src="threeballoon.jpg" alt="Three Balloons" width="400" height="300" /
>Our Balloon Museum computers . . .
```

Several changes must be made in the CSS. Start with `#nav`. Change the rule to:

```
#nav {
   width: 25%;
   margin-left: 70%;
}
```

This creates a `nav` element that will have 70 percent of the page to the left of it open and empty. If there was no width declaration on the `nav` element, it would completely fill the right 30 percent of the page. (Using a width of 25 percent, instead of the full 30 percent, allows a little whitespace room on the right so things won't bump into the right side of the viewport.) Visualize this; you have filled the right 30 percent of the page with an element. The rest of the page is not spoken for yet.

Adding a light gray background (`#E4E4E4`) to `#content` will help visualize the two-column effect, and it will clearly show where the other elements fall when the content is changed to `float: left`. Here's the rule:

```
#content {
   background-color: #E4E4E4;
   width: 65%;
   float: left;
}
```

This rule makes `content` move to the left. Other elements, the `nav` to be precise, will sit next to it. The `nav` would actually wrap around the content like the text around the three-balloon image, except for one big difference. That difference is the `margin-left: 70%` holding the `nav` to the right 30 percent of the page. Even if the `nav` grew to be longer than the content, it couldn't wrap under it like the text under the three balloon image because it is constrained to the right 30 percent of the page. In effect, it is a column filling 30 percent on the right.

`Content` will stay to the left. It has 70 percent of the page to itself. (Setting a `width` of 65 percent for content means that there will be a bit of whitespace to the right of the content before any text in the `nav` begins—a gutter, in print terminology.) The floated content is, in effect, a column filling 70 percent on the left. Voilà, a two-column layout.

Change the images in the `content` box back to their original left floating position, like this:

```
#content img {
   float: left;
   padding-right: 5px;
padding-bottom: 5px;
}
```

Finally, don't completely eliminate the `clear: both` in the `#footer`, because as you'll quick
see, it's needed. For now, just comment it out, like this:

```
#footer {
   font-size: 80%;
   /*clear: both;*/
   }
```

Save everything and take a look in the browser. The `nav` element, which is part of the `contain`
and has a white background inherited from the `container`, now appears to be only as large as t
textual content it contains. See Figure 5.13. Most designers who use background colors to help d
tinguish a two-column layout want both columns to contain the appropriate background color
the way down the page to the footer. The lack of white background filling the entire right "colum
becomes a problem.

Furthermore, as you see in Figure 5.13, the footer now appears under the `nav`, and not at the fo
of the page at all! Another problem. Both problems result from floating the `content` element on t
left. The solution, in this particular configuration of elements, is to give the footer the `clear` proper

The possible declarations for the `clear` property are `clear: left`, `clear: right`, or `clear`
`both`. Using `clear:left` or `clear: right` forces your content past anything floating on the left
on the right, respectively. Using `clear: both` forces material past anything floating on *either* si

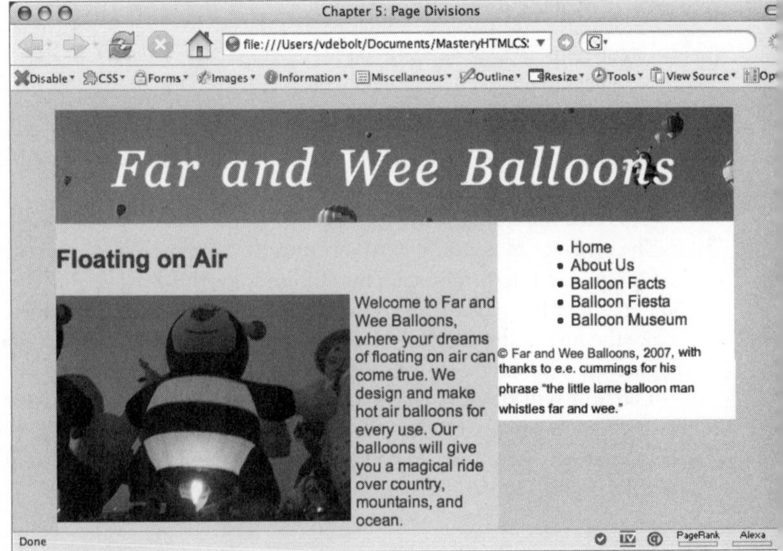

FIGURE 5.13
The `nav` element doesn't extend the white background of the container all the way down the right column, and the footer sits directly under the `nav` without a `clear: both` rule.

Remove the comment marks from the `#footer` rule. That forces the footer to clear all the content on both sides before it appears. The rule looks like this:

```
#footer {
    font-size: 80%;
    clear: both;
    }
```

The effect makes the right "column" background color appear to extend all the way down the page and to place the footer under both the `content` and `nav` boxes, right where you want it to be. See Figure 5.14.

Because `footer` is nested inside `container`, when `footer` is set to `clear: both`, the container has to stretch down to a `clear: both` position along with `footer`. The `background-color` of `container` stretches down with it.

The `clear` property can be assigned to any element such as `img`, `p`, `h3`, and `table`.

There may be design situations where a clear is needed after some element, but for whatever reason, the clear cannot be assigned to the following element. Sometimes designers use an empty, nonsemantic, extra element to create a clear. A common solution involves creating a `class` declaration and using it in a `div`. First create the `class` in a style sheet. Use an explanatory name, such as `clearer`.

```
.clearer {
   clear: both;
}
```

Then add an empty element such as `<div class="clearer"> </div>` to the XHTML in the spot where you need to clear a float. With no content except the nonbreaking space (` `), this element is not an example of good XHTML structure and would fall into the category of a flawed-but-useful workaround.

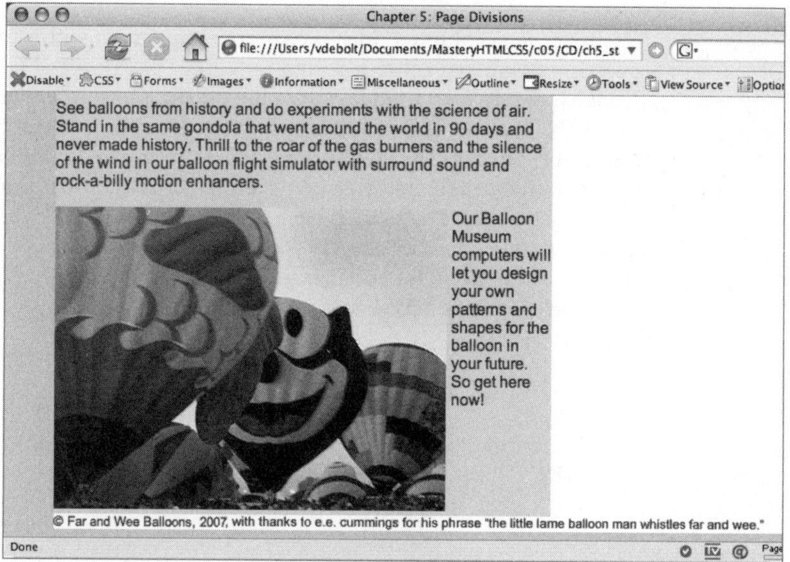

FIGURE 5.14
With `clear:both` applied to the footer, both the right side of the page and the position of the footer are as desired.

ANOTHER WAY TO CLEAR

One way to clear floats without extra structural markup is the easy clearing method at `http://positioniseverything.net/easyclearing.html`. It uses a technique that involves the pseudo-elements `:after` and `visibility: hidden`. IE6 and below do not support pseudo-elements, so hacks are involved in getting the technique to work cross-browser. The pseudo-element `:after` may not be supported in IE7. One of the hacks used to make this work, the Holly hack, isn't going to work in IE7, so any use of this method would best be separated into a specific hacks style sheet and linked to in a conditional comment targeting IE. I expect `positioniseverything.net` to offer revisions when IE7 is available, so keep an eye on that site for updates. There are a couple of useful resources about the future of easy clearing here: `www.456bereastreet.com/archive/200603/new_clearing_method_needed_for_ie7` and `www.stuffandnonsense.co.uk/archives/clearing_floats_without_structural_markup_in_ie7.html`

USING FAUX COLUMNS IN A FIXED TWO-COLUMN LAYOUT

With a floated layout, background colors used in various divs creating the column effects don't always carry all the way down the "column" to the footer. The `clear` property can't always fix th problem. Dan Cederholm came up with the idea of using a background image to create the appea ance of a full-length background color. He dubbed it "faux columns" and published an article abo it in A List Apart at `http://alistapart.com/articles/fauxcolumns`.

As with any good idea, other CSS developers have run with it, polished it, improved it, and p it to all sorts of uses. My esteemed colleague and the technical editor of this book, Zoe Gillenwate described how to create liquid faux columns here:

```
www.communitymx.com/content/article.cfm?cid=AFC58
```

I urge you to read the article and try adding a faux column to one of the liquid designs in thi chapter.

The basic "faux columns" idea is easiest to implement with a fixed-width design. You'll add faux column to the two-column design.

Percentages created a fluid layout in the previous example. You'll switch things around agai to a fixed pixel layout. This time the `nav` will float on the left, and the `content` will be on the rig with an ample `margin-left` to keep it from wrapping under the floated `nav` element.

I mentioned that a floated element is removed from the document flow. But its position in th source order matters. The floated element must appear in the source prior to elements that wi wrap around it. In order for the `nav` element to appear in the document flow in the proper pla for the element to float left and create a "left column," it needs to move back up to the spot between the `sitename` and the `content` (where it's been before; you're sending it back home It goes here:

```
<!-- end of the sitename div -->
  </div>
  <div id="nav">
    <ul>
```

```
      <li>Home</li>
      <li>About Us</li>
      <li>Balloon Facts</li>
      <li>Balloon Fiesta</li>
      <li>Balloon Museum</li>
    </ul>
    <!-- end of the nav div -->
  </div>
  <div id="content">
```

Now go through the CSS rules to change over to the new layout. Give `#container` a fixed width:

```
#container {
   width: 800px;
   background: #FFFFFF;
   margin: 0px auto;
}
```

Change the `width` and `float` rules for both the `#nav` and `#content`, like this:

```
#nav {
   width: 200px;
   float: left;
}
#content {
   background-color: #E4E4E4;
   width: 550px;
   margin-left: 225px;
}
```

Save both files and look at the page with a browser. The top of the page looks good. See Figure 5.15. The bottom of the page has a problem with the floated image. See Figure 5.16.

Containing Floats and IE

In Internet Explorer for Windows, if an element `hasLayout` then the containing element will automatically expand to contain a floated element. In IE/Win, the floated image in Figure 5.16 will not extend out of the containing element as you see in the screen capture.

These properties give an element hasLayout in IE/Win:

`position: absolute`

`float: left or float: right`

`display: inline-block`

`width:` any value

`height:` any value

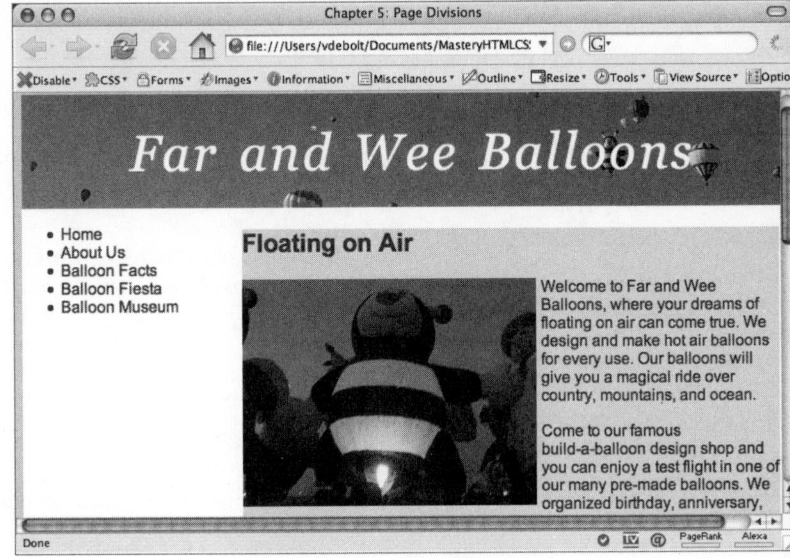

FIGURE 5.15 The upper part of the page with a fixed pixel layout. The `nav` element is floated on the left. The content element has a large `margin-left`.

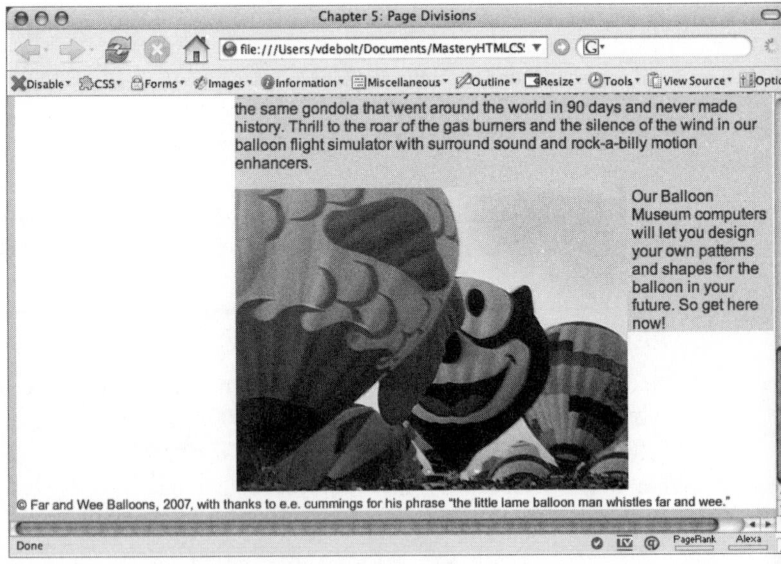

FIGURE 5.16 The lower part shows how the floated image sticks out of the content element containing it.

Time for faux columns. You'll resolve this problem with a `background-image` in the container that creates the illusion of columns. The `fixed800.gif` on the accompanying CD is the background graphic. This image is exactly 800 pixels in width, a thin graphic that will repeat along the y-axis of the container. The 200 pixels on the left are a light blue, and the 600 pixels on the right are the same light gray used as background in the `content` div.

First, add the `background-image` to the container:

```
#container {
    width: 800px;
    background: #FFFFFF url(fixed800.gif) repeat-y left;
    margin: 0px auto;
}
```

ANOTHER FAUX POSSIBILITY

A workable faux alternative in the two-column design in this exercise is to use a GIF with 200 blue pixels on the left and 600 transparent pixels on the right. Then change the background color of the `container` to `#E4E4E4`, so the light gray shines through the transparent part of the GIF.

A 2-pixel line separates the blue from the gray in this background graphic. To match that design element, add a 1-pixel border to the bottom of `#sitename`.

```
#sitename {
    background: url(multi_bg_1000.jpg) no-repeat left top;
    border-bottom: 1px solid #666666;
height: 113px;
letter-spacing: .2em;
    text-align: center;
    word-spacing: .3em;

}
```

You see the top of the page in Figure 5.17, the bottom in Figure 5.18. The blue column extends all the way to the bottom; the gray column does the same. The floated divs can end anywhere along the y-axis, but the background image continues for the entire container, creating the column appearance. Note that the `footer` has the same two-column appearance now. To overcome that effect, the `footer` would need to be moved out of the container. The `sitename` div, also in the `container`, has the faux column effect as well, but the `background-image` in `sitename` hides it.

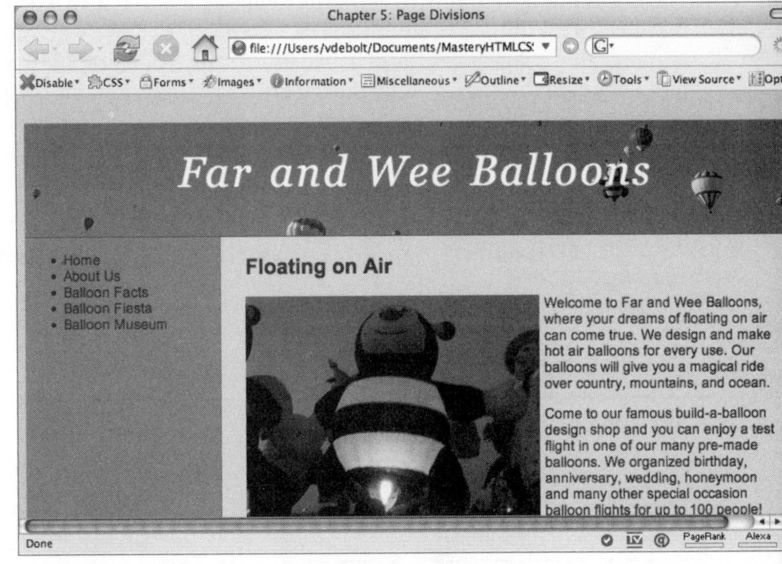

FIGURE 5.17 A `background-image` in the container creates the faux column effect.

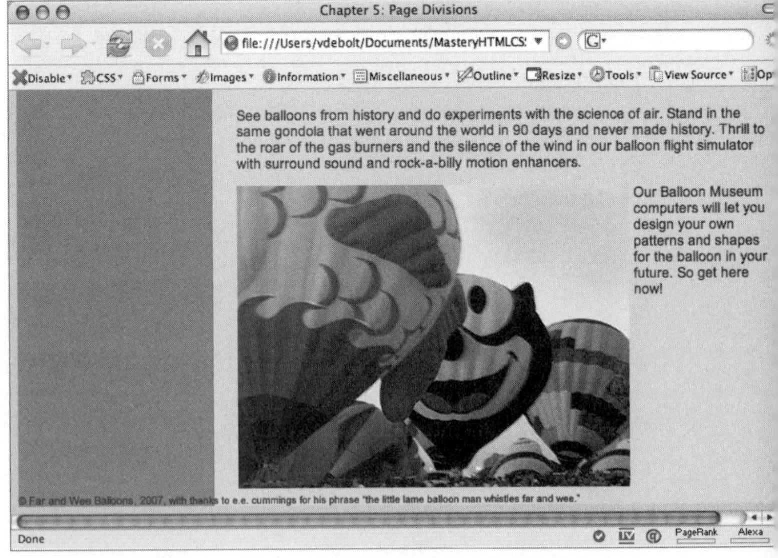

FIGURE 5.18 The faux column effect carries all the way to the end of the container, regardless of where the floated divs come to an end.

A Flexible Three-Column Floated Layout

There are many ways to create a three-column layout. There is a property in CSS, `display: table`, that creates columns, although it's not supported by Internet Explorer. IE7 will not support it, either. If this property ever gains support by this major browser, it will quickly replace most other methods of creating layouts with columns. For now, many three-column solutions build on floats, margins, and positioning.

Figures 5.19–5.21 show the basic XHTML and CSS needed for three possible ways to achieve a three-column layout. You will work with the example shown in Figure 5.19: the *liquid, all floated, content first* layout. Use Figures 5.20 and 5.21 to help you put together the other two examples on your own.

There's a page using that structure, but filled out with a bit of text and images, on the accompanying CD: `ch5_threecol.html`. Images used in the file include `header.jpg`, `content.jpg`, `right1.jpg`, `right2.jpg`, and `right3.jpg`. The contents of that XHTML file are shown in Listing 5.4. Note the attached `ch5_threecol.css`.

Figure 5.19
The content comes first in the document flow in this layout, giving it an accessibility and search engine advantage. The three main columns are floated, the two on the left inside a container `div` that is itself floated.

Three-Column Layout 1: Liquid, all floated, content first

```
<div id="wrapper">
   <div id="header"></div>
   <div id="main-body">
      <div id="content"></div>
      <div id="left"> </div>
   </div>
   <div id="right"></div>
<div id="footer"></div>
</div>
```

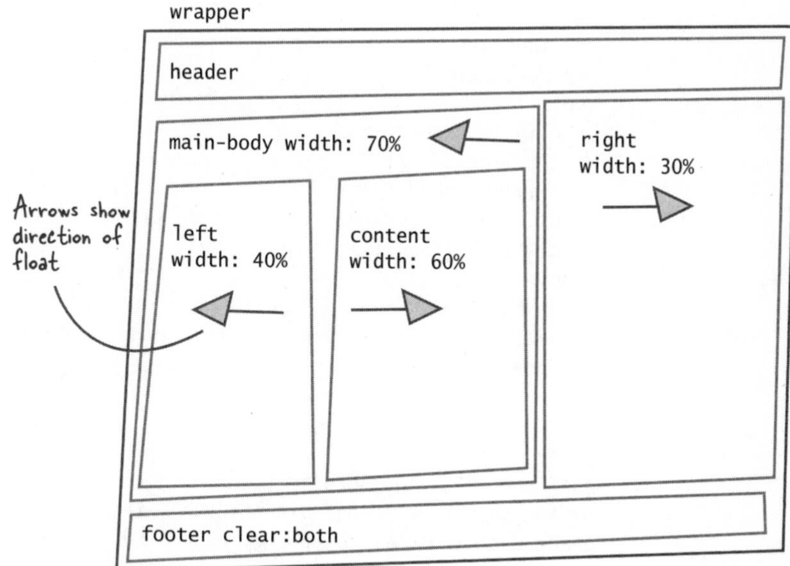

LISTING 5.4: The *ch5_threecol.html* Page

```
<!DOCTYPE html PUBLIC "-//W3C//DTD XHTML 1.0 Transitional//EN" "http://www.w3.org/
TR/xhtml1/DTD/xhtml1-transitional.dtd">
<html xmlns="http://www.w3.org/1999/xhtml">
<head>
<title>Ch5: Three-Column</title>
<link href="ch5_threecol.css" rel="style sheet" type="text/css" />
</head>
<body>
<div id="wrapper">
  <div id="header">
    <h1>The Flower Page</h1>
  </div>
  <div id="main-body">
    <div id="content">
      <h2>Flower of the Week</h2>
      <img src="content.jpg" alt="White Iris" width="300" height="225" />
      <p>This week's featured flower is the white iris. This flower is white. It's
an iris. You can trust me to tell the truth about that.</p>
      <p>It grows in the ground. It blooms in the spring. It's known as a spring
bulb. It grows from a bulb and the bulbs multiply and if you aren't careful you'll
have a whole field full of iris after a few years, because these bulbs are busy
being prolific down there in the dark.</p>
      <p>Don't forget to cut some and take them inside because they smell really
nice and they don't make you sneeze all that much.</p>
    </div>
    <div id="left">
      <p>Navigation</p>
      <ul>
        <li>link one</li>
        <li>link two</li>
        <li>link three</li>
        <li>link four</li>
        <li>link five</li>
      </ul>
      <h3>News Items</h3>
      <p>All the latest flower news and blurbs about specials and stuff and
nonsense goes here.</p>
    </div>
  </div>
  <div id="right">
    <h3>Flower Highlights</h3>
    <p><img src="right1.jpg" alt="Cactus" width="150" height="113" /></p>
    <p>The cactus blooms in spring. Here's how to encourage your cactus to bloom:
water it.</p>
    <p><img src="right2.jpg" width="150" height="113" /></p>
```

```
    <p>A cactus in your garden can brighten up the scene in early spring. The rest
of the year feel free to ignore it.</p>
    <p><img src="right3.jpg" alt="White flowers" width="150" height="113" /> </p>
    <p>Masses of flowers make good ground cover.</p>
  </div>
  <div id="footer">The Flower Page footer </div>
</div>
</body>
</html>
```

The three columns in this layout, `content`, `left`, and `right`, are all floated. The layout is based on percentages (hence the flexible or fluid name) and the `footer` is cleared using `clear: both`. Those rules and a few more are in the `ch5_threecol.css` file. See Listing 5.5.

Listing 5.5: The Basic Rules with a Few Embellishments for the Liquid, All Floated, Content First Layout

```
body {
   font: 100%/125% Verdana, Arial, Helvetica, sans-serif;
   background: #FFF;
   margin: 0px; /*remove all the margins, add them where you want later*/
   padding: 0px; /*remove all the padding, add it where you want later*/
}
#wrapper {
   margin: 0px;
   padding: 0px;
   width: 100%;
}
#main-body {
   float: left;
   width: 70%;
}
#content {
   float: right;
   width: 60%;
}
#left {
   float: left;
   width: 40%;
}
#right {
   float: right;
   width: 30%;
}
#footer {
   clear: both;
   text-align: center;
```

```
}
#header {
   background: url(header.jpg) no-repeat left top;
}
#header h1 {
   font: 200%/150% Verdana, Arial, Helvetica, sans-serif;
   color: #FFF;
   text-align: right;
   padding-right: 1em;
}
#right img, #content img {
   border-right: 2px solid #CCC; /*creates a drop shadow effect*/
   border-bottom: 3px solid #CCC; /*creates a drop shadow effect*/
   margin-left: 3px;
}
```

Another three column layout (see Figure 5.20) uses absolute positioning and still achieves a fluid layout in the middle column.

The third example three-column layout (see Figure 5.21) shows three divs, all floated left. Negative margins are used to place the last div in the source order on the left visually.

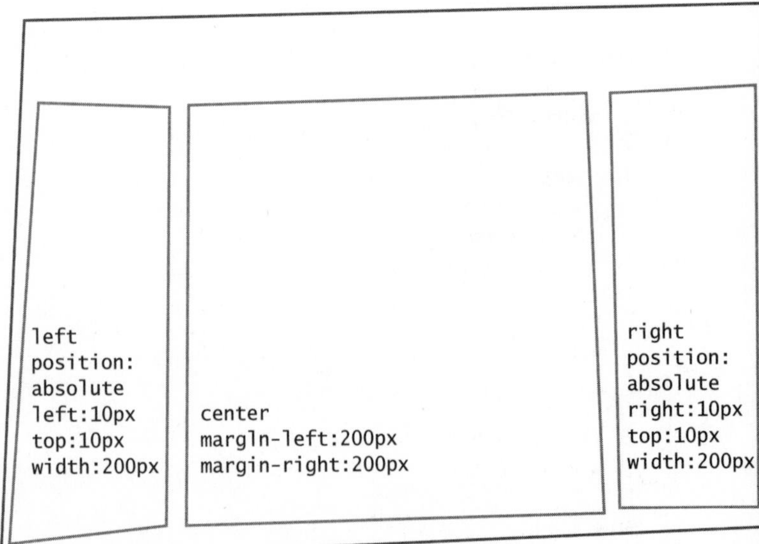

FIGURE 5.20 While the left and right columns have a set width, the center column in this design can expand or contract with the viewport. Designs using position: absolute may not hold up if the user enlarges the text size.

Three-Column Layout 3: Fixed width, all floated, negative margins

```
<div id="wrapper">
   <div id="header"></div>
   <div id="content"></div>
   <div id="right"></div>
   <div id="left"></div>
   <div id="footer"></div>
</div>
```

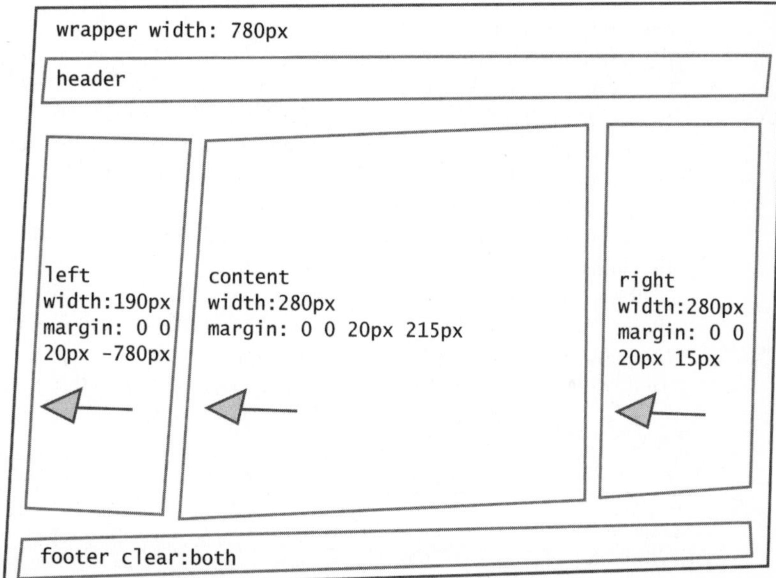

FIGURE 5.21 Another design with the content first in the document flow, this layout uses floats and a large negative margin to put the last element in the document flow at the left of the presentation.

THREE COLUMNS: EVERYBODY WANTS 'EM

Since the W3C first came out with the recommendation that layouts should be built with CSS, many talented designers have struggled to come up with the best way to get to that "holy grail," the three-column layout. The number of variations on this theme is astounding. Here are a few places where you can learn more ways to create three-column layouts:

- The CSS Discuss Wiki: `http://css-discuss.incutio.com/?page=ThreeColumnLayouts`
- Glish (originator of the phrase "holy grail"): `www.glish.com/css/7.asp`
- Blue Robot: `www.bluerobot.com/web/layouts`
- Salia: `www.saila.com/usage/layouts`
- Position Is Everything's One True Layout: `http://positioniseverything.net/articles/onetruelayout`
- Eric Meyer's Multi Unit: `http://meyerweb.com/eric/thoughts/2005/11/09/multi-unit-any-order-columns`

- Max Design: `www.maxdesign.com.au/presentation/page_layouts`
- A List Apart:
  - `www.alistapart.com/articles/holygrail/`
  - `www.alistapart.com/articles/negativemargins/`

Of the three layouts shown, you'll do some work with the liquid, all floated, content first layou and CSS shown in Listings 5.4 and 5.5. You will get a chance to work with it in the exercises at t end of the chapter. Take a look at `ch5_threecol.html` in the browser. You should see a page si ilar to Figure 5.22.

There's a lot to like about this layout. The `content div` comes first in the XHTML source. The fore it's screen reader (and search engine) friendly and more accessible. The percentage-based desi holds up well when a user alters the browser width or reduces/enlarges the text size to suit his or h own visual requirements. A picky drawback to the design is the requirement of an extra nonseman div (`main-body`) to contain the `content` and `left` boxes.

Three-column layouts always present some sort of compromise choice. Some need skip naviga tion links to help screen reader users bypass divs full of links prior to the content. Some don't hold well cross-browser. Some require several hacks. The layouts in Figures 5.19–5.21 are good choice though not perfect. The accompanying CD does not contain prebuilt XHTML and CSS pages for t *left and right absolute—center fluid* layout or for the *all floats with negative margin—fixed width* layou That's so you can build them yourself! The information in the figures will get you started.

The final layout scheme you will use is `z-index`.

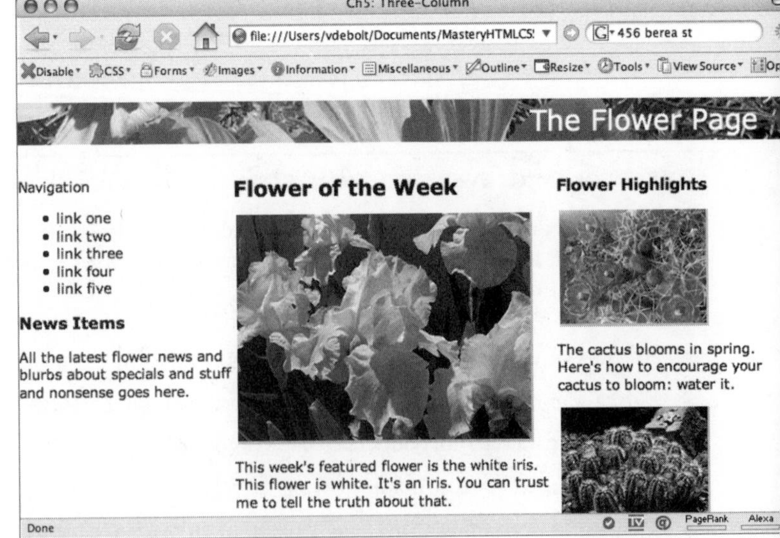

FIGURE 5.22 This fluid three-column design uses three floated columns, with the content element first in the source.

Using *z-index* to Arrange Content

Basically, z-index is the third dimension of a web page. One dimension is the x-axis, which places elements on the horizontal axis. The second dimension is the y-axis, which places elements on the vertical axis. The final dimension is front-to-back, or z-index.

Some of the most interesting reasons for using `z-index` rely on JavaScript (or some similar scripting language) to do things such as make one element visible and another hidden when the user clicks a link or rolls over an element with a pointing device or mouse. Since explaining scripting languages is beyond the scope of this book, I will not do anything like that here, but you will take a look at a simple page that will help you understand `z-index`.

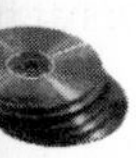

Open `ch5_z-index.html` and `ch5_z-index.css` in your text editor, and open `ch5_z-index.html` in the browser. In the browser, you should see something like Figure 5.23.

The XHTML page is very simple (Listing 5.6).

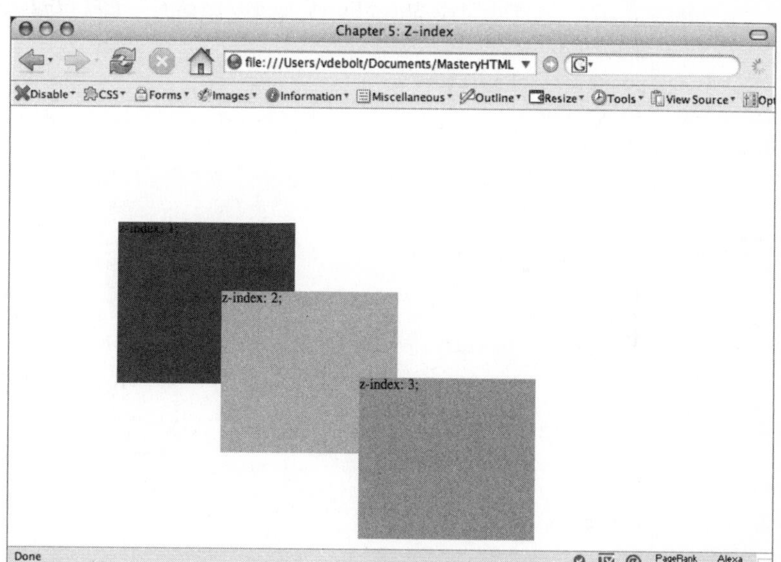

FIGURE 5.23
The starting `ch5_z-index.html` file

LISTING 5.6: A Simple Page Demonstrating *z-index* for Layout

```
<!DOCTYPE html PUBLIC "-//W3C//DTD XHTML 1.0 Transitional//EN" "http://www.w3.org/
TR/xhtml1/DTD/xhtml1-transitional.dtd">
<html xmlns="http://www.w3.org/1999/xhtml">
<head>
<title>Chapter 5: Z-index</title>
<link href="ch5_z-index.css" rel="stylesheet" type="text/css" />
</head>
```

```
<body>
<div id="one">z-index: 1; </div>
<div id="two">z-index: 2; </div>
<div id="three">z-index: 3; </div>
</body>
</html>
```

The XHTML page contains three `div` elements, each with a bit of text giving you a visual clu as to the `z-index` value of the `div`. The page includes a link to a style sheet. The style sheet contair the rules shown in Listing 5.7.

LISTING 5.7: The Style Sheet Rules Used with *ch5_z-index.html*

```
#one {
position: absolute;
left:111px;
top:114px;
width:180px;
height:160px;
z-index:1;
background: #FF0000;
}
#two {
position: absolute;
left:217px;
top:182px;
width:180px;
height:160px;
z-index:2;
background: #FFCC00;
}
#three {
position: absolute;
left:358px;
top:267px;
width:180px;
height:160px;
z-index:3;
background: #66CCCC;
}
```

You already understand most of these rules. Each `div` is absolutely positioned, using slight different pixel offsets from the `left` and `top`—to place them in different positions. Each `div` shares the same `width` and `height`. There are different background colors. The only new CS property for you to learn here is `z-index`. An element with a higher `z-index` is closer to the viewer. So the element with `z-index: 1` is the farthest back, the element with `z-index: 2` overlaps that and is closer to the viewer, and the element with `z-index: 3` is the closest of the three. This concept is often referred to as *stacking order*, with the highest `z-index` value putting an element on the top of the stack.

ACT NATURALLY

Elements in a document have a natural z-index based on document flow and position values, even when a z-index order is not declared. To understand this, simply use CSS comments to disable the three z-index declarations in the style sheet, like this: `/*z-index:1;*/`. In a browser, the page should look exactly like Figure 5.23. Only when you want to manipulate that natural stacking order do you need to include a z-index declaration in the CSS. You will be manipulating that natural stacking order in the following exercises, so remove comment marks from the three z-index declarations before proceeding.

Values with `z-index` don't have to start from 1 and progress in unbroken order. The elements in this example could have had `z-index` values of 10, 20, and 30, or 3, 7, 9, and the results would have been the same. If you have several stacked elements on a page and want to add a new one that you are sure will be at the very top of the stacking order, you can give it some high `z-index` value like 100.

In the style sheet, change the values for the `position` of all three elements to be exactly the same:

```
position: absolute;
left: 111px;
top: 114px;
```

With all three elements in the same position on the page, which one should you see? The answer is element `three`, the one with the highest `z-index`, as shown in Figure 5.24. The other two are there. You just can't see them at the moment.

Move elements `two` and `three` a few pixels, as shown in this snippet:

```
#two {
position:absolute;
left:116px;
top:118px;
[...]

#three {
position:absolute;
left:120px;
top:122px;
[...]
```

With this shift of a few pixels down and to the right, you get an appearance similar to what you see in Figure 5.25.

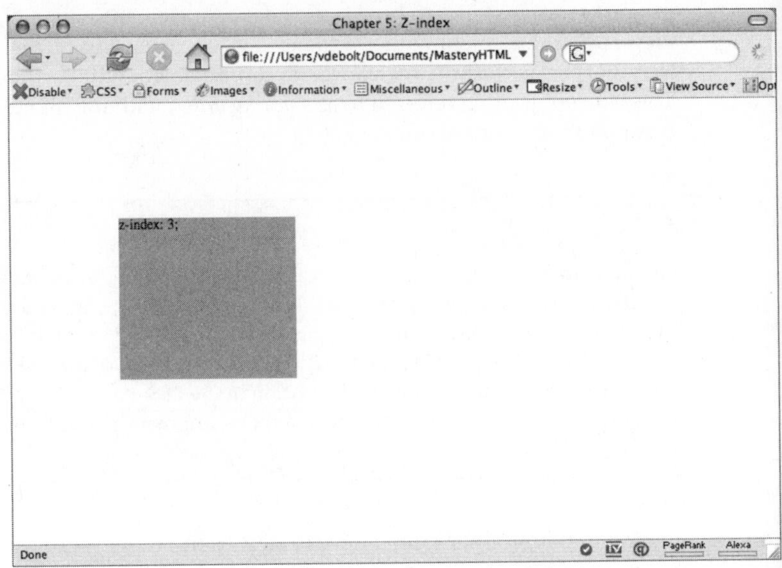

FIGURE 5.24 Three elements in the same absolute position. Only the topmost one is visible.

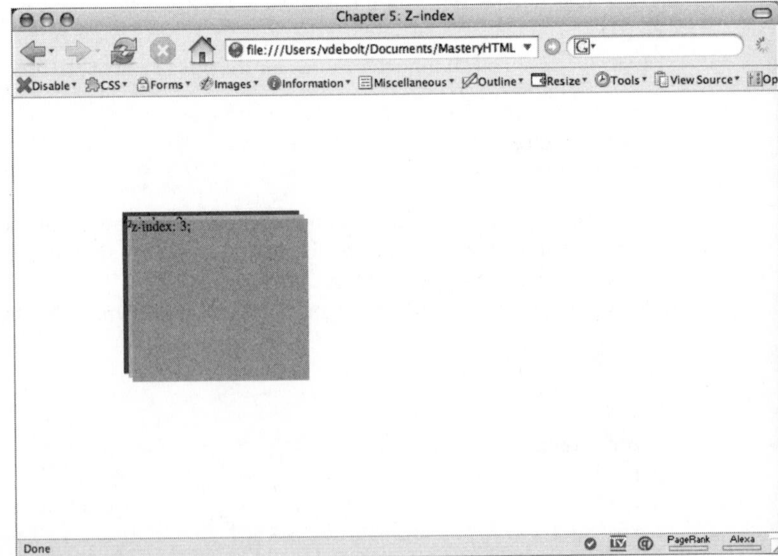

FIGURE 5.25 Elements shifted down and to the right. You see bits of the elements with a z-index of one and two behind the topmost element.

By using `z-index` to overlap part or all of an element you can create interesting visual effect Adjusting the position a few pixels in a different direction could create a look like a drop shadov As I mention in the sidebar "JavaScript and the Visibility Property," `z-index` is seldom used, bu when it is, it's usually with a JavaScript to hide or reveal elements stacked in the same positio on a page.

JAVASCRIPT AND THE *VISIBILITY* PROPERTY

Visibility is a CSS property often used with stacked elements. Its possible values are `visibility: visible;` or `visibility: hidden;`. As you would guess, when the declaration is `visible`, the element can be seen, and when it's `hidden`, the element cannot be seen.

On the example page, if selectors `#two` and `#three` were set to `visibility: hidden;` you would see element `div id="one"`, even if all three elements were stacked in the same position, as in Figure 5.24.

Without JavaScript to switch visibility from `visible` to `hidden` or from `hidden` to `visible` based on some user action such as clicking a link, there isn't much use for this property at this point in your learning.

When you are ready to learn JavaScript, there is a site called JavaScript Source (`http://javascript.internet.com`) that offers hundreds of free scripts with instructions about how to add them to the page. There are also many excellent books on the topic, including *JavaScript and Ajax for the Web: Visual QuickStart Guide, 6th edition* by Tom Negrino and Dori Smith (Peachpit Press, 2007) and *Mastering JavaScript: Premium Edition* by James Jaworski (Sybex, 2001).

In Chapter 6 you will learn the XHTML and CSS to format text elements such as paragraphs, headings, and block quotes.

Real-World Scenario

A three-column layout creates the look and feel for the SEOMOZ home page at `seomoz.org`. A version of the site's home page appears in Figure 5.26. The site uses valid XHTML and CSS. Interesting features of this home page include the use of large images to attract attention and convey information. Numerous heading elements are given the `h1` designation, creating a heading hierarchy in each column of the layout.

A glance at View Source shows this snippet:

```
<div id="background">
<div id="container">
<div id="sidebar">
  <div id="what_is_seo">
    <h1><span>What is SEO?</span></h1>
    <p>SEO, a subset of website marketing
```

A textured and shadowed background for the page is given its own `div`. The global navigation appears in the header, so the smaller sidebar column gets treated as significant content with an `h1` heading. The image replacement technique used hides the text from visual browsers and screen readers with this rule:

```
h1 span, h2 span, a span {
  display: none;
}
```

Search engines index the content of a site without using CSS. So the hidden text in the `h1` and `h2` is read by search engines.

The inner pages of the site use a two-column layout to list the featured information in each of th main areas of the site. See Figure 5.27. If you click a link to one of the articles listed, the article di plays in a full screen one-column layout.

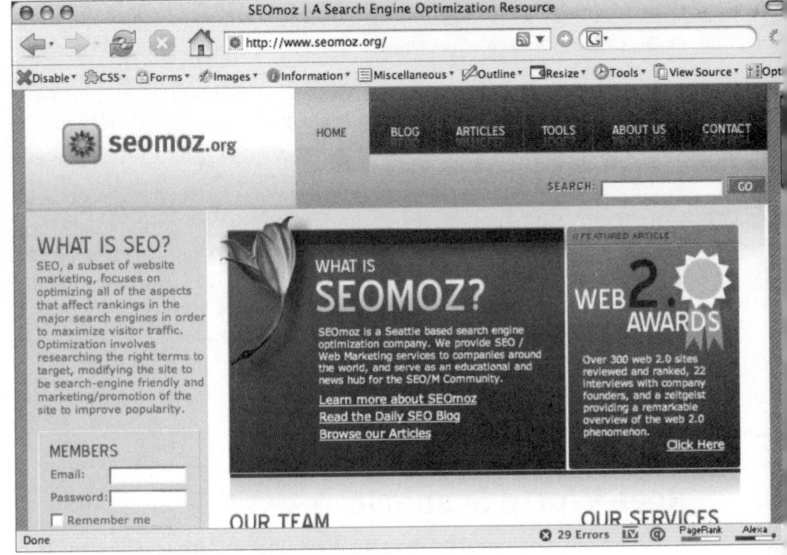

FIGURE 5.26
The main page of SEOMOZ uses a three-column layout.

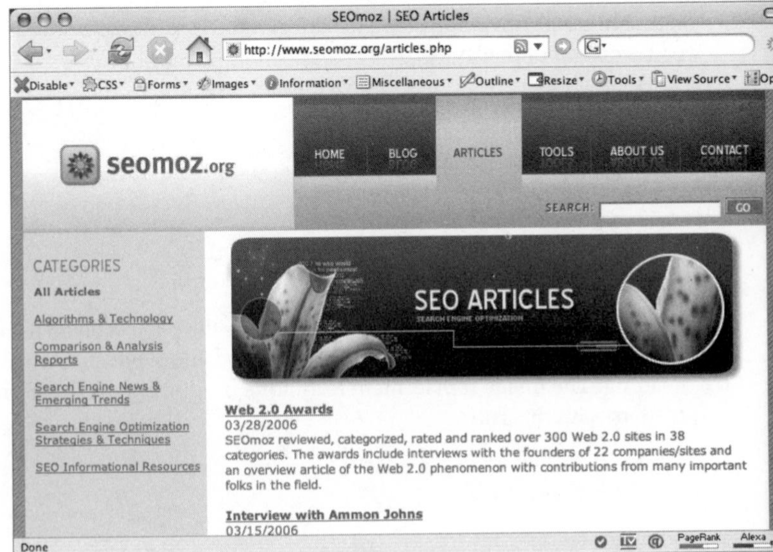

FIGURE 5.27
A two-column layout on the main Articles page of SEOMOZ

The site does not use a single style sheet with an `id` or `class` in the `body` element, as you've seen in previous Real World Examples. Instead, a unique style sheet for each area of the site is placed in the cascade following the main style sheet. You can see this in the source of the main Articles page:

```
<link rel="style sheet" href="/css/main.css" type="text/css" media="all" />
<link rel="style sheet" href="/css/articles.css" type="text/css" media="all" />
```

The SEOMOZ site is an example of a business model very common on the Internet. The profit making business of this company is selling search engine optimization reports, training, and other SEO services. In addition, they publish articles and free information, tips, and allow limited use of their tools. The helpful advice and articles build a reputation, good will, and a brand name for SEOMOZ that earns rewards in the form of paying customers.

Online businesses have learned the hard way that if nothing of value is available free on a site, customers don't stay around long enough to buy. If you visit `kodak.com` you can buy a camera, but you can also read a free online magazine telling you how to take better photos. If you visit `adobe.com` you can buy software, but you can also learn about design and development in virtual centers with free educational resources.

CSS Properties

The CSS properties that were used to position or arrange content in this chapter include `position`, `float`, `clear`, and `z-index`.

CSS *integers* are whole numbers. Integers can be either positive or negative numbers for many properties, including `z-index`.

TABLE 5.1: CSS Properties for Arranging Content

SELECTOR	PROPERTY	POSSIBLE VALUES
all block-level elements	`position`	`static`, `relative`, `absolute`, `fixed`, `inherit`
	`float`	`left`, `right`, `none`, `inherit`
	`clear`	`left`, `right`, `both`, `none`
	`z-index`	<*integer*>, `auto`, `inherit`
	`visibility`	`visible`, `hidden`, `collapse`, `inherit`
all elements	`letter-spacing`	<*length*>, `normal`, `inherit`

The Bottom Line

Use *div* and *id* to create structure for styling. XHTML elements such as headings, paragraphs, lists, and block quotes create structure in a document. That basic semantic information can be grouped into content blocks that share a common purpose in a `div` element. With an `id` creating a unique identifier for the content block, CSS can be used to present the content block in numerous ways.

Master It On `ch5_threecol.html` and `ch5_threecol.css` make modifications to do the following:

1. Create a "navbar" `div` and a "news" `div` within this element on the page:

```
<div id="left">
      <p>Navigation</p>
      <ul>
        <li>link one</li>
        <li>link two</li>
        <li>link three</li>
        <li>link four</li>
        <li>link five</li>
      </ul>
      <h3>News Items</h3>
      <p>All the latest flower news and blurbs about specials and stuff and
nonsense goes here.</p>
    </div>
```

2. Create CSS rules for the two new divs. The two new structural elements should have different appearances. Be ready to demonstrate you results in a browser.
3. Make changes to `ch5_threecol.css` to improve the padding, headings, and other features of the presentation. Be prepared to demonstrate your work in a browser.

Create layouts with *absolute* and *relative* positioning. Absolute positioning removes an element from the document flow and positions it with regard to its nearest positioned ancestor. Relative positioning maintains the element's orientation to the document flow but offsets its position within its container relative to its spot if it were in the flow.

Master It Change some style rules in two CSS files to create specific effects.

1. On `ch5_start.css`, use `position: absolute` to place the `div id="content"` element in a precise location along with an absolutely positioned nav element. Then enlarge the text several times using the browser menu. What happens?
2. On `ch5_threecol.css`, use `position: relative` to shift the new "navbar" you created a few pixels to the left or right. Demonstrate your results in a browser.

Create layouts based on *float, margin,* and *z-index*. Text wraps around a floated element. To create the illusion of columns, an element next to a `float` can be given a margin value that will prevent it from wrapping around the floated element. Z-index deals with the fact that more than one element can occupy the same position on a page. The elements can be stacked in a particular order using `z-index`.

Master It Create a layout of your own using some guidelines and try out some new numbers with z-index.

1. Using Figure 5.21 as your guide, create the *all floats with negative margin—fixed width* layout. Alternatively, create your own version of a two- or three-column design using `float`. Demonstrate your results in a browser. (Feel free to use content and images from the Far and Wee Balloon page or from the Flower Page to fill in some content.)
2. On `ch5_z-index.css`, change the `z-index` value of the selector `#two` to a higher value such as 10. What happens? Now change the `z-index` value of the selector `#two` to —2. What happens? Demonstrate your results in a browser.

Understand *float* for images and other floated elements The purpose of the `float` property is to move an element to either the right or left side of its parent element. Elements such as images, callouts, pull quotes, and other page layout features are often used with `float`. The text next to the floated element wraps around it, unless it is cleared. If it is cleared, it appears beneath the float.

Master It There are three small images in the `right` element on the page `ch5_threecol.html`. Apply a CSS `float` property to them and add any other rules need to make the images display nicely. Demonstrate your results.

Use *clear* with floated elements The `clear` property forces an element to move below any float on the left or right sides, or both.

Master It Use `ch5_threecol.css` to float the image in the `content` div. Then force the paragraph text that follows it to the floated element.

Chapter 6

Paragraph and Text Styles

XHTML contains many elements to format text. You already have some experience with headings and paragraphs from previous chapters. In this chapter you'll work with a variety of additional elements specifically for formatting text.

CSS allows effective techniques to make large areas of text on the Web more reader friendly. Readability and appearance are affected by line length, line height, white space, font choice, and other formatting. Use CSS for visually grouping material into content blocks that reflect its organization and semantic distinctions, and to make the text easier to read and use.

If your site will provide long documents or documents readers may want to print for reference, you may want to create a print style sheet. Reading from a printed page makes different demands on a reader than reading from a computer screen. Adding a print-media style sheet to your web page helps your users get the best results when printing your pages.

In this chapter you will:

- Identify helpful XHTML elements for formatting text, including `em`, `strong`, `acronym`, `abbr`, `cite`, `q`, `blockquote`, `sub`, `sup`, `code`, `var`, `dfn`, and others.
- Understand and use CSS selectors including child selectors, adjacent selectors, and attribute selectors.
- Create generated content.
- Create codes for special characters such as copyright symbols.
- Write a print style sheet.

XHTML: Formatting Text

You will use an example file from the CD to learn more about formatting text. In the Chapter 6 folder on the CD, find `ch6_start.html` and copy it to your computer in the `Mastering Integrated HTML and CSS` folder.

If you look at this file in your browser, you see a long, all-text page. Figure 6.1 shows the browser view; the file is very long, so Listing 6.1 shows only a portion of the XHTML code.

EXPANDING INTO REALITY

If this page were not a stand-alone document but were instead part of a larger site, you might need other elements such as navigation and site identification on the page that would require more structuring and more context building with additional `id` and `class` selectors.

Things have been simplified here, and as a result the CSS selectors you will use later in the chapter to style the page can be basic element selectors.

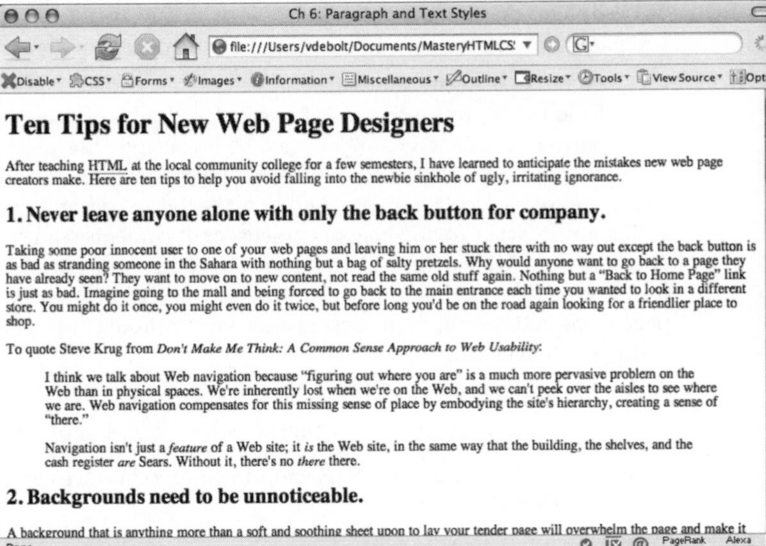

FIGURE 6.1 The `ch6_start.html` text file in the browser

LISTING 6.1: The Starting Text-Formatting Page

```
<!DOCTYPE html PUBLIC "-//W3C//DTD XHTML 1.0 Transitional//EN"
   "http://www.w3.org/TR/xhtml1/DTD/xhtml1-transitional.dtd">
<html xmlns="http://www.w3.org/1999/xhtml">
<head>
 <title>Ch 6: Paragraph and Text Styles</title>
</head>
<body>
<h1>Ten Tips for New Web Page Designers</h1>
<p>After teaching <acronym title="Hypertext Markup Language">HTML</acronym>
  at the local community college for a few semesters, I have learned to
  anticipate the mistakes new web page creators make. Here are ten tips to
  help you avoid falling into the newbie sinkhole of ugly, irritating
  ignorance.</p>
<h2> 1. Never leave anyone alone with only the Back button for company.</h2>
<p> Taking some poor innocent user to one of your web pages and leaving him
  or her stuck there with no way out except the Back button is as bad as
```

```
    stranding someone in the Sahara with nothing but a bag of salty pretzels.
    Why would anyone want to go back to a page they have already seen? They
    want to move on to new content, not read the same old stuff again. Nothing
    but a &#8220;Back to Home Page&#8221; link is just as bad. Imagine going
    to the mall and being forced to go back to the main entrance each time you
    wanted to look in a different store. You might do it once, you might even
    do it twice, but before long you'd be on the road again looking for a
    friendlier place to shop.</p>
  <p>To quote Steve Krug from <cite>Don't Make Me Think: A Common Sense
    Approach to Web Usability</cite>:</p>
  <blockquote>
    <p>I think we talk about Web navigation because &#8220;figuring out where
      you are&#8221; is a much more pervasive problem on the Web than in
      physical spaces. We're inherently lost when we're on the Web, and we
      can't peek over the aisles to see where we are. Web navigation
      compensates for this missing sense of place by embodying the site's
      hierarchy, creating a sense of &#8220;there.&#8221;</p>
    <p>Navigation isn't just a <em>feature</em> of a Web site; it <em>is</em>
      the Web site, in the same way that the building, the shelves, and the
      cash register <em>are</em> Sears. Without it, there's no <em>there</em>
      there. </p>
  </blockquote>
  [...]
  <div class="callout"><p>If you don't have much design experience, you can
    learn the basics of good design in <cite>The Non-Designer's Design
    Book</cite> by Robin Williams. She describes the four basic principles
    of design: contrast, repetition, alignment, and proximity.</p>
  </div>
  [...]
  <div id="footer">
    <p>&#169; Virginia DeBolt<br />
    This article first appeared at <a href="http://www.vdebolt.com/ht/
  tentips.html">vdebolt.com</a>. It has
    been modified slightly to add XHTML elements not present in the original
    version.</p>
  </div>
  </body>
  </html>
```

This is a real article, something I wrote several years ago to help beginning HTML students. It contains advice for beginning designers, so you may want to take the time to read it while you are working with it.

Your design goal in this chapter is to make this long text article easy to read on the screen by improving the formatting of the text elements on the page. You also will make it easy to read in print.

Before you can begin trying to change this page visually with CSS, there are several new XHTML elements to learn. Open `ch6_start.html` in your text editor and examine the XHTML. Note that there's no style sheet `link` element in the document `head`. You will add some style rules later.

First, you will work your way down the page and look at each new element in the XHTML.

TYPOGRAPHY RESOURCES

Here are two great sources for anyone who needs to learn about effective typography:

- Five Simple Steps to Better Typography: `www.markboulton.co.uk/journal/comments/five_simple_steps_to_better_typography`
- *The Non-Designer's Type Book* (2nd Edition) by Robin Williams (Peachpit Press, 2005)

Acronyms and Abbreviations

The first new element is acronym. Look for it here:

```
<h1>Ten Tips for New Web Page Designers</h1>
<p>After teaching <acronym title="Hypertext Markup Language">HTML</acronym>
```

The acronym element includes a title attribute. In the title you provide the actual meaning of the words that create the acronym. The default display of this element varies from browser to browser. In some browsers, the acronym will be displayed in italics or with a dotted underline. Other browsers may not show any visual clue that the acronym element exists. See Figure 6.2.

FIGURE 6.2 Various browser default displays of the acronym element

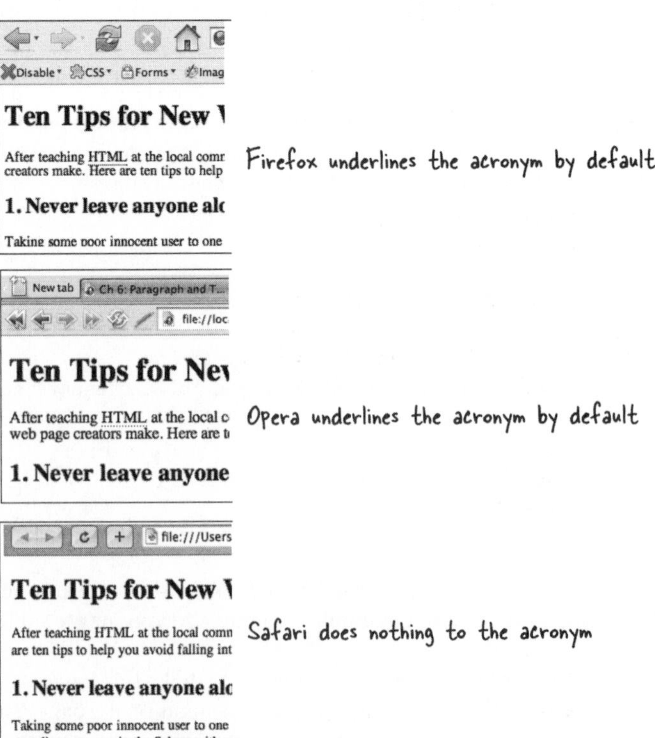

All browsers should display the information in the `title` attribute if the user's cursor hovers over the `acronym`. Most browsers show it as a tool tip, but some display the information at the bottom of the browser window in the status bar. See Figure 6.3.

The `title` attribute can be used with more than just acronyms. Its effect is the same with any element: a visual clue provides additional information or clarification about the element. The `title` attribute may be read aloud by a screen reader, so `title` provides helpful information about textual elements, hyperlinks, and other objects to users surfing with assistive devices.

When using acronyms, it's considered adequate to identify the acronym with an `acronym` element including a `title` attribute on *first* use. The acronym can be used after that without being identified as an `acronym` element in the XHTML. In the following example, *SPCA* is marked up as an acronym only when first used.

```
<p>Mr. Jones is a member of the <acronym title="Society for the Prevention of
Cruelty to Animals">SPCA</acronym>. The SPCA encourages the humane treatment of
animals. The local SPCA meets the second Monday of each month at the Community
Center.</p>
```

MARKUP VS. WRITING WELL

Neither the `acronym` nor the `abbr` element (discussed next) replaces the need to be clear about what things mean in the plain text of your information. There are two ways of clarifying meaning when acronyms or abbreviations are first used in text.

- The first method is to give the full version of the text and immediately follow it with the acronym or abbreviation in parentheses. For example, "In this book you will learn about Cascading Style Sheets (CSS)."
- The second method is to give the acronym or abbreviation first, and immediately follow it with the full version in parentheses. For example, "In this book you will learn about CSS (Cascading Style Sheets)."

With an `acronym` or `abbr` element added to the XHTML applied to the example about Mr. Jones and the SPCA, the complete text would be like this:

```
<p>Mr. Jones is a member of the <acronym title="Society for the Prevention of
Cruelty to Animals">SPCA</acronym> (Society for the Prevention of Cruelty to
Animals). The SPCA encourages the humane treatment of animals. The local SPCA
meets the second Monday of each month at the Community Center.</p>
```

This example of good writing plus appropriate markup provides the information to any reader and is carried over into print. (The information in the title attribute of an `acronym` or `abbr` element isn't printed.) No particular browser is required, no hovering over an element with the pointing device is required—the only requirement is clear writing. Like using an `acronym` or `abbr` element in the markup, explaining what an acronym or abbreviation means in plain English in your text is only necessary when a term is first used. After that, you assume people understand what the term means.

In actual practice, it seems redundant to do both. On a web page, the `title` attribute on first use is probably sufficient.

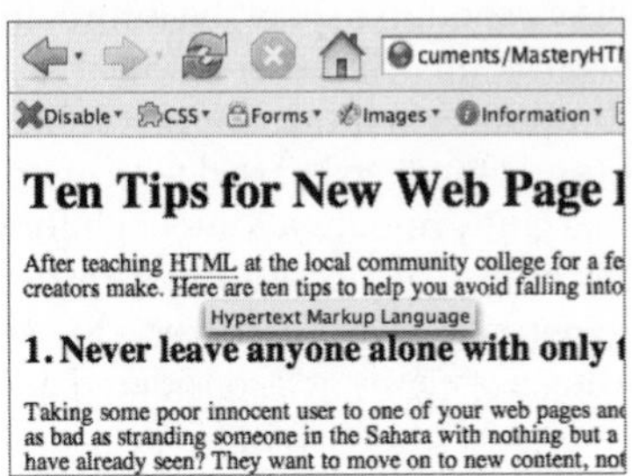

FIGURE 6.3
The `title` attribute displays when the cursor hovers over the acronym.

THE *ABBR* ELEMENT

Related to `acronym` is `abbr` (for abbreviation). Like `acronym` elements, the `abbr` element needs a `title` attribute. For example,

```
<abbr title="Limited">Ltd.</abbr>
```

Default rendering of the `abbr` element varies by browser, similar to the various browser interpret- tions of `acronym`. Since browsers may vary in the default style for `abbr`, you can set it to your likir with a CSS rule. Like `acronym`, you only need to fully identify an abbreviation on first use.

WILL *ACRONYM* AND *ABBR* MERGE?

The use of `acronym` and `abbr` is subject to change. Internet Explorer does not currently support `abbr`, so many developers use `acronym` for both acronyms and abbreviations. The W3C, however, is considering dropping `acronym` from the next version of XHTML and using only the `abbr` element for both purposes. While the W3C works on new specifications, they use the term *working draft*. A completed and adopted set of standards is identified as *recommended*. At the time of this writing, the W3C is still in the working draft stage with XHTML 2; the working draft states, "The `abbr` element indicates that a text fragment is an abbreviation (e.g., W3C, XML, Inc., Ltd., Mass., etc.); this includes acronyms."

To see what actually happens with the `acronym` and `abbr` elements, keep an eye out for both IE7 and the W3C final recommendation for XHTML 2 when they are released.

Special Characters

There are many symbols, marks, and characters needed in writing that are not among the letter and numbers on a keyboard. There are also symbols on the keyboard that have specific functio in XHTML and therefore need to be encoded to display on a screen, such as the angle brackets use to type XHTML tags. These are called *character entities* and *special characters*. A code number is assigned to each of these symbols or characters. Look at this example from `ch6_start.html` in yo text editor:

```
They want to move on to new content, not read the same old stuff again.
Nothing but a &#8220;Back to Home Page&#8221; link is just as bad.
```

Notice the `“` and `”`. These are special codes (which I'll tell you how to look u in a minute) for English language opening and closing double quotation marks, respectively. Special character codes must have the ampersand (&), the hash sign (#), a code number, and a semicolon (;). If you forget any of these, the symbol or character won't display properly. In the browser, you should see something like Figure 6.4 when using `“` and `”` correctly.

But wait, you say! You can create a quotation mark using my computer keyboard. You have been using them in XHTML attributes, such as `title="Hypertext Markup Language"`.

The important distinction here is that quotation marks produced by using the keyboard are *straight quotes*. Straight quotes are required in XHTML code. Straight quotes are the only type of quotation marks most simple text editing tools make, which is one reason basic text editing software is used to write XHTML code.

Straight quotes are often used as inch marks when viewed in the browser, however. For example:

```
<p>The photo is 8" by 10" in size.</p>
```

For quotation marks in text, you want to be able to create quotes that curve, sometimes called *curly quotes*. Using the character codes `“` and `”`, you can create a genuine curvy quotation mark instead of a straight inch mark.

FIGURE 6.4
Quotation marks displayed in the browser

MORE QUOTATION MARKS

The `q` (for quote) element also creates quotation marks in browsers that support it. (IE up to and including version 6 simply ignores a `q` element.) The value of the `q` element comes from the fact that it should create the correct style of quotation mark for the language, be it English, French, or some other language, and it should also change the quotation marks used when one quote is nested within another. The `lang` attribute is used to specify the language for the style of quotation mark wanted.

You may recall seeing an unexplained `q` element in Chapters 4 and 5 (minus a `lang` attribute). Remember this?

```
<div id="footer">&copy; Far and Wee Balloons, 2007, with thanks to e.e. cummings
for his phrase <q>the little lame balloon man whistles far and wee</q>.
```

If you tested your pages in a browser other than Internet Explorer, you no doubt noticed that the marked-up phrase was in quotation marks. To specify that the quotation marks would be the curly, double-quote marks used in English, you could add a `lang` attribute to the `q` element, like this:

```
<div id="footer">&copy; Far and Wee Balloons, 2007, with thanks to e.e. cummings
for his phrase <q lang="en">the little lame balloon man whistles far and wee</q>.
```

While special characters such as `“` and `”` serve well, they are restricted to English language style quotation marks. Different numeric codes are needed to produce other languages' quotation marks. When `q` is supported by all the major browsers, it will be an excellent alternative. Until then, you probably want to insert the proper quotation marks into the text itself and avoid the `q` element.

More Special Characters

Web pages can be written in any language by using the multitude of special codes available. A com plete list of XHTML Latin character entities can be found here:

```
http://www.w3.org/TR/2000/REC-xhtml1-20000126/DTD/xhtml-lat1.ent
```

Special characters, such as ampersands and angled brackets, are listed here:

```
http://www.w3.org/TR/2000/REC-xhtml1-20000126/DTD/xhtml-special.ent
```

When looking at these pages or the previous URL to the W3C, you will see long lists of characte entities and special characters written in a form like this:

```
<!ENTITY ldquo   "&#8220;"> <!-- left double quotation mark, U+201C ISOnum -->
```

I'll decipher that for you. You are looking at the listing for left double quotation mark (`ldquo`), which is the code `“` mentioned previously. With an ampersand (&) and semicolon (`;`)—like this: `“`—you also have a character entity that would be rendered in the browser as a left doubl quote. There are 252 *named* entity references similar to `“`. These names can be used instead o the numeric code (in this case `“`) with what should be equivalent results in the browser. If yo test in various browsers and see inconsistent results using named entity references, try it with the numeric code, as browser support for some of the named entity references is unreliable. For now, yo don't need to worry about the meaning of the `U+201C ISOnum` part of the character entity listing.

More character entity resources

More reader-friendly lists of character entities can be found at:

- Evolt: `www.evolt.org/article/ala/17/21234`
- The Web Standards Group: `http://webstandards.org/learn/reference/charts/entities/named_entities`
- Character entities for language types other than Latin-based languages are at `www.unicode.org`

En Dashes and Em Dashes

Another special character code in `ch6_start.html` is the em dash. Look for it in Rule 4 in the exampl XHTML file:

```
Okay, sometimes the animated gifs are cute&#8212;for about three
seconds&#8212;but do they add meaning or significance to what you're saying?
```

An em dash is a dash the width of the character *M* for the font size in use; it's usually used to set o a phrase within a sentence, as in the preceding example, or to mark an emphatic break in a sentenc Many novice writers try to achieve this effect with one or two hyphens, but the correct character for th job is the em dash. The code to create an em dash is `—`. In the browser, an em dash looks like th ones in Figure 6.5.

There is a slightly shorter dash called an en dash. An en dash is the width of the character *N* fo the font size in use. Its purpose is indicate a range of numbers, as in "pages 32–45," or to join proper names within a phrase, as in "the Canada–United States border." The code for an en das is `–`. Table 6.1 provides a few additional codes.

FIGURE 6.5
A pair of em dashes sets off the phrase "for about three seconds."

4. Blinking text, scrolling t looping animated gifs are i

Would you read a book if it constantly fla people won't read your web page if it doe anything to do with your message and yo are cute—for about three seconds—but d you're saying? Those animated "under co inexperienced web newbieness. The entir and immediate. People expect change and

MIND YOUR EMS AND ENS

For more about how to use these punctuation marks correctly, see the following:

www.mtannoyances.com/?p=218

http://alistapart.com/stories/emen/

http://en.wikipedia.org/wiki/Dash

An en or em dash for a font like Arial might be relatively shorter than an en or em dash for a font like Verdana, because Arial is a rather narrow font while Verdana is a rather wide font.

TABLE 6.1: Selected Character and Symbol Codes

SAMPLE	CHARACTER	NUMERIC CODE	ALPHA CODE
–	En dash	–	–
—	Em dash	—	—
“	Left or opening double quote	“	“
”	Right or closing double quote	”	”
<	Less than or opening angle bracket	<	<
>	Greater than or opening angle bracket	>	>
&	Ampersand	&	&
¢	Cent	¢	¢
£	Pound	£	£
™	Trademark	™	™
©	Copyright	©	©

THE *EM* AS A *FONT-SIZE* MEASURE

In CSS, an `em` is the value of a `font-size` for a given font. It is not the same thing as an em dash, although both relate to the size of the font in use.

One `em` for a heading with a `font-size` of 18 pixels is different from one `em` for a paragraph with a `font-size` of 12 pixels. For that reason, ems are considered a relative measure. In terms of accessibility, relative measures are considered a very good thing indeed. This is because relative measures allow users to resize for better viewing with the browser controls.

> **WANNA SEE 264 EXAMPLES?**
>
> More information about relative measurement of font sizes can be found at The Noodle Incident at `www.thenoodleincident.com/tutorials/box_lesson/font/index.html`, where you can see 264 screen shots of various `font-size` options in different browsers. Keep in mind that this information was posted in 2002 when there was a raging battle among web designers over whether pixels (not a relative measure) or ems/percentages (both relative measures) were preferable. Since 2002, every browser except Internet Explorer has upgraded several times, but the basic results shown in the 264 screen shots remain relevant, even if not entirely up to date.

The *cite* Element

An XHTML element in `ch6_start.html` that you haven't seen before is the `cite` element. You see an example here:

```
<p>To quote Steve Krug from <cite>Don't Make Me Think: A Common Sense Approach to
Web Usability</cite>: </p>
```

The `cite` element is intended to be used for citations such as book and magazine names. Sometimes `cite` elements contain a reference to another source, with a `cite` attribute giving the location of the original document. The example in `ch6_start.html` indicates that the words within the `cite` element tags are a book title. On the other hand, if something was quoted from the website that supports the book cited, the `cite` element might look like this instead:

```
<cite cite="http://www.sensible.com">Don't Make Me Think: A Common Sense Approach
to Web Usability</cite>
```

You are not seeing double. That is a `cite` element with a `cite` attribute. Most browsers render the `cite` element in italics. See Figure 6.6. The `cite` attribute may also be used with the `q` and `blockquote` elements.

When listing the source of information, be it a book, magazine, or person, you can indicate that source with a `cite` element. As you are about to see in the following section, there are other ways to make a browser render text in italics. But keep in mind the accessibility requirement for logical formatting. None of the other ways to create italic text for a book or magazine title carry the logical element characteristics inherent in the `cite` element, which is expressly intended to be used for citations.

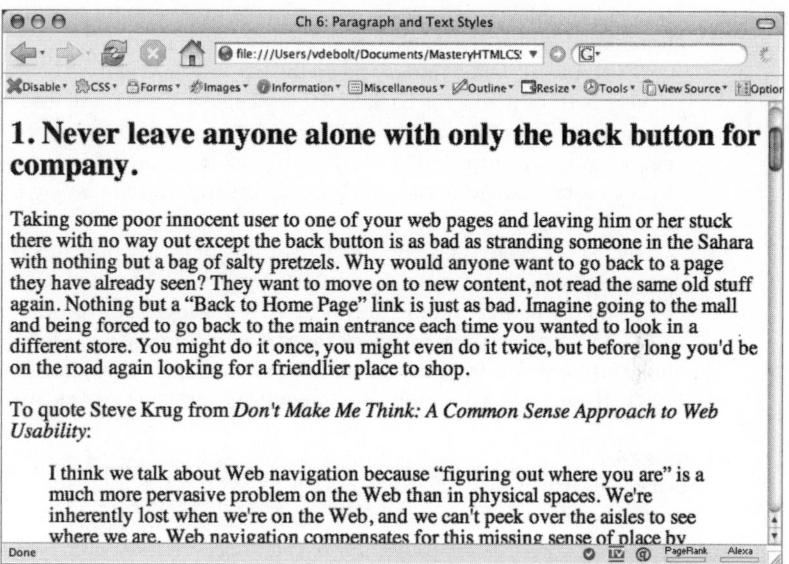

FIGURE 6.6
The `cite` element renders in italics in many browsers.

Block Quotes

When you quote more than a few words directly from a book or other resource in your writing, you ordinarily indent the quoted material to set it off as a *block quote.* The same principle applies to XHTML, where the `blockquote` element is used for the same purpose. In `ch6_start.html`, you see this example in Listing 6.2.

LISTING 6.2: The Blockquote Element from *ch6_start.html*

```
<blockquote>
  <p>I think we talk about Web navigation because &#8220;figuring out where
    you are&#8221; is a much more pervasive problem on the Web than in
    physical spaces. We're inherently lost when we're on the Web, and we
    can't peek over the aisles to see where we are. Web navigation
    compensates for this missing sense of place by embodying the site's
    hierarchy, creating a sense of &#8220;there.&#8221;</p>
  <p>Navigation isn't just a <em>feature</em> of a Web site; it <em>is</em>
    the Web site, in the same way that the building, the shelves, and the
    cash register <em>are</em> Sears. Without it, there's no <em>there</em>
    there.</p>
</blockquote>
```

Visually, all browsers indent the `blockquote` element on both the right and left margins anc treat them as block-level elements, as shown in Figure 6.7.

The browser default indenting on the left and right margin of a `blockquote` led to some exampl of very bad coding habits back in the days before CSS. There was no good way to add white spac around elements then, and the `blockquote` was sadly misused to move text about a bit, add whi space, and give emphasis. The semantic result was a disaster, with `blockquotes` nested inside `blockquotes` nested inside of `blockquotes` in order to display text that was in no way an actu block quote.

By using CSS to set up margins, padding, or positioning, it's possible to create indented text. you want to indent text, use CSS rules. Do not use a `blockquote` element merely to indent text. Tl `blockquote` element should only be used for its logical purpose, namely to quote a block of materi

The material quoted in a `blockquote` element may include paragraphs, lists, and other bloc level elements. At least one block-level element is *required* in a blockquote when the DOCTYPE XHTML strict. The opening `blockquote` tag can have a `cite` attribute.

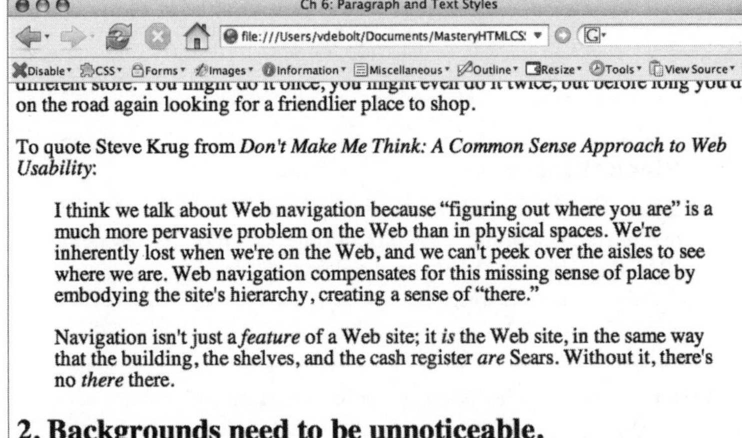
Ch 6: Paragraph and Text Styles
file:///Users/vdebolt/Documents/MasteryHTMLCS
Disable CSS Forms Images Information Miscellaneous Outline Resize Tools View Source
on the road again looking for a friendlier place to shop.
To quote Steve Krug from Don't Make Me Think: A Common Sense Approach to Web Usability:
I think we talk about Web navigation because "figuring out where you are" is a much more pervasive problem on the Web than in physical spaces. We're inherently lost when we're on the Web, and we can't peek over the aisles to see where we are. Web navigation compensates for this missing sense of place by embodying the site's hierarchy, creating a sense of "there."
Navigation isn't just a feature of a Web site; it is the Web site, in the same way that the building, the shelves, and the cash register are Sears. Without it, there's no there there.
2. Backgrounds need to be unnoticeable.
A background that is anything more than a soft and soothing sheet upon to lay your tender page will overwhelm the page and make it so hard to read that, guess what? No one will
Done
PageRank
Alexa

FIGURE 6.7
A block quote is indented on the right and left.

Formatting for Meaning: The *em* and *strong* Elements

The `blockquote` in Listing 6.2 contains several `em` elements—for example, `<em>feature</em>` ar `<em>there</em>`. If a person (or an assistive device such as a screen reader) read those words aloud, the words would be given extra vocal emphasis to clarify the meaning of the sentence. T `em` (for emphasis) element is usually rendered in the browser as italics. See Figure 6.8.

A few browsers render an `em` element in bold. Since `em` is a logical element, any browser (ev an aural screen reader) will give some sort of emphasis to the `em` element. If you want to be sure th an `em` element will appear visually as italics rather than bold, you can always write a CSS rule f `em`. You will do exactly that later in the chapter.

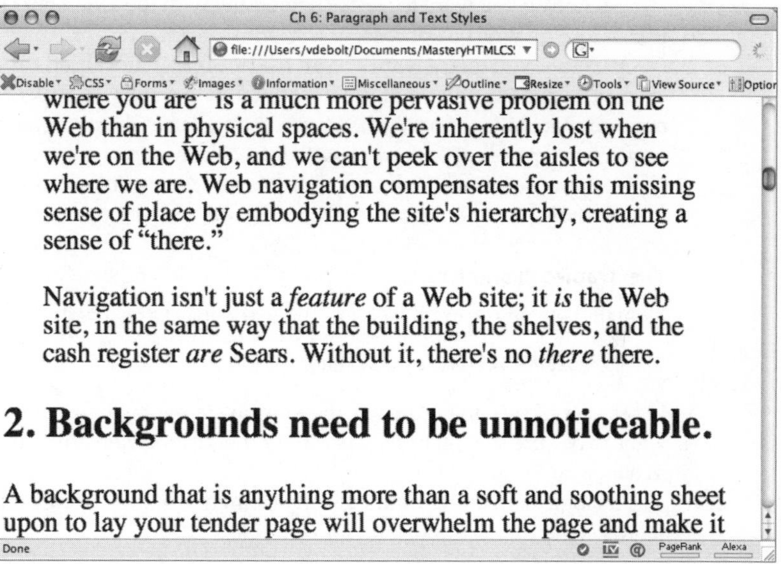
Ch 6: Paragraph and Text Styles
file:///Users/vdebolt/Documents/MasteryHTMLCS
Disable CSS Forms Images Information Miscellaneous Outline Resize Tools View Source
where you are" is a much more pervasive problem on the Web than in physical spaces. We're inherently lost when we're on the Web, and we can't peek over the aisles to see where we are. Web navigation compensates for this missing sense of place by embodying the site's hierarchy, creating a sense of "there."
Navigation isn't just a feature of a Web site; it is the Web site, in the same way that the building, the shelves, and the cash register are Sears. Without it, there's no there there.
2. Backgrounds need to be unnoticeable.
A background that is anything more than a soft and soothing sheet upon to lay your tender page will overwhelm the page and make it
Done
PageRank
Alexa

FIGURE 6.8
There are several emphasized words in the second paragraph of the `blockquote`. Visually, they are emphasized with italics.

The `cite` element is often rendered in italics. The `em` element is often rendered in italics. You can also create italics using the `i` (for italic) element. So `<i>feature</i>` renders *visually* exactly like `<em>feature</em>` or `<cite>feature</cite>` does. However, the `i` element is strictly a visual rendering; it doesn't carry any logical underpinning that gives meta-meaning to an element, the way `em` or `cite` do.

EM AND EMS

The `em` (for emphasis) element is not the same `em` (for sizing) unit of measurement. And it isn't the same as an em dash. We are beset by swarms of ems!

When you first read the words in Figure 6.7, you didn't have any problem realizing that *Don't Make Me Think: A Common Sense Approach to Web Usability* was a book title, and that the words *feature, is, are,* and *there* were meant to be emphasized. As a reader, you have been trained in the visual conventions since first grade, and recognizing titles and emphasis are second nature. On the Web, however, there are ways to distinguish between italics used to indicate something like a movie title versus italics used for emphasis versus italics used to indicate a citation. In addition to the visual clue, there is an underlying semantic clue.

The Web is not merely visual. For the approximately 10 percent of people who access the Web by some means other than visually, the distinction is clear between `em` and `i` or between `cite` and `i`, because aural screen readers give different voice inflections to the logical elements. In terms of structuring your XHTML for meaning, the logical element (`em` or `cite`) may be a better choice than a visual element (`i`).

So when do you want to format something with the `i` element? It is used to indicate a publicatio title, a foreign word or phrase, or a scientific term.

Of course, you might want a word to appear in italics strictly as a decorative design decision. Fo example, suppose you want the introduction to a story to appear in italics. Use CSS to style the paragraph in italics. If needed, you can use a `span` in the paragraph with a `class` or `id` that provid a means to target that paragraph with the CSS. Be wary, however, of too much italic type as a desig choice, because it is difficult to read, especially in large blocks. Large blocks of decorative italic typ (say a whole paragraph) can affect box model calculations in Internet Explorer in quirks mode.

THE *STRONG* ELEMENT

A related element can be seen in Rule 3 of `ch6_start.html`: the `strong` element.

```
<strong>Click Here!</strong>
```

As you can see in Figure 6.9, the `strong` element usually renders as bold in the browser. If yo want to be sure that all browsers render the `strong` element as bold, you can create a CSS rule fo `strong`.

The logical meaning of the `strong` element implies strong emphasis. It's often used to make words stand out as important, for example,

```
<p><strong>Do not</strong> light a match if you smell gas.</p>
```

The `strong` element is preferred over its purely visual counterpart, the `b` (for bold) element, fo the same reasons that `em` is preferred over `i`. An aural screen reader will read `strong` in a differen voice from normal text and in a different voice from that used for `em`. These contextual clues hel users of assistive devices make sense of your content.

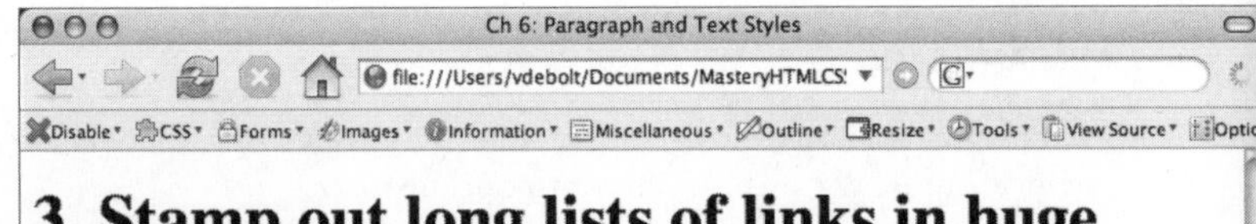

Ch 6: Paragraph and Text Styles
file:///Users/vdebolt/Documents/MasteryHTMLCS
Disable CSS Forms Images Information Miscellaneous Outline Resize Tools View Source
3. Stamp out long lists of links in huge bold fonts.
Who wants to scroll through fifteen feet of over-large links (preceded by exclamations of Click Here!) when the same information could fit into a neat three inch long div? Where do all those links go in the first place? If they lead away from your site, you are drop kicking people out the back door as soon as they come in the front door. If you must link to places outside your site, do it deep into your site so viewers will have had a good look at your content first.
4. Blinking text, scrolling tickertapes and
Done

FIGURE 6.9
An example of the `strong` element

Like the i element, the b element can correctly achieve visual effects that are strictly for appearance's sake and do not carry any underlying logic or meaning of strong emphasis. Don't confuse bold (b) text with heading text. For example:

```
<p><b>1. Never leave anyone alone with only the back button for company.</b></p>
```

Visually, that might resemble a heading in appearance, but it carries no semantic meaning as a heading with it to any assistive device. An actual heading (bold by default) would be a much better practice.

U CAUTIONS

Another strictly visual element is u (underline). I suggest you ban it from your formatting repertoire because underlined text on the Web is misunderstood to be a link. Many print conventions have survived the journey to the Web intact; underlining has not.

Other Useful Text Formatting Elements

There are several text formatting elements not used in ch6_start.html that you need to know about.

Sometimes you may wish to display monospaced fonts (like those produced by old-fashioned typewriters) on your web page. Several elements display their contents, by default, in monospaced fonts:

- code (for "computer code"), as in <code>your code</code>
- kbd (for "keyboard"), as in <kbd>your text</kbd>

Each of these text formatting elements has a purpose, although their display results are sometimes the same. For example, kbd is used for formatting keyboard instructions. If you need to display computer code, use code. These are logical elements.

Normally, when you type more than one space or create a new line with the Return (Enter) key in your XHTML code, the browser ignores it. However, there is one element you can use that will maintain spaces and line breaks from an original document. Even the original font is retained. This is the pre (for preformatted) element. It is often used for poems, ASCII art, and simple column construction, as in

```
<pre>some    preformatted    text</pre>
```

The pre element is sometimes used to display long code blocks on a page. The pre element is a block-level element, while kbd and code are used inline.

Examples of code, kbd, and pre are shown in Figure 6.10.

In order to create footnotes or street names or numbers like 1st, 2nd, and 3rd, use the sup (for superscript) element. The code would look like: <p>I live at 1st and York.</p>

For chemical formulas such as H_2O, use the sub (for subscript) element: H₂O.

The del element (for delete) is used to delete text. <p>Chaucer <del>lives</del> lived in England.</p> The original text is left with a strikethrough in most browsers.

When writing about computer programming or mathematics, the var element (for variable) may be useful. For example: <p>To find twice a number, double(<var>x</var>) = <var>x</var> + <var>x</var>, where x is a variable.</p>

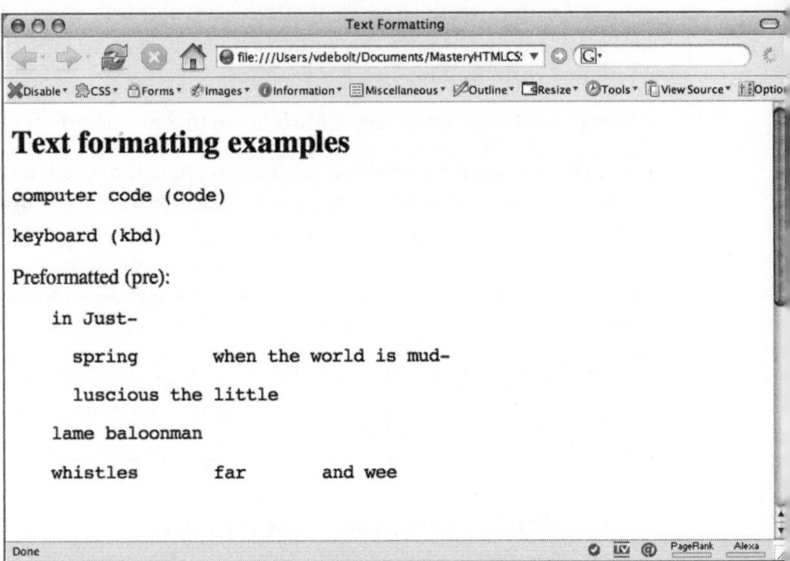

FIGURE 6.10 Browser rendering of text formatted as code, keyboard, or preformatted

The `dfn` (for definition) element contains the defining instance of a term. Like `acronym`, it is only necessary to use it the first time a term is used. It usually renders in italics by default. A `dfn` element may contain a `title` attribute that defines the term, or it may contain an `id` that creates a landing point for an anchor element somewhere else that refers to the definition. Here's an example with a title attribute:

```
A  <def title="a variable represents a place where a quantity can be
stored">variable</def> is used in computer science.
```

Figure 6.11 shows browser rendering of these elements.

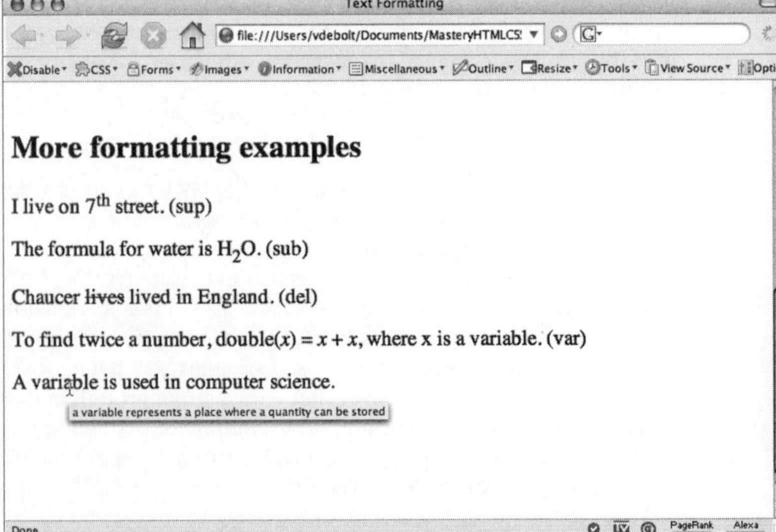

FIGURE 6.11 The `sup`, `sub`, `del`, `var`, and `def` elements. Without some CSS to style the `dfn` element, Firefox renders it as plain text; however, the definition is displayed by the `title` attribute when the element is hovered over.

Making Your XHTML Text CSS-Ready

Most of the CSS rules needed to make this long text document (`ch6_start.html`) easy to read will be applied to XHTML elements such as `h2` and `p`. (You will also use some advanced selectors such as child selectors to create styles. These advanced selectors don't need any special markup in the XHTML.)

Structurally, this simple page consists only of headings and paragraphs. When it is possible to style a page using only the XHTML elements themselves, such as `p`, `h2`, `blockquote`, and so on, that is the best way to do the job. Don't add complexity to the markup or to the style sheet unless it is needed. For this example, the majority of the CSS heavy lifting can be done with simple selectors. In previous chapters, not-strictly-necessary descendant selectors were used as a learning exercise. This chapter will stick to the basic selectors needed to fit this simple document.

There are exceptions to this general rule, however. You may have noticed that there are two divs in `ch6_start.html` identified with the class name `callout`. The two `div class="callout"` elements contain a single paragraph. The `class="callout"` attribute *could* be used with the `p` element, so this seems to contradict what I just said about adding unnecessary complexity to the markup. See Listing 6.3.

However, when you get to the styling of the callout, you will see why it's necessary to have both a `div` and a `p` element for these two text items.

LISTING 6.3: A Paragraph Wrapped in a *div* with a Class Assignment

```
<div class="callout">
 <p>If you don't have much design experience, you can learn the basics of good
design in <cite>The Non-Designer's Design Book</cite> by Robin Williams. She
describes the four basic principles of design: contrast, repetition, alignment,
and proximity.</p>
</div>
```

The final structural element on the page is one `div` element at the very end of the page with the `id="footer"` attribute.

There is no need to go beyond the added `callout` and `footer` elements with more named classes or IDs, because the XHTML elements that make up the page can be styled quite well without further structuring.

CSS: Stylish Text

You already know much of the CSS that will be used to style this document. You will use background, font, color, margin, and other style attributes you have already learned. The new CSS you will learn will be for creating a print style sheet and for using advanced selectors such as the adjacent selector.

First you will create a style sheet for all media and link to it in the XHTML document head. Then you will create a print-media style sheet and link to it after the all-media style sheet in the XTHML document.

Think about the cascade and the position of the print style sheet after the all-media style sheet. Because of the cascade, the *only* CSS rules the print style sheet will need are rules that must be different from the declarations in the first all-media style sheet.

Start Your Style Sheet

Open a blank document in your text editor of choice and save it in the same folder where `ch6_start.html` is saved. Name the new document `ch6_allmedia.css`.

One of the first rules for making text readable on the Web is to use short lines. Reading on a screen is difficult in comparison with reading on paper, and longer lines of text are harder for th eye to track.

There's no hard and fast rule that establishes the perfect line length or an exact number of characters a line should contain. In print, there is the natural limit of the paper size. Large paper for example, newspapers, often divide the text into columns to create more readable line lengt Readability is affected by factors such as `font-size` and `line-height`. Computer monitors, unlike books or printer papers, seem to keep getting wider and wider. At the same time, mor of us use smaller and smaller devices like cell phones to read web pages. We'll look at some way to contain the number of words that appear in the viewport with percentage.

An easy way to reduce number of words in any given line in the `ch6_start.html` document to constrain the width of the `body` element. On this page, everything in the `body` is main conten except for the footer.

> **SIZE CONSTRAINTS**
>
> In Chapter 5, you used a `div` named `"container"` at a set pixel width. Nested in the `"container"` was a `div` named `"content"` with a wide margin to control line length and readability. See Figure 5.18 in Chapter 5 for a reminder of how you finally laid out that page. The number of words in each line in the layout in Chapter 5 was further reduced by the use of floated images to cause the text to wrap around the images.

One way to accomplish the goal of narrowing the `body` element is to set a specific width for th `body` in pixels, perhaps 400 or 500 pixels. A more flexible way is to set wide margins on the left ar right sides using percentages. An example using percentages:

```
body {
 margin-right: 10%;
 margin-left: 10%;
}
```

If you use the same margin width on both the left and right sides, the document will be centere in the viewport. Using percentages for the margins allows more flexibility for users who might want to resize the text using the browser's View menu.

You'll use this method, but before you get to it, I want to point out another way to constrain th `body` element. You could set the `body` to a width in percent—say, perhaps 70 percent or 80 percer If you didn't want the default left alignment for the `body` element, you could center it using `margi right: auto` and `margin-left: auto`. In fact, any block element, including a `div`, can be centere by assigning it auto margins on the left and right sides.

Here's an example of this:

```
body {
 width: 70%;
 margin-right: auto;
 margin-left: auto;
 }
```

A layout that uses percentage to adjust to the size of the window is called a liquid layout. If the user resizes the text, all the text remains within the viewport, even if it's only a very large word or two. No scroll bars will appear. A layout similar to this, but using ems for font and width measurements instead of percentages would behave differently if the text were enlarged by the user. The number of words per line (or actual line length) would remain the same. As the text grew larger and larger, a horizontal scroll bar would appear, allowing the user to read across a line of the same length that others might be viewing at a more standard small or medium text size.

Is it better to use percentages to allow the words to wrap within the viewport, or ems to retain the actual word count per line with scrolling to the right for reading text that is enlarged beyond the viewport? There's no hard data from users who must resize text to provide an answer. Either percentage or ems will allow the user to resize the text without having to worry about one element overlapping another, as would happen with a set pixel size layout.

Using *min-width* and *max-width*

Two CSS properties that can be helpful when you are constraining the size of page elements are `min-width` and `max-width`.

- Use `min-width` to set a minimum size for the element. In browsers that support `min-width` (Internet Explorer 6 and below for Windows does not, while Firefox, Opera, Mozilla, Safari, and other more standards-compliant browsers do), the element can get no narrower than the `min-width` setting allows.
- Use `max-width` to set a maximum size for the element. In browsers that support `max-width` (you guessed it, IE 5/6 does not), the element will get no wider than the `max-width` allows.

A free JavaScript that will fix IE's lack of implementation for `min-width` and `max-width`, including directions for how to use it, is here:

```
www.doxdesk.com/software/js/minmax.html
```

Time to get that `ch6_allmedia.css` page going! Begin with this rule for the body element:

```
body {
  margin-right: 20%;
  margin-left: 20%;
}
```

Save your `ch6_allmedia.css` document again. If you look at `ch6_start.html` in the browser now, nothing has changed. Eek! Why?

You have a style sheet with a rule in it, but there's nothing to connect the style sheet to the XHTML document. You must add a `link` to the style sheet in the XHTML document. (Give yourself a pat on the back if you knew that.) You should include a `media` attribute in this `link` element because you are planning more than one style sheet for different media. Your link element should be placed in the head and look like this:

```
<title>Ch 6 Start</title>
<link href="ch6_allmedia.css" rel="stylesheet" type="text/css" media="all" />
</head>
```

In this situation, `media="screen"` would also be effective. A value of `screen` for the `media` attribute is for viewing on a computer monitor. See Table 6.2 for more `media` attributes. Be warned some of these media types are not supported by any browsers yet, although there is good current support for `all`, `screen`, and `print`. Support for `handheld` is growing rapidly, as is the market for such devices. If you don't specify a media type, current browsers assume you have specified `all` and apply your styles to both screen and print.

With the link to the style sheet included, save the XHTML file and reload the browser. You should now see something similar to Figure 6.12.

Because you used percents rather than pixels to size the body element, when the browser window is resized (either larger or smaller) the lines of text reflow easily according to the user's window size. So if one user actually wanted to read long lines of text in the browser, it would be possible to stretch the browser window to its full width and read that way. Conversely, if another user wanted to read shorter lines of text, the browser window could be made less wide and the text would reflow accordingly.

Had you instead set the body width to 500 pixels, it would never be any wider or narrower than that, no matter what the user did with the browser window. There are situations in web design when you must have a set pixel size to make a design work, typically because you have images arranged in a way that resizing the browser window would ruin the layout, but exact measurements hold the images together in the desired proximity to one another.

In this example, however, it's better to stay loose and use percentages. Designs using percentages are often termed *fluid* or liquid and are considered more accessible than fixed pixel designs. The fact that liquid designs can be resized to suit the user's needs is a perfect example of accessible design.

When starting a new website and making early plans for your design, often one of the first decisions you make is whether to use a fluid or fixed plan for your layout. Such decisions are made on a case-by-case basis, depending on the site goals. As with a good many design decisions, there's no one right answer to the question of fluid versus fixed.

TABLE 6.2: *media* Attributes for Style Sheets

ATTRIBUTE	USE
`all`	In all presentational media
`aural`	In speech synthesizers, screen readers, or any audio rendering
`Braille`	With Braille devices
`embossed`	When printing with a Braille device
`handheld`	With cell phones and personal digital assistants
`print`	When printing
`projection`	When presenting a slide show with a projector
`screen`	For screen media such as desktop computers
`tty`	For teletype printers
`tv`	For television

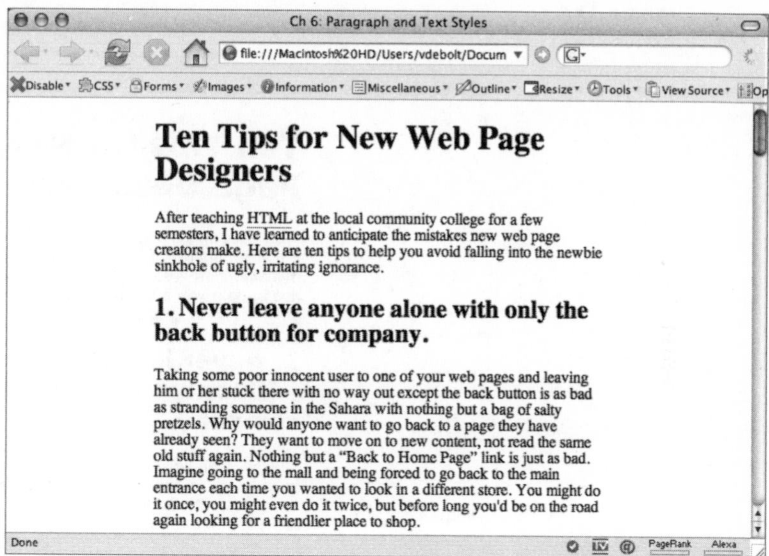

FIGURE 6.12 Margins narrow the entire page, improving readability immediately.

More Body Rules

You can do a lot more to your page while working with the `body` element selector. One declaration you always want to include in your body rule is background color. You want the text to be easy to read, so white (`#fff`) is a good choice for the background.

If you have your own browser set with a white background color as the default, it is easy to forget to set the background color on elements such as the `body`. A trick many web designers use to remind themselves to set background colors is to change the browser default background color to something out of the ordinary like bright pink or lime green. The first browser check you perform on a page instantly reminds you of a forgotten background color declaration. Remember to set a foreground color for the text when you set a background color, to be sure you have enough contrast. We'll use black (`#000`).

You should also declare a font. Common wisdom is that sans-serif fonts are easier to read on a screen. (You'll see an interesting exception to this rule in the Real-World Scenario for this chapter.) Verdana is easy to read, and you haven't used it yet, so give it a whirl. As usual, you should add a couple of other common sans-serif fonts in case users don't have Verdana. Finally, you want to declare a `font-size` of 100 percent for accessibility reasons. Even if you plan to use ems for `font-size` later in the style sheet, it's a good idea to use percentage in the body rule to avoid problems with Internet Explorer. Here is the new body rule:

```
body {
  margin-right: 20%;
  margin-left: 20%;
  color: #000;
  background: #fff;
  font: 100% Verdana, Arial, Helvetica, sans-serif;
}
```

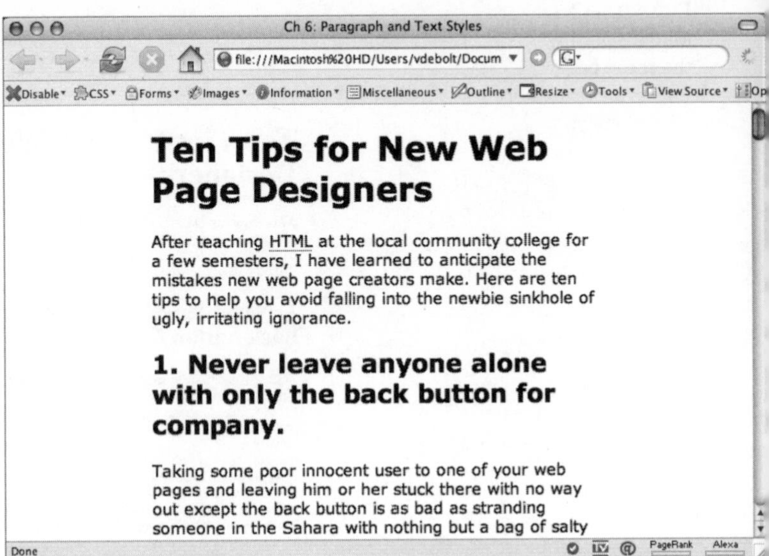

FIGURE 6.13
Background and font settings appear.

Save that change, and reload the page in the browser. The text should look like Figure 6.13, reflecting the change in the body font. The font size should not change much, other than to refle the fact that Verdana appears "large and wide." It's a font meant for easy reading on a compute screen and it has the appearance of being bigger than fonts such as Arial.

Black text on a white background provides the contrast needed for easy readability. There's r need to restrict yourself to this combination of colors, however. If you choose other colors for th background and the text, just be sure you have sufficient contrast between the colors to make th text readable for people with color perception problems.

A free tool at `www.vischeck.com/vischeck/vischeckURL.php` will check a web page and show you how the page looks to various types of color-blind users. Checks like this will help yc make sure there is enough contrast between the foreground and background colors of your pag for good readability. Juicy Studio provides free tools for analyzing color contrast and other colc issues at `http://juicystudio.com/services/colourcontrast.php`.

Heading Rules

The `h1` looks too large, in my opinion. In previous chapters, you got some experience setting `fon size` with ems, so in this chapter you'll use percentages. Declare a `font-size` value of 130% for th `h1`. In addition, the `h1` can be a dark gray (#333) instead of completely black. The `h1` selector ru

```
h1 {
  font-size: 130%;
  color: #333;
}
```

Note that `font-size: 130%;` is equivalent to `font-size: 1.3em;`.

You have used `margin` before but not negative margins for "outdenting" text. Well, it's time to get negative. Put –1.5em of negative margin on the `h1`. It might also look nice to add a 2-pixel dotted border on the right and bottom in a light gray (#CCC) color. The complete `h1` rule:

```
h1 {
  font-size: 130%;
  color: #333;
  margin-left: -1.5em;
  border-right: 2px dotted #CCC;
  border-bottom: 2px dotted #CCC;
}
```

Save and reload the browser to see something similar to Figure 6.14. You have used `margin` and `border` several times already in the book and should be getting comfortable with these CSS properties. Try my suggestions as to ways to style the text and check your work against the screen captures in the figures. Then stretch yourself and have fun writing some rules of your own design.

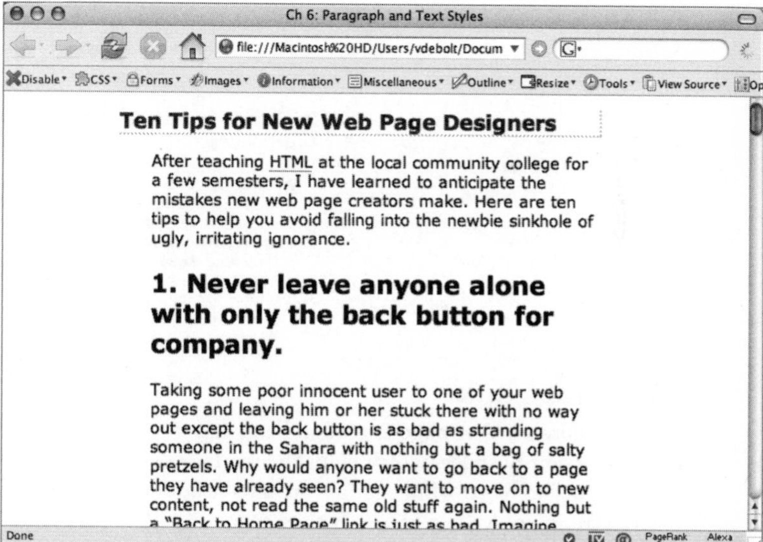

FIGURE 6.14 The styled `h1` element with a negative `margin-left` and dotted borders

The `h2` elements can be treated in a similar way. Make them a little smaller than the `h1`—say, 120 percent. You can use a slightly less negative margin—say, –1em. Match the color and border styles used on the `h1` element but apply borders to the top and bottom to set off the numbered tips in a frame-like arrangement. Add some padding to the top of the `h2` to push the heading into a more apparent proximity with the paragraph it heads. Here's the `h2` selector, the results of which are shown in Figure 6.15:

```
h2 {
  font-size: 120%;
  color: #333;
```

```
    margin-left: -1em;
    border-top: 2px dotted #CCC;
    border-bottom: 2px dotted #CCC;
    padding-top: 1.5em;
  }
```

Every h2 on the page will change to reflect the style for the h2 selector. Scroll down the page to be sure you like the way this looks.

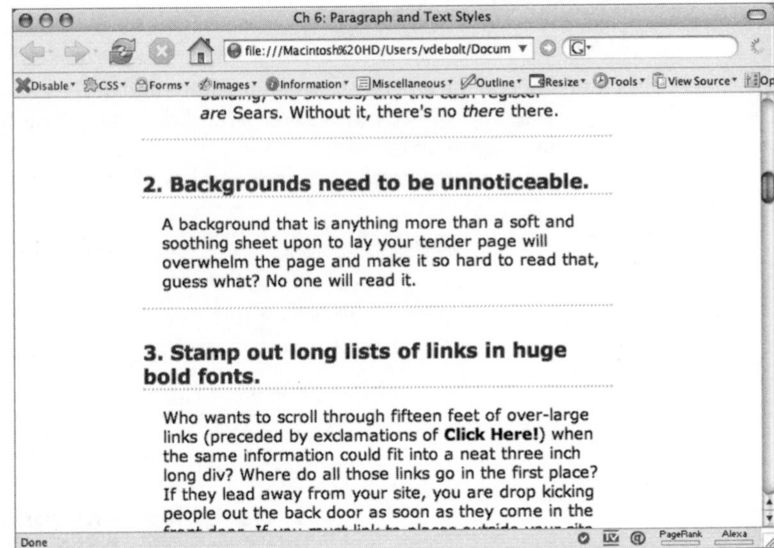
Ch 6: Paragraph and Text Styles
file:///Macintosh%20HD/Users/vdebolt/Docum
Disable CSS Forms Images Information Miscellaneous Outline Resize Tools View Source
are Sears. Without it, there's no there there.
2. Backgrounds need to be unnoticeable.
A background that is anything more than a soft and soothing sheet upon to lay your tender page will overwhelm the page and make it so hard to read that, guess what? No one will read it.
3. Stamp out long lists of links in huge bold fonts.
Who wants to scroll through fifteen feet of over-large links (preceded by exclamations of Click Here!) when the same information could fit into a neat three inch long div? Where do all those links go in the first place? If they lead away from your site, you are drop kicking people out the back door as soon as they come in the
Done
PageRank
Alexa

FIGURE 6.15 Style the h2 elements to look similar to the h1 but recognizably distinct from it.

Paragraph Rules

When there's a long page to read, it helps to put what I call "air" on the page. Air refers to white space or empty space, which helps the reader's eye separate and identify layout units and track from word to word while reading. You have added quite a bit of white space with your wide margins, but it would help to also have some white space *between* the lines of text.

> **THE IMPORTANCE OF NOTHINGNESS**
>
> White space is also called *negative space* in design terms. The empty space around parts of a design is often as important to the success of the design as the actual images or text used in the design. The negative space does more than increase readability; it adds contrast and emphasis to the items that *do* fill the space. An award for good negativity?
>
> Apple Computer's website at `www.apple.com` frequently wins design awards, in no small measure due to the brilliant use of negative space on its pages. An iPod ad with nothing more than a solid silhouette of someone dancing with an iPod against a large contrasting block of negative space is another example of effective use of negative space.

Inserting space between lines of text is easy to accomplish with a `line-height` declaration. Since you are using percentages for the `font-size`, use percentages for the `line-height` as well. A `line-height: 150%;` rule should create a very nicely spaced paragraph. The rule would be:

```
p {
  line-height: 150%;
}
```

Viewed in the browser, you see an increase in the amount of space between each line in the paragraphs. See Figure 6.16. If you know anything about typographical conventions in print, you recognize this characteristic as *leading*. `Line-height` is the distance between baselines of lines of text. Increasing the `line-height` increases the extra space above the font, or the leading. When `line-height` is expressed as a percentage, it is calculated in relation to the font size of the element. `Line-height` may also be expressed in absolute values such as pixels.

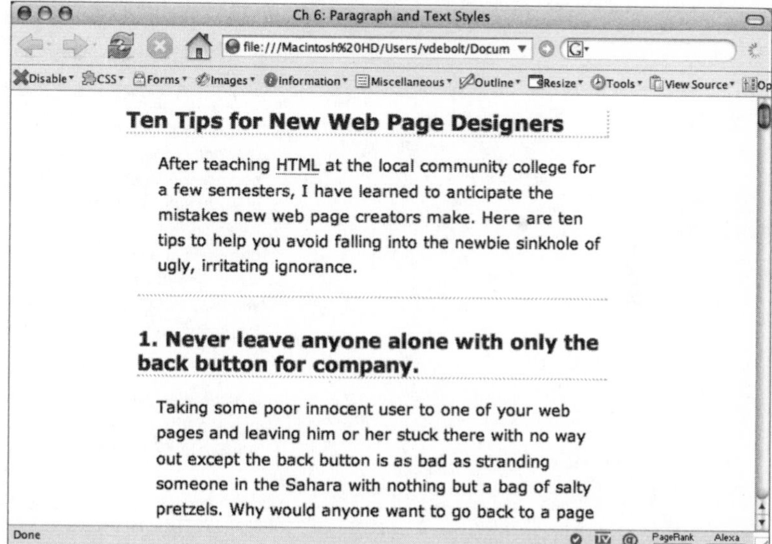

FIGURE 6.16
Paragraphs with `line-height` declared

Block Quote Rules

The paragraphs in the block quote inherit all the body and paragraph rules already set up in the style sheet, so it looks pretty good. You could leave the block quote alone, and it would be just fine. But let's write a style declaration for it anyway, just to give you more practice in styling XHTML elements.

Why not use the `2px dotted` #CCC border again but this time only on the left side?

```
blockquote {
  border-left: 2px dotted #CCC;
}
```

If you look at that in the browser, the text is too scrunched up next to the border. You want whi space! A few pixels of `padding-left` will solve the problem:

```
blockquote {
  border-left: 2px dotted #CCC;
  padding-left: 2px;
}
```

With the new rule in place, the block quote is set off with subtle distinction. See Figure 6.17. F more contrast to emphasize the `blockquote`, many additional style rules could be used, for examp a `background-image` or a `color` change.

The `blockquote` contains two paragraphs, a good place to learn about child and adjacent sibli selectors.

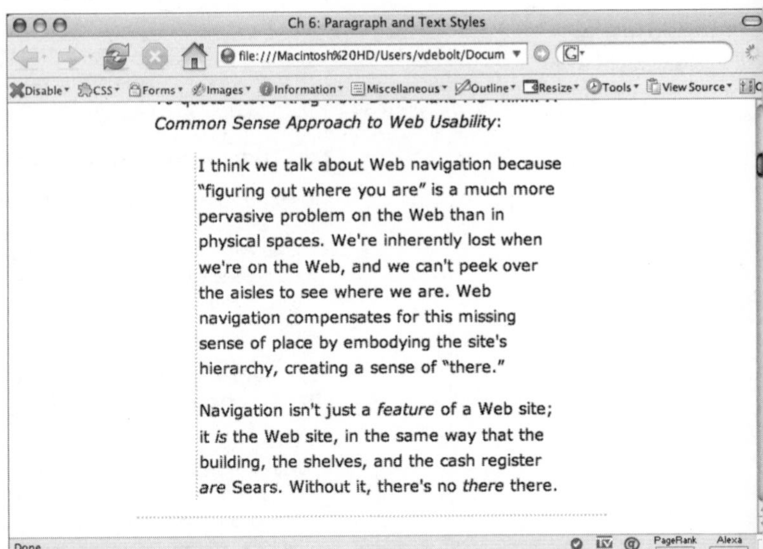
Ch 6: Paragraph and Text Styles
file:///Macintosh%20HD/Users/vdebolt/Docum
Disable CSS Forms Images Information Miscellaneous Outline Resize Tools View Source
Common Sense Approach to Web Usability:
I think we talk about Web navigation because "figuring out where you are" is a much more pervasive problem on the Web than in physical spaces. We're inherently lost when we're on the Web, and we can't peek over the aisles to see where we are. Web navigation compensates for this missing sense of place by embodying the site's hierarchy, creating a sense of "there."
Navigation isn't just a feature of a Web site; it is the Web site, in the same way that the building, the shelves, and the cash register are Sears. Without it, there's no there there.
Done
PageRank
Alexa

FIGURE 6.17
The styled block quote

The Child Selector

You know that the descendant selector `#content p` would select every `p` element that was descend from a `content` element. A child selector is similar, except it doesn't select every descendant, it selects only immediate descendants or children. The syntax is *`element > element`*. For exampl to select only those paragraphs that are immediate descendants of a `blockquote` element, you c use the child selector `blockquote > p`.

In the XHTML, the structure of the `blockquote` is:

```
<blockquote>
   <p></p>
   <p></p>
</blockquote>
```

The `p` elements are immediate descendants, or children, of the `blockquote`. Try this rule in the style sheet to see child selectors in action, as illustrated in Figure 6.18.

```
blockquote > p {
   color: red;
   }
```

Suppose the structure of the `blockquote` was slightly different, for example:

```
<blockquote>
   <p></p>
   <div>
      <p></p>
   </div>
</blockquote>
```

In this scenario, the second `p` element is not an immediate child of the `blockquote` but instead is the immediate child of a `div` element. With this structure, the first paragraph would be styled according to the `blockquote > p` child selector rule but not the second.

The red text does nothing to improve the readability of this page, so now that you understand what a child selector does, feel free to change the text back to black.

Internet Explorer 6 and before do not recognize child selectors.

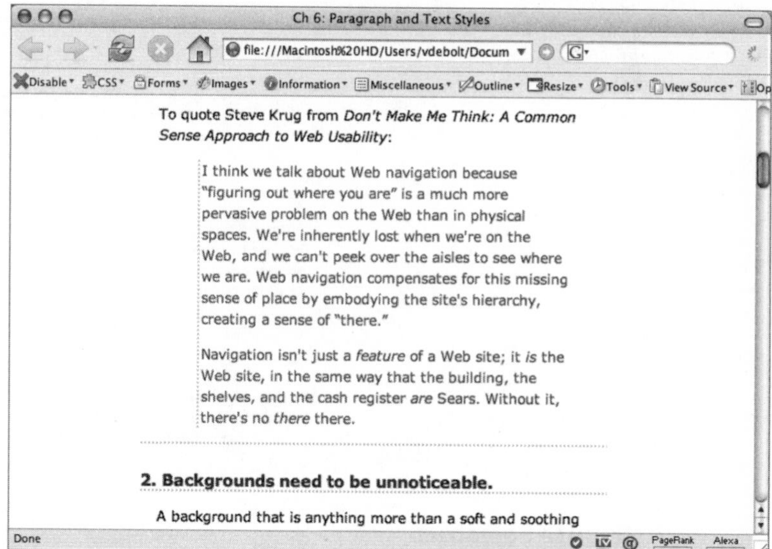
Ch 6: Paragraph and Text Styles
file:///Macintosh%20HD/Users/vdebolt/Docum
Disable CSS Forms Images Information Miscellaneous Outline Resize Tools View Source
To quote Steve Krug from Don't Make Me Think: A Common Sense Approach to Web Usability:
I think we talk about Web navigation because "figuring out where you are" is a much more pervasive problem on the Web than in physical spaces. We're inherently lost when we're on the Web, and we can't peek over the aisles to see where we are. Web navigation compensates for this missing sense of place by embodying the site's hierarchy, creating a sense of "there."
Navigation isn't just a feature of a Web site; it is the Web site, in the same way that the building, the shelves, and the cash register are Sears. Without it, there's no there there.
2. Backgrounds need to be unnoticeable.
A background that is anything more than a soft and soothing
Done
PageRank
Alexa

FIGURE 6.18 The immediate children of the `blockquote` are affected by the `blockquote > p` selector rule.

Adjacent Sibling Selectors

An adjacent sibling selector targets an element that is preceded by another element with the same parent. The syntax is *`element + element`*. The two elements must be at the same level in the document tree (with the same parent). The second element cannot be nested within the first. For example `ul + li` would not work, because the `li` element is nested within the `ul` element.

In this document, `h2 + p` would select every `p` element that was preceded by an `h2` element.

In this document, `p + p` would select every `p` element that was immediately preceded by a `p` element. Or, `p + p + p` would select every paragraph that was preceded by two paragraphs.

You created quite a bit of white space between the headings and the paragraphs with the `line-height` rule. It's always a good idea to place headings in close proximity to the material they head. An adjacent sibling selector will let you snuggle the paragraphs following each `h2` element a bit closer again, so you'll write a rule for the selector `h2 + p`. Some negative `margin-top` will close the gap between the `h2` and the `p` elements. Make the paragraph blue, too, to make the effect of this rule really obvious. Figure 6.19 shows the result.

```
h2 + p {
   margin-top: -15px;
   color: blue;
   }
```

The blue does nothing for the page either, so now that you understand what an adjacent selector does, feel free to change the text back to black.

Internet Explorer 6 and below do not support adjacent sibling selectors.

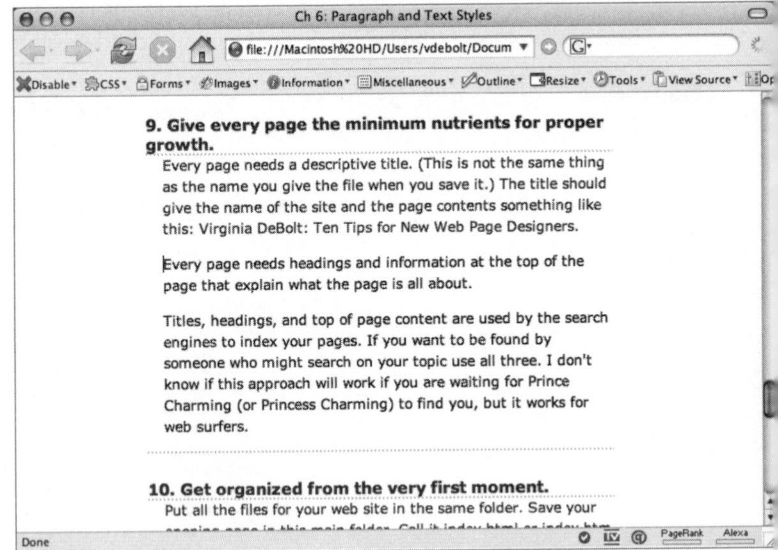

FIGURE 6.19 Using an adjacent sibling selector, the paragraph following each `h2` can be styled differently from other paragraphs.

Attribute Selectors

You select an element based on its attributes using an attribute selector. The syntax is `element[attribute]`. A few examples, not all applicable to this document, are: `h1[class]`, `img[alt]`, and `acronym[title]`. Attribute selectors can match elements in several ways:

h2[class] Matches `h2` elements that have a `class` attribute, regardless of its value.

h2[class=news] Matches `h2` elements that have a `class` attribute with a value of exactly news.

td[headers~=col1] Matches `td` elements whose `header` attribute value contains a list of space-separated values, one of which is exactly `col1`. (You'll work with XHTML like this in Chapter 10.)

p[lang|=en] Matches `p` elements whose attribute value is a hyphen-separated list that begins with `en`. (The main use for this is to match language subcodes specified by the `lang` attribute, for example, `en-us`, `en-gb`.)

In this document, there are only a few places you can test the attribute selector. Two possibilities are `acronym[title]` and `div[class=callout]`. Add this rule:

```
div[class=callout] {
   font-style: italic;
   }
```

Both of the callouts in the document should be affected by the rule. See Figure 6.20. Internet Explorer 6 and below do not support attribute selectors.

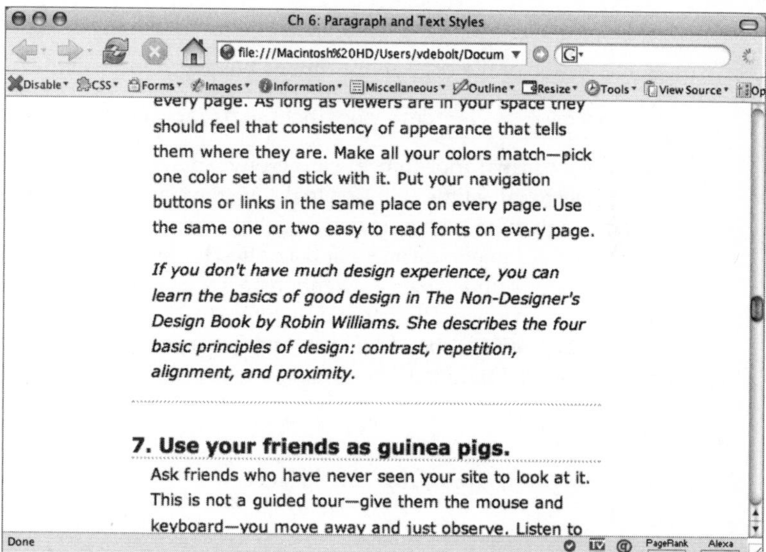

FIGURE 6.20
Using an attribute selector, `div` elements identified with the `class` callout are styled with an italic font.

em and His Buddy *strong* Once Again

As mentioned in the XHTML section, most browsers render `em` as italics and `strong` as bold, but some reverse these. You want to be sure that any browser will interpret these elements the way you want them. A couple of quick rules for `em` and `strong` will make sure the decision is yours.

Use `font-style` for `em`, like this:

```
em {
  font-style: italic;
}
```

Use `font-weight` to declare bold fonts for `strong`, like this:

```
strong {
  font-weight: bold;
}
```

Depending on the browser you are using to check your work, you may not see any difference i the appearance of the page with these two new rules in your style sheet. But it will ensure consisten appearance across all browsers to have them among your CSS rules. If you were so inclined, yo could add all sorts of CSS rules to your `em` and `strong` selectors, such as background colors and bo ders, but you don't need them for `ch6_start.html`.

There's no `dfn` element in `ch6_start.html`, but if you ever have need of one, you'd probabl want to write a CSS rule to control its display, too.

Acronym

There are two `acronym` elements in `ch6_start.html`. Earlier you looked at this one:

```
<acronym title="Hypertext Markup Language">HTML</acronym>
```

In the section of the page about "image busting," you will find another:

```
<acronym title="dots per inch">dpi</acronym>
```

Because the visual appearance of an acronym may vary from browser to browser, add a rule to you style sheet to call a little attention to the `acronym` and give it a consistent cross-browser appearanc

Although there is no iron-clad rule that says you must style an acronym in a particular way, s many web designers use italics and a dotted bottom border for acronyms that it has become one c those generally understood conventions: a dotted underline is a visual clue to a defined or expande term, such as a glossary entry, and therefore to an `acronym` element. Since dotted border rules (as i `2px dotted #CCC;`) abound in your style sheet already, it would be consistent with your design t continue in that tradition. You should already know how to write this rule:

```
acronym {
  font-style: italic;
  border-bottom: 2px dotted #CCC;
}
```

View the page in the browser; it will look like Figure 6.21. Hovering over the `acronym` should produce a visible rendering of the `title` attribute.

Callout

In a magazine, a *callout* or *pull quote* is extracted from the text and set in display type. Sometimes th pull quote is displayed at quite a distance from the source of the material in the text.

In `ch6_start.html` there are two divs identified with the `class="callout"` attribute. These will be styled to resemble pull quotes. You won't attempt to create the effect you might see in a magazine, but you will set off the text in this class to make it visually distinct.

You will reduce the font size, move the callout to the right and right-align the text, and use bac ground images to create a visual accent for the callout.

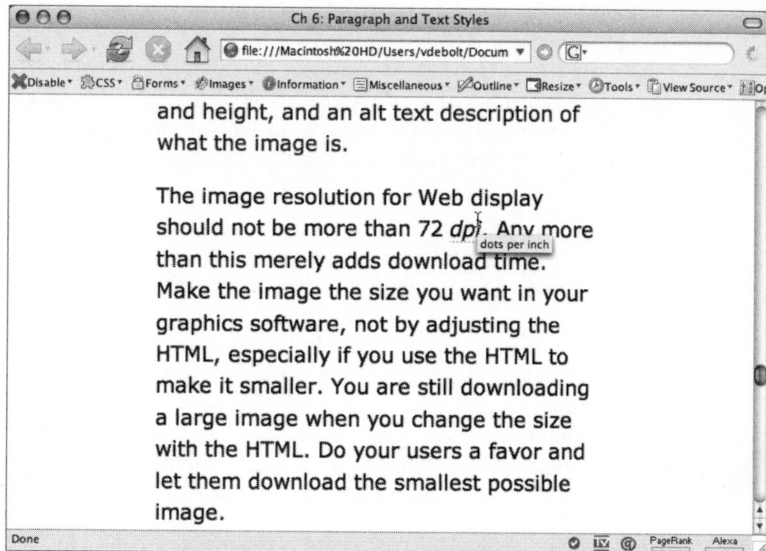

FIGURE 6.21
An italic acronym with a tool tip revealing the contents of the `title` attribute

GENERAL CONVENTIONS

People who use the Internet and the Web frequently come to understand some of the unspoken conventions that help to navigate and interpret web pages. I mentioned the convention of using a dotted bottom border to offer a clue to the presence of an acronym, but there are many more. Here are a few others.

- When a word is underlined, it is understood to be a link.
- A small graphic with a word on it is usually a link.
- When a site logo in the upper-left corner of a web page is clicked, it usually leads to the home page.
- A phrase in large type is usually a heading.
- Lists of links are often displayed in a colored bar down the left or right side of a page.
- Main site navigation links will be consistent from page to page within a site.
- Most large sites have an easy-to-find search box. (Searching is a function that requires a script and will not be covered in this book.)
- Some icons, such as those representing mailboxes and shopping carts, have an agreed-upon meaning. (There are not many icons that are immediately understood without textual help.)

Of course, people can and do break free from these conventional notions when designing websites. However, it pays to be careful when breaking conventions lest your visitors become confused or regard your site as unusable and go elsewhere.

Start by creating a `.callout` selector in the style sheet. Add declarations for `font-size` and `tex` `align`. Align the text to the right and reduce the width of the callout by adding margin to the left. If y add a `margin-left: 30%;` declaration, the callout will be 70 percent of the width of the normal par graphs. Keep in mind that you have a previous rule targeting the callout using an attribute selector th made the font italic. (Since IE6 and below won't recognize the attribute selector, a simple class select is probably a more sensible way to style the callouts at the current time.) The rule so far:

```
.callout {
  font-size: 90%;
  text-align: right;
  margin-left: 30%;
}
```

You have something like Figure 6.22 at this stage. The callout is set off mostly by means o white space.

You aren't finished yet, however, because I intend to teach you a nice effect using two background images. On the CD in the Chapter 6 folder, you will find two GIF images: `callout_l.g` and `callout_r.gif`. Copy these two images into the same folder on your computer where you have the HTML and CSS files for Chapter 6. The two GIFs are thin gray bars with a drop shadc and curved ends that will sit under the text of the callout like a tray.

Both callouts are formatted similar to the example in Listing 6.4.

LISTING 6.4: The Structure of the Callouts

```
<div class="callout">
  <p>If you don't have much design experience, you can learn the basics of good
design in <cite>The Non-Designer's Design Book</cite> by Robin Williams. She
describes the four basic principles of design: contrast, repetition, alignment,
and proximity.</p>
</div>
```

The `div` is assigned to a class and the paragraph is a descendant of the `div`. Since an XHTML e ment can only have one background image, you need two elements here to make this work: bc the `div` and the `p`.

One GIF image will be used for the `.callout` class selector. After that, you will create an additional style for a `.callout p` descendant selector and assign a GIF to it. The two graphic backgrour will combine to create a single visual effect accenting the callout element.

You need to add the background image to the callout rules—use `callout_r.gif` first. The ba ground image should not repeat, and it should be located horizontally at the right and vertically the bottom of the `div`, like this:

```
.callout {
  font-size: 90%;
  background: url(callout_r.gif) no-repeat right bottom;
  text-align: right;
  margin-left: 30%;
}
```

FIGURE 6.22
Using `margin-left` and `text-align:right`, you achieve a unique look for the callout text.

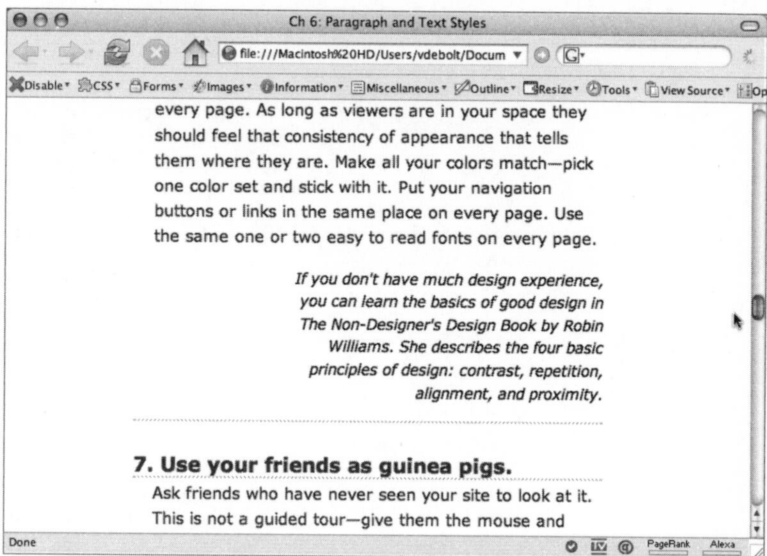

You can look at it at this point, but it looks better with a little padding, so why not go ahead and add some? (You'll pad the bottom in just a minute, be patient.) The rule should be like this:

```
.callout {
  font-size: 90%;
  background: url(callout_r.gif) no-repeat right bottom;
  text-align: right;
  margin-left: 30%;
  padding-right: 4px;
}
```

Save your style sheet and take a look in the browser to see something like Figure 6.23.

The callout is almost finished. But the accent graphic on the bottom needs to curve up on the left side, too. If you had a fixed width for the callout, you could have easily made a single graphic in the exact width you wanted and just used that to do the job. But your callout is a percentage width and putting a fixed-size graphic under it just won't work.

You will use a technique that combines the effects of two backgrounds. This fluid technique allows the backgrounds to slide over each other and appear to grow or shrink to fit the size of the user's viewport.

STANDING ON THE SHOULDERS OF . . .

One of the first descriptions of multiple background designs was published in A List Apart by writer Douglas Bowman at `www.alistapart.com/articles/slidingdoors/`. Thanks to Bowman, the technique has come to be called "sliding doors."

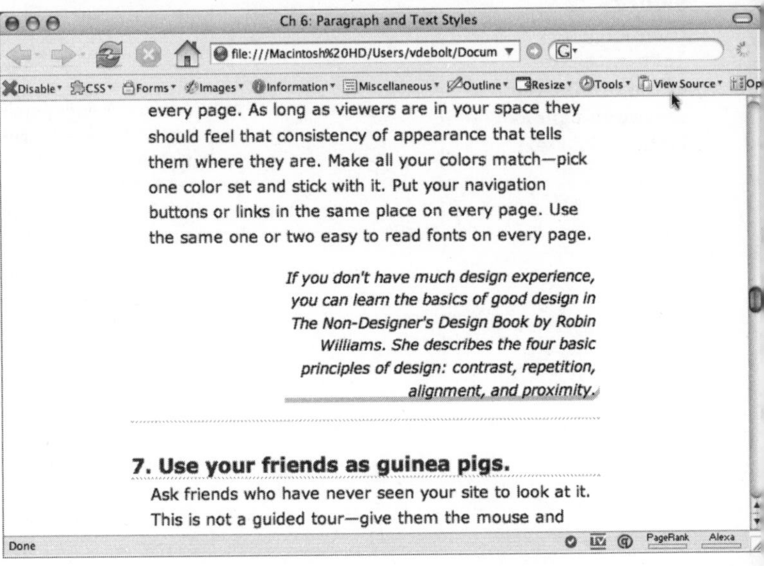

FIGURE 6.23
The callout with right bottom background

I hinted at this earlier, but the complete process works like this. You already have a background o the class named `callout`. You have to find a place to add another background. Look at the XHTM

```
<div class="callout"><p>If you don't ...</p></div>
```

In the `div` element there is a `p` element. You can create a selector in your CSS that will allow yo to use a background for the `p` element descended from the `div class="callout"` element. The selector would be `.callout p`. You want to use the GIF with the left curve (`callout_l.gif`) as background. You want the image not to repeat and to be placed horizontally on the left and ver cally on the bottom. As noted, some padding at the bottom would be welcome, too. Here's the ru

```
.callout p {
  background: url(callout_l.gif) no-repeat left bottom;
  padding-bottom: 8px;
}
```

Save that and refresh the browser view. See Figure 6.24. Be sure to put it to the test by resizing yo browser window and admiring the graphic as it shrinks or grows according to the browser width

There are two `callout` elements on the page; both should have the same presentation. Scroll dow the entire page to see the second callout. Remember that a class can be used multiple times, so you c add as many callouts as you want to this page. If you used the <div class="callout"><p> structu to create them, they would all look the same.

PUSHING AROUND A PULL QUOTE

The text of a pull quote or callout can often be styled effectively using `float` to remove the quote from the normal document flow, move it to the left or right, and allow the remaining text to flow around it. It isn't particularly effective on this page, but keep `float` in mind for future reference with other possible page designs.

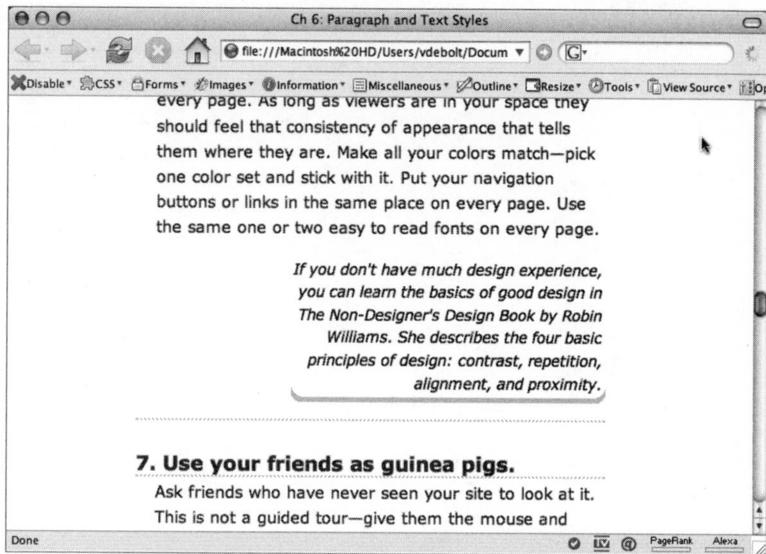

FIGURE 6.24
The callout with a finished curve under it created with two separate background images

To get rounded corners on elements on the Web, which is restricted to a box model that puts everything in a square-cornered rectangular box, it's necessary to use multiple images as in this exercise. (There are also techniques using JavaScript rather than images and CSS.) A source of many rounded corner techniques is the CSS Discuss Wiki at `http://css-discuss.incutio.com/?page=RoundedCorners`.

Footer Rules

The footer is another web page convention inherited from print. It holds information tucked away at the bottom (or foot) of the web page.

Most footer material is meant to be unobtrusive. Footers may contain legal information such as links to privacy policies or copyright notices. Footers also often contain a link to the site designer's home page or a webmaster's e-mail link. Unless a user is specifically looking for such information, footers are generally not given much attention.

One way to make this information unobtrusive is to use a smaller font size and make the text a light gray. Something like this:

```
#footer {
  font-size: 80%;
  color: #999;
}
```

Your view in the browser should be like Figure 6.25. The footer is less obtrusive with the lighter gray text and the smaller size and is clearly not meant to be part of the main content. Be careful with a gray that light against a white background: the text may not have enough contrast for many users to comfortably see and read.

That helps define the footer, but there's a proximity issue with it snuggled up next to the last of the main content. It needs some visual separation to clarify the distinction between the main content and footer content. In other situations on this page you have used `padding` to move things around, so move the footer down and away from the last paragraph with `padding-top`.

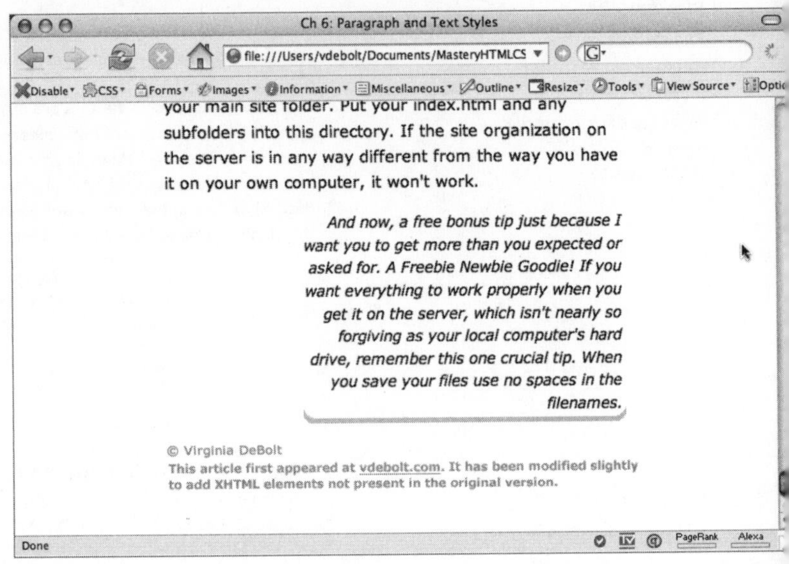

FIGURE 6.25
The styled footer

Use a `border-top` as well, to create a visual separator between the content and the footer. Wh change your design now? Use a `2px dotted #CCC` border once again. The changed rule:

```
#footer {
  font-size: 80%;
  color: #999;
  padding-top: 3em;
  border-top: 2px dotted #CCC;
}
```

Figure 6.26 shows the results of the additional change.

You have another proximity problem now, apparent in Figure 6.26. The `border-top` is too fa away from the `footer` text. This is because `padding` comes between the content of your elemen and the `border`. (See the diagram in Figure 4.21 for a refresher on the box model.) You need a wa to keep the `footer` content where it is but make the `border-top` appear closer to the content of th `footer`.

Have you figured out how yet? Understanding the box model is the key. You *don't* want `padding`, because `padding` comes between `content` and `border`. You *do* want `margin`, becaus `margin` is beyond the `border`. I purposely had you try it the "wrong" way first in this exercise, because mixing up the uses for padding and margin is a common mistake. Learn from your mi takes, I say.

Instead of using `padding-top`, use `margin-top`, like this:

```
#footer {
  font-size: 80%;
  color: #999;
  border-top: 2px dotted #CCC;
  margin-top: 4em;
}
```

Finally, the footer is satisfactory: unobtrusive and visually distinct. See Figure 6.27.

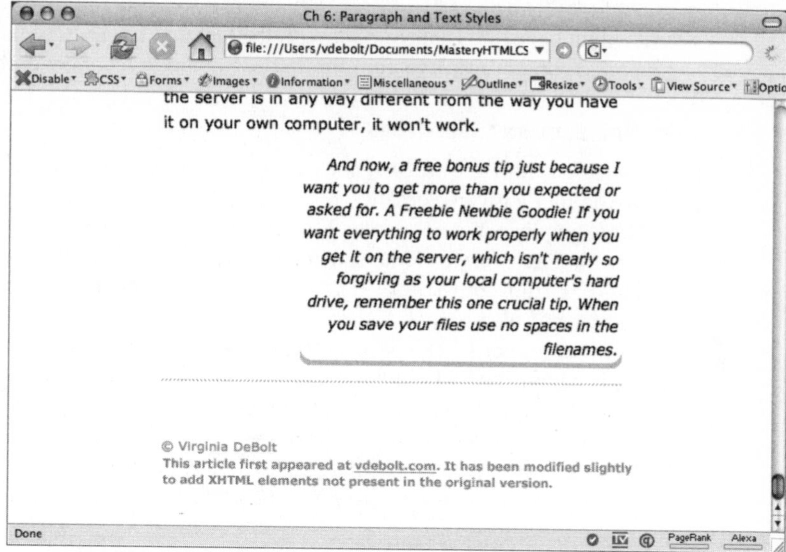

FIGURE 6.26 The changed footer with a `padding-top` of `3em`. You can clearly see how padding comes between the content and the border.

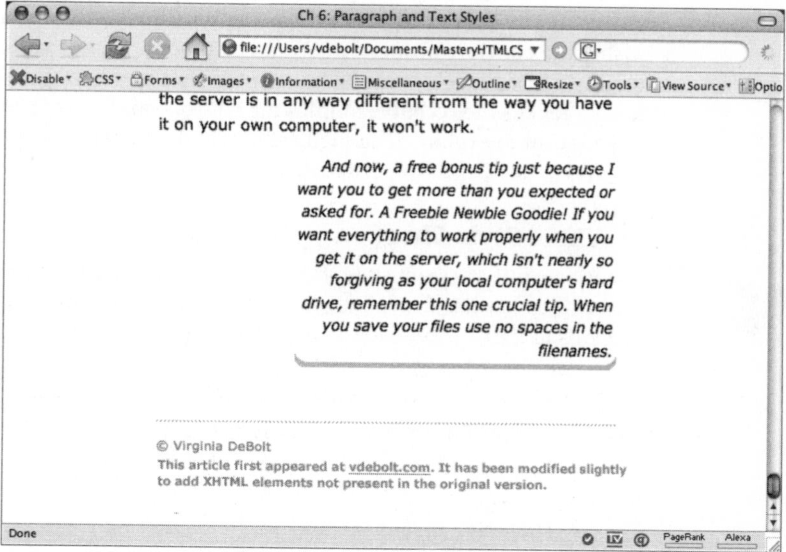

FIGURE 6.27 The footer with `margin-top`

This exercise with `padding` versus `margin` wasn't designed to be a trick. It's merely a way to point out that just because you used `padding` several times on this page to move content a bit, it doesn't mean that `padding` is the only tool at your disposal, or even the right tool for every situation.

Generated Content

There are a number of ways to use *generated content*, or content created by the browser rather than in the markup. I'll briefly explain some types of generated content here; later in the chapter you'll add generated content in the print style sheet. Since generated content is not in the XHTML, if a user with CSS turned off or a device that does not display styles finds your page, the generated cc tent will not appear. That coupled with the fact that Internet Explorer 6 and below do not suppc generated content result in very limited use of any type of generated content at this time.

Pseudo-Element Selectors

The selectors `:before` and `:after` allow `content` specified in a style sheet to be inserted either before or after a given element.

For example, `p.note:before { content: "Note: " }` in a style sheet inserts the text conte "Note: " before every `p` element whose `class` attribute has the value `note`.

This CSS rule, `container:after { content: "The End"; }` inserts the text `"The End"` aft the `container` element.

Any CSS properties can be assigned to `:before` and `:after` pseudo-elements, including background images. The background images that you used earlier in the chapter to create a visual effect `blockquote` required the addition of a nonsemantic extra `div` to the markup. Once pseudo-eleme selectors are supported by all major browsers, you will see designers rushing to create all sorts of be tifully styled presentations such as the `blockquote` presentation exercise, using `:before` and `:aft` to insert background images. No extra nonsemantic elements required.

Generated Quotation Marks, List Markers, and More

Several other uses for generated content exist as possibilities for the future. Until full browser su port arrives, you don't need to know much more than the fact that these mechanisms exist.

Using the `content` property, CSS can be used to insert markers and lists, to open and clos quotation marks, and for automatic counters and numbering—all in addition to the insertion strings of text as the recent examples for `:before` and `:after` indicated.

If you want to explore generated content in depth, the W3C provides information here: `www.w3.org/TR/CSS21/generate.html`.

The Whole Style Sheet

Before we get into the print style sheet, look at your completed `ch6_allmedia.css` file. A versio named `ch6_allmedia_finished.css`, which you can use for comparison with your `ch6_allmec .css` file, is in the Chapter 6 folder on the accompanying CD and is reproduced in Listing 6.5.

Listing 6.5: The Finished All-Media Style Sheet

```
body {
   margin-right: 20%;
   margin-left: 20%;
   background: #fff;
    font: 100% Verdana, Arial, Helvetica, sans-serif;
}
h1 {
  font-size: 130%;
  color: #333;
  margin-left: -1.5em;
```

```
  border-right: 2px dotted #CCC;
  border-bottom: 2px dotted #CCC;
}
h2 {
  font-size: 120%;
  color: #333;
  margin-left: -1em;
  border-top: 2px dotted #CCC;
  border-bottom: 2px dotted #CCC;
  padding-top: 1.5em;
}
p {
  line-height: 150%;
}
blockquote {
  border-left: 2px dotted #CCC;
  padding-left: 2px;
}
blockquote > p {
   color: red;
   }
h2 + p {
   margin-top: -15px;
   color: blue;
   }
div[class=callout] {
   font-style: italic;
   }
em {
  font-style: italic;
}
strong {
  font-weight: bold;
}
acronym {
  font-style: italic;
  border-bottom: 2px dotted #CCC;
}
.callout {
  font-size: 90%;
  background: url(callout_r.gif) no-repeat right bottom;
  text-align: right;
  margin-left: 30%;
  padding-right: 4px;
}
.callout p {
  background: url(callout_l.gif) no-repeat left bottom;
```

```
    padding-bottom: 8px;
  }
  #footer {
    font-size: 80%;
    color: #999;
    margin-top: 4em;
    border-top: 2px dotted #CCC;
  }
```

Print Preview

You have an all-media style sheet. If you print the page as it's now styled, the rules you set will b used on the printed page. If no print media style sheet is linked to a file, the all-media style she will be used for exactly what it says: all media.

You have an option in your browser's File menu that allows you to preview a printed page wi out using the paper and ink to actually print it. Use that to see how the page would print with on the current `ch6_allmedia.css` style sheet attached.

Feel free to make use of the browser's print preview in the next section. There's no reason to print this page over and over as you go through the exercises when you can preview the chang instead.

Let's Go into Print

If you previewed the printed version of the current page as I suggested, you may have thought looked readable enough and wondered why there was any need for a print style sheet. A valid point; however, in a more realistic situation when you are posting an article such as this to a we site, there would be more on the page than this text. There would be images, navigation elemen perhaps ads, search boxes, and other elements.

Often there are elements on the page that the reader doesn't need or want in print. For examp what benefit is there in having a search form printed on a sheet of paper? It can't be used and mere eats into someone's ink budget to print. The visitor may grumble and eventually decide not to co back to your site. Therefore, one of the things you will learn to do with print style sheets is how n to print selected elements on a page.

Start Your Style Sheet

Open a new blank document in your text editor. Save it in the same folder on your computer a `ch6_start.html`. Name it `ch6_print.css`.

Even though it's a blank document right now, go ahead and add a link to it in your `ch6_start.html` document. Put the new link *after* the existing style sheet link, like this:

```
<link href="ch6_allmedia.css" rel="stylesheet" type="text/css" media="all" />
<link href="ch6_print.css" rel="stylesheet" type="text/css" media="print" />
```

Notice that the `media` value is set to `print` in this case. Setting a `media` value of `print` means th style sheet will be ignored by devices other than printers. As mentioned earlier, putting the link to t print style sheet after the all-media style sheet means that the print rules come last in the cascade

As discussed in Chapter 2, the cascade is affected by proximity. The last rule read is in the closest proximity to the element and is the rule applied. For example, if the `font-size: 130%;` rule in `ch6_allmedia.css` were followed by a `font-size: 16pt;` rule in `ch6_print.css`, the `16pt` rule would be the one used when printing.

Using the *display* Property to Remove Content

The `display` property is a handy one for print style sheets. You will use it again in Chapter 9 to declare `display: block` or `display: inline` rules for lists. In this chapter, you will work with the value `none` for the `display` property, to hide the elements that should not be printed.

A declaration of `display: none` completely removes the element from the visual display—but not from the document. (One of the image replacement techniques you looked at in Chapter 4 used this property and value.) With `display: none`, the space closes up, and the page is shown as if the element did not exist. Using `display: none` removes elements from the view of some aural screen readers too, which is why it cannot be used to hide things visually while still leaving them available to users with assistive devices.

SAVE THAT SPOT

The `visibility: hidden;` property and value used to show or hide `divs` does not remove the element from the document. It merely hides it temporarily while holding open a position for it.

A good example of something you might not want to print is a search box. The document `ch6_start.html` does not have a search form, but if it did it might be contained like this: `<div id="search">search form here</div>`. The style sheet selector `#search` could be used like this:

```
#search {
  display: none;
}
```

In a print style sheet, this would keep the `search div` from displaying and printing.

There aren't actually elements in `ch6_start.html` that you can logically use to try `display: none;`. You want all the headings and paragraphs to display. For the sake of the exercise, I've arbitrarily picked the `footer` to not display. In your `ch6_print.css` document, add your first rule:

```
#footer {
  display: none;
}
```

Save that and reload the browser. If you look at the browser you'll still see the footer. It's only been removed from view in the print style sheet. Use the browser's File menu to preview the print results. Keep in mind as you do the following exercises that you'll need to reload the browser after you change a style rule, but you can only see the results of a change to the print style sheet when you look at print preview.

Your print preview may look very different from the screen capture in Figure 6.28, depending on your particular operating system, browser, and setup. But in every setup, the footer should not be visible at the end of the document. Figure 6.28 is a Mac print preview taken from a Firefox browser view. (The Mac creates a PDF document for print previews.)

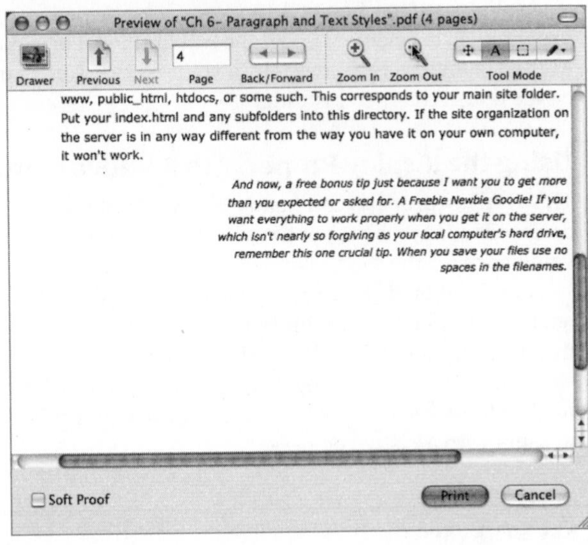

FIGURE 6.28
Using Firefox and print preview on a Mac, you see the footer isn't displayed in the print version of the page.

Remember, this rule only applies to print, so if you look for the footer in the normal browser window, you should still see it.

The footer really should be there in print. I had you remove it to make a point. If you use co ments around the rule in the CSS, it will still be there for your future reference, but it will not affe the display.

One of the nice things about using comments is that you can leave notes to yourself or to othe with whom you might work. Wrap the whole rule in a comment something like this:

```
/*this rule stops an element from displaying
#footer {
  display: none;
}*/
```

If you save this in the style sheet, but commented out, the footer will indeed display when pri ing, but the rule will be saved to remind you at some later date how to stop elements from displayin If you don't think you'll need the reminder, delete the entire `#footer` rule from the style sheet.

If you wrote a print style sheet for an article from a three-column page layout, such as Chapter The Flower Page, you might use `display: none` to eliminate most or all of the two side columns a print only the `masthead`, `content`, and `footer` information.

Back to Black

I retained the red and blue color rules in my `ch6_allmedia.css` styles. You may have changed those colors earlier, as I suggested. I don't want this to print in red and blue, so I'll write a rule usi a *universal selector* that will make the page print with all black text. The universal selector uses th symbol: *. A universal selector matches any element.

To use it in the print style sheet, add this:

```
* {
color: #000 !important;
}
```

By using a universal selector and the `!important` rule, I overruled earlier declarations in the cascade that created red and blue text. You don't need this rule if you've already changed your text back to black.

Setting Print Margins

The need for short line lengths is not so important in print. It's easier for the eye to track across a long line and then find its way back to the next line without getting lost when reading a printed page.

`ch6_allmedia.css` has the body set with margins of 20 percent on both the left and right. You can change that rule in the `ch6_print.css` style sheet to allow the page to print the full width of a sheet of paper.

Exact measures like inches and points aren't used on web pages because screen resolution and size can make a measurement like inches to meaningless. However, print is an exact medium. Printers understand measurement in inches (`in`) and points (`pt`), so use those units in your print styles. First, change the `body margin` to `0.5in` to apply to top, right, bottom, and left:

```
body {
  margin: 0.5in;
}
```

If you use the browser's print preview to view this change, you'll see the wider page layout. You may notice that the printed version will use fewer pages (on my setup it's four pages long instead of five) with the wider margins for print. See Figure 6.29.

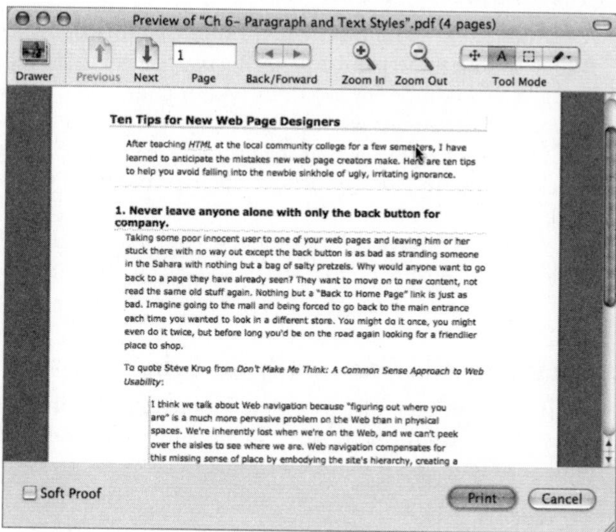

FIGURE 6.29 Half-inch (0.5 in) margins in a print preview

Changing the Font Size for Print

Another change you should make for print is to set `font-size` values in points. You will need a ru for `h1`, `h2`, and `p`. A reasonable point size for most printed text is `12pt`. Make the headings slight larger than that. Add these rules to the style sheet:

```
p {
  font-size: 12pt;
}
h1 {
  font-size: 18pt;
}
h2 {
  font-size: 16pt;
}
```

Viewing the print preview now, you may or may not notice much of a change visually. Eve though the print appears to be about the same size as you see on the screen, you may notice that t number of pages that will print with the `font-size` expressed in points has changed.

POINTS ABOUT POINTS

A point is an actual physical measurement in print: it is 1/72 of an inch. Twelve points equal one pica in the print world. There is no corresponding physical measurement with pixels on a computer screen that can be guaranteed across platforms, screen resolutions, and browsers. Therefore, points are not a good choice for screen-media styles, but they are perfect for print-media styles.

PRINTING MEANS "USER'S CHOICE"

One thing to keep in mind with print is that the user has options that you have no control ove When setting up to print a page, the user decides whether or not to print background colors a images, whether or not to print URLs or page numbers in header or footer sections of the print page, and sometimes what margins to use.

It is safest to assume that the user will not print backgrounds. If you designed a page with a black background and white text, the user might get white text on a white paper when printing. sure to test colors for print.

Not all users have color printers, so you may need to rethink all your color choices in your pr style rules to ensure good contrast in black and white.

If a background image is used, it may not appear on the printed page.

Changing the *font-family* for Print

Serif fonts are generally considered more readable in print. You originally set the font in the bo selector. Revisit the `body` selector and add a declaration changing to a serif font. Georgia is a re able serif font, so list it as first choice:

```
body {
  margin: 0.5in;
  font-family: Georgia, Times, serif;
}
```

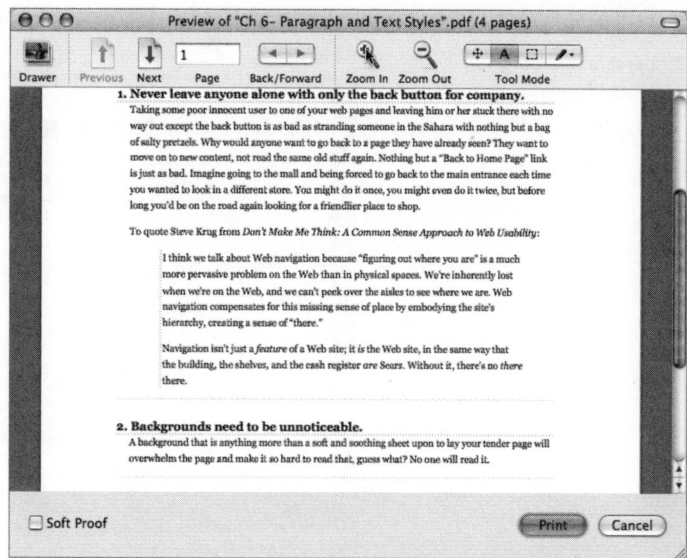

FIGURE 6.30
Print preview with serif fonts

Your print preview should reveal something similar to Figure 6.30.

Changing the *text-indent* for Print

Although the first line of a paragraph may or may not be indented on the Web, readers expect a printed paragraph to be indented. The property that will indent the first line of a given element is `text-indent`.

Revisit the `p` selector and add a couple of ems of indented space at the beginning of your paragraphs:

```
p {
  font-size: 12pt;
  text-indent: 2em;
}
```

A preview of the printed page reveals nicely indented paragraphs. See Figure 6.31.

You create indented paragraphs for the screen in the same way, using `text-indent`, which indents only the first line of an element.

A common print convention is not to indent the first paragraph after a heading. If you set `text-indent` for all paragraphs with the `p` selector, you could remove the `text-indent` from the first paragraph after the `h2` headings with the selector `h2+p`.

Print a URL

Hyperlinks on a sheet of paper just don't work. Material printed from the Internet is often stuffed full of hyperlinks. Instead, you can use generated content to insert the URL (also called URI) of a hyperlink after the link text. Then the printed document is a useful resource for readers who want to follow the links in the text.

> **URLS**
>
> URL means uniform resource locator, URI means uniform resource indicator. Chapter 7 is about URLs!

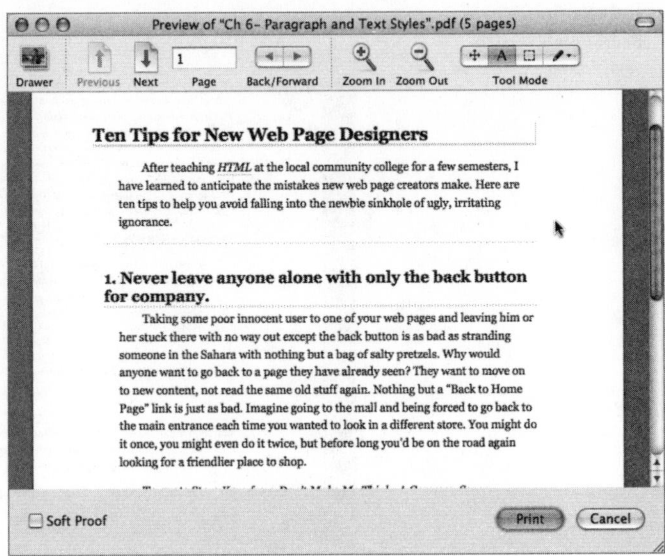

FIGURE 6.31 Create indented paragraphs using `text-indent`.

There's one hyperlink in the document. See Listing 6.6.

LISTING 6.6: The Document Footer Contains a Hyperlink

```
<div id="footer">
  <p>&#169; Virginia DeBolt <br />
  This article first appeared at <a href="http://www.vdebolt.com/ht/
tentips.html">vdebolt.com</a>. It has been modified slightly to add XHTML elements
not present in the original version. </p>
</div>
```

The selector that will add generated content after the hyperlink (an a element) is this: `a:link:after`. Here's the rule:

```
a:link:after {
   content: " (" attr(href) ") ";
   }
```

This rule takes the content of an element's `attr` (attribute)—in this case the `content` is the `href` (`hypertext reference`)—and generates the `href` text after the link, in parentheses.

Look at the print preview of this using some browser other than Internet Explorer. See Figure 6.32.

The Whole Style Sheet

That's it! You now have a document ready for reading on screen or in print. The completed style sheet is shown in Listing 6.7. Note that this version of the style sheet has the commented out `#footer` declaration and the * rule. Your style sheet may not have either of these rules.

FIGURE 6.32
The URL of the hyperlink appears in parentheses following the link when the page prints.

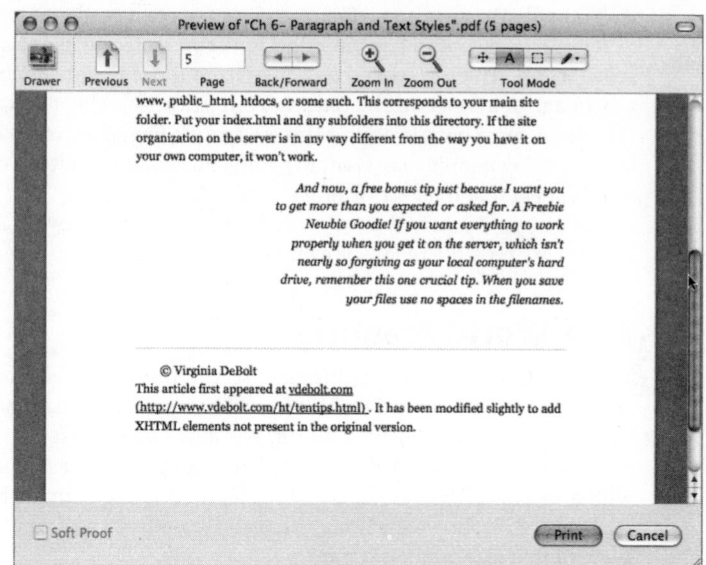

LISTING 6.7: The Print Stylesheet

```
* {
color: #000 !important;
}
body {
   margin: 0.5in;
   font-family: Georgia, Times, serif;
}
/*this rule will remove the footer from any display
#footer {
  display: none;
}*/
p {
  font-size: 12pt;
  text-indent: 2em;
}
h1 {
  font-size: 18pt;
}
h2 {
  font-size: 16pt;
}
a:link:after {
   content: " (" attr(href) ") ";
   }
```

You will also find a version of `ch6_print.css` on the accompanying CD.

The key concept to keep in mind for print style sheets is that it's only necessary to include th selectors and rules that need a change from those in your main style sheet—as long as you take advantage of the cascade by placing your print style sheet link after your all-media style sheet lin Of course, most people don't print every web page they read. But if you think your content mig be something people may want to print, you can see that it isn't much more work for you to incluc a style sheet that makes printing easy for your users.

In Chapter 7 you will work with links, discovering how to incorporate them into your XHTM document and style them so readers of your page can easily use them.

Real-World Scenario

The *New York Times* (`www.nytimes.com`) recently switched from an old-fashioned table-based la out to an all CSS layout. The *New York Times* is an old-fashioned news outlet, but they were ear to go online in the publishing world. The new makeover isn't perfect, but it's quite an achieveme nevertheless. The *New York Times* is a newspaper that has overwhelming amounts of text to dea with every day. They use every typographic technique in the book to help readers keep track of all. Figure 6.33 shows the home page and points out a few of the ways they found to help reade keep all that information organized.

FIGURE 6.33 The home page of the *New York Times* newspaper online

One of the most interesting choices the *New York Times* made, in my opinion, was to retain serif fonts for the actual articles. This is a well-established company with a long history of publishing with serif fonts. It seems entirely in keeping with their image and reputation to publish on the Internet with serif fonts, although most people consider sans-serif fonts easier to read on the Web. Not everything you see is a serif font; some headings are in a sans-serif font, an example of good use of typography to achieve contrast.

You can't see the whole page in the screen capture, but the *New York Times* managed to retain the newspapery look and feel of this site by squeezing six columns into this layout. Something important, like the image for the lead story, covers more than one column. Yet you have no problem tracking where to read the next line of any article you select, nor do you have problems running headings, menus, and article text together.

Each section from the global nav area, for example, Technology, has its own main page. See Figure 6.34.

In the main sections of the inner pages, the featured articles are moved completely to the left with sidebars on the right that feature favorite technology columns, blogs, and writers and also show advertising. If you look carefully, you see the same techniques here you saw on the home page: all caps nav text, color contrast, borders between columns, white space, and so on all put into practice on the inner pages of the site.

The technology section has a subnavigation bar, again in capitals, immediately under the global nav. It begins with CAMCORDERS, CAMERAS, and so on, in the screen capture. These menu items are set off with a faint background color. They take the reader to `cnet.com` reviews of various technology products, but the reviews are shown in the *New York Times* pages. The articles below that, for example the one with the heading "Was It Done With a Lens, or a Brush?" are material from within the *New York Times*.

FIGURE 6.34
The main page of the *New York Times* Technology section

CSS Properties

Most of the CSS properties used in Chapter 6 were explained earlier in the book.

TABLE 6.3: Properties for Element and Text Display

SELECTOR	PROPERTY	POSSIBLE VALUES
all elements	`display`	none, `inline`, `block`, `inline-block`, `list-item`, `run-in`, `table`, `inline-table`, `table-row-group`, `table-row`, `table-column-group`, `table-column`, `table-cell`, `table-caption`, `inherit`
all block-level elements	`text-indent`	*<length>*, *<percentage>*, `inherit`
all block-level elements except tables	`min-width`	*<length>*, *<percentage>*, `inherit`
all block-level elements except tables	`max-width`	*<length>*, *<percentage>*, none, `inherit`
`:before` and `:after` pseudo-elements	`content`	`normal, <string>, <uri>, <counter>, attr<identifier>, open-quote, close-quote, no-open-quote, no-close-quote, inherit`

The Bottom Line

Identify helpful XHTML elements for formatting text, including `em`, `strong`, `acronym`, `abb` **`cite`, `q`, `blockquote`, `big`, `small`, `sub`, `sup`, `code`, `var`, and others.** Long strings of letters an words must be formatted in ways that help readers understand organization, content, and pu pose. Adding to the heading and paragraph elements from past chapters, this chapter provide a number of other helpful text formatting elements.

Master It Find the document `mark_me_up.html` on the accompanying CD. Use all the things you have learned up to this point to format and style the document.

Understand and use CSS selectors including child selectors, adjacent selectors, and attribu selectors.

Master It Make the following changes to `mark_me_up.html` and its accompanying style sheet:

1. Add an `em` element to one of the headings. Then write a CSS child selector rule that wi style only that `em` element and no other `em` elements on the page.
2. Assign the first paragraph a `class` or `id` of "intro" and use an attribute selector to crea a style for the first paragraph.

Create generated content. Although not widely used, it's possible to generate content from the CSS rather than the XHTML. The `:before` and `:after` pseudo-elements are examples of generated content.

Master It Include this in the work on `mark_me_up.html`. Add generated content to either the all media or print styles.

Create codes for special characters such as copyright symbols. Literally hundreds of special characters have unique codes for display in XHTML.

Master It Include special characters in `mark_me_up.html` by using character codes where appropriate.

Write a print style sheet. Reading large blocks of text online is difficult. Designers must take special care to ensure that their content is readable and that various elements on a page are easy to distinguish. Reading in print is less demanding on the reader in terms of eye tracking from line to line and line length. Material from the online world can be formatted to more closely resemble print from magazines and books when styling text for print.

Master It Make a print style sheet for `mark_me_up.html`.

Chapter 7

Links and Link Styles

So far you've worked with individual pages completely detached from each other. The real Web is composed of sets of multiple files and folders, organized and connected with each other through elements called *hyperlinks* or simply *links*. Linking from site to site and page to page is what the Web is all about. You write links to allow navigation among all the files within a given site, to web pages outside the site, and to resources beyond XHTML pages: e-mail links, links to sound clips, and links to PDF documents, for instance.

CSS can help you to style links in various ways based on color and state (that is, whether a link has been visited or whether the pointer is hovering over the link).

Now that you're moving up to look at more than one page at a time, this chapter also introduces organizing and managing the various files that are assembled in the making of a website.

In this chapter you will:

- Write relative and absolute hyperlinks.
- Write hyperlinks for e-mail and to MP3 and PDF files.
- Use images to create hyperlinks.
- Use CSS to style hyperlinks.
- Use CSS to create pop-up text.

Organizing a Site

Before you get into writing the XHTML for links, you need to look at some of the basics of how a site is organized and stored. When you begin working on a new site, create a new folder (directory) on your computer where you will save every document that will be transferred to the server when the site is complete. This includes all the XHTML files, all the images, and other material such as sound files, multimedia files, and any material that will eventually be transferred to a server as part of the site. You can add as many subfolders (subdirectories) to this folder as you need, so long as all your files are kept within the main site folder.

I will discuss this again in Chapter 12 when you learn how to put a website on a server, but it is important enough to say here, too: you must organize the files for your website on your own computer in exactly the same way you put your files on the server. That is because of the way hyperlinks work. A link is like a path or a map to a file's location. If the file isn't in the exact location that you write in the link, then the computer returns one of those "File Not Found" errors that make users leave your site at warp speed.

DATABASES

Many websites connect with databases so that visitors can do things like order products from catalogs. Although working with databases is not covered in this book, if you plan to build such a site, you need to be aware that databases are stored on computers and servers in different locations from the main site folder where you store documents related to your site. Many hosting companies offer a free database called MySQL. When you create a MySQL database for your site, the hosting company sends you instructions about how to access it and where it's stored.

On the CD, you will find a small sample site. In the Chapter 7 folder on the CD, find the fold called `flowerpagesite`. Copy this entire folder and everything in it. Save it on your computer i the folder with your other files for this book. You should see a folder named `flowerpagesite` wh you are finished copying.

Displaying the folder in an icon view, you see something like Figure 7.1. Depending on wheth you are using Windows, Linux, or Mac, there may be slight differences in your view and the ico used for the files compared what you see in Figure 7.1, but the files and folders should have th same names. In Figure 7.1, you see an XHTML file and a CSS file that aren't in a subfolder. The are subfolders named `cactus`, `groundcover`, `img`, and `iris`.

Another way of looking at the `flowerpagesite` files is the conceptual tree view, as diagramm in Figure 7.2. Here you see the relationship of the subfolders to the home page (or `index.html` pag and the folders and files that are subordinate to it.

On your computer, you can expand each folder in the list to reveal the contents of all the sub folders. See Figure 7.3. The `img` folder contains all the images, and each of the other subfolders cc tains one XHTML page. A real world website would have more files than this, but you can learn write hyperlinks with just these few.

No matter which view of the site contents you take, you can see that it has room to grow. Add tional pages could be added in each of the subfolders. Additional subfolders could be added for oth types of flowering plants. Apply some forethought to not only what your site will contain at its inc tion, but also what growth you anticipate. Organize and structure for the long term possibilities.

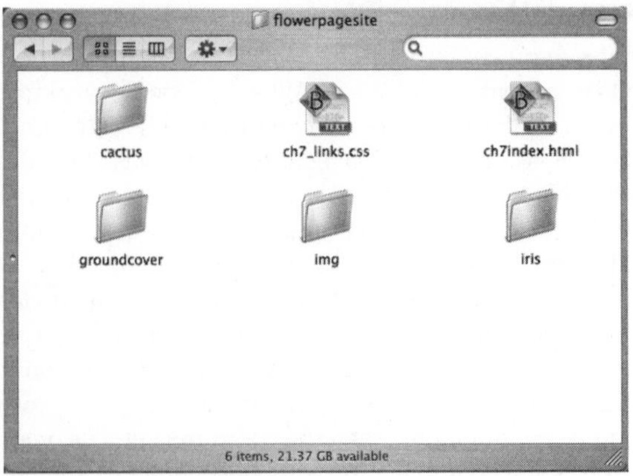

FIGURE 7.1
The `flowerpagesite` in icon view

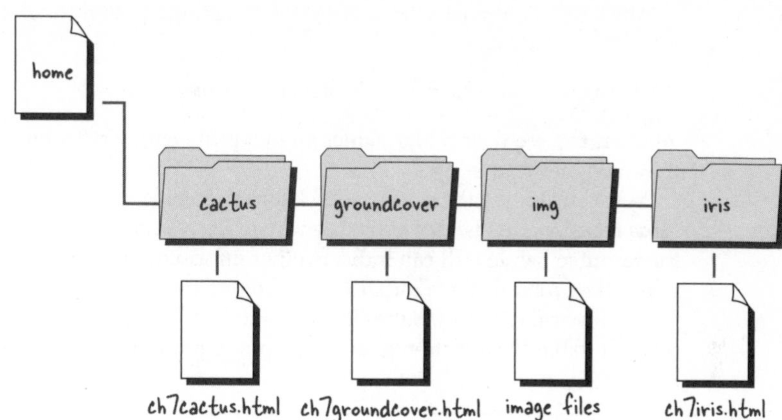

FIGURE 7.2
A tree view diagram of the relationship of the files in the site

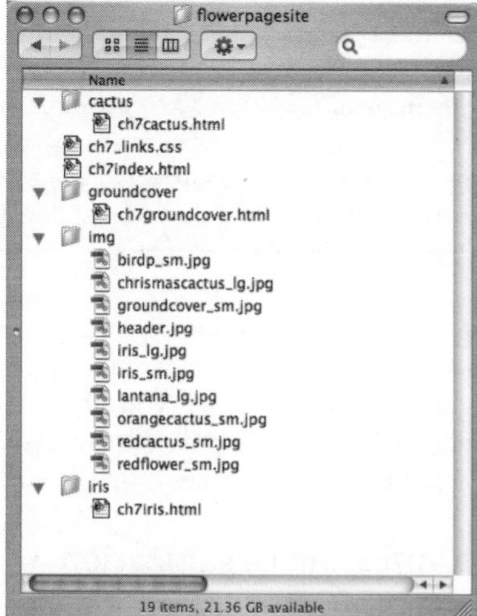

FIGURE 7.3
The `flowerpagesite` expanded into list view

In the sample site, the CSS file is at the top level along with the `ch7index.html` file. This is not a hard and fast rule. Many sites use a subfolder for CSS files and may have more than one CSS document there.

Anatomy of a URL

A *uniform resource locator* (URL) locates servers and files and is a mirror of your site organization. The first part of a URL is a *protocol* (or scheme) such as the Hypertext Transfer Protocol (`http`). Immediately after the protocol, you see the server name:

```
http://www.aserver.com/
```

The URL might go deeper into a website, listing a path through folders and filenames to find a exact file to display:

```
http://www.aserver.com/folder/file.html
```

Users can see your folder names and your filenames in the browser location (or address) bar a they navigate your site.

You will also see the acronym *URI*, for Uniform Resource Indicator. URL and URI perform th same function; that is, they point the way to the resource in question. The URL gives the *location* o the resource, while URI can indicate other information besides location, such as a resource nam URI is the umbrella term for URLs and other Uniform Resource Identifiers.

An important part of planning a site is to imagine all the files the completed site will contain s that a suitable organization plan can be put in place from the beginning.

ANNOUNCING SUBDIRECTORIES

The Internet is growing up. I have recently noticed that several advertisers assume a certain level of Internet savvy from the general public and include subfolders in URLs that they use in ads. I've heard TV ads urging me to "Visit `www.sbc.com/details` for more information," or to "Visit `www.bravotv.com/queereye` for more information." At one time, the prevailing wisdom was to make everyone enter a site through the home page so as not to miss any advertising along the way. Now the idea seems to be to acknowledge that users are in a hurry and want the fastest route to the information and to assume that users are so well-versed in using the Internet that a URL that includes a subfolder won't confuse them.

Getting well organized in the beginning is much easier than going back after a site has grown o expanded and moving files around or reorganizing the folder structure, because the relative links (I explain relative links a little later) you already have built into your site will not work properly if fil are moved. If you move files and folders after a site is already on a server, it will change URLs withi your site, and bookmarked pages might not be found by users who were familiar with your site.

Folder Names and Organization

Websites frequently contain a folder named `images`. (I've shortened that to `img` in the sample site Notice that in the `flowerpages` site, images appear on all the pages, but all the image files are store in the `img` folder, not the individual page folders.

Depending on the size of the site, HTML documents "behind" the home page might be organize into subfolders, as `cactus`, `groundcover`, and `iris` are in this example.

Subfolder names—and the need for further subfolders—depend on the site. If a site has a large number of sound clips, it might be wise to organize them in a folder named `music` or `sound` or a simil name. If a site has a large number of PDF files, it might be wise to store them all in a folder named pd

The subfolder name should be short and reflect its purpose. Keep in mind that folder names might end up in a web address you want someone to remember and use. If the coach stood on th football field and announced, "Just go to the website at `xhs.edu/football` for our next game date," more people would remember and find the site than if he said, "Just go to the website at `xhs.edu/ph_f_c2`." (The information after the forward slash in `xhs.edu/football` is a subfold on the `xhs.edu` server.)

If you organize a site for an elementary school, you might create subfolders named `calendar`, `grade1`, `grade2`, `staff`, and so on. If you organize a site for an ice skating rink, you might create folders named `classes`, `shop`, or `events`.

Do not use spaces in folder names. The hyphen (-) and the underscore (_) are allowed but should be avoided for folder names that might be released to the public in situations like the football example just mentioned. You can use numbers as long as the number is not the first character in the name. For example, a folder named `mp3` is acceptable. Capitals are allowed, but again, it pays to be careful. If the link is not capitalized in exactly the same way as the folder name and the server happens to be case sensitive (as some are), the link won't work. For example, `showdates/gigs.html` is different from `showDates/gigs.html` on case-sensitive servers.

FRIENDLY URLS

You are in control of your URLs, because you are in control of your domain name and subfolder names. There's been considerable study on the topic of what makes a URL "friendly" and how a friendly URL can help you with getting your site remembered and found by search engines.

If you use software to generate a site, for example a blog, or if you use a database to store your site pages, you lose some of that URL naming control. However, you can still take steps to make sure your URLs are friendly.

You'll find links to several articles on this topic at `brainstormsandraves.com/archives/2003/08/08/friday_feast_55_friendly_lasting_urls`.

The Home Page

Notice the file called `ch7index.html`. This file is the site's home page. For a real world site, the name would be simply `index.html`. The site's home page must not be placed inside any of the subfolders.

You probably know dozens of web addresses: `www.google.com`, `www.cnn.com`, `www.dell.com`, or any site you visit regularly. Most sites have a home page with the filename `index.html`. A visitor doesn't have to remember or type in the name of this particular page in the website, such as `www.google.com/index.html`, because the browser will automatically look for a file called `index.html` and open it. If the home page has a nonstandard filename like `home.html`, it must be included in the URL when advertising the site or giving potential users the site address. A home page file named `home.html` will *not* be automatically opened by the browser unless there is a link specifically written that targets it.

TAKE ME HOME

The home page may be named `index.html`, `index.htm`, or `default.htm`, depending on the server. The browser will automatically open whichever of these is present on the server in any site or folder. See Chapter 12 for more information on publishing your site on a server and on finding help and information from the server company about whether the server is configured to use `index.html`, `index.htm`, or `default.htm`.

More complex websites, such as large commercial sites, may use a database and some form of scripting to interact with the database. In sites like that—for example, Starbucks Coffee—when you type www.starbucks.com in the browser address bar, it quickly and automatically changes, to something like:

```
http://www.starbucks.com/Default.asp?cookie%5Ftest=1
```

From this, you can conclude that Starbucks is using Active Server Pages (ASP) technology and a database to produce web pages.

For the work you will be doing in this book, and for most small sites that aren't connected to a database, the home page will be named index.html.

This is true as you go deeper into a website as well. When the browser goes into any subfolder or directory, it looks for a file called index.html to open if no other filename is given in the link. If your flowerpagesite site had so many pages in the cactus folder that you wanted a main page for that folder, you could make an index.html page for the cactus folder. It would serve as the main page for all the other pages that might be placed in the cactus folder. There may be several files in a site named index.html, each one tucked away inside its own subfolder.

XHTML: The Anchor Element

When you click a link on the Web, the link uses the a (for anchor) tag with an href (for hypertext reference) attribute. An example:

```
<a href="somefile.html">Click me</a>
```

The default display for <a href="somefile.html">Click me</a> is for the words "Click me" to appear in blue and to be underlined. If you click the link and get whisked away to the page named somefile.html, then the next time you see <a href="somefile.html">Click me</a> rendered in the browser, the default display will be in the "visited" link color and still be underlined.

For years, all links were underlined, all unvisited links were blue, and all visited links were a reddish purple. With CSS, you can change those defaults. It is good to be careful when altering normal browser renderings, however, so your users don't get confused and not realize that a word is a link. And although you may be accustomed to underlining words in print for emphasis, it is not a good idea on the Web, because users think it indicates a link.

Links, Anchors, and Terminology

The a tag is one of the few tags that hindsight tells us could have been better named. One of its first purposes was to allow users to jump around to various points (anchors) on a single page. The word "anchor" makes sense there, but calling a tag an anchor when it allows you to jump to another page in your site or to some completely different site does not make the same semantic sense. Some people resort to incorrectly calling the anchor tag "a link tag" although there is a real link tag that you have used to link your style sheets to your XHTML pages in previous chapters. Still others call it an "an href" tag, even though the href is an attribute, not an element. You use a tags to *anchor* links to other documents or locations on a page, but a tags are not link tags.

You create a hyperlink to another web page using an a tag. You link to a style sheet using a link tag. In everyday usage, the a tag used to link to another web page is often referred to as "a link," even though it is technically "an anchor."

Linking within the Same Directory

Open the ch7index.html page both in your text editor and in the browser. You will add some links to this page. In the browser, the page looks like Figure 7.4.

The ch7index.html page, along with the other pages in the flowerpagesite folder, is based on the three-column Flower Page you worked with in Chapter 5. There have been a few changes to the CSS: different width measurements of the divs to allow for some padding, no margin-top on the h1 to move it to the top of the viewport, and a few other small adjustments.

To this point, everything you've linked to your XHTML page (you've had style sheet and image links up to now) has been a link to a file in the same directory as the XHTML page.

Look at this link element in ch7index.html.

```
<link href="ch7_links.css" rel="stylesheet" type="text/css" />
```

This is an example of a reference (or href, hypertext reference) to a file within the same directory as the XHTML file where the link element is. Since the file is in the same directory as the XHTML file, all that is needed as a referenced pathway to that file is merely to give the filename: "ch7_links.css". That's enough instruction for the browser to find it.

You may have noticed when working on this page in Chapter 5 that the image elements looked like this:

```
<img src="content.jpg" alt="White Iris" width="300" height="225" />
```

In Chapter 5, the images were in the same folder as the XHTML. So the path to the source (src) of the image was a simple "content.jpg", which gave the name of the image and nothing more.

FIGURE 7.4
The prebuilt ch7index.html page

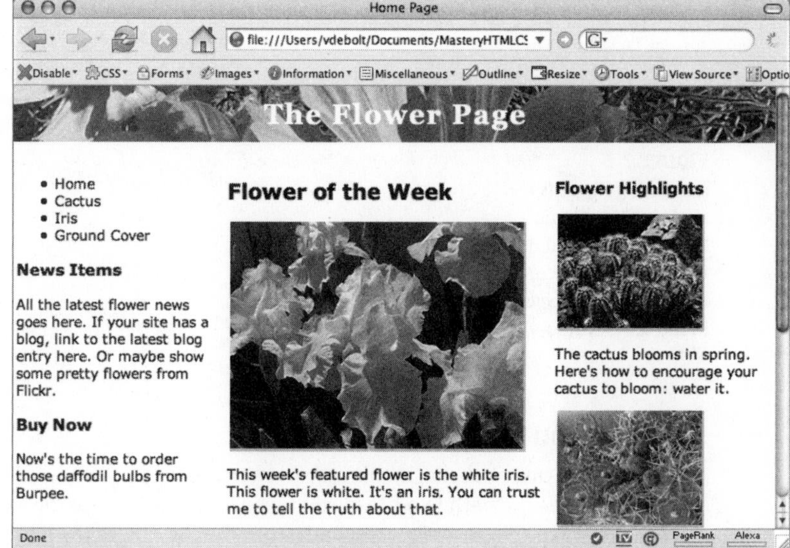

In Chapter 7, within `flowerpagesite`, there are no files except the CSS document in the top lev folder with `ch7index.html`. Let's imagine there is one, perhaps an About page named `aboutus.htm` How do you write a hyperlink from `ch7index.html` to `aboutus.html`? If the words the user clicks reach the page are "About Us," then the a element is:

```
<a href="aboutus.html">About Us</a>
```

The element opens with the a tag. The `href` attribute gives the path to the file, which is in th same directory as the XHTML page where the link is placed, the "About Us" is the clickable lin text, and the </a> tag closes the element.

In the browser, an unvisited link is blue and underlined. See Figure 7.5. When a user hovers ov a link element (a word or an image), the browser displays a pointing finger to indicate "clickability See Figure 7.6.

It is possible to remove the default underline from a link with CSS. If you do, be sure there i some other clue to the fact that the word is, in fact, a link. If a more obvious clue that clearly co municates clickability, such as an underline, fails to appear on a web page, users might start de perately running the mouse around a page searching for a clue to the existence of a link in the for of a pointing finger. Or even worse, visitors might just leave because the page seems unusable.

The basics of the a element are simple, but there are some slightly more intricate things you ne to know when the two files are not in the same folder. But before you can finish linking all the sit pages, you need to learn about relative and absolute links.

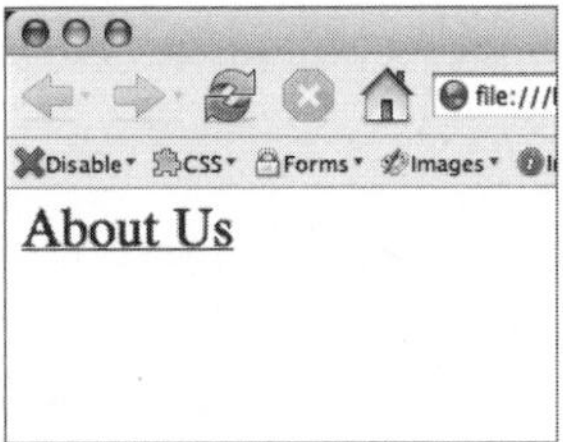

FIGURE 7.5
By default, an unvisited link displays with an underline in blue.

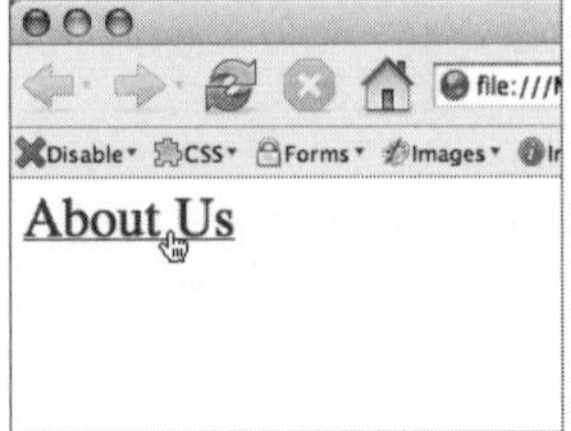

FIGURE 7.6
A pointing finger is a clue that this text is a link. When clicked, it is expected behavior for a new page to open in the same window.

Relative and Absolute Links

Within your own website, in this case `flowerpagesite`, you generally write *relative* links. A relati link describes the path to a file in reference to the file where the link is located. It is a type of "y are here" map that describes the path from the file where the link is located to the destination fi The example link to the About Us page

```
<a href="aboutus.html">About Us</a>
```

is a relative link.

You can write a relative link to anything within the main site folder. Hold on to this thought about what a relative link is, and let's find out what an absolute link is.

If you write a link to a file outside your own site folder, you must write an *absolute* link. An absolute link gives the complete URL, or path, to a file. `http://www.google.com/` and `ftp://somesite.com/` are examples of absolute URLs. The absolute link must include the protocol, server, and possibly a folder or filename. An absolute URL with a scheme, server, folder, and file looks something like this:

```
http://www.example.com/folder/file.html
```

An absolute link will always be exactly the same, no matter where in a site it is located. You have a section requiring absolute links on your practice pages. You will write those links before we go back to relative links.

BOOK LINKS VS. WEB LINKS

When writing an absolute link in XHTML that ends with a server or folder name, include the trailing slash: `http://www.example.com/`. When I give a URL to you, the reader, to visit, I sometimes provide an abbreviated version without the slash or even without the protocol, such as `google.com` or `www.wiley.com`. This is fine for readability in print, but you should be complete when writing code.

LINKING TO PAGES OUTSIDE YOUR SITE: WRITING ABSOLUTE LINKS

Each of your pages awaits links to `www.burpee.com`—a real flower company—and `www.flickr.com`—a real photo-sharing site. These require absolute URLs. Since you don't have Burpee.com or Flickr.com within your site folder, a relative link to these pages will not work.

The XHTML is here is shown in Listing 7.1. Note the highlighted words. They will become the clickable link text.

LISTING 7.1: The News Items Section of the Page Has Two Possible External Links

```
<p>All the latest flower news goes here. If your site has a blog, link to the
latest blog entry here. Or maybe show some pretty flowers from Flickr.</p>
<h3>Buy Now</h3>
<p>Now's the time to order those daffodil bulbs from Burpee.</p>
```

Normally it might not be the best idea to have links leading away from your site on every page. After all, you want people to stay on your site and sample your content. Links to external sites are a plus when using weblogs, however. (See Chapter 13 for more about weblogs.)

Every one of the practice pages has the same lines of XHTML code for these links. If you complete the changes on one of the pages, you can copy it and paste it over the appropriate line on the remaining pages. That way you won't have to retype the same links several times.

To define an absolute link, you use the a element again, as with a relative link. The `href` attribute contains the absolute value for the URL. Here's a link to Burpee:

```
<a href="http://www.burpee.com/">Burpee</a>
```

Write the link with a forward slash after the server name, as in "http://www.burpee.com/ The page will open without the trailing forward slash, but using it is considered best practice. Th new page will open faster with the forward slash in the URL, too. Save this and reload the brows to test it out. See Figure 7.7. Notice that you have the default blue link text with an underline. Aft you click the Burpee hyperlink and go to burpee.com, use the Back button to come back to you exercise page.

Be sure to look at the underlined Burpee text in your browser after you've used the Back butto to come back from the Burpee site. The link text color changes. It is now the default visited link color, purple.

Open the other XHTML files in the site, ch7cactus.html, ch7groundcover.html, and ch7iris.html, and add the link to Burpee; it will be exactly the same href. It doesn't matte what directory or website the hyperlink is in when it's written, because it's an absolute link. A links to pages external to your website must be absolute links.

Once you have the Burpee link in the other site pages, look at one or all of them in the browse Notice that even when you first open the page, the color of the clickable text in the link is the visite link color. Your browser knows you've just been to that URL, and it applies that knowledge to every page you want to test. If you want to force the browser to "forget" that you've already visite burpee.com, you must empty the browser's history. This is done in various ways, depending o the browser. Sometimes the menu under "Tools" has an Advanced section where you select Emp Cache or perhaps Clear History. Other browsers might have it in the Preferences menu. Whereve you find it, delete all the saved versions of your page stored by the browser in order to return th display to the nonvisited state when you need to test your unvisited link colors.

Under Cache, you can select Always Update Pages so that your changed pages will be display instead of a cached version when you revisit or test a page. This is very helpful in the design pr cess. You frequently make a change and reload the page to test the results; selecting Always Upda Pages forces the browser to load the new page, not a cached version.

FIGURE 7.7
Shown is an absolute link to a real flower company. Clicking it should take you the home page of the Burpee Company.

The photo-sharing site Flickr allows users to tag their photos. (Flickr's tags are words, not XHTML tags.) You can use tags to drill down into the millions of photos and find only those that are of flowers. If you went to Flickr and explored by searching the photos for the tag "flower" you would arrive at this URL: `http://www.flickr.com/photos/tags/flowers/`.

Link to that on the exercise page. Add this absolute URL in the same way you did the first. The new link will be:

```
<a href="http://www.flickr.com/photos/tags/flowers/">Flickr</a>
```

The `ch7index.html` page should look like Figure 7.8 in the browser when the external links are complete.

If you click any of the new links to test them, you can use the Back button to return to your page. Note again that the color of the link changes after you visit a page.

Copy the completed set of anchor elements and paste them in the proper spot on each of your other XHTML pages to replace the nonlinked text that is there.

Specifically, every page should have the code you see in Listing 7.2.

LISTING 7.2: The External Links Section of the Page with Completed Links

```
<p>All the latest flower news goes here. If your site has a blog, link to the
latest blog entry here. Or maybe show some pretty flowers from <a href="http://
www.flickr.com/photos/tags/flowers/">Flickr</a>.</p>
 <h3>Buy Now</h3>
 <p>Now's the time to order those daffodil bulbs from <a href="http://
www.burpee.com/">Burpee</a>.</p>
```

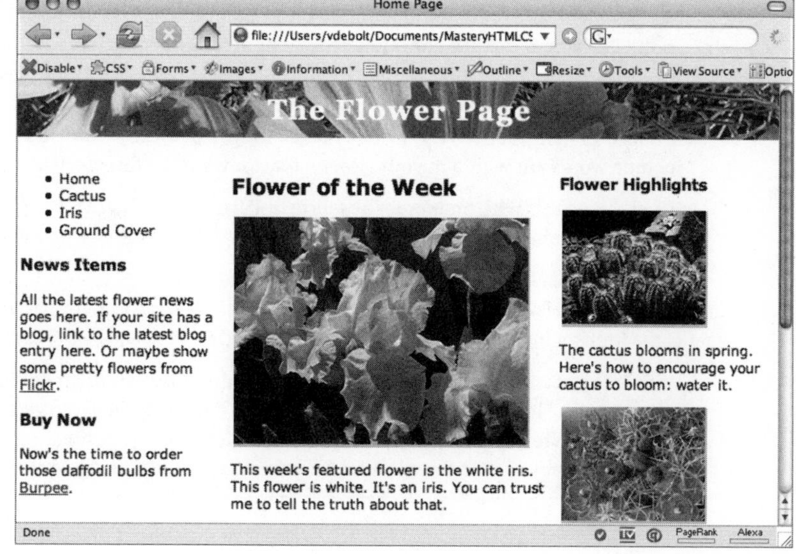

FIGURE 7.8
The two external links are complete. In this view, Flickr has not been visited yet and is a different link color from Burpee, which has been visited.

SERVER ABSOLUTE LINKS

There is one other type of absolute link that is slightly different from the absolute URL links such as `<a href="http://www.burpee.com/">Burpee</a>` described earlier.

The other absolute link is a *server absolute*, also called *root relative*. It can be used with Apache servers, if the server is configured for it. It uses a forward slash at the beginning (with no dots) to force the path to start from the site's root level on the server, like this: `<a href="`**/index.html"**`>Home</a>`. That link can be used in any directory or subdirectory, and when it is clicked the server will start the path to the file at the root level of the server, rather than relative to the location of the file where the link is anchored.

As another example, suppose you have a subfolder called `legal` and in it is a privacy policy page called `privacy.html`. Further, suppose you want this link to the privacy policy to be on every single footer on every single page in the site, no matter where the page is located in the site structure. With a server absolute link like this

```
<a href="/legal/privacy.html">Privacy Policy</a>
```

you can use the same element on every page anywhere in the site. It works anywhere in your site, because the path to the file begins at the site root level on the server.

SERVER ABSOLUTE URLS + SSIS = TIME SAVED

Server absolutes are often used with Server Side Includes (SSIs), which are beyond the scope of this book but are great time savers that I'll describe very briefly. An SSI is a single file to control any number of web pages. In that sense, it is like a CSS file. If you change one SSI file on the server, every page in the site that uses that include changes instantly. Includes are little snippets of HTML code, sometimes no more than this:

```
<a href="/legal/privacy.html">Privacy Policy</a>
```

That snippet is saved on the server as an include file, perhaps called `privacy.inc` or `privacy.txt`. Instead of putting the actual a element on the page in places where you want a link to the privacy policy, you put an include command, which says in plain English, "Put the HTML from `privacy.inc` in this spot." The actual include command code might look like this:

```
<!--#include virtual="/includes/privacy.inc"-->
```

Because the snippet of HTML that makes up the `privacy.inc` file uses a server absolute link, the include works anywhere in your site, no matter what the directory location is.

If you can do this with one server absolute link, you can do it with a whole nav bar full of server absolute links, or a whole footer, or a whole masthead. To update a thousand web pages that use a nav bar placed on a page with an include command, you need only update *one* include file.

Once the page is rendered in the browser, the user has no idea whether the XHTML they see in View Source came from an include directive or was hand typed on the page by the designer. The results are the same.

Within the scope of what you are learning in this book, you are most likely building and testing your pages on your local machine, not on a server. Therefore, relative links within a site will be what you write and use for now. In Chapter 12, when you learn about publishing on a server, keep in mind that a big plus in favor of choosing an Apache server is its ability to use server absolute links.

Linking to Pages in Different Directories

In this chapter's example, the images are organized into a subfolder named `img`. Notice something new in the `src` attribute of the `img` elements now—a folder name:

```
<img src="img/iris_lg.jpg" alt="White Iris" width="300" height="225" />
```

Because the image is no longer in the same directory as the XHTML file, the name of the directory to look in must be given as part of the pathway to the source of the image. The same thing happens when using an anchor element to create a hyperlink to a page in a different directory than the one holding the XHTML page.

As noted, a relative link gives a pathway from one place in your website to another place in your website. There has to be some code to use to explain this pathway to the computer, and there is: two periods (`..`) and the forward slash (/). The two periods are pronounced "dot dot." These two symbols, used separately, together, or in multiple combinations, give the computer the needed instructions to navigate your file and folder organization and find any file. Whether or not a relative link requires any, or one, or more `../` codes depends on where the files being linked together are *in relation to each other*. You are going to get some hands-on practice in a bit, which will help you understand relative links.

The two periods tell the computer to move up a level in the folder (directory) structure. The forward slash tells the computer to move into a folder (directory) or it separates a folder name from a filename.

Here are a few specific examples, translated into plain English.

```
href="iris/ch7iris.html"
```

Move down into the `iris` folder and find the file `ch7iris.html`.

```
href="../iris/ch7iris.html"
```

Move up out of the folder this file is in, go into the `iris` folder, and find the file `ch7iris.html`.

```
href="../../iris/ch7iris.html
```

Move up two directory levels from the folder this file is in, go into the `iris` folder, and find the file `ch7iris.html`.

Look at your folder setup again, and then you will write some hyperlinks yourself. Figure 7.9 shows the paths and links you will implement.

The next few subsections give you practice linking documents in various places throughout a site's folder structure.

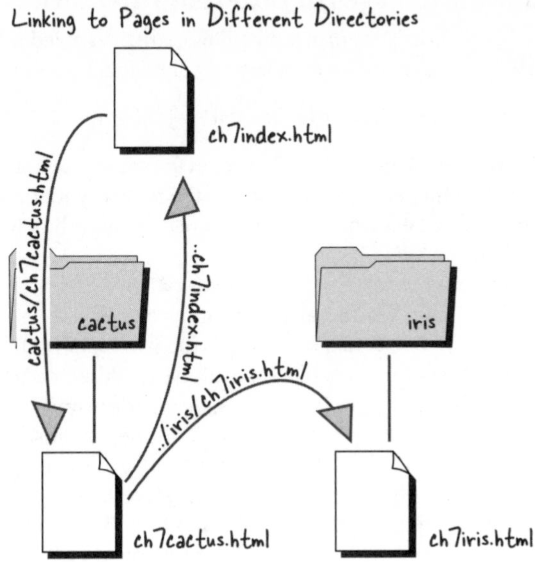

FIGURE 7.9
The site organization with some path examples

LINKING DOWN ONE LEVEL

Open `ch7index.html`. The links from the home page to a file inside a subfolder will be similar f each subfolder. The path is to enter `iris` (or another subfolder on the same level such as `cactu` and find the file `ch7iris.html` (or `ch7cactus.html`). Find the list, which looks like this:

```
<ul>
   <li>Home</li>
   <li>Cactus</li>
   <li>Iris</li>
   <li>Ground Cover</li>
</ul>
```

To link `ch7index.html` to `ch7iris.html`, the path is `href="iris/ch7iris.html"`, which te the browser to move into the named subfolder and find the named file. Create a similar hyperli for the Cactus and Ground Cover items. Leave the Home link alone for now. Here's the set of anchor elements so far:

```
<ul>
   <li>Home</li>
   <li><a href="cactus/ch7cactus.html">Cactus</a></li>
   <li><a href="iris/ch7iris.html">Iris</a></li>
   <li><a href="groundcover/ch7groundcover.html">Ground Cover</a></li>
</ul>
```

See Figure 7.10. Each link should take you to the proper page. Use the Back button to retu to Home.

FIGURE 7.10
The Home page with hyperlinks to the pages in the subfolders

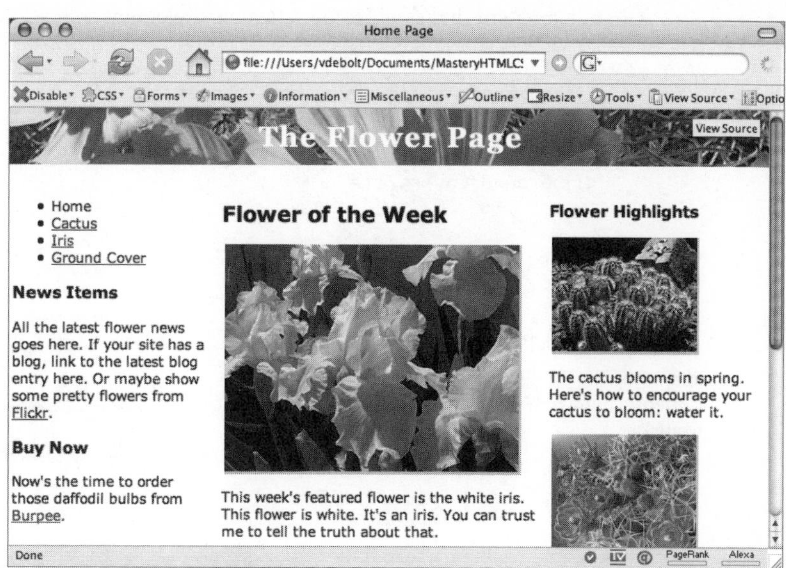

GOING DOWN

What if there were deeper levels of subfolders to navigate to from the home page? For example, what if the `iris` subfolder held a subfolder named `bulbcare`? To get from the home page to a file in the `bulbcare` folder you just keep naming the folders to pass through on the pathway. Here's how to get to a file called `thinning.html` in the `bulbcare` folder from the home page.

```
<a href="iris/bulbcare/thinning.html">Thinning your bulbs</a>
```

Drill deeper and deeper into as many folders as you must pass through in a path by naming each folder to enter as the path goes further and further.

LINKING UP ONE LEVEL

The file `ch7iris.html` is located in the subdirectory `iris`. To link to `ch7index.html` from inside `iris`, the path in the link must lead out of `iris` and then give the filename. You use the `../` path to get from `ch7iris.html` to `ch7index.html`, like this:

```
<a href="../ch7index.html">Home</a>
```

Open `ch7iris.html` in your text editor and add the link. Find the list, which looks like this:

```
<ul>
   <li>Home</li>
   <li>Cactus</li>
   <li>Iris</li>
   <li>Ground Cover</li>
</ul>
```

Change the item that says Home. The new a element is:

```
<ul>
   <li><a href="../ch7index.html">Home</a></li>
   <li>Cactus</li>
   <li>Iris</li>
   <li>Ground Cover</li>
</ul>
```

Your page should look similar to Figure 7.11.

FIGURE 7.11
The `ch7iris.html` page has a functioning Home anchor, ready to click.

Link the other files to the Home page. The other two pages in subfolders on the site have the same relative relationship in terms of the pathway to Home. In both cases, the link path is `../ch7index.html`, which is a route up and out of the subfolder to the named file.

Open `ch7cactus.html` and `ch7groundcover.html` and add the link to the home page to each or

```
<li><a href="../ch7index.html">Home</a></li>
```

Keep all three subfolder XHTML pages open in your text editor until the hyperlinks are complete

GOING UP

Here's an example of a longer upward path, this time from the imaginary `thinning.html` file in the `bulbcare` subfolder of the `iris` folder. To get from this file to the Home page, you would have to instruct the browser to move up and out of two levels of subfolders with `../../`. Here's how the link would look from `thinning.html`:

```
<a href="../../ch7index.html">Home</a>
```

You can move up as many levels as need by adding `../../../` until you reach the destination folder.

LINKING TO A PAGE IN A PARALLEL FOLDER

Start from `ch7iris.html` again. You want to link `ch7iris.html` to `ch7cactus.html`, but `href="../ch7cactus.html"` won't work. It would lead out of `iris`, but there is no file called `ch7cactus.html` to be found once you are out of `iris`.

Instead, you have to add the name of the folder where `ch7cactus.html` is located to your pathway. The path must translate to "go out of `iris`, then go into `cactus`, then look for a file called `ch7cactus.html`." The path is `../cactus/ch7cactus.html`.

Now the list looks like this:

```
<ul>
    <li><a href="../ch7index.html">Home</a></li>
    <li><a href="../cactus/ch7cactus.html">Cactus</a></li>
    <li>Iris</li>
    <li>Ground Cover</li>
</ul>
```

You now have two working a elements on the Iris page. See Figure 7.12.

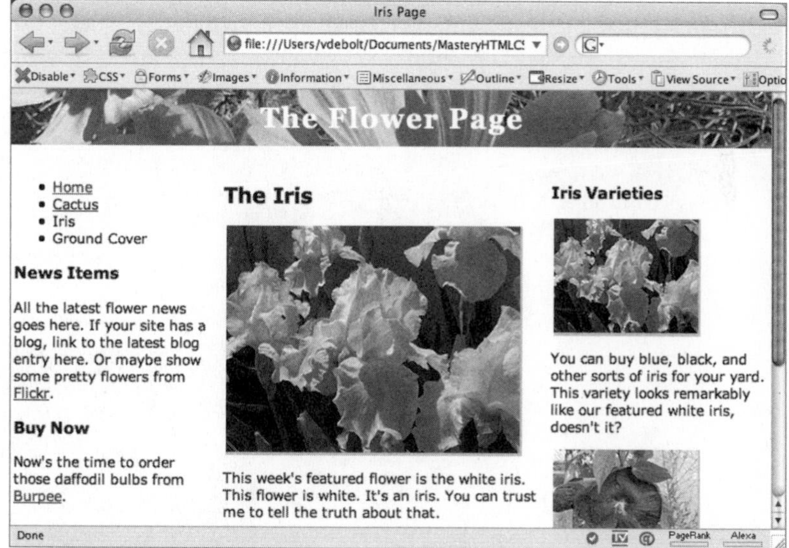

FIGURE 7.12 The `ch7iris.html` page now has a link to the Cactus page.

The relative pathway from `ch7groundcover.html` to `ch7cactus.html` is the same. It must go out of `groundcover`, into `cactus`, and find `ch7cactus.html`. Add the same link to the `ch7groundcover.html` page that you just added to the `ch7iris.html` page. Don't do anything to `ch7cactus.html` yet.

Go to `ch7iris.html` once again. You'll finish up the parallel links for this page with a hyperlink to `ch7groundcover.html`. The path is similar: out of `iris`, into `groundcover`, find the file `ch7groundcover.html`. Try to write it yourself before you look at this code snippet:

```
<ul>
    <li><a href="../ch7index.html">Home</a></li>
    <li><a href="../cactus/ch7cactus.html">Cactus</a></li>
    <li>Iris</li>
```

```
        <li><a href="../groundcover/ch7groundcover.html">Ground Cover</a></li>
    </ul>
```

Except for a link to itself, the Iris page is now complete. See Figure 7.13. Linking a page to itse is a special case, which I will address in a moment.

Complete the other two subpages with links to any pages other than the page itself. Test all yo links. You should be able to move around all the pages without using the Back button now.

> ### GOING UP *AND* DOWN
>
> Here's another *what if* game for the imaginary `thinning.html` file. How do you link `thinning.html` to `ch7cactus.html`? You must go up out of `bulbcare`, up out of `iris`, then down into `cactus` to find the file `ch7cactus.html`. Here's how:
>
> ```
> <a href="../../cactus/ch7cactus.html">Cactus</a>
> ```
>
> Computer pathways are like drawing your route on a map. You go here, then there, follow this way, then that way, and you reach your destination. But instead of drawing lines on a map you give instructions consisting of `..` and / and folder names and filenames to describe the path. These basic directional instructions can lead the browser through an infinite number of up and down pathways to suit your exact site organization.

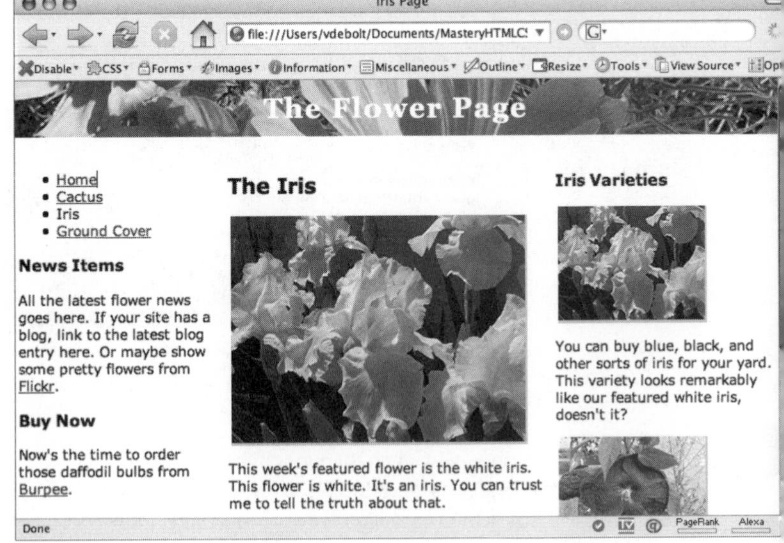

FIGURE 7.13
The almost complete `ch7iris.html` page has links to other pages in the site but not a link to itself.

INDICATING THE CURRENT PAGE

When writing links on `ch7index.html`, you did not add a link in the menu area for Home. The `ch7iris.html` page does not have a working hyperlink to itself. That is one way to indicate to t user that Home is the current page. There are other more effective and attractive ways to give a visual clue in the menu area that the user is currently on a particular page. You will use CSS for th later in the chapter.

Whether or not it's a working link, it is important not to remove the word "Home" from the main navigation. New designers sometimes think, "Well, I'm on the Home page where I don't need a link to the Home page, so I'll just take that word out of the menu." Don't fall into this type of thinking. Once users see your main navigation, they expect it to be consistent from page to page within the site. When words appear or disappear on different pages, or the order of the words in the menu changes, users can get lost.

The first visit to a site is like the first visit to a new town. You look around town, read a map, get oriented, find the main roads, the landmarks, and quickly go where you want. When a visitor looks at your home page and decides to have a further look inside, he or she studies the map (your menu) and the landmarks and gets going. If the map or the landmarks change, the visitor is lost.

Linking to Non-HTML Files

Many types of files can be put on web servers for display in a browser or for download. Here is a quick exercise creating hyperlinks to a sound file and a PDF file.

In addition to MP3 and PDF documents, you might link to various sound formats besides MP3, QuickTime movies, Flash files, Microsoft Word or PowerPoint documents, executable files, or other types of files. Some of these types of hyperlinks require nothing more than the a `href` element and attribute. Flash or other movies require more than that and are discussed in Chapter 8.

LINKING WITH PROTOCOLS OTHER THAN HTTP

A browser cannot open or display every type of document or file. But a user may want to download such a document and open it with the appropriate software on their computer. For example, a browser cannot open a PowerPoint (PPT) file. Sometimes download sites for such documents are on FTP servers. The user downloads the file by FTP (file transfer protocol) and opens it with the appropriate software. For links to FTP sites, use ftp in the `href` attribute, similar to this:

```
<a href="ftp://www.someserver.com/somefile.ppt">a PowerPoint file</a>
```

Note that PowerPoint files, Zip files, Microsoft Word files, and so on can also be downloaded by http. They do not have to be on FTP servers.

Mady Kaye, a jazz vocalist from Austin, Texas, kindly agreed to allow the use of a sound clip and PDF file related to a jazz trio she sings with called The Beat Divas.

Move the following files from the accompanying CD to your hard drive. Do not put them in the `flowerpagesite` folder, merely in the Chapter 7 folder.

```
beatdivas_girlsjustgottaswing.mp3
beatdivas_liveatreeds.jpg
beatdivas.pdf
extralinkexamples.html
```

Open `extralinkexamples.html` in your text editor and in your browser. It's a simple page meant to suggest the beginnings of a Links page. See Figure 7.14.

A few CSS rules for `extralinkexamples.html` are embedded, so there's no external style sheet. The complete page is shown in Listing 7.3.

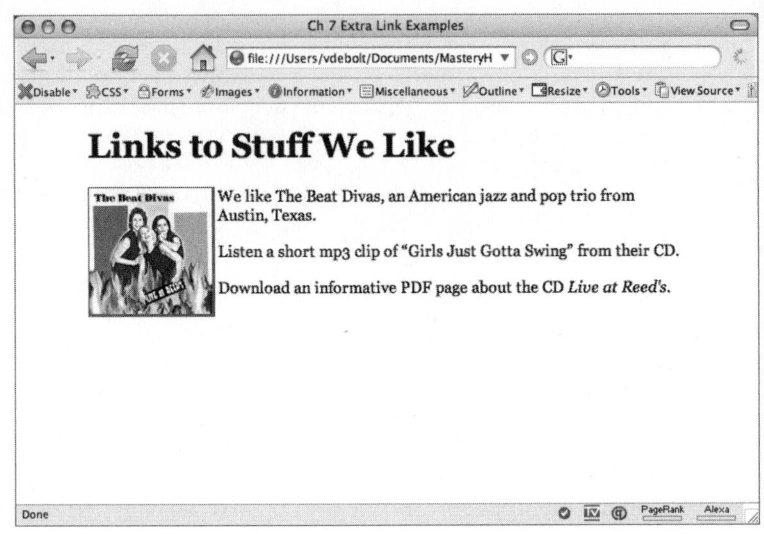

FIGURE 7.14
The `extralink-examples.html` page before any hyperlinks are added

LISTING 7.3: The *extralinkexamples.html* Page

```
<!DOCTYPE html PUBLIC "-//W3C//DTD XHTML 1.0 Transitional//EN" "http://www.w3.org/
TR/xhtml1/DTD/xhtml1-transitional.dtd">
<html xmlns="http://www.w3.org/1999/xhtml">
<head>
<title>Ch 7 Extra Link Examples</title>
<style type="text/css">
body {
      font: 100% Georgia, "Times New Roman", Times, serif;
      margin-right: 10%;
      margin-left: 10%;
      background: #FFF;
}
.floatleft {
      float: left;
      margin-right: 3px;
      margin-bottom: 3px;
}
img {
      border-top: 1px solid #666;
      border-right: 3px solid #666;
      border-bottom: 3px solid #666;
      border-left: 1px solid #666;
}
</style>
</head>
```

```
<body>
<h1>Links to Stuff We Like</h1>
<p><img src="beatdivas_liveatreeds.jpg" alt="The Beat Divas Live at Reed's"
width="125" height="125" class="floatleft" />We like The Beat Divas, an American
jazz and pop trio from Austin, Texas.</p>
<p>Listen to a short mp3 clip of &#8220;Girls Just Gotta Swing&#8221; from their
CD.</p>
<p>Download an informative PDF page about the CD <cite>Live at Reed's</cite>. </p>
</body>
</html>
```

The first hyperlink to add is one you already know how to write, an absolute link to The Beat Divas website at `http://www.madykaye.com/divas/`. In the line, "We like The Beat Divas," make the group name the clickable text. Here's the relevant snippet:

```
We like <a href="http://www.madykaye.com/divas/">The Beat Divas</a>, an
```

That change gives you the results shown in Figure 7.15.

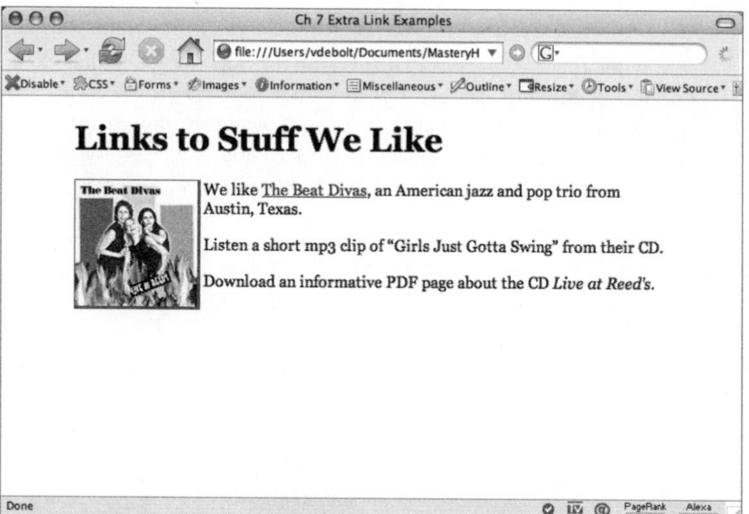

FIGURE 7.15
An absolute hyperlink to The Beat Diva's website is added.

LINKING TO SOUND FILES

There are a number of ways to deal with sound files. They can be embedded in Flash movies made to look like jukeboxes, they can be made to play in the background when an HTML page loads in the browser (an annoying surprise), or they can be offered as an ordinary hyperlink. The latter is what you are going to do. Pick the text you want to have clickable from this sentence:

```
<p>Listen to a short mp3 clip of &#8220;Girls Just Gotta Swing&#8221; from their
CD.</p>
```

Use an a element with an `href` attribute that points to the sound file. That's all there is to it. Yc may have selected different words for the link text, but here's one way to do it:

```
<p><a href="beatdivas_girlsjustgottaswing.mp3">Listen to a short mp3 clip</a> o
&#8220;Girls Just Gotta Swing&#8221; from their CD.</p>
```

As you see in the browser (see Figure 7.16), it looks exactly like any other hyperlink.

When a user clicks the MP3 link, the sound could be played by one of many sound players, depending on the user's setup. It might play in Windows Media Player, Real Player, or QuickTim Player. It is a good idea to offer a link to a download site for one of these players, although mo computer users already have an MP3 player.

On my particular setup, MP3 files play in QuickTime, which opens in a new page. After I he the clip, I use the Back button to return to the original page. See Figure 7.17.

A clever user knows that an MP3 file can be downloaded to the user's own computer with a option from a contextual menu. You see a contextual menu with a right mouse click (or Ctrl-Clic on a Mac). Once the file is on the user's hard drive, a double-click to the filename opens it in Wi dows Media Player, iTunes, or some other application where the MP3 file is stored permanently b the user. This is one reason why many sites that offer sound clips only give you a few seconds of song, rather than the whole tune. See Figure 7.18.

LINKING TO PDF DOCUMENTS

When the user clicks a PDF link, the file may open in Adobe Reader (Mac OS X might open it in Pr view). Some modern computers may open it in the browser. On the same computer, one brows may open it one way and a different browser may open it another way.

It's a good idea to provide a link to `adobe.com` so the user can download Adobe Reader, although most computers already have it.

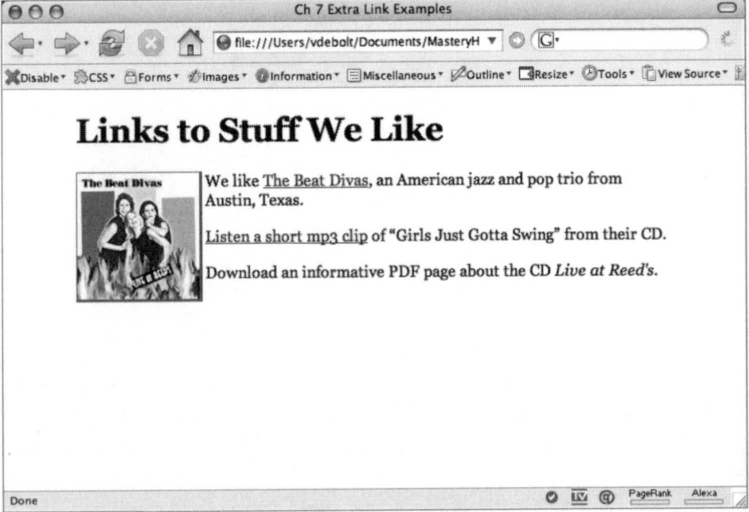

FIGURE 7.16
The hyperlink to the sound clip looks like any other link.

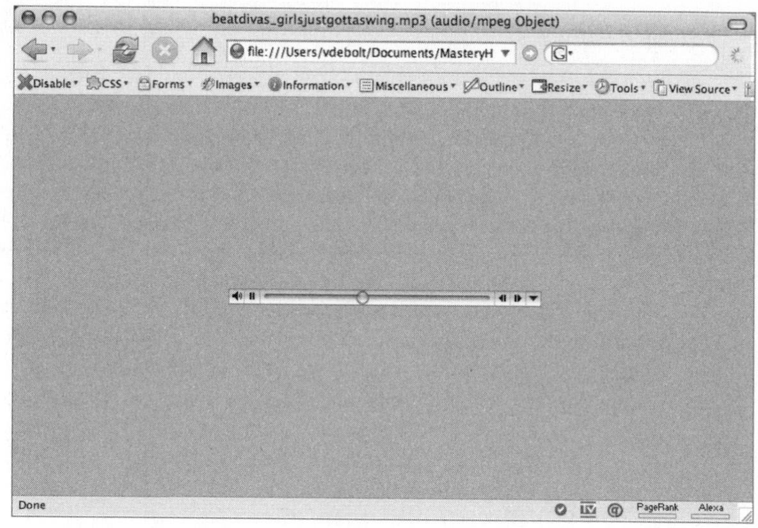

FIGURE 7.17 Depending on the user's setup, a sound file may play in QuickTime, like this, or in one of several other ways, perhaps in Windows Media Player or RealPlayer.

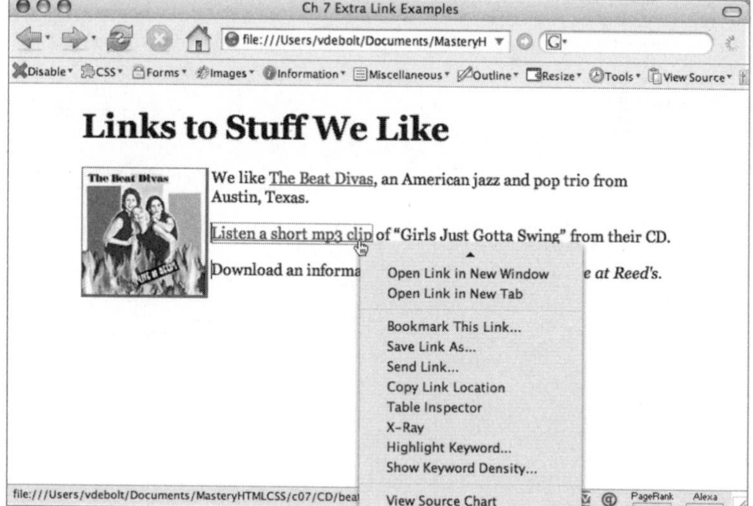

FIGURE 7.18 A right mouse click (or Ctrl-Click on a Mac) reveals a contextual menu that allows users to download and save an MP3 file to their own hard drive.

To hyperlink to the PDF file, add the a element to this sentence in `extralinkexercises.html`:

```
<p>Download an informative PDF page about the CD <cite>Live at Reed's</cite>.
```

Again, use the basic a element you know how to write, but make the `href` point to the `beatdivas.pdf` file rather than an XHTML file. Here's how:

```
<p>Download an <a href="beatdivas.pdf">informative PDF page</a> about the CD
<cite>Live at Reed's</cite>.
```

> **CLOSE BUT NO CODE**
>
> Web designers sometimes save web pages as PDF files during the design process to allow clients to view and approve design ideas. The PDF file looks and feels like a web page, but there's no XHTML code, CSS code, or other code you might not be ready to reveal to a client. PDF files include the images and colors and can be e-mailed easily. To save XHTML files as PDF files, you need to own the full version of Adobe Acrobat (as opposed to the free Adobe Reader), or your computer must have built-in software that allows you to print pages as PDF files.

The clickable text on the page looks like any other link. (You may have selected different words to use as the link text.) See Figure 7.19. In Firefox on my setup, clicking this hyperlink opens the PDF file in the full Adobe Acrobat program on my computer. See Figure 7.20. In oth setups, the PDF file may automatically download. The user must double-click the filename aft it downloads, and it will open in Acrobat Reader or some similar software.

As with MP3 files, a right-click (Ctrl-Click on a Mac) on the PDF hyperlink provides options th allow a user to download the file to their own computer no matter what the default behavior fo opening PDF files is in their setup.

Since browsers vary so widely in how they handle links to PDF files, you may need to incluc some instructions to the user to make sure of a particular response to the clicked hyperlink. For example, if you want to make sure the user actually downloads and saves the PDF file, you ma need to include a sentence or two explaining how to do that.

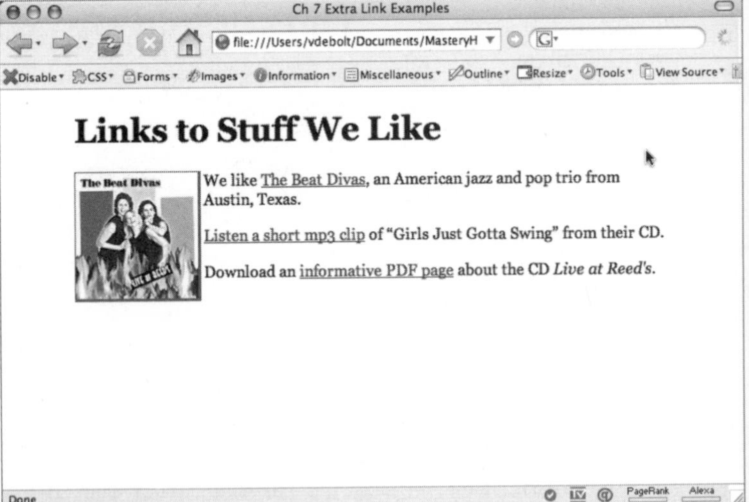

FIGURE 7.19
The link to the PDF file, when clicked, will open the file in whatever program is configured in the user's setup.

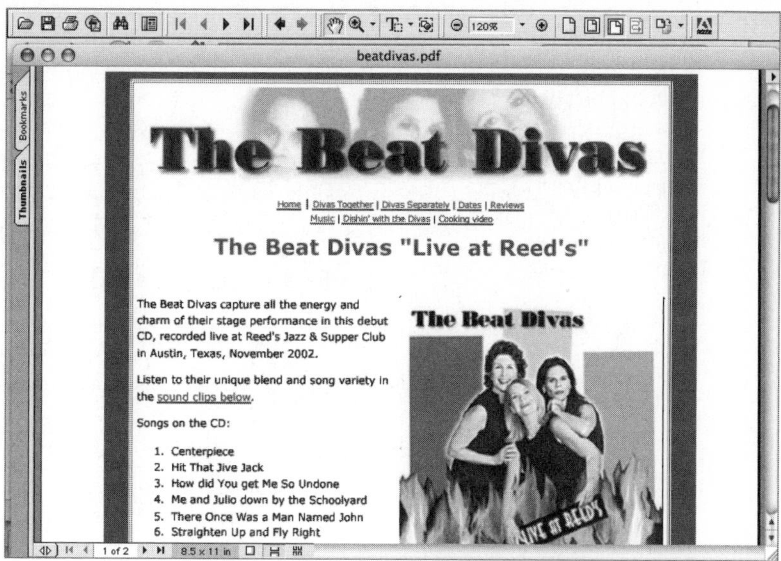

FIGURE 7.20
A PDF file may open in Adobe Acrobat Reader (similar to this example), the browser itself, or in Preview (Mac OS X).

Images as Links

When creating an a element, you can insert more than words into the clickable area. You can also insert images. To try that, make the image of The Beat Divas' album cover into a link to the sound clip. Find the `img` element:

```
<img src="beatdivas_liveatreeds.jpg" alt="The Beat Divas Live at Reed's"
width="125" height="125" class="floatleft" />
```

To make the image a link, the a element must enclose the `img` element. The `img` element then becomes the clickable portion of the link (Figure 7.21):

```
<a href="beatdivas_girlsjustgottaswing.mp3"><img src="beatdivas_liveatreeds.jpg"
alt="The Beat Divas Live at Reed's" width="125" height="125" class="floatleft" /
></a>
```

Clicking the album cover image should do exactly what clicking the text link to the song did on your particular computer setup.

By default, an image used as a link is ringed in blue rather than underlined. The embedded `img` styles in the head of the page are overriding that default behavior. Temporarily disable them with comment marks, like this:

```
/*img {
   border-top: 1px solid #666;
   border-right: 3px solid #666;
   border-bottom: 3px solid #666;
   border-left: 1px solid #666;
}*/
```

I've zoomed in on the image to demonstrate the default image-as-link border. See Figure 7.22.

Remove the comment marks from the `img` selector in the styles in the head and let it return to the light gray, drop shadow–like border. If you didn't want borders of any kind, the correct CSS rule would be `border: none`.

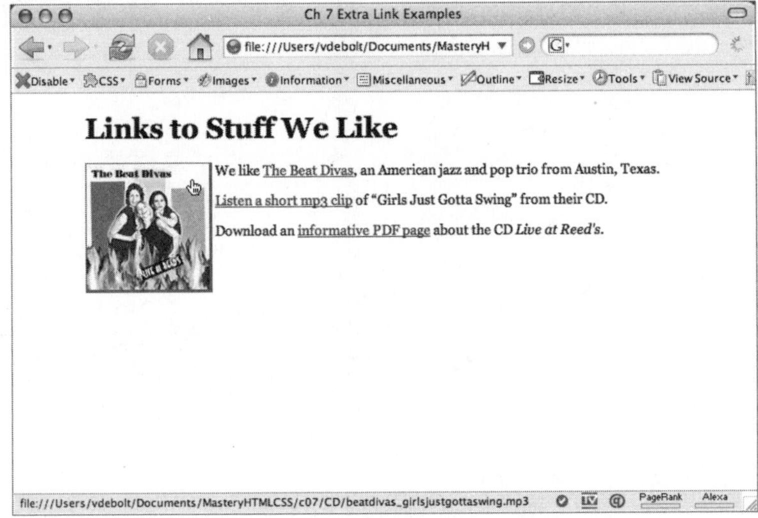

FIGURE 7.21
The pointing finger indicates that the image is a clickable hyperlink.

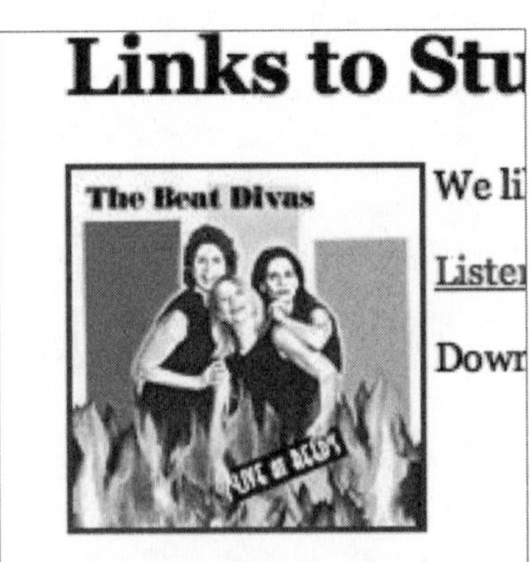

FIGURE 7.22
With no style rules to override the default link color, the image is ringed by a blue (or purple, if visited) border when used as a hyperlink.

CLUELESS

It is important to point out that there is nothing on this page that gives you any clue that the album image is a link to a sound file. It does not look clickable. If you do something like this on a real web page, it's a good idea to include some explanatory text, such as "Click the image to hear a sound clip." In Chapter 8 you will use images as links and add a text link under the image so that the purpose of the image will be absolutely clear.

E-mail Links

An e-mail link is an absolute link, but it doesn't use http; it uses the mailto protocol.

You can add an e-mail link to `extralinkexamples.html`. Add this paragraph after the last paragraph in the XHTML:

```
<p>Email Me</p>
```

Create the link like this:

```
<p><a href="mailto:someone@somewhere.com">Email Me</a></p>
```

GOT MAIL?

I suggest you use your own e-mail address instead of the fake `someone@somewhere.com`. That way you can test it out by sending yourself mail. Don't say I never let you have any fun!

Save that and reload the browser. You see the new link, waiting to be clicked. See Figure 7.23.

Click the e-mail link. A new mail document in your default e-mail program should open with the TO: line filled in with the address you used. It should look like Figure 7.24, with minor variation depending on what e-mail program you use.

You can create your own subject line in the blank e-mail by adding `?subject=some subject` to the end of the URL in your `mailto` attribute, like this:

```
<p><a href="mailto:someone@somewhere.com?subject=web site mail">Email Me</a></p>
```

Notice that there is no space either before or after the question mark. Save that and reload the browser. Try the link. You should see a subject line already in place in the blank e-mail document. See Figure 7.25.

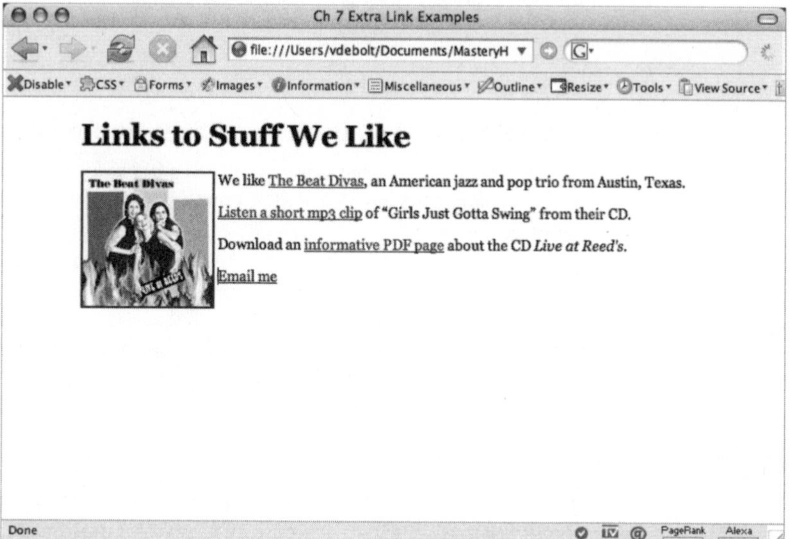

FIGURE 7.23 A hyperlink using the mailto protocol creates an e-mail link.

FIGURE 7.24
When you click an e-mail link on the Web, your system's e-mail program should open with the address of the recipient filled in.

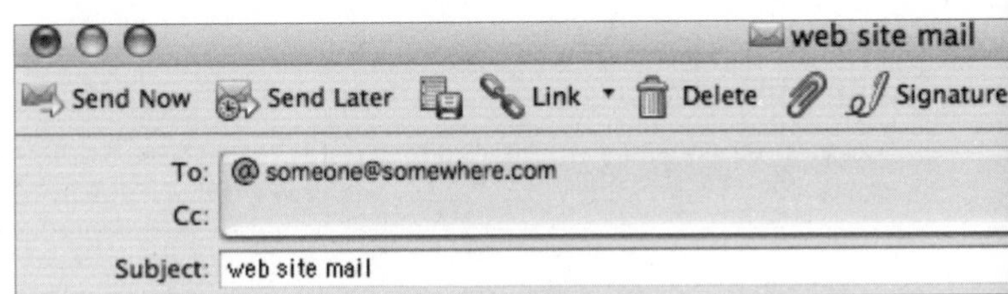

FIGURE 7.25
The e-mail contains a subject line of your own choosing.

GOT SPAM?

Using a mailto protocol to add your e-mail to a web page is so easy, it's a snap. Unfortunately it's also a snap for the spambots to "harvest" your e-mail address from a hyperlink like this on your web page. To protect yourself from floods of spam it is necessary to obscure the address somehow with JavaScript or special character encoding or to use a form tied to a script that will block attempts at spam. You'll learn about creating forms in Chapter 11, but the scripting needed is beyond the scope of this book.

Helpful research sources for a solution to this problem include:

www.netmechanic.com/news/vol4/design_no21.htm

javascript.internet.com/miscellaneous/hide-e-mail-address.html

Linking to a Specific Location in a Page: Named Anchors and IDs

By giving an anchor tag a name, you can allow a browser to find that specific location in your document. A *named anchor* is simply an a element with a name attribute; it looks like this: <a name="somename"></a>.

Don't type anything inside these a tags, because this is not something you click. It will actual be invisible on the page. You can use any name you want, but it must be unique. Names can be words or numbers.

To link to a named anchor, you write an ordinary a tag elsewhere and, in the href attribute, include a hash sign (#) and the name of the anchor. Thus, <a href="#somename"> is a link from o spot on a web page to another location on the same page where name="somename" occurs.

Practicing with named anchors requires a longer page, so you need a new practice page. Loo in the Chapter 7 folder on the accompanying CD for a page called namedanchors.html and cop it to your computer. Open it in your text editor and in the browser.

You're forgiven if you suddenly groan, "Oh, no! Not that again!" Unfortunately, you need a ni long page to help you understand named anchors.

A common practice on a long page of text is to put links near the top of the page that take you instantly down the page to the relevant sections. These links work using named anchors. You will make three.

1. In `namedanchors.html`, after the introductory paragraph but before the first tip, insert the paragraph highlighted here:

```
<p>After teaching <acronym title="Hypertext Markup Language">HTML</acronym> at
the local community college for a few semesters, I have learned to anticipate
the mistakes new web page creators make. Here are ten tips to help you avoid
falling into the newbie sinkhole of ugly, irritating ignorance.</p>
<p>Quick Links: Tip 3 | Tip 6 | Tip 9</p>
<h2>1. Never leave anyone alone with only the back button for company.</h2>
```

   You can see this text in the browser but without any hyperlinks. See Figure 7.26.

   You will use the Quick Links to navigate to Tip 3 or Tip 6 or Tip 9. In a real site, you would make a quick link to every tip, but doing three of them will give you plenty of experience with it for now. If you find it so exciting you just can't stop, go ahead and make quick links for all ten tips.

   You can't write the a element markup yet. First you have to insert something near those tips to navigate to: the named anchor. (You can also use an ID for this, I'll get to that in just a bit.)

2. Start with Tip 3 and name the anchor "3". Normally a word might make more sense than a number as a name; however, in this case, a number matching the number of the tip makes a clear connection that will hold up over time if you edit this page again at a later time. Put the anchor right before the beginning of Tip 3:

```
<a name="3"></a><h2>3. Stamp out long lists of links in huge bold fonts.</h2>
```

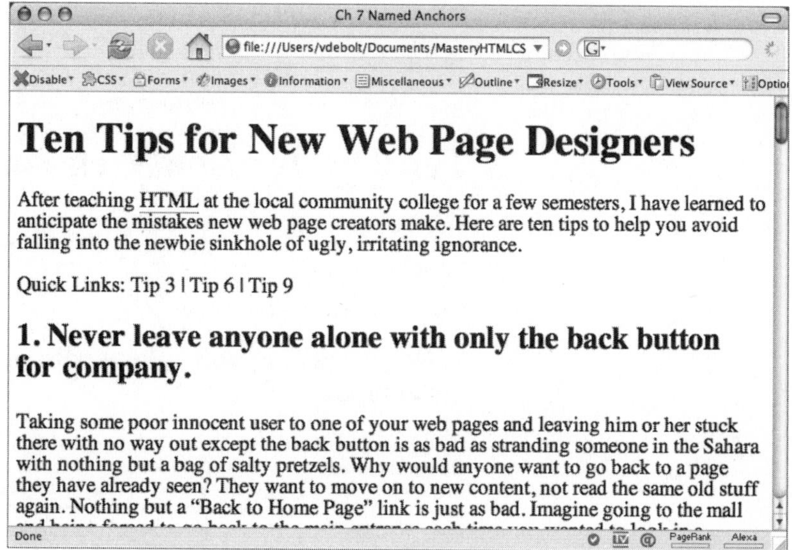

FIGURE 7.26 The text is ready and waiting to be linked to named anchors farther down the page.

3. Move on down to Tip 6. Name this anchor "6".

```
<a name="6"></a><h2>6. Create a sense of place.</h2>
```

4. Move down to Tip 9. Use "9" for a name for this one.

```
<a name="9"></a><h2>9. Give every page the minimum nutrients for proper
growth.</h2>
```

5. Look at the page in the browser. The named anchors are invisible elements. You see nothir added in front of Tips 3, 6, and 9.

6. Now write the links. Go back to the "Quick Links" paragraph you added at the top of th page and link the "Tip 3" text to the "3" named anchor. Remember, the link `href` attribu includes a hash sign and the name of the anchor. The link to Tip 3 is

```
<a href="#3">Tip 3</a>
```

7. Add similar links to the "Tip 6" and "Tip 9" text. The completed set is

```
<p>Quick Links: <a href="#3">Tip 3</a> | <a href="#6">Tip 6</a> | <a
href="#9">Tip 9</a></p>
```

Figure 7.27 shows the links in the browser, ready to take you quickly to the named anchors, ar Figure 7.28 shows the result of clicking the Tip 6 link.

You can also link directly to a named anchor from another page. For example:

```
<a href="namedanchors.html#3">Tip 3</a>
```

The page would open with Tip 3 at the top of the browser window.

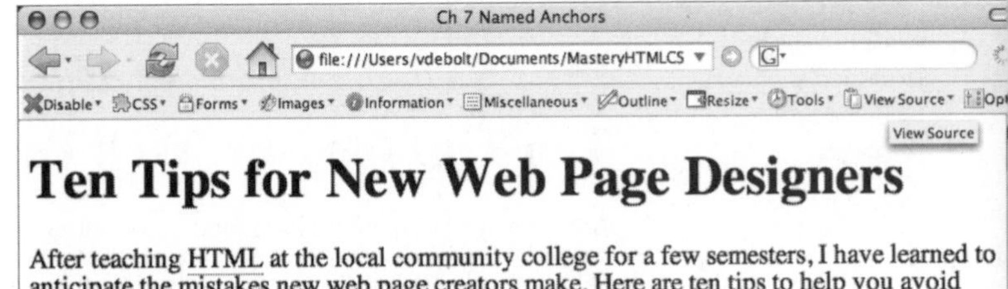

FIGURE 7.27
The hyperlinks, when clicked, will take you down the page to the named anchors.

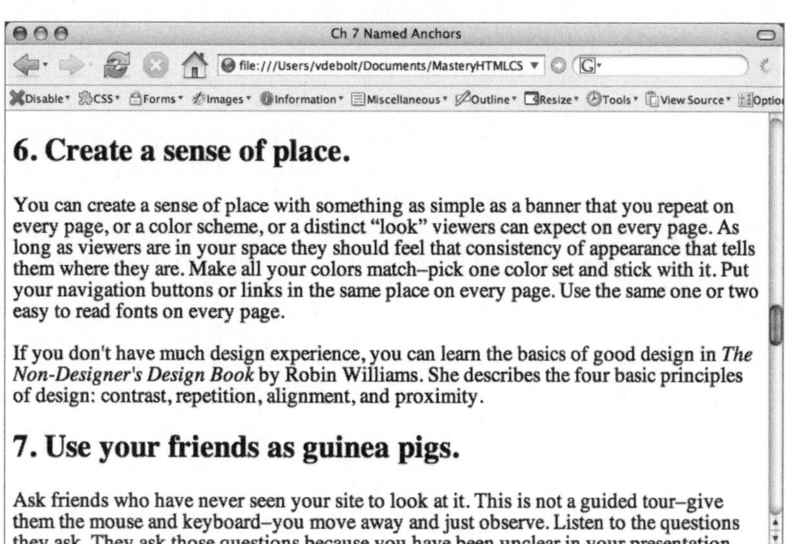

FIGURE 7.28 Clicking the Tip 6 link near the top of the page brings you immediately down the page to the name anchor beside Tip 6.

USE AN ID

The same process you used to link to named anchors also works for IDs. And when you use an `id`, you don't have to add the extra named anchor element, you merely give the element an `id`.

For example, look at the heading for Tip 3.

```
<h2>3. Stamp out long lists of links in huge bold fonts.</h2>
```

By assigning an `id` to the `h2` element, you have a landing spot for the link in the Quick Link section. Here's how it would look:

```
<h2 id="3">3. Stamp out long lists of links in huge bold fonts.</h2>
```

Try it. Take out the named anchors and add `id`s. Your links will work exactly as before.

Links on long pages don't always have to jump down a page: they can move up a page as well. You can jump back to the top of the page from anywhere in the page with a link like `<a href="# ">Back to Top</a>`.

SKIP NAVIGATION LINKS

An often-used accessibility feature of a site is to put a "skip navigation" link at the beginning of a web page. Clicking this link allows the user to skip directly to a named anchor or id marking the beginning of the main content of the page.

One of many barriers to accessibility is lack of a pointing device or mouse. This is the case with certain types of Internet-capable devices, such as personal digital assistants and mobile phones, and especially with aural screen readers that read a page aloud to the user. In such situations, or if the user suffers from mobility impairments, the user must use the Tab key (or the A key in the Opera browser) to navigate a page. With no skip navigation link, users may have to press Tab dozens of times to finally reach the part of the page they want. The skip navigation link provides a welcome opportunity to jump directly to the page content.

You can also link to a specific location identified with an id attribute. A named anchor isn't required. That's how most "skip to main content" links you see work. If there was an element wit id="content" on the page, this anchor element <a href="#content">Skip to Main Content< a> would take you there.

Although not as accessible as using real text displayed on the page, transparent graphics are sometimes used to create skip navigation links. The transparent graphic does not appear to the visual user but can be tabbed to or read aloud by an aural screen reader. There must be alt text explaining that the image is a link to the main content.

If you had one of these invisible skip links selected, you might see something like this in the browser.

When found with the Tab key, the image outline may appear to a user with a visual browser. A screen reader would announce the alt text when the tiny graphic was the object of focus. The XHTML for this is a link to a named anchor or an id. If the transparent graphic used is named skip.gif and the main content named anchor is marked a name ="content", then the hyperlink

```
<a href="#content"><img src="/images/skip.gif" width="10" height="1" alt="Skip t
main content" /></a>
```

This image may create the appearance of a blue rectangle on the screen if you forget to use a CS rule to remove the borders on img as a link.

Test results have shown that having visible text for the skip navigation is better than using a tran parent GIF as a link. If your design would be totally ruined by a visible skip navigation link, you ca hide it using CSS. Some of the techniques discussed for image replacement in Chapter 4 could be use to hide skip navigation links: absolute positioning outside the viewport, negative margins, display none, and other hiding techniques are some of the CSS options. See the "Resources" sidebar for mo information about screen reader support for various hiding techniques.

RESOURCES

Accessibility expert Jim Thatcher has a tutorial on skip navigation at jimthatcher.com/skipnav.htm that contains more information.

Accessibility expert Joe Clark outlines reasons why using visible text instead of transparent graphics is a good idea in this excerpt from his book *Building Accessible Websites* at joeclark.org/book/sashay/serialization/Chapter08.html#h4-2020. Note that this URL contains a link to a named anchor or an id (#h4-2020), thereby serving as a real-world example for you.

Access-Matters runs tests on various scenarios and reports the results. The visibility tests show how screen readers and other assistive technology react to different methods of hiding information from visual display. Find them at

```
www.access-matters.com/screen-reader-test-results
```

Tab Index

As I've noted, it is possible to navigate a web page using the Tab key. The user presses Tab to move from link to link (and also to move from one form field to the next). (In Opera, the A key moves from link to link, and the Tab key moves between form elements.) If the web designer does not explicitly set a Tab index value (sometimes called Tab order), it begins with the browser's location bar and moves through the page in the order that items appear in the XHTML source. If your browser has a search form in the address bar, the second Tab stop may be in the search form field.

If the page would be more usable or more accessible to Tab through the links or form elements in some order other than that of the XHTML source, a specific value can be set for `tabindex`. It is an attribute of the a element, like this:

```
<a href="index.html" tabindex="3">Home</a>
```

Tab index values must be whole number integers: 1, 2, 3, 4, and so on.

Tab index might be used in conjunction with a skip link to allow users to Tab immediately into the main content area.

As with any change you make in expected default browser behavior, you must be careful if you change tab order from its normal progression through the XHTML source order. Be careful to let users know what you are doing and what to expect when using the Tab key.

CSS: Pizzazz for Anchors

Turn your attention back to the files in the `flowerpagesite` folder. You will write some styles for the links on those pages. You've created hyperlinks with an a element, therefore, the a selector is used in CSS to style rules for the a elements.

CSS rules often target the a element combined with a *pseudo class selector*. CSS uses pseudo class selectors to style links based on their state. Links fall into pseudo classes because the state of a link is not written into the XHTML; it depends on the user's interaction. The four most common pseudo classes use these selectors:

```
a:link
a:visited
a:hover
a:active
```

The selectors need to be listed in link-visited-hover-active order (or L-V-H-A) in the style rules for most common uses. A link can actually be in more than one state at the same time—for example, both visited and hover. The cascade requires the selectors to be in that order for the links to display reliably in normal use.

There is another less frequently used pseudo state, `:focus`. The `:focus` pseudo class applies while an element has the focus. When an element has focus, it accepts keyboard events or other forms of text input. If you add an `a:focus` rule to your CSS, it should come in the cascade as L-V-F-H-A. The `:focus` pseudo class also applies to elements other than anchors, such as form input fields.

Open the `ch7index.html` page. The current structure has all the a elements in the sidebar `left`. See Listing 7.4.

LISTING 7.4: The *<div id="left">* Element Contains All the Ccurrent Hyperlinks

```
<div id="left">
   <ul>
        <li>Home</li>
        <li><a href="cactus/ch7cactus.html">Cactus</a></li>
     <li><a href="iris/ch7iris_vd.html">Iris</a></li>
     <li><a href="groundcover/ch7groundcover_vd.html">Ground Cover</a></li>
   </ul>
   <h3>News Items</h3>
      <p>All the latest flower news  goes here. If your site has a blog,  link t
the latest blog entry here. Or maybe show some pretty flowers from <a href="http
/www.flickr.com/photos/tags/flowers/">Flickr</a>.</p>
   <h3>Buy Now</h3>
      <p>Now's the time to order those daffodil bulbs from <a href="http://
www.burpee.com">Burpee</a>.</p>
</div>
```

You could write style rules for the `a:link`, `a:visited`, `a:hover`, `a:active` selectors now. They would apply globally to every link on the page, including any that you might place in other areas o the page such as the sidebar `right` or the `footer`. To style the links in various areas of the page mo effectively, the page needs more context so that descendant selectors can be used. Wrap the `ul` eleme in a new `div`. Give the new div the `id` `"mainnav"`. (Note that with the current structure of the page th `id` could be assigned to the `ul`, and the additional `div` would be unnecessary.) Then wrap the two h elements following the `ul` in another new `div` with the `id` `"news"`. See Listing 7.5 for the changes.

LISTING 7.5: Added Structure in the Left *div* Creates Context for Descendant Selectors

```
<div id="left">
   <div id="mainnav">
      <ul>
           <li>Home</li>
           <li><a href="cactus/ch7cactus.html">Cactus</a></li>
        <li><a href="iris/ch7iris_vd.html">Iris</a></li>
        <li><a href="groundcover/ch7groundcover_vd.html">Ground Cover</a></li>
      </ul>
    </div>
    <div id="news">
       <h3>News Items</h3>
       <p>All the latest flower news  goes here. If your site has a blog,  link t
the latest blog entry here. Or maybe show some pretty flowers from <a href="http
/www.flickr.com/photos/tags/flowers/">Flickr</a>.</p>
       <h3>Buy Now</h3>
       <p>Now's the time to order those daffodil bulbs from <a href="http://
www.burpee.com">Burpee</a>.</p>
   </div>
</div>
```

Here are some examples of contextual selectors with the added structure:

```
#mainnav a:link
#mainnav a:visited
#mainnav a:hover
#mainnav a:active
```

or

```
#news a:link
#news a:visited
#news a:hover
#news a:active
```

Setting Link Colors

Most designers want link colors that complement the site's color scheme. That might suggest a green or a pink for this page. I'll use various shades of gray, but feel free to try other colors.

In the `ch7_links.css` document, add this selector and rule. The CSS comment labeling this section of rules is an organizational help. You can add it or omit it as you prefer.

```
/* mainnav styles */
#mainnav a:link {
   color: #333;
}
```

When altering the default link colors, an accepted convention is to use a faded or lighter shade of the color selected for the `a:link` color to represent the `a:visited` color. Try this:

```
#mainnav a:visited {
   color: #666;
}
```

With these two rules in place, you will notice several things in the browsers. You should see a small difference in the colors of links that have been visited versus those that have not. (In Figure 7.29, Iris is a visited link.) If all your links are in the visited state, you can clear the browser's history to bring them back to the unvisited state. The links after the list in the `news` div should be unaffected and display in the default blue or purple.

An accepted convention for :`hover` pseudo classes is to brighten them up and make them stand out. The `hover` state is created when the user holds a pointing device such as a mouse over an a element. The `active` state occurs at the actual instant that the user clicks. A group selector can be used to style these two pseudo states with the same rule. Remember, a group selector lists a comma-separated list of selectors, like this:

```
#mainnav a:hover, #mainnav a:active {
color: #000;
}
```

You must hover over a link or click a link to see the resûlts of this rule in the browser, shown in Figure 7.30. When you hover over any link, whether visited or unvisited, the color should change to the hover color.

FIGURE 7.29 Styles for the `a:link` and `a:visited` are apparent in the `mainnav` area. Links in the news area are the default colors.

FIGURE 7.30 The pointing finger shows the link being hovered over and the resulting darker color. Even a visited link would change to the darker color on hover, if the rules were in L-V-H-A order in the style sheet.

Styling Links with *background-image*

These graphics should be on your hard drive in the `flowerpagesite/img` folder:

```
hoverbg.jpg
linkbg.jpg
visitedbg.jpg
```

Using background graphics for these hyperlinks without also styling the list (as you'll do in Chapter 9) is not the best way to style a menu. For now, treat this as a learning exercise only.

As you probably guessed from the names of the images for this exercise, they are meant to use with the `:link`, `:hover`, and `:visited` pseudo states.

RELATIVE PATHWAYS AND CSS

Background images use the same relative pathway scheme as links. The important distinction to keep in mind when writing a relative pathway in a CSS rule is that the path is relative to the CSS document location. Up to this point, all the background-image rules you've written have been to images in the same folder as the CSS file. Now the images are in a subfolder just below the CSS file, called `img`, hence the pathway: `url(img/linkbg.jpg)`.

Change the `#mainnav a:link` rule to add a background image:

```
#mainnav a:link {
   color: #333;
   background: url(img/linkbg.jpg);
}
```

The background image will appear behind the text. In Figure 7.31, Iris is a visited link, and it has no background image as yet. Depending on whether or not you have visited links in your display, you may see something slightly different than shown here.

FIGURE 7.31 With a background image behind the `a:link` elements, you see this effect.

Add the background image to the `:visited` pseudo class next:

```
#mainnav a:visited {
   color: #666;
   background: url(img/visitedbg.jpg);
}
```

Look closely in the browser and you will see that the background color and image for the visited links are both slightly faded when compared with nonvisited links (see Figure 7.32). Again, your own display will depend on which links are visited and which are not.

Complete the exercise by adding a background to the group selector for `#mainnav a:hover, #mainnav a:active`, like this:

```
#mainnav a:hover, #mainnav a:active {
   color: #000;
   background: url(img/hoverbg.jpg);
}
```

Again, hold the cursor over a link to check the results of this rule. The hovered link's color should be black and its background image slightly darker than the rest. See Figure 7.33.

The `:active` pseudo state should be exactly like the `:hover` pseudo state. Click a link to test it.

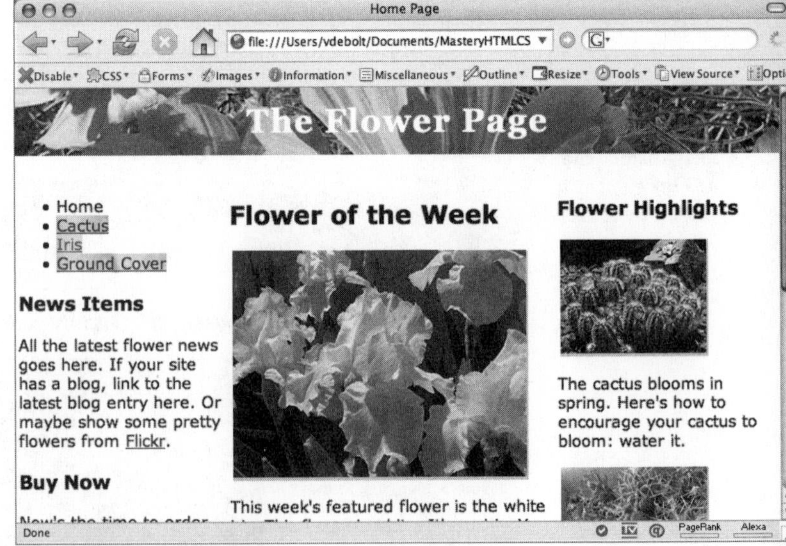

FIGURE 7.32
The visited link, Iris, is lighter in text color, and the background image is slightly less saturated in color as well.

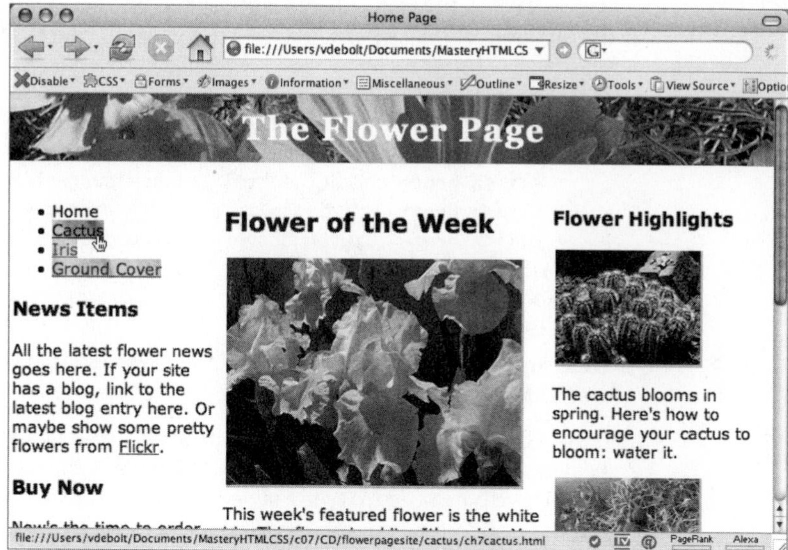

FIGURE 7.33 With the Cactus link in the hover state, the background image and the link color change.

Styles to Indicate the Current Page

Earlier in this chapter there was a discussion about deliberately omitting a link to the current page in the navigation, as a reminder to the site visitor. Here you will try another way of making the current page stand out. You will create a link to the current page and use a class to serve as a current page indicator. You'll also get some practice using the most complex selector you've tried thus far.

1. First you need to write the hyperlinks. You will link each of the four pages *to themselves*, and add a class to the a element while you're at it. The class will be named "current." Here's how it looks in the `ch7index.html` page:

```
<div id="mainnav">
   <ul>
      <li><a href="ch7index.html" class="current">Home</a></li>
      <li><a href="cactus/ch7cactus.html">Cactus</a></li>
      <li><a href="iris/ch7iris_vd.html">Iris</a></li>
      <li><a href="groundcover/ch7groundcover_vd.html">Ground Cover</a></li>
   </ul>
</div>
```

2. Add a hyperlink to make `ch7cactus.html`, `ch7groundcover.html`, and `ch7iris.html` all connect to themselves when clicked. Add the `class="current"` to each of the links. While

you are in each file, remember to add the new mainnav and news divs that you are using fo the selectors. The changes to the list portion of ch7cactus.html are

```
<div id="mainnav">
   <ul>
      <li><a href="../ch7index.html">Home</a></li>
      <li><a href="ch7cactus.html" class="current">Cactus</a></li>
      <li><a href="../iris/ch7iris.html">Iris</a></li>
      <li><a href="../groundcover/ch7groundcover.html">Ground Cover</a></li>
   </ul>
 </div>
```

The changes to ch7groundcover.html and ch7iris.html should be the same except for th href values.

3. Write a CSS rule for the class. When applying a class to a specific element such as this element, the selector needs to select an a element in the class current and give the pseud state. There is no need to write a style for the selector .current before you write a style fo your link, although you certainly could. Once you are on the page, it will be a visited lin The selector is

   ```
   #mainnav a.current:visited
   ```

   Make it look different from the other links by changing the color slightly (to #F00 or red) ar removing the underline:

   ```
   #mainnav a.current:visited {
      color: #F00;
      text-decoration: none;
   }
   ```

The ch7index.html page now looks like Figure 7.34. The other pages should show a simil current page indicator with red link text and no underline. As current page indicators go, tha one doesn't thrill me much. The background images displaying at all different sizes create alig ment issues, too. Things will improve in Chapter 9 when you work with lists.

An online tool named Select Oracle at http://gallery.theopalgroup.com/selectoracle can help you distinguish between very similar selectors. Enter your style rule or provide the sty sheet's URL, and it will tell you what you've got. For example, Select Oracle defines .current a:visited as, "Selects any a element whose target has been visited that is a descendant of any e ment with a class attribute that contains the word current." (In the example page, the a eleme is not a descendant, so this selector wouldn't match anything.) It explains a.current:visited "Selects any a element with a class attribute that contains the word current and whose target h been visited."

Try some other rules with what you have now; perhaps background color, borders, padding, lett spacing, or other CSS rules could make it more impressive. The important concept is that you can u a class indicator to provide a visual clue to the current page and at the same time have every item i your navigation a working link.

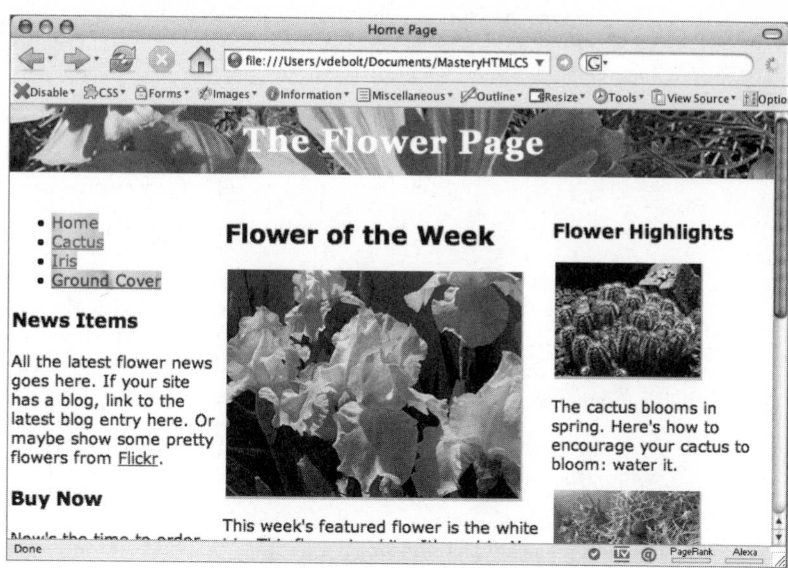

FIGURE 7.34 The current page (Home) has a different style in the menu, indicating that it is the current page.

> **UBER WHAT?**
>
> Project Seven is a site that offers tutorials and code samples aimed mainly at Dreamweaver users. However, many of their tutorials contain useful information for hand coders. Their excellent tutorial on what they call by the peculiar name "uberlinks" at `www.projectseven.com/tutorials/css/uberlinks/` explains how to create a button rollover with CSS and doesn't require Dreamweaver to use. It teaches some of the list styles you'll learn in Chapter 9. And it includes a lovely way to indicate the current page, too.

An *id*-Based Current Page Indicator

Many sites, as you have seen in the Real-World Scenarios, use an `id` in the body element. Combine that with an `id` in each `li` element (instead of a `class` attribute in the a element) and you have an alternative system for indicating the current page.

I'll briefly describe how it's done. Every page needs an `id` in the body element; for example the index page might have:

```
<body id="home">
```

Each `li` needs a related `id`. For example:

```
<ul>
   <li id="nav-home"><a href="ch7index_vd.html">Home</a></li>
   <li id="nav-cactus"><a href="cactus/ch7cactus.html">Cactus</a></li>
   <li id="nav-iris"><a href="iris/ch7iris_vd.html">Iris</a></li>
```

```
<li id="nav-gc"><a href="groundcover/ch7groundcover_vd.html">Ground Cover</
a></li>
</ul>
```

Those ids relate to a group of body ids such as home, cactus, iris, and gc.

The CSS then targets the link to be styled as the current page with group selectors such as these examples:

```
#home #nav-home a, #cactus #nav-cactus a, #iris #nav-iris a, #gc #nav-gc a
```

The group selector covers all the possibilities, since only one selector out of the group would match any given link for any given page. For example, the selector #home #nav-home a would only match an a element descended from an element with the id #nav-home, which was descended from an element with the id #home. The other selectors in the group list would simply be ignored.

Similar selectors would be used for the :hover state rules. For example:

```
#home #nav-home a:hover, #cactus #nav-cactus a:hover, #iris #nav-iris a:hover,
#gc #nav-gc a:hover
```

The rules for the various pseudo states could be very similar to those used for the example with class="current". The difference is the selector chosen to implement the rule. If you use some sort of server side scripting or server side includes for your navigation menu, the body-id-based system makes it possible to indicate the current page, since you cannot edit the class attribute of any elements in the nav include on individual pages.

CURRENT PAGE INDICATOR BY *ID*

Two good sources of further information and examples with ids to indicate current pages are

- 456 Berea Street "Setting the Current Menu State with CSS" at www.456bereastreet.com/archive/200503/setting_the_current_menu_state_with_css
- Hicks Design "Highlighting Current Page with CSS" at www.hicksdesign.co.uk/journal/highlighting-current-page-with-css

CSS Pop-ups

Using CSS with no JavaScript, you can add text to a link that will pop up in a remote position on the page. It's done with a span element in a hyperlink. There are other possible ways to achieve the pop-up without JavaScript, as you'll see later in this chapter's Real-World Scenario.

Begin with ch7index.html. You need some empty space for the pop-ups, so the first thing to do is add a margin-top rule for the #news selector. Although you have a news div in the XHTML, you don't have any rules for it in the style sheet yet. Create this style rule:

```
#news {
   margin-top: 12em;
}
```

That gives you some white space, as shown in Figure 7.35.

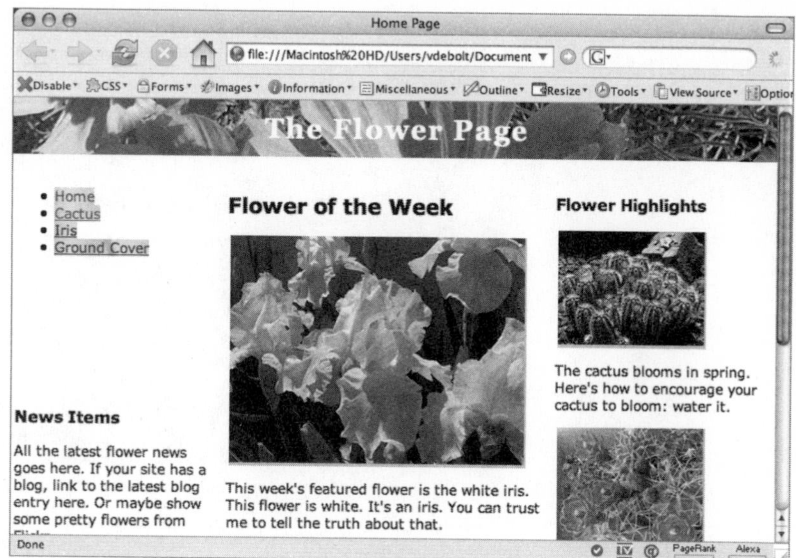

FIGURE 7.35 `margin-top` is used on the `news div` to create a blank area on the page.

Next you must add the span element with some text for the pop-up. Each hyperlink in the menu gets its own `span` element. The `span` element begins after the link text and ends just before the closing </a> tag. Here's an example for the Home link:

```
<a href="ch7index_vd.html" class="current">Home<span>You are here</span></a>
```

Each anchor needs to be given a span element in the same manner. With some suggested text for the spans, a completed `mainnav` element is shown in Listing 7.6.

LISTING 7.6: The Text for Each Span Added to the *a* Element

```
<div id="mainnav">
   <ul>
      <li><a href="ch7index_vd.html" class="current">Home<span>You are here</
span></a></li>
         <li><a href="cactus/ch7cactus.html">Cactus<span>Learn all about the care
and propagation of the cactus.</span></a></li>
       <li><a href="iris/ch7iris_vd.html">Iris<span>Learn about planting, thinning
and caring for iris.</span></a></li>
        <li><a href="groundcover/ch7groundcover_vd.html">Ground Cover<span>Learn
about dozens of useful ground covers.</span></a></li>
   </ul>
</div>
```

If you look at this in the browser now (Figure 7.36), you see the text in the span as part of the link text. This is not what you want to have happen.

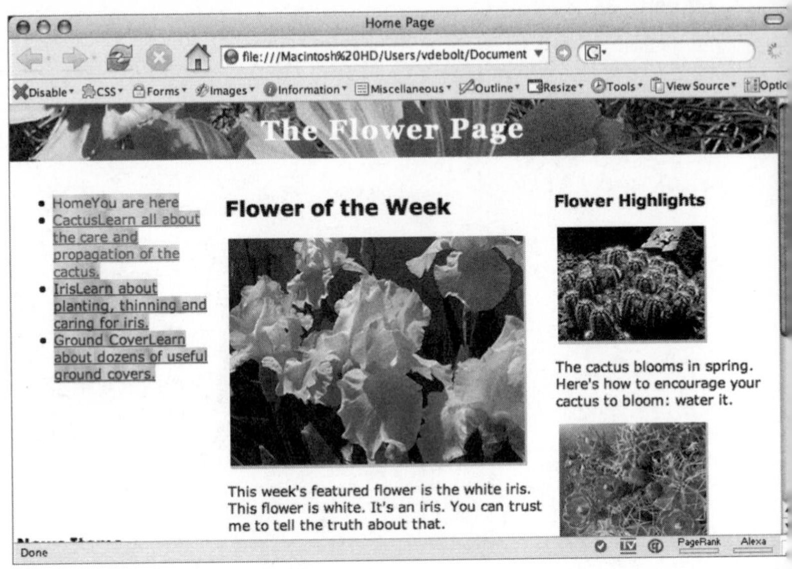

FIGURE 7.36
Text added to the span nested in each link is clearly visible as part of the hyperlink; you'll fix that next.

Instead of showing up as part of the clickable link text, you want the text in the `span` to pop u somewhere else on the page (the blank area). So you must keep it from displaying in the menu. You'll use `display: none` to accomplish this, with this rule:

```
#mainnav a span {
   display: none;
}
```

The selector `#mainnav a span` targets the `span` in any a element in the `mainnav`, regardless o link state. You don't want them appearing unexpectedly in the visited state, or some other state yo haven't planned for. This rule will prevent that from happening.

At this stage, the `span` text is hidden, so when you hover over a link, nothing pops up. Se Figure 7.37.

To make this work in Internet Explorer, add this rule:

```
#mainnav a:hover {
height: auto;
   }
```

Without this rule for the `a: hover` that assigns `height`, nothing will pop up in IE5/6. This what is lovingly referred to as a known bug. It doesn't have to be `height: auto`; several othe declarations can also be used in the additional `:hover` rule. You can read more about this bug `www.tanfa.co.uk/css/articles/pure-css-popups-bug.asp`.

The final step is a rule for the selector `#mainnav a:hover span`. You can use this selector make the text in the span pop up when the user hovers over the hyperlink. This rule involves se eral CSS properties. First, to overrule the `display: none` rule you used to hide the span, mal the `#mainnav a:hover span` use `display: block`. You want the span to pop up in the space y made for it below the menu. Use `position: absolute` to achieve that. Add position values o `top: 12em` and `left: 2em` to move the span where you want it in the containing block (`mainnav`). Give the pop-up a `width: 125px` to keep it within your `left` column with no overlaps. That's all the CSS you need to make the pop-up work. With a few optional niceties for color, padding, and background, a suggestion for the complete rule is shown in Listing 7.7.

LISTING 7.7: The Completed Rule for *#mainnav a:hover span*

```
#mainnav a:hover span {
      display: block;
      position: absolute;
      top: 12em;
      left: 2em;
      width: 125px;
      padding: 5px;
      margin: 10px;
      color: #FFF;
      background: #9C4071;
      text-decoration: none;
}
```

The completed pop-up in your browser should resemble Figure 7.38.

Using a relative measurement (in this case ems) to create the white space and the positioning values needed means that the pop-up will appear below the navigation text, with no overlaps, even if the user must increase the text size dramatically in order to read the page. See Figure 7.39.

You will work further with links in Chapter 8 and in Chapter 9.

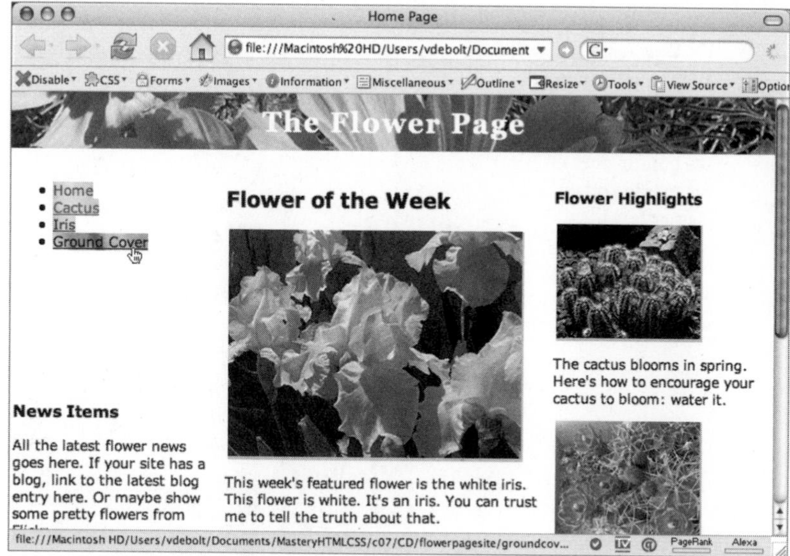

FIGURE 7.37 The text in the span does not display, even when hovering over a link. Since you do want the span to display when hovering over a link, more CSS work is needed.

> **POP-UP RESOURCES**
>
> Eric Meyer first wrote about the CSS pop-up technique at his experimental CSS Edge site at `meyerweb.com/eric/css/edge/popups/demo.html`. Andy Budd describes a way to create pop-ups with two `span` elements nested in a hyperlink in *CSS Mastery: Advanced Web Standards Solutions* (Friends of Ed, 2006). Budd calls them "remote rollovers."

FIGURE 7.38 The completed pop-up shows when a hyperlink is in the hover state.

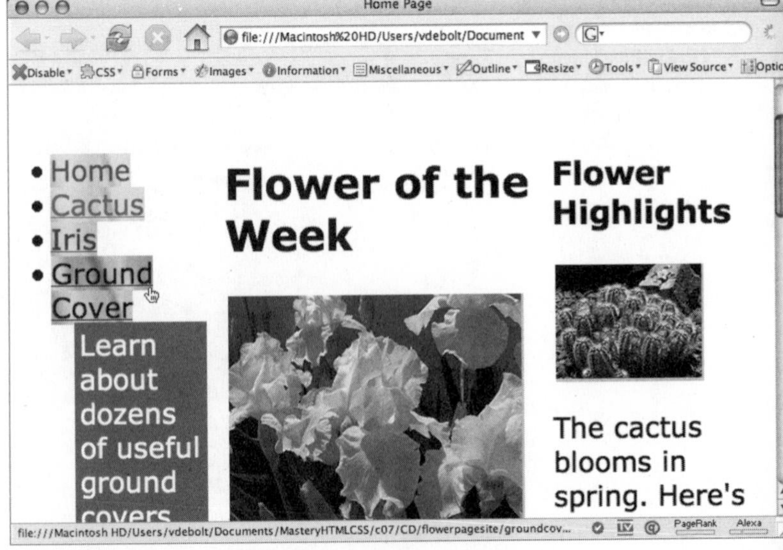

FIGURE 7.39 Even when significant enlargements of the text are needed, the pop-up does not overlap other elements.

Real-World Scenario

Black Eagle Limousine, based in Washington, D.C., is an example of interesting links. Figure 7.40 shows their site, at `www.blackeaglelimo.com`.

Compared with some of the big sites we've examined in the Real-World Scenarios, Black Eagle Limousine is a small site. The site focuses with laser-like concentration on two things: showing the vehicle choices they offer and taking reservations for their limo services.

If you check the site with online XHTML and CSS validators, you find that the XHTML validates. The CSS has a few errors caused by the use of the underscore hack to target rules specifically for Internet Explorer. The underscore hack uses a selector name preceded by an underscore (such as `_margin`) to write rules only for certain versions of IE. (IE7 is not going to recognize the underscore hack.)

The main nav bar that runs horizontally across the top of the right column is a list. The three images of the fleet vehicles in the left column are also a list. Actually the fleet vehicles images are more than a simple list, because each list item contains a nested list used to create a CSS pop-up. See Figure 7.41.

These pop-ups aren't created with `span` elements; they use nested lists. Here's the code for the Bus hyperlink:

```
<ul id="fleetApp">
   <li id="fa-bus"><a href="/content/bel_fleet.html" title="Bus">Bus</a>
      <ul id="fa-busDetails">
         <li><b>Coach Bus</b><br />Our Coach Bus' are ideal for group trips,
executive meetings, and conferences.  With seating up to 47 or 57 passengers, a
lavatory, televisions, plush seats, and drop-down shades on every window, this is
true luxury on wheels.  And with our special rates, you can't go wrong.
         </li>
      </ul>
   </li>
```

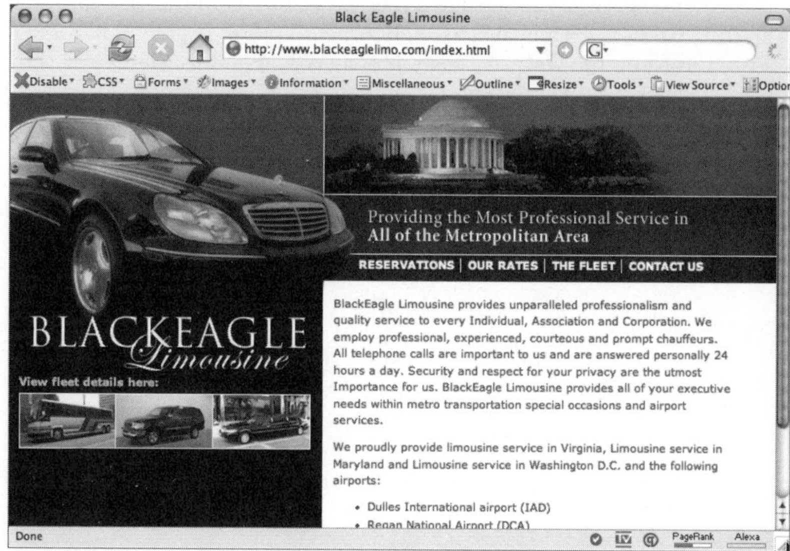

FIGURE 7.40 The home page of Black Eagle Limousine. Global links are in all caps in a bar across the masthead area. The vehicles in the fleet in the small photos on the left are also links.

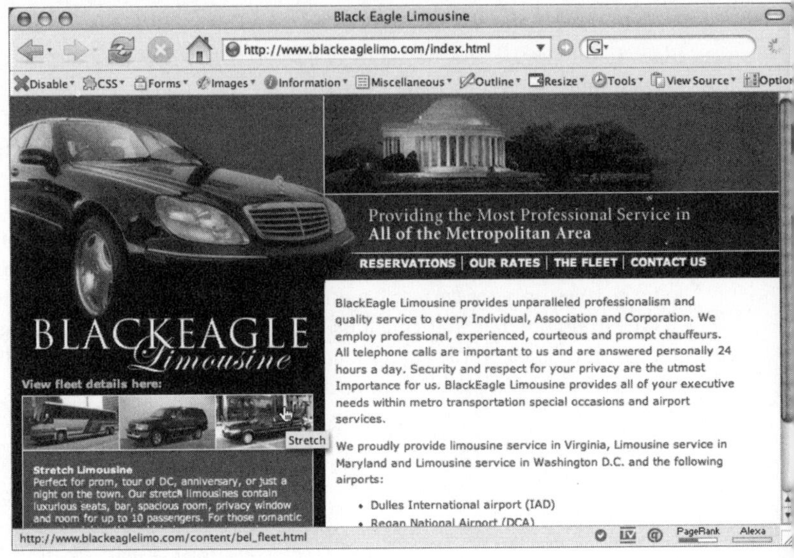

FIGURE 7.41
Hovering over one of the fleet vehicle images triggers a pop-up with more information about the particular vehicle.

Nor are the pop-ups hidden with `display: none`, as in the preceding exercises. Instead they use a technique similar to that used to hide text for image replacements. Here's the relevant hiding CSS:

```
#fleetApp li ul {
   position: absolute;
   left: -999em;
}
```

When an unordered list descended from a list item is hovered over, the position of the nested list is changed to a visible position on the page. Note that the pop-ups use an unordered list (`ul`). That brings up an Internet Explorer problem. IE 6 and below do not recognize `:hover` on anything but an `a` element. The W3C standard states that `:hover` should be applicable to any element. (IE 7 will recognize `:hover` on all elements.) To make the `:hover` work on the `ul` in IE5/6 on this site, a small amount of JavaScript was used. Despite this minor complication, this Real-World Scenario should make you aware that `:hover` most certainly offers interesting ways to create all CSS pop-ups.

On the inner pages of the site, only the global navigation in the masthead area is used. See Figure 7.42.

FIGURE 7.42
The inner pages have navigation at the top, but the fleet vehicle links are not used. The width of the two columns is changed on the inner pages as well.

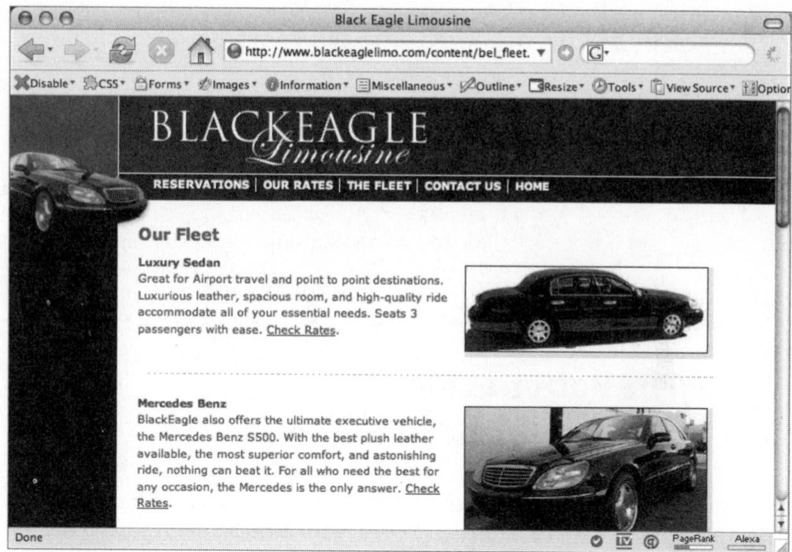

CSS Properties

Most of the CSS properties used in Chapter 7 were explained earlier in the book. Only one new CSS property is used in Chapter 7; it's shown in Table 7.1.

Dynamic pseudo classes create styles that are dependent on the user's interaction with the page. Pseudo class selectors are listed in Table 7.2.

TABLE 7.1: CSS Properties in Chapter 7 for the a Selector

PROPERTY	POSSIBLE VALUES
`text-decoration`	`none, underline, overline, line-through, blink, inherit`

TABLE 7.2: Pseudo Class Selectors

CLASS	USE
LINK PSEUDO CLASSES	
`:link`	Use with any anchor with an `href` attribute.
`:visited`	Use with any anchor that has been visited.

TABLE 7.2: Pseudo Class Selectors *(CONTINUED)*

CLASS	USE
DYNAMIC PSEUDO CLASSES	
`:hover`	Use with any anchor the mouse is hovering over.
`:active`	Use with any anchor element while the mouse is held down.
`:focus`	Use with any anchor element while the element has focus.

The Bottom Line

Write relative and absolute hyperlinks. Relative links are used only within your own site. Any link to pages outside your site needs an absolute URL.

Master It Assume that the `flowerpagesite` has a subfolder in the `cactus` folder. The su folder is named `pricklypear`. Write a link from the document `pricklypearjam.html` in that subfolder to the home page.

Also write a link from the `pricklypearjam.html` page to this Prickly Pear Sweets and Treats Page:

```
http://www.desertusa.com/magoct97/oct_pear.html
```

Write hyperlinks for e-mail and to MP3 and PDF files. E-mail uses the `mailto` protocol. A e-mail link is an a element with the `mailto` protocol in the `href` attribute. An a element with a `href` attribute is all that is needed to link to files in the MP3 and PDF formats.

Master It Create a new line in the footer of `ch7index.html` and create an e-mail link to yourself there.

Master It Write a link to this music clip on the Internet:

```
http://madykaye.com/girlsjustgotta.mp3
```

Use images to create hyperlinks. An `img` element is enclosed in an a element to create a clic able image.

Master It In the right column of `ch7index.html` there are three images. Link them to th appropriate site subpages.

Use CSS to style hyperlinks. The a element can be styled with any CSS property you have learned thus far, including `color`, `margin`, `padding`, `border`, `background-color`, and `backgroun image`. Its different states can be targeted with pseudo class elements.

Master It Create a completely different presentation for the links in `flowerpagesite` from the styles used in the exercises. Create rules for the different pseudo class selecto and for the current page indicator. Be prepared to demonstrate your results in a browse Create a backup copy of your current style sheet before you begin making changes.

Use CSS to create pop-up text. By nesting a `span` element in an a element, you can cause text to pop up in various locations on the page when the a element is in the hover state.

Master It Remove the `margin-top` from the `#news` selector. Then add a `z-index` rule to the `#mainnav a:hover span` selector to keep it on top even if it overlaps other text. When would you consider this a good use of a pop-up? Demonstrate in the browser.

Chapter 8

Multimedia, Images, and Image Styles

Exercises in previous chapters have included images that were already placed on the exercise pages for you. In this chapter, *you* will add images to pages.

Browsers can display only a few image formats. In this chapter, you will work with GIF (for Graphic Interchange Format) and JPEG or JPG (for Joint Photographic Experts Group) documents. There is growing support among browsers for another file type, PNG (for Portable Network Graphics). Although PNG graphics have some advantages that will be discussed, they will not be used in these exercises. Any graphic you might have in some format other than GIF, JPEG, or PNG is not a web graphic and needs to be saved into a web format.

Multimedia objects are a bit more complex to add to a page. Some prepared multimedia examples will help you learn how to work with Flash and QuickTime on a web page.

In this chapter you will:

- Understand basic functions of graphics software.
- Place images on web pages.
- Build horizontal and vertical navigation bars with images.
- Use images to create a photo gallery.
- Understand how to add multimedia objects to web pages.

Creating and Editing Images

Specialized software is required to create and edit web graphics. There is a definite learning curve involved in mastering graphic design tools, and this book is not going to address that issue at all. However, if you have such tools at hand, you can manage basic tasks such as cropping and resizing images without much training in the software. In this section, I'll walk you through a few basic web-related actions in graphics software programs.

In the Chapter 8 folder on the companion CD are two files named `banner.png` and `button.png`. They can be found in the `img_exercises/images` folder. These are the original Macromedia Fireworks PNG files that created the banner and button images in the exercises. In the event that you have software that can open and work with PNG images, feel free to study these files as examples and change them to suit your own needs.

It is a good idea to keep the original files used to create buttons or other web graphics. If you need to change or add to them later, you'll have the original information at hand. It's much easier to go back to the original file in Fireworks or Photoshop, add a new layer with the same dimensions, colors, fonts, and so on, and export another GIF or JPEG to add to your site graphics than it is to tr to match an existing GIF or JPEG image from scratch.

In addition to Macromedia Fireworks and Adobe Photoshop, programs that can be used to creat web graphics include Adobe Illustrator, Jasc Paint Shop Pro, and others. Some computers come wit a basic graphics program, such as Paint, which can produce simple web graphics.

WEB-READY GRAPHICS

Graphics software such as Photoshop and Fireworks can convert images in formats such as TIFF, PICT, and BMP into formats that are more usable on the Web. There are also very inexpensive tools designed just for this, such as Graphic Converter (`www.graphic-converter.net`).

Most monitors or viewing devices display at a resolution of 72 *ppi* (pixels per inch). There is no rea son to save a web graphic with a resolution of more than 72 ppi, because the vast majority of monito cannot display the additional pixel detail. Even though the monitor cannot display the additional pi els, it takes time to download them, so images with a resolution higher than 72 dpi force your user to wait unnecessarily long for images to appear. Some Windows monitors display 96 dpi, so this re olution is often used as well. Either choice is acceptable, although I refer more often to 72 ppi here.

You may use your digital camera, or you may scan snapshots to use on the Web. The camera migh take a photo at 300 ppi, which would be perfect for a printed photo, but not for the Web. Your scanne might be set to scan photos at 150 ppi or 300 ppi. When processing these images for web graphics, it is essential to reduce the image resolution to 72 ppi. In terms of download speed, a 72 ppi image download is like a speedy jackrabbit in a race with a snail-like 300 ppi download. And once a user si there for the agonizing seconds or minutes it takes a 300 ppi image to finally download, they'll onl see 72 ppi in the monitor anyway!

Keep a high-resolution original of your photos. You might need the additional pixels of infor mation at some point. Save a low-resolution copy for any web work.

Any of the graphics software programs allows you to make changes in resolution to a document's image size. Reducing an image's resolution to 72 ppi is one facet in the process known as *image optimization*.

JPEG, GIF, and PNG

Each image format has its unique virtues.

JPEG (pronounced "jay-peg") stands for Joint Photographic Experts Group, the committee tha defined the format. JPEG images are often used for photographs or art with many subtle color var ations. A JPEG image can contain millions of colors but is compressed so that its file size is far les than other image formats, such as TIF, that are used for photos. When many colors are required most people are happier with the way a JPEG image looks in a browser than with a GIF image.

When saving a JPEG, you'll have options about setting the image quality to a range of high, mediur or low. A low quality JPEG will download faster than a medium or high quality JPEG, and a mediu quality JPEG will download faster than a high quality JPEG. Sometimes you have to play around wit it a bit to determine which quality level will produce the best results and the smallest file size.

Selecting the lowest acceptable quality for a JPEG image is another facet in the process of imag optimization.

Most people pronounce GIF with a hard *g*, as in "gift"; some use a soft *g*, as in "giraffe." At any rate, a GIF (Graphics Interchange Format) image can have a transparent background. A JPEG cannot have a transparent background. The GIFs used in some of the practice exercises in this chapter have transparent backgrounds, so you will get a clear idea of what that means as the chapter progresses.

Although the GIF format can display as many as 256 colors, one of its virtues is that the number of colors used in the image can be reduced to only the essential colors. For example, a solid red button with a white triangle on it to indicate a link to the next page has only two colors: red and white. Saving that button as a GIF with the number of colors reduced to two makes for a very small file size and hence a very fast download. When solid colors for graphics such as buttons, banners, logos, and headings are required, a GIF can generally be used and will have a smaller file size than a JPEG.

Saving a GIF with the fewest acceptable number of colors is another image optimization technique.

The PNG (Portable Network Graphic) format allows various levels of transparent backgrounds, a feature known as alpha transparency. Internet Explorer has not supported alpha-channel transparency for PNG graphics, but it's coming in IE 7. PNGs can be given a single transparent background color, which *does* work on older versions of IE, and is similar to the type of transparency available with a GIF.

PNG text for buttons and headings may appear to have smoother edges than text made in other formats, and PNG files optimize well. Many modern browsers already display alpha-channel transparency PNG files, but with IE holding a dominant position in the browser market, the PNG format has not come into common use yet. When IE 7 is released, the PNG format surely will be more widely used on web pages.

Like a JPEG, PNG files can display millions of colors. JPEG is a *lossy* data format, whereas a PNG is *lossless*. Lossy means that if you resave a JPEG, particularly if you resize to make it smaller, you lose some pixels in the process. In fact, even without resizing, every time you save a JPG, you lose some image data. If you need to make the JPEG bigger at a later time, those pixels are lost forever and you may get a grainy or blurry image as a result. No pixels are lost when resaving PNG images, whether enlarging or reducing the file size.

DID YOU SAY ALPHA-CHANNEL?

Alpha-channel transparency is a variable level of transparency. It's also known as a mask channel. It is a way to associate variable transparency with an image. Whereas GIF supports simple binary transparency—any given pixel can be only fully transparent or fully opaque—PNG allows up to 254 levels of partial transparency.

Basic Graphics Software Tips

If you are a beginner with graphics software tools such as Adobe Photoshop or Fireworks, I can give you a few very basic tips that will help you get web pages of your own going.

Cropping Images

Images may have unwanted elements or unnecessary background material that can be eliminated by cropping the image. In both Photoshop and Fireworks, the icon for the Crop tool looks like a draftsman's square, as shown at left. With the Crop tool selected, you simply drag a marquee around the area you want to keep and press Return (Enter), and the image is croppe Figure 8.1 shows an example in Photoshop.

FIGURE 8.1
The Crop tool was used to create a marquee around the part of the image I wanted. Pressing Return (Enter) crops the image to only the portion inside the marquee.

SIZING IMAGES

Sizing images can change both the resolution and the actual measurement of the image in pixel Sometimes you want to do both: reduce the resolution and change the pixel dimensions. Sometim you merely want to reduce the resolution to a level suitable for the Web, but leave the actual pix dimensions as large as possible. You may also want to save an image at two or three sizes, each wi different pixel dimensions, to use for different purposes. It's always a good idea to retain the ori inal high resolution image. Do the sizing you need with copies of the original.

In the Image Size options for both Photoshop and Fireworks you can do both operations at o time: you can reduce the overall dimensions of the image in pixels, and you can reduce the reso tion to 72 ppi.

In Figure 8.2, you see Photoshop's Image menu, which allows you to select Image Size. The Image Size window (Figure 8.3) shows Pixel Dimensions at the top and Resolution as pixels/in under Document Size.

I find it easiest to change the resolution to 72 first, because the overall pixel dimensions of th image will change when the resolution is changed. Before you change the pixel dimensions, sele the Constrain Proportions option. You only need to change one of the pixel dimensions (either width or height) and the other will automatically change in proportion.

In Fireworks, you must select Modify ➤ Canvas ➤ Image Size to get to the Image Size optio (Figure 8.4). The Fireworks Image Size dialog window is very similar to the one in Photoshop, you can see in Figure 8.5.

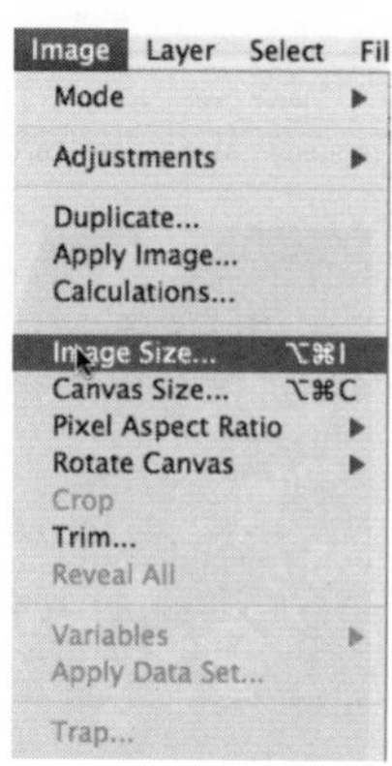

FIGURE 8.2
The Photoshop Image Size command is under the Image menu.

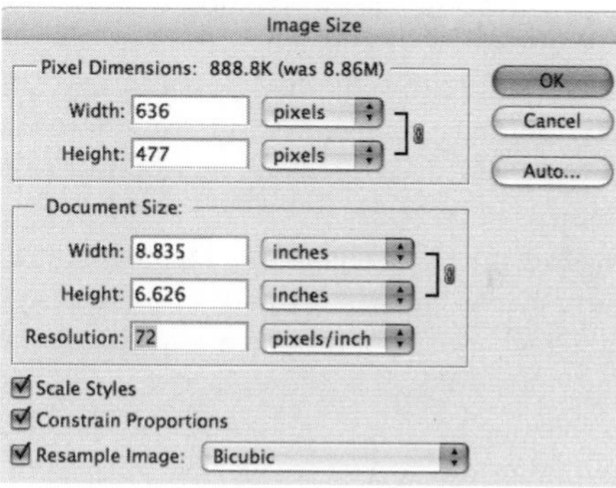

FIGURE 8.3
The Photoshop Image Size options let you resize overall pixel dimensions and the resolution in pixels/inch.

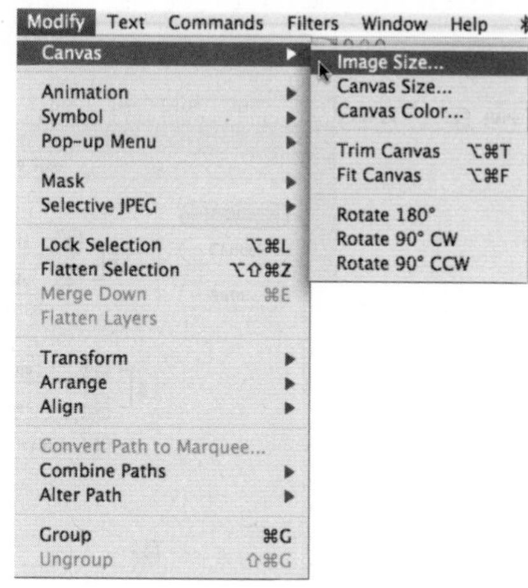

FIGURE 8.4
The Fireworks Image Size menu is under Modify ➢ Canvas ➢ Image Size.

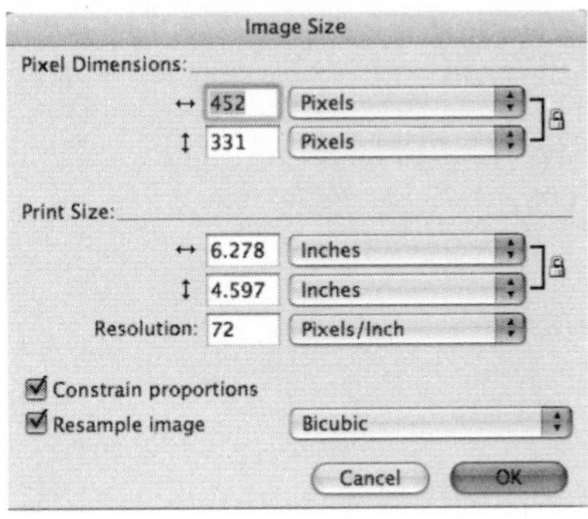

FIGURE 8.5
The Fireworks Image Size pop-up window works exactly like the one in Photoshop.

OPTIMIZING GIFS

Optimizing an image means finding a balance between quality and file size. Each type of imag format is optimized in a slightly different way. The goal is always to reduce the file size (and th download time) to the smallest possible size while still maintaining acceptable image quality.

To save an image in a web format in Photoshop, start with the File ➤ Save for Web menu com mand (Figure 8.6). This opens up an optimization window in Image Ready, the web optimizatio companion to Photoshop.

Photoshop opens a special Save for Web optimization palette that lets you see the image in eithe two or four views. Each view can be optimized individually for the best choice. In Figure 8.7, you se the right panel selected, optimized as a GIF containing 128 colors. You can see that for this image saving as a GIF with a 128-color selective palette greatly reduces the file size without affecting imag quality. Clicking Save at this point saves it as a GIF, or you can change the number of colors (fewe colors would mean an even smaller file but at some point would sacrifice accuracy), or see if you lik it better as a JPEG.

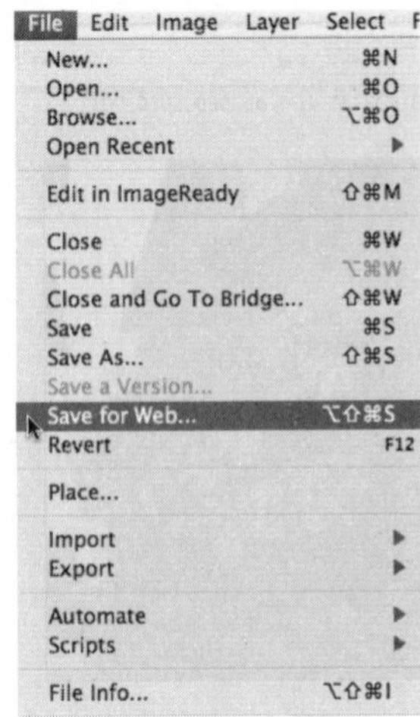

FIGURE 8.6
The Photoshop Save for Web command

Fireworks keeps the web optimization palette options right at the top of any image, as you see in Figure 8.8. Once you have a 2-Up or 4-Up view open in Fireworks, as in Figure 8.9, you can compare optimizations at various settings for GIF (or JPEG) to find the best options.

When optimizing a GIF, reduce the number of colors until you begin to lose quality, then back up to the number with no quality loss. The ideal is to reduce the image size to no larger than 10 to 20Kb.

FIGURE 8.7
The Photoshop Save for Web options with the 2-Up view selected. If you want more choices to compare, select the 4-Up tab to see more optimization options.

FIGURE 8.8
The Fireworks optimization options are always visible. Select either 2-Up or 4-Up to begin optimization.

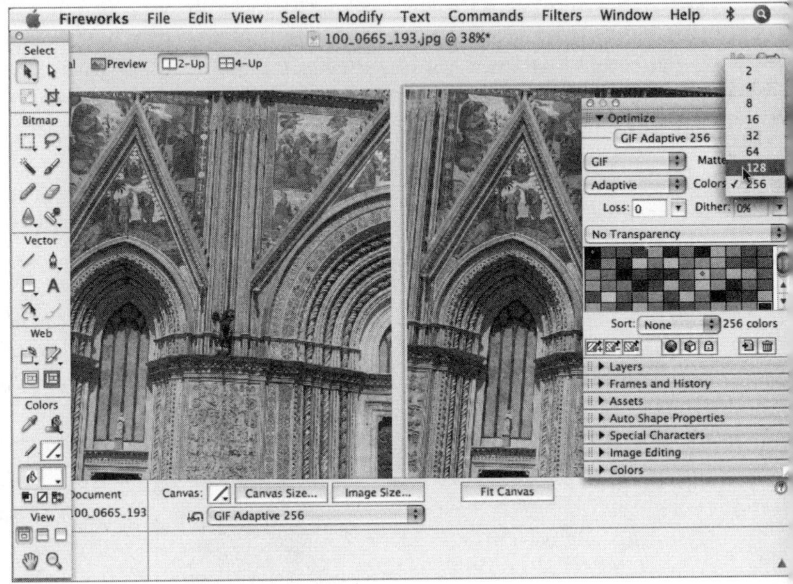

FIGURE 8.9
The Fireworks GIF optimization options are similar to those in Photoshop.

OPTIMIZING JPEGS

JPEGs are optimized by quality, not by number of colors.

In Photoshop (Figure 8.10), you once again begin with File ➢ Save for Web. On a 2-Up Save fo Web window, you view the options for JPEG. These options in Photoshop include a Low, Mediun or High quality setting and also a sliding scale for raising or lowering the quality of the JPEG in small increments.

In Fireworks (Figure 8.11), a 2-Up menu allows you to select JPEG with quality choices listed o a pull-down menu such as the JPEG – Better Quality you see displayed. There is also a sliding scal to allow small incremental adjustments in quality.

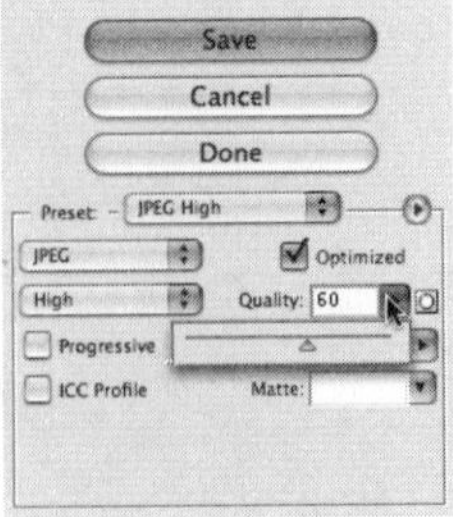

FIGURE 8.10
Photoshop's JPEG optimization choices

FIGURE 8.11
Fireworks' JPEG optimization choices

As you can see, both tools have a similar way of doing things. Some of the menu choices to get to what you want are slightly different, but the basic chores you want to do are similar. This applies to Jasc Paint Shop Pro as well, although the jobs are accomplished perhaps by slightly different names or with slightly different menu options.

Because of these similarities, I'm only going to show you screen shots from one tool (Fireworks) for the remainder of these graphics software tips. I trust that you realize that whichever tool you are using has similar options available somewhere in its menu choices.

MAKING BACKGROUND IMAGES

To serve as a background, an image needs to be inconspicuous so that text placed over it will be legible. There are several techniques you can use to tone down an image in a background. One is to adjust the image's hue and saturation.

In Figure 8.12, above the Fireworks Hue/Saturation palette, you see the results of my adjustments in the image (enabled by checking the Preview check box). A live preview of the change helps you make small adjustments until you are satisfied. I not only reduced the saturation by quite a bit, I also increased the lightness.

Another way to lighten an image so it can be used as a background is to reduce the opacity. To use the Opacity tool, select the layer holding the image and use the Opacity sliding scale to reduce the opacity. You see an example in Fireworks in Figure 8.13.

Transparency is represented by a checkerboard effect in image editing tools. As you reduce opacity, you increase transparency. The checkerboard effect you see in Figure 8.13 demonstrates that.

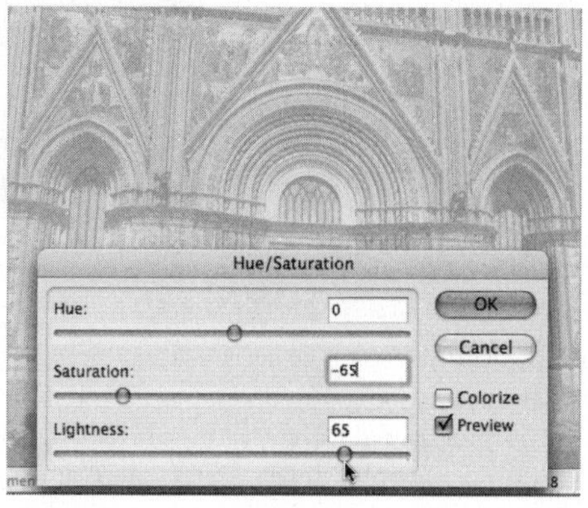

FIGURE 8.12
One way to lighten up a background image is with Hue/Saturation settings.

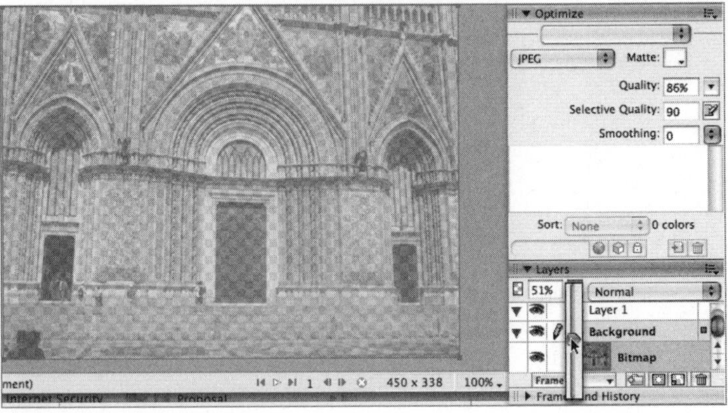

FIGURE 8.13
Reducing the opacity makes the image much less intense when it's used as a background. You don't want a background image to compete with the text elements that are in the foreground.

USING GRAPHICS SOFTWARE TO GET A COLOR CODE

Often you want to select colors from an image and build them into other page elements. Whole color schemes for backgrounds, link colors, heading colors, and such can be taken from an imag

Graphics software programs use an Eyedropper tool to select a color. When you hover over a color with the Eyedropper tool, you see information about the spot where you are hovering, inclu ing RGB values for the color; you can then incorporate this color code into CSS style rules for pag elements. In Figure 8.14, you see the color of a bit of the flowers registering in either the Photoshc Info panel or the Color panel as both decimal RGB values and the hexadecimal #FBEDFE.

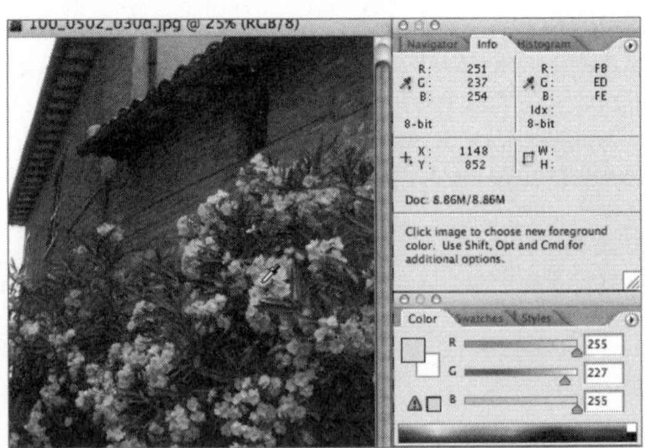

FIGURE 8.14
The Eyedropper tool selects a color. You can find the code for the color in the Info panel as separate RGB values, in this case #FBEDFE.

SELECTING PNG TRANSPARENT COLORS

Create a file in Photoshop and it's saved as a PSD (Photoshop document). Create a file in Firewor and it's saved as a PNG. The PNG format is the native format for Fireworks. Either program wor with PNG alpha transparency. Here's how to select different colors to be transparent in Firewor

With a PNG file open, select either 2-Up or 4-Up. In the optimize panel, set the file to PNG 8 ar set the transparency to Alpha Transparency (Figure 8.15).

The Color Table will show the colors in the image. At the lower left of the color table, there a three eyedropper icons. One has a plus sign, one a minus sign, and one has an equal sign. Use o of these three eyedroppers to either add colors to the transparency or remove them. The eyedropper with the equal sign selects transparent colors (Figure 8.16).

Transparency is used in the following exercises to allow a background color to show through headings created with text. But there are more uses of transparency. It can create effects where one object or image is allowed to partially shine through another image that sits atop it. Partially transparent images can slide over each other to create seamless transitions between one image and the next. Don't limit yourself to thinking about transparency only with text.

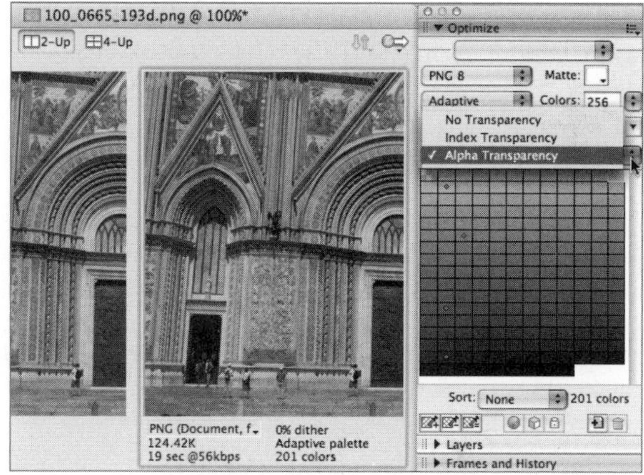

FIGURE 8.15
In Fireworks, with the Optimize file format set to PNG 8, use the transparency options to select Alpha Transparency.

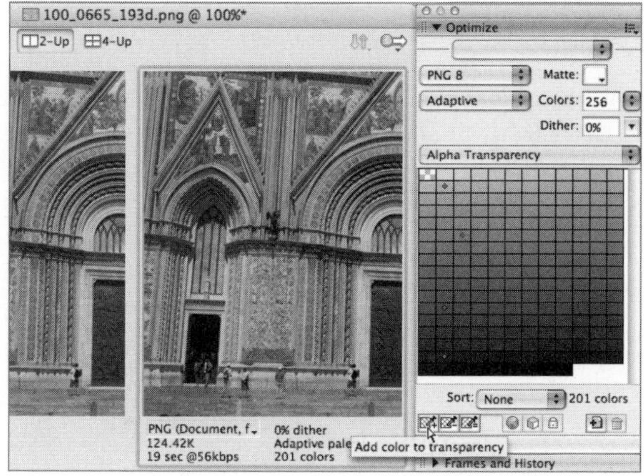

FIGURE 8.16
In Fireworks, three eyedropper icons below the color table can be used to add or remove colors from the alpha transparency color selections.

XHTML: Add Images to a Page

To begin learning how to incorporate images into your HTML pages, start by copying the entire `img_exercises` folder from the Chapter 8 folder on the CD to your computer. This folder includes several HTML files, a CSS file, and a subfolder with some images.

The *img* Element

For your own images, you need to know the size of each graphic in pixels. If you have image editing software, you can open an image in that software to get the image size. If you don't yet have any graphics software, here's a trick that will work with Netscape, Mozilla, Firefox, or Safari browsers. Open the file `creek_sm.jpg` in one of the aforementioned browsers, as you see in Figure 8.17. You can jot down the image width and height shown in the browser title bar.

This image is 200 pixels in width and 109 pixels in height. Now, *that* is some information you can use.

The `img` element has several must-have attributes. The first is `src` (for source). A `src` attribute is a lot like an `href` attribute because it gives the path to the location of the image. Like `href`, the path used for the `src` attribute can be relative or absolute. If you are on one of the XHTML pages in `img_exercises` writing a `src` value for the `creek_sm.jpg` image in the `images` subfolder, the `img` element is

```
<img src="images/creek_sm.jpg" />
```

The `img` element is an empty element. As I explained in Chapter 1, an empty element is one that doesn't include any text to be displayed on screen. In the case of `img`, you don't need a second tag to close the element (the slash at the end of the `img` tag does the closing for you in XHTML).

That tag will get the image to display in the browser, but I strongly recommend you also include the optional `width` and `height` attributes, which help the browser render the page. If the browser knows how much width and height to allow on the page for images, it can render the text immediately instead of waiting for the images to download.

WIDTH AND HEIGHT AND EXCEPTIONS

You can set `width` and `height` for the `img` selector in a style sheet. That works well if a particular page element uses a series of images that are all the same size. An example is a nav bar with a series of buttons that share the same dimensions. A selector in the CSS for `#navbar img` could be used to set the image size on all of them. That would reduce the file size of the XHTML document and still instruct the browser about the amount of room to allot for the images while rendering the page. You'll set size in the XHTML in these exercises, but keep in mind that image size can be set in a style sheet.

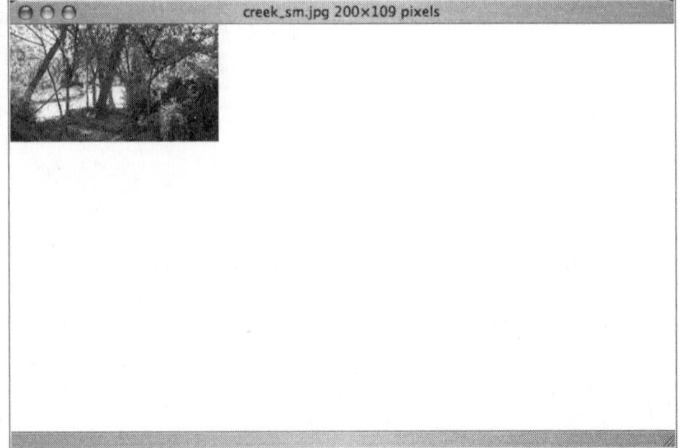

FIGURE 8.17
Certain browsers display the pixel size of the image in the title bar.

With the width and height added, the img element looks like this:

```
<img src="images/creek_sm.jpg" width="200" height="109" />
```

You aren't finished yet. The final requirement is alt (for alternative) text. This is the single most important thing you need to ensure accessible information, as well. The alt text provides the textual message that the image is trying to portray. If the user is unable to see the image, the alt text will display. The use and purpose of the image is explained by the alt text.

There are a number of reasons why a user of your page might not see an image. There might be a network connection problem. The user might prefer to surf with images not showing because of slow dial-up service. The user might have a browser that doesn't display images. The alt text is an aid in such cases.

CONFUSED ABOUT TOOL TIPS?

If you have never used any browser but Internet Explorer on Windows, you may think that the primary purpose of alt text is to display as a tool tip when you mouse over an image. This is not what alt text is supposed to do, and it doesn't appear as a tool tip in other browsers. Alt text is supposed to be visible when the image is *not* visible—that is, it is an alternative to the image.

If you want a tool tip to appear, use a title attribute in the img element.

For this image, suitable alt text might be something like "See the creek."

```
<img src="images/creek_sm.jpg" width="200" height="109" alt="See the creek" />
```

Figure 8.18 shows how the preceding img element would display in the Firefox browser if the image didn't appear. Note that different alt text is used in the screen capture from that in the preceding example. The browser treatment is the same, no matter what the alt text might be. In some browsers, a rectangle the size of the actual image is shown with the alt text, rather than a rectangular outline matching the size of the alt text.

If the img element is used as a button, the alt text should match the button text. In other words, if the button says Home, the alt text should say Home, too. When an image used as a link does not display, the alt text is clickable. So if the Home button wasn't visible, the visitor could still navigate by reading and clicking on the alt text.

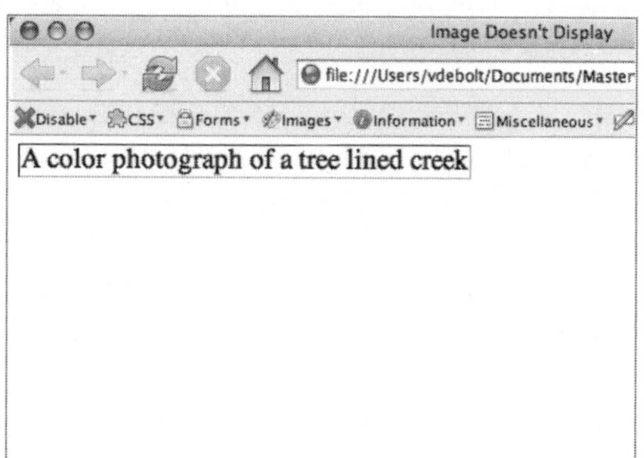

FIGURE 8.18
The alt text appears if the image does not.

The `img` element as you have it in the last example has all the necessities: `src` and `alt`, whi are both required, and `width`, `height`, which is not required but is needed in either the XHTM or the CSS.

If an image conveys no content, then the `alt` text should not convey content either; it shou be coded as `alt=""`. Don't write descriptive `alt` text for an image that is merely descriptive. there's no meaningful content associated with the image, don't use anything between the quo tion marks.

There are other attributes allowed in XHTML transitional for an `img` element: `name`, `id`, `tit` `longdesc`, `border`, `hspace`, `vspace`, `usemap`, and `ismap`. You don't need to worry about the na attribute because you would use `id` instead if a unique identifier were needed for the image. You do need to worry about `border`, `hspace`, and `vspace` because those are handled better with CSS. `usem` and `ismap` relate to image maps, and you are not going to make an image map in these exercises.

That leaves `longdesc` and `title`.

EQUIVALENT VS. DESCRIPTIVE

Images can contain important content, link to other areas of a site, or create visual enhancements that provide no content. In the first two cases, equivalent `alt` text is required. Equivalent text communicates the purpose of the graphic rather than its appearance. Here's how the W3C defines equivalent text:

> "Content is 'equivalent' to other content when both fulfill essentially the same function or purpose upon presentation to the user.... The equivalent must fulfill essentially the same function for the person with a disability... as the primary content does for the person without any disability. For example, the text 'The Full Moon' might convey the same information as an image of a full moon when presented to users. Note that equivalent information focuses on fulfilling the same function. If the image is part of a link and understanding the image is crucial to guessing the link target, an equivalent must also give users an idea of the link target."

The *longdesc* Attribute

Complex images such as charts and graphs often need a `longdesc` (for long description) attribu If the image contains informational content that would make the page meaningless if the imag were not seen, then `longdesc` is essential. The `longdesc` attribute points to a separate HTML f that gives a detailed description of the content of the image. It looks something like this:

```
<img src="images/chart.jpg" height="400" width="400" alt="monthly sales figures
longdesc="sales.html" />
```

Browser support for `longdesc` is still somewhat problematic. Many web page designers us workaround that involves putting a D after the element, which is made into a link to the long description. This practice is understood by people who need the long description information. With a `longdesc` D indicator added to the preceding snippet, you get this:

```
<img src="images/chart.jpg" height="400" width="400" alt="monthly sales figures
longdesc="sales.html" /><a href="sales.html">[D]</a>
```

For the images you will use in `img_exercises`, `alt` text is adequate; there will be no need for `longdesc`.

The *title* Attribute

The `title` attribute can be used with `img` elements. All browsers show the text of a `title` attribute to all users if the element is hovered over; most browsers show it as a tool tip. The `title` attribute can include further description of an image or a link and often gives accessibility hints such as key combinations for access keys or tab index numbers or points to the location of long description (`longdesc`) files.

Again, there is no need for `title` attributes on the images in this chapter.

The Image Stockpile

Figure 8.19 shows the contents of the `images` subfolder in the `img_exercises` folder.

There are five button images that will be used in the basic nav bars. There are also five main images saved at three different sizes each: `lg` (large), `sm` (small), and `tn` (thumbnail). There is a banner and a heading graphic. As I explained earlier, the two PNG files are examples for you but won't be used in an exercise.

The five images saved in various sizes are photos I took while out walking near my home, like all the other photos in this book. You are going to use them to create a small photo gallery. They aren't great art, but since I took them myself, we don't have to deal with copyright problems when using them, which makes them very attractive photos indeed.

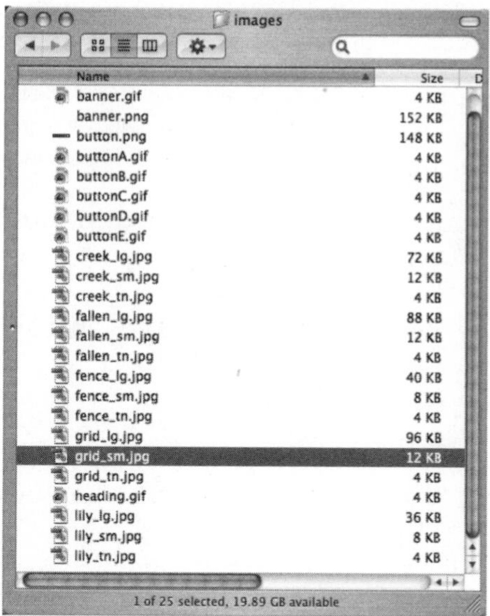

FIGURE 8.19
The images subfolder

INTELLECTUAL PROPERTY RIGHTS

Images on the Web are easy to copy and save. That does not mean that the image is copyright free and available for your use, however. Always check for copyright information and permission before using any graphic you obtain from a website.

Whether it's graphic art, music, or writing, the product of a person's creative endeavor is, in fact, a product. It has value. It's only free to take when the creator says it is.

Build Some Basic Button Nav Bars

Find the file `Ch8_navbars.html`. Open it in your text editor and in the browser. You will see that it is a partially completed page similar to Figure 8.20.

Look at the XHTML for the `horiz` division:

```
<div id="horiz">
  <h1>Insert images in horizontal line in this div</h1>
  <div><img src="images/buttonA.gif" width="100" height="18" alt="Button A" />
    <img src="images/buttonB.gif" alt="Button B" width="100" height="18" />
    more here... </div>
</div>
```

Each button is 100×18 pixels, and each is in the `images` subfolder. Notice that the `img` elements are separated only by a space. To finish the `horiz` nav bar, remove the words `more here` and insert `img` elements for `buttonC.gif`, `buttonD.gif`, and `buttonE.gif`. When you finish, the browser should look like Figure 8.21.

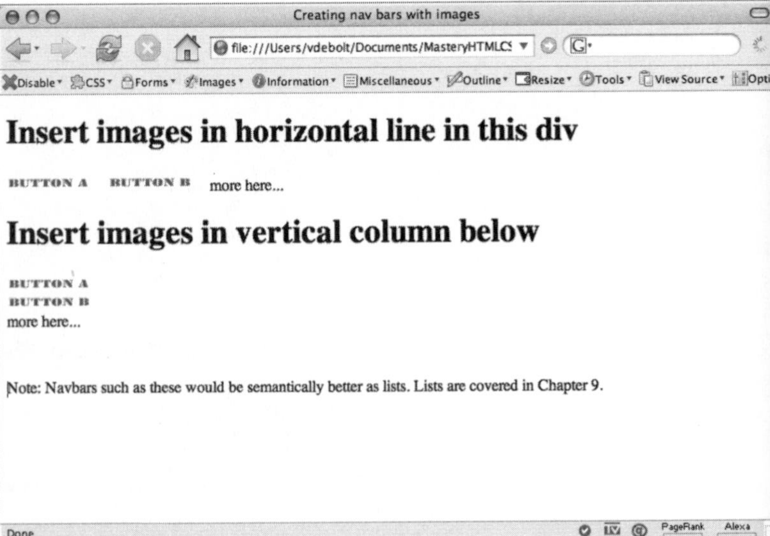

FIGURE 8.20 The beginning `Ch8_navbars.html` page

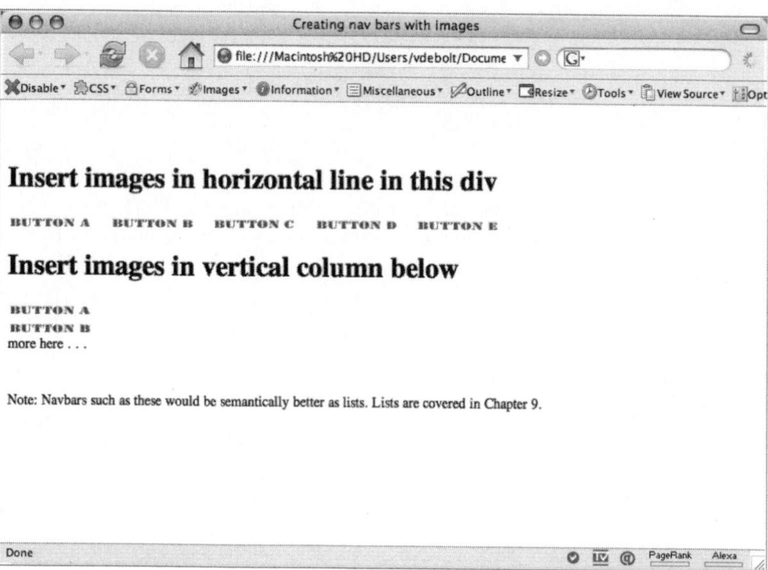

FIGURE 8.21 Completed `horiz` nav bar

The completed `div` with the `img` elements in it is

```
<div>
  <img src="images/buttonA.gif" alt="Button A" width="100" height="18" />
  <img src="images/buttonB.gif" alt="Button B" width="100" height="18" />
  <img src="images/buttonC.gif" alt="button C" width="100" height="18" />
  <img src="images/buttonD.gif" alt="button D" width="100" height="18" />
  <img src="images/buttonE.gif" alt="button E" width="100" height="18" />
</div>
```

With no styles attached to provide a set width for this nav bar, the images will wrap just like words in a line of text if the user has a very narrow browser viewport, as shown in Figure 8.22. This makes the point, once again, that an image is an inline element. When discussing `float` in Chapter 5, you moved images in and out of a paragraph, both with and without `float` to see how images behaved with other inline elements, namely words in a paragraph. Here the images behave just like a line of words strung across the page.

A style for the selector `#horiz` specifying a width for the `div` of 525px would prevent the images from wrapping. With five images, each 100 pixels in width, and a space between each image, 525px is an adequate width to hold the nav bar and prevent wrapping.

Of course, the whole notion of a button means that the image serves as a link. There are five HTML files in the folder that you can link to, or you can link these buttons to external sites such as Google. Here is an example of the buttons linked to the files in the `img_exercises` folder:

```
<div>
  <a href="fallen.html"><img src="images/buttonA.gif" alt="Button A"
  width="100" height="18" /></a>
  <a href="fence.html"><img src="images/buttonB.gif" alt="Button B" width="100"
height="18" /></a>
  <a href="grid.html"><img src="images/buttonC.gif" alt="button C" width="100"
```

```
    height="18" /></a>
    <a href="index.html"><img src="images/buttonD.gif"
    alt="button D" width="100" height="18" /></a>
    <a href="lily.html"><img src="images/buttonE.gif" alt="button E" width="100"
  height="18" /></a>
  </div>
```

You've succeeded in getting some images (and hyperlinks) on a page, but this nav bar leaves a to be desired (Figure 8.23). There's no separator between the hyperlinks—a vertical bar or some oth character—to interrupt the inline flow of `alt` text that would be announced like a sentence by an au screen reader. And, of course, you have the "newbie curse," the default blue border around an ima used as a hyperlink. Using a list to separate each of the menu items semantically would make the more accessible. You'll learn how to do that in Chapter 9.

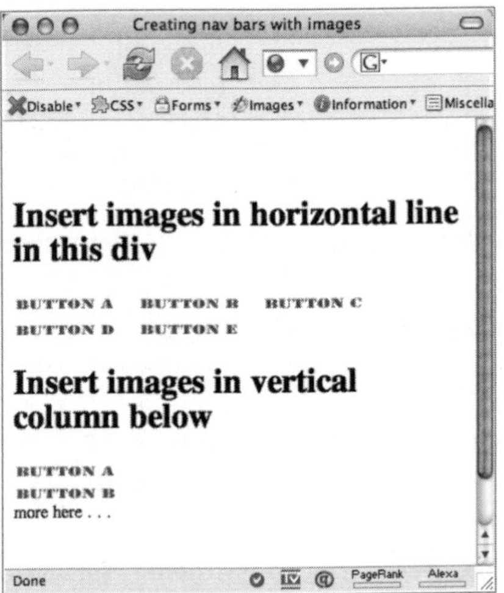

FIGURE 8.22
The images wrap just like a line of text if the window is resized.

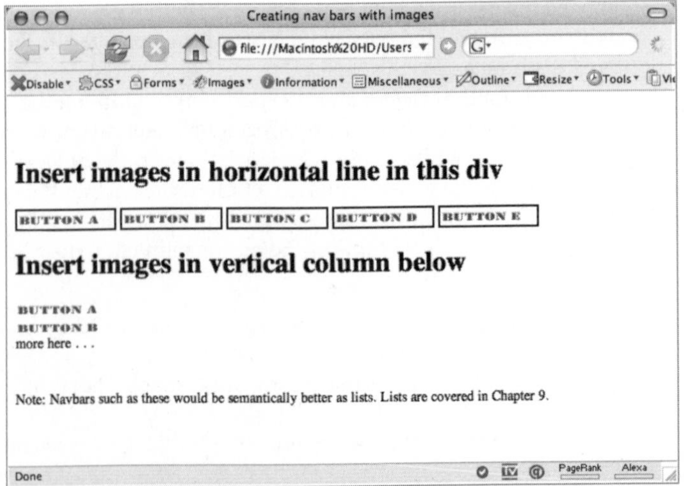

FIGURE 8.23
With no styles to remove the default blue border, these images are clearly hyperlinks.

Turn your attention to the `<div id="vert">` element. It uses the same buttons but this time in a vertical arrangement. The markup is the same as in the horizontal nav bar, except that instead of a single space between buttons, there is a `<br />` tag after each button image, which moves the next button down a line.

For this vertical arrangement, each image could also be in its own `div` or paragraph instead of using a `br` to move down a line. Again, stay tuned for Chapter 9, because a list for a vertical nav bar would be the best option.

```
<div id="vert">
  <h2>Insert images in vertical column below</h2>
  <div>
  <img src="images/buttonA.gif" alt="Button A" width="100" height="18" /><br />
  <img src="images/buttonB.gif" alt="Button B" width="100" height="18" /><br />
  more here...
  </div>
</div>
```

Add the remaining images where it says `more here`. You should see a page like Figure 8.24 in the browser.

Before adding the a elements to the vertical display, the new XHTML is

```
<div>
  <img src="images/buttonA.gif" alt="Button A" width="100" height="18" /><br />
  <img src="images/buttonB.gif" alt="Button B" width="100" height="18" /><br />
  <img src="images/buttonC.gif" alt="button C" width="100" height="18" /><br />
  <img src="images/buttonD.gif" alt="button D" width="100" height="18" /><br />
  <img src="images/buttonE.gif" alt="button E" width="100" height="18" />
</div>
```

Add links to these button images in the same manner that you did for the horizontal nav bar. Use files from the `img_exercises` or absolute links of your own choosing.

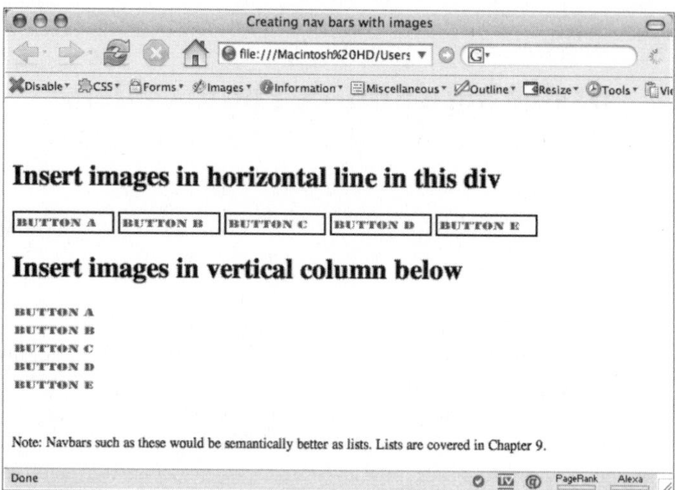

FIGURE 8.24
The images for the vertical nav bar are completed but are not yet hyperlinks.

These simple graphic nav bars illustrate two ways in which images can be strung together ir a navigation structure. Generally when you create a graphic as a button for a hyperlink, you crea different buttons for different hyperlink *pseudo states* (so called because they don't exist in the XHTML but are created based on user interaction). You might have a slightly different looking graphic for the `a:hover` state, another for the `a:visited` state, and so on. Rules in the CSS wou change the button image at the appropriate time. With completely different graphics for each pseudo state, one of the graphics could be designed to indicate the current page.

You might produce three or four versions of the Home button and three or four versions of eve other button. The number of specific graphic images you create, organize, store, and upload to g a graphic nav bar to function properly grows quickly. I don't recommend this as the best way to c ate a nav bar, so I'm not going to explain the various steps involved in doing this. You know enou about adding images to a page and styling the pseudo states to do it yourself if you have the ne

This section has given you some good practice getting images on a page and making them ser as buttons. You will benefit from learning several more ways to use images.

Tie Background Images to Hyperlink Pseudo States

Any element can have a background image, including text hyperlinks like those you learned abc in Chapter 7.

Background images are not page content; they are presentational features created in a style she But background images can be used with text hyperlinks and the various pseudo states to creat something that looks and acts like a graphic button element inserted on a page.

The XHTML merely needs a link, for example:

```
<a href="index.html">Home</a>
```

The CSS rules set different background images for the different pseudo states of that hyperli You did something similar to this in Chapter 7, so I won't go into details except to point out tha is another way to create horizontal or vertical nav bars using images.

The distinction to keep in mind when using images this way is that there is no `alt` text or a thing else related to the image on the page when it's a CSS background image. Of course, in the ca of a text link like the preceding example, `alt` text is unnecessary.

Designing a Simple Photo Gallery

You will use these pages to create a small photo gallery:

```
creek.html
fallen.html
fence.html
grid.html
lily.html
```

Notice the similarity of the HTML page names to the image names. That's a clue as to whic image goes with which page!

Some of the page basics have been prepared in advance for you. Open `creek.html` in your te editor and in the browser (Figure 8.25). You will add a number of images to the page, used in v ious ways, to get extensive practice working with images.

Notice that this page uses an imported style sheet, `layout.css`:

```
<style type="text/css">

@import url(layout.css);

</style>
```

Look at `layout.css` (Listing 8.1). It contains four rules to lay out the page and set some body properties. There isn't yet a rule for the body background color, so depending on your browser's default background color setting, you may see a different color from the white in Figure 8.25.

FIGURE 8.25
The beginning `creek.html` page

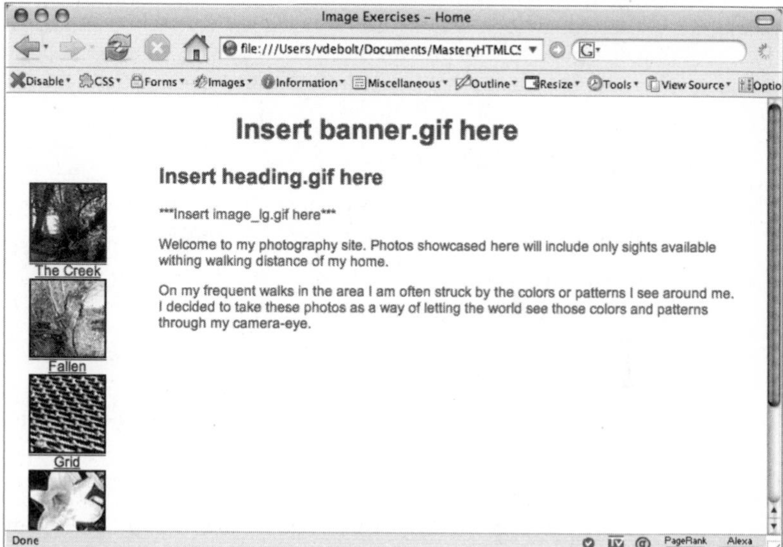

LISTING 8.1: *layout.css*

```
#navbar {
  float: left;
  width: 15%;
  top: 20px;
  position: relative;
  text-align: center;
}
#content {

  margin-left: 20%;
}
body {
```

```
    font: 100.01% Arial, Helvetica, sans-serif;
    color: #369;
    width: 95%;
  }
  #banner {
    text-align: center;
  }
```

You will create a link to a new style sheet and write new styles affecting the images as you procee

The pages also contain a working nav bar using the thumbnail-sized images. This nav bar is co structed in the same way as the one you built earlier using `buttonA.gif`, `buttonB.gif`, and so on Under each thumbnail image there is also a text link. If an image or icon is not perfectly clear in mea ing, it is good idea to provide a text equivalent as well. Look at the rules for the selector `#navbar` i `layout.css` to see what CSS rules are already determining the way the nav bar displays.

Adding a Banner

You'll use some transparent GIF images for the headings. In the `creek.html` page, find this in th XHTML:

```
<div id="banner">
  <h1>Insert banner.gif here</h1>
</div>
```

Replace the words "Insert banner.gif here" with an `img` element for `banner.gif` found in the `images` folder. Be sure to find out the width and height of this image.

The changed banner element should be:

```
<div id="banner">
<h1><img src="images/banner.gif" alt="Image Exercises" width="642" height="40" /
></h1>
</div>
```

With `banner.gif` in place, the page should look like Figure 8.26. Notice that the banner imag is centered.

If you replace only the text with the `img` element, the image is nested inside an `h1` element, ma ing this graphic into the logical equivalent of the most important heading on the page.

STRETCH YOURSELF

Feel free to use one of the image replacement techniques from Chapter 4 for the banner and heading graphics in this chapter. These are transparent GIFs, so the Gilder/Levin method isn't the best choice in this situation.

FIGURE 8.26
The graphic in the banner division

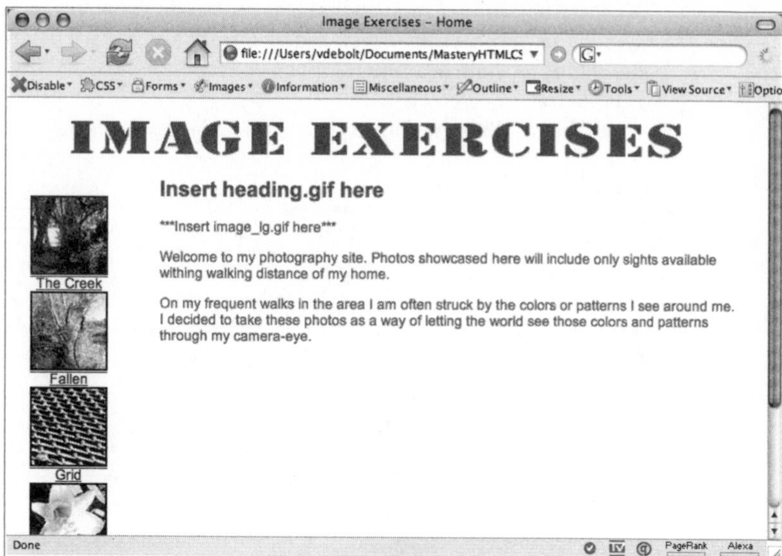

Adding Other Headings

Look farther down the page and find this:

```
<div id="content">
  <h2>Insert heading.gif here</h2>
```

Remove the words in the h2 element and replace them with an img element for heading.gif. The new code is:

```
<div id="content">
<h2><img src="images/heading.gif" alt="same words as heading" width="156"
height="20" /></h2>
```

GETTING GRAPHIC

If a heading uses a font commonly found on most users' Internet-capable devices, there is no reason to create a graphic representing the heading. When an unusual font is wanted—such as this one called Stencil—a graphic may be the only way to ensure its appearance. The file heading.gif is 4K in size—not huge, but using graphics to create text can add up quickly. Using graphics for text also creates a maintenance issue, since each change requires time in a graphics program and new image uploads to the server.

Graphic text can't be resized. However, one of the image replacement techniques referred to briefly in Chapter 4, Scalable Inman Flash Replacement (sIFR), does use scalable images. Information is available here:

```
www.mikeindustries.com/sifr/
```

The `alt` text should reflect whatever the heading actually says. Like the `buttonA`, `buttonB` graphics, this graphic can be replaced by a graphic of a word that relates to the page content. On th page, an appropriate heading might be A Tree-Lined Creek. The `alt` text should be the same words: "a tree-lined creek."

With the heading graphic in place, the page should appear in the browser like Figure 8.27.

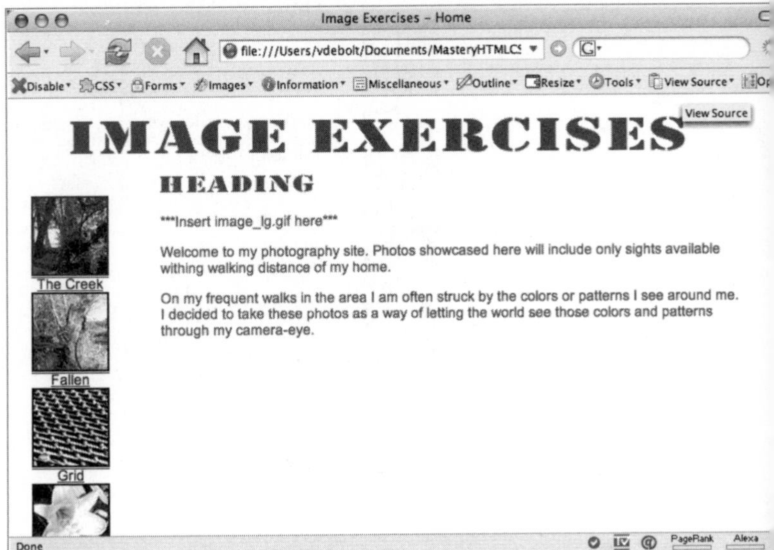

FIGURE 8.27
With a graphic heading in the h2 element, the page appears like this.

Inserting a Photo in Your Gallery

You are ready to add a large photo to the page. You will be replacing this text on the page with image element:

```
***Insert image_lg.gif here***
```

On the page `creek.html`, the large image you want is `creek_lg.jpg`.

The large images are all 600px in width, but the height varies. Check each one for height befo writing the `width` and `height` attributes for each `img` element.

You don't want the image to be part of the paragraph following it. Insert it before the `p` eleme The `img` element for the `creek_lg.jpg` is:

```
<img src="images/creek_lg.jpg" alt="A tree-lined area of Gilleland Creek"
width="600" height="328" />
```

Once you refresh, the browser will look like Figure 8.28.

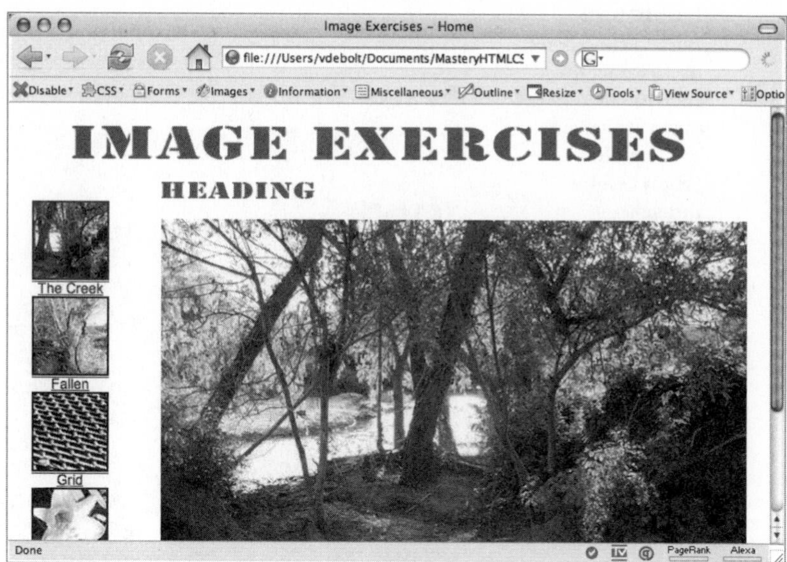

FIGURE 8.28
The large image that is the focal point of the page is added.

Transparent GIFs

Earlier in the chapter, I promised to show how to use images that have transparency. Here's where I do that:

1. Open a blank text document and save it in the `img_exercises` folder as `ch8.css`.
2. Link `creek.html` to the new style sheet by adding this tag within the `head` element:

```
<link href="ch8.css" rel="stylesheet" type="text/css" media="screen" />
```

3. The first style will be a background color for the body. You can use any color you want. This is for yellow:

```
body {
  background: #FF9;
}
```

4. Save everything and refresh the browser (Figure 8.29): The two transparent GIFs, `banner.gif` and `heading.gif`, allow the yellow background to shine through between the letters.

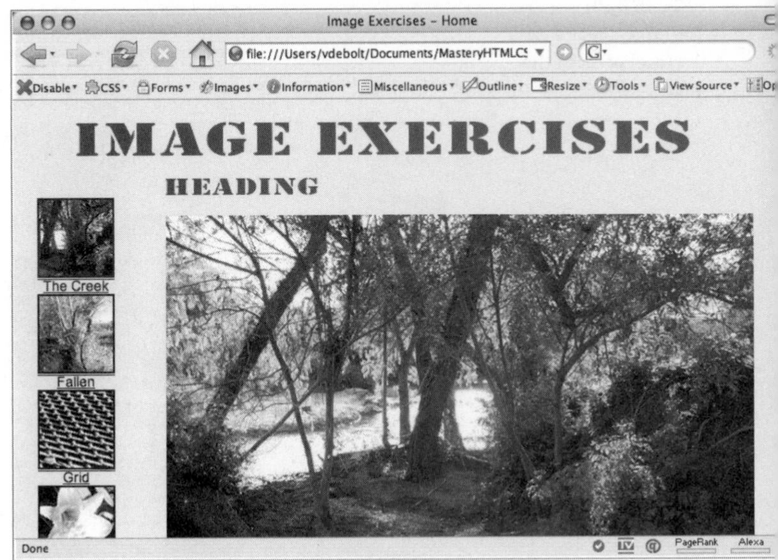

FIGURE 8.29
With a yellow body background, the transparent graphics in the banner and heading allow the yellow to shine through.

5. If you didn't already, try a darker color, like this dark green:

```
body {
  background: #330;
}
```

In the browser you see the page shown in Figure 8.30.

But something is amiss in Figure 8.30. The background color does shine through, but few white pixels appear in what is called a halo (or pixilation or jaggies) around the lett of the transparent GIF. They were there on the yellow background too but weren't as noticeable.

Here's why. When I made these transparent GIFs in Fireworks, I selected white as the *matte color* (Figures 8.31 and 8.32). That was because I intended these transparent graph to end up on a white background. If I had intended to use #330 as the page backgroun color, I would have made the matte color #330, too. Choosing a matte color for a GIF i needed, because it creates a smooth (rather than jagged) transition between the color a the transparency. In PNG alpha transparency, the pixels around the edge of an image object are partially transparent, so the choice of a matte color isn't necessary.

6. Get rid of those ugly, jagged halo effects by changing the body style once again:

```
body {
  background: #FFF;
}
```

Ahh, white. No jaggies.

The moral of this story is that even when you use transparency, you have to have some idea of your color scheme in advance when using GIFs. If you completely change your mind after the image is finished, you may have to go back into your graphics software and change the matte color.

FIGURE 8.30
A white "halo" shows around the letters when the dark background shows through the transparent GIF.

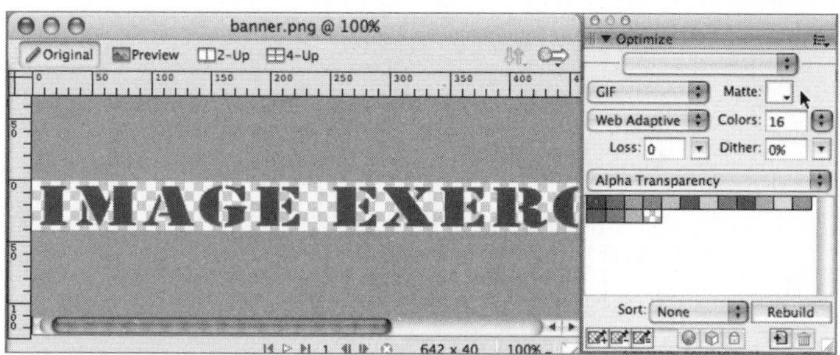

FIGURE 8.31
In Fireworks, select a matte color for the transparent GIF. The matte color should be the same or close to the color you intend to have shine through the transparent GIF to avoid the pixilated halo effect.

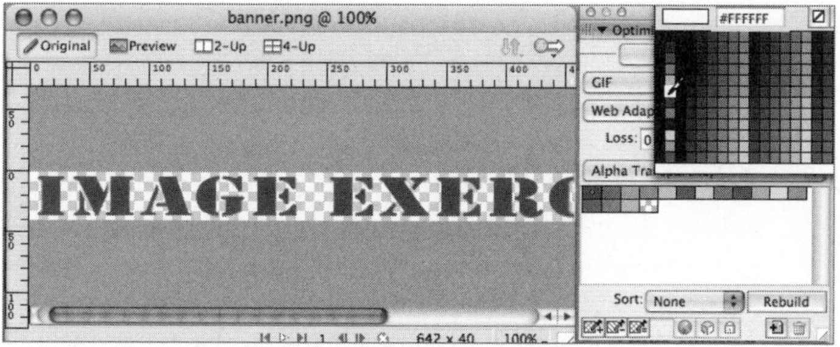

FIGURE 8.32
In Fireworks, selecting the Matte menu pops up a color box to use when choosing a matte color.

A Complete Site

You have some work to do before you can make any more progress on the ch8.css style rules. Yo need to insert the images into the other four pages in the same way that you just did for creek.htm

Repeat these steps on each page:

1. Within <div id="banner">, replace

```
<h1>Insert banner.gif here</h1>
```

with

```
<h1><img src="images/banner.gif" alt="Image Exercises" width="642" height="40
/></h1>
```

2. Replace

```
<h2>Insert heading.gif here</h2>
```

with

```
<h2><img src="images/heading.gif" alt="same words as heading" width="156"
height="20" /></h2>
```

3. Replace the large image on every page. The large image is different for every page:
   - fallen.html gets fallen_lg.jpg
   - fence.html gets fence_lg.jpg
   - grid.html gets grid_lg.jpg
   - lily.html gets lily_lg.jpg

Don't stop until every page has a banner, a heading, and a large image. Then take a moment t click around through the pages and enjoy your work.

GROWTH SPURT

Our little site has only five images. With more images, you might have a whole page of thumbnails as your main page. Each thumbnail is linked, as in the example, to a page with more information about the image and a larger version of the image.

CSS: Dress It Up

Use the ch8.css style sheet you made earlier for all the new styles. You've probably noticed the default blue line around the linked thumbnail images. If you change the default colors for the a el ments, the image border reflects that color change. As you learned earlier, the way to eliminate tha border is write a style to eliminate the border across the whole site.

The thumbnail images are in this division:

```
<div id="navbar">
<a href="creek.html"><img src="images/creek_tn.jpg" alt="Creek" width="75"
  height="75" /><br />
Creek</a><br />
```

The CSS selector you need is `#navbar img`. Set a value of `none` for the `border` property of that selector. Add this rule to `ch8.css`:

```
#navbar img {
  border: none;
}
```

Poof, just like that the borders are gone for any `img` element within the `navbar` section, as shown in Figure 8.33.

Sometimes you *want* borders. You could use a border around the large image like a frame for the great photographic art.

The selector `#content img` selects every image in the `content` division: not what you want. There's nothing structural in the XHTML that will let you distinguish between the image in the heading and the large photo that is the topic of the page.

You need some class: apply it to the `img` you want to have a border. Remember that a class name in a style sheet must be preceded by a period. Call the class `.photo`. Now the border will only be applied to elements in the class `photo`. The new rule is

```
.photo {
  border: 6px ridge #369;
}
```

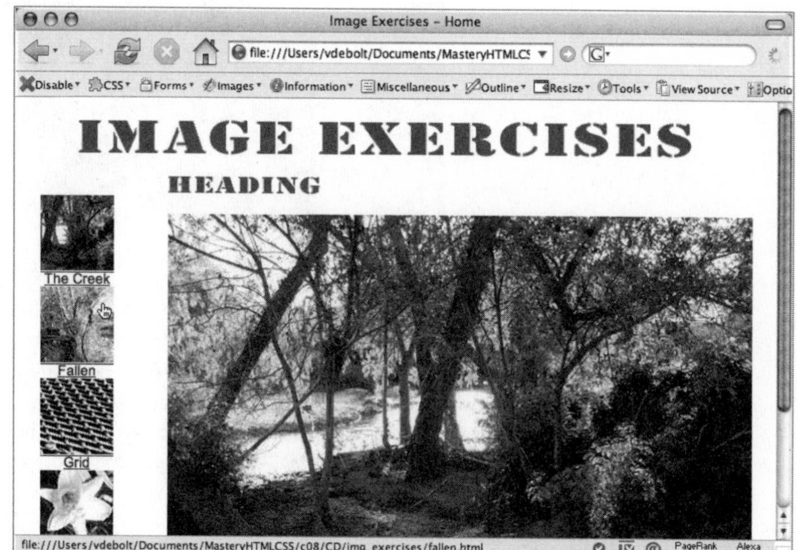

FIGURE 8.33
No more borders on the image, although they are still clickable. You still see underlines on the images and text links.

Next go into the XHTML and add the class attribute to the `img` element, like this:

```
<img src="images/creek_lg.jpg" alt="Creek" width="600" height="328"
  class="photo" />
```

The results in the browser look similar to Figure 8.34.

If you want this effect on every large photo page, you have to add the `class` attribute to ea `img` element.

> **OTHER BORDERS**
>
> Remember, the `border-style` values are `dotted`, `dashed`, `solid`, `double`, `groove`, `ridge`, `inset`, and `outset`. Play around with these to see if you can design a frame-like effect you like better than the one I suggested. The `border-width` can vary on each of the `top`, `right`, `bottom`, and `left` sides, as can the `color`, or even the `border-style`.

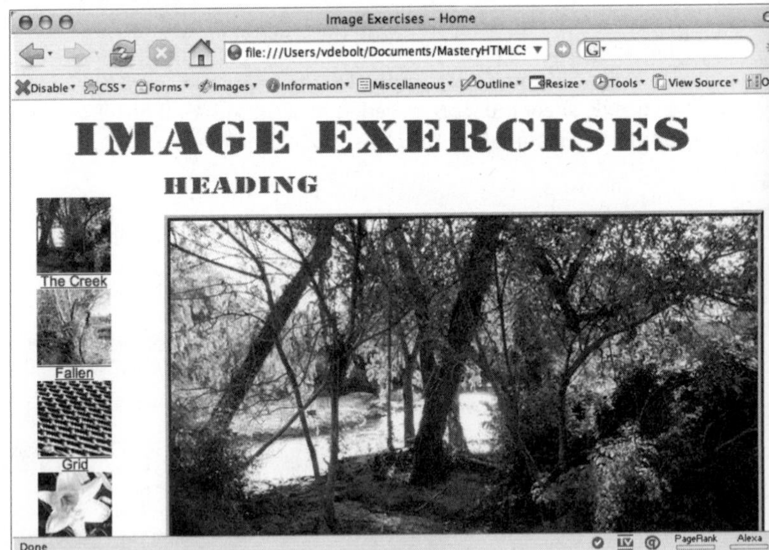

FIGURE 8.34 The image in the class `.photo` has a border that gives it a framed effect.

Link Color and Decoration

The nav bar link text would look better if it were not underlined and had some white space arou it. The font size could be reduced a bit, to 85 percent (or .85em). The blue color could also be chang to match the other blue on the page (#369). A different color on hover would be nice for the link t

Start with the `#navbar img` style you already have. (Remember that `text-align: center` w applied to the nav bar in `layout.css`.) Add some `margin-top` to the `img`. I think 8px looks goc but you can try other amounts. The changed style is

```
#navbar img {
  border: 0px;
  margin-top: 8px;
}
```

You can use a comma-separated group selector for all the pseudo states of the a selector, except `:hover`, like this:

```
#navbar a:link, #navbar a:visited, #navbar a:active {
  font-size: 85%;
  color: #369;
  text-decoration: none;
}
```

If you write a style after this one for the `a:hover` pseudo state, it will inherit the font-size and text-decoration rules. All you need is a new color value. With all these rules in place, the page looks similar to Figure 8.35.

```
#navbar a:hover {
  color: #C36;
}
```

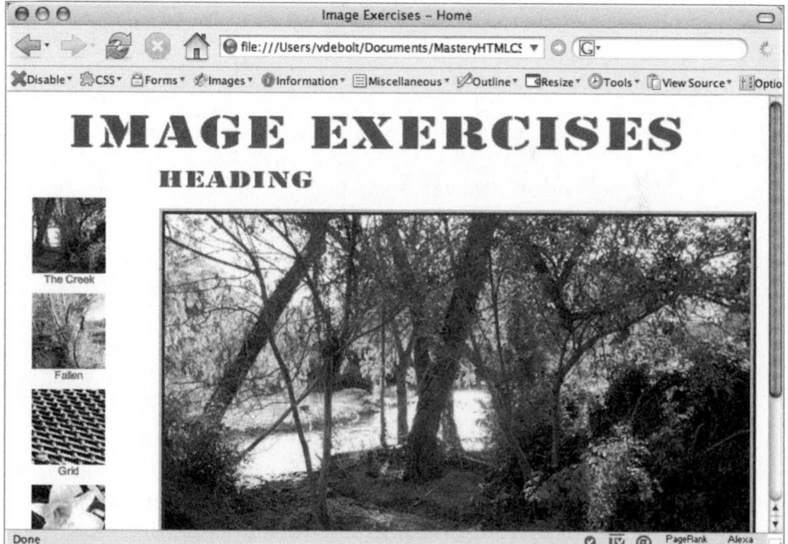

FIGURE 8.35
The nav bar styles are reflected.

Add a Pop-up

On a layout like this, there are some drawbacks to using pop-ups with the menu because it scrolls down the page vertically. But it would be a very nice feature if you had a large number of small thumbnails and you wanted to give viewers a somewhat larger view of the image to help them decide whether to click for the largest image.

Try it using the technique you learned in Chapter 7, except instead of inserting text in the `span` element in the hyperlinks, insert an `img` element.

In `img_exercises/images`, use the images with `sm` in the filename (for example, `creek_sm.jpg`) for the pop-up.

This is a three-step process.

1. Add span elements containing the appropriate `img` element to each link in the `navbar`. Here's the first one:

```
<a href="creek.html"><img src="images/creek_tn.jpg" alt="See the creek"
width="75" height="75" /><span><img src="images/creek_sm.jpg" /></span><br /
  The Creek</a><br />
```

2. Hide the images with this rule in the CSS:

```
#navbar a span {
   display: none;
}
```

3. Add this to make it work in IE:

```
#navbar a:hover {
   height: auto;
}
```

4. Show the pop-up on hover with this rule in the CSS:

```
#navbar a:hover span {
   display: block;
   position: absolute;
   z-index: 10;
   width: 200px;
   top: 10em;
   left: 60px;
}
```

See Figures 8.36 and 8.37. Some of the value choices, for example `left: 60px`, are strictly su gestions. Take some time to adapt this to your own liking.

As you scroll down the page and the pop-up image remains fixed in its absolute position, y see that a long vertical page could run into problems. There are ways to solve that problem. If y added a few more CSS hooks, perhaps an `id` for each image in the `navbar`, you could easily gi each pop-up a unique style and position on the page.

GALLERY RESOURCES

A lovely example of CSS pop-ups in an image gallery is Nathan Smith's hoverbox: `http:// host.sonspring.com/hoverbox`. He provides a tutorial on how he made it.

A second stunning example is the sliding photograph gallery at CSS Play: `www.cssplay.co.uk/menu/ gallery31.html`. This site gives you the CSS rules needed to make it work and grants permission for you to use the technique on your site.

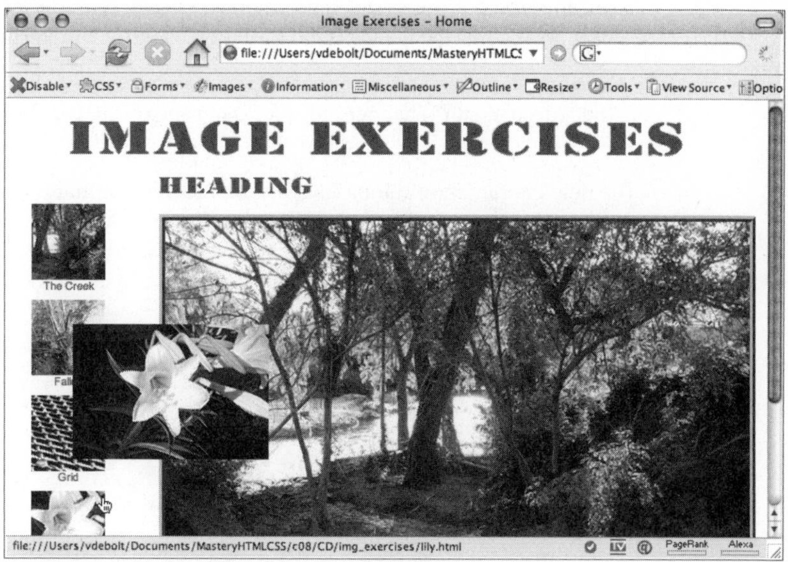

FIGURE 8.36
The small image of the lily pops up when the hyperlink for the lily page is hovered over.

FIGURE 8.37
The small image of the fence pops up in the same position the lily image did, pointing out one of the difficulties in using this presentation with a long vertical page.

Backgrounds

An image in the foreground can be placed over an image in the background. You'll use `banner_bg.jpg` in the `img_exercises/images` folder as a background for the banner. (The original Fireworks file, `banner_bg.png`, is there for your inspection, also.)

This image is 1200 pixels in width. At this size it should be wide enough for most monitors. It gives a fluid quality to the banner at that width because the image seems to grow or shrink as the browser window is resized.

To add this background, use the `#banner` selector, with declarations to set the background fc no-repeat and center the background both horizontally and vertically:

```
#banner {
  background: url(banner_bg.jpg) no-repeat center center;
}
```

The new banner should look like Figure 8.38. Notice that the transparency of the GIF used fo the banner allows the background image to shine through the transparent areas of the banner.

On the CD, you will find a file named `ch8_finish.css`. It is the completed style sheet for th Photo Gallery pages that you just completed. You can use it for reference or comparison.

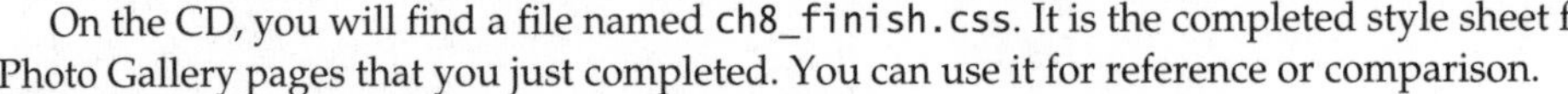

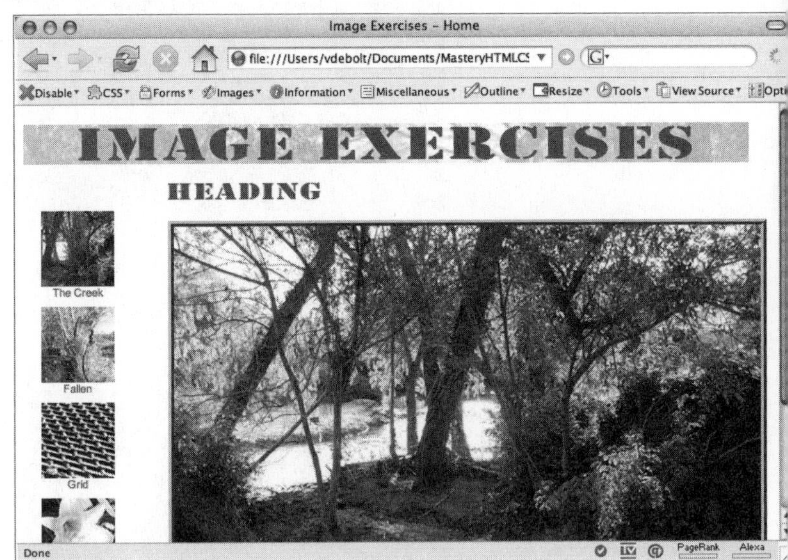

FIGURE 8.38 A graphic background centered behind the transparent GIF in the banner seems to expand or contract when the browser window is resized.

Size Matters

Throughout this chapter I have stressed the importance of figuring out the correct size in width an height of an image before writing the `img` tag. Generally, it is a good practice to match the actua width and height of the image to the width and height attributes you use in the XHTML, but the are exceptions.

You can use the `width` and `height` attributes of an `img` element to make an image any size yo want. Sometimes it is a good idea to change the visual display of an image using `width` and `heigh` values. Sometimes it is terrible idea.

Sizing Images via XHTML: The Good

Try changing width and height values for images. Open the page you haven't touched yet: `Ch8_smallimage.html`, as shown in Figure 8.39.

Note that there are a couple of embedded styles in the document head that create the `float: left` for these images. Each image is in a `div` with the class attribute `images`. The entire page is shown in Listing 8.2.

LISTING 8.2: The Beginning *Ch8_smallimage.html* Page

```
<!DOCTYPE html PUBLIC "-//W3C//DTD XHTML 1.0 Transitional//EN" "http://www.w3.org/
TR/xhtml1/DTD/xhtml1-transitional.dtd">
<html xmlns="http://www.w3.org/1999/xhtml">
<head>
<title>Image Exercises: Small Images</title>
<style type="text/css">
.images {
   clear: left;
   }
.images img {
   float: left;
   padding-right: 5px;
   padding-bottom: 5px;
}
</style>
</head>
<body>
<div id="banner">
   <h1><img src="images/banner.gif" alt="Image Exercises" width="642" height="40"
/>
 </h1>
</div>
<div class="images"><p><a href="images/creek_lg.jpg"><img src="images/creek_
sm.jpg" alt="See the creek" width="200" height="109" /></a>
  Tangled growth along the banks of Gilleland Creek create a pattern of light and
shadow.</p>
</div>
<div class="images">
  <p><img src="images/fallen_sm.jpg" alt="See the fallen tree" width="200"
height="130" /> Raging flood waters uprooted and knocked over a clump of shallow
rooted trees along the creek bed.</p>
</div>
<div class="images">
  <p>Add more images and text in structures like this. Link the sm image to the lg
image similar to the way the first one was done.</p>
</div>
</body>
</html>
```

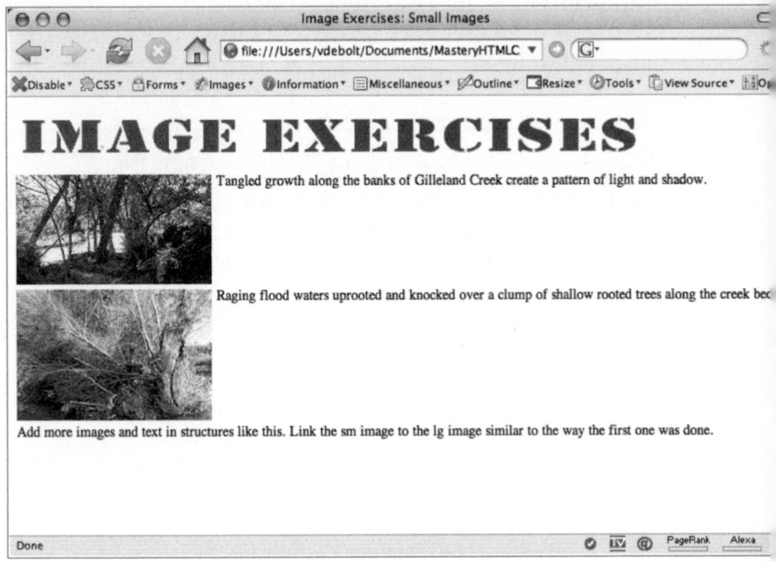

FIGURE 8.39
The beginning `Ch8_smallimage.html` page

You will resize an image in the XHTML using `bluebar.gif`. This GIF is 5×1 pixels and less th 1K in file size. It is a solid bit of blue (color #369) and will download almost instantly. You will ins it immediately under the `banner.gif`, but instead of using the real dimensions of `width="5"` a `height="1"`, use `width="642"` (to match the banner above it) and `height="2"`. The solid blue co will stretch to fit these dimensions (Figure 8.40).

This `bluebar.gif` is strictly for decoration. It adds nothing to the content of the page. Peop using screen readers or people surfing with images off don't need `alt` text for this image. Leave t `alt` attribute in the `img` element, but put nothing (not even a space) between the quotation mar for the value. This tells the user that the image is not part of the content and no `alt` text is need

The entire banner code is now:

```
<div id="banner">
  <img src="images/banner.gif" alt="Image Exercises" width="642"
    height="40" /><br />
  <img src="bluebar.gif" width="642" height="2" alt="" />
</div>
```

Often, decorative images such as this blue bar can be background images inserted in the sty sheet and don't have to be part of the XHTML at all. For example, you could add it to the #bann selector rule.

Enlarging graphics this way works fine for solid blocks of color.

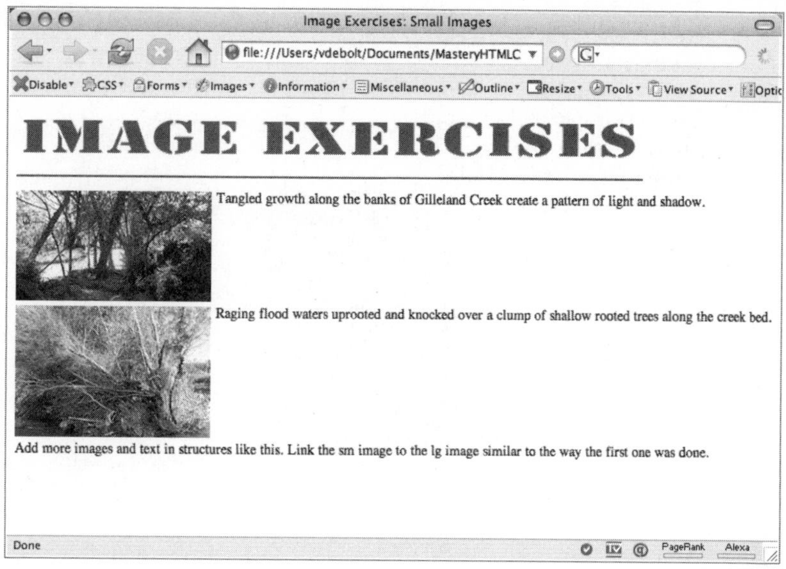

FIGURE 8.40
The tiny blue graphic creates a wide horizontal line by changing the actual image dimensions with width and height values in the XHTML.

Sizing Images via XHTML: The Bad

Unless you are actually trying to distort an image, any other kind of playing around with the true size of an image by changing `width` or `height` is probably a bad idea.

Find this in `Ch8_smallimages.html`:

```
<div class="images">
  <p><a href="images/creek_lg.jpg"><img src="images/creek_sm.jpg"
    alt="Creek" width="200" height="109" border="0" /></a>
```

Change the image size in the code to `width="400",height="125"`. As you can see in Figure 8.36, the browser displays the image in the size specified. But if you look closely at the image, it has a bad case of the jaggies (also called pixilation) and looks bad, bad, bad. Quick, change those values back to 200×109 (Figure 8.41). If you want a large version of an image, it is best to make it in Photoshop or some similar software so it will look its best.

As you might have guessed, this process can work to make images appear smaller as well. For example, the 72Kb image, `creek_lg.jpg`, could be inserted in the position on the page where `creek_sm.jpg` currently is. With the width and height values set to 200×109, the large image would look exactly like the small one on the page now, except for one important thing: the user will have waited through the download of a 72Kb image. The small image at 12Kb appears exactly the same but downloads much more quickly.

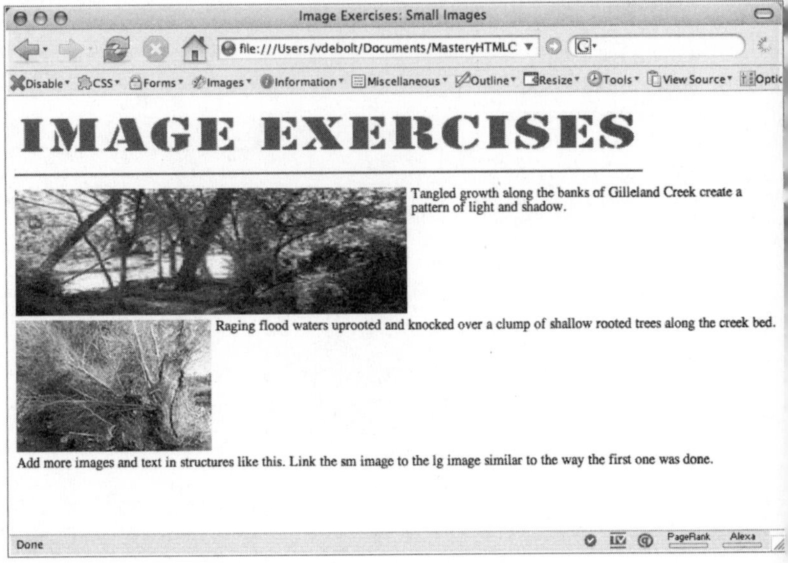

FIGURE 8.41 By changing the image measurement values in the XHTML, you can make it appear larger, but the image quality is very low.

Now you understand why there are three different-sized versions of each image in the image folder for this set of exercises. Except for the few instances just mentioned, it is best for quality and download time to match the real image size to the display size on the page. It takes a bit more time to prepare the images, but it pays off.

Linking Directly to Images

`Ch8_smallimage.html` is an example of another way to link to and display photos.

Here the small image is linked directly to the large image. When the user clicks the link, the image opens in the browser with no XHTML page holding it. Therefore, the web designer has no control over background colors or any other aspect of what the user sees. They simply see the image. There is no navigation on the image, so the user must use the Back button to come back to the XHTML page. You may have noticed that the first image, The Creek, is already linked to the large version as an example.

Displaying images in this simple fashion is fine for jobs such as quickly putting up photos from your nephew's birthday party so the other members of your family can see them. Sometimes a direct link to a high-resolution graphic is used to provide press or publicity images. This allows the user to download a print-quality image. For example, a direct link to a high-resolution photo of Saturn from the Cassini space mission might be found at the NASA site.

Notice that each image and its accompanying text is in a `div` assigned to the class `images`. The prewritten style rules for this page are in the `head`. Be sure to take a look at them so you will understand what rules are already being applied to the images as you place them in the new `div` elements on the page.

Finish the page. You need five `<div class="images">` elements in all. One is already finished for you. Another has an image but no link to the large image yet. One more such `div` is already on the page but contains text telling you to replace the text with an image and the descriptive paragraph.

1. Start by copying the following `div` and pasting it on the page two more times so you have the needed five `divs`:

```
<div class="images">
<p>Add more images and text in structures like this. Link the sm image to the
lg image similar to the way the first one was done.</p>
```

2. In the second, partially completed `div`, add a link to the `fallen_lg.jpg` to this element:

```
<img src="images/fallen_sm.jpg" alt="See the fallen tree" />
```

3. In the next three `divs`, insert the `img` element for each of the three remaining small images: `fence_sm.jpg`, `grid_sm.jpg`, and `lily_sm.jpg`.

   In each of the three incomplete `divs`, add the paragraph text. The text for each of the paragraphs in Listing 8.2 is in `img_exercises` in a file called `image.txt`, if you would like to copy and paste the text sections.

4. Link each of the small images to its corresponding large image.

The four changed image links, with the suggested text to describe each image, are shown in Listing 8.3.

LISTING 8.3: The Changes to the *.images* Divs on the *Ch8_smallimage.html* Page

```
<div class="images">
  <p><a href="images/fallen_lg.jpg"><img src="images/fallen_sm.jpg" alt="See the
fallen tree" /></a> Raging flood waters uprooted and knocked over a clump of
shallow rooted trees along the creek bed.</p>
</div>
<div class="images">
  <p><a href="images/fence_lg.jpg"><img src="images/fence_sm.jpg" alt="See the
fence" width="200" height="122" /></a>This is a fence with a peculiar pattern of
markings. I always wonder how these marks appear. Are they from a weed cutter gone
amok? Insects? A kid banging the fence with a stick?</p>
</div>
<div class="images">
  <p><a href="images/grid_lg.jpg"><img src="images/grid_sm.jpg" alt="See the grid"
width="200" height="92" /></a>Picnic tables in the park are constructed of a
reinforced metal gridwork and covered in some sort of rubberized coating to
prevent rusting. It makes for an interesting pattern.</p>
</div>
<div class="images">
  <p><a href="images/lily_lg.jpg"><img src="images/lily_sm.jpg" alt="See the lily"
width="200" height="134" /></a> The Easter lily burst into bloom in June. This is
a two year old plant that was planted last spring.</p>
</div>
```

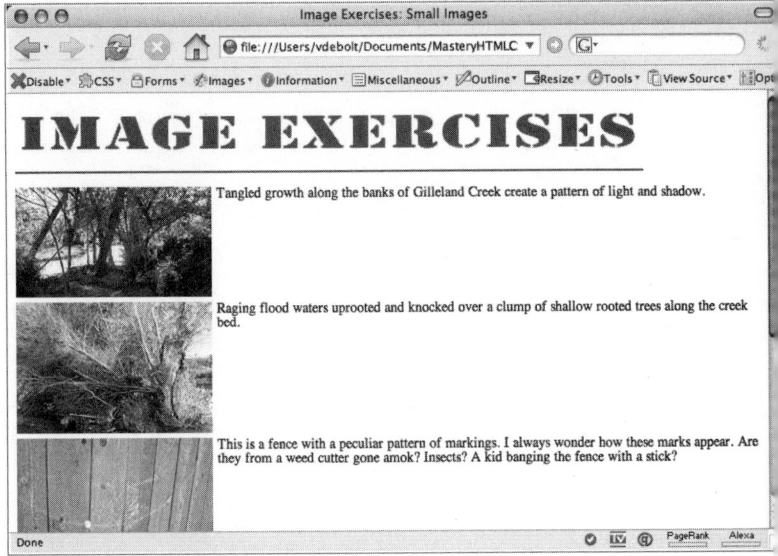

Image Exercises: Small Images
file:///Users/vdebolt/Documents/MasteryHTMLC
Disable CSS Forms Images Information Miscellaneous Outline Resize Tools View Source
IMAGE EXERCISES
Tangled growth along the banks of Gilleland Creek create a pattern of light and shadow.
Raging flood waters uprooted and knocked over a clump of shallow rooted trees along the creek bed.
This is a fence with a peculiar pattern of markings. I always wonder how these marks appear. Are they from a weed cutter gone amok? Insects? A kid banging the fence with a stick?
Done
PageRank
Alexa

FIGURE 8.42
All the small images are in place, with links to open the larger images in a plain browser window.

In the browser, you should see something like Figure 8.42.

Body Talk

Dress up the appearance of the `Ch8_smallimage.html` file a bit with a `body` style. Give the `body` set width of about 650px; the `banner.gif` is 642px, so 650px is enough. I think a centered body would look good; with `margin-right` and `margin-left` set to `auto`, the body will be centered i most browsers (see the sidebar "Centering Issues" for more information about this). And don't fo get a background color.

While a set width will produce cleaner looking alignment, a fixed width of 650px for the boc is a potential barrier to anyone with accessibility issues requiring extra large text sizes.

Add the new CSS rule to the embedded `style` element in the document `head`. The `body` sty is this:

```
body {
  width: 650px;
  margin-right: auto; margin-left: auto;
  background: #FFF;
}
```

This rule has the effect of reining in the lines of text that describe each image and preventing them from growing unreadably long (Figure 8.43). The completed `Ch8_smallimage.html` page shown in Listing 8.4.

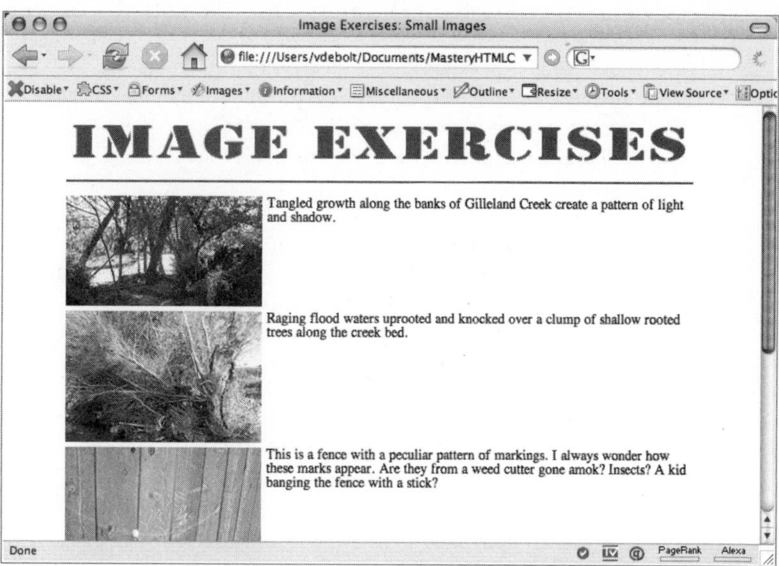

FIGURE 8.43
The size-constrained and centered body

LISTING 8.4: The Completed *Ch8_smallimage.html* Page

```
<!DOCTYPE html PUBLIC "-//W3C//DTD XHTML 1.0 Transitional//EN" "http://www.w3.org/
TR/xhtml1/DTD/xhtml1-transitional.dtd">
<html xmlns="http://www.w3.org/1999/xhtml">
<head>
<title>Image Exercises: Small Images</title>
<style type="text/css">
.images {
   clear: left;
   }
.images img {
   float: left;
   padding-right: 5px;
   padding-bottom: 5px;
}
body {
  width: 650px;
  margin-right: auto; margin-left: auto;
  background: #FFF;
}
</style>
</head>
<body>
<div id="banner">
<h1><img src="images/banner.gif" alt="Image Exercises" width="642" height="40" /
></h1>
```

```
<img src="bluebar.gif" width="642" height="2" alt="" />
</div>
<div class="images">
  <p><a href="images/creek_lg.jpg"><img src="images/creek_sm.jpg" alt="See the
creek" width="200" height="109" /></a>
  Tangled growth along the banks of Gilleland Creek create a pattern of light and
shadow. </p>
</div>
<div class="images">
  <p><a href="images/fallen_lg.jpg"><img src="images/fallen_sm.jpg" alt="See the
fallen tree" /></a> Raging flood waters uprooted and knocked over a clump of
shallow rooted trees along the creek bed.</p>
</div>
<div class="images">
  <p><a href="images/fence_lg.jpg"><img src="images/fence_sm.jpg" alt="See the
fence" width="200" height="122" /></a> This is a fence with a peculiar pattern of
markings. I always wonder how these marks appear. Are they from a weed cutter gone
amok? Insects? A kid banging the fence with a stick? </p>
</div>
<div class="images">
  <p><a href="images/grid_lg.jpg"><img src="images/grid_sm.jpg" alt="See the grid"
width="200" height="92" /></a> Picnic tables in the park are constructed of a
reinforced metal gridwork and covered in some sort of rubberized coating to
prevent rusting. It makes for an interesting pattern. </p>
</div>
<div class="images">
  <p><a href="images/lily_lg.jpg"><img src="images/lily_sm.jpg" alt="See the lily"
width="200" height="134" /></a> The Easter lily burst into bloom in June. This is
a two year old plant that was planted last spring. </p>
</div>
</body>
</html>
```

Centering Issues

I mentioned that you center a block horizontally on a page with a rule like:

```
#content {
  margin-left: auto;
  margin-right: auto;
}
```

This is what the W3C standards deem correct. However, browser support for this standard is not uniform. In Windows Internet Explorer 5.0 and 5.5, and in IE 6.0 when running in Quirks rendering mode, you must center a `div` (as well as the text that is in the `div`) like this:

```
#content {
  text-align: center;
}
```

It centers your text, which you must overrule later in the cascade if you don't want the text centered.

The solution is to use both rules at the same time. Browsers missed by one rule will be caught by the other. Like this:

```
#content {
  margin-left: auto;
  margin-right: auto;
  text-align: center;
}
```

Now, of course, if you don't want the centered text in your centered `div`, you come along after this rule with another rule to set the text-align to what you want. You probably want left alignment, so the rule would be:

```
#content p {
  text-align: left;
}
```

This would left-align paragraphs in the content `div`. But you might also have lists, block quotes, or other elements in the content `div` that you wanted left-aligned. In actual practice, you might want to put the content `div` in a container (`#container`) `div`. Center the container `div` in the way I described, and then left-align every element in the content `div` with a second rule.

```
#container {
  margin-left: auto;
  margin-right: auto;
  text-align: center;
}
#content {
  text-align: left;
}
```

Technically, this is a hack. It is called the Horizontal Centering Hack, but it will survive a trip through a CSS validator with no ill effects, since all the rules used are valid rules. It becomes a hack because the need to combine the rules in this fashion to achieve horizontal centering in all browsers is not the method the standard specifications stipulate.

Adding Multimedia to Your Page

If you love web pages that pop and sizzle with sound and motion, multimedia is where it's at. Mult media involves images, but a multimedia file is much more than the static images you have workec with up to this point. Multimedia usually involves movement, possibly sound and user interaction. You will learn how to add Flash and QuickTime to your XHTML.

Creating the Flash or QuickTime file is beyond the scope of this book. Creating files in either o these formats requires software and skills that take time and study to master.

If you already have the needed skills, you can create your own multimedia files. If you haven' started down that particular learning path yet, you can find samples and examples of multimedia o numerous websites that you can use on your web pages to add a bit of that illusive coolness facto

The `object` tag is the current recommendation from the W3C for adding multimedia objects to web pages. However, the `object` tag is often coupled with the older `embed` tag in a double-whamm approach needed to ensure that your multimedia element shows up in every browser. Eventually, a browsers will interpret the `object` tag correctly and the `embed` tag will no longer be needed.

Changes in the way Internet Explorer 7 handles active content have brought about a change i the way Flash and other active content are added to a page and how they work when included i an XHTML page. This new twist creates the need for a triple-whammy approach to multimedia, which is what you will learn.

There is limited support for CSS within Adobe's most recent version of Flash. QuickTime doe not make use of CSS.

FINDING MULTIMEDIA RESOURCES

A good resource for both stock photos and Flash movies is iStockphoto at `www.istockphoto.com`. You can buy excellent quality photos or Flash movies at a very reasonable price, with a license agreement that allows use on personal sites.

Another source of stock photos, often free, is Stock.XCHNG at `www.sxc.hu/index.phtml`.

Both sites have search features that let you narrow down your hunt for the perfect photo or movie for your needs. Here are a few more sites I've seen recommended:

`http://www.morguefile.com/`

`http://openphoto.net/`

`http://www.imageafter.com/`

`http://commons.wikimedia.org/wiki/Main_Page`

`http://www.pixelperfectdigital.com/free_image_archive/`

The Plug-in Problem

An issue with the multimedia formats for some web surfers is the fact that they must download an install a plug-in in order to play the files involved. The situation is improving, with many browser automatically including certain plug-ins in their installation. Flash is widely supported because it now installed with the browser. However, as you will see in the section on Flash, the web designe can specify a particular version of Flash, which might mean a new download and install for the use or the user can install browser add-ons that block all Flash content, such as the Flashblock extensio for the Firefox browser.

All new Windows operating system computers come with Windows Media Player installed, and most new computers with Mac operating systems have QuickTime installed. This means that in cases where WMP is the only option for playing a multimedia file, Mac users will have to download a plug-in; when QuickTime is the only option, Windows users will have to download a plug-in. Windows users with iTunes may have QuickTime already, because it is part of the iTunes installation. Linux users will have to download a plug-in to view any multimedia effects.

Another common plug-in for multimedia playback is the RealPlayer. As with the Windows Media Player, the RealPlayer will play many file formats for both sound and movies.

Viewers may be so irritated by the fact that they need to download something in order to see your content that they simply leave. On the other hand, they may be quite willing to download and install a new plug-in to see your content. The timeworn but sage advice to "know your audience" will help you balance your desire for sound and motion with the goals your audience has when visiting your site.

Flash

An entire website can be created in Flash. There are several software programs that write Flash files, but the best known is from Macromedia, now owned by Adobe. Flash can be used to write applications, connect to a database, gather form data, play movies and music, or simply animate something small such as a banner ad or a button.

For years there was a raging debate over Flash. Flash designers loved it because they had complete control over appearance and it allowed them to generate a lot of razzle-dazzle on the Web. Accessibility gurus hated it because it was inaccessible. At one time there was no text anywhere for a screen reader to read with Flash. Some implementations of Flash trapped users of screen readers in loops from which they couldn't escape.

To Flash's credit, there have been many improvements in Flash to make it more accessible. Careful use of the latest versions of Flash can create quite acceptably accessible multimedia.

A Flash file is saved with the file extension `.fla`. When it is exported for use on the Web, the file extension becomes `.swf`, which is pronounced "swiff."

Find in the Chapter 8 folder the `multimedia` folder on the accompanying CD. Copy the entire folder to your computer.

Recent events involving Microsoft have resulted in a change in the way Internet Explorer deals with what Microsoft calls "active content." When Flash or some other type of embedded content is on a page of XHTML, IE will pop up an alert asking you to OK the use of an Active X plug-in. To prevent this—in other words, to have the page open and simply work with no need for confirmation—some JavaScript can be used. This is what Adobe recommends for Flash content, and it works with other types of multimedia such as QuickTime as well.

The subfolder `scripts` in the `multimedia` folder contains two JavaScripts provided by Adobe for use with Flash. (The `scripts` folder has to be uploaded along with all the XHTML, SWF, or other files needed to make these exercises work on a server. Chapter 12 explains how to put your site on a server.) With the `scripts` folder on your hard drive, the pages should work fine locally.

The `ch8_flash.html` page is a finished page. You can look at it in the browser to see what the Flash will look like when you are finished adding it to your page. It can also be used to copy and paste some of the more complicated bits of scripts and codes that you are going to use to create your new page. You'll have fewer typos that way.

Begin a new XHTML document and prepare it to be ready to add the Flash element. Save it with a filename such as `myflash.html`. When you're finished, you'll have JavaScript elements and both an `object` and `embed` element on the page. The `embed` element is deprecated but is included in case your visitor has an older browser. Basically, it takes three different methods—the JavaScripts, the `object` element, and the `embed` element—all of which do the exact same thing: make sure the SW file will play in any situation. The Flash you'll add to your page is `abitofflash.swf`. Included the `multimedia` folder is the original FLA file. It is there for your reference only. If you have Fla software you can open it and see how it was put together. If you put the page you're about to ma on a server, the FLA file does not need to be uploaded, only the SWF file.

Begin by adding a script element to the document `head`:

```
<script src="scripts/AC_RunActiveContent.js" type="text/javascript"></script>
```

That `script` element tells the browser where to find the needed script when it is called for lat in the `body`.

In the `body` of the document, in the position where you intent to place the Flash, insert th JavaScript:

```
<script type="text/javascript">
AC_FL_RunContent( 'codebase','http://download.macromedia.com/pub/shockwave/cabs
flash/swflash.cab#version=6,0,29,0','width','350','height','350','title','A Bit
of
Flash','src','abitofflash','loop','false','quality','high','pluginspage','http:
www.macromedia.com/go/getflashplayer','movie','abitofflash' ); //end AC code
</script>
```

I'll attempt to translate that into English. It uses the script `AC_FL_RunContent` that you give t source for in the `head`. It gives the URL to a `codebase` which still bears the macromedia name. (Adobe bought Macromedia and its suite of products, which included Flash, Fireworks, and Dreamweaver. The `macromedia` URL still works.) It's looking for at least `version` 6 of the Flas player—not the latest version but fairly recent, so it's a safe compromise. The `width` and `heig` of the movie are given in pixels. The file `title` and source are listed. The looping is set to `fal` (it won't loop). It gives a URL to a plug-in page in case the user does not have Flash 6 or above. T `//end AC code` is a JavaScript-style comment.

Of course, JavaScript instructions only work if the user has enabled JavaScript, so backup method #1 is to include the `object` element. The `object` element is nested in a `noscript` eleme It only gets called upon if the user does not have JavaScript enabled. Further, if the JavaScrip cannot do its magic, users of Internet Explorer 7 will see a pop-up window asking if they wa to use Active X to run the content. They will be required to click OK to see the movie run usi the elements in the `noscript` section. Here's the `noscript` element:

```
<noscript>
   <object classid="clsid:D27CDB6E-AE6D-11cf-96B8-444553540000" codebase="http:
download.macromedia.com/pub/shockwave/cabs/flash/swflash.cab#version=6,0,29,0"
width="350" height="350" title="A Bit of Flash">
     <param name="movie" value="abitofflash.swf" />
     <param name="quality" value="high" />
     <param name="LOOP" value="false" />
   </object>
</noscript>
```

The `object` element has several attributes when using Flash that do the same functions the Ja Script does, for example, set parameters for the movie name and the loop setting.

A new item is classid. This is a long string of code numbers that must be typed correctly, so you might consider using copy and paste. The second attribute needed is codebase. This attribute sends people to Macromedia to download the Flash plug-in if they don't have it. Note version=6. This refers to the Flash 6 player. If the user doesn't have a Flash Player at version 6 or above, they will be prompted to download the latest version. (See Figure 8.46 later in this chapter for an example of a message about a missing plug-in.)

A width and height are needed. The title is there for accessibility, since the object element does not use an alt attribute.

Each param (for parameter) element has a name and a value. The param elements give the source file location, set the quality, and set the value for loop to false.

FEELING LOOPY?

A loop in a computer program means that the program plays, then goes back to the start and plays again. Loops can be set to play a specific number of times and then stop, or to repeat endlessly. The value="false" is the same as "no" in plain English, meaning, "No, the file will not loop but will only play once." If you want it to play over and over, set the value to "true." A number, say 3, would cause it to repeat three times and then stop looping.

The object element by itself won't work in every possible browser, so on to backup method #2. Repeat some of the same information using an embed element. It appears immediately after the object element as part of the noscript section:

```
<noscript>
   <object classid="clsid:D27CDB6E-AE6D-11cf-96B8-444553540000" codebase="http://
download.macromedia.com/pub/shockwave/cabs/flash/swflash.cab#version=6,0,29,0"
width="350" height="350" title="A Bit of Flash">
     <param name="movie" value="abitofflash.swf" />
     <param name="quality" value="high" />
     <param name="LOOP" value="false" />
     <embed src="abitofflash.swf" width="350" height="350" loop="False"
quality="high" pluginspage="http://www.macromedia.com/go/getflashplayer"
type="application/x-shockwave-flash"></embed>
   </object>
</noscript>
```

The embed element repeats the information about the source of the movie, the width and height, the loop value, and the quality value. Instead of codebase, it uses an attribute called pluginspage to point users who don't have the Flash Player to the download site. Finally, the embed element includes a type attribute.

The type shockwave-flash is a peek into history where Shockwave was once a bigger technology than Flash. Some say the file format SWF stands for "small web file" while others claim it stands for "shockwave flash." Whether it actually means small web file or not, in a contest for the smallest file size between video saved as a MOV file and a SWF file, the SWF would come out smaller.

The completed bits for the movie abitofflash.swf are shown in Listing 8.5. Remember you need the script element in the head, too.

Listing 8.5: The Completed Section of the *body* Element to Place the Flash Content in the XHTML

```
<script type="text/javascript">
AC_FL_RunContent( 'codebase','http://download.macromedia.com/pub/shockwave/cabs/
flash/swflash.cab#version=6,0,29,0','width','350','height','350','title','A Bit of
Flash','src','abitofflash','loop','false','quality','high','pluginspage','http://
www.macromedia.com/go/getflashplayer','movie','abitofflash' ); //end AC code
</script>
<noscript>
  <object classid="clsid:D27CDB6E-AE6D-11cf-96B8-444553540000" codebase="http://
download.macromedia.com/pub/shockwave/cabs/flash/swflash.cab#version=6,0,29,0"
width="350" height="350" title="A Bit of Flash">
    <param name="movie" value="abitofflash.swf" />
    <param name="quality" value="high" />
    <param name="LOOP" value="false" />
    <embed src="abitofflash.swf" width="350" height="350" loop="False"
quality="high" pluginspage="http://www.macromedia.com/go/getflashplayer"
type="application/x-shockwave-flash"></embed>
  </object>
</noscript>
```

With all that in place, take a look in the browser (Figure 8.44).

Figure 8.44 The end of the Flash movie

FLASH RESOURCES

An article in the support section of the Adobe site offers a zip download of the JavaScripts needed to make Flash and QuickTime work without a hitch with Active X. It is part of an informative page at `www.adobe.com/devnet/activecontent/articles/devletter.html`. Most people who own Flash also own Dreamweaver. If you download the latest Dreamweaver updater, the product updates included will automatically add the JavaScripts needed when adding active content like Flash and QuickTime to a web page.

There's also an attractive alternative system for Flash (but not QuickTime) available at `http://blog.deconcept.com/swfobject`. This site provides a script that will do more than simply bypass the new Active X consent pop-up. The `swfobject.js` script adds the Flash object, detects the Flash plug-in, is search engine friendly, and is valid XHTML (no deprecated elements are used).

QuickTime

QuickTime was once the major technology for movies on the Web. Most recent computers include software for processing movies imported from the owner's camera. Once you have edited the movie into what you want, you have the option to export it in a format that can be played on a web page. QuickTime is still a standard choice. However, nowadays movies exported as QuickTime are frequently imported into Flash before they are used on the Web.

As for playback and plug-ins for QuickTime, one playback choice is Windows Media Player, which comes loaded on any Windows computer. (QuickTime comes loaded on any Apple computer.) Some versions of Windows Media Player will play QuickTime movies. Of course, with the proper plug-in, Windows computers can play QuickTime movies, and Apple computers can play Windows Media format files. The RealPlayer, which is available as a free download, can play QuickTime movies, too. QuickTime movies can be added to Flash, which results in a movie with a smaller file size that will download and play with less wait for the user.

Not just camcorders, but digital cameras and even phones take movies now. The very popular home movie sharing site `www.youtube.com` accepts movies from most digital cameras, camcorders, and cell phones in the AVI, MOV, and MPG file formats. `Youtube.com` converts all these formats to Flash and shows the videos as SWF files.

You can use a QuickTime movie provided in the `multimedia` folder to practice using QuickTime. QuickTime movies are saved with the file extension `.mov`.

The `ch8_qt.html` page is a finished page. When you have created your own page for the movie, it should work like this page. The movie file is `newzealandQT.mov`.

Begin a new XHTML page. Save it with a name such as `myqt.html`. You will add the movie to this page. The same redundant process of giving the information in three ways applies here, too.

CAPTIONING

The Media Access Generator (MAGpie) tool can create captions for QuickTime, Flash, and other media. It is available at `http://ncam.wgbh.org/webaccess/magpie/`.

Two `script` elements are needed in the document head for QuickTime. Both are in the `multimedia/scripts` folder. Here are the two elements:

```
<script src="scripts/AC_ActiveX.js" type="text/javascript"></script>
<script src="scripts/AC_RunActiveContent.js" type="text/javascript"></script>
```

These scripts are combined with the `object` and `embed` elements to play the movie. As with Flash, first use the `script`, then in a `noscript` section, add the `object` and `embed` elements. The complete code is shown in Listing 8.6.

LISTING 8.6: The Complete *body* Elements to Add a QuickTime Movie to an XHTML Page

```
<!-- START QUICKTIME CONTENT -->
<script type="text/javascript">
AC_AX_RunContent( 'classid','clsid:02BF25D5-8C17-4B23-BC80-
D3488ABDDC6B','width','320','height','256','codebase','http://www.apple.com/
qtactivex/
qtplugin.cab','src','newzealandQT.mov','autoplay','false','controller','true','bo
der','0','pluginspage','http://www.apple.com/quicktime/download/
indext.html','target','myself','type','video/quicktime' ); //end AC code
</script>
<noscript>
   <object classid="clsid:02BF25D5-8C17-4B23-BC80-D3488ABDDC6B" width="320"
height="256" codebase="http://www.apple.com/qtactivex/qtplugin.cab">
    <param name="autoplay" value="false" />
    <param name="controller" value="true" />
    <param name="pluginspage" value="http://www.apple.com/quicktime/download/
indext.html" />
    <param name="target" value="myself" />
    <param name="type" value="video/quicktime" />
    <param name="src" value="newzealandQT.mov" />
   <embed src="newzealandQT.mov" width="320" height="256" autoplay="false"
controller="true" border="0" pluginspage="http://www.apple.com/quicktime/downloa
indext.html" target="myself" type="video/quicktime">
   </embed>
   </object>
</noscript>
```

In the JavaScript, `'autoplay','false','controller','true'` mean that the movie will no play automatically—the user must start it by clicking the triangle in the controller on the bottom The controller appears because the value for `controller` is set to `true`. If it were set to `false`, n controller would appear, in which case you would definitely want the movie to play automaticall The `target myself` means that the movie will open on this page, not in a new window.

In the `object` element, you will recognize some of the attributes needed for QuickTime object Most of them repeat the same instructions provided in the JavaScript. You also need to include

```
classid="clsid:02BF25D5-8C17-4B23-BC80-D3488ABDDC6B"
```

Note that the `classid` is specific to QuickTime and is not the same set of numbers as those used for the Flash Player. You must give Apple's Active X plug-in codebase for the player,

```
codebase="http://www.apple.com/qtactivex/qtplugin.cab"
```

A few more of the parameters in the object element need explanation. The movie does not begin to play until the user clicks the triangle play icon. That is because of the `param name="autoplay" value="false"` element in the `object` element. If that value were set to `true`, the movie would begin to play automatically.

The `param name="controller" value="true"` means that there will be controllers with the movie. Since the movie doesn't start playing automatically, it is unusable without the controller.

If the user does not have a QuickTime Player, this `param` points out the download site:

```
<param name="pluginspage" value="http://www.apple.com/quicktime/download/
indext.html"
```

The QuickTime Player can launch as a separate application window or play right on the web page using `param name="target" value="myself"`.

The `param name="type"` tells the browser what type of object is being played (`value="video/quicktime"`).

The source file URL is given in `param name="src" value="newzealandQT.mov"`.

The attributes in the embed element provide the same information.

Your page may not have the explanatory text that `Ch8_qt.html` has, but the *movie* should appear something like Figure 8.45 in the browser. The completed page, including the script elements and the body elements used for Figure 8.45, are shown in Listing 8.7.

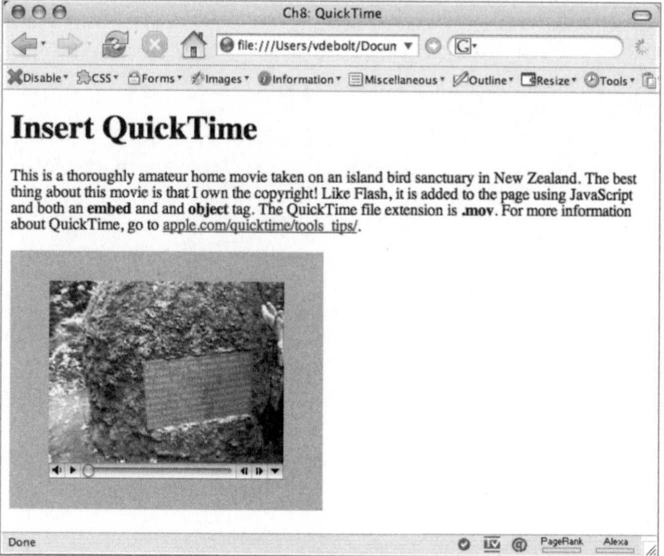

FIGURE 8.45
The opening screen of the QuickTime movie

LISTING 8.7: The Complete QuickTime Page

```
<!DOCTYPE html PUBLIC "-//W3C//DTD XHTML 1.0 Transitional//EN"
       "http://www.w3.org/TR/2000/REC-xhtml1-20000126/DTD/xhtml1-
transitional.dtd">
<html xmlns="http://www.w3.org/1999/xhtml">
<head>
   <title>Ch8: QuickTime</title>
    <script src="scripts/AC_ActiveX.js" type="text/javascript"></script>
    <script src="scripts/AC_RunActiveContent.js" type="text/javascript"></script
</head>
<body>
<h1>Insert QuickTime</h1>
<p>This is a thoroughly amateur home movie taken on an island bird sanctuary in
New Zealand. The best thing about this movie is that I own the copyright! Like
Flash, it is added to the page using JavaScript and both an <strong>embed</strong
and an<strong>object</strong> tag. The QuickTime file extension is <strong>.mov<
strong>. For more information about QuickTime, go to <a href="http://
www.apple.com/quicktime/tools_tips/">apple.com/quicktime/tools_tips/</a>. </p>
<p>
<!-- START QUICKTIME CONTENT -->
<script type="text/javascript">
AC_AX_RunContent( 'classid','clsid:02BF25D5-8C17-4B23-BC80-
D3488ABDDC6B','width','320','height','256','codebase','http://www.apple.com/
qtactivex/
qtplugin.cab','src','newzealandQT.mov','autoplay','false','controller','true','b
der','0','pluginspage','http://www.apple.com/quicktime/download/
indext.html','target','myself','type','video/quicktime' ); //end AC code
</script>
<noscript>
   <object classid="clsid:02BF25D5-8C17-4B23-BC80-D3488ABDDC6B" width="320"
height="256" codebase="http://www.apple.com/qtactivex/qtplugin.cab">
    <param name="autoplay" value="false" />
    <param name="controller" value="true" />
    <param name="pluginspage" value="http://www.apple.com/quicktime/download/
indext.html" />
    <param name="target" value="myself" />
    <param name="type" value="video/quicktime" />
    <param name="src" value="newzealandQT.mov" />
   <embed src="newzealandQT.mov" width="320" height="256" autoplay="false"
controller="true" border="0" pluginspage="http://www.apple.com/quicktime/downloa
indext.html" target="myself" type="video/quicktime">
   </embed>
   </object>
</noscript>
</p>
</body>
</html>
```

QUICKTIME RESOURCES

The same site I referred to for an additional Flash resource also offers a QuickTime detect and embed script. This script has the virtue of being standards compliant, like the Flash script. Download the files and read the instructions here:

```
http://blog.deconcept.com/2005/01/26/web-standards-➥
compliant-javascript-quicktime-detect-and-embed/
```

Windows Media Player and RealPlayer

Windows Media Player and RealPlayer will play all sorts of multimedia files: sound files, movies, radio channels, and various video formats. Windows Media Player can play files in all of these formats: AVI, ASF, ASX, RMI, WAV, WMA, WAX, MPG, MPEG, M1V, MP2, MP3, MPA, MPE, QT, AIF, AIFC, AIFF, MOV, and others.

Because Windows Media Player will play MOV files, a Windows user may have their computer set to automatically open MOV files in Windows Media Player. Similarly, the user can set preferences to open MOV files in RealPlayer.

Browser Help if There's No Plug-in

If you arrive plug-in-less at a page where a particular file format demands a particular plug-in, the browser will pop up an error message offering suggestions about where the plug-in can be found. (You provide this information in the parameters of the `object` element.)

For example, suppose there's a file in the WMA format (strictly a Windows Media format) viewed by a user with the Mac Safari browser. The Mac doesn't come with a preinstalled Windows Media Player plug-in, so the user sees a message telling where to find the plug-in (Figure 8.46). While other browsers or operating systems might display the message in a slightly different way, the offer to find the needed download page would be the same.

Coming in the next chapter: the super-useful list. The wait is almost over.

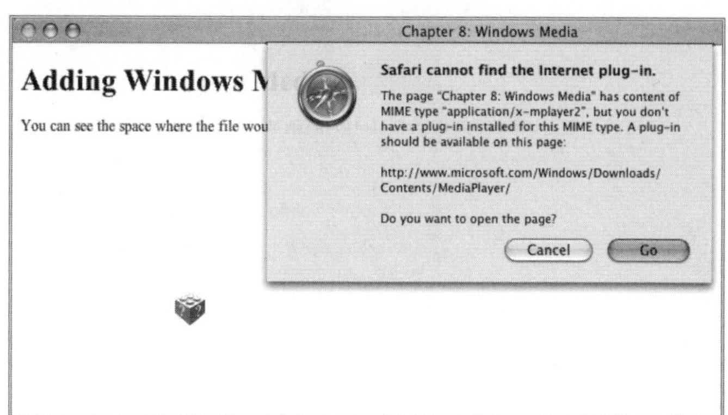

FIGURE 8.46 The little icon with the question mark in the space reserved for the Windows Media object indicates a missing file or plug-in. The browser offers to help you download the needed software.

Real-World Scenario

Images do many jobs on a web page. They add interest, color, and information. The create emotior On some sites that's all images are required to do. On other sites, multimedia images create mov ment and interesting user interactions with the site.

University of Missouri-Columbia

The University of Missouri-Columbia (`www.missouri.edu`)website is an example of a well-designed, standards-based site with a vast amount of information to organize and a sparing us of images to add interest and color. The images change each time you revisit the page, so there' always something new and interesting to attract your eye. The home page (Figure 8.47) has a large banner-like image at the top. The three-column layout uses two global menu areas, variou typographical and layout techniques, and sectional lists of links to specific pages to keep you oriented and to organize the information.

About halfway down each right column on the University of Missouri site is another image—also changed on each new visit—featuring a student or faculty member (Figure 8.48).

You can resize the text, resize the viewport, disable JavaScript or disable CSS, and the Unive sity of Missouri site is still completely usable. This is an important factor for a public institutio where a wide range of visitors including students, parents, visitors, and alumni will come for information.

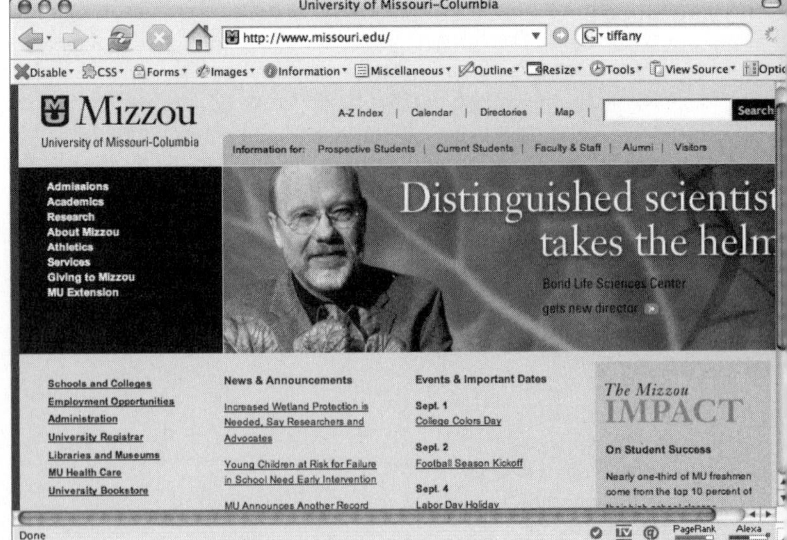

FIGURE 8.47 The home page of the University of Missouri-Columbia site. The top image is large, with explanatory text, and may relate to current university news.

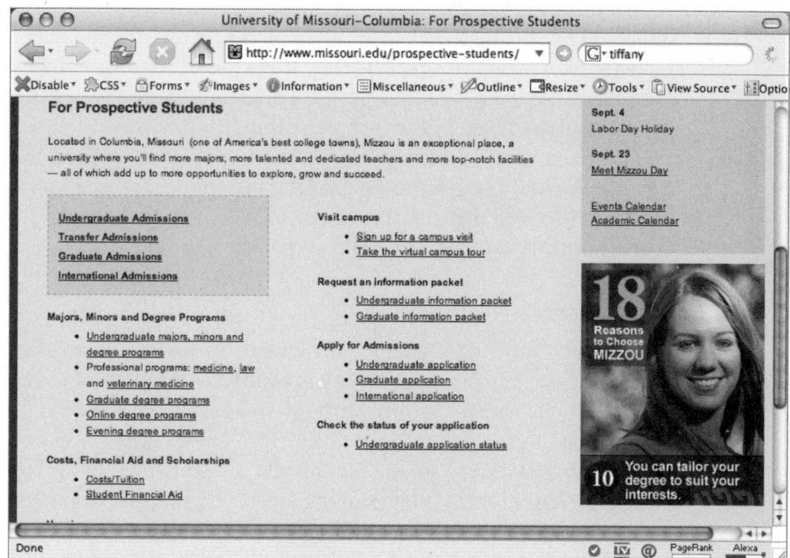

FIGURE 8.48
The right column on the University of Missouri-Columbia site has varied images of students or faculty with appropriate text or a quote. This image is about halfway down the page. A large image in a banner similar to the one in Figure 8.47 tops the page.

David Bowie

With rocker David Bowie at `www.davidbowie.com`, however, coolness matters and glitz is a definite plus. Whether the site is open to the range of visitors who might want information about a university is less important in his site.

David Bowie's site uses Flash extensively. In Figure 8.49, you see the home page, which includes a Flash jukebox and other Flash features.

David Bowie is known for being one of the first musicians to understand and tap into the power of the Internet to build rapport with his fans. His site has been redesigned a number of times, always with an eye on the coolness factor.

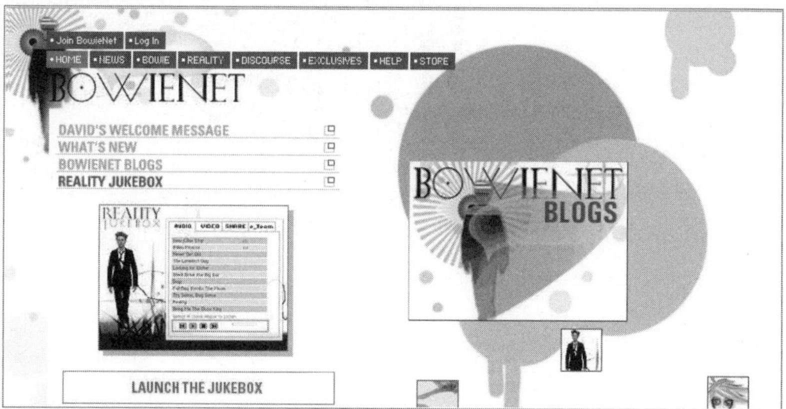

FIGURE 8.49
David Bowie's site is full of glitzy features including a Flash jukebox.

The choice of Flash means that Bowie's aging baby boomer fans with declining eyesight will b unable to resize the text used in many places on the site, the way they would be able to do with th University of Missouri site. Will they leave the site because of that? Probably not. It is likely that hi long-term and very loyal fans will keep coming back and will be willing to overlook such detail in search of the latest in concert and album news.

These sites demonstrate the importance of knowing your audience. A site like the University c Missouri's would be a hopeless dud if it were David Bowie's site. A site like David Bowie's woul be distracting and difficult if it were a university site. Yet each site uses images and multimedia i a way perfectly appropriate to its audience.

River Rock

The final example is a site where the images are an important sales tool. Everything about the Rive Rock site (`www.riverrocknc.com`) is created to emphasize the beauty and serenity of this privat community in North Carolina through imagery (Figure 8.50).

The headings support the emotional pull of the images with phrases like "River Rock is a place...River Rock is a time...River Rock is a spirit." The Galleries link takes you to inside page with even more lovely images of the area to further convince you that it's a beautiful natural env ronment in which to build your dream home (Figure 8.51). The site uses good design practice, bu its impact comes from superb imagery.

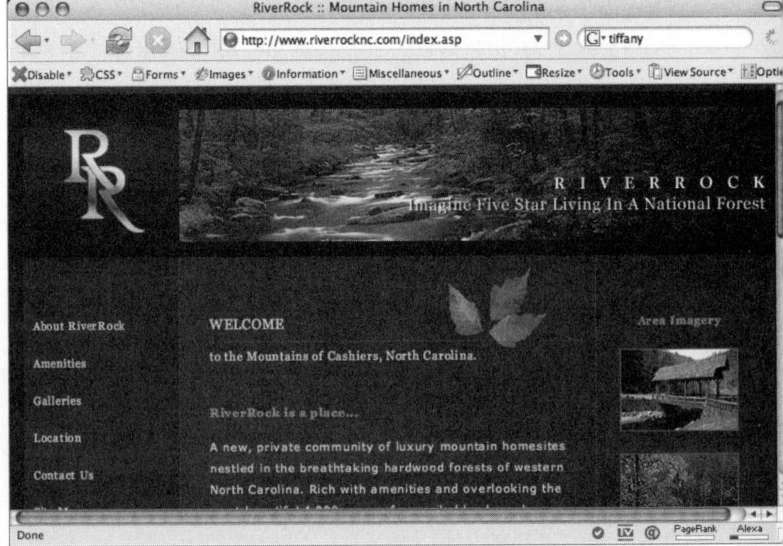

FIGURE 8.50 The color scheme, the page layout, everything about the River Rock page emphasizes the images, which draw you in and convince you of the beauty of the location.

FIGURE 8.51
Galleries of small images can be clicked to open a larger version below the thumbnails. The galleries are so vital that separate image galleries were created for area photos, home examples, and a proposed additional development.

CSS Properties

No new CSS properties were harmed in the making of this chapter.

The Bottom Line

Understand basic functions of graphics software. Image skills essential for web pages including cropping, sizing, changing resolution, and understanding transparency.

Master It If you have a way to create a new background graphic or to crop the 1200-pixel file provided on the CD, try using a background graphic of about 600px for the background image of the banner (see Figure 8.38). Instead of using `no-repeat`, have it repeat on the horizontal axis only. Compare the results with what you did for Figure 8.38.

Place images on web pages. The `img` element requires two attributes: `src` and `alt`. Other attributes may include `width`, `height`, `title`, and `longdesc`.

Master It Go to a site like `www.freeimages.co.uk` and download some images. Create an XHTML page and some CSS styles to use one or more images. Be ready to demonstrate your work in a browser.

Build horizontal and vertical navigation bars with images. Images used as hyperlinks are common practice on the Internet. Images in a navigation bar are often called buttons and may change for various link states such as `:hover` and `:visited`, depending on the CSS rules used.

Master It Find or create a few button images to use as navigation on the page you created in the previous exercise. Since you only have one page to work with, you can link the buttons to other pages you have in Chapter 8 or to external sites like `yahoo.com`. Be prepared to demonstrate your results in a browser.

Use images to create a photo gallery. Photo galleries come in a multitude of formats but generally employ a series of small or thumbnail images as links to larger images.

Master It On the `Ch8_smallimage.html` page, reverse the position of the photo and th text. Put the text on the left and the image on the right in each `div`.

Instead of centering the body of `Ch_smallimage.html` using a fixed width, try centering with a `body` width set to a percentage value to create a more accessible `body` size.

Understand how to add multimedia objects to web pages. Because of varying browser su port and legal restrictions placed on Microsoft, three redundant types of code are needed to ac multimedia to a web page.

Master It Set the Flash file to `value="true"` for the loop `param` and see what happens. T other changes. Demonstrate your results in a browser.

Chapter 9

Lists and List Styles

Lists are extremely useful on the Web. Users are often in a hurry and scan pages rapidly in search of a particular tidbit. Organizing important points in a bulleted or numbered list helps users find information quickly. Lists are easy to read because the lines are short and there is usually considerable white space around each item.

In XHTML there are three types of lists, depending on their purpose. Ordered lists (`ol`) have a sequence or hierarchy, marked with Arabic numerals, Roman numerals, or upper- and lowercase letters of the alphabet. Unordered lists (`ul`) have no sequence and typically use bullets or other markers. Definition lists (`dl`) consist of one or more terms and their definitions.

With CSS, you can determine what type of bullet or number to use (if any) with a list, whether the list will display horizontally or vertically, and how the list will be positioned with regard to the bullets or markers.

Using the structure of a list to create menus is both logical and accessible. With the addition of CSS to set background and hover rules, lists of links can be made to appear very much like buttons with rollovers.

In this chapter you will:

- Write every type of list.
- Use CSS to control the presentation of lists.
- Use lists as vertical, horizontal, and CSS pop-up navigation elements.

XHTML: List Basics

Both ordered and unordered lists use the `li` (for list item) tag for individual items, but they use different tags to begin and end the whole list. A simple unordered list (`ul`) would be constructed like this:

```
<ul>
  <li>Bread</li>
  <li>Milk</li>
  <li>Eggs</li>
</ul>
```

The browser displays something like Figure 9.1 for this list.

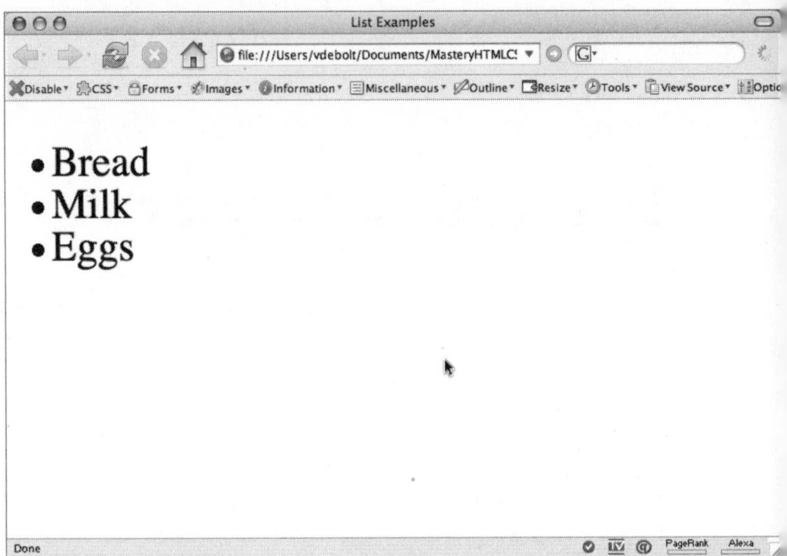

FIGURE 9.1
A simple unordered list. The default marker is a disk.

Lists can be nested. An outline is a good example of a nested ordered list. If you want several types of bread, you can list them under the Bread list item. The nested list is a complete unordered list element, *nested within* the "Bread" list item. Look at this example:

```
<ul>
  <li>Bread
    <ul>
      <li>Whole wheat</li>
      <li>Hot dog buns</li>
      <li>Bagels</li>
    </ul>
  </li>
  <li>Milk</li>
  <li>Eggs</li>
</ul>
```

Notice that the opening and closing nested `ul` tags fall within the opening and closing `li` tags for "Bread." Properly nested lists must follow this example. With the nested list of bread types, the list looks like Figure 9.2. Notice that the browser indents the second-level list.

You can carry on nesting lists as deeply as you need to go, as long as you remember to keep the nested list inside the `li` element it is describing. For example, you can add an item for "2 pkg Foot Long" and a second item for "5 pkg Regular" as a nested list under the "Hot dog buns" item.

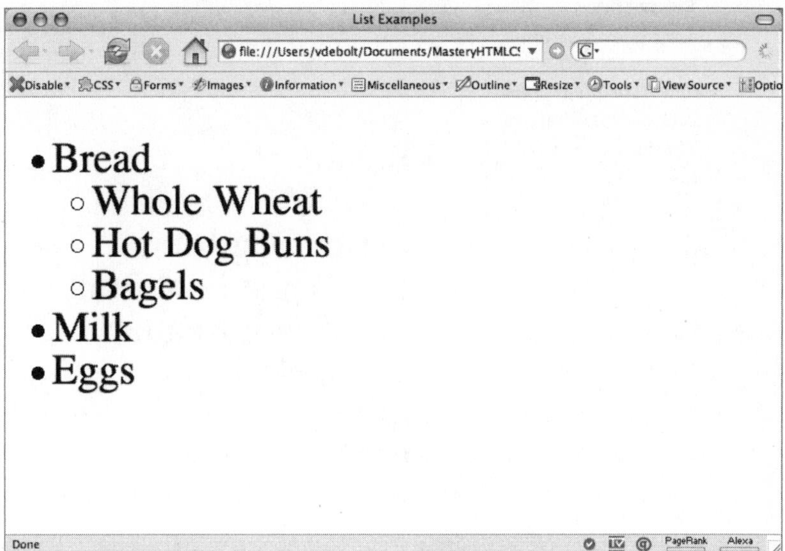

FIGURE 9.2
The types of bread are a nested list. The default marker for the second-level list is a circle.

Here's the code:

```
<ul>
  <li>Bread
    <ul>
      <li>Whole wheat</li>
      <li>Hot dog buns
        <ul>
          <li>2 pkg Foot Long</li>
          <li>5 pkg Regular</li>
        </ul>
      </li>
      <li>Bagels</li>
    </ul>
  </li>
  <li>Milk</li>
  <li>Eggs</li>
</ul>
```

In the browser, you should see something like Figure 9.3. Notice that the browser makes a distinction in the type of bullet it uses to mark second- and third-level nested lists.

FIGURE 9.3
A third-level nested list. Note that the default list marker for each level is different. The third-level default is a square.

Ordered lists use exactly the same XHTML as unordered lists, except that the opening list tag <ol> and the closing list tag is </ol>.

To create an example, save a copy of your unordered list file with a new name. You will us to make a quick-and-dirty ordered list. On your newly saved page, change all the lists to orde lists. To accomplish that, simply change all the <ul></ul> tags in the shopping list to <ol></o Suddenly you have ordered lists instead of unordered lists.

Here is the code:

```
<ol>
  <li>Bread
      <ol>
        <li>Whole wheat</li>
        <li>Hot dog buns
            <ol>
              <li>2 pkg Foot Long</li>
              <li>5 pkg Regular</li>
            </ol>
        </li>
        <li>Bagels</li>
      </ol>
  </li>
  <li>Milk</li>
  <li>Eggs</li>
</ol>
```

You should see something similar to Figure 9.4.

FIGURE 9.4 Nested ordered lists shown with the default decimal number markers.

You saved a lot of typing in this exercise by converting an unordered list to an ordered list, but perhaps you noticed something a bit odd about a numbered grocery list. There is no reason for a grocery list to be an ordered list, because there is no ordered series of steps. A true ordered list would list steps in chronological order or in a required sequence, for example:

```
<ol>
  <li>Turn off computer</li>
  <li>Remove battery</li>
  <li>Wash screen with damp, lint-free cloth</li>
</ol>
```

Unordered lists are perfect for navigation elements, since menus are really nothing more than a list of links.

Both unordered and ordered lists can have various types of markers beyond the default ones just shown. You'll learn to control that in the CSS section of the chapter, so save the lists you are making for future use.

Definition Lists

Definition lists are different from ordered and unordered lists because they are meant to list terms and their definitions. The opening tag is `dl` (for definition list). The list contains terms, tagged with `dt` (for definition term). Each term may be defined with a `dd` (for definition data) element.

The structure of a definition list is the following:

```
<dl>
  <dt>definition term</dt>
  <dd>definition data</dd>
</dl>
```

If you have more than one term, you add more dt and dd elements to the list, like this:

```
<dl>
  <dt>definition term</dt>
  <dd>definition data</dd>
  <dt>definition term</dt>
  <dd>definition data</dd>
</dl>
```

Make a definition list defining the terms "Ordered Lists" and "Unordered Lists." When you finis
it should look like Figure 9.5.

Start a new page for this list. See if you can use Figure 9.5 and the preceding examples to wri
the code yourself.

Here it is:

```
<dl>
  <dt>Ordered Lists</dt>
    <dd>Ordered Lists use numerical or alphabetical markers to organize lists o
information by sequence or chronological order</dd>
  <dt>Unordered Lists</dt>
    <dd>Unordered Lists use bullets or markers to itemize items in a list</dd>
</dl>
```

If you study Figure 9.5, you will notice that the browser indents the dd by default.

Definition lists can be nested within other dl elements or within ul or ol elements. You can u
more than one dd following a dt, if the term has more than one meaning. Or, if there is more tha
one spelling of a term or several terms with the same definition, you may have more than one d
per dd. It is also possible to nest other block-level elements within either a dt or dd.

FIGURE 9.5
A definition list

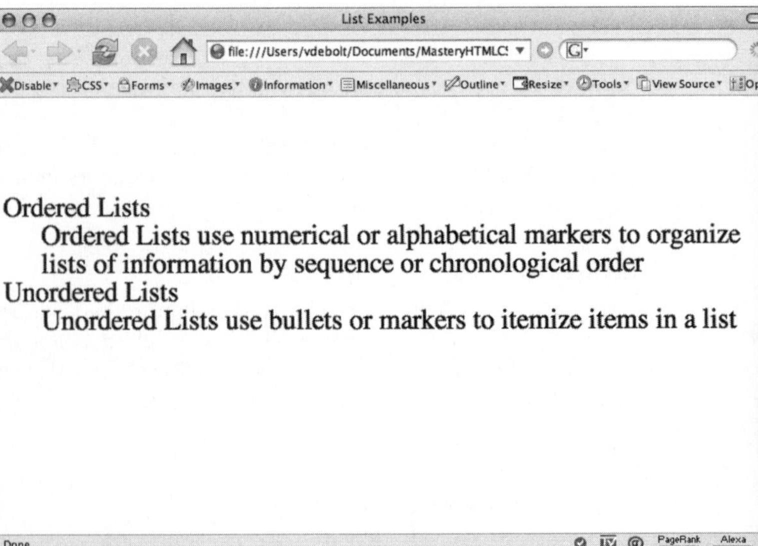

DEFINITIONS PLUS

A definition list is meant for a list of terms and definitions, but isn't limited to that. The W3C rather vaguely suggests that it can be used for other purposes. If you're posting a screenplay, it's perfect for dialog:

```
<dl>
<dt>Jane</dt>
<dd>Is there something you want to tell me?</dd>
<dt>John</dt>
<dd>I... I... I guess not.</dd>
</dl>
```

It can be used in navigation, lists of frequently asked questions, lists of links with their descriptions, or any situation where you have a list of values paired with their descriptions. I've even seen it used in photo galleries. For example, in a photo gallery, the user might hover over a `dt` (Grand Canyon) and cause a dd (a Grand Canyon photo) to pop up. This seems to fit the semantic logic of what a `dl` element is, and so seems to be a reasonable use of a `dl`. The nested structure of the `dt` and dd elements invite all sorts of `display`, `:hover`, and `position` presentations. When experimenting with definition lists, maintain the semantic underpinning for what you are doing.

CSS: Presentation Is Powerful

As you saw earlier, the default marker style for ordered lists is an Arabic numeral. The Arabic numerals—1, 2, 3, 4, and so on—in CSS terms are `decimal` values. The CSS property that is used to change the type of marker is `list-style-type`. For CSS shorthand, use `list-style`. When using shorthand for list styles, the `list-style` possible values in order would be `list-style-type`, `list-style-image`, and `list-style-position`.

For ordered lists, the `list-style-type` choices, other than the default `decimal` type, are `upper-alpha`, `lower-alpha`, `upper-roman`, `lower-roman`, and `none`. More possibilities are available in CSS 2 and are listed in the table of CSS properties at the chapter's end; however, they are not all well supported by browsers at this time.

We'll use the ordered list in Listing 9.1 and add some CSS to control the list markers.

LISTING 9.1: An Ordered List

```
<p>Set up equipment </p>
<ol>
  <li>Computer
    <ol>
      <li>Cable modem</li>
      <li>Wireless base station
        <ol>
          <li>Check firewall</li>
          <li>Check reception strength</li>
        </ol>
      </li>
      <li>Check network connections</li>
```

```
      </ol>
    </li>
    <li>Printer</li>
    <li>Speakers</li>
  </ol>
  <p>Install software </p>
  <ol start="4">
    <li>Install Photoshop from CD</li>
    <li>Download Firefox </li>
  </ol>
```

Notice the `start="4"` attribute in the `ol` element after "Install Software." This list was interrupt by a nonlist element (the paragraph). When opening the new list element after this interruption, i makes sense to continue numbering the steps in order. The `start` attribute is used to achieve this Even if you are using Roman numerals or alphabetical markers, you still express the start numbe with a standard Arabic numeral.

For example, if you want an alphabetical list to start with the letter D, you use `start="4"`. To g a Roman numeral IV, you use `start="4"`.

Transitional XHTML allows the `start` attribute with an `ol` element. Strict XHTML does not CSS2 has several `counter` properties that should be used with XHTML Strict. Browser support still spotty, so use the `start` attribute allowed by the Transitional DOCTYPE.

In the browser, Listing 9.1 displays like Figure 9.6.

If you haven't already typed the preceding ordered list example about setting up a compute start a new XHTML page and type that list example. You will write CSS selectors for that page. T top-level list selector is `ol`. The second-level list selector (containing the items "Cable modem," "Wireless base station," and "Check network connections") is `ol ol`. The third-level list select (containing the items "Check firewall" and "Check reception strength") is `ol ol ol`.

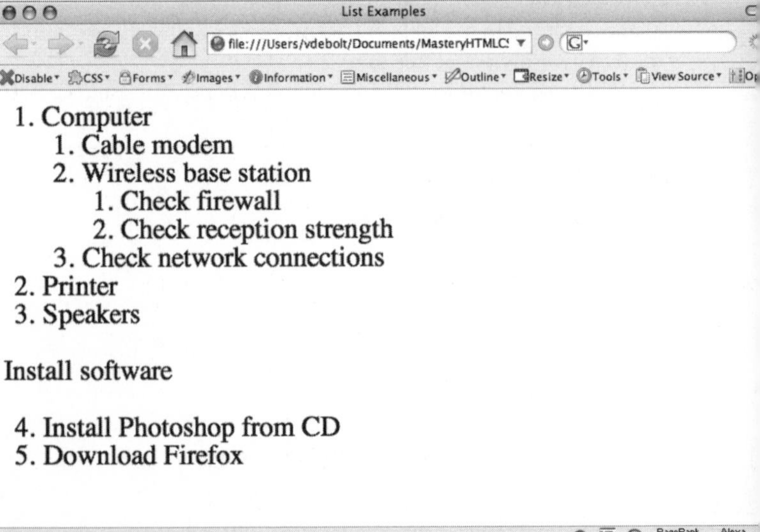

FIGURE 9.6
Setting a start value of 4 in a list

Armed with the proper selectors for your nested lists, make this list start with capitalized Roman numerals, change to capitalized alphabet letters at the second level, and then change to decimal numbers at the third level.

As you know, `decimal` is the default marker. However, if the second-level list (`ol ol`) is set to `upper-alpha`, the third-level list (`ol ol ol`) will inherit the `upper-alpha` value. Therefore, you must explicitly set it back to `decimal`.

You won't do anything to this page beyond writing some CSS rules for lists, so embed the styles in the head. The complete style element to be added to the head is shown in Listing 9.2, and Figure 9.7 shows the result.

LISTING 9.2: CSS Rules Set Marker Styles for Ordered Lists

```
<style type="text/css">
ol {
  list-style: upper-roman;
}
ol ol {
  list-style: upper-alpha;
}
ol ol ol {
  list-style: decimal;
}
</style>
```

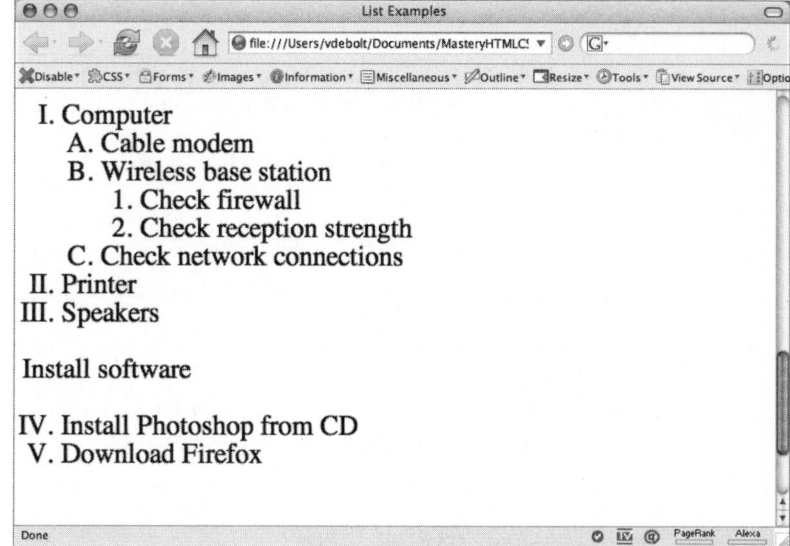

FIGURE 9.7 List-style-type set to `upper-roman`, `upper-alpha`, and `decimal`. Notice that the item "Install Photoshop from CD" is item IV in `upper-roman` because of the `start="4"` attribute and value.

OF COURSE

Everything you know about CSS applies to lists. You can write styles for fonts, colors, line heights, margins, and other style properties you already know about for `ol`, `ul`, and `li` elements.

Unordered List Markers

Not all browsers have the same defaults for nested unordered lists. In the browser used for Figure 9 the browser's built-in style is

```
ul {
list-style: disc;
}
ul ul {
list-style: circle;
}
ul ul ul {
list-style: square
}
```

These three—`disc`, `circle`, and `square`—are the only bullet types for unordered lists. You can change the default bullet by writing rules such as:

```
ul {
list-style: square;
}
ul ul {
list-style: disc;
}
```

For even more fun with an unordered list and CSS, use an image as a bullet. On the CD, fin `star.gif` in the Chapter 9 folder. Save it in the same folder where you have the practice list pag for this chapter.

The CSS property you want is `list-style-image` (in CSS shorthand, `list-style`). Here's h it works:

```
list-style-image: url(somegraphic.gif);
```

If the graphic happened to be in a subfolder named `images`, the `url` might be like this: `url(images/somegraphic.gif)`.

Remember, when writing a `url` value in a style sheet, the path to the file is relative to the locati of the style sheet.

Use the grocery shopping unordered list to try this. To make one rule that will be inherited every unordered list on the page, embed it in the `head`:

```
<style type="text/css">
ul {
  list-style: url(star.gif);
}
</style>
```

FIGURE 9.8
Graphic list markers

That change should look like Figure 9.8 in the browser.

In the same way that the ordered list selectors worked, different graphic markers can be used with each level in the unordered list with the selectors `ul`, `ul ul`, or `ul ul ul`.

GRAPHIC LIST MARKERS IN THE BACKGROUND

When you use `list-style: url(star.gif)` you have limited control over how the star or other graphic you might use gets positioned on the text baseline. For this reason, you may prefer to use a `list-style: none` rule in the CSS and insert a graphic in the `li` element as a `background-image`.

If the list contains navigation, `background-image` can also be used with the anchor element. You did something similar to this in Chapter 4 with a heading, where you used a bit of padding to move the heading element out of the way of the background. The same technique works with lists.

List-Marker Positions

Using the property `list-style-position`, you can alter the default `list-style-position` from `outside` to `inside`. `list-style-position: inside` moves the marker into the list item content. It can be declared in the shorthand `list-style` property. The computer setup list is a good one for demonstrating this.

The changed rule for the `ol ol ol` selector is

```
ol ol ol {
list-style: decimal inside;
}
```

Add some text to the third-level list (see Figure 9.9) so it takes up more than one line. That makes the hanging `list-style-position` of the list more obvious.

FIGURE 9.9
The second-level list is in the default position: `outside`. The third-level list is positioned `inside`.

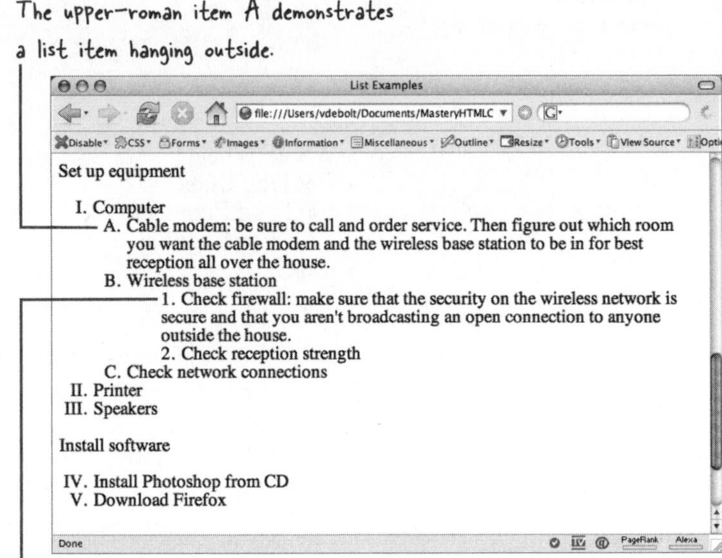

The decimal item 1 demonstrates a list item hanging inside.

Make the second-level list item longer also (see Figure 9.9). It uses `list-style-position: outside`, but there is no need to include the rule in your style element in this situation since `outsid` is the default display value. This helps you see how an outside position marker hangs outside the li item's content.

Back to Definition Lists

The CSS you can use with definition lists is familiar to you. Font, color, padding, background, bc der, and other CSS properties you are familiar with can be applied to definition lists. Here's a simp example. Make the `dt` bold with 1em of `margin-top` to give it air. Make the `dd` a small font size. I you wrote style rules for that, it would look something like Figure 9.10.

Those two rules for your definition list are

```
dt {
  font-weight: bold;
  margin-top: 1em;
}
dd {
  font-size: small;
}
```

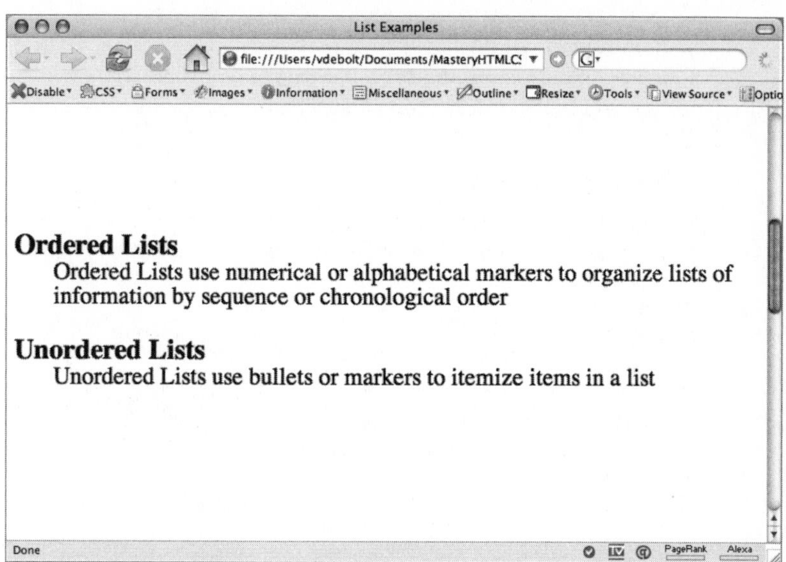

FIGURE 9.10
The styled definition list

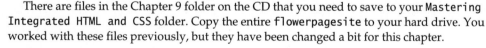

> **RESOURCE**
>
> An article at Max Design explores some of the semantic issues involved in using definition lists for more than definitions: `http://maxdesign.com.au/presentation/definition`. It also has a series of links to examples of definition lists used as image galleries, tables, calendars, and boxes.

Lists of Links

Here's the information you've been promised for several chapters: styling lists of links to serve as nav bars or menus.

A web page menu logically fits the idea of lists. A menu is, in fact, a list of links. Lists of links satisfy accessibility concerns perfectly because they are constructed of text. For years, designers combined JavaScript with images to create nav bars; today, most designers make them with lists and CSS. The text in a list item can be resized as needed by the user, screen readers easily delineate between one list item and another making aural rendering more sensible sounding, and fancy visual effects can be achieved using CSS properties. The switch from images and JavaScript to lists and CSS has been a positive one in many ways but also can present drawbacks if JavaScript is eliminated completely. I'll point out some of the drawbacks as we go through the exercises.

There are files in the Chapter 9 folder on the CD that you need to save to your `Mastering Integrated HTML and CSS` folder. Copy the entire `flowerpagesite` to your hard drive. You worked with these files previously, but they have been changed a bit for this chapter.

Note that there are now two versions of the main page: `ch9index_vert.html` and `ch9inde` `horiz.html`. You will use these two pages to make a vertically configured nav bar from a list ar a horizontally configured nav bar from a list. There's a new page, `cactus/ch9cactusfaq.html` that will be used when you add a CSS pop-up menu. There are also a few new images.

Vertical Lists

Open `ch9index_vert.html` in a text editor and in the browser. Also open `ch9_lists.css`, whi contains the familiar rules that create the layout for this page (see Figure 9.11).

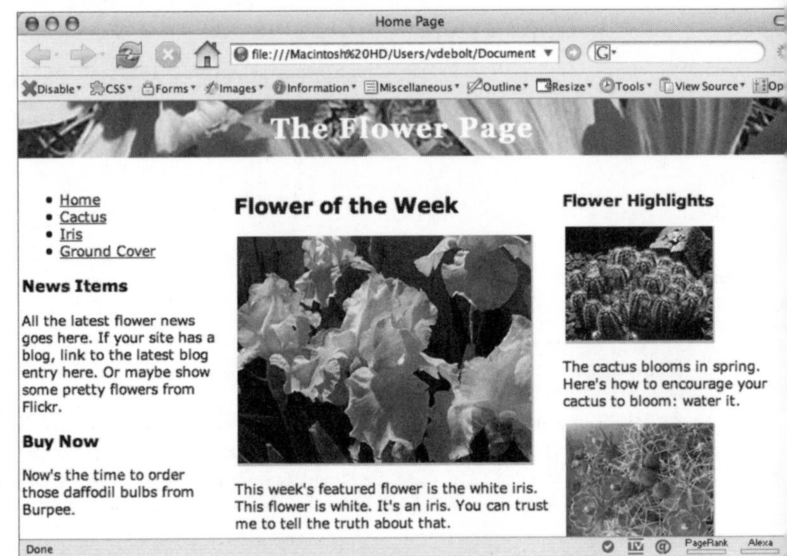

FIGURE 9.11 At this point, `ch9index_vert.html` displays the main flower page with an unstyled vertical list for navigation.

Before you begin styling the list, you need to assign an `id` to the `ul` element so you have a s cific selector to work with. Add **`id="navlist"`** to the `ul` element, as shown in Listing 9.3.

LISTING 9.3: Add an *id* to the List to Create a Hook for a CSS Selector

```
<ul id="navlist">
   <li><a href="ch9index_horiz.html">Home</a></li>
   <li><a href="cactus/ch9cactus.html">Cactus</a></li>
   <li><a href="iris/ch9iris.html">Iris</a></li>
   <li><a href="groundcover/ch9groundcover.html">Ground Cover</a></li>
</ul>
```

Add a comment at the bottom of ch9_lists.css to indicate that the new rules will create the vertical nav bar. You'll add several new rules to style the nav bar.

When you work with lists, it's a good practice to zero out the margins and padding at the start. That way you don't have to worry about browser defaults, which vary; then you can set your own margins and padding to suit your needs. The navlist needs a width and a background-color. Here's the opening rule:

```
/* vertical navbar */
#navlist {
padding: 0 1px 1px;
margin-left: 0;
font: bold 0.9em;
background: #DDDDDD;
width: 95%;
}
```

Note that I suggest reducing the font-size a bit and making the font bold. Keep in mind that the 95% is a percentage of the parent element, in this case the left div. I'll suggest some colors that are fairly neutral or that match some color elsewhere on the page—feel free to try others (see Figure 9.12).

Note that the list markers seem to have vanished in Figure 9.12. They are actually still there, but because the margin-left is set to 0, they are beyond the left edge of the viewport and are not visible. If this list was somewhere else, say in the right div, you would see the markers, probably in a place where you didn't want them to be, such as in the way of the text in the content div.

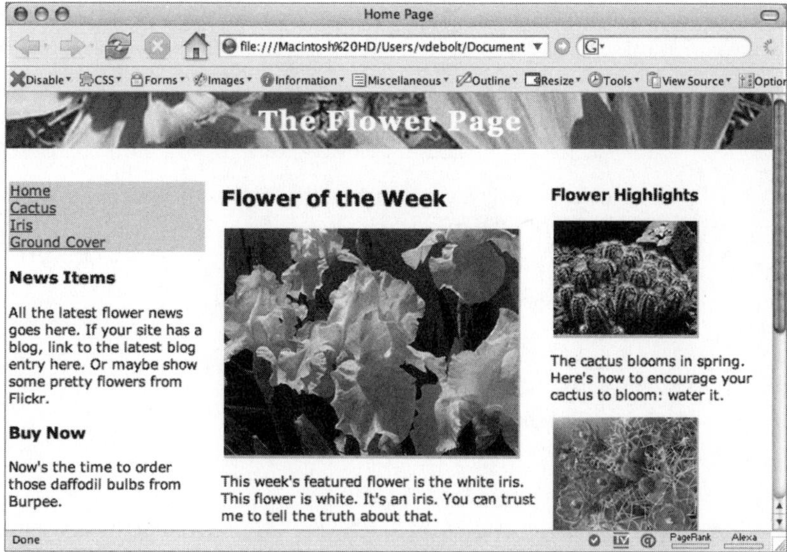

FIGURE 9.12
The list with changes to padding, margin, width, and background color

The list markers need to be explicitly set not to display; to do that, use `list-style: none` wi a `ul` selector. You will zero the margins on the list items, too. A border at the top of each list ite will add a separator to each list item (see Figure 9.13). Here are the rules:

```
#navlist ul {
list-style: none;
}
#navlist li {
margin: 0;
border-top: 1px solid gray;
}
```

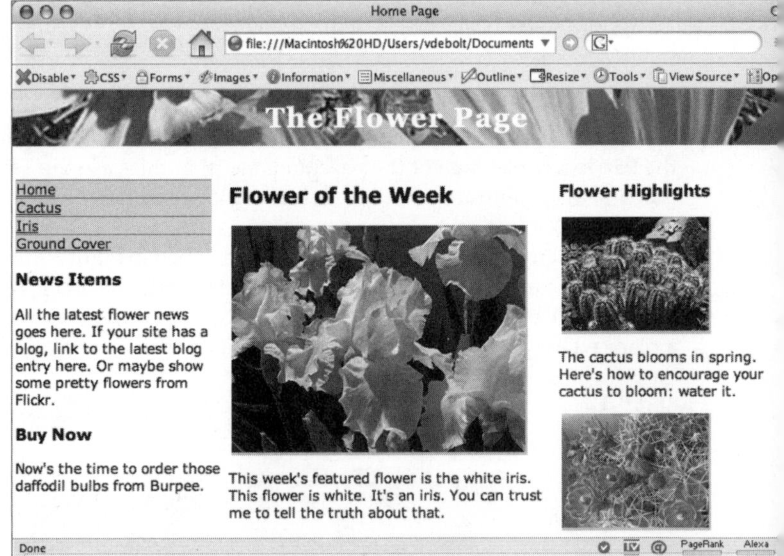

FIGURE 9.13 The list markers are truly not on display now. The border creates the beginnings of a button-like nav bar appearance for the list.

The next rule is the crucial one that makes the nav bar truly effective. Use the `#navbar li a` selector. Here's the rule:

```
#navlist li a {
display: block;
width: auto;
padding: 0.25em 0.5em 0.25em 0.75em;
border-left: 1em solid #AAB;
text-decoration: none;
}
```

The key is `display: block`. This makes the a element (normally an inline element) behav like a block-level element and fill the entire width of the list item. The list item at 95% of the `wid` of the `left` column is wider than the mere text within the a element. The entire width of the now becomes clickable, providing a much larger target. Having the entire `li` clickable, rather than just the text, creates the sense that there is a clickable graphic there, further enhancing the nav bar look and feel.

The `width: auto` is needed to prevent IE6 from creating large gaps between your newly created block-level anchor elements. Other properties (anything that creates hasLayoutin the a element) such as height would work for IE 6 also.

With the preceding rule, you've put in some `padding`. Keep in mind you're padding the a element, not the `li` or the `ul`. A colored `border` on the left also adds to the graphic nav bar feel. You get rid of the underlines on the a elements with `text-decoration: none` (see Figure 9.14).

You'll use three rules to style the pseudo states and change colors on hover to finish the styles. Here are all three:

```
#navlist li a:link {
   color: #80386A;
}
#navlist li a:visited {
   color: #666;
}
#navlist li a:hover {
border-color: #80386A;
color: #FFF;
background: #666;
}
```

The effect is complete with new colors for the link text and background color and border color changes on hover (see Figure 9.15).

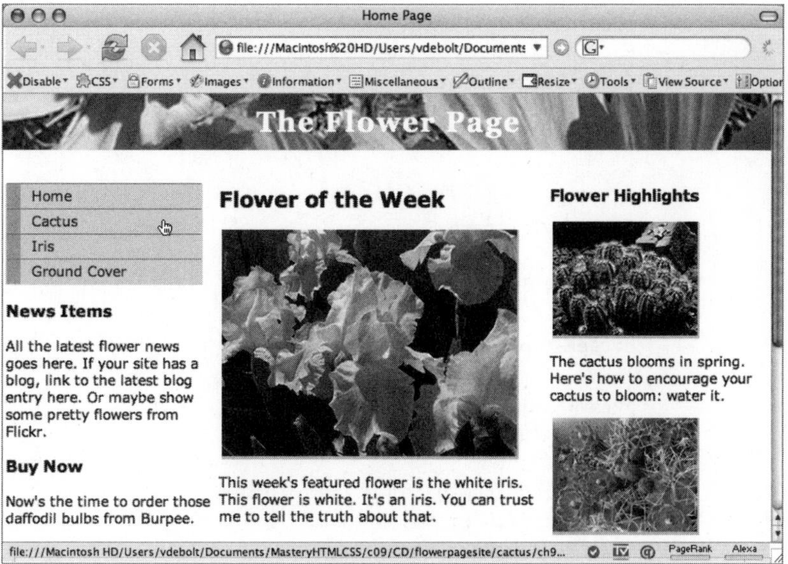

FIGURE 9.14
The pointing finger indicates that the user can now click anywhere within the list item and the link will work. With no underline on the link text and a bit of left border, the nav bar appearance is very like a traditional image-based nav bar.

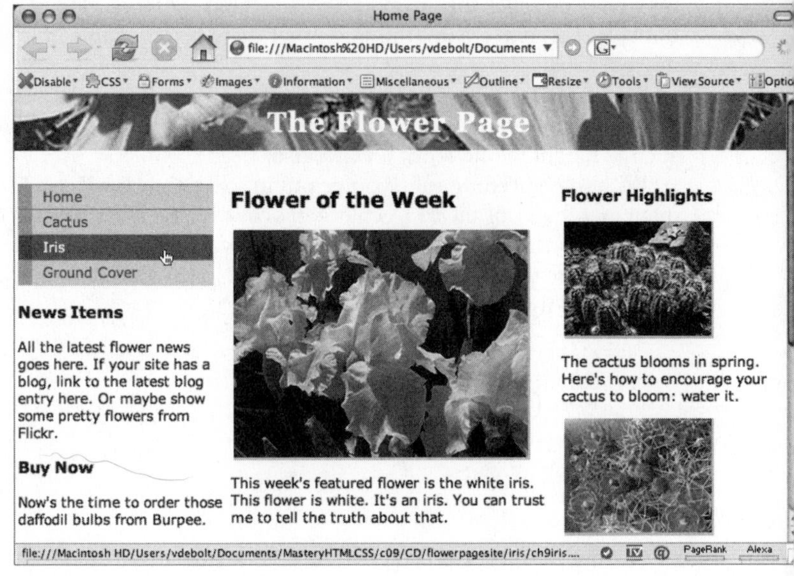

FIGURE 9.15 With the pseudo states styled, the rollover colors appear, the link text colors change, and the vertical nav bar is complete.

The completed rules for the vertical nav bar are shown in Listing 9.4.

LISTING 9.4: The Entire Set of Rules to Style the Vertical List as a Nav Bar

```
/* the vertical nav */
#navlist {
padding: 0 1px 1px;
margin-left: 0;
font: bold 0.9em;
background: #DDDDDD;
width: 95%;
}
#navlist ul {
list-style: none;
}
#navlist li {
margin: 0;
border-top: 1px solid gray;
}
#navlist li a {
display: block;
width: auto;
padding: 0.25em 0.5em 0.25em 0.75em;
border-left: 1em solid #AAB;
text-decoration: none;
}
```

```
#navlist li a:link {
   color: #80386A;
}
#navlist li a:visited {
   color: #667;
}
#navlist li a:hover {
border-color: #80386A;
color: #FFF;
background: #666;
}
```

A Vertical Nav bar with Pure CSS Pop-ups

I'll start this section with a big disclaimer. Pure CSS pop-ups don't work in IE5/6 because they use the `:hover` pseudo class on a `li`.

There are ways to make IE5/6 work with the `:hover` pseudo class on a `li` that require JavaScript. There is a list of good resources for such scripts at the end of this section.

Obviously, you don't want to use IE as your test browser when you work through this section.

There are a number of sources of information on how to create this type of menu. I'll model this exercise on the original pure CSS pop-up article published at `http://meyerweb.com/eric/css/edge/menus/demo.html` that got the whole trend toward drop-down and pop-up menus using CSS started.

Continue with `ch9index_vert.html` and `ch9_lists.css`. You'll add to both documents. In the XHTML, add a couple of nested lists to the menu. Remember, when you nest a list inside a list item, the complete new element must be enclosed by the opening and closing `li` tags (see Listing 9.5).

LISTING 9.5: Two New Nested Lists for the Menu

```
<ul id="navlist">
   <li><a href="ch9index_horiz.html">Home</a></li>
   <li><a href="cactus/ch9cactus.html">Cactus</a>
        <ul class="subnav">
         <li><a href="cactus/ch9cactusfaq.html">Cactus FAQ</a></li>
         <li><a href="#">Link B</a></li>
      </ul>
   </li>
   <li><a href="iris/ch9iris.html">Iris</a>
      <ul class="subnav">
         <li><a href="#">Link A</a></li>
         <li><a href="#">Link B</a></li>
      </ul>
   </li>
   <li><a href="groundcover/ch9groundcover.html">Ground Cover</a> </li>
</ul>
```

Note that the two new nested lists are assigned to a `class` called `subnav`. You need a selector f the `display` rules, and `.subnav` will be it. Another selector that works without the addition of class is `#navlist ul`. If you'd like to use that one, remove the class from the preceding code ar use the `#navlist ul` selector in the following exercises instead.

There is a real page for the `Cactus FAQ` hyperlink. The other hyperlinks are fakes and onl look like links because `href="#"` creates something that looks close enough to make the exerci understandable.

Before you add the CSS to hide the nested lists and make them pop out when you want, the appear as part of the menu (see Figure 9.16).

Add a comment to your style sheet such as `/* pure CSS popups */` and write a rule after it hide the nested lists. The selector is `#navlist .subnav`. The `display: none` rule hides the list Here's the rule:

```
/* pure CSS popups */
#navlist .subnav  {
display: none;
}
```

That hides the `subnav` (see Figure 9.17), but there is no visual clue to the fact that two of the me items have submenus.

The user needs a hint that certain items in the menu contain more links. Well-understood ico for this include plus signs, triangles, and arrows. The `li` elements that need an icon can be assign to a class, for example `arrow`. Listing 9.6 shows where to add that class attribute.

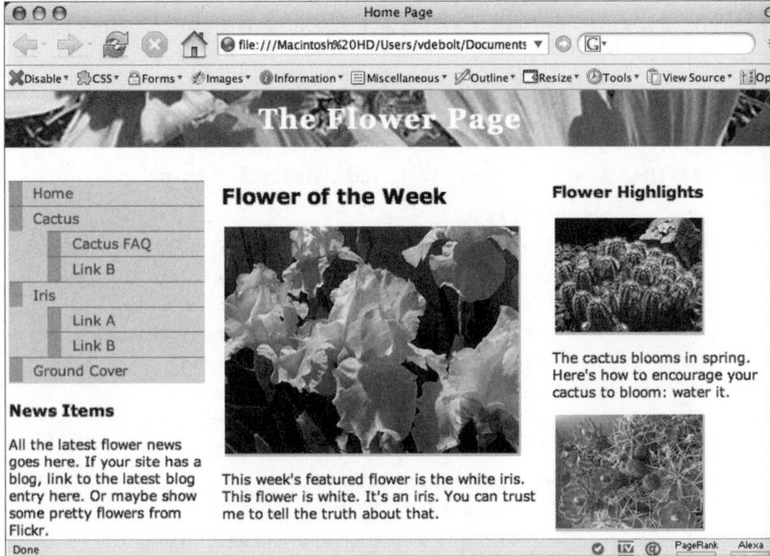

FIGURE 9.16 With no CSS to style the presentation of the nested lists, they are clearly visible in the menu.

FIGURE 9.17
With `display: none` for the subnav, the nested lists are hidden, but there is no clue that they exist.

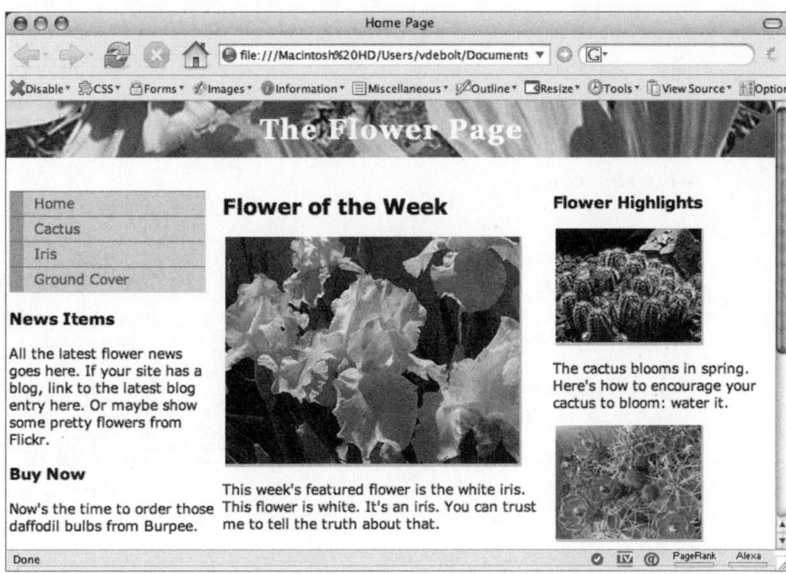

LISTING 9.6: Add the *class="arrow"* Attribute to the Hyperlinks with Subnavigation

```
<ul id="navlist">
   <li><a href="ch9index_horiz.html">Home</a></li>
   <li class="arrow"><a href="cactus/ch9cactus.html">Cactus</a>
        <ul class="subnav">
         <li><a href="cactus/ch9cactusfaq.html">Cactus FAQ</a></li>
         <li><a href="#">Link B</a></li>
      </ul>
   </li>
   <li class="arrow"><a href="iris/ch9iris.html">Iris</a>
      <ul class="subnav">
         <li><a href="#">Link A</a></li>
         <li><a href="#">Link B</a></li>
      </ul>
   </li>
   <li><a href="groundcover/ch9groundcover.html">Ground Cover</a> </li>
</ul>
```

You will write a rule for the class that inserts an arrow in the list item as a background image. Add the arrow at `img/arrow.gif` with this rule:

```
#navlist li.arrow {
   background: url(img/arrow.gif) no-repeat right center;
}
```

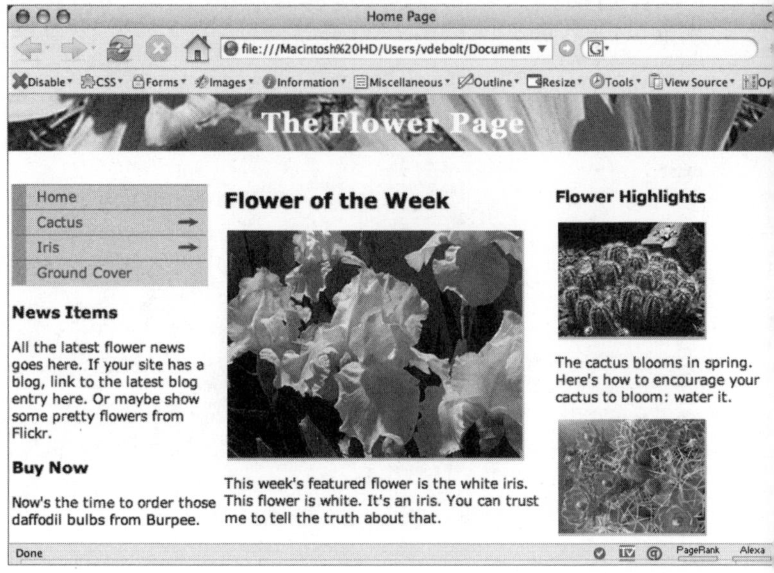

FIGURE 9.18
The arrows convey the idea that the menu items have submenu items that can be seen when the item is hovered over.

Note that the arrow is set for `no-repeat` and is positioned at the `right` and centered vertica (see Figure 9.18).

An absolutely positioned element is positioned with respect to its nearest positioned ancestor. Sir you want to position the pop-ups, you need to assign `position: relative` to the `li` elements—t parents of the `subnav` elements. There's no need to apply any offsets, you're just enabling the childr of the `li` elements to be positioned absolutely. Here's the rule:

```
#navlist li {
   position: relative;
}
```

This rule has no visible effect on the browser display. It makes a difference in what happen when you add the last style rule.

To make the nested list appear, use `display: block`. The selector is `#navlist li:hover u` The selector targets a `ul` descended from a list item when it is in the `:hover` pseudo state.

When positioning the pop-up, you must not let any space appear between the parent list ite and its descendants. If the cursor passes over space that isn't part of the list item, the pop-up w disappear. Pop-up (and drop-down) menus present difficulties for users with motor impairmen making them a bit controversial. However, *no one* can use a pop-up menu that is separated from parent by even one pixel of empty space.

I suggest some `position` values that make the `subnav` actually overlap the `navlist` by a bi (hence the `z-index`). You can fudge the numbers if you don't like the effect; just remember not go too far. Here's the rule:

```
#navlist li:hover ul {
   display: block;
   position: absolute; top: 5px; left: 55%;
   width: 10em;
   z-index: 100;
}
```

Add some rules to style the subnav items that will pop out. First the `.subnav a:link` needs a color and background:

```
.subnav li a:link {
   color: #80386A;
   background: #DDDDDD;
}
```

Give the visited links a different color. Use a group selector for `.subnav li a:hover, .subnav li a:active` to style both these with the same rules. Here's a suggested color scheme:

```
.subnav li a:visited {
   color: #FFFFFF;
   background: #DDDDDD;
}
.subnav li a:hover, #subnav li a:active {
   border-color: #80386A;
   color: #FFF;
   background: #666;
}
```

You now have a complete working CSS pop-up menu (see Figure 9.19). I'll end this section with another disclaimer. Even in a browser like Firefox, this technique isn't perfect. But you have an understanding of the principles involved. If you extend your web design skills to add JavaScript, which is intended to create browser behavior, you can make pop-ups that are easier to use. For example, a script can create a delay so that if the cursor moves off the menu item for a second, the menu does not disappear. CSS pop-ups only work if the user has a mouse and can hover over the item. JavaScript can use several keyboard event handlers and even recognize which key is currently pressed, making a scripted pop-up menu work with keyboard alone. Websites use XHTML for content, CSS for presentation, and scripts for behavior. Each has a place, even though scripting is not covered in this book.

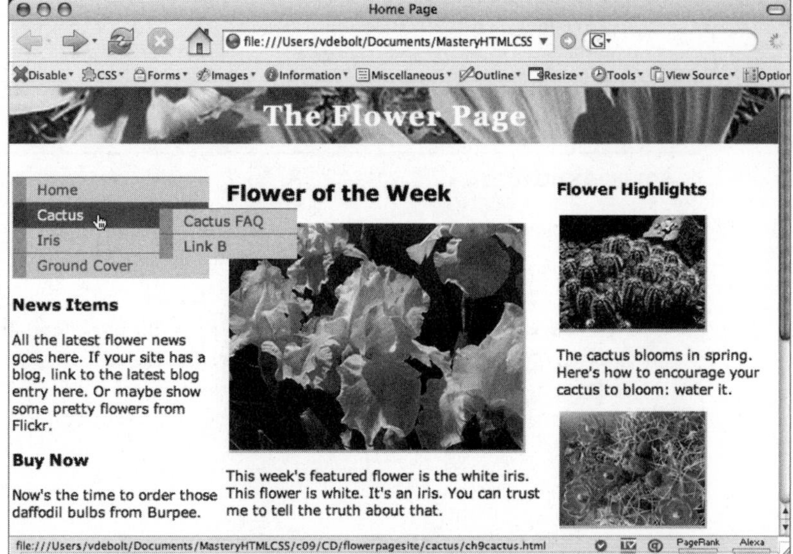

FIGURE 9.19
The CSS pop-up menu appears on hover.

Listing 9.7 shows the completed styles for the pop-up menu .

LISTING 9.7: The Complete Set of Styles That Create the Pure CSS Pop-ups

```
/* the popup CSS menu */
#navlist .subnav  {
display: none;
}
#navlist li.arrow {
   background: url(img/arrow.gif) no-repeat right center;
}
.subnav li a:link {
color: #80386A;
background: #DDDDDD; }
.subnav li a:visited {
color: #FFFFFF;
background: #DDDDDD;
}
.subnav li a:hover, #subnav li a:active {
border-color: #80386A;
color: #FFF;
background: #666;
}
#navlist li {
   position: relative;
}
#navlist li:hover ul {
   display: block;
   position: absolute; top: 5px; left: 65%;
   width: 10em;
   z-index: 100;
}
```

SOME RESOURCES

Internet Explorer versions 6 and below do not understand `li:hover`. Therefore, pure CSS pop-ups don't work for most people. Most designers add a bit of JavaScript to make IE do what other modern browsers do. Here are some sources;

- Project Seven's CSS Express Drop-Down Menus (for horizontal drop-downs only) complete with tutorial, CSS, and JavaScript at `www.projectseven.com/tutorials/navigation/auto_hide/index.htm`. This is a free tutorial from Project Seven, but they also have some very well tested Dreamweaver pop-up menus for sale that use scripting and CSS with excellent results.

- A script called `whatever:hover` makes hover work on just about anything. It's available at `www.xs4all.nl/~peterned/csshover.html`.
- Dean Edwards offers a whole library of JavaScripts that do much more than fix `:hover`. They make IE5/6 act standards-compliant in all kinds of ways. The library is available at `dean.edwards.name/IE7`.

Horizontal Lists

The `display` property can make elements that are not actually block level behave as block-level elements, a rule you just used to create vertical list menus. Conversely, the `display` property can make elements that are not actually inline elements behave as inline elements. The magic bullet of horizontal list display is `display: inline`. Keep in mind that if the user does not have a CSS-capable browser, the block (or inline) elements will still be what they actually are in the XHTML. You only change the display, not the document. You cannot nest a block-level element in an inline element in XHTML, no matter what you declare as a display value in the CSS.

To create a horizontal menu, work with `ch9index_horiz.html`.

Save a copy of `ch9_lists.css` with a new name, for example `ch9_lists_horiz.css`. Take it back to its original state by deleting all the vertical menu and pop-up rules, and change the `link` element in `ch9index_horiz.html` to link to your new style sheet. The new link element is

```
<link href="ch9_lists_horiz.css" rel="stylesheet" type="text/css" />
```

Take a look at the code for `ch9index_horiz.html`. The list has been moved. It's now nested in the `header` div; see Listing 9.8.

LISTING 9.8: The Menu Is a Nested Div in the Header on *ch9index_horiz.html*

```
<div id="header">
   <h1>The Flower Page</h1>
   <div id="horiznav">
     <ul id="navlist">
       <li><a href="ch9index_horiz.html">Home</a></li>
       <li><a href="cactus/ch9cactus.html">Cactus</a></li>
       <li><a href="iris/ch9iris.html">Iris</a></li>
       <li><a href="groundcover/ch9groundcover.html">Ground Cover</a></li>
     </ul>
   </div>
</div>
```

Note that the new menu is in a div called `horiznav` and the `ul` element again has the `id` `navlist`.

As you can see in Figure 9.20, things look pretty awful before you do anything with the CSS when first viewing `ch9index_horiz.html` in a browser.

ID WATCH

If you use both a horizontal and a vertical menu on the same page—a common practice on large sites—you cannot use the `id="navlist"` for both lists, since an `id` must be unique. Use a sensible name for the two `id` attributes: `globalnav`, `mainnav`, `secondarynav`, `subnav`—you get the idea.

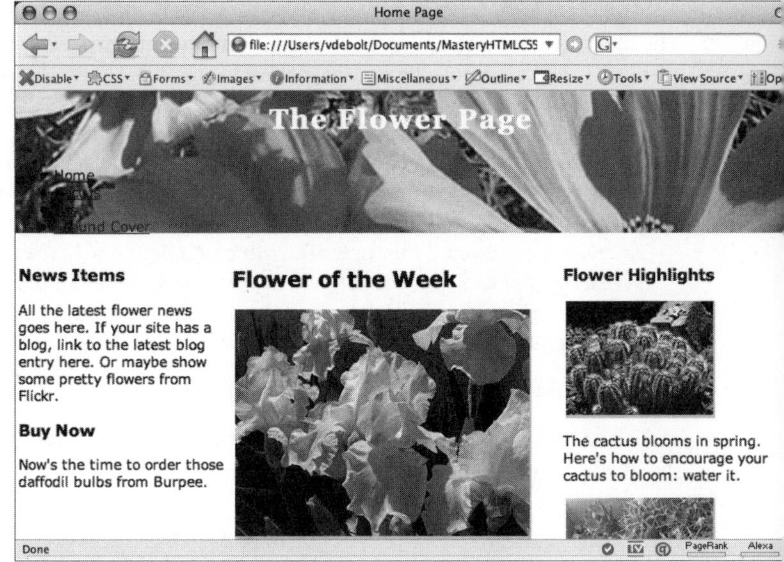

FIGURE 9.20 The unstyled menu, obscured by the background image in the header, is barely visible on the left.

The first rule creates a style for the `horiznav` element that sets up `margin`, `padding`, `width`, a `background` color, and a `border-bottom`.

```
/* horizontal nav list */
#horiznav {
   margin: 0;
   padding: 1px 0 0 12px;
   width: 100%;
   background: #DDDDDD;
   border-bottom: 2px solid #666666;
}
```

This rule defines an area for the menu and covers the flowers with a light gray background (s Figure 9.21).

As with the vertical `ul`, you want to zero out the `margin`. Use `text-align: center` to center the list. Just a touch of `padding` at the top and bottom will keep the menu items from sticking out of the gray bar. Here's the rule:

```
#horiznav ul {
text-align: center;
margin: 0
padding-top: 3px;padding-bottom: 3px;
}
```

You see the center alignment, although it is more difficult to see the margin and padding changes visually at this point (see Figure 9.22).

Move on to the list item rules. Here is where you use `display: inline` to line the list items up horizontally. You'll remove those bullet markers now and again zero out any margin and padding. Here's the rule:

```
#horiznav li {
display: inline;
list-style: none;
margin: 0;
padding: 0;
}
```

With the `display; inline` rule, you're starting to look pretty good (see Figure 9.23).

FIGURE 9.21
You've defined an area where your styled menu will sit when it's complete.

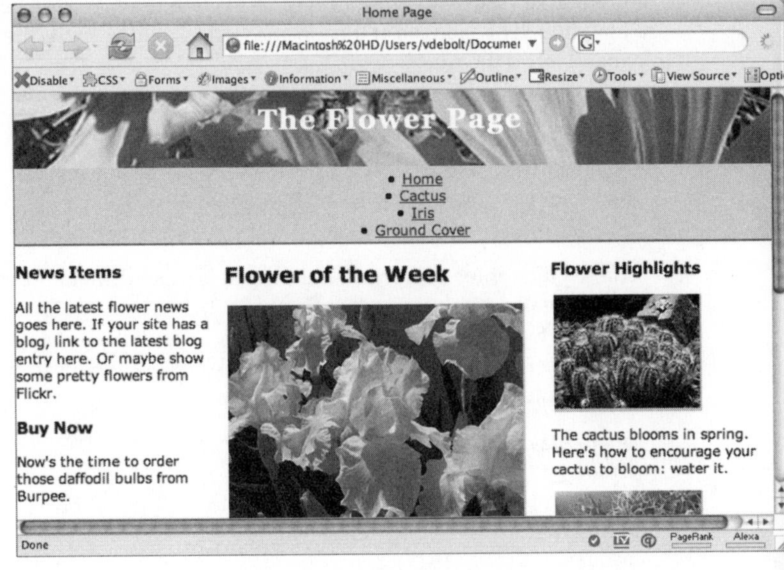

FIGURE 9.22
The list is centered and has no margin and a bit of top and bottom padding.

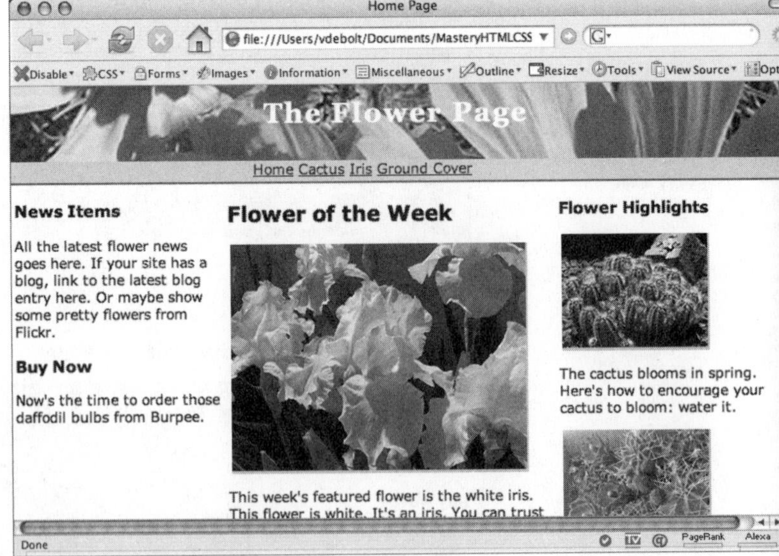

FIGURE 9.23
The list items display like inline elements flowing across a line because of `display: inline`.

FLOAT THAT LIST

The gorgeous and brilliant sliding doors horizontal menu, found at `http://alistapart.com/articles/slidingdoors`, relies on floats and background images to create a tabbed appearance. A floated item can have a width, needed for a technique like sliding doors. But floats cannot be centered.

Ethan Marcotte at 24 Ways found a way to center the tabs *and* use the sliding doors technique, too: `http://24ways.org/advent/centered-tabs-with-css`.

Turn your attention to the a elements. The selector `#horiznav a` will style all the anchor elements, regardless of pseudo state. Add a rule for `color`, `text-decoration`, `background`, `padding`, and `border`. Note that I suggest borders only on the top, right, and left, and that they are not all the same color.

```
#horiznav a {
color: #80386A;text-decoration: none;
background: #DDDDDD;
margin: 0;
padding: 2px 10px;
border-top: 1px solid #fff;
border-right: 1px solid #aaa;
border-left: 1px solid #fff;
}
```

That gives more control over the link colors and creates a bit more of a button-like appearance (see Figure 9.24).

FIGURE 9.24
All the anchor elements have the same rules applied to remove the link underline and change the link colors.

The final touches will create the rollover effects and set colors for the other link states. Add subtle `color` change for the `:visited` links and a different `color` and `background` for the `:hov` and `:active` pseudo states, and you're finished. Here are the two rules:

```
#horiznav a:visited {
   color: #B54F99;
}
#horiznav a:hover, #horiznav a:active {
   color: #333333;
   background: #BBBBBB;
}
```

As in Figure 9.25, you should see a background color change as a rollover. It may be a bit ha to tell in Figure 9.25 that "Cactus" is a visited link, but in your browser you should detect a slig color change for visited links. If the visited link color change is too subtle to suit you, experime with other colors to achieve more contrast.

The entire set of rules needed to create the horizontal menu is shown in Listing 9.9.

FIGURE 9.25
When hovering over an item, the background color changes.

LISTING 9.9: The Rules Used to Create the Horizontal List

```
/* horizontal nav list */
#horiznav {
   margin: 0;
   padding: 1px 0 0 12px;
   width: 100%;
   background: #DDDDDD;
   border-bottom: 2px solid #666;
}
```

```
#horiznav ul {
   margin: 0;
   padding-top: 3px;
   padding-bottom: 3px;
   text-align: center;
}
#horiznav li {
   display: inline;
   list-style: none;
   margin: 0;
   padding: 0;
}
#horiznav a {
   color: #80386A;
   text-decoration: none;
   background: #DDDDDD;
   margin-top: 3px;
   padding: 2px 10px;
   border-top: 1px solid #fff;
   border-right: 1px solid #aaaaaa;
   border-left: 1px solid #fff;
}
#horiznav a:visited {
   color: #B54F99;
}
#horiznav a:hover, #horiznav a:active {
   color: #333;
   background: #BBBBBB;
}
```

You did a number of things to style the lists. They were all important parts of the end result, but boil it down to the essentials and you end up with just a couple of things that create the effect: a `list-style` rule and a `display` rule (see Figure 9.26).

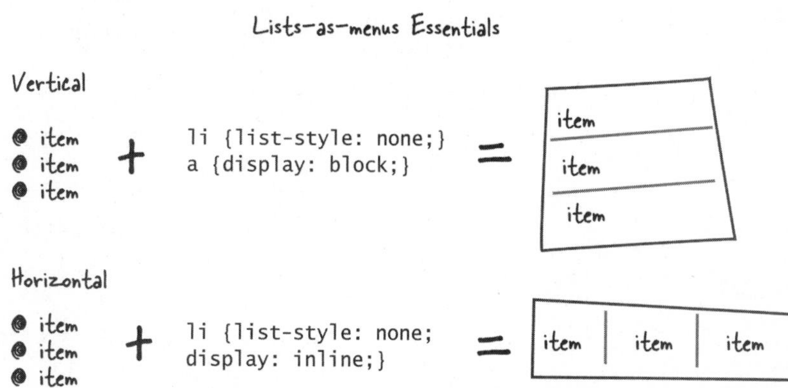

FIGURE 9.26
The key elements in creating styled menus of lists

THE JOY OF WIZARDS

A couple of sites offer excellent resources that either provide or automatically generate both the XHTML and CSS for either a vertical or horizontal nav bar list.

Listamatic at `http://css.maxdesign.com.au/listamatic` has helpful information about lists with examples various of CSS styling options. Be sure to check Listamatic2 at `http://css.maxdesign.com.au/listamatic2` also. In addition to numerous code samples for the list examples in the gallery, there are links to other list examples and list resources.

Listamatic inspired List-O-Matic at `http://accessify.com/tools-and-wizards/developer-tools/list-o-matic`. This wizard will let you fill in your link information and then generate a horizontal or vertical menu of your choosing automatically. This site has other helpful wizards besides List-O-Matic, so look around while you're there.

Coming up next in Chapter 10, you will learn how to create and style a table.

Real-World Scenario

Here are two sites that demonstrate effective use of lists: Digital Web and Accessify.

Digital Web

Digital Web Magazine is a publication for web designers. It includes tutorials, articles, interviews, book reviews, and software reviews at `www.digital-web.com`. This nonprofit publication is created by a worldwide network of volunteers. A view of the home page is shown in Figure 9.27.

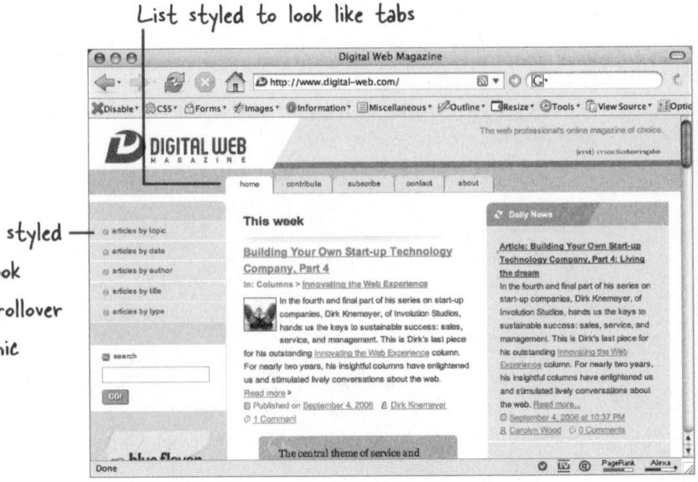

FIGURE 9.27
Digital Web Magazine is an online magazine for web designers.

Across the top of the page you see menu items that look like tabs with links to articles pages where the user can contribute or subscribe, and the usual Contact and About pages. These links are marked up in a list.

On the left side, you see links that look like buttons with rollover effects that lead to articles by date, articles by author, and so on. These links are also contained in a list.

A glance at the source code reveals that there are several style sheets in use on this site. There's an `id` in the `body` tag that provides a CSS hook for rules specific to the home page. The first `div` in the document flow is the main `content` div. The navigation elements come later in the document flow and are placed in the layout with absolute positioning.

In addition to serving as an example of attractive and functional use of lists in the real world, Digital Web Magazine also uses valid XHTML and passes online accessibility testing by Cynthia Says. (You will learn more about testing your sites for accessibility in Chapter 12.)

I recommend Digital Web Magazine as a source of good reading as you continue to develop your skills as a web designer.

Accessify

Accessify (`www.accessify.com`) is another site making good use of a list for its navigation (see Figure 9.28).

This site uses CSS to create a current page indicator, a good reminder of the value of this practice. You learned how to create a current page indicator in Chapter 7; the point demonstrated here is that it is good practice to include this feature with all menus, whether they are made of styled lists or not. In Figure 9.28 the current page is Home. Note that the link being hovered over changes using the same blue bar that styles the current page indicator. There is also additional information about the link in a title attribute that shows as a tool tip when you hover over it.

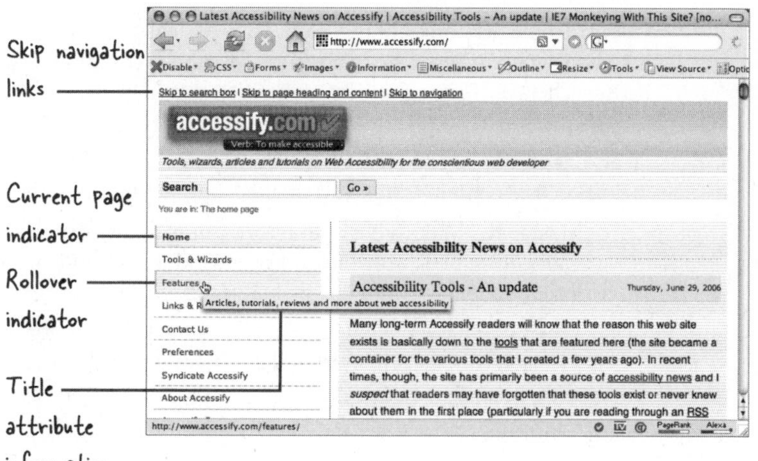

FIGURE 9.28
Accessify uses a list for navigation. Note the use of the title attribute on the link text, the current page indicator for the Home page, and the rollover effect on hover.

If you checked out the resources mentioned in the sidebar "The Joy of Wizards," you recogniz this site as the source of the recommended wizard for creating navigation elements from lists.

There are three skip navigation links at the top of the page: to the search box, to the content, an to the navigation. The navigation on Accessify, like the navigation on Digital Web Magazine, is the end of the document flow.

CSS Properties for Lists

New CSS properties for list display were covered in this chapter. Table 9.1 shows the new CSS properties you learned.

TABLE 9.1: CSS Properties for the *ul*, *ol*, and *li* Selectors

PROPERTY	POSSIBLE VALUE
`list-style-type`	`disc`, `circle`, `square`, `decimal`, `decimal-leading-zero`, `upper-alpha`, `lower-alpha`, `upper-roman`, `lower-roman`, `lower-greek`, `hebrew`, `armenian`, `georgian`, `cjk-ideographic`, `hiragana`, `katakana`, `hiragana-iroha`, `none`, `inherit`
`list-style-image`	`uri`, `none`, `inherit`
`list-style-position`	`inside`, `outside`, `inherit`

The Bottom Line

Lists are the workhorses of the Web. They are easy to read, make finding information go quickl help you set up ordered steps or processes, and accommodate a myriad of marker types and nu bering schemes. This versatility makes lists popular for many different situations.

Write every type of list. There are three types of lists in use on the Web: ordered, unordere and definition. Ordered and unordered lists are constructed of a simple series of list items. D inition lists contain terms and their accompanying definitions.

Master It Make a list with information about your friends, family, CD collection, produ warranties, pets, or some other type of information you are interested in. Nest the list to least two levels, more if it makes sense with your topic.

When you have the list built, write some CSS rules for it. Be as creative as you can in you presentation. Be prepared to demonstrate your list in a browser.

Use CSS to control the presentation of lists. Any CSS property can be applied to the prese tation of lists.

Master It Instead of making the `star.gif` apply to every marker on your page of unorder lists, see what happens if you do this: `ul ul {list-style: url(star.gif);}`. Where do the star first appear in the list? When is it inherited? What happens if the `ul ul` rule has the s as a background image rather than a `list-style-type`? Is the star inherited?

Use lists as vertical, horizontal, and CSS pop-up navigation elements. A list can contain any textual element, including links. Because navigation menus on web pages are often a list of links, lists are often used to create menus and nav bars. Using `display: block` or `display: inline` or `floats`, lists can be styled with CSS rules that make them appear in a button-like vertical or horizontal display.

Master It Pick either the horizontal or the vertical list exercise and try using background images instead of background colors to create the rollover effect. Use `hoverbg.jpg`, `linkbg.jpg` or `visitedbg.jpg` from the accompanying CD if you need images for this (or make your own). You did something like this in Chapter 7 with `background-image`, but the knowledge you gained from Chapter 9 makes it a much more attractive option for a menu. Demonstrate your results in a browser.

Chapter 10

Tables and Table Styles

You shouldn't use a table for layout if your goal is a site accessible to everyone.

If you're lucky enough to be learning XHTML, CSS, and site design together, that warning may seem odd. In print, a table is a specialized format for a certain kind of information, and why would anyone use it to lay out a whole page? Because until CSS came along, they had to. Many designers spent years learning to create web pages using table-based layouts, and the transition to CSS-based layouts has been rocky. There are still millions of websites built with table layouts on the Web, but that is slowly changing. You should use tables only to display tabular data—that is, where you need to present the same categories of information (the columns) for two or more related things (the rows), such as comparing NFL player stats or features available in different software versions.

The tables you make should be accessible to all users. If you use web standards and accessibility guidelines when you create a table, all the *shoulds* in the preceding sentences will be accomplished.

In this chapter you will:

- Write the XHTML for a table.
- Use elements and attributes to make a table accessible.
- Write CSS to control the presentation of a table.

A Tangled Table Tale

The topic of tables requires a brief history lesson. In versions of HTML prior to 1996, CSS was not available. Even when the first recommendation for CSS was released by the W3C, there was very limited support for the standard in browsers available at that time. Without CSS to lay out a page, designers took what they knew about publishing in print and applied that to web page design. When laying out a magazine or newspaper page, the designer thinks in terms of a grid, an arrangement of columns and rows. Often accustomed to improvising solutions and thinking of document content visually rather than structurally or functionally, these designers saw the table as the equivalent grid layout tool for web pages. For quite some time, tables were the only layout tool in town. There were tables nested within tables, tables beside tables: tables, tables everywhere. Page headings, navigation, and main content were all shoehorned into table cells.

About the same time that designers grew really masterful at creating complicated arrangements of myriad numbers of nested tables, it became apparent that nested table layouts were a serious barrier to users with accessibility needs because they often rendered as senseless gibberish when not accessed visually. More and more people were using the Internet, and more and more people were finding barriers to accessing the Internet in the process.

Limited support for CSS appeared in Internet Explorer 3 (1996) and Netscape Navigator 4. Designers began using CSS in limited ways, while still mostly misusing tables to achieve page lay outs. The W3C responded with improved versions of HTML and CSS. The W3C also responde with the Web Accessibility Initiative (WAI), which provided guidelines for content accessibilit and authoring tool accessibility as well as other accessibility information. Designers, frustrated with the lack of browser support for these new technologies, raised their cries for browser suppo for the W3C standards to a fever pitch, and the Web Standards Project (`www.webstandards.org` began aggressively urging standards support on the browser makers.

The U.S. government added Section 508 to the Americans with Disabilities Act, which required ce tain accessibility features to be integrated with the website of any federal agency or federal contract

The WAI and the Section 508 requirements cover a range of web-based technologies, including audible screen readers and Braille readers. They also address issues relating to site graphics, frame animations, image maps, scripting languages, plug-ins, and forms. Try as they might, without prop implementation of the standards by the browser makers, it was very difficult for people making we pages to comply with these accessibility requirements.

In the flurry of activity around the notion of making web-based information accessible to all people, tables received a lot of attention. Most of that attention was negative. Finally, however, standards-compliant browsers began to appear on the scene, and a rush to lay out with CSS and remove table layouts from web pages began—a process that is still ongoing.

The negative attention to tables gave some people the impression that they should never use table, ever, for any reason. Since you are about to read the chapter in this book that teaches you ho to build a table, you probably realize that the idea that tables are nothing but bad is not correct. Tables have a real purpose on the Web. They do the job of displaying data in an organized grid be ter than any other structure. Such tables are called *data tables*, a naming convention that has arise to distinguish them from layout tables. This chapter explores data tables.

You could say that the `table` element is going through an adolescent phase and is suffering fro growing pains. The uses for tables are changing and may evolve even more in the future becaus CSS now has ways to make elements that are not actually tables behave as if they were using th `display` property.

ACCESSIBILITY RESOURCES

Two excellent sources of accessibility information and training are WebAIM at `www.webaim.org` and Knowbility at `www.knowbility.org`.

Knowbility, in particular, offers outstanding training programs in a growing list of cities. Knowbility sponsors an Accessible Internet Rally (AIR) event for web design teams each year, with an awards event that occurs during the annual South by Southwest Interactive Conference (`www.sxsw.com`).

XHTML: Creating the Rows and Columns

The `table` element is composed of a number of horizontal table rows (`tr`) that are filled with cel of table data (`td`). As rows are added to the table, the cells in each row create a vertical colum Both rows and columns in a table can contain table header elements (`th`) as row or column label Figure 10.1 illustrates a completed table element.

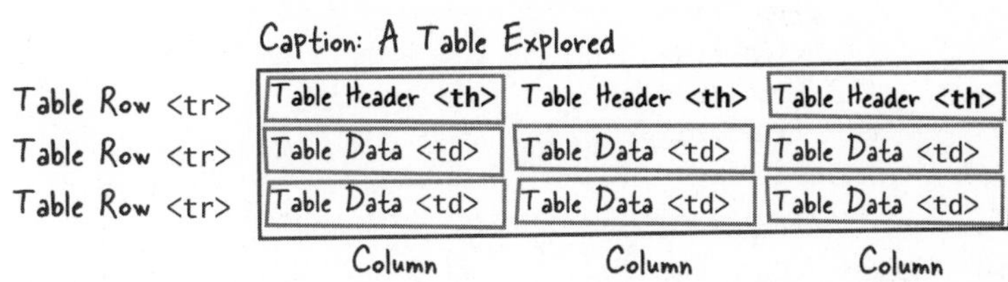

FIGURE 10.1
A diagram of a table's structural parts

Begin a new XHTML document and type along as you go though the steps of building a table.

Begin by typing **<table>**, press Return (Enter) a few times, then type **</table>**. This gives you both the opening and closing tags for the table, so you can view it row by row as you go along, and it will be properly terminated to display in the browser correctly.

```
<table>

</table>
```

For a while, ignore the idea of headings for the rows or columns and just make a row (`tr`) of table data (`td`) elements. The number of `td` elements you put in a row ultimately determines the number of columns your table will have. You'll use three. Type **<tr>** to begin the row, press Return (Enter) a few times and type the closing **</tr>**:

```
<table>
  <tr>

  </tr>
</table>
```

That gives you the row structure, but there is nothing in it. You need `td` elements for that. Since you want three data cells in your row, type **<td></td>** three times, like this:

```
<table>
 <tr>
  <td></td>
  <td></td>
  <td></td>
 </tr>
</table>
```

You don't have any content yet, of course, but that is basically the structure of a table. To add more data cells to a row, you add more `td` elements. To add more rows, you add more `tr` elements. Here is an example of the table with two rows and three data columns:

```
<table>
 <tr>
  <td></td>
  <td></td>
  <td></td>
  </tr>
```

```
  <tr>
   <td></td>
   <td></td>
   <td></td>
  </tr>
 </table>
```

Notice that the number of data cells in each row is the same. Look at Listing 10.1 for a complete table with some content in `th` and `td` elements. The completed file is available on the accompanyin CD: `ch10_table1.html`.

LISTING 10.1: The XHTML to Create the *table* Element in Figure 10.1

```
<table>
   <caption>
   A Table Explored
   </caption>
   <tr>
      <th>Table Header</th>
      <th>Table Header</th>
      <th>Table Header</th>
   </tr>
   <tr>
      <td>Table Data</td>
      <td>Table Data</td>
      <td>Table Data</td>
   </tr>
   <tr>
      <td>Table Data</td>
      <td>Table Data</td>
      <td>Table Data</td>
   </tr>
</table>
```

In the browser, Listing 10.1 displays like Figure 10.2.

Notice the `caption` element. The `caption` element appears in the code immediately after th opening table tag. The caption describes the nature and purpose of the table. The `caption` isn a required element, but its use will help visitors grasp the meaning and purpose of the table With the help of CSS, it can be made to appear at either the top or the bottom of the table, bu it must appear in the XHTML immediately following the opening table tag. You'll get to the CS in just a bit.

The default unstyled table display should also be noted. The `caption` is at the top of the table, th table cells expand to whatever width is needed to hold the content and no further, the `th` elements a in bold. There are no borders.

Obviously, you need some CSS to improve on the browser's default display of a `table` elemen but you'll use a more complex table for those exercises.

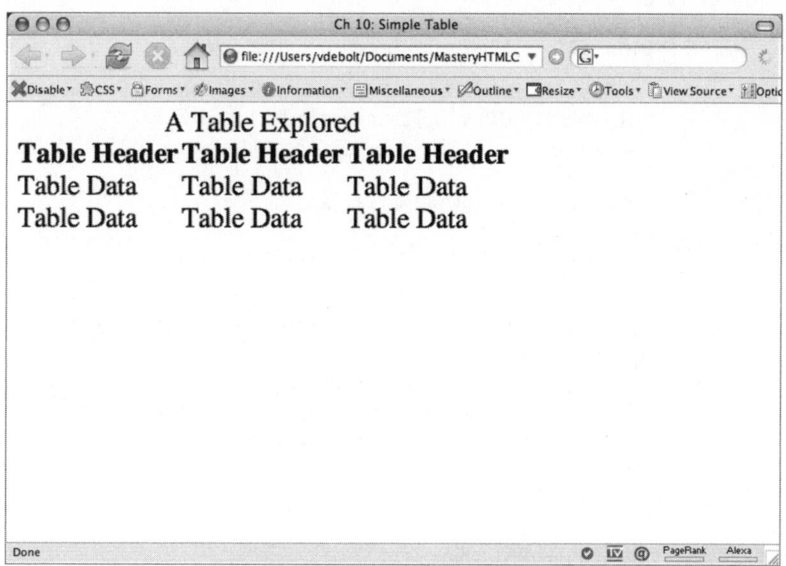

FIGURE 10.2 An unstyled table with the code from Listing 10.1

Making a More Complex and Accessible Table

On the CD, there's a file named `ch10_table2.html`. You'll use it to learn more about tables and how to make them accessible. Open it in your text editor and in your browser. The table looks like Figure 10.3 in the browser. Note that the text size of the tables from the exercises has been increased for the screen captures. Your table may not appear as large as the ones in Figure 10.3 or the following figures.

The complete page for `ch10_table2.html` is shown in Listing 10.2.

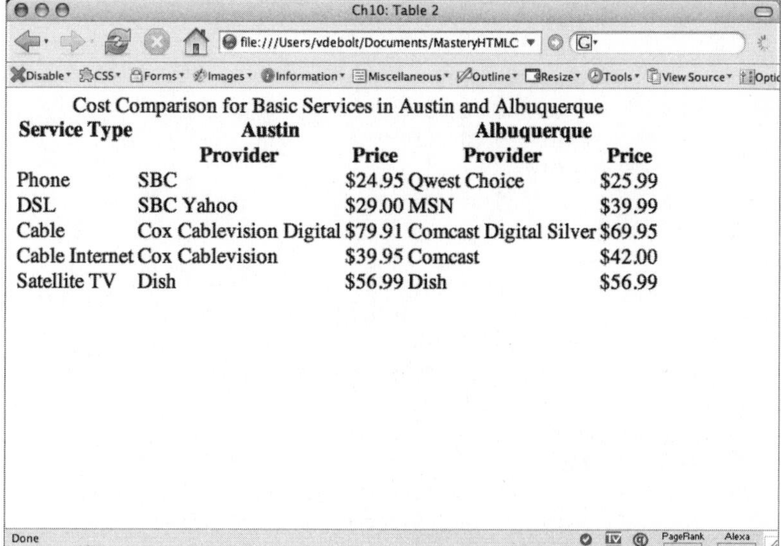

Cost Comparison for Basic Services in Austin and Albuquerque

Service Type	Austin		Albuquerque	
	Provider	Price	Provider	Price
Phone	SBC	$24.95	Qwest Choice	$25.99
DSL	SBC Yahoo	$29.00	MSN	$39.99
Cable	Cox Cablevision Digital	$79.91	Comcast Digital Silver	$69.95
Cable Internet	Cox Cablevision	$39.95	Comcast	$42.00
Satellite TV	Dish	$56.99	Dish	$56.99

FIGURE 10.3 The unstyled `ch10_table2.html` page

LISTING 10.2: The Beginning *ch10_table2.html* Page

```
<!DOCTYPE html PUBLIC "-//W3C//DTD XHTML 1.0 Transitional//EN" "http://www.w3.o
TR/xhtml1/DTD/xhtml1-transitional.dtd">
<html xmlns="http://www.w3.org/1999/xhtml">
<head>
<title>Ch10: Table 2</title>
</head>
<body>
<table>
   <caption>Cost Comparison for Basic Services in Austin and Albuquerque</capti
   <tr>
     <th>Service Type</th>
     <th colspan="2">Austin</th>
     <th colspan="2">Albuquerque</th>
   </tr>
   <tr>
     <th> </th>
     <th>Provider</th>
     <th>Price</th>
     <th>Provider</th>
     <th>Price</th>
   </tr>
   <tr>
     <td>Phone</td>
     <td>SBC</td>
     <td>$24.95</td>
     <td>Qwest Choice</td>
     <td>$25.99</td>
   </tr>
   <tr>
     <td>DSL</td>
     <td>SBC Yahoo</td>
     <td>$29.00</td>
     <td>MSN </td>
     <td>$39.99</td>
   </tr>
   <tr>
     <td>Cable</td>
     <td>Cox Cablevision Digital</td>
     <td>$79.91</td>
     <td>Comcast Digital Silver</td>
     <td>$69.95</td>
   </tr>
   <tr>
     <td>Cable Internet</td>
     <td>Cox Cablevision</td>
     <td>$39.95</td>
```

```
      <td>Comcast</td>
      <td>$42.00</td>
    </tr>
    <tr>
      <td>Satellite TV</td>
      <td>Dish </td>
      <td>$56.99</td>
      <td>Dish </td>
      <td>$56.99</td>
    </tr>
</table>
</body>
</html>
```

One of the th elements (<th> </th>) has nothing in it but a nonbreaking space. You actually need a blank cell there, but to get some older browsers to treat this table cell like all the others in terms of styling borders and other properties you have to put *something* there; a blank space will do.

This table already has one of the accessibility requirements: it uses th elements as column headers. This is essential for accessibility and proper interpretation of the table. If headings are needed for the rows, th elements can also be used in the first cell of each row. The column headings are: Service Type, Austin, Albuquerque.

SPANNING ROWS AND COLUMNS

Note especially this table row:

```
<tr>
  <th>Service Type</th>
  <th colspan="2">Austin</th>
  <th colspan="2">Albuquerque</th>
</tr>
```

As you see in Figure 10.3, the column headings Austin and Albuquerque span two columns. The XHTML creating that span effect is colspan="2".You can make a table cell span any number of columns by specifying this attribute with the number of columns to be spanned in a th or td element.

There is a similar attribute for spanning multiple rows: rowspan. Use rowspan as an attribute in the th or td that you wish to have span more than one row, in a similar fashion to using colspan. For example, <td rowspan="3"> creates a table cell that spans three rows.

CSS: Table Presentation

It's easier to see what you're doing with a table if you use borders. Even if you don't want them in the table when you're finished, they're a help while you're designing.

Start a new style sheet. Save it with the name ch10_table2.css. Add a link to it in your ch10_table2.html document. Add this rule to the new style sheet:

```
table {
   width: 90%;
   border: 1px solid #333;
}
```

The width value will stretch the table out a bit so the table cells are not shrink-wrapped aroun the text. The border property will apply to only the table, not the cells (see Figure 10.4).

For borders around the table cells, add this rule:

```
th, td {
   border: 1px solid #333;
}
```

Now you have *two* borders, because each element—`td`, `th`, and `table`—has individual borde (see Figure 10.5).

The doubled borders can be fixed with the `border-collapse` property. Apply it only to the `table` selector to affect all the borders. The possible values are `separate`, `collapse`, `inherit`. Yo want `collapse`. Add this to the table rule:

```
table {
   width: 90%;
   border: 1px solid #333;
   border-collapse: collapse;
}
```

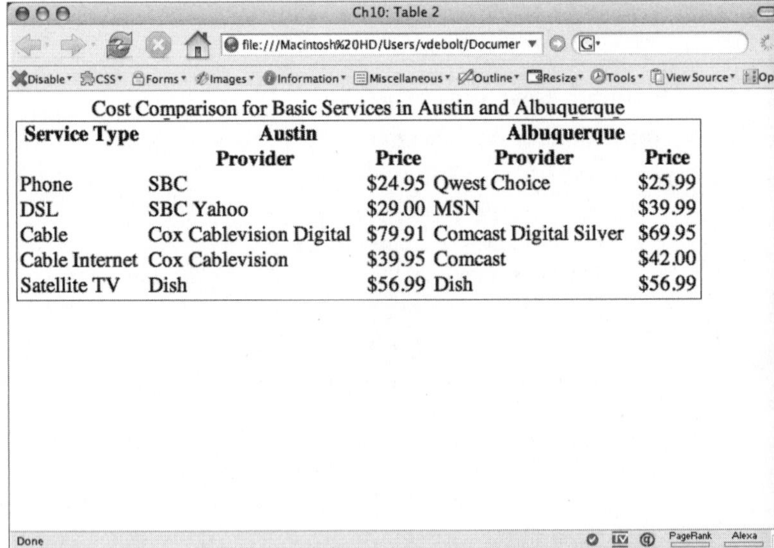

FIGURE 10.4
Using CSS to set a width and add a border to the table element changes the appearance of the table.

You now have a clean and simple single gray border between the cells and around the table itself (see Figure 10.6).

Notice that th cell where you put nothing but a nonbreaking space? It is treated like all the other cells with borders showing.

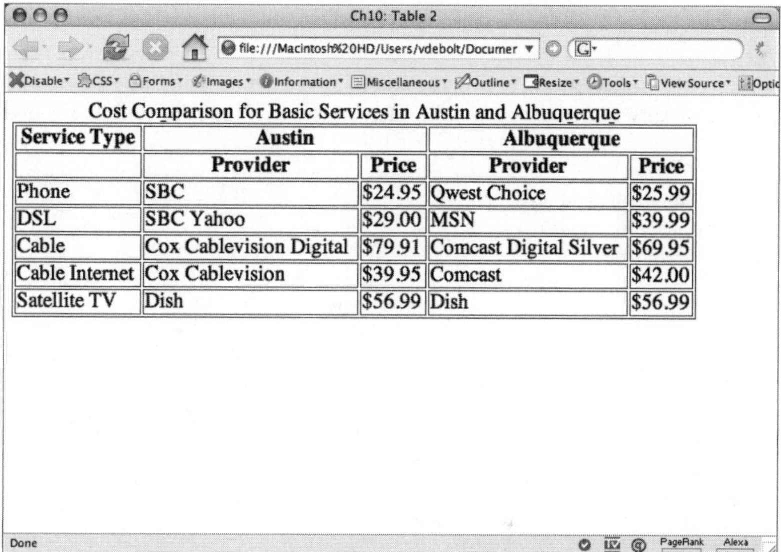

FIGURE 10.5 With borders assigned to the th and td elements, you now have two borderlines visible.

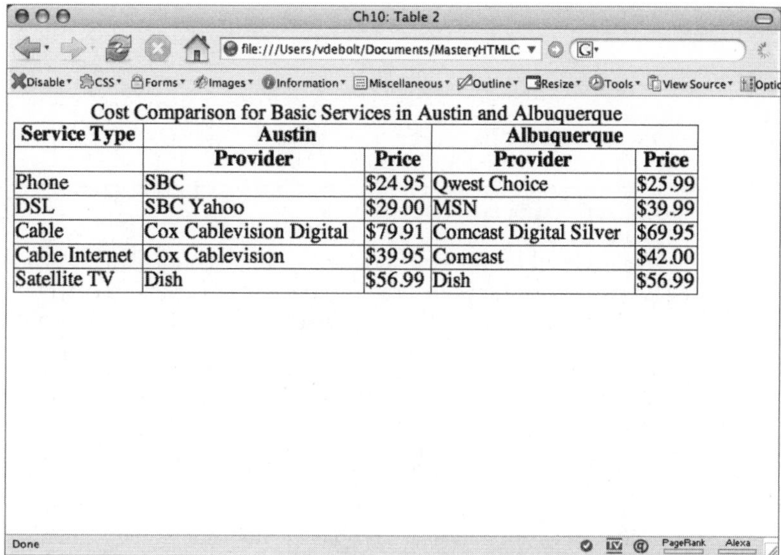

FIGURE 10.6 The border-collapse: collapse declaration creates a single border between cells.

Now that you have the borders in place, it's easier to see that the text in each cell is rubbing u against the cell walls. Provide a bit of `padding`. Add it to the `th, td` selector:

```
th, td {
   border: 1px solid #333;
   padding: 3px;
}
```

That much CSS makes the table easier to read and understand (see Figure 10.7). Before you d any more styling, you'll return to the XHTML needed to achieve accessibility.

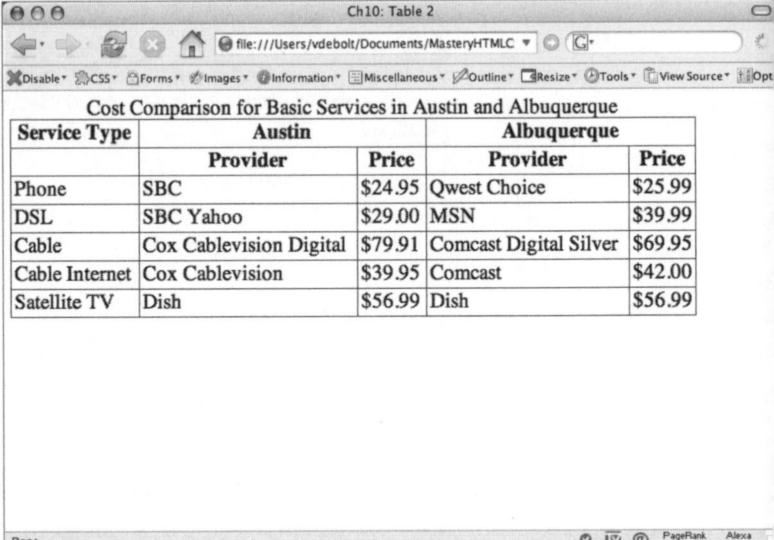

Cost Comparison for Basic Services in Austin and Albuquerque

Service Type	Austin		Albuquerque	
	Provider	Price	Provider	Price
Phone	SBC	$24.95	Qwest Choice	$25.99
DSL	SBC Yahoo	$29.00	MSN	$39.99
Cable	Cox Cablevision Digital	$79.91	Comcast Digital Silver	$69.95
Cable Internet	Cox Cablevision	$39.95	Comcast	$42.00
Satellite TV	Dish	$56.99	Dish	$56.99

FIGURE 10.7 Some cell padding makes the table look less crowded.

TABLE FRAMES AND RULES

When you use the `border` property, a border appears around an entire table or cell. Two less-often used `table` attributes are `frame` and `rule`. You can fine-tune which borders you want to display with the `frame` attribute. The `frame` attribute is applied to the `table` element. Possible values are: `void|above|below|hsides|lhs|rhs|vsides|box|border`.

To describe a few of these values, `lhs` adds a single border on the left side, `rhs` adds a single border on the right side, and box and `border` add a border on all sides.

This example, `<table frame="below">` places a single border on the bottom.

The attribute `rule` can also be applied to a `table`. A `rule` is an internal border. The possible values are: `none | groups | rows | cols | all`. The value rows adds horizontal rules between rows; the value `cols` adds vertical rules between columns.

Much like the `thead` or `tbody` elements discussed in detail later in the chapter, a group of columns can be grouped for styling purposes with a `colgroup` attribute (discussed later in the chapter). If a `table` has designated `colgroup` elements, then the `rule="groups"` attribute and value would place rules between column groups.

Before using these XHTML attributes, however, consider that the same effects can—and usually should—be controlled with CSS.

Headers

Care must be taken with a complex table using a `colspan` (or a `rowspan`). Under the table heading `Austin`, there are two columns: `Provider` and `Price`. The table heading for `Albuquerque` is similar. It's easy enough to visually track across from a service and down in a column to see a particular service and price for a particular city. But users with assistive devices such as screen readers need more help to associate the various `th` elements with the proper data cells. The `headers` attribute is used for this.

KEEP IT SIMPLE

In general, a data table using a simple grid without any spanned rows or columns is more accessible to a device like a screen reader. A table with only one level of row or column headers is better than a more complicated one. If the table needs more than one header element for each row or column, it might be better to divide it into two or more simpler tables.

The `headers` attribute is used to associate specific data cells with specific headers. An `id` is assigned to each `th` element. Find the two rows in your table that use the `th` element. Suggested `id` names to add to each of the `th` elements are shown here:

```
<tr>
  <th id="service">Service Type</th>
  <th colspan="2" id="austin">Austin</th>
  <th colspan="2" id="albuquerque">Albuquerque</th>
</tr>
<tr>
  <th> </th>
  <th id="txprovider">Provider</th>
  <th id="txprice">Price</th>
  <th id="nmprovider">Provider</th>
  <th id="nmprice">Price</th>
</tr>
```

Now that each `th` has an `id`, turn your attention to the `td` elements. Each `td` is associated with the relevant `th` using a `headers` attribute, like this:

```
<td headers="service">Phone</td>
```

More than one of the named IDs can be listed in the `headers` attribute, if more than one `th` applies to the particular data cell. Leave a space between the names when more than one ID na is listed. For example:

```
<td headers="austin txprovider">SBC</td>
```

Each `td` in the table needs these attributes. Try adding them yourself to make sure you und stand the concept. Then check yourself using the code in Listing 10.3.

Listing 10.3: The *td* Elments with Headers Included

```
<tr>
  <td headers="service">Phone</td>
  <td headers="austin txprovider">SBC</td>
  <td headers="austin txprice">$24.95</td>
  <td headers="albuquerque nmprovider">Qwest Choice</td>
  <td headers="albuquerque nmprice">$25.99</td>
</tr>
<tr>
  <td headers="service">DSL</td>
  <td headers="austin txprovider">SBC Yahoo</td>
  <td headers="austin txprice">$29.00</td>
  <td headers="albuquerque nmprovider">MSN</td>
  <td headers="albuquerque nmprice">$39.99</td>
</tr>
<tr>
  <td headers="service">Cable</td>
  <td headers="austin txprovider">Cox Cablevision Digital</td>
  <td headers="austin txprice">$79.91</td>
  <td headers="albuquerque nmprovider">Comcast Digital Silver</td>
  <td headers="albuquerque nmprice">$69.95</td>
</tr>
<tr>
  <td headers="service">Cable Internet</td>
  <td headers="austin txprovider">Cox Cablevision</td>
  <td headers="austin txprice">$39.95</td>
  <td headers="albuquerque nmprovider">Comcast</td>
  <td headers="albuquerque nmprice">$42.00</td>
</tr>
<tr>
  <td headers="service">Satellite TV</td>
  <td headers="austin txprovider">Dish </td>
  <td headers="austin txprice">$56.99</td>
  <td headers="albuquerque nmprovider">Dish</td>
  <td headers="albuquerque nmprice">$56.99</td>
</tr>
```

With that added to the XHTML, you won't see anything in a browser check. It will continue to look like Figure 10.7. If you have a way to check the page with an aural screen reader such as JAWS, you'll hear a noticeable difference, however.

Some screen readers read tables in the order of the HTML, others read across the page line by line as if the table cells weren't even there. Either way you hear nonsense. Modern screen readers have a "table reading mode," which is helped by the care you take with `th`, `scope`, `id`, `headers`, `summary`, and `caption`.

RESOURCES FOR TABLES

An excellent article at WebAIM (`www.webaim.org/techniques/tables`) provides helpful information about how screen readers interpret tables. WebAIM provides an online tool called WAVE (`www.wave.webaim.org`) that tests pages for all sorts of accessibility features and provides especially helpful information about tables. The WAVE tool is an important tool for testing your site for accessibility, along with a number of other online tools that will be explained in more detail in Chapter 12.

SCOPE

The `scope` attribute is used with simple data tables where there is no need for headers. It associates the `td` cells with the appropriate `th`.

You can use `scope` with colspans and rowspans. The appropriate values for the `scope` attribute in these cases would be `colgroup` and `rowgroup`.

Open `ch10_scope.html` in your text editor; see Figure 10.8.

Note that the CSS file `ch10_table2.css` is linked to `ch10_scope.html` and affects the presentation you see in Figure 10.8.

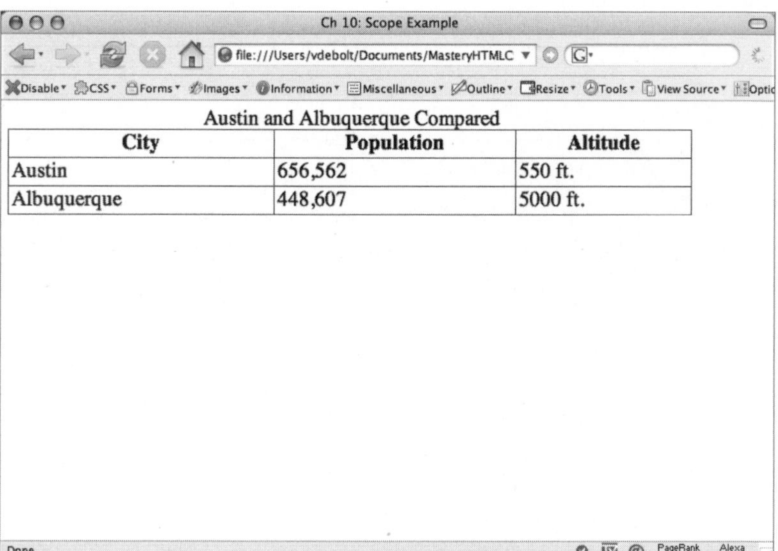

FIGURE 10.8
The only `th` elements in this table identify columns.

In `ch10_scope.html`, the only `th` elements are for columns. There are no data cells with two o
more associated headers. In this simple table, there's no need for an `id` for each `th` element. The
attribute `scope="col"` in each `th` element is enough information to associate the heading with th
entire column of data cells beneath it.

The table element from `ch10_scope.html` is shown in Listing 10.4.

LISTING 10.4: A Table Using the *scope="col"* Attribute in the *th* Elements

```
<table>
  <caption>
  Austin and Albuquerque Compared
  </caption>
 <tr>
    <th scope="col">City</th>
    <th scope="col">Population</th>
    <th scope="col">Altitude</th>
  </tr>
  <tr>
    <td>Austin</td>
    <td>656,562</td>
    <td>550 ft.</td>
  </tr>
  <tr>
    <td>Albuquerque</td>
    <td>448,607</td>
    <td>5000 ft.</td>
  </tr>
</table>
```

WHAT ABOUT ROWS?

If you are also using `th` elements for each row, the correct `scope` attribute in each row `th` is `scope="row"`. A table might have `scope` attributes for both columns and rows if you use a `th` element in both columns and rows.

The `scope` attribute tells a browser or screen reader that the contents of the data cells in each co
umn are related to the heading of the column or row.

Whether you use `headers` or `scope` to identify the `td` with its related `th`, when you view the
table with a visual browser such as Internet Explorer or Safari, it will still look like Figures 10.7 a
10.8. Even though you don't "see" the information, it is there in the code, and a browser or scree
reader that does present such information to the user can use it.

Mastering Integrated HTML and CSS in Color

This full-color section augments and expands the XHTML and CSS techniques taught throughout the book. The first portion shows winning entries in the StyleMe Challenge. A similar StyleMe Challenge is available on the accompanying CD. Next, compare your work in various chapters with these color examples of how the finished exercise pages look. Finally, I've collected some examples of real websites that demonstrate the concepts taught in the book.

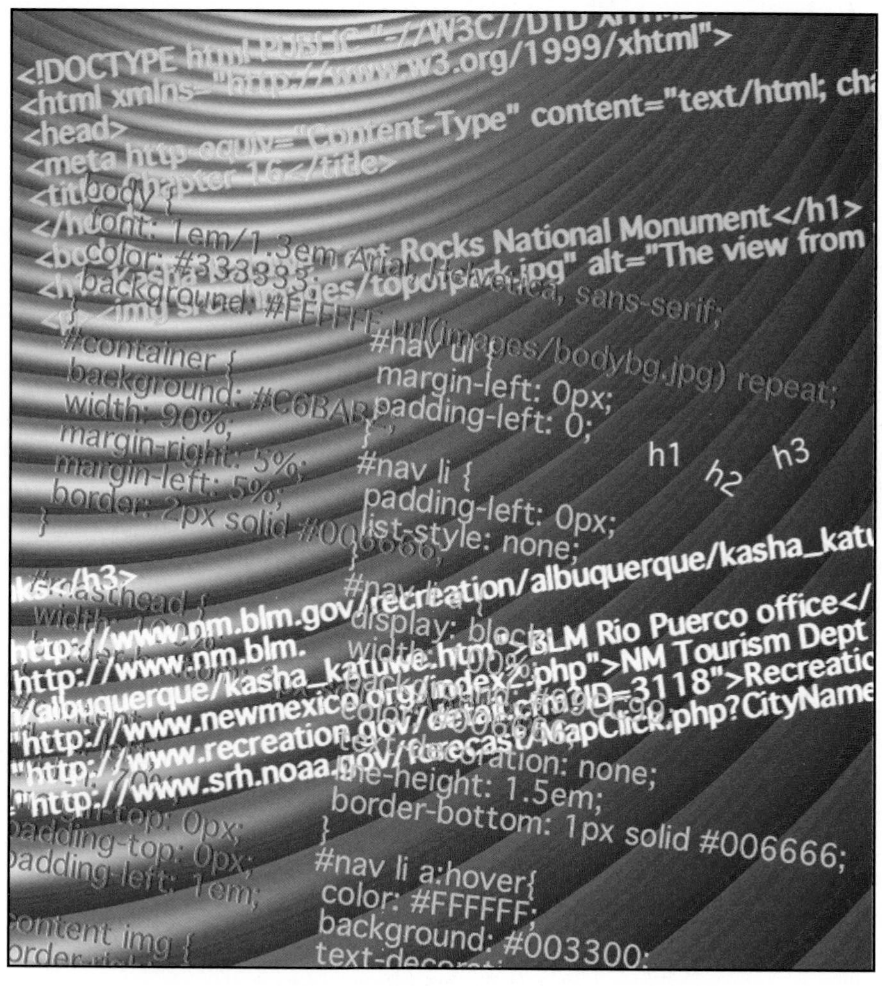

StyleMe Challenge Winners

The six winning designs are shown in random order. Each design uses the HTML provided for the StyleMe Challenge to create unique and exciting presentations with CSS.

These two winners are from Donna Jones of Portland, Maine. She develops and maintains sites locally, mainly for non-profits. You can see some examples of her work by visiting `www.westendwebs.com`.

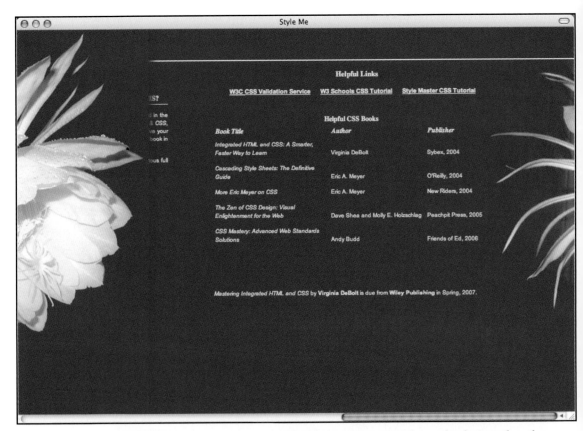

Figure 1 This design by Donna Jones scrolls horizontally. The screen capture shows the design when the design elements at the right end of the horizontal scroll are visible.

Figure 2 Look carefully at the initial "s" in the word "style me" and you'll see how a subtle transparent PNG was used to smooth out the transition between the image on the left and the text that scrolls beneath it.

The horizontal scrolling was achieved with a combination of absolute and fixed positioning. The two flowers framing the design are held in place with clever use of background image positions.

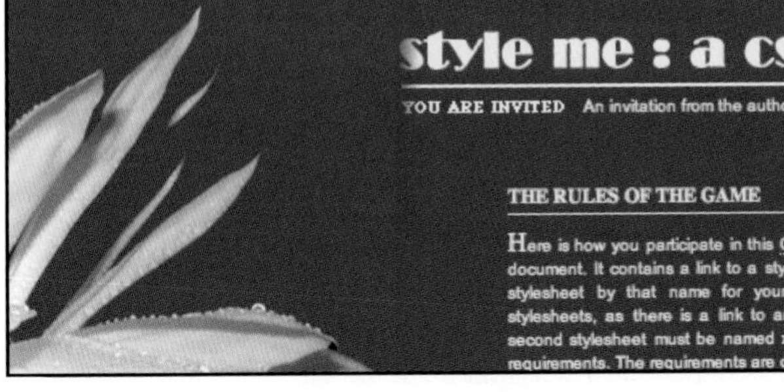

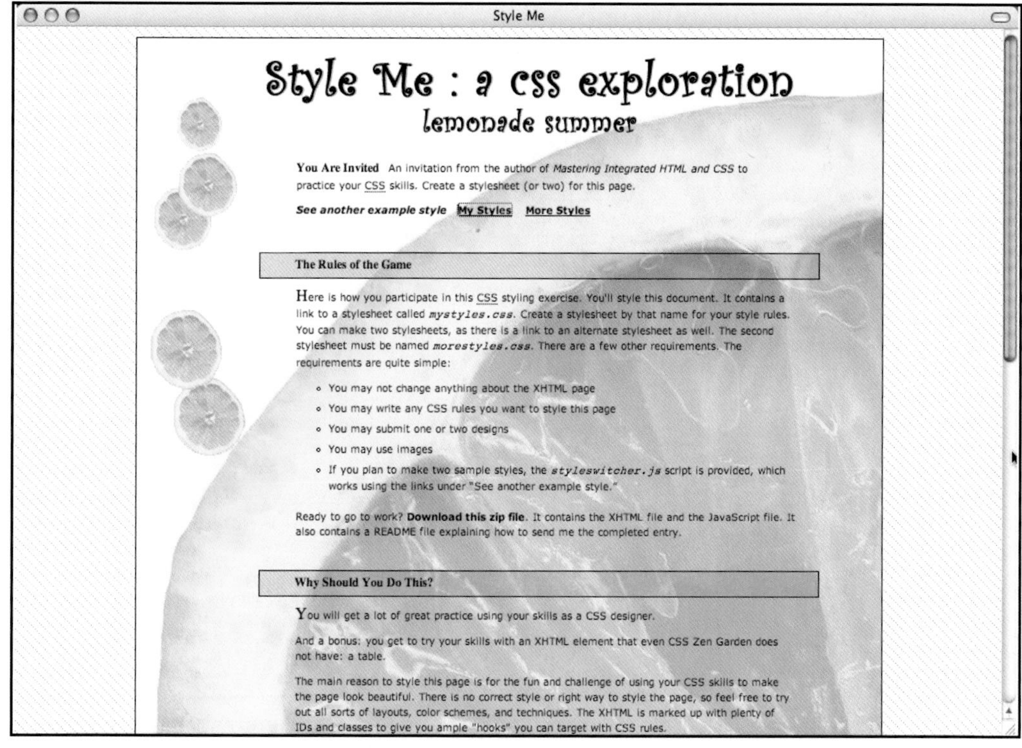

Figure 3 Another Donna Jones design with a bright and sunny presentation.

Donna Jones' Lemonade Summer design uses background images and careful attention to typographic detail to achieve this refreshing and crisp appearance.

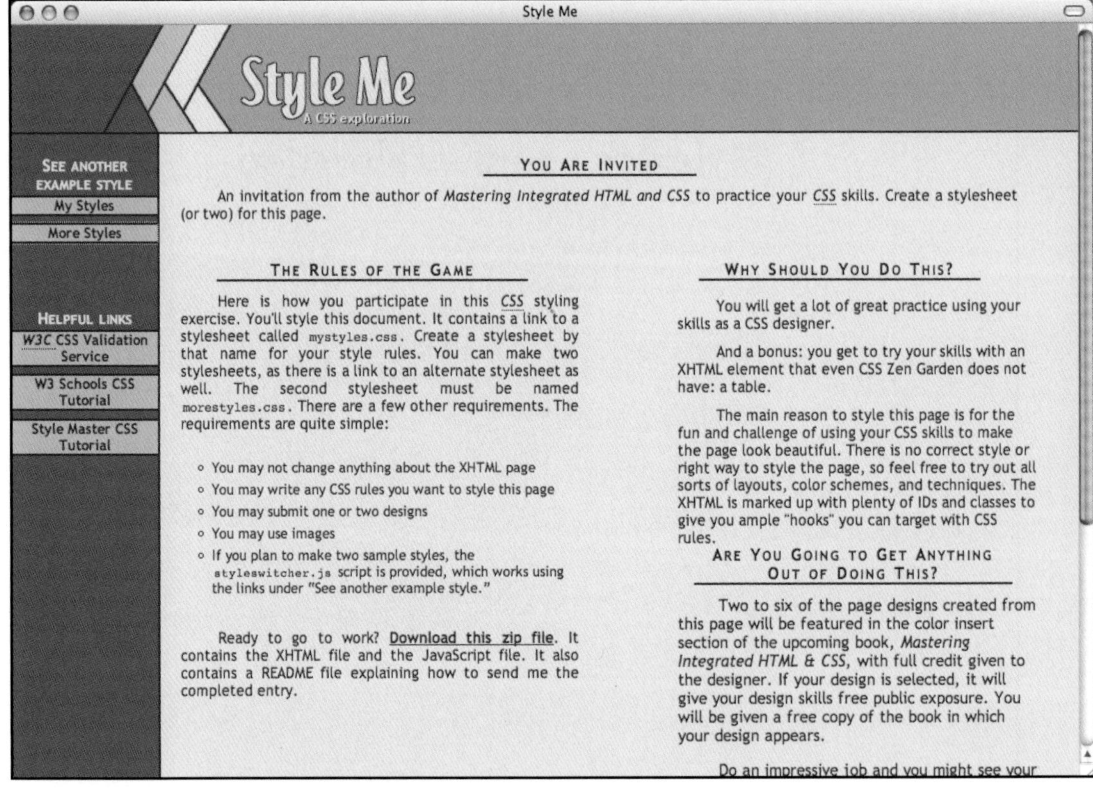

Figure 4 B. C. Bass created this design with image replacement and background image positioning

B. C. Bass for Butterfly Dezignz at `http://butterflydezignz.com` entered this design. The styles are customized for a number of different browsers using CSS filters. The design look is created with image replacement and positioned background images. Bunny Bass, owner of Butterfly Dezignz, started in 2D and 3D graphic design, and switched to web design after receiving certifications in Web Graphics and Multimedia, Web Programming, and Web Technologies from the International Web Masters Association. Ms. Bass graduated Magna Cum Laude from City University of New York, where she earned a degree in Computer Information Systems and Programming.

Style Me

STYLE ME

A CSS EXPLORATION

you are invited

An invitation from the author of *Mastering Integrated HTML and CSS* to practice your CSS skills. Create a stylesheet (or two) for this page.

the rules of the game

Here is how you participate in this CSS styling exercise. You'll style this document. It contains a link to a stylesheet called mystyles.css. Create a stylesheet by that name for your style rules. You can make two stylesheets, as there is a link to an alternate stylesheet as well. The second stylesheet must be named morestyles.css. There are a few other requirements. The requirements are quite simple:

- You may not change anything about the XHTML page
- You may write any CSS rules you want to style this page
- You may submit one or two designs
- You may use images
- If you plan to make two sample styles,

See another example style

my styles more styles

why should you do this?

You will get a lot of great practice using your skills as a CSS designer.

And a bonus: you get to try your skills with an XHTML element that even CSS Zen Garden does not have: a table.

The main reason to style this page is for the fun and challenge of using your CSS skills to make the page look beautiful. There is no correct style or right way to style the page, so feel free to try out all sorts of layouts, color schemes, and techniques. The XHTML is marked up with plenty of IDs and classes to give you ample "hooks" you can target with CSS rules.

are you going to get anything out of doing this?

Two to six of the page designs created from this page will be featured in the color insert section of the upcoming book, *Mastering Integrated HTML & CSS*, with full credit given to the designer. If your design is selected, it will give your design skills free public exposure. You will be given a free copy of the book in which your design appears.

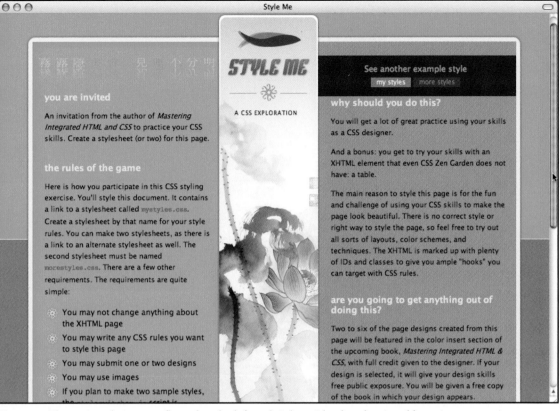

Figure 5 The main columns are floated to the left and right, with a hand-painted lotus image creating a focal point.

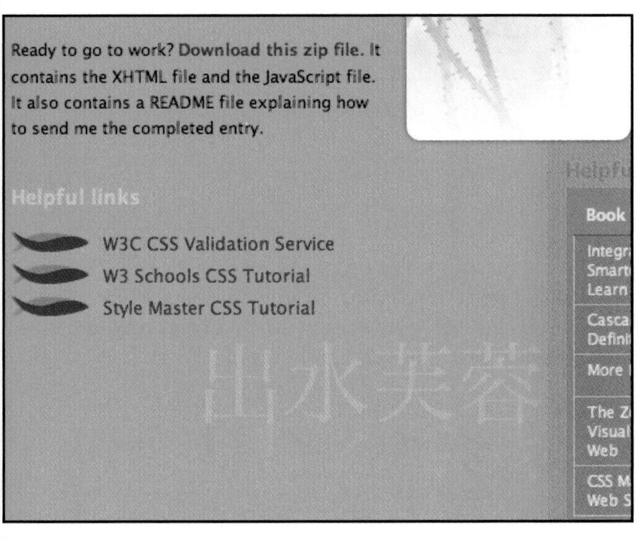

Figure 6 Design details created with background images are shown in this close-up.

This entry includes lovely design details that unite and give meaning to the presentation. The designer, Tee G. Peng, can be found at `www.lotusseedsdesign.com`. Tee is a self-taught web designer who crosses over from traditional print media.

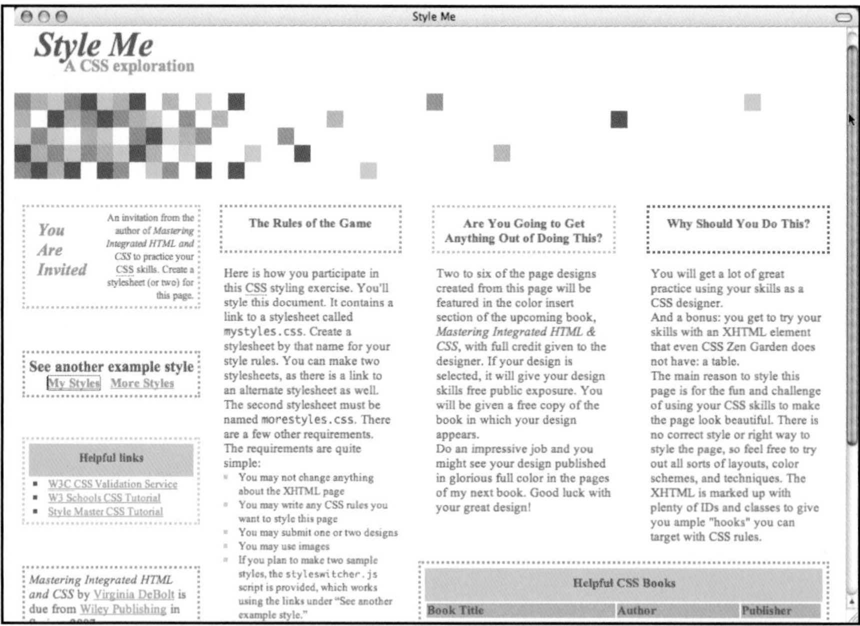

Figure 7 You can see a bit of the table in the lower right of this four-column CSS design. The table is given two "columns" of display area.

This bright four-column layout is the work of Leslie Hastings. The proprietor of Kodiak Web Designs at `www.kodiak-web-design.com`, Leslie has been developing for the Web since 1998, and started her own business in 2003. Kodiak specializes in CSS-based design for small and medium-size businesses with an emphasis on accessibility, and also provides print and graphic design services as well as Web training.

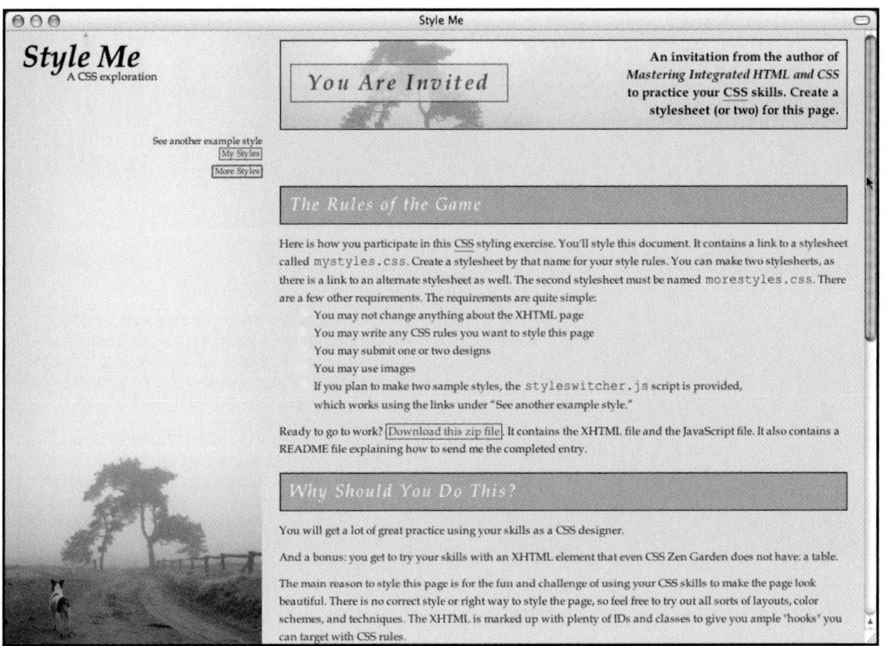

Figure 8 This is the second winning design by Leslie Hastings. The column on the left and the banner remain fixed in place as you scroll down the page.

This design keeps the imagery in view with fixed positioning as the page is read. The tree motif from the left column is repeated in the banner with a partially transparent heading placed over it.

Web Color in Practice

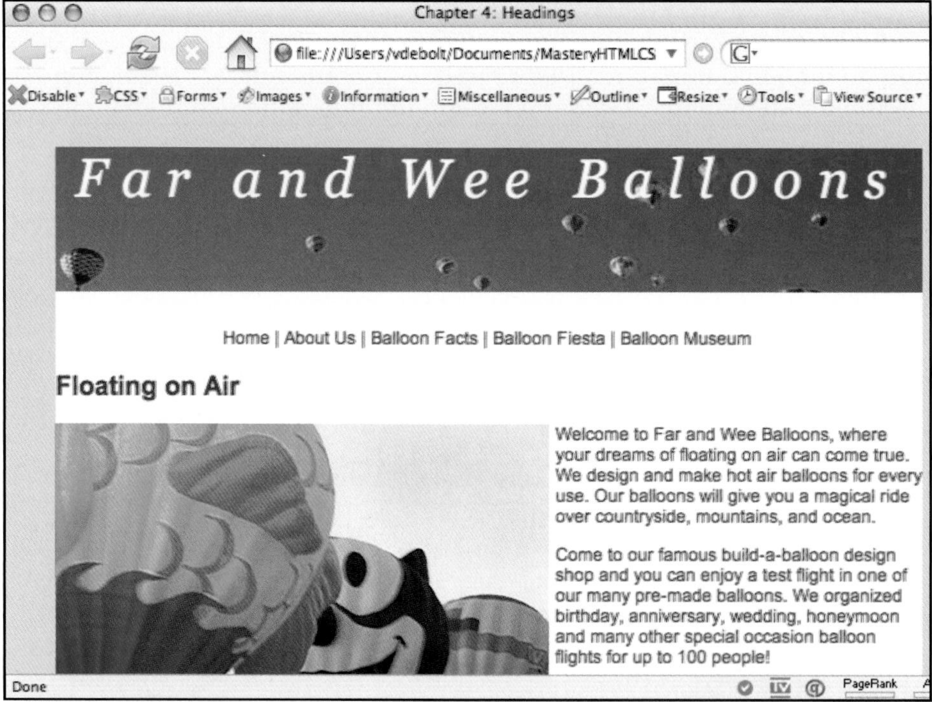

Figure 9 The Far and Wee Balloon practice page uses shades of blue from the sky and balloons, as well as the primary colors of the balloons themselves.

Practice exercises use a number of repeated page designs in various fixed and fluid layouts throughout the book. These practice designs may be used to learn CSS layouts in one chapter, image replacement techniques in another, and to style a list of hyperlinks in a different chapter.

Here you'll look at the color schemes used in the practice pages. The color schemes selected for the practice exercises are often taken from the images planned for the presentation of the site. The image might be a masthead or page title, or it might be a focal point for the page.

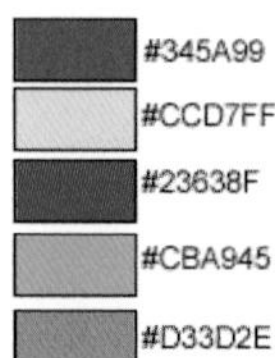

Figure 10 The color palette for the page in Figure 9. Black and white are also used, but not shown in the color palette.

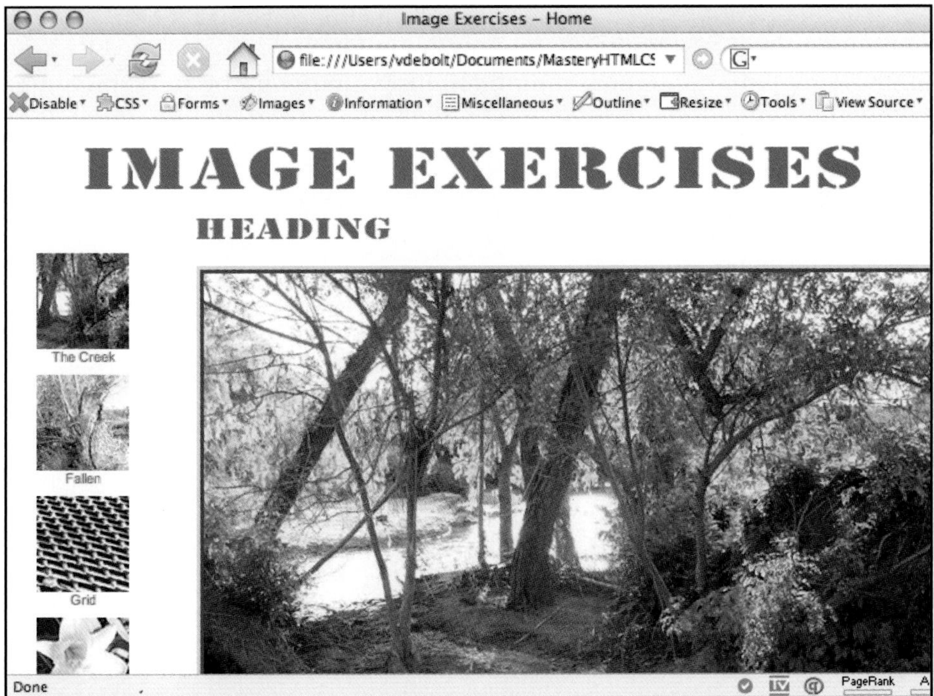

Figure 11 The image gallery practice pages use a neutral background and heading colors. This lets the image featured become the focal point.

For this image gallery practice page, there was no common color scheme to the images, so a neutral blue on a white background was used for the repeating page elements. Image galleries often use a dark background, rather than a white background, to allow to images to "pop" out from the background.

Figure 12 The blue in the heading graphics is a web-safe color.

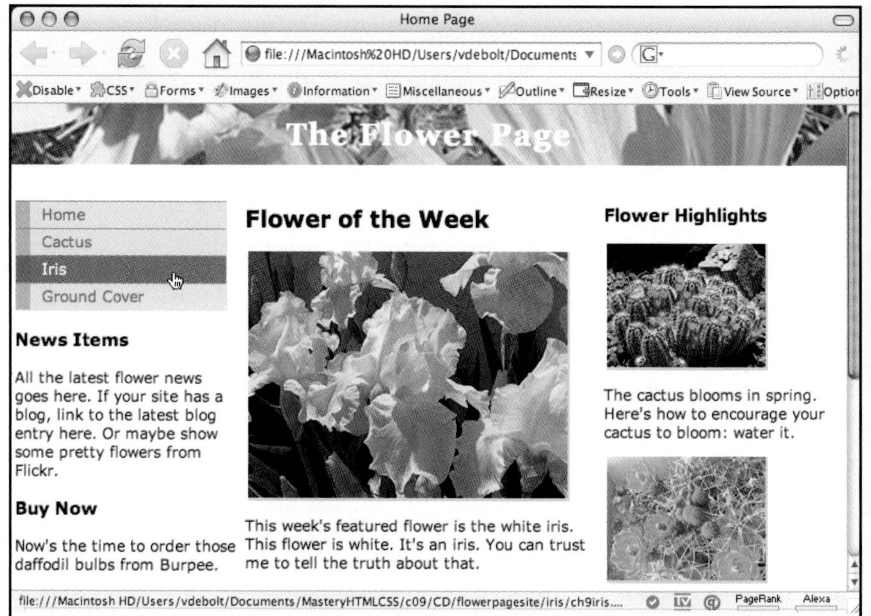

Figure 13 A three-column design used on several practice pages. Here you see it with a set of styled hyperlinks in a list on the left.

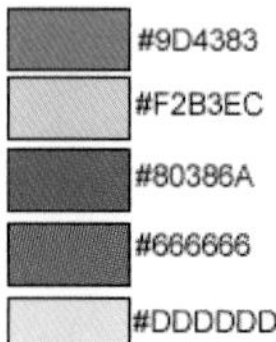

Figure 14 The pinks from the image at the top of the page cover a wide range of "pinkness" so specific sections of the image were used for the colors chosen. To achieve good contrast, a dark pink is needed.

Figure 15 The three-column design is reworked to use a horizontal navigation bar, but the color scheme remains the same.

In this practice site, the images in the content area may change on each page, but the masthead image repeats sitewide. The pinks for the styled navigation element were taken from the masthead image, contrasted with some neutral grays.

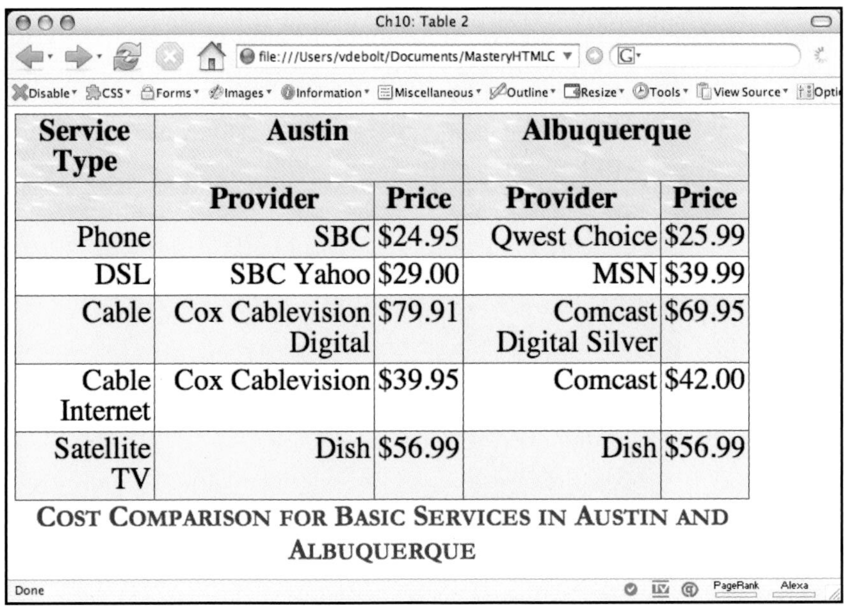

Service Type	Austin		Albuquerque	
	Provider	Price	Provider	Price
Phone	SBC	$24.95	Qwest Choice	$25.99
DSL	SBC Yahoo	$29.00	MSN	$39.99
Cable	Cox Cablevision Digital	$79.91	Comcast Digital Silver	$69.95
Cable Internet	Cox Cablevision	$39.95	Comcast	$42.00
Satellite TV	Dish	$56.99	Dish	$56.99

COST COMPARISON FOR BASIC SERVICES IN AUSTIN AND ALBUQUERQUE

Figure 16 A complex and accessible table is one of the practice exercises.

A script example

Personal Information

Your Name:

Your E-mail:

Your support password:

Your Support Question

Describe Your Problem:

Select your camera type Sony

Is your camera still under warranty?

Figure 17 The accessible forms exercise uses color and a background image to create a clear and attractive form.

Creating a complex, accessible table is one of the practice exercises in the book. The exercise is a stand-alone page, so the color scheme for the table doesn't have to take other page design colors into consideration. The blue behind the top two rows of table header elements is an image, and a background color is used to create the alternating row color effect.

The practice page used for the accessible form is also a stand-alone page. You see a background image and colors used to present the form.

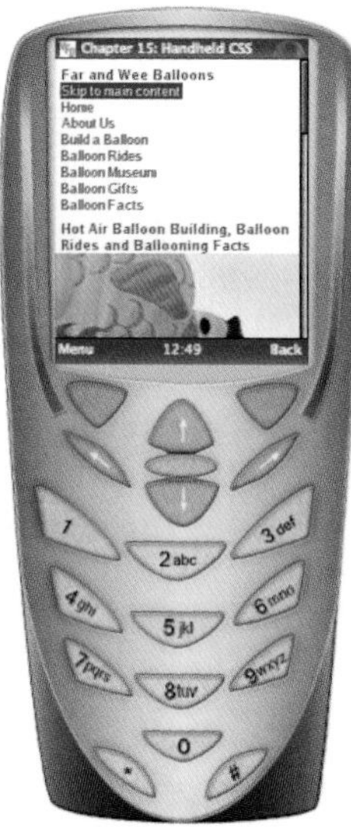

Figure 18 This Opera Mini Simulator view shows how a page displays before any handheld CSS is linked to the page.

The Opera Mini online simulator was helpful in working with the practice exercises for the handheld CSS chapter. Here you see a page without a handheld style sheet.

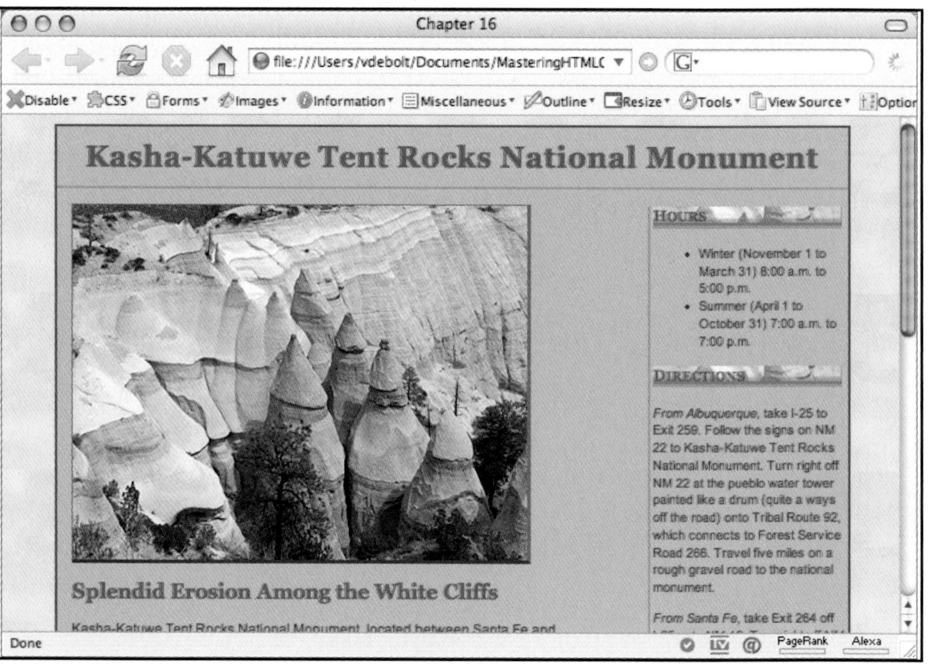

Figure 19 This practice page is used to write CSS with Dreamweaver.

Figure 20 The earth tone palette used for Figure 19

In the chapter explaining how to write styles with Dreamweaver, the practice pages uses a color scheme derived from an image. The image is of eroded rocks. The earth tones are offset with a strong green for contrast.

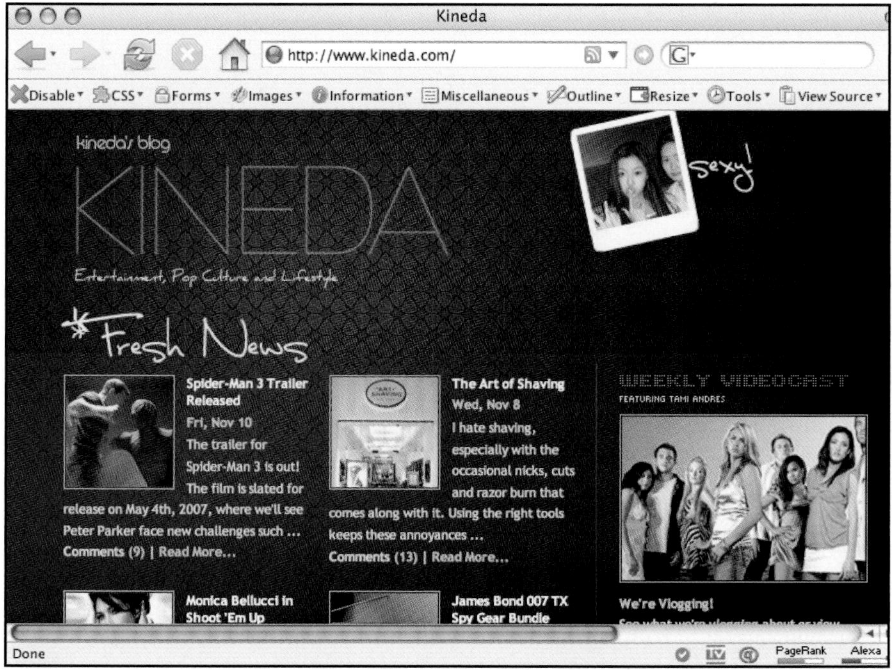

Figure 21 Kineda (`www.kineda.com`) began as an entertainment site for Asian Americans, but has switched focused to a general entertainment site. The dark background makes the images focal points. The contrasting colors are pink and blue, with pastel shades of green and peach used for link text.

Figure 22 Vitamin (`www.thinkvitamin.com`) is a magazine about web design. The basic palette is a mix of green, oranges, and browns in backgrounds that help organize content into meaningful chunks.

Figure 23 The Vitamin color palette

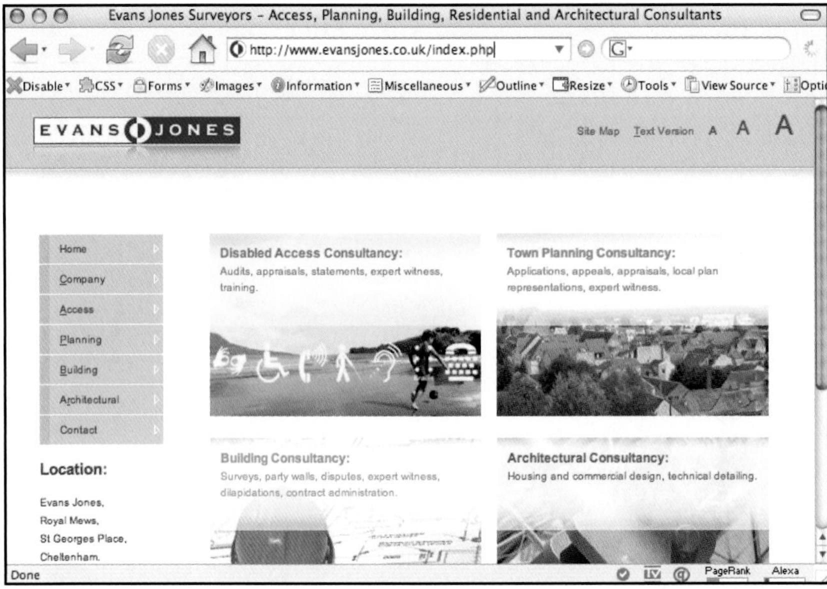

Figure 24 Evans Jones (`www.evansjones.co.uk`) is a company specializing in disability access in building, architecture, and town planning. The palette is muted grays with white. Light shades of blue, orange, and green create focal points and hierarchy.

Figure 25 SEOMOZ (`www.seomoz.org`) offers search engine optimization services. Most of the site's functional areas are gray or beige, while bright background colors of blue and green create focal points on the page.

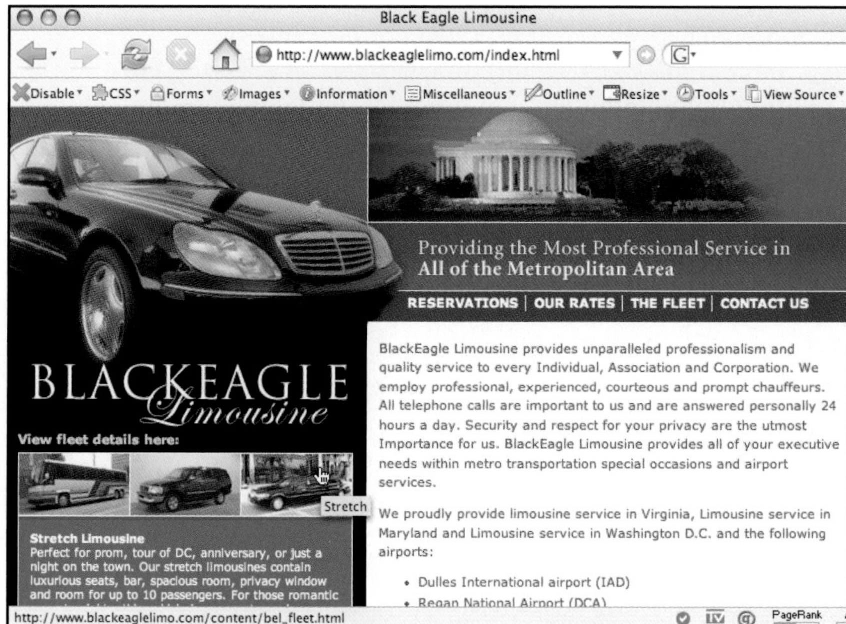

Figure 26 Black Eagle Limousine (`www.blackeaglelimo.com`) uses an interesting combination of reds for the tagline and navigation at the upper right. The other colors on the page are accented by blue on black.

#970000

#6D0000

Figure 27 The Black Eagle Limousine red palette.

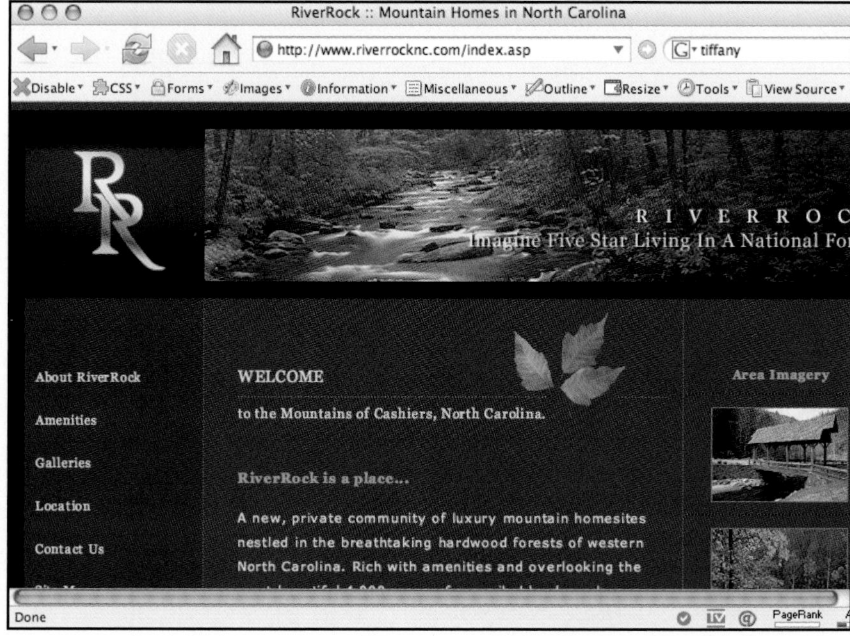

Figure 28 River Rock (`www.riverrocknc.com`) promotes a North Carolina community of luxury homes. Dark gray and black create a background that allows the color in the images to dominate the page and draw the eye.

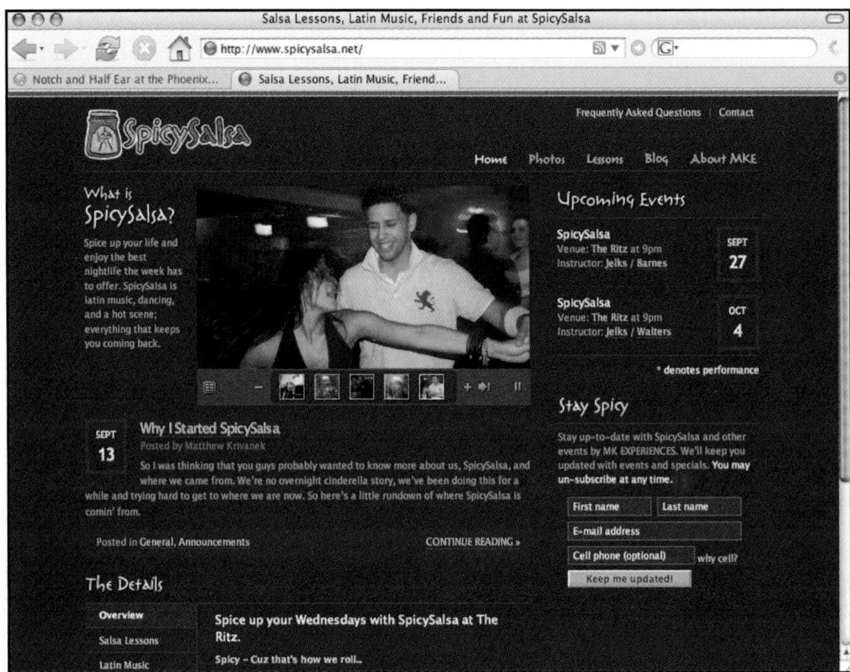

Figure 29 Spicy Salsa (`www.spicysalsa.net`) is a site for salsa dancers. Bright yellow on dark gray is the predominant color scheme, with a touch of red in the logo.

Figure 30 The most visited blog at the time of this writing is Engadget (`www.engadget.com`). Blue text on a white background provides a clean page on which to showcase the photos of the latest gadgets.

The *summary* Attribute

Go back to working with `ch10_table2.html` and `ch10_table2.css`.

The `summary` attribute is part of the `table` element. `Summary` is another accessibility attribute that is not seen visually in browsers but can be used to provide information to users with screen readers. A `summary` emphasizes important aspects of the table and helps the user understand and interpret the information in the data cells. The `summary` attribute is not a required attribute.

Add this to the table element:

```
<table summary="The cost of services for phone, TV, and Internet service in
Austin is compared with the cost of similar services in Albuquerque.">
```

In a visual browser, you still see something like Figure 10.7.

JUDGMENT CALLS

As mentioned, the `caption` and `summary` are optional in tables. You have to use your own good judgment to decide whether none, one, or both of these are needed. While a `caption` is an identifier, rather like a title, a `summary` can explain in more depth about how to interpret the data given.

Do you need to describe the nature of the table? Use a `caption`. Does a `caption` alone provide enough identifying information for both visual and aural browsers? Would it be helpful to explain the relationship among cells, especially if there are nested headings, cells that span multiple columns or rows? Would it be helpful to explain how the table fits into the context of the current document? Use a `summary`.

Your answers to these questions will depend on your table.

You've learned everything needed to make your table accessible. You can use the brief checklist in Figure 10.9 as a reminder. Keep in mind that the last item in the checklist is only needed if the table has `th` elements that span rows or columns and associate the data in a particular cell with more than one `th`.

FIGURE 10.9
Check yourself. 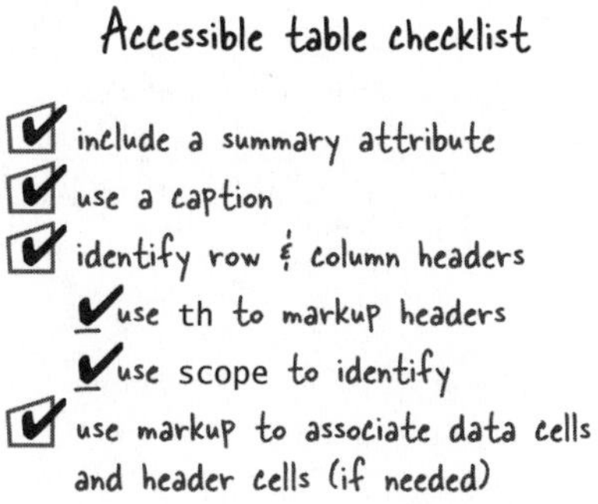

Accessible table checklist

- [x] include a summary attribute
- [x] use a caption
- [x] identify row & column headers
  - ✔ use th to markup headers
  - ✔ use scope to identify
- [x] use markup to associate data cells and header cells (if needed)

Style the Caption

The caption-side property specifies the position of the caption box with respect to the table bo Possible values are top or bottom. In theory, caption-side should also work with the values le or right, but there's no browser support for that yet. Nor does Internet Explorer for Windows su port any value for caption-side.

Start with some styles for the caption. Here's a suggested new rule:

```
caption {
   font-family: Garamond, Georgia, "Times New Roman", serif;
   font-weight: bold;
   font-variant: small-caps;
   color: #0000FF;
}
```

That change in the browser looks like Figure 10.10.

Add caption-side: bottom to your rule if you want, like this:

```
caption {
   font-family: Garamond, Georgia, "Times New Roman", serif;
   font-weight: bold;
   font-variant: small-caps;
   color: #0000FF;
   caption-side: bottom;
}
```

The result is shown in Figure 10.11. (In Internet Explorer for Windows, the caption would n move to the bottom.)

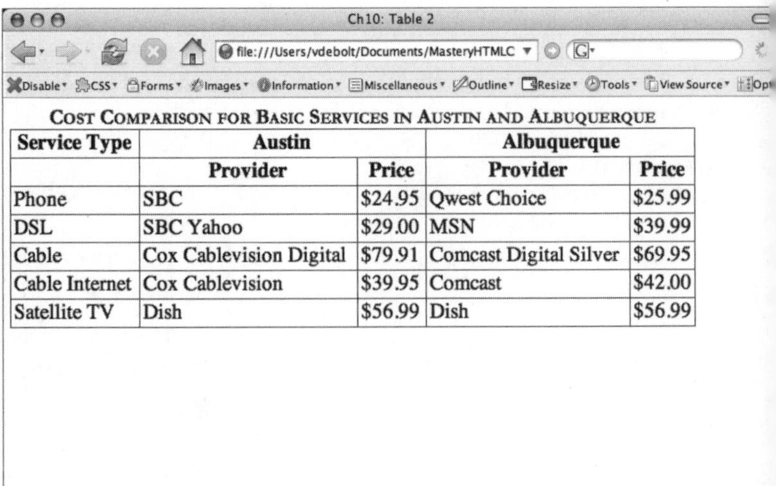

COST COMPARISON FOR BASIC SERVICES IN AUSTIN AND ALBUQUERQUE

Service Type	Austin		Albuquerque	
	Provider	Price	Provider	Price
Phone	SBC	$24.95	Qwest Choice	$25.99
DSL	SBC Yahoo	$29.00	MSN	$39.99
Cable	Cox Cablevision Digital	$79.91	Comcast Digital Silver	$69.95
Cable Internet	Cox Cablevision	$39.95	Comcast	$42.00
Satellite TV	Dish	$56.99	Dish	$56.99

FIGURE 10.10 The caption reflects several new CSS properties.

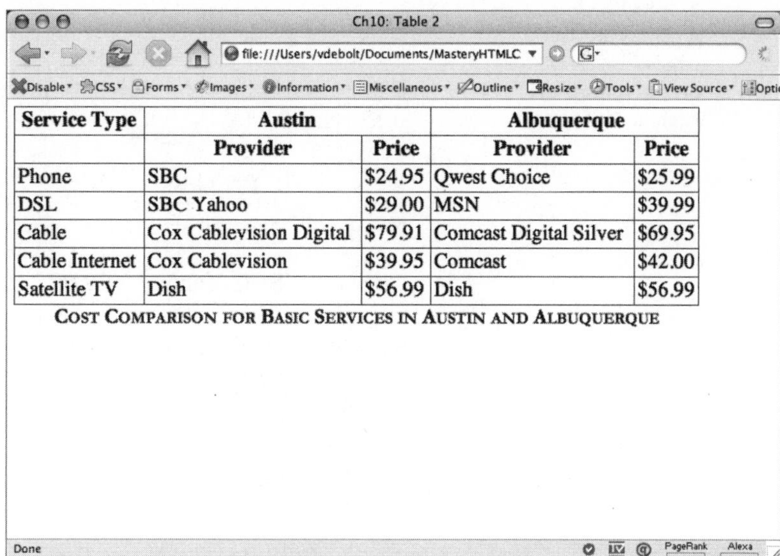

Service Type	Austin		Albuquerque	
	Provider	Price	Provider	Price
Phone	SBC	$24.95	Qwest Choice	$25.99
DSL	SBC Yahoo	$29.00	MSN	$39.99
Cable	Cox Cablevision Digital	$79.91	Comcast Digital Silver	$69.95
Cable Internet	Cox Cablevision	$39.95	Comcast	$42.00
Satellite TV	Dish	$56.99	Dish	$56.99

COST COMPARISON FOR BASIC SERVICES IN AUSTIN AND ALBUQUERQUE

FIGURE 10.11 With `caption-side: bottom` in the rule, the caption moves below the table box.

CSS for Cell Alignment and Color

The property `vertical-align` is used to align text vertically in table cells. If you narrow the browser window so that the text in some of the table cell wraps, you will notice that the default vertical alignment for table cells is `middle`. The wrapping of content in the table cells is automatic (see Figure 10.12).

The content of table cells can be aligned vertically with the values `top`, `middle`, or `bottom`. Change the rule for the `th, td` selector to include `vertical-align: top` and see what happens (see Figure 10.13).

```
th, td {
  border: 1px solid #333;
  padding: 3px;
  vertical-align: top;
}
```

If you expect the contents of even one of the table cells to wrap, it is a good idea to use `vertical-align` to control placement.

The horizontal alignment of material in table cells uses the `text-align` property that you have seen before.

As I mentioned earlier, in terms of horizontal alignment, `th` elements are set at `text-align: center` by default. Leave them as they are and look at the `td` elements. They are set at `text-align: left` by default. Change the `td` element to `text-align: right` so you can see a change, as shown in Figure 10.14. The new rule for the style sheet is

```
td {
  text-align: right;
}
```

FIGURE 10.12
A narrow browser window reveals the default vertical cell alignment as `middle`.

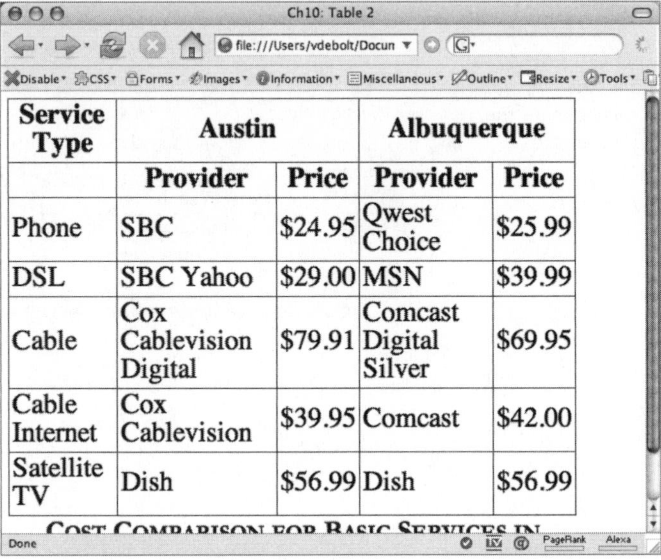

Service Type	Austin		Albuquerque	
	Provider	Price	Provider	Price
Phone	SBC	$24.95	Qwest Choice	$25.99
DSL	SBC Yahoo	$29.00	MSN	$39.99
Cable	Cox Cablevision Digital	$79.91	Comcast Digital Silver	$69.95
Cable Internet	Cox Cablevision	$39.95	Comcast	$42.00
Satellite TV	Dish	$56.99	Dish	$56.99

FIGURE 10.13
Cell contents are moved to the top with `vertical-align: top`.

Service Type	Austin		Albuquerque	
	Provider	Price	Provider	Price
Phone	SBC	$24.95	Qwest Choice	$25.99
DSL	SBC Yahoo	$29.00	MSN	$39.99
Cable	Cox Cablevision Digital	$79.91	Comcast Digital Silver	$69.95
Cable Internet	Cox Cablevision	$39.95	Comcast	$42.00
Satellite TV	Dish	$56.99	Dish	$56.99

While `text-align: right` doesn't always improve the interpretation of a table, in this parti ular table it groups the columns together visually in a way that aids readability.

There are many choices when it comes to adding color to a table. You can add a background color (or image) to the entire table. You can add background colors (or images) to the `thead`, `tbod` and `tfoot` elements that you will learn about in just a bit. You can add background colors to the `th` elements and/or the `td` elements.

In lengthy tables with many rows to keep track of, it's common to use a color on every other row to help the eye track across each row. That's usually done by assigning a `class` to every other row in the table. (There are advanced selectors that apply a rule to every other row, but they aren't well supported by the browsers yet, so you'll stick with the `class` idea for now.) First, you need a class name. The name "rowshade" will work. Go through the XHTML and assign the class to these three rows:

```
<tr class="rowshade">
   <td headers="service">Phone</td>
...snip...
<tr class="rowshade">
   <td headers="service">Cable</td>
...snip...
<tr class="rowshade">
   <td headers="service">Satellite TV</td>
```

Everything but the essentials is snipped out of the preceding code. Add the class to the rows indicated.

In the CSS, create the new class with a light color for the background, perhaps a light yellow:

```
.rowshade {
   background: #FFC;
   }
```

Figure 10.15 shows the results in a browser.

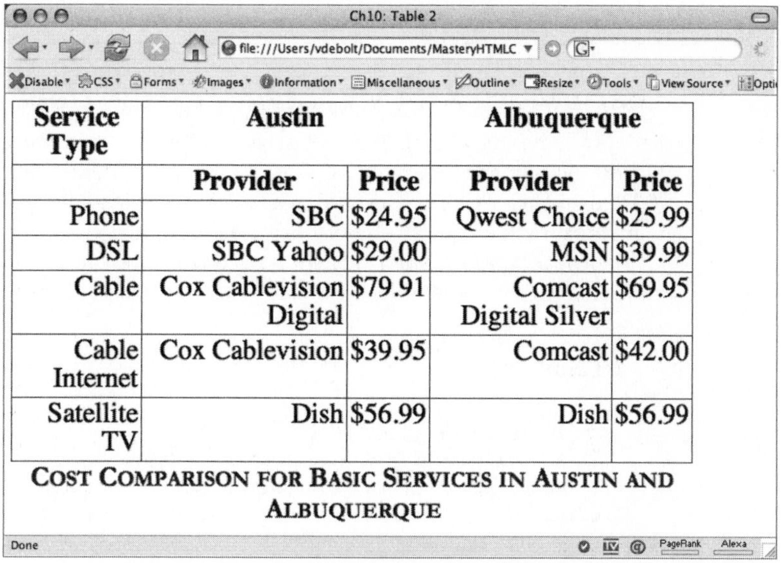

Service Type	Austin		Albuquerque	
	Provider	Price	Provider	Price
Phone	SBC	$24.95	Qwest Choice	$25.99
DSL	SBC Yahoo	$29.00	MSN	$39.99
Cable	Cox Cablevision Digital	$79.91	Comcast Digital Silver	$69.95
Cable Internet	Cox Cablevision	$39.95	Comcast	$42.00
Satellite TV	Dish	$56.99	Dish	$56.99

COST COMPARISON FOR BASIC SERVICES IN AUSTIN AND ALBUQUERQUE

FIGURE 10.14
The contents of the `td` elements are aligned right, while the `th` elements remain at the default center-aligned position.

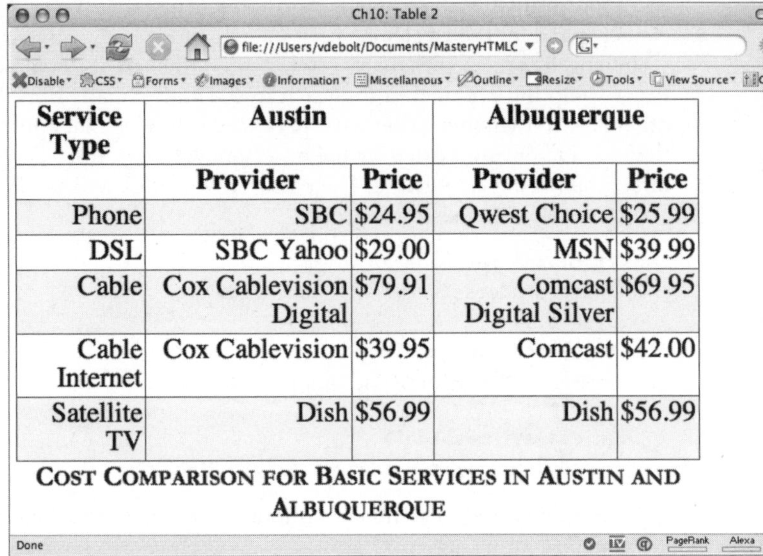

Service Type	Austin		Albuquerque	
	Provider	Price	Provider	Price
Phone	SBC	$24.95	Qwest Choice	$25.99
DSL	SBC Yahoo	$29.00	MSN	$39.99
Cable	Cox Cablevision Digital	$79.91	Comcast Digital Silver	$69.95
Cable Internet	Cox Cablevision	$39.95	Comcast	$42.00
Satellite TV	Dish	$56.99	Dish	$56.99

COST COMPARISON FOR BASIC SERVICES IN AUSTIN AND ALBUQUERQUE

FIGURE 10.15
Alternating rows with a class assignment to create a background color

SAVE TIME AND TROUBLE

Have a really big table? There are JavaScript solutions to alternating row colors that automate the task for you. Here are a couple of popular resources (I haven't had a chance to use them myself, however):

- At DHTML Dev: `http://dhtmldev.com/content/view/12/26`
- At Site Point: `www.sitepoint.com/article/background-colors-javascript`

Learn More XHTML: *thead, tbody, tfoot*

Let's finish the study of tables by going back to XHTML for more table elements. Although it soun like the instructions for a child's dance activity, `thead`, `tbody`, and `tfoot` are actually additional XHTML elements that can be used in a table. These elements are handy because they give you fu ther structure that you can style within a table.

The `thead` (for *table head*) element is used to format one or more `tr` elements. Using `ch10_table2.html` as an example, the `thead` element encloses the rows containing the `column head` elements, like this:

```
<thead>
 <tr>
    <th id="service">Service Type</th>
    <th colspan="2" id="austin">Austin</th>
    <th colspan="2" id="albuquerque">Albuquerque</th>
  </tr>
  <tr>
    <th> </th>
    <th id="txprovider">Provider</th>
    <th id="txprice">Price</th>
```

```
    <th id="nmprovider">Provider</th>
    <th id="nmprice">Price</th>
  </tr>
  </thead>
```

There can only be one thead element in a table.

The tbody (for *table body*) element adds structure to the table rows that make up the body of the table. In the example table, Listing 10.5 shows how it can be used.

LISTING 10.5: An Example Showing the *tbody* Element

```
<tbody>
  <tr class="rowshade">
    <td headers="service">Phone</td>
    <td headers="austin txprovider">SBC</td>
    <td headers="austin txprice">$24.95</td>
    <td headers="albuquerque nmprovider">Qwest Choice</td>
    <td headers="albuquerque nmprice">$25.99</td>
  </tr>
  <tr>
    <td headers="service">DSL</td>
    <td headers="austin txprovider">SBC Yahoo</td>
    <td headers="austin txprice">$29.00</td>
    <td headers="albuquerque nmprovider">MSN</td>
    <td headers="albuquerque nmprice">$39.99</td>
  </tr>
  <tr class="rowshade">
    <td headers="service">Cable</td>
    <td headers="austin txprovider">Cox Cablevision Digital</td>
    <td headers="austin txprice">$79.91</td>
    <td headers="albuquerque nmprovider">Comcast Digital Silver</td>
    <td headers="albuquerque nmprice">$69.95</td>
  </tr>
  <tr>
    <td headers="service">Cable Internet</td>
    <td headers="austin txprovider">Cox Cablevision</td>
    <td headers="austin txprice">$39.95</td>
    <td headers="albuquerque nmprovider">Comcast</td>
    <td headers="albuquerque nmprice">$42.00</td>
  </tr>
  <tr class="rowshade">
    <td headers="service">Satellite TV</td>
    <td headers="austin txprovider">Dish </td>
    <td headers="austin txprice">$56.99</td>
    <td headers="albuquerque nmprovider">Dish</td>
    <td headers="albuquerque nmprice">$56.99</td>
  </tr>
  </tbody>
```

The `tfoot` (for table footer) formats the table row containing the table footer. The example tab does not have a footer; however, the element is used in exactly the same way as `thead` and `tbod` There can only be one `tfoot` element in a table. The `tfoot` element is added in the source imme diately below the `thead` element, although it should still appear beneath the `tbody` element in th browser. Adding the `thead` and `tfoot` elements to the beginning of the table enables browsers preload the header and footer rows so that they can be repeated across every page that a table spa when the web page is printed.

Browsers are very literal in their interpretation of `thead`, `tbody`, and `tfoot`. If you mark up th first row in this table as `tfoot`, the browser will display it at the foot of the table.

With the `thead` and `tbody` elements in your `ch10_table2.html` page, you can add a style for th `thead` element. Table elements can be styled with `background-image`, so try that.

You will find `background-image.gif` in the Chapter 10 folder on the CD. With the graphic i the same folder as your current style sheet, add this rule to the style sheet:

```
thead {
  background: url(background-image.gif) repeat;
}
```

In most browsers, the background image should repeat to fill the entire `thead` element. Diff ent browsers interpret the `background-image` property differently, so you may not see the sam result as in Figure 10.16.

Some browsers fill an entire `table` or `thead` with a `background-image`. Others apply the ima to each table cell. This is one of those properties you use with caution after a lot of testing in vario browsers.

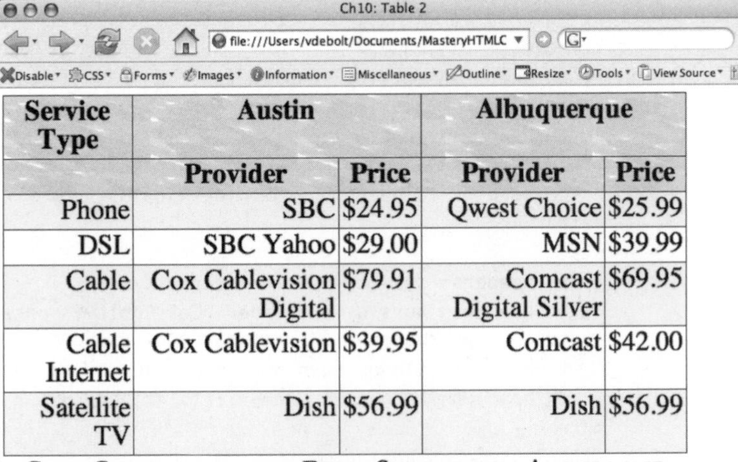

Service Type	Austin		Albuquerque	
	Provider	Price	Provider	Price
Phone	SBC	$24.95	Qwest Choice	$25.99
DSL	SBC Yahoo	$29.00	MSN	$39.99
Cable	Cox Cablevision Digital	$79.91	Comcast Digital Silver	$69.95
Cable Internet	Cox Cablevision	$39.95	Comcast	$42.00
Satellite TV	Dish	$56.99	Dish	$56.99

COST COMPARISON FOR BASIC SERVICES IN AUSTIN AND ALBUQUERQUE

FIGURE 10.16
A `background-image` style added to the `thead` element

There are more options for styling this table. You have many possible selectors with `table`, `th`, `td`, `thead`, `tbody`, `caption`, and the class you created. More classes and ids could certainly be added to create even more finely aimed CSS selectors. However, you've learned all the relevant XHTML, and the CSS you know from previous chapters can all be applied here, giving you the skills to experiment on your own. The complete `ch10_table2.css` is shown in Listing 10.6.

LISTING 10.6: The Complete Style Sheet in *ch10_table2.css*

```
table {
   width: 90%;
   border: 1px solid #333;
   border-collapse: collapse;
}
th, td {
   padding: 3px;
   border: 1px solid #333;
   vertical-align: top;
}
td {
   text-align: right;
}
caption {
   font-weight: bold;
   font-variant: small-caps;
   color: #0000FF;
   font-family: Garamond, Georgia, "Times New Roman", serif;
   caption-side: bottom;
}
.rowshade {
   background: #FFC;
   }
thead {
   background: url(background-image.gif) repeat;
}
```

Using *colgroup* and *col*

A `colgroup` is a table column group. The two chief attributes associated with `colgroup` are `span` and `width`. The `span` attribute represents the number of columns in the group, with one being the default. If the number is anything other than one, use `span="n"` to set a particular value.

If you use `colgroup`, it goes immediately after the opening `table` tag and any `caption` elemen like this:

```
<caption>
  Cost Comparison for Basic Services in Austin and Albuquerque
</caption>
<colgroup />
<colgroup span="2" />
<colgroup span="2" />
<thead>
```

Since the first `colgroup` only has one column, there's no need for a `span` attribute in that `colgroup`. The `width` attribute gives the default width for any enclosed cols. For example:

```
<caption>
  Cost Comparison for Basic Services in Austin and Albuquerque
</caption>
<colgroup width="20%" />
<colgroup span="2" width="20%" />
<colgroup span="2" width="20%" />
<thead>
```

Width can also be set in the CSS. If you wanted each column in the table to be equal in widtl and there were five columns as in this example, then this rule in the CSS would set the width fo all five columns.

```
colgroup {
   width: 20%;
   }
```

With colgroups added to the XHTML and the CSS rule setting the width to 20 percent, `ch10_table2.html` changes to an appearance like Figure 10.17 in compliant browsers, such as Firefo (Some browsers ignore both `colgroup` and `col`.)

Other attributes that may be used with `colgroup` are `class`, `id`, and `title`.

When it is necessary to single out a column for style information or to specify width informatio you must identify that column with a `col` element.

When the `colgroup` contains `col` elements, you must use an explicit closing tag, like this:

```
<colgroup span="2">
<col width="30%" />
<col width="10%" id="gimmestyle" />
</colgroup>
```

Attributes in a `col` element override attributes in a `colgroup` element.

The `col` element is most useful as a styling hook. The possibilities are limited, however. Pro erties supported include `width`, `border`, `background`, and `visibility`. These properties are su ported by IE/Win but not by Firefox.

In Chapter 11, you will learn how to create forms so that you can collect data from your site visito

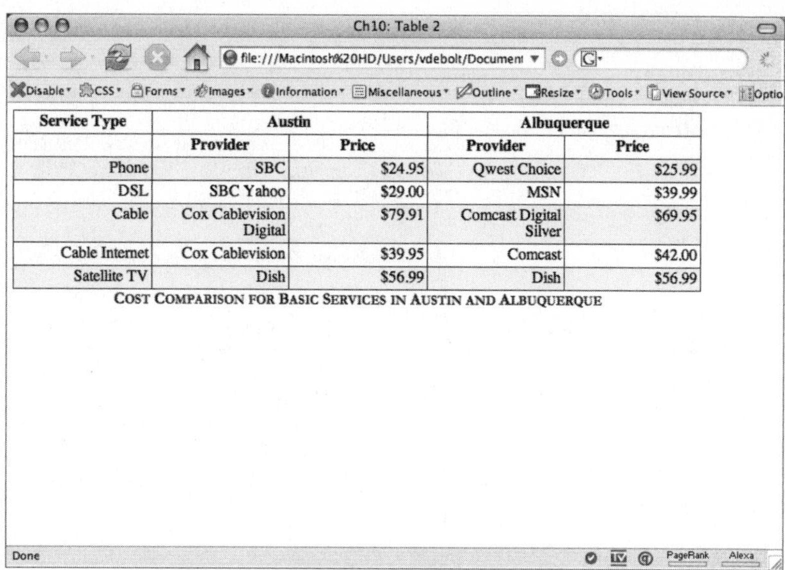

Service Type	Austin		Albuquerque	
	Provider	Price	Provider	Price
Phone	SBC	$24.95	Qwest Choice	$25.99
DSL	SBC Yahoo	$29.00	MSN	$39.99
Cable	Cox Cablevision Digital	$79.91	Comcast Digital Silver	$69.95
Cable Internet	Cox Cablevision	$39.95	Comcast	$42.00
Satellite TV	Dish	$56.99	Dish	$56.99

COST COMPARISON FOR BASIC SERVICES IN AUSTIN AND ALBUQUERQUE

FIGURE 10.17 Firefox renders the width of each column based on a `colgroup` rule in the CSS.

INSPIRATION FOR TABLES

A site that invites readers to submit style sheets for a table is at `http://icant.co.uk/csstablegallery`. You can get good ideas for ways to style all elements of a table by looking at the different designs that have been submitted. A few that are particularly creative, in my opinion, are "Inset Cells," "Two Times Table," and "Second Revolution." You can download the CSS for any of the example table styles.

The Style Me Challenge on the accompanying CD contains a table as part of the page you style for additional practice and skill building.

Real-World Scenario

All sorts of information is easier to understand when it's organized in a tabular display. Stock information, climate information, and other statistical data are the stuff of tables.

Quik n Simple Trade Manager

Quik n Simple Trade Manager is software meant to track and manage stock trades. I've never used the software, but I've admired the data table designed to compare the features of two versions of the software. This data table is accessible as well as functional; you can see it at `www.quiknsimple.com/features/compare.html`. The table is part of a larger site (see Figure 10.18).

You can understand how it was built by viewing the source code. The table includes `summary`, `caption`, `thead`, `tbody`, and `scope` elements and attributes.

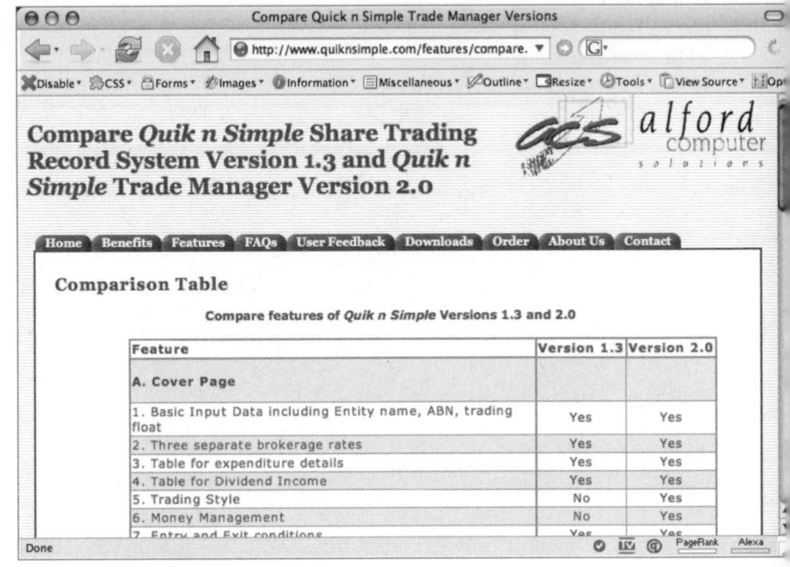

Feature	Version 1.3	Version 2.0
A. Cover Page		
1. Basic Input Data including Entity name, ABN, trading float	Yes	Yes
2. Three separate brokerage rates	Yes	Yes
3. Table for expenditure details	Yes	Yes
4. Table for Dividend Income	Yes	Yes
5. Trading Style	No	Yes
6. Money Management	No	Yes
7. Entry and Exit conditions	Yes	Yes

FIGURE 10.18
A data table comparing Quik n Simple Trade Manager versions

ESPN

Sports stats. Data tables. The two belong together. Schedules are presented as tables on `espn.co` Look at the NFL schedule shown on `http://sports.espn.go.com/nfl/schedule` (see Fig ures 10.19 and 10.20).

The tables in Figures 10.19 and 10.20 are on the same page, one under the other. They use th same styles and look but change the data after the week has passed. Both tables are easy to und stand visually, although the underlying code is not as accessible as it should be.

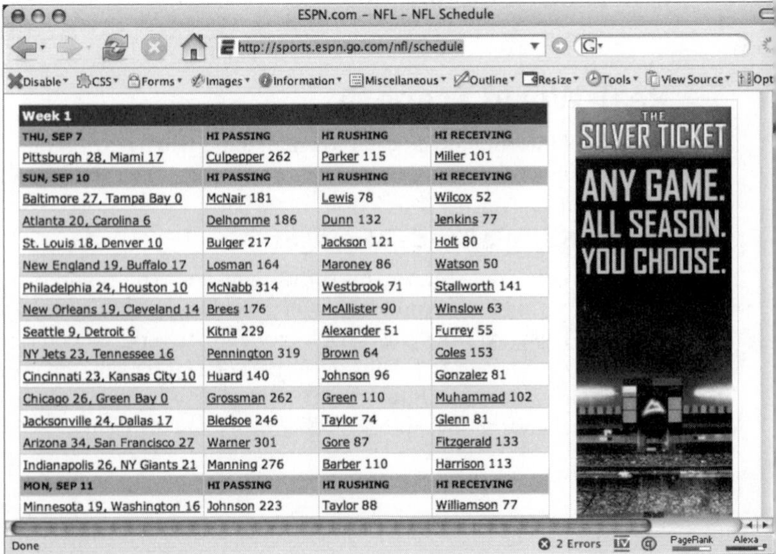

Week 1			
THU, SEP 7	HI PASSING	HI RUSHING	HI RECEIVING
Pittsburgh 28, Miami 17	Culpepper 262	Parker 115	Miller 101
SUN, SEP 10	HI PASSING	HI RUSHING	HI RECEIVING
Baltimore 27, Tampa Bay 0	McNair 181	Lewis 78	Wilcox 52
Atlanta 20, Carolina 6	Delhomme 186	Dunn 132	Jenkins 77
St. Louis 18, Denver 10	Bulger 217	Jackson 121	Holt 80
New England 19, Buffalo 17	Losman 164	Maroney 86	Watson 50
Philadelphia 24, Houston 10	McNabb 314	Westbrook 71	Stallworth 141
New Orleans 19, Cleveland 14	Brees 176	McAllister 90	Winslow 63
Seattle 9, Detroit 6	Kitna 229	Alexander 51	Furrey 55
NY Jets 23, Tennessee 16	Pennington 319	Brown 64	Coles 153
Cincinnati 23, Kansas City 10	Huard 140	Johnson 96	Gonzalez 81
Chicago 26, Green Bay 0	Grossman 262	Green 110	Muhammad 102
Jacksonville 24, Dallas 17	Bledsoe 246	Taylor 74	Glenn 81
Arizona 34, San Francisco 27	Warner 301	Gore 87	Fitzgerald 133
Indianapolis 26, NY Giants 21	Manning 276	Barber 110	Harrison 113
MON, SEP 11	HI PASSING	HI RUSHING	HI RECEIVING
Minnesota 19, Washington 16	Johnson 223	Taylor 88	Williamson 77

FIGURE 10.19
The table for a week already past gives scores, passing, rushing, and receiving stats.

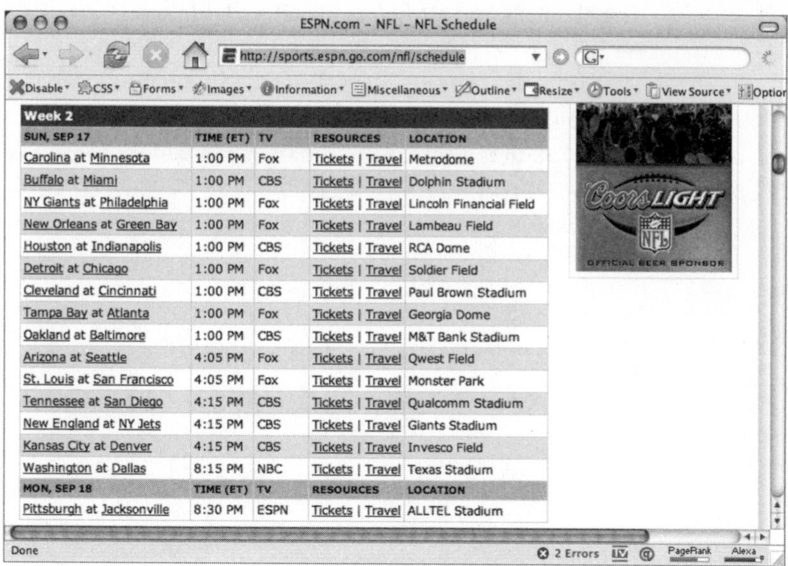

Week 2				
SUN, SEP 17	TIME (ET)	TV	RESOURCES	LOCATION
Carolina at Minnesota	1:00 PM	Fox	Tickets | Travel	Metrodome
Buffalo at Miami	1:00 PM	CBS	Tickets | Travel	Dolphin Stadium
NY Giants at Philadelphia	1:00 PM	Fox	Tickets | Travel	Lincoln Financial Field
New Orleans at Green Bay	1:00 PM	Fox	Tickets | Travel	Lambeau Field
Houston at Indianapolis	1:00 PM	CBS	Tickets | Travel	RCA Dome
Detroit at Chicago	1:00 PM	Fox	Tickets | Travel	Soldier Field
Cleveland at Cincinnati	1:00 PM	CBS	Tickets | Travel	Paul Brown Stadium
Tampa Bay at Atlanta	1:00 PM	Fox	Tickets | Travel	Georgia Dome
Oakland at Baltimore	1:00 PM	CBS	Tickets | Travel	M&T Bank Stadium
Arizona at Seattle	4:05 PM	Fox	Tickets | Travel	Qwest Field
St. Louis at San Francisco	4:05 PM	Fox	Tickets | Travel	Monster Park
Tennessee at San Diego	4:15 PM	CBS	Tickets | Travel	Qualcomm Stadium
New England at NY Jets	4:15 PM	CBS	Tickets | Travel	Giants Stadium
Kansas City at Denver	4:15 PM	CBS	Tickets | Travel	Invesco Field
Washington at Dallas	8:15 PM	NBC	Tickets | Travel	Texas Stadium
MON, SEP 18	TIME (ET)	TV	RESOURCES	LOCATION
Pittsburgh at Jacksonville	8:30 PM	ESPN	Tickets | Travel	ALLTEL Stadium

FIGURE 10.20
The table for a week not yet played gives games, times, TV info, travel info, and location.

CSS Properties

All the CSS properties you have learned in previous chapters can be applied to tables, table cells, and the content of tables. Classes and IDs can be used with tables to increase specificity when writing style rules. New CSS properties learned in Chapter 10 are shown in Table 10.1.

TABLE 10.1: Properties for Tables

PROPERTY	POSSIBLE VALUES
`border-collapse`	`collapse`, `separate`, `inherit`
`vertical-align`	`top`, `middle`, `bottom`

The Bottom Line

Write the XHTML for a table. The `table` element is composed of a number of horizontal table rows (`tr`) that are filled with cells of table data (`td`). As rows are added to the table, the cells in each row create a vertical column. Both rows and columns in a table can contain table header elements (`th`) as row or column labels.

Master It Make a new table with your own information, perhaps something like the names, ages, birthplaces, and favorite movies of people you know. Use this table for all the exercises that follow.

Use elements and attributes to make a table accessible. A caption element, a summary attribute, scope attributes, or `id`s for header elements add to a table's accessibility.

Master It Add a caption element, a summary attribute, scope attributes, or `id`s for heade attributes to ensure your table's accessibility.

Write CSS to control the presentation of a table. Tables can be styled with possible selectc such as `table`, `th`, `td`, `thead`, `tbody`, `caption`, and any classes or `id`s you create.

Master It Use styles to give your table an attractive appearance.

Chapter 11

Forms and Form Styles

Forms are used to allow visitors to contact you, to collect information from visitors, to search, to subscribe to newsletters, to complete sales transactions and do many other web-based tasks. When a visitor completes a form and presses the Submit or Search button, a script processes the information. In a search, the script might return information to the visitor. A contact or sales form might take the data from the form and send it to a person (or a database) for appropriate action.

This chapter is a bit different from the others in the book because you won't get all the foundation information you need about collecting data with forms by reading this chapter. Other chapters have helped you build that solid foundation, but forms generally require an associated script in order to execute the command to submit the data collected in the form fields.

Scripts and programming are beyond the scope of this book. You *will* learn where to find some free scripts and helpful resources that will get you started on the subject of using scripts, but you won't learn how to write scripts in this book.

In this chapter you will:

- Write XHTML for form elements.
- Create style rules for forms.
- Use XHTML elements and attributes to ensure accessible forms.

Script Matters

The purpose of this brief section is to direct you to scripts that you can download and use and to information about the scripting languages used in web authoring.

Scripts that format and e-mail form data are often written in Perl and have the file extension `.pl`. Sometimes you see this as `.cgi` (for Common Gateway Interface). There are many places on the Internet that offer up free Perl and CGI scripts for various functions such as submitting e-mail or creating guest books. Consider using the scripts available from the open source outfit called SourceForge. The Perl scripts in question are located at

```
http://nms-cgi.sourceforge.net/scripts.shtml
```

A script often used to submit form data is called FormMail. SourceForge has a version called TFMail. There is an extensive README file with each script at SourceForge that explains in detail what needs to be done in your form and to your script in order to make it all work together.

PHP (Hypertext Preprocessor) is a general-purpose scripting language that can be embedded into HTML. PHP can create entire websites. PHP is also excellent for form processing. SourceForge has thousands PHP projects listed at

```
http://sourceforge.net/softwaremap/trove_list.php?form_cat=183.
```

FORM RESOURCES

A book with a good chapter on using FormMail, including how to put it on your server and set permissions to execute it, is *Dreamweaver MX 2004 Savvy* by Christian Crumlish and Lucinda Dykes (Sybex, 2004). Use their directions, but get the script at `nms-cgi.sourceforge.net` that I referred to previously. Do not use the original FormMail script they suggest, as it is not secure.

Another possible source of scripts is here:

```
www.bebosoft.com/products/formstogo
```

Bebosoft provides software called Forms To Go that will generate a script for your forms. This is not a free service like that offered by SourceForge, but it is inexpensive. You can select PHP, ASP, or Perl for the programming language of the script.

Community MX has an inexpensive ColdFusion form handler at

```
www.communitymx.com/abstract.cfm?cid=A20192B2481B9136
```

If you search within those results for "form handlers", you find several useful scripts for sendir mail and other form handling chores.

Some web hosting companies will let you use your version of FormMail.pl or some other forr handling script. Others will not. Those who do not want you to use your own scripts often provic a script located on their server that you are allowed to use. Hosting companies that supply scrip provide support information about how to use them. For example, if the hosting company provid a script, they will give you the URL for the `action` attribute in your `form` element. More on the `action` attribute is coming later.

Hosting companies are picky about letting you use your own scripts because the script that sends mail is actually an executable file. It can pose security risks or can be misused to send spa e-mail if it is not handled with the proper security. See Chapter 12 for an explanation of how to u your FTP software to set permissions to execute a file.

Learn the XHTML

In the following exercises, you will create a fairly typical web form: a page on a camera tech suppo site where the user enters contact and other information, including a description of the problem selects a camera type; and optionally uploads a sample image. This example provides an opport nity to work with each type of `form` element. You will make a second abbreviated form that de onstrates a single concept that differs from the way the main form functions.

On the CD, find these files: `ch11_forms_start.html`, `ch11_forms.css` and `camera.jpg`. Listing 11.1 shows the complete `ch11_forms_start.html` page. The page uses two `div` elemen with named `id` attributes to establish the colors and widths of the containers that will hold th two forms.

LISTING 11.1: The *ch11_forms_start.html* Page

```
<!DOCTYPE html PUBLIC "-//W3C//DTD XHTML 1.0 Transitional//EN"
        "http://www.w3.org/TR/xhtml1/DTD/xhtml1-transitional.dtd">
<html xmlns="http://www.w3.org/1999/xhtml">
<head>
<title>Ch11: Forms Start Page</title>
<link href="ch11_forms.css" rel="stylesheet" type="text/css" />
</head>
<body>
<div id="script">
  <h1>A script example</h1>
</div>
<div id="mailto">
  <h1>An example using a mailto action </h1>
</div>
</body>
</html>
```

The `ch11_forms_start.html` is linked to `ch11_forms.css`. The style sheet sets up a few basics for the page. The complete file is shown in Listing 11.2. You'll add to these two documents as the chapter evolves.

LISTING 11.2: The *ch11_forms.css* Page

```
body {
   font: 100% Arial, Helvetica, sans-serif;
   color: #000;
   background: #FFF;
}
#script {
   width: 599px;
   background: #FFC;
   border: 1px dotted #3FF;
}
#mailto {
   width: 80%;
   background: #CDE8B7;
   border: 1px dotted #606;
   margin-top: 2em;
}
```

Figure 11.1 shows the initial page in a browser. The main form will be contained by the div id="script" element. The mailto example will show you how to submit a form without a scrip The #script selector uses an exact width because that is the width of a camera image you will ad later as a background. The #mailto selector is set for a percentage width.

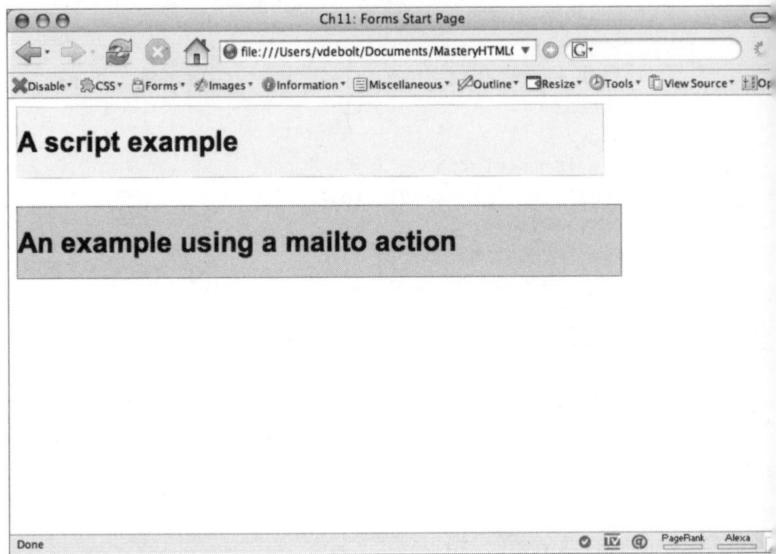

FIGURE 11.1
The start page in the browser

The *form* Element

Following the <h1>A Script Example</h1>, type the opening **<form>** tag, then press Enter (Retur a few times and type the closing **</form>** tag:

```
<h1>A Script Example</h1>
<form>

</form>
```

The form element can have several attributes: method, action, name, and id.

The values for method are either get or post. All get does is retrieve the data. However, po may store or update data, order a product, or send e-mail. The value for action is usually a UR pointing to the location of the script that will do the actual work on submitting the form. While na and id are not required form attributes, they are useful as unique identifiers. You will give it th name and id of scriptex, since this form is the example that uses a script. Add these to your fo element, like this:

```
<form name="scriptex" id="scriptex">
```

Decide on a method. Because get limits the amount of data and the manner of formatting th incoming e-mail, post is normally used. Add **method="post"** to your form attributes.

The final attribute is `action`, which points to the location of the script. It might be a relative link such as `action="../cgi-bin/somescript.pl"`, or `action="submit.php"`. The value might be an absolute link such as `action="http://www.example.com/somescript.pl"`. Use the absolute URL in your example form, which is now:

```
<form name="scriptex" id="scriptex" method="post"
  action="http://www.example.com/somescript.pl">
```

At this point, you don't see any evidence of the form in the browser because none of the visible `form` elements nor the Submit button are there yet. And, of course, the action will not execute because it is an example URL and not a real URL.

CGI-BIN, SAY WHAT?

Many servers use a specific directory called `cgi-bin`, where CGI or Perl scripts are isolated and stored. This is a security measure. Whether you upload your own script or use one provided by your hosting company, if you use Perl it will probably be located in a directory named `cgi-bin`. PHP and other scripts can be stored in the `cgi-bin` directory, but they are not required to be.

Hidden Fields

Speaking of things you don't see in the browser, forms often use `hidden` fields, so you'll add one to this form. Common uses of hidden fields include holding temporary values, primary keys (for a database), and values that are passed to the page. Following the opening `form` element, type this `hidden form` element:

```
<input name="subject" type="hidden" value="Your form results" />
```

As you continue creating `form` elements, you will see that many `form` elements are `input` elements. Each `input` element is given a `type` attribute, in this case, `type="hidden"`. Note that the `input` element is an empty element and requires the XHTML closing forward slash.

Text Boxes

Enough with the things you can't admire in the browser! Let's get started creating the fields where the user will provide information. Make a text box asking for the user's name.

NAME-VALUE PAIRS

A `name` is assigned to each `form` element. When you receive the data that the user typed in the form, the e-mail is formatted in what are called *name-value pairs*. That is to say, you see the `name` of the `form` element and the `value` that the user typed or selected. It is good practice to give `form` elements names that will help you interpret the data you received from it in the form of name-value pairs. For example, a `form` element asking for a first name to be input could use `name="firstname"`, or a `form` element asking for postal code input could use `name="zipcode"`. Do not use spaces in `form` element names.

There are two parts to the form elements you will make: the label and the form element itse The label is what makes the form accessible to any type of browser. The label text is visible a does what the name implies—labels the form field. A label tells you what information to enter the field. The label text can also be tied to its particular form field so that nonvisual users can as ciate the label text with the proper form field.

To create a one-line text box, type **<input type="text" />**. You also need to name this eleme and since it will be asking for a person's name, name it "name". With that added, you have <inp type="text" name="name" />. Finally, you need to add the label element.

ALL TYPES OF INPUT

The complete list of input types includes text | password | checkbox | radio | submit | reset | file | hidden | image | button. The name attribute is required for all of them except submit and reset.

The label element with the for attribute, coupled with an id matching the value of the for attribute in the input element, creates an accessible text prompt for each form field. Since this inp form is asking for a name, you can use the value "name" in the for attribute. Type this before t input element: **<label for="name">Your name: </label>**. Next, add the id to the input eleme that matches the value of the for attribute, making the input element now read:

```
<input type=text" name="name" id="name" />
```

The value of the for attribute and the id attribute *must match.* The value of the name attribu does not have to be the same as the value used for the for and id, although it is in this example. T space after Your Name: is merely to keep the text box from bumping into the label text.

The complete code is

```
<label for="name">Your Name: </label><input type="text" name="name" id="name" /
```

PASSING THE VALIDATION TESTS

As of this writing, the accessibility validators will not give a form an acceptable rating without the for attribute. (See Chapter 12 for information about validators.) However, my friends at www.knowbility.org, who are experts in accessibility training and advocacy, inform me that label without the for attribute is fully supported by the aural screen readers Jaws, Window Eyes, and Home Page Reader, but only when the form element is wrapped in the label element, as explained next under "Create a Big Target."

If you build a site for any government entity, or for a client who specifically requests proof of accessibility, you will no doubt use the online validators to show that you have met the requirements. To help you achieve acceptable validation results, you'll use the for attribute for all form labels in this chapter.

CREATE A BIG TARGET

It's also technically correct to nest the entire form element inside the `label`, like this:

```
<label for="name">Your Name: <input type="text" name="name" id="name" /></label>
```

Nesting the entire form element in the `label` has the effect of creating a large target for the mouse or other pointing device to bring focus to the form field. In other words, if you click anywhere in the `label` "Your Name" in the previous example, the input field for that label receives focus. When a form field has focus, the field outline is highlighted and the cursor is in position ready for your input. You also no longer need the `for` attribute when the label wraps around the entire form element. Sounds like a great idea. Except for the bugaboo known as unreliable browser support.

Tabbing from one form field to another also moves the focus, whether a `label` wraps the entire form element or not.

To sum up, it's best to use the `for` attribute in the way described throughout the chapter if you want reliable results and successful validation.

You could use a `<br />` after the closing label tag to move down to the next line for the text box, for a neater looking alignment. Feel free to do that if you like the appearance better. Nest each new form element in a `p` element. The paragraph elements will space out the form fields a bit. Add this:

```
<p><label for="name">Your Name: </label><input type="text" name="name" id="name"
/></p>
```

Now you can take a look in the browser because you finally have a `form` element you can see (Figure 11.2).

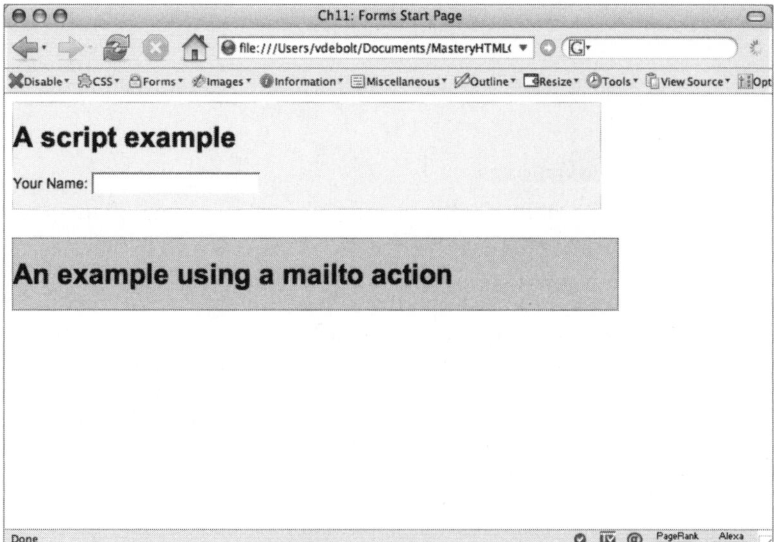

FIGURE 11.2
A text box with a label is your first visible form element.

Of course, you may want to ask for first and last name, or even middle initial, in separate for elements. Each would be like the one you just made, except that you would use unique `name` an `id` attributes for each `input` element, and each unique `label` would have a `for` attribute matchir the `id` of its corresponding input element.

To make a text box asking for the user's e-mail, you use the same formatting, except the `labe` will say Your Email: and the `name` will be `"email"`. Use `email` as the value of the `for` and `id` attributes as well.

```
<p><label for="email">Your Email: </label><input type="text" name="email"
id="email" /></p>
```

Figure 11.3 shows this input box in the browser.

FIGURE 11.3
The input box requesting an e-mail address is shown.

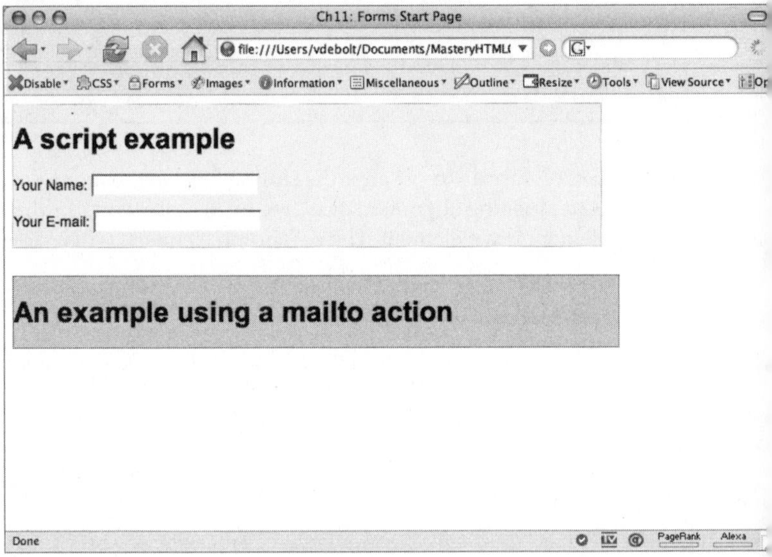

PASSWORD BOXES

The form you are building is for an imaginary camera support site. Often when you return to a si where you are a registered user, a password is required.

Make another text box so you can use `type="password"`. When the user types something in th password form field, only asterisks or dots appear. This prevents other people from reading the pa word information. Make the `label` read `Your support password:`. Make the `for` and `id` attribu values `"password"`. Use `input type="password"` and think of a great `name` for this `form` elemen such as `name="password"`. All that, together with the `p` element, will look like this:

```
<p><label for="password">Your support password: </label><input type="password"
name="password" id="password" /></p>
```

See Figure 11.4. For even more thrills, try typing in the browser password box to see if asterisks appear.

In a real-world situation where a password is required, the password field would probably appear on a login screen before you reached a form where you could input information about a camera problem. That login form would be submitted to a script that would verify that you were a registered user and send you on to a form similar to the one you're building now. Keep in mind that while this is the way to create the password form field, a password field probably wouldn't be smack in the middle of a real-world form as it is in this exercise.

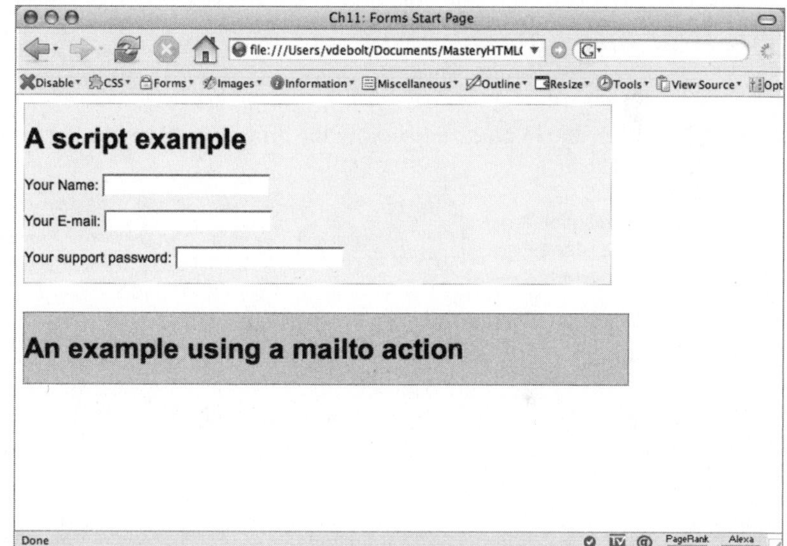

FIGURE 11.4
Three text boxes are complete.

The *fieldset* Element

One of the most useful elements recently added to the form designer's options is the `fieldset` element. The `fieldset` element organizes `form` elements into related groups. The default appearance of a `fieldset` element is to box in the group of `form` elements and provide a `legend` that identifies the particular grouping.

You have three `form` elements asking for personal information about the user, so enclose them in a `fieldset` element.

Before the first `p` element in your form, type **`<fieldset>`**. Following the closing `p` tag after the third `p` element, type **`</fieldset>`**. That wraps all three of your existing `form` elements in the `fieldset`. Next, add the `legend`. After the opening `fieldset` element, type **`<legend>Personal Information</legend>`**. The `legend` is used as an accessibility tool to provide information about the grouping, to indicate the type of choices to be made in the grouping, or to clarify the purpose of the grouping. The completed `fieldset` element is shown in Listing 11.3, and Figure 11.5 shows the current form.

LISTING 11.3: Wrap the Three Text Boxes in a *fieldset* Element with a *legend*

```
<fieldset>
<legend>Personal Information</legend>
<p><label for="name">Your Name: </label><input type="text" name="name" id="name"
></p>
<p><label for="email">Your E-mail: </label><input type="text" name="email"
id="email" /></p>
<p><label for="password">Your support password: </label><input type="password"
name="password" id="password" /></p>
</fieldset>
```

With that in place, the view in the browser will be like Figure 11.5.

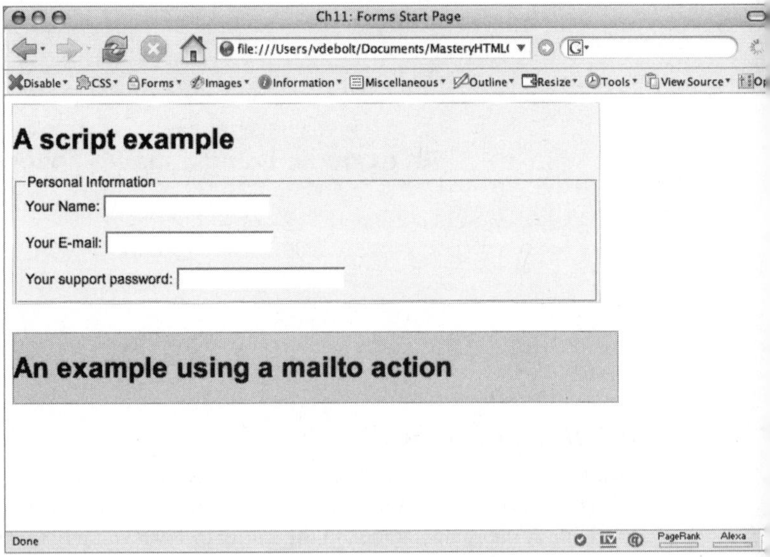

FIGURE 11.5 The personal information `fieldset` organizes the form elements.

The *textarea* Element

The `form` element that allows for several lines of text to be entered is a `textarea` element.

Before you make a `textarea` element, add another `fieldset` to organize this new section of the form. Remember, this form is for an imaginary support page, so make a group of form elements about the support question. Type this:

```
<fieldset><legend>Your Support Question</legend>

</fieldset>
```

The next few `form` elements you learn will be nested in this `fieldset`.

ADDITIONAL TEXT BOX ATTRIBUTES

Several optional attributes are allowed with text boxes. If you use `value="somevalue"` in an `input type="text"` element, the `value` will display in the `form` element as text before the user begins typing their own input. The initial value is replaced by whatever the user types. For example, you might see a search form with the initial value "search our site" in the input field. Or a field asking for name might use `value="Your full name"` as an initial value. You can use `size="n"` where *n* is the desired width of the box in characters, such as 30 or 40. The default width for a text box is 20 characters, but the size does not limit the number of characters that can actually be typed in the box. If you have an input box asking for a street address that is the default 20 characters in width and the user's address requires more than 20 characters, the complete address can still be typed in the box. The CSS `width` property can be used instead of `size`. The form field has an `id`, so you have a perfect selector already built into the code to target with the CSS. The size is a visual decision, rather than a factor affecting the amount of input the field can hold, so it is more properly controlled by CSS.

You can use `maxlength="n"` where *n* is the maximum number of characters that can be typed in an input box. Sometimes this is useful when you are asking for information that has a specific number of characters such as a postal code or a phone number. If the user tries to type more than the allowed number of characters, nothing appears after the maximum is reached.

You can help your users understand what they need to type with `size` and `maxlength`. For example, if you asked for a three-digit area code, the `size` attribute (or a width rule in the CSS) shows the user a small `input` field. And `maxlength` permits only three characters to be entered, as in this snippet:

```
<input type="text" size="3" maxlength="3" ...
```

A `textarea` can be as large as you want. You will make a rather small one in this exercise. Again, to help with line spacing, start by typing a **`<p></p>`** element. Nested inside the `p` element, type the label:

```
<label for="problem">Describe Your Problem:</label><br />
```

I suggest a `<br />` after the label, but that isn't required. Finally, type the `textarea`. You will give a size in `cols` (for columns) and `rows` right off the bat as well. You must name the element; you are asking the user to describe a problem, so use `name="problem"`. Type the following:

```
<textarea name="problem" cols="30" rows="5" id="problem"></textarea>
```

Notice that the `textarea` element requires a closing tag. Here is the complete snippet:

```
<p><label for="problem">Describe Your Problem:</label><br />
<textarea name="problem" cols="30" rows="5" id="problem"></textarea></p>
```

Look at your page in the browser (see Figure 11.6).

In the browser, type a couple of paragraphs in that `textarea` box to see what happens. A scrollbar automatically appears when the user types more than the `cols="30"` and `rows="5"` size will accommodate (see Figure 11.7).

Of course, you can adjust the size values of the `cols` and `rows` attributes to suit your needs. There is a limit to how much text a user can enter in a `textarea` field, but it is quite large.

FIGURE 11.6
A textarea inside a new fieldset.

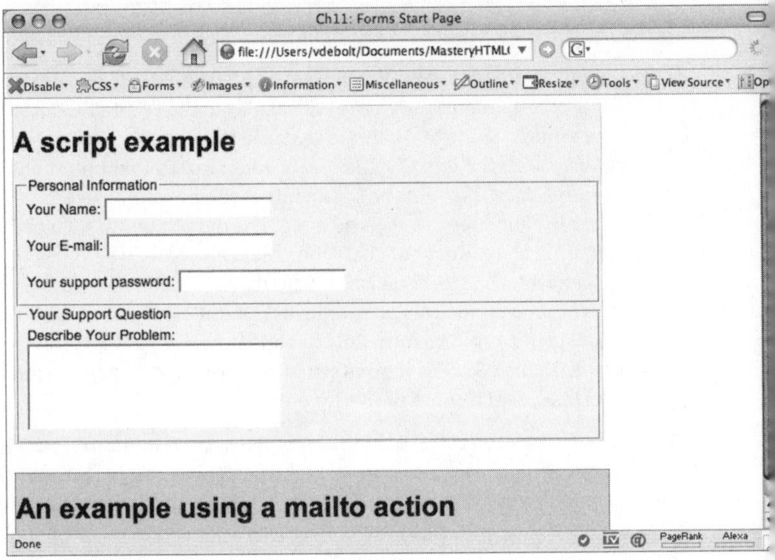

FIGURE 11.7
When the user types more than the number of columns and rows set for the text area, a scroll bar appears and the user can continue to type.

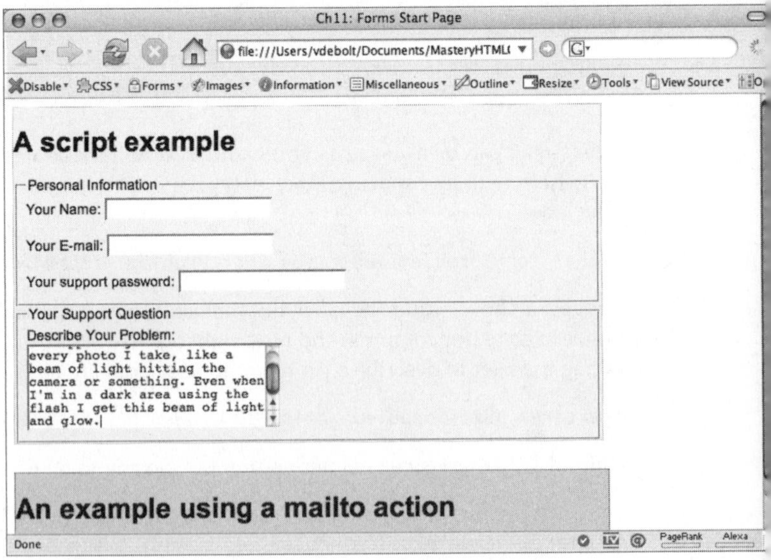

The *select* Menu

Use the select element when you need to display a list of choices for the user to select from. In t example, the user will select from a list of camera types, and the select element will be nested the current fieldset, immediately following the textarea element. Start by typing this:

```
<p><label for="camera">Select your camera type</label>
```

You will close the paragraph element after you insert and close the select element. You will ask the user to select a camera, so open the select element with this:

```
<select name="camera" id="camera">
```

As with the paragraph, the select element will be closed following the last of the options. A select element contains several option elements. Start with just one:

```
<p><label for="camera">Select your camera type</label>
   <select name="camera" id="camera">
      <option value="sony" selected="selected">Sony</option>
```

Notice the selected="selected" attribute in the code? That option appears in the pull-down list of options as selected. If you don't want an option to be preselected, simply leave that attribute out. If you leave it out, the first option in the select element will be shown in the drop-down menu of the select in the browser by default.

The entire select menu uses name="camera". Each individual option will have a different value. Add option elements for Kodak, Polaroid, and Canon. Then close the select element and close the paragraph, like this:

```
<p><label for="camera">Select your camera type</label>
   <select name="camera" id="camera">
      <option value="sony" selected="selected">Sony</option>
      <option value="kodak">Kodak</option>
      <option value="polaroid">Polaroid</option>
      <option value="canon">Canon</option>
   </select>
</p>
```

Take a look at that in the browser (Figure 11.8).

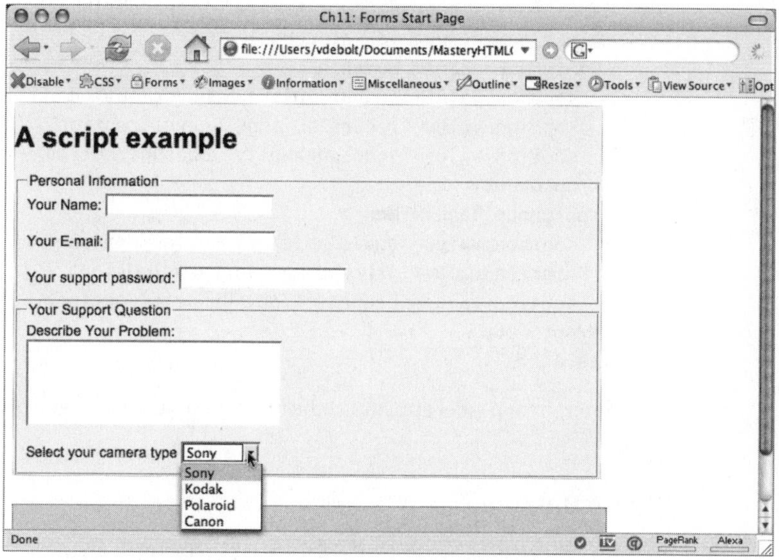

FIGURE 11.8
The select menu form element shown with the select menu options expanded

You are probably familiar with form elements like this that list all 50 states or numerous count codes in forms you have filled out yourself on websites. Forms often feed information into data bases, and sometimes the database is set up to receive the information in a particular way. For example, a database might be set up to store a state name only as a two-character code, such as C(In that case, if the user entered **Colo** or **Col** instead, the database might not accept the informatio Using preset `option` elements in a `select` menu is one way to control what is sent to a databas which is why such form elements are popular for certain kinds of data collection.

The `select` element can have several other attributes that are not needed in this example. O is `size="n"` where *n* is the number of lines the menu displays at one time. When the size is mo than 1, a scrollbar will appear to allow the user to see all of the options, instead of the pull-dow menu you currently have. That code would look like this:

```
<select name="camera" id="camera" size="2">
```

You may want to allow users to select more than one option from an option menu. It wouldr make sense to choose more than one camera in the camera menu, but here's how the code wou work, as an example. The `multiple` attribute is used for this, as in:

```
<select name="camera" id="camera" size="2" multiple="multiple">
```

If users are allowed to select more than one option, you need to add a note somewhere near th select menu instructing them how to do it. Normally this is accomplished by holding down the C key (the Command key on a Mac) while clicking the desired options. Job sites often use the `multip` attribute in `select` menus to let people search for jobs in more than one field at a time, or to indica more than one area of expertise when submitting a resume.

OPTGROUP

A select menu can be organized internally using `optgroup`. You won't add `optgroup` to the for for this exercise, but here's an example of how it works.

```
<label for="singers">Favorite Jazz Singers</label>
<select name="fav" id="singers">
  <optgroup label="Women">
    <option value="schuur">Diane Schuur</option>
    <option value="reeves">Dianne Reeves</option>
    <option value="johnson">Molly Johnson</option>
  </optgroup>
  <optgroup label="Men">
    <option value="buble">Michael Buble</option>
    <option value="jarreau">Al Jarreau</option>
    <option value="bennett">Tony Bennett</option>
  </optgroup>
</select>
```

The `optgroup` label appears in the menu and can help organize select menus with large numb of options.

Radio Buttons

Radio buttons offer a variety of responses to a question, only one of which may be selected at a tin You will make a set of radio buttons that say Yes and No. If the user selects Yes and then chang the selection to No, the Yes radio button automatically becomes deselected. Clicking the label will also select the radio button.

Each radio button in the set has the same `name` attribute. If you asked the user, "Is your camera still under warranty?" you could use `name="warranty"` for every radio button in the set. However, each radio button in the set gets an individual `value`. This is the code:

```
<p>Is your camera still under warranty?<br />
<input name="warranty" type="radio" value="Yes" id="yes" /><label for="yes">Yes
</label><br />
<input name="warranty" type="radio" value="No" id="no" /><label for="no">No </
label>
</p>
```

The preceding snippet includes the `p` element, a `br` after the question and the first radio button, and a `label` after each of the radio buttons (see Figure 11.9).

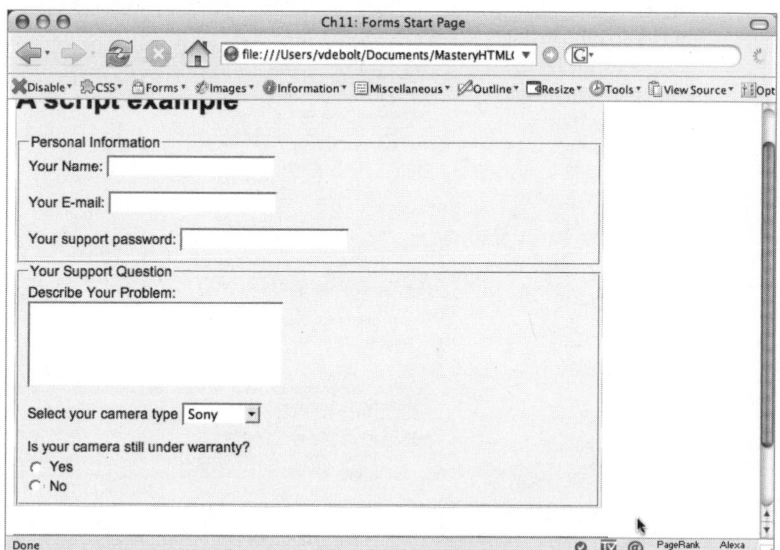

FIGURE 11.9
In a set of radio buttons, only one may be selected.

Letting Visitors Upload Files

A page like this might include an option for users to upload a photograph as an example of the problem with the camera. To make this happen, the following attribute would have to be included in the opening `form` element:

```
enctype="multipart/form-data"
```

This attribute specifies the content type used to submit the form to the server. Go back to the beginning form tag and add this to the list of attributes:

```
<form name="scriptex" id="scriptex" method="post"
  action="http://www.example.com/somescript.pl" enctype="multipart/form-data">
```

The `method` must be `post` for uploading files.

The particular form element you need for the user to be able to upload a file is input type="file An explanatory line of text will tell the user what you are asking them to upload. Find your place agai in the form and add this after the radio buttons. An example paragraph and form element of this type

```
<p>Do you have a photograph taken with your camera that shows an example of the
problem? If so, you can upload it.</p>
<p><label for="photo">Select a photo from your computer:</label><br />
<input type="file" name="photo" id="photo" /></p>
```

A browse button automatically appears next to the form field when using the type="file" attribute. The user browses their computer to find the file. When it is selected, the location of the fi on the user's computer appears as a directory path in the form field box.

The way a file input element is rendered varies widely depending on operating system an browser, but you should see something similar to Figure 11.10.

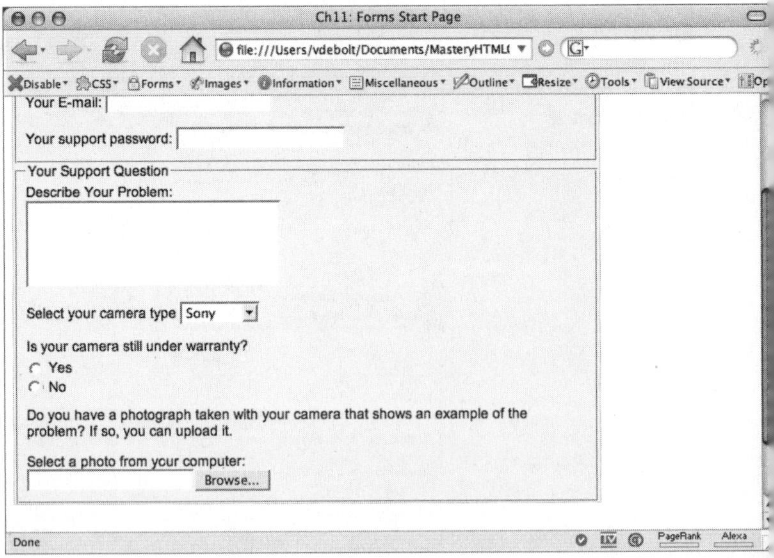

FIGURE 11.10
The file upload field and its accompanying browse button let the user upload an image or other file.

YOU MAY EXPERIENCE SOME LOSS OF CONTROL

Because rendering of form control elements can vary widely, you may notice slight differences between the figures shown here and the results on your browser and operating system. As the designer, you have no control over the way the different operating systems and browsers render certain form elements, even with CSS. A browse button, for example will be styled and named according to the browser and operating system requirements.

At 456 Berea St. you will find a number of examples of form control styles and how they appear in various browsers. A must-read article!

www.456bereastreet.com/archive/200410/styling_even_more_form_controls

It's interesting to check the page with two or three browsers, because the linked styled form control test pages appear according to whatever browser and setup you are using to view them.

That finishes the area that should be contained within the `fieldset` element for "Your Support Question." Move beyond the `fieldset` terminating tag, so you can create one last `fieldset` for the `input type="checkbox"` element.

The *checkbox*

Businesses often take advantage of the fact that users are submitting a form to establish a way to keep in contact with the user. There might be questions about whether special offers or product information would be welcomed by the user, or there might be an offer to receive a regular newsletter. Often the user will select more than one option from a set of related choices. You need a `form` element that allows for multiple options to be selected. That `form` element is the familiar `input` where `type="checkbox"`.

Before you add the checkboxes, create one more `fieldset` element to set off the last section of the form. The `legend` should be something that lets the user know what the section is about. Type the following, pressing Enter (Return) once or twice before typing the closing tag:

```
<fieldset><legend>Please send me the following information</legend>

</fieldset>
```

The new `fieldset` element will be the container for the checkboxes. Some explanatory text might be good to begin:

```
<p>Indicate which of the following you would like to receive:<br />
```

The `input` element for a checkbox looks like this:

```
<input name="groupname" type="checkbox" value="uniquevalue" id="someid" />
```

Like radio buttons, checkboxes are grouped. The set of related checkboxes all have the same `name` and a unique `value`. Since you are asking what you can send the user, use `name="send"` for the group name.

It makes sense to have the text in the label appear after the checkbox, so with a label added, a single checkbox element for New Product Information would look like this:

```
<input name="send" type="checkbox" value="newProd" id="newProd" /><label
for="newProd">New Product Information</label><br />
```

You will complete three checkboxes, asking for users to select whether they want to receive the previously completed new product information (`value="newProd"`), money saving offers (`value="offers"`), and a monthly tips newsletter (`value="newsletter"`).

If you want to have a checkbox automatically selected when the user sees the form, use the attribute `checked="checked"`. Put that attribute in the `input` element for Monthly Tips Newsletter. If the user does not want it checked, they must manually deselect it. Clicking either the label or the checkbox itself will select or unselect the checkbox.

ATTRIBUTE ORDER

The order of the attributes does not matter. For example, the `input` element could be coded as `<input type="checkbox" id="someid" name="somename" value="somevalue" />` instead of in the order shown in the example.

With <br /> elements after each line, the whole new section, including the `fieldset`, is show in Listing 11.4.

LISTING 11.4: The New *fieldset* with *checkbox* Fields

```
<fieldset><legend>Please send me the following information</legend>
   <p>Indicate which of the following you would like to receive:<br />
   <input name="send" type="checkbox" value="newProd" id="newProd" /><label
for="newProd">New Product Information</label><br />
   <input name="send" type="checkbox" value="offers" id="offers" /><label
for="offers">Money Saving Offers</label><br />
   <input name="send" type="checkbox" value="newsletter" checked="checked"
id="newsletter" /><label for="newsletter">Monthly Tips Newsletter</label></p>
 </fieldset>
```

In the browser, your view should be similar to Figure 11.11. Note that the Monthly Tips New letter checkbox is selected because of the `checked="checked"` in the `input` attributes. Play with in the browser to see what happens if you deselect Monthly Tips Newsletter or if you select mo than one checkbox.

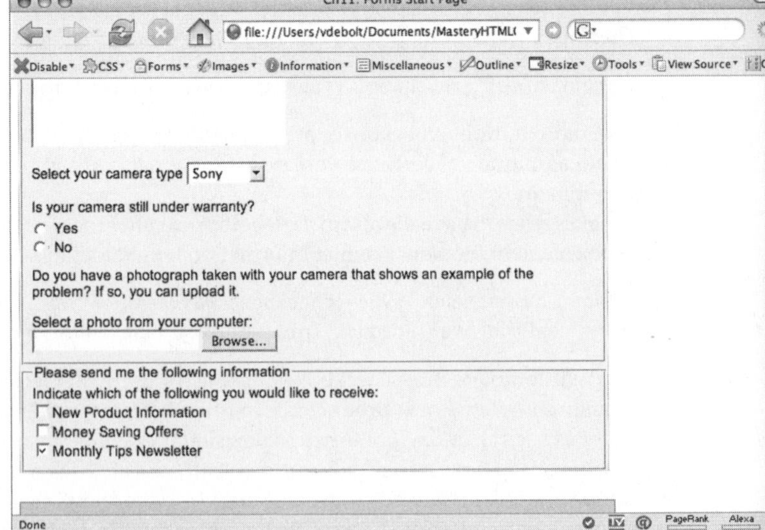

FIGURE 11.11
Users may select more than one checkbox. If the visitor does not want the preselected item sent to them, they must manually deselect it.

The *tabindex* Attribute

Users can move from one form field to the next with the Tab key, in a manner very similar to what was discussed in Chapter 7.

As with hyperlinks, the `tabindex` attribute used with `form` elements alters the normal tab order of form fields in the flow of the XHTML. To change the tab order, use `tabindex="n"` as an attribute of a specific element, where *n* is a number.

The `tabindex` attribute is not needed in this form. I caution you to use it only when it is absolutely needed to make the page more usable and understandable. Make sure the user moves from one form field to another in the most logical manner when changing the tab order in any way.

TITLE HELP

A `title` attribute can be used with any form element. Often when the normal tab order is disrupted with `tabindex`, hints about `tabindex` values are included in the form element as `title` information.

The `title` attribute can be helpful in other situations involving forms, particularly if the situation, for whatever reason, just doesn't lend itself to including a `label`. In that case a `title` attribute can be used to provide supplemental information that might have been in a `label` if one could have been used. I'm not recommending a `title` attribute as a substitute for the `label` as an everyday practice—only in unusual cases where a `label` simply cannot be included.

To see an example of a case where no label is needed, look at question 14 near the end of this form: `www.walktoschool.org/survey`. If you look at the source of this page (which was made by this book's technical editor, Zoe Gillenwater; please don't actually submit this form), you'll note that the radio buttons for question 14 are in a table. The `th` elements at the head of each column use a `scope` attribute and create the context needed for the radio buttons, thereby eliminating the need for labels in this situation. Even a `title` is not needed in this case.

The Submit Button

The last element to include in this form example is the Submit button. The Submit button is another `input` element, with the attribute `type="button"`. The text that you use for the attribute `value` (e.g., `value="Send Form"`) is the text that appears on the button. A label is not needed on a button. The control creates the needed text.

Move beyond the closing `fieldset` tag that encloses the checkboxes. Put the Submit button on a line of its own, with no surrounding `fieldset`. The element looks like this:

```
<input name="submit" type="button" value="Submit" />
```

See Figure 11.12.

The size of the Submit button will change depending on the assigned `value`. To see an example, change to this value:

```
value="Send this baby on its way"
```

The browser then displays a button like Figure 11.13. While "Submit" is the logical choice f this form, other forms may logically use a value like "Search" or "Go" on the input button.

Since "Submit" is the best choice for this form, change the value back to "submit" on your pa

The form is complete! The terminating `</form>` and `</div>` elements should be immediatel after your new Submit button. Of course, the form won't actually submit because it isn't linked a real script in the form `action`.

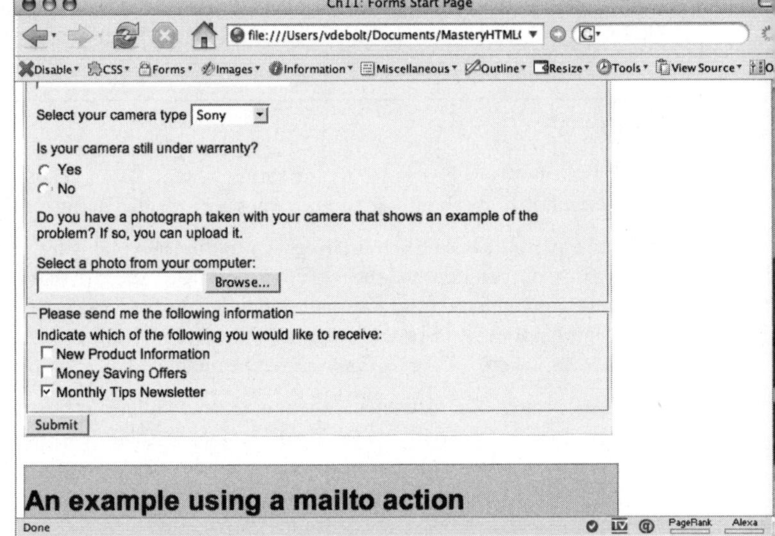

FIGURE 11.12 The form is complete with the addition of the Submit button.

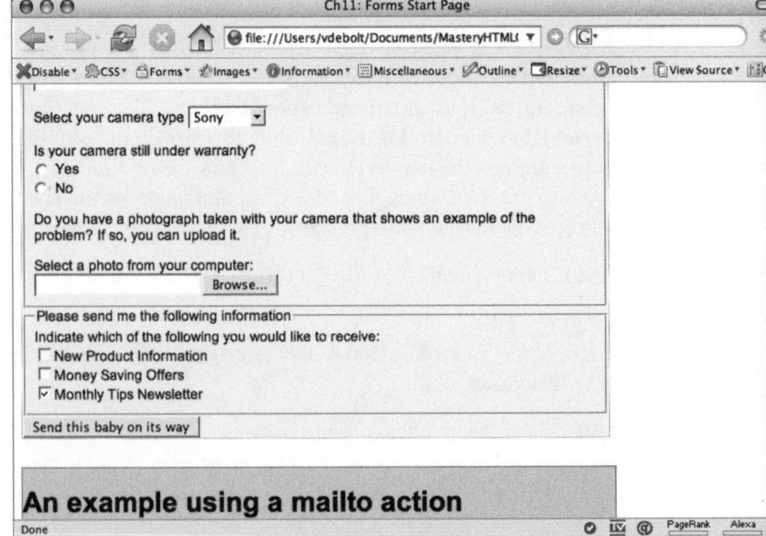

FIGURE 11.13 The value of the Submit button may be changed to something offbeat. Often the words "Go" or "Search" are used as the value on Submit buttons.

SUBMIT BY IMAGE

As an alternative, you can use a graphic as a Submit button. The `input type` is `image`, with a `src` attribute giving the path to the image. Be sure to include `alt` text if you use an image. Here's an example of how to do it:

```
<input type="image" src="somegraphic.gif" name="submit" alt="submit" />
```

Keep in mind that using an image as a Submit button will change the normal appearance of the form control and may be confusing to some users.

Before you move on to using CSS to style this page, there's one other thing about XHTML for forms that you need to know. You won't make a large form for the following example, merely enough for you to learn the new information.

Using a *mailto* Action

If you don't have a script, you can still collect information by pointing to your e-mail address in the form `action` attribute.

On the page `ch11_forms_start.html`, find this code:

```
<div id="mailto">
  <h1>An Email Example using a mailto action</h1>

</div>
```

Remember that there is a style rule in `ch11_forms.css` that sets a background color and width for the `div id="mailto"` section.

You will put a new `form` element in this `div` immediately after the `h1` element. When using `mailto` in the `action` attribute you must also use this attribute: `enctype="text/plain"`. The method must be `post`.

For the action, use your own e-mail address in the `mailto:` value. Press Enter (Return) a couple of times and type **`</form>`**. The complete snippet looks like this:

```
<form name="mailex" method="post" enctype="text/plain"
  action="mailto:someone@example.com">

</form>
```

That is the only difference in what you need to do between the script submission and the e-mail submission forms. However, copy and paste the first two text boxes from the earlier form so there is something to see here. Remember that an ID must be unique on the page, so the `for` and `id` attributes will have to change a bit to reuse the same two form fields:

```
<p><label for="name2">Your Name: </label><input type="text" name="name2"
id="name2" /></p>
<p><label for="email2">Your Email: </label><input type="text" name="email2"
id="email2" /></p>
```

Add a Submit button:

```
<p><input type="submit" name="Submit" value="Submit" /></p>
```

The completed form is shown in Listing 11.5.

Listing 11.5: The Completed *mailto* Example

```
<h1>An example using a mailto action</h1>
<form name="mailex" method="post"  enctype="text/plain"
action="mailto:someone@example.com">
  <p><label for="name2">Your Name: </label><input type="text" name="name2"
id="name2" /></p>
  <p><label for="email2">Your Email: </label><input type="text" name="email2"
id="email2" /></p>
  <p>and more . . . </p>
  <p><input type="submit" name="Submit" value="Submit" /></p>
</form>
```

There is no visible difference to indicate that the form will submit by e-mail (see Figure 11.1 However, when you click the Submit button, the effect is to open an e-mail document containi the data from the name-value pairs in the form. To see this, click Submit on the page in a brows

A form using `action="mailto:someone@somewhere.com"` may seem like the solution to all your problems—after all, no script is needed. However, there are issues with this method. First some older browsers don't know what to do with `enctype="text/plain"`, and this won't wor with them. Second, the formatting of the e-mail leaves a lot to be desired in terms of readability. won't work for people who use a web mail account instead of a desktop mail client. Finally, an worst of all, it exposes your e-mail address to spammers.

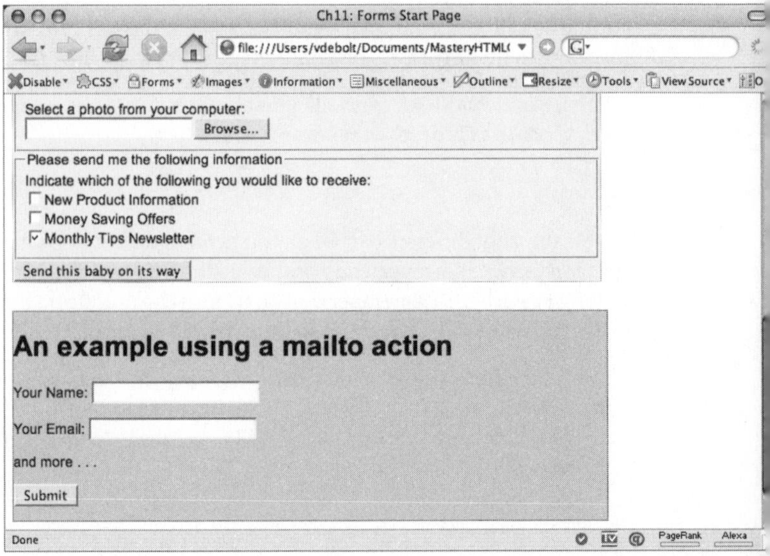

Figure 11.14 The completed `mailto` example. When the user clicks Submit, an e-mail document opens to send the form data.

If I put a silly name and e-mail address in this form and click Submit, Figure 11.15 shows what would be sent in my default e-mail application. If there were more form fields in this form, they would all be formatted in this rather hard-to-read manner.

Using a `mailto action` is fine if you just want a small amount of information, but for processing large amounts of data, a script becomes necessary. Keep in mind that your e-mail address is exposed to spammers using this method.

You can compare your finished page with `ch11_forms_finished.html` from the CD or with the complete page in Listing 11.6.

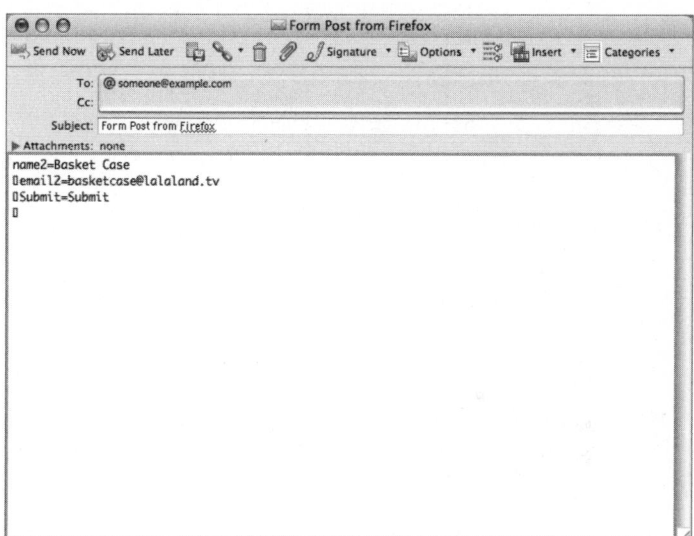

FIGURE 11.15 A formatted e-mail from a `mailto` submission

LISTING 11.6: *ch11_forms_finished.html*

```
<!DOCTYPE html PUBLIC "-//W3C//DTD XHTML 1.0 Transitional//EN"
        "http://www.w3.org/TR/xhtml1/DTD/xhtml1-transitional.dtd">
<html xmlns="http://www.w3.org/1999/xhtml">
<head>
<title>Ch11: Forms: Finished Page</title>
<link href="ch11_forms.css" rel="stylesheet" type="text/css" />
</head>
<body>
<div id="script">
  <h1>A script  example</h1>
  <form name="scriptex" id="scriptex" method="post" action="http://
www.example.com/somescript.pl" enctype="multipart/form-data">
  <input name="subject" type="hidden" value="Your Form Results" />
  <fieldset><legend>Personal Information</legend>
   <p><label for="name">Your Name: </label><input type="text" name="name"
id="name" /></p>
```

```
    <p><label for="email">Your E-mail: </label><input type="text" name="email"
id="email" /></p>
    <p><label for="password">Your support password: </label><input type="password
name="password" id="password" /></p>
   </fieldset>
   <fieldset><legend>Your Support Question</legend>
     <p><label for="problem">Describe Your Problem:</label><br />
        <textarea name="problem" cols="30" rows="5" id="problem"></textarea></p>
      <p><label for="camera">Select your camera type</label>
        <select name="camera" id="camera">
          <option value="sony" selected="selected">Sony</option>
          <option value="kodak">Kodak</option>
          <option value="polaroid">Polaroid</option>
          <option value="canon">Canon</option>
        </select>
        </p>
    <p>Is your camera still under warranty?<br />
     <input name="warranty" type="radio" value="Yes" id="yes" /><label for="yes">
Yes </label><br />
     <input name="warranty" type="radio" value="No" id="no" /><label for="no">No
label>
     </p>
    <p>Do you have a photograph taken with your camera that shows an example of th
problem? If so, you can upload it.</p>
    <p><label for="photo">Select a photo from your computer:</label><br />
    <input type="file" name="photo" id="photo" /></p>
    </fieldset>
    <fieldset><legend>Please send me the following information</legend>
    <p>Indicate which of the following you would like to receive:<br />
    <input name="send" type="checkbox" value="newProd" id="newProd" /><label
for="newProd">New Product Information</label><br />
    <input name="send" type="checkbox" value="offers" id="offers" /><label
for="offers">Money Saving Offers</label><br />
    <input name="send" type="checkbox" value="newsletter" checked="checked"
id="newsletter" /><label for="newsletter">Monthly Tips Newsletter</label></p>
    </fieldset>
    <input id="submit" name="submit" type="button" value="Submit" />
  </form>
</div>
<div id="mailto">
  <h1>An example using a mailto action </h1>
  <form name="mailex" method="post"  enctype="text/plain"
action="mailto:someone@example.com">
     <p><label for="name2">Your Name: </label><input type="text" name="name2"
id="name2" /></p>
     <p><label for="email2">Your Email: </label><input type="text" name="email2"
id="email2" /></p>
```

```
    <p>and more . . . </p>
    <p><input type="submit" name="Submit" value="Submit" /></p>
  </form>
</div>
</body>
</html>
```

FORMS IN TABLES

Accessibility issues arise when a table is used to lay out a form. It is debatable whether a form is really a valid use for a data table. It's a judgment call and depends on the situation. One such situation was mentioned in the previous sidebar "Title Help."

Separating the `label` from the `input` element by putting these two items in two different `td` elements creates a disconnect in logic for some types of screen readers. This is where the `label for="somename"` markup really shines, because it creates a logical connection between the information in the two table cells. Using the `for` attribute is the only way to logically connect the `label` to the `input` element when tables are involved.

As an example, suppose a table uses two columns. One column has text telling the user what to type into the form, perhaps their name. Then in the next column there is the `input` element where the user types. The two parts of the form are in separate `td` cells.

Here is an example, in a couple of `td` elements, showing how it's done accessibly:

```
<tr>
<td><label for="email">Your Email:</label></td>
<td><input type="text" name="email" id="email" /></td>
</tr>
```

As you can see, the markup is exactly what you learned previously, just separated into table cells. The `label` text is connected to the input element by the `for` and `id` attributes.

Add CSS to Your Form

Certain things about `form` elements fall into the realm of browser control rather than web designer control. For example, if you are using `z-index` on a page to position elements one atop another, in IEWin/5–6, select elements are always going to be on top of everything else. In addition, many form elements cannot have their colors, border styles, or other visual properties changed no matter how much CSS you throw at them. `Form` element controls should and do remain consistently rendered by browsers. This is really about usability and accessibility—if designers were allowed to use CSS to completely change the way form controls looked, the form might become difficult or confusing to use.

Even so, there is still plenty you can do with `background-color`, `color`, `font`, `border`, `padding`, `text-align`, and other CSS properties to make a form's looks remain in keeping with your overall site design and color scheme. With these goals in mind, you'll add new rules to `ch11_forms.css`.

Styling the *fieldset*

The `fieldset` elements are bumping into one another vertically, and they are of the same `wid` as the `form` element. Reduce them to `width: 90%`. A dark blue border, 2 pixels in width would distinctive, and a bit of `padding` would help separate them vertically.

The rules I suggest are

```
fieldset {

   width: 90%;
   border: 2px solid #00F;
   padding: 1em;
}
```

With that in your style sheet, your browser should display a page similar to Figure 11.16.

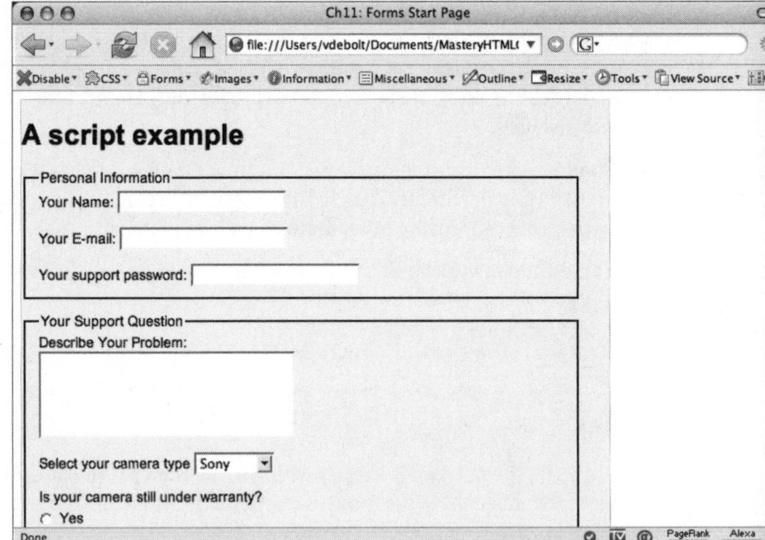

FIGURE 11.16
A few rules applied to the `fieldset` make it stand out.

The Legend

I think the blue border would look good matched by a blue background color (#00F) for the leger contrasted with a bright yellow (#FF0) for the legend text. A `bold` font with `letter-spacing: 0.2` will make the legend text stand out even more. Padding of `0.5em` on the top and bottom and `1em` the right and left will make the dark blue background shine through a larger area.

```
legend {
   color: #FF0;
   letter-spacing: 0.2em;
   font-weight: bold;
```

```
    background: #00F;
    padding: 0.5em 1em;
}
```

See Figure 11.17.

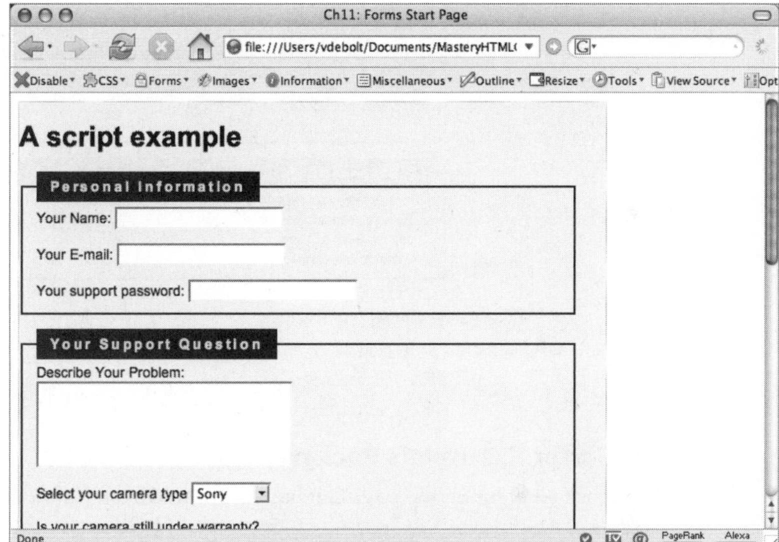

FIGURE 11.17
The legend with a style added

FORM RESOURCES

The site `www.aplus.co.yu/css/forms` has several interesting CSS examples for styling a form. Use the links in the right sidebar to see the form with different styles applied.

The Web Standards Group has a well-illustrated guide to best practices in form building at `www.webstandards.org/learn/tutorials/accessible-forms/beginner`.

There are many valuable accessibility resources at Jim Thatcher's site, including this excellent explanation of accessible forms: `www.jimthatcher.com/webcourse8.htm`.

The Submit Button

You can't do much to change the appearance of the Submit button because of limitations I described previously. But I think it seems a bit lost under those newly distinctive looking `fieldsets`. Giving it more room with a 1em margin all around would make it stand out. Try this:

```
#submit {
    margin: 1em;
}
```

See Figure 11.18.

FIGURE 11.18
Some margin around the Submit button makes it more noticeable.

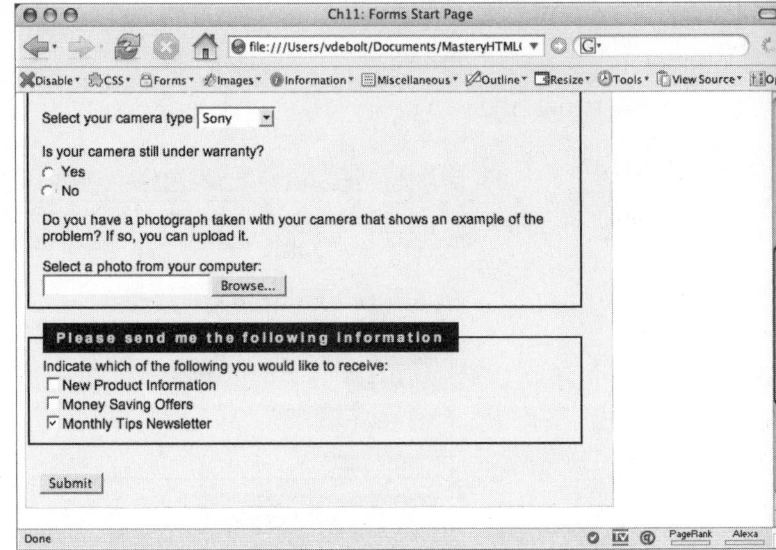

The Script Example's Background

Any block element on the page can have a graphic background, including the body element, th various div elements, the form elements, or the fieldset elements. Just to pick one and see ho it works, use the camera.jpg image as a background-image for the div id="script" element

As you recall, there is already a style rule for the #script selector. You'll add a background image to the existing rule. You want the image to repeat on the y-axis and to be placed at the le top. Note that the semicolon you previously had after the #FFC will move to the end of the back ground declaration.

```
#script {
   width: 599px;
   background: #FFC url(camera.jpg) repeat-y left top;
   border: 1px dotted #3FF;
}
```

See Figure 11.19.

SHOWING REQUIRED FIELDS

Some kind of indicator, often an asterisk, is used to indicate required fields. If the script requires a field, the form won't submit if it isn't completed. Let visitors know which fields are required so they don't try to submit an incomplete form and then have error messages to decipher. Adding the asterisk (or other indicator) is usually done as part of the label or immediately before the label. For example:

```
<p><label for="name">*Your Name: </label><input type="text" name="name" id="name"
/></p>
```

```
<p>*<label for="name">Your Name: </label><input type="text" name="name" id="name"
/></p>
```

If you use the asterisk, it's good to explicitly state something like, "An asterisk (*) indicates a required field" at the beginning of the form.

You *don't* want to use color as an indicator, or at least not color alone, because many web surfers cannot distinguish color. So a `class` applied to a `label` that changes the label color of a required field to red will not work. While an asterisk is part of the XHTML—the content—a color change is part of the CSS—the presentation. Under some circumstances, the CSS may not appear even for users who are not colorblind.

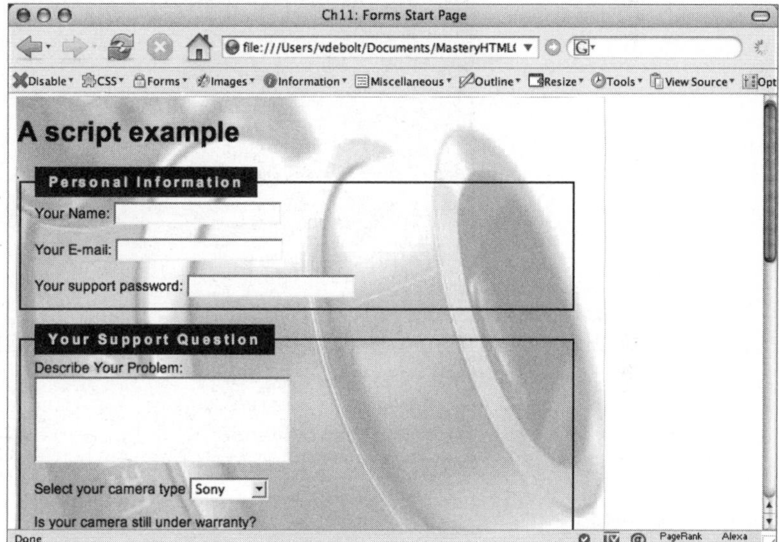

FIGURE 11.19
A background image in the `#script div` repeats on the y-axis.

In Chapter 12, you will learn how to put the web pages you make in a place where the rest of the world can see them! You are ready for the World Wide Web.

Real-World Scenario

The real-world scenarios for this chapter are interesting in terms of styling, and both use valid XHTML.

Spicy Salsa

Spicy Salsa at `www.spicysalsa.net` is about the salsa dance scene, not the foodstuff. They don't waste a minute in getting you to sign up for their newsletter. The form is right on the home page (see Figure 11.20). This form uses the `value` attribute to insert an initial value in the form field, which will disappear when the user moves to the field to type.

Because the page background is dark, this site has extensive styling of the form elements, including a background color for the text fields. When you click inside a field, the border color changes. This effect is created with the `:focus` selector. They use a graphic image for the Submit button.

The contact form, on an inner page of Spicy Salsa, uses a similar style (see Figure 11.21). The Spicy Salsa form uses a `fieldset` and proper `label` elements.

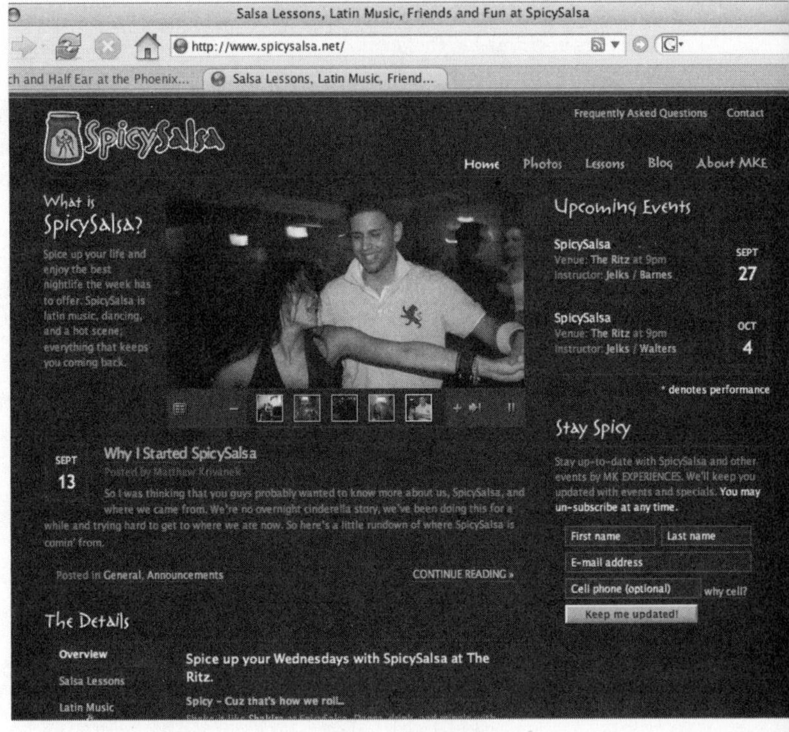

FIGURE 11.20
The Spicy Salsa homepage has a form at the right for signing up to receive a newsletter.

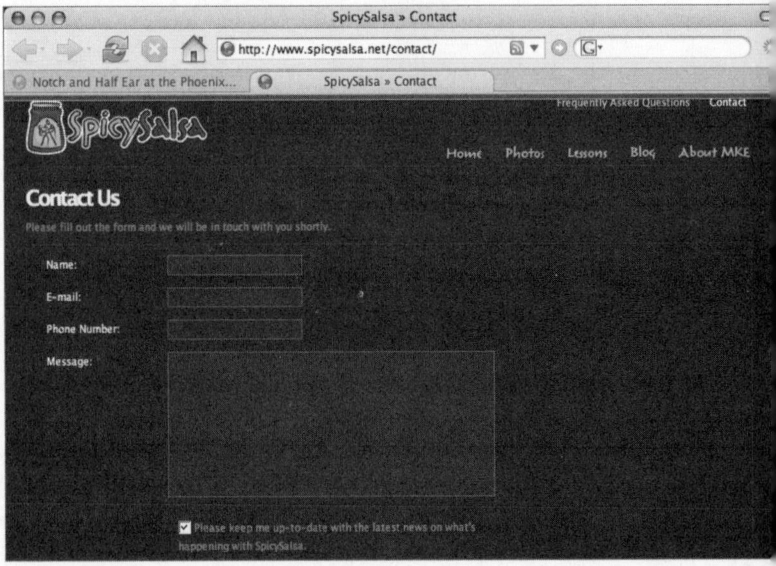

FIGURE 11.21
The contact form at Spicy Salsa uses an asterisk to designate required fields, a prechecked checkbox for the user to subscribe to a newsletter, and a graphic Submit button.

Follow the Rhinos

Follow the Rhinos at `www.followtherhinos.com` traces the trip of two white rhinos across the country on their way to the Phoenix Zoo. The home page describes the trip and has links to information and videos (see Figure 11.22).

The contact form on an inner page is shown in Figure 11.23. The screen capture is zoomed in on the area of the form. Notice that there is a select menu allowing you to designate who you want to receive the e-mail, with one of the choices being the rhinos themselves! There's no indication of required fields, but on a simple form like this it's safe to assume every field is required. This site also uses a graphic as the Submit button.

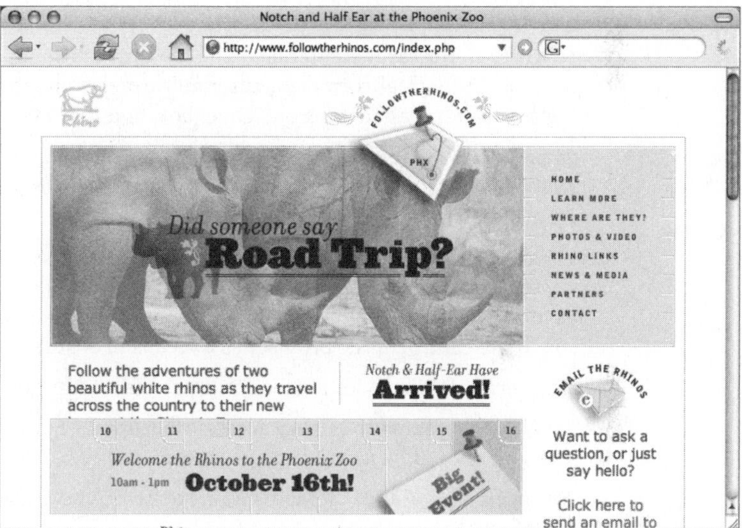

FIGURE 11.22 The home page of Follow the Rhinos

FIGURE 11.23 The contact form allows you to decide who will receive your mail.

Although it's written in valid XHTML, the Follow the Rhino site does not use the `label` eleme at all. There's a class called `.label` which is used to style text, but the text styled is not `label` te

CSS Properties

No new CSS properties were introduced in this chapter.

The Bottom Line

Forms allow interaction with visitors. They are used to take orders, gather information, solicit fe back, collect votes, search, and interact with web applications or databases.

The three Master It exercises for this chapter are to be completed together as a single assignme

Write XHTML for form elements. The essential attributes of the `form` element include `meth` and `action`. Individual `form` elements you learned to create include `fieldset`, `legend`, `input` `textarea`, `select`, `radio button`, `checkbox`, and the `Submit button`.

Master It Create a form of your own design. You can work it into the Far and Wee Ballo or the Flower Page designs, or you can create something completely original. Use all of t form elements you learned about.

Create style rules for forms. Any CSS rules you have learned up to this point for `font`, `background`, `color`, `border`, `padding`, `alignment`, `position`, and `width` can be used to wri styles for forms. However, certain things about the appearance and function of `form` elemer remain in the control of the browser as a means of ensuring accessibility and usability in for

Master It Write styles for the form you created in the previous exercise.

Use XHTML elements to ensure accessible forms. `Form` elements need a `label`. The `labe` `for` markup should be used for clarity and usability.

Master It Use `label` elements with `for` attributes and input elements with `id` attributes your form.

Chapter 12

Publishing and Testing Your Pages

You can make web pages 24 hours a day, but until you move them from your computer onto a server that can be reached on the World Wide Web, no one else will see what you have done. In this chapter you will learn to:

- Use FTP to put files on a server.
- Get a domain name and server space.
- Test your site.
- Identify search engine submission tools.

The Big Picture

There are five broad steps to publishing a website:

1. Create the XHTML, CSS, and image files on your computer.
2. Set up an account with a web hosting company
3. Use FTP software to transfer the completed files to the server provided by the hosting company.
4. Launch a browser to view and test your pages on the WWW.
5. If needed, edit or revise your files and upload the changed versions to the server.

Step 1, of course, has been the subject of the previous chapters, and I'll add some refinements in later chapters. Step 5 also relies on techniques that have been covered elsewhere. So the main focus of this chapter is on the second, third, and fourth steps. And although it's not really part of a sequence, there's a sixth step to publishing a site:

6. Help your audience find the site.

As you'll see, there are two aspects to this: identifying your audience and tailoring your site content to them, and letting the search engines know you are there.

Finding Free Server Space

The companies that offer server space are called web hosts or web hosting companies. These companies usually have hundreds of servers. For a small monthly fee you can get space on one of these servers that will be for your exclusive use and will serve your web pages to any visitors to your URL.

If you just want to practice and try out your new skills, you don't have to spend any money. These places have free web hosting plans:

- `www.netfirms.com/`
- `geocities.yahoo.com/`
- `www.tripod.lycos.com/host`

You have to look carefully for the free option, but these places do have one. While there are drawbacks and irritations (chiefly unwanted advertising) involved with using one of the free ho ing outfits, it does give you some practice getting your pages and images where they can be see If you are not ready for your own domain but just want to learn how to post pages on the Web, fr hosting is a good first step. You can learn the basics of using FTP (File Transfer Protocol), revisi pages and reuploading them, and making sure images show up and links work properly. You c check your pages with various testing strategies that will be detailed in this chapter. The free se vices are merely a first step and are not adequate for a professional web presence.

If you pick one of the companies listed previously, you need to read their instructions on ho to manage your account and use FTP. The free hosting plans may include a browser-based interfa that lets you upload files and see your server space in a browser window rather than with a se rate FTP application as described in the next section. There will also be information there tellin you what the URL for your pages will be so other people can find them.

Another free option you may have is with your *Internet service provider (ISP)*. Your ISP is the co pany you pay for your Internet connection service and e-mail account at your home. There are a m titude of choices among ISPs, but some of the larger ones include Earthlink, SBC Yahoo!, Roadrunn AOL, and MSN. Sometimes your ISP provides you with a small amount of space on a server as p of your package. If that is the case with your ISP, there should be information on their website telli you how to FTP to your space and what your URL will be.

Blogs are often hosted free. A blog hosted free by Blogger has an address like `http://somena` `.blogspot.com`. A free Wordpress blog has an address like `http://somename.wordpress.co` Blogs hosted free don't require FTP. You can buy a domain name and put a blog on your own server, but that is not free. You'll learn more about blogs in Chapter 13.

If a free hosting plan doesn't meet your needs, the next section explains how to buy a doma name and find a host for it.

Your Own Domain

The free services won't fill your needs permanently. You will need to purchase web hosting se vices and a domain name. (However, a blog can be highly successful when hosted at blogspot.co or wordpress.com.)

You can buy a domain name fairly inexpensively. A domain name is the part of a web addre after the www; for example, in `www.wiley.com`, "wiley" is the domain name. There are a multitu of companies that will register your domain name. Often the same company that provides web ho ing space for you will provide a domain name registration service as well. If you used any of the fr hosting plans described in the previous section, you probably noticed that the companies were se ing hosting and domain name registration as you searched for the offer of free hosting space.

There are many factors to consider when choosing a hosting company. Cost is important, of cour but you may have other needs. If you specifically want a Linux server or a Windows server, look f that. You may want to be sure you have access to MySQL databases and can use PHP. You may want a lot of e-mail accounts with your site. Perhaps you are looking for a particular type of shopping cart for an e-commerce site. Perhaps you will need extra storage space or bandwidth because you have very large files such as movies or music that you'll be serving to visitors. Determine in advance what your needs are so that you can sign up with the right host and for the right plan.

Some popular domain name registration and web hosting companies with good reputations are

- `www.godaddy.com`
- `www.pairnic.com` with `www.pair.com`
- `www.register.com`

Sometimes people feel that a local company will provide more accessible customer support, so you might check the reputations of the local companies in your area when you make a decision about hosting and domain name registration. Physical location is not an important factor in cyberspace, in my opinion, but some people like a local connection.

COMPARISON SHOPPING

A site that offers ratings and all sorts of comparisons of web hosting companies is Find My Hosting at `www.findmyhosting.com`. Other helpful comparison sites are Web Hosting Talk at `www.webhostingtalk.com/`, Hosting Review at `www.hosting-review.com/`, and Web Hosting Jury at `www.webhostingjury.com/`.

Many of the big-name Internet companies that you might already be familiar with, such as Yahoo!, also provide hosting and domain name registration.

Any domain name registration company, or *registrar*, will let you search *whois*, the index of names that are already registered, to see if a name you want is available. At certain sites, simply showing interest in a domain name may get it bought up with the intent to offer to sell it to you at an inflated price later, a practice known as "domain kiting." To be safe, search *whois* at `www.internic.net/whois.html`.

Although it is not necessary, it is often easier to sign up for both web hosting and domain name registration with the same company. That way, all your information is available in one location.

The domain registrar must know the *DNS (Domain Name Server)* information about your server, or web host, so that the domain name can be associated with the correct server. When someone types `www.`*`yourdomain`*`.`*`com`* in their browser location bar, the DNS information is what connects that someone to your particular server out of all the millions of servers that are delivering web pages to the Internet. When you open a web hosting account, you get DNS information about the server you'll be using. When you buy a domain name, provide the DNS information to the domain registrar so that they know where the domain will be located. If you buy the domain name before you've decided on a hosting company, you can always revisit the registrar later to supply the DNS information.

After you get going with a site, you may decide to move a site to a new hosting company. Or the hosting company you are using may go out of business. When you change the location of the server for any reason, let the registrar for the domain know what the new DNS information is, so people will find the site as usual.

SAVE YOUR INFO

When you buy a domain name, keep good records about who the registrar is and where you go to change your account information, renew the domain name, or change the DNS information if your move the domain to different servers. Your name and address as the domain owner is public information. When your domain name is near its expiration date you get all sorts of mail from various outfits wanting to renew your domain name, usually for far more money than it would cost to go straight to your registrar and renew it there.

Using FTP Software

There are trial versions of several FTP software tools on the CD accompanying this book. The Fil Transfer Protocol is really simple. You can *put* files somewhere, or you can *get* files from somewhe

If you are familiar with using the command prompt on Windows or the terminal window Mac OS X, you can FTP directly from that interface. You don't need any particular software to However, using a software tool such as those provided on the CD often makes much more sen visually to nonprogrammers who aren't familiar with command-line work. You can FTP with browser. The address in the location bar begins with `ftp://` rather than `http://` when you'r using an FTP server. The Firefox browser has an extension for FTP called Filezilla.

FTP software tools are very easy to use and often let you drag and drop files from a window r resenting your computer to a window representing the server.

When you sign up for web hosting, you'll receive an e-mail from the hosting company with yo FTP information, including the FTP address, your username, your password, and the directory path. You'll need this information when setting up your FTP software to connect to the server. Lo at Figure 12.1 to examine the way you use the information in your FTP software.

Figure 12.1 shows an FTP application called Transmit. Other FTP tools may look slightly diff ent or use slightly different terms. However, the basic information the tool needs will be the sa no matter what terms are used or how the software looks.

In Figure 12.1, you see your own computer on the left side. Transmit calls it "your stuff." Oth tools may call it "local" or "your computer." In the figure, the view on the left side shows a part ular folder on the computer. The folder name is `phoebehome`. The connection to be made will be the server where the files from the folder `phoebehome` will be put.

The server information goes on the right side of the figure. Put the FTP address in the for field where it says Server. Other tools might label this box FTP Address or URL. The informati you put here depends on the particular server; it might be something like `ftp.example.com` `www.example.com` or even the IP address of the server. When you open a web hosting accoun the address that goes in the server form field will be sent to you with the initial e-mail from t hosting company.

Next are form fields where you enter your username and password. These two fields probab use the same terms no matter what software you are using.

The Initial Path form field might be called Directory or Directory Path in a different FTP too The information you put in this field is the name of the folder that contains your files. Most of t time, servers use names such as `public_html`, `www`, or `htdocs` for this path name. This is another important piece of information sent to you in the initial e-mail you receive from the hosting company. It is the root level of your site on your server space. If you open a browser and go to your URL, the files you see when you type `www.yoururl.com` in the location bar are the files in the `public_html` or `www` directory on the server. That directory name does not become part of your URL, it is merely the way your particular server designates the space for the root folder of your domain.

In the example in Figure 12.1, there is a subfolder in the path. The main site is located in `public_html`, but this particular set of files will be put into a subfolder called `phoebehome`. Depending on what files you are working on, you can set up different connections to different parts of a site with initial path values that reflect your destination.

There's also a field where a port number can be entered. (In most situations, the default port is used to FTP, and there is no need to indicate any other choice.) In the next field down, this particular software allows you to choose between standard FTP and secure FTP for the file transfers. Secure FTP is used for encrypted file transfers, which you most likely won't need for simple web page transfers.

The Transmit 2 FTP software does not have a form field for a proxy server, but some FTP tools do. If you are working for a company that requires you to use a proxy server to get to the `www`, they will provide you with the address of the proxy server. As with the port number, if you don't need to enter a proxy address, simply leave it blank.

When all the information regarding the server has been filled in, click the Connect button. Other FTP software might label this button Choose or OK. If you did everything properly, when you click this button, you should be connected to the server.

After you connect, the view changes to show you the files on the server, as in Figure 12.2.

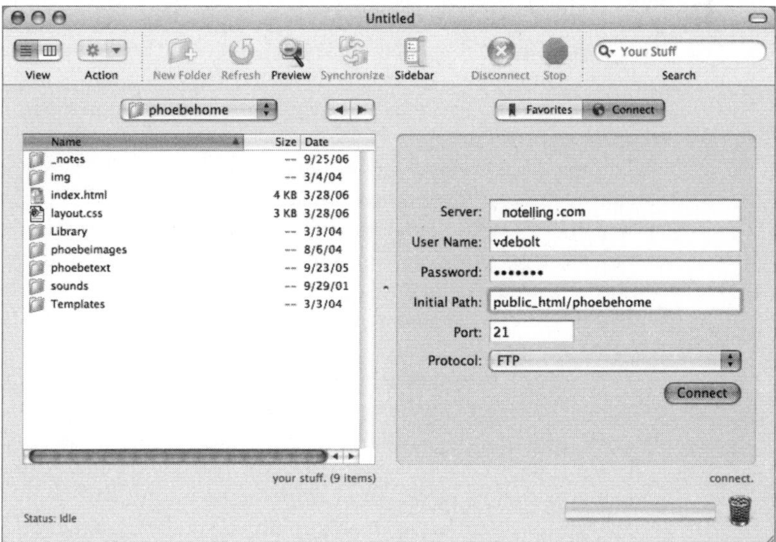

FIGURE 12.1
The server connection information screen in the Transmit 2 FTP tool

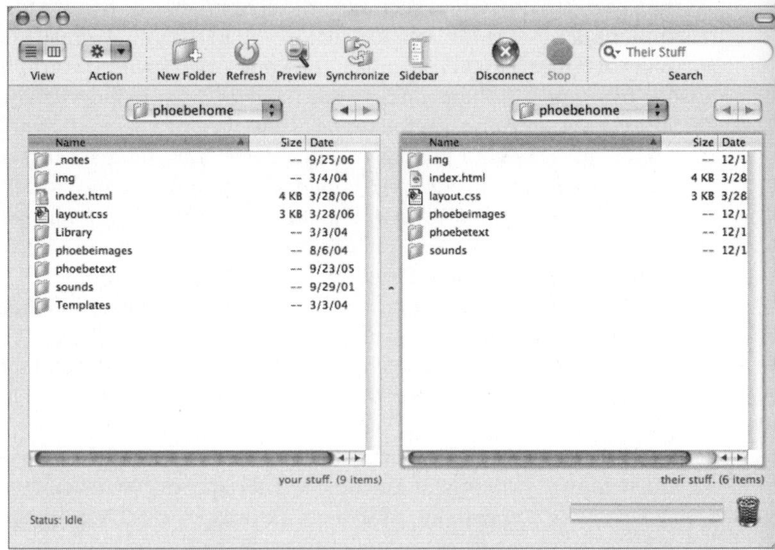

FIGURE 12.2
Local files are on the left and remote files are on the right. Other FTP tools may reverse this or ask you to set it up as you want it in Preferences.

The first time you connect, there may not be any files on the server, or there may be one file the named `index.html` that the hosting company put in that space. This file usually says somethin like "Coming Soon" and will be overwritten by your own `index.html` page.

Figure 12.2 shows a website that already has files and folders uploaded from the local comput (your stuff) to the remote computer (their stuff). Notice that not everything from the *your stuff* si was uploaded to the *their stuff* side. For example, there are folders called Library and Templates th were used in the making of this site but that are not needed on the server. Also notice that the fold names that are on the server exactly match the folder names in the local site folder. Your links w break and your images may not display if you don't match up filenames, subfolder names, and structure exactly.

To copy a file from your computer to the server in Transmit, simply drag and drop the file (an entire folder when you first upload the folder) from the local side to the remote side. This is known in FTP lingo as *put*. Other FTP applications may require you to click a button labeled "pu or with an arrow pointing to the other side of the screen to put the files. You can transfer more th one file at a time. For example, putting an entire folder creates the folder and all the files in the folder on the server in one operation. Or you can select several files simultaneously and transfe them in one operation.

Files can also be copied from the server to your computer. Simply drag and drop a file from t remote window into the local window. This is known in FTP lingo as *get*. Again, other progran may require that you click a button instead of dragging and dropping to get files.

When you get a file from the server and bring it to your computer, it overwrites the existing fi you have by that name on your computer. Be careful!

To transfer files to or from an individual subfolder, simply double-click to open the folder o both your computer and the server, then put or get the individual files. Figure 12.3 shows a vie inside one of the subfolders in the example site.

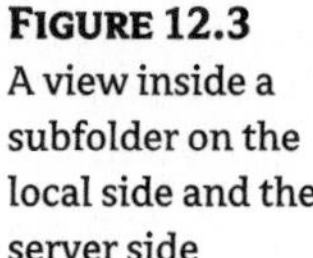

FIGURE 12.3
A view inside a subfolder on the local side and the server side

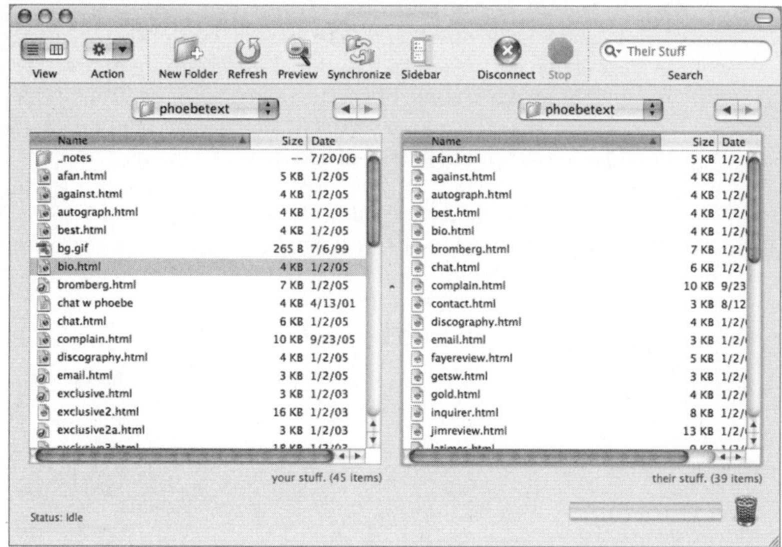

FILE NOT FOUND

If you forget to put a needed file on the server, the user will see some sort of error such as a "File Not Found" message or an icon representing a missing image. This will also happen if you don't match the site structure on the server with your local site structure.

You can create your own File Not Found page to replace the default one. This is a good practice because it gives you the opportunity to include some menu options on the page the user is served when the requested file is not found. There's more information about this in the sidebar "A Handy Server Control File" near the end of the chapter.

Setting Permissions

Most FTP software provides a measure of security by letting you *set permissions*. This means you can specify who has permission to read a file, write to a file, and execute a file. Permissions can also be set on an entire folder.

For XHTML or CSS files, there is no need to set permissions. To make a form submit, however, you must set permissions on the script used with the form so that it can be executed. See Chapter 11 for more on forms.

A script is often kept in a special directory on the web server called `cgi-bin`. The `cgi-bin` directory is at the same level as the `public_html` or the `www` directory. Therefore, if your FTP connection information is set to open in the `public_html` or `www` directory, you won't be able to see the `cgi-bin` directory or to upload files into it. If you are uploading a script, you need to temporarily leave the FTP connection directory field blank so you are able to see the `cgi-bin` directory when you connect to the server. The `cgi-bin` directory is often the only place you are allowed to store executable files such scripts, and it is the directory where you will be working if you need to set permissions.

Permission is given to an individual user, a group of users, or to the whole world when spe fying who can read, write, or execute a file.

In your FTP software, you can look at the properties (or choose Get Info) for an individual f or folder to see options such as those shown in Figure 12.4. An XHTML file won't execute, but script will.

As you see in Figure 12.4, this individual XHTML file is set to let the world read it, but only t user (that's you) can write it. This is the normal setting. The only time you need to think about s ting permissions is when you want to change the normal setting, which is normally something y do with scripts, not XHTML files.

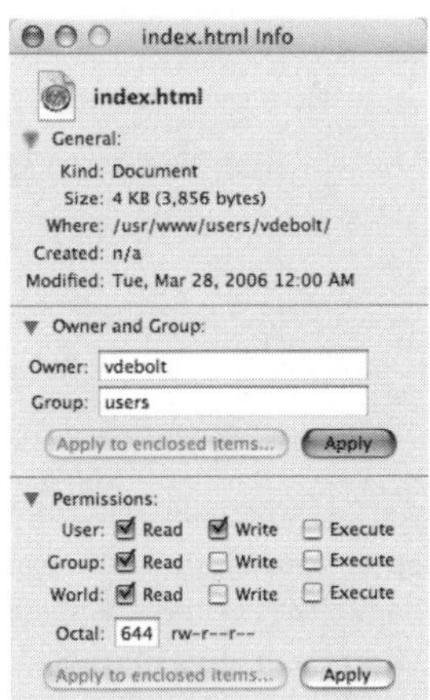

FIGURE 12.4
Setting permissions for an individual file

C-PANEL

Some hosting companies provide a secure spot on their servers with an interface called C-panel (for control panel). You can use it to do all sorts of tasks to your site. You can upload files, create directories, and set permissions, just as you do with some FTP software. You can also set up e-mail accounts and arrange to have each e-mail address you set up forwarded to the appropriate person. You can set up MySQL databases (if your host provides them) and view site statistics. You manage your account information with your hosting company here. If the hosting company provides any CGI scripts, you can set up which ones you want to use from the C-panel.

If all you need to do is upload a few files to update your site, an FTP application is much faster and more efficient than doing it with the C-panel.

The username and password for your account C-panel sign-in may or may not be the same as the username and password for your FTP logon. Be sure to save all the information about your account in a safe place with good backups.

Testing and Validating the Site

As you are designing the site, you check pages on your local computer. But it is also important to test everything about the site once it is on the Internet. Sometimes things seem to work on your local computer but are broken on a server. All sorts of problems may arise, including these and other major or minor disasters:

- Incorrect file paths
- Incorrect links
- Site organization not being copied properly when you upload to the server
- Files served with the incorrect MIME type (for example, if you see an unstyled page in a Mozilla-based browser, the server may not have the correct MIME setting for CSS files)
- Forgotten files that never get uploaded
- Filenames with spaces or typos in them

Typos are a problem when writing XHTML and CSS by hand. If something doesn't look the way you expect, check your typing for spacing, colons, semicolons, curly braces, and other syntax issues. If you are sure the part that doesn't seem to work is correct, work backward through the code looking for an error, perhaps a forgotten semicolon or a missing bracket. Often the error occurred somewhere before the place where things appear to break down. This type of error is easy to find with an XHTML validator.

Make it a habit to check every page of a site after you put it on the WWW. Check all the links, look for missing images, play any sound files, check to make sure the styles are working: test everything. If something is not working right, you need to find it and fix it immediately.

If an image does not appear, try these troubleshooting steps:

- Check the file path.
- Make sure the image is on the server in the place the `src` attribute points to.
- Make sure you are using a JPEG, GIF, or PNG file format instead of one that a browser won't display.

If a page cannot be found, check that the page is on the server in the place the `href` attribute points to and make sure the file has the correct file extension.

If you included sound or any type of multimedia such as Flash with your page, verify that the file plays when it is supposed to play. Check on the server to be sure the sound files or other multimedia files are in the place where they are supposed to be. If a special plug-in is needed to play multimedia files, have it installed in your browser.

Test the site in a variety of browsers and with different operating systems if you can. If you don't have access to more than one computer and operating system, send out a request to your colleagues and friends asking them to check the site using their systems. If they find something wrong, ask them to send you a screen shot and tell you what browser, what operating system, and what screen resolution they used to view the site.

You also want to test for appearance to make sure that a site looks the way you intend across a browsers and operating systems. A for-fee service called BrowserCam (`www.browsercam.com`) w create a screen shot of your web page using any operating system or browser you want tested. Yo can also test pages at various screen resolutions (see Figure 12.5).

FIND A BROWSERCAM GROUP

BrowserCam is not cheap, but it performs a multitude of browser tests that are impossible to reproduce yourself, even with several computers at your disposal. Luckily, it currently allows groups of people to share a subscription. Often web design mailing list members or forum members band together to get a shared BrowserCam subscription. There's a site that helps people organize fund-raising for things like this at `www.fundable.org`.

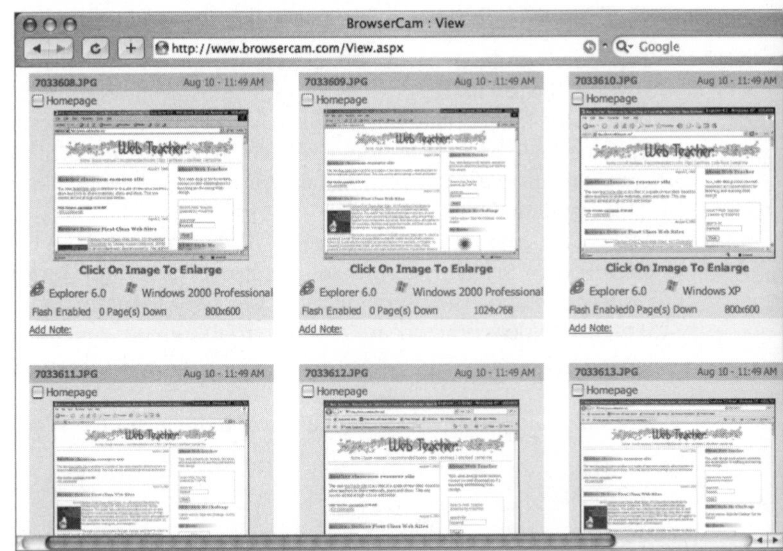

FIGURE 12.5
A BrowserCam results page shows small images (which can be enlarged) of the page you're testing in the browsers, operating systems, and resolutions you specify.

SPELLING MATTERS

Grammar and spelling are very important. Don't forget to check them. A misspelled word can make people decide you're not a professional and they won't do business with you. Visiting a site with basic errors in spelling and grammar is like going into a restaurant with roaches crawling up the walls. Not a good first impression.

The Validators

An important part of testing your site is making sure you have valid code. XHTML is valid when it follows the rules for the DTD declared in the page's DOCTYPE declaration, and CSS is valid when it follows the rules set out in one of the approved CSS specifications. You can use the free validation services offered by the W3C to check your XHTML and your CSS for correctness.

The XHTML validator is at `http://validator.w3.org/`. The CSS validator is at `http://jigsaw.w3.org/css-validator/`. In both validators, you simply enter the URL of your XHTML or CSS file on the server and let the tool check your page.

The tool reports back with a detailed list of any problems you have in your code. It points out the exact line where the problem is and gives some help in explaining what you need to do to correct the error.

Make changes to your original file, upload it to the server, and then run the validator again. Do this as many times as you need to until every error has been evaluated and/or corrected.

CHARACTER ENCODING AND VALIDATION

Use the validators while still in the design process to test your markup and style rules. When you are sure you are writing correct and valid pages, it is easier to get pages to display as you want. Validation helps you spot your problems early. If you don't have the page on a server yet, the W3C lets you upload a file from your computer using one of those dandy `input type="file"` forms you learned about in Chapter 11. The character encoding is added to the web page on the server, so if you upload a file from your computer for validation and there is an error about character encoding, don't worry.

If you get an error about character encoding when testing a page using a URL from your server, then you need to check with the hosting company to see what type of encoding is set on the server. If for some reason the server does not have encoding set, you can add a `meta` element to your page. A common character encoding for English: `iso-8859-1`. The `meta` element goes in the document head. It is:

```
<meta http-equiv="Content-Type" content="text/html; charset=iso-8859-1" />
```

VALID ISN'T THE SAME AS GOOD

There are a few important points about validity that are worth mentioning.

Validity does not mean quality. The validator can't check to see if you've used HTML semantically or efficiently or accessibly. The validator can't tell if you created a nice-looking, well-functioning, and usable page. It just checks to make sure the "grammar" is correct; it can't tell if it's a well-written "sentence."

Validity is a means, not an end. Producing valid pages is a goal, but that shouldn't be your end goal. Producing "good" pages should be your goal, and as stated, validity is not a measure of "goodness." There will be times when you have a piece of invalid code and choose not to fix it because you need it and know it's not messing anything up. This is fine. Validity is just a tool to help you catch your mistakes and make it more likely that your page will render as you want it to across browsers and in the future.

Accessibility Testing

When you have tested all your links and pages yourself and you have used the HTML and CSS va idators to make sure your code is pristine, you still need to test for accessibility. There are differen types of testing. Determine whether you need to comply with the W3C's WCAG guidelines, Sectic 508 (a federal guideline) or other government accessibility guidelines. Then test for those standard

It is a good idea to use more than one tool, since they return slightly different information. Online accessibility testing is available with WebXACT at

```
http://webxact.watchfire.com
```

Like the validators at the W3C, the WebXACT tool checks an online page using a URL. Imm diately under the form field where you enter your URL, there is a link to Show Advanced/Acce sibility Option. Click that before you begin and you can specify which set of accessibility guidelin you want to test your page against (see Figure 12.6).

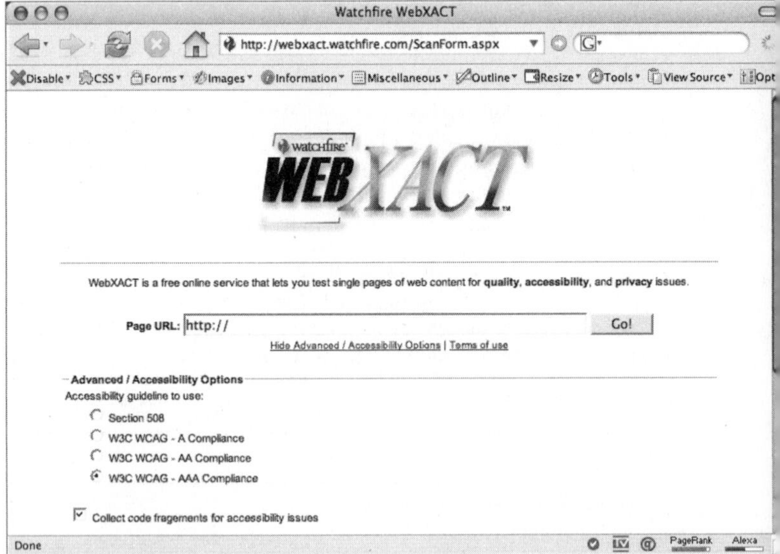

FIGURE 12.6 The WebXACT tool with advanced options selected, ready for the input of a URL for testing

The W3C guidelines evaluated by WebXACT check that you do the following on your page:

1. Provide equivalent alternatives to auditory and visual content.
2. Don't rely on color alone.
3. Use markup and style sheets and do so properly.
4. Clarify natural language usage.
5. Create tables that transform gracefully.
6. Ensure that pages featuring new technologies transform gracefully.
7. Ensure user control of time-sensitive content changes.
8. Ensure direct accessibility of embedded user interfaces.

9. Design for device-independence.
10. Use interim solutions.
11. Use W3C technologies and guidelines.
12. Provide context and orientation information.
13. Provide clear navigation mechanisms.
14. Ensure that documents are clear and simple.

Each of these guidelines from the W3C has several checkpoints. Some checkpoints are assigned a priority. WebXACT reports point out any problems with your page according to the priority level.

GET YOUR PRIORITIES STRAIGHT

This is how the W3C explains the accessibility priorities:

Priority 1 A web content developer *must* satisfy this checkpoint. Otherwise, one or more groups will find it impossible to access information in the document. Satisfying this checkpoint is a basic requirement for some groups to be able to use web documents. For example, although some people cannot use images, movies, sounds, or applets directly, they may still use pages that include equivalent information to the visual or auditory content. The lack of such equivalent information would be a Priority 1 failure.

Priority 2 A web content developer *should* satisfy this checkpoint. Otherwise, one or more groups will find it difficult to access information in the document. Satisfying this checkpoint will remove significant barriers to accessing web documents. For example, link text should be meaningful enough to make sense when read out of context. Using link text such as "click here" is a Priority 2 error.

Priority 3 A web content developer *may* address this checkpoint. Otherwise, one or more groups will find it somewhat difficult to access information in the document. Satisfying this checkpoint will improve access to web documents. For example, if you don't create a style of presentation that is consistent across pages it is considered a Priority 3 error.

The complete document on guidelines, checkpoints, techniques for each checkpoint, and priorities is at `www.w3.org/TR/WCAG10`.

When you read through the report, you should fix any Priority 1 problems you have. Priority 2 and 3 problems require some judgment on your part as to whether or not they really require changes. Don't let the Priority 2 and 3 errors scare you. They aren't necessarily a problem. They could *potentially* be a problem, and you are asked to make sure that no such problem exists on your page.

Another online testing tool is Cynthia Says. Since it is used by Firefox in the Web Developer Toolbar extension, you'll find out more about it in the next section.

Another way to test for accessibility is to answer this question: "If style sheets are ignored or unsupported, are pages still readable and usable?" Certain browsers may allow you to look at web pages with the CSS turned off. Of course, you can test this on your own pages by simply temporarily removing the links to any style sheets and seeing how the page looks in the browser. Remember, it doesn't have to look good without CSS, it only has to be readable and usable.

You can test what your pages will look like in a text-only browser (even the images won't appe in this simulation) by using the Lynx viewer here:

```
http://www.delorie.com/web/lynxview.html
```

If you can read, understand, and navigate your page in a text-only browser, that is a good in cation that the page will be usable in various accessibility devices such as screen readers.

Another excellent online accessibility testing tool was mentioned in Chapter 10: the WAVE to at `www.wave.webaim.org`. In Chapter 10, it was suggested for testing tables, but the WAVE to evaluates much more than tables.

However, no tool is a substitute for manually testing pages for accessibility. The tools cannot t you whether your `alt` text is good, whether you're using color to indicate information, whethe your page hierarchy aids comprehension, whether the semantics of elements like `em` and `strong` helpful, and so on.

Getting Help from Browser Extensions

One point about using Firefox and the other browsers I'm about to mention is that most of the tir your page must be on a server. You cannot validate pages with tools like Cynthia Says while th are still on your hard drive.

You *can* test drive local XHTML and CSS files in Firefox (or any other browser) while the pag are still on your hard drive. You have been checking your pages that way throughout this book Since Firefox is a browser that follows the standards quite well, it is a good browser to use as yo test browser when you are first planning and designing your pages.

Open source projects provide source code for software to programmers and developers w are interested in working to improve a software application. One of the better known such projects is Mozilla, at `www.mozilla.org`. This open source project created the Mozilla brows which eventually became a version of the Netscape browser. Mozilla is also the source of th Firefox browser, which has Web Developer extensions that are very helpful in testing and debugging your web pages.

Mozilla is a complete suite of products, including an advanced e-mail and newsgroup client, IRC chat client, and an HTML editor. Firefox is a web browser.

You can download the latest version of Firefox at `www.mozilla.com`. Once you have Firefo installed on your computer, you can download extensions. There are over 100 extensions for Mozilla and Firefox, but the one you need is at `https://addons.mozilla.org/firefox/60`. (Note the `https`, with an "s" indicating that this download is on a secure server.) With the We Developer extensions installed in Firefox, you have a toolbar with invaluable help in testing a validating your pages.

You've been seeing the Web Developer Toolbar in this book in all the screen shots made with the Firefox browser. It appears directly under the address bar. Here's a close up view of t toolbar.

Disable ▾ CSS ▾ Forms ▾ Images ▾ Information ▾ Miscellaneous ▾ Outline ▾ Resize ▾ Tools ▾ View Source ▾ Optio

Look at some of the tools available to you in some of the choices in the toolbar. Figure 12.7 sho an expanded view of the Validation menu.

FIGURE 12.7
The Validation menu expanded

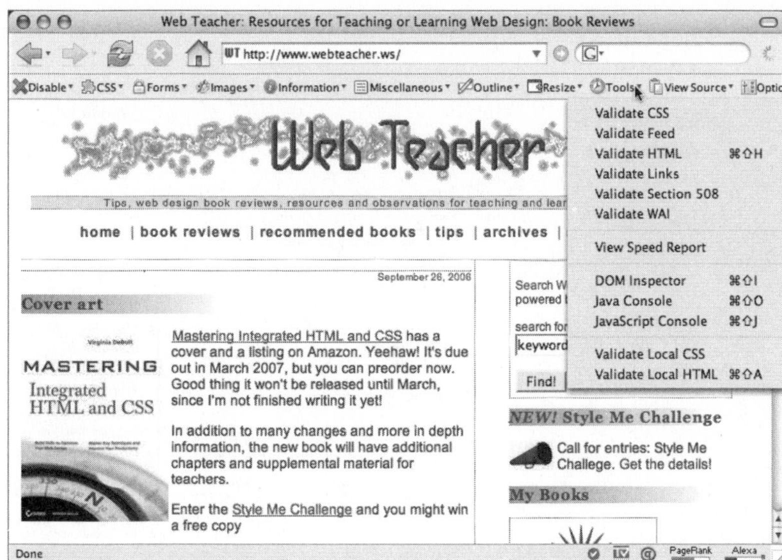

> **RESOURCES**
>
> As noted in Chapter 10, the WAI was developed in response to the addition of Section 508 to the Americans with Disabilities Act (ADA) by the U.S. Congress. See Chapter 10 for more Section 508 accessibility resources.

As you can see, there are built-in tools to validate CSS, HTML, links, and accessibility. The accessibility options include validation against the rules of Section 508 or the W3C's WAI (Web Accessibility Initiative) rules.

I selected the Validation ➢ Validate Section 508 Accessibility menu command, and my page was tested using the validation tool Cynthia Says. This tool is similar to the WebXACT tool discussed earlier, although the report returned from Cynthia Says is slightly different from—and easier to interpret than—WebXACT's. Figure 12.8 shows a bit of the Section 508 Validation Report, which is returned by opening the window in another tab, leaving my original page open in a tabbed window as well.

You can go straight to Cynthia Says at `www.cynthiasays.com` for accessibility validation if you do not have the Firefox Web Developer extensions.

Another of the useful tools can be seen in Figure 12.9, which shows the expanded Images menu.

You can find missing `alt` attributes, hide images, or replace images with `alt` text to see what a user browsing without images visible would see. I picked the Replace Images with Alt Attributes option, and you can see the results in Figure 12.10.

The options in the Information menu, which include revealing all the div and class information on a page, are shown in Figure 12.11.

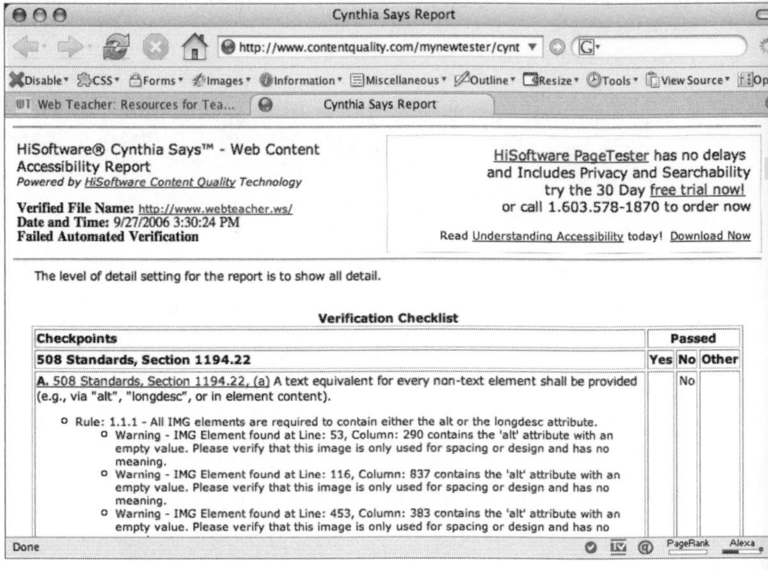

FIGURE 12.8
The results of the Section 508 Accessibility test are returned in a new tabbed window.

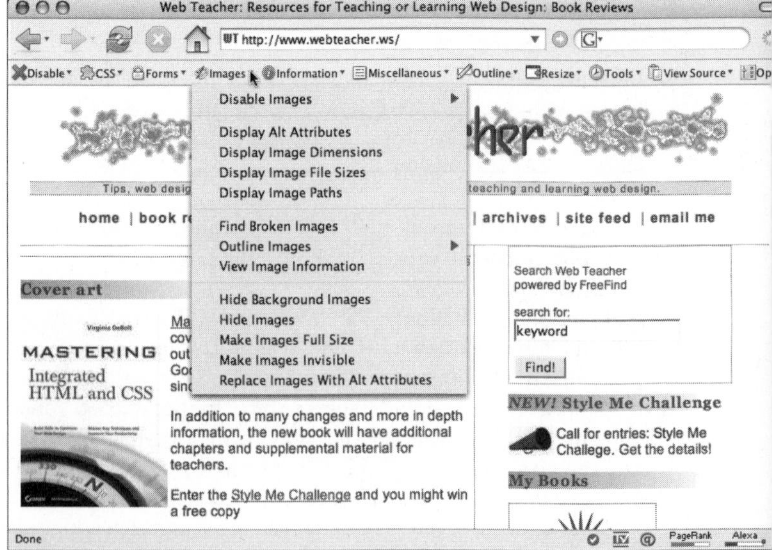

FIGURE 12.9
The expanded Images menu in the Firefox Web Developer toolbar

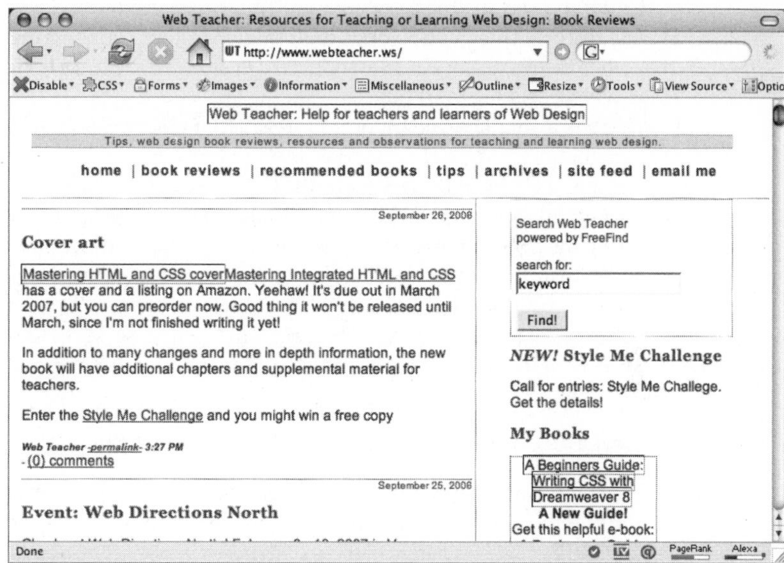

FIGURE 12.10 The graphic banner and other images have been replaced by the `alt` text in a simple box.

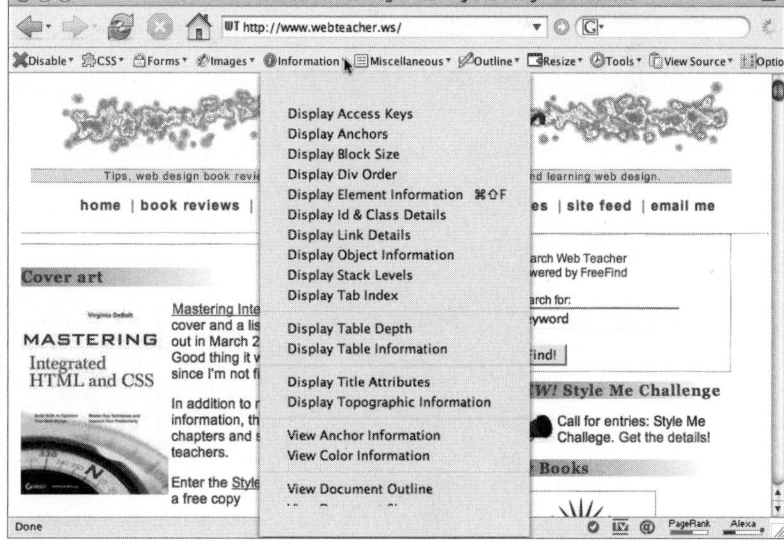

FIGURE 12.11 The expanded Information menu. These are very useful options that can show you the entire cascade affecting a particular element and other useful facts.

Under the Outline menu (see Figure 12.12), you can outline block level elements, deprecated el ments, and other elements. Notice the Outline Custom Elements menu option. You may have notice that other menus also include an option to customize the tools to do whatever you particularly nee done when checking your pages.

There is also a Disable menu in Firefox that allows you to disable the CSS or the colors on web page.

The menu CSS ➢ Edit CSS opens the CSS used for any page in a sidebar (see Figure 12.13). This a very helpful tool. You can edit the CSS and the changes appear on the page. You aren't actually changing the CSS on the server, only the presentation at the moment. If you make a change you lil and want to incorporate it, you have to change the actual CSS file involved and upload it to the serv

If you are a Mac user, the Safari browser has what it calls enhancements that include a Debu menu. To get it to appear in your Safari menu, first close Safari. Open a Terminal window. You w find the Terminal in Applications ➢ Utilities ➢ Terminal. When the prompt is blinking for your entry, type

```
defaults write com.apple.Safari IncludeDebugMenu 1
```

Close the Terminal. When you reopen Safari, the Debug menu will be there.

Some of the options, including the Show Tree options to determine page structure, are shown Figure 12.14.

Netscape includes a Tools ➢ Web Development menu with a JavaScript debugger and other tools, as shown in Figure 12.15.

FIGURE 12.12
The Outline menu is expanded.

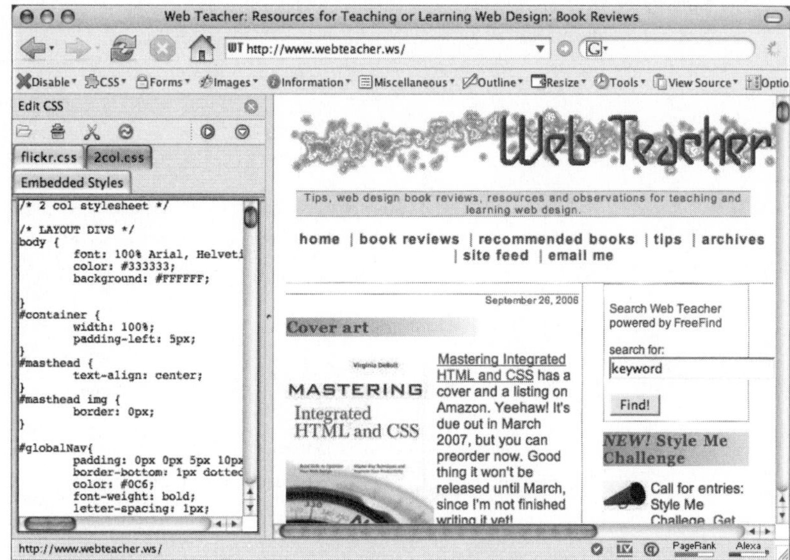

FIGURE 12.13 The Edit CSS sidebar is open, allowing real-time editing. The changes appear in the window on the right as they are made.

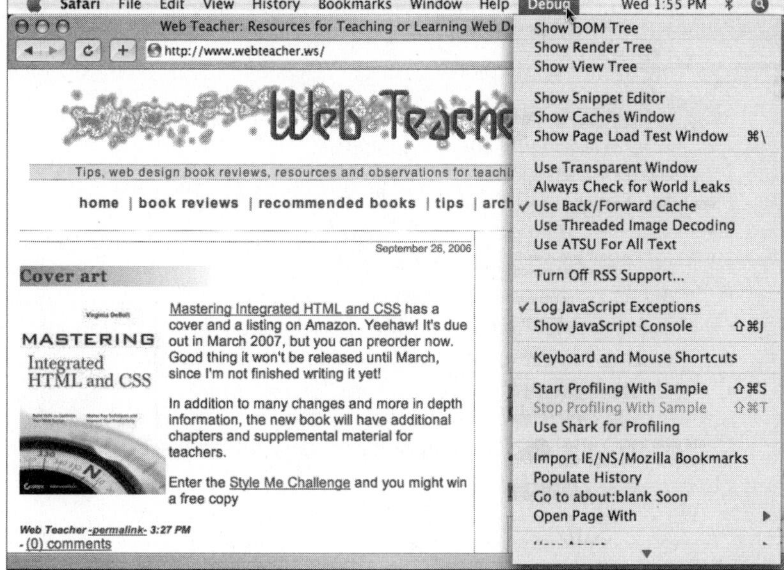

FIGURE 12.14 The Safari browser with Debug enhancements installed

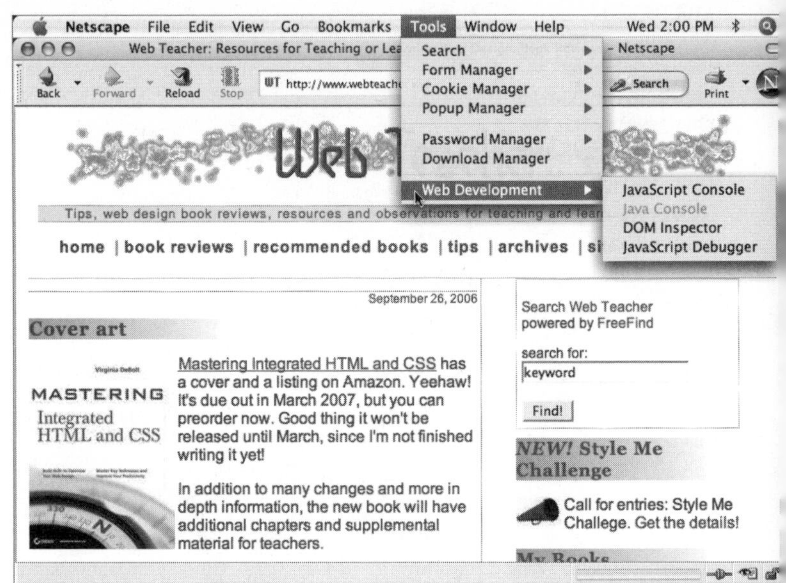

FIGURE 12.15
Netscape tools for web development

Internet Explorer provides a Web Developer Toolbar. It appears directly under the address b in the browser. A close up view is shown here. Note that the screen captures for this tool were ma using a beta version of IE7, so the view may be somewhat different from what you are used to s ing in Internet Explorer. You can download the IE Web Developer Toolbar at:

```
http://www.microsoft.com/downloads/details.aspx?familyid=e59c3964-672d-4511-bb3
2d5e1db91038&displaylang=en
```

The IE Web Developer Toolbar has some options similar to those in the Firefox Web Develop tools, and some that are different. Under the View menu, for example, you can see Class and II details (see Figure 12.16).

When View ➤ Class and ID Information is selected, you see where each class or id is located. you hover over one of these markers, a tool tip gives information about the particular element (s Figure 12.17).

The Opera browser has a similar toolbar. Opera is also useful when testing for small screen applications such as handhelds because the browser has a View ➤ Small Screen option. You wi make use of this option in Chapter 15.

SQUISH IT, SQUEEZE IT

Some designers like to compress or optimize their style sheets by removing unneeded line breaks and spaces before uploading them to the web server, thus speeding up download time and saving money on bandwidth charges. You can do it manually, but if a site uses an Apache server, there's an Apache Module called mod_gzip that compresses not only CSS but also HTML right on the server.

CSS file compression can also be achieved using PHP.

Learn more about mod_gzip at www.sitepoint.com/article/web-output-mod_gzip-apache. For information about compressing CSS with PHP, a good resource is www.fiftyfoureleven.com/sandbox/weblog/2004/jun/the-definitive-css-gzip-method/.

You can test your site for rendering time. There's an online tool that calculates document weight and load time at www.webpageanalyzer.com. Following the speed report of your page, the site also offers recommendations about ways to optimize download time.

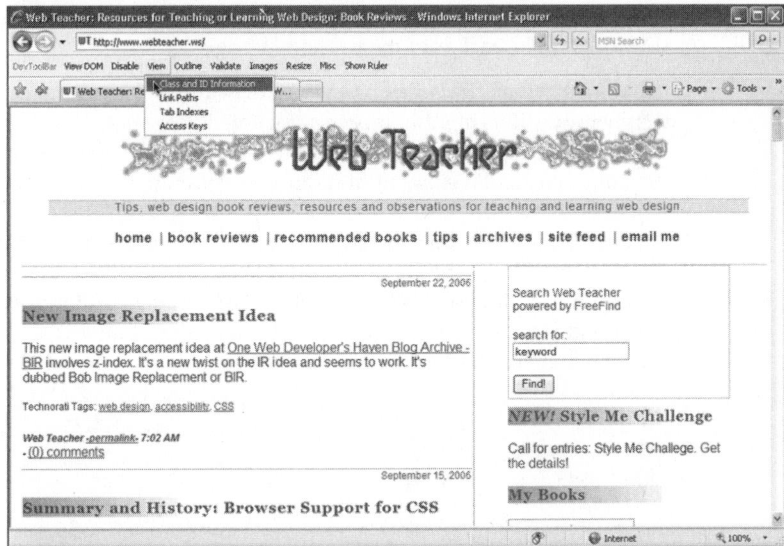

FIGURE 12.16
The IE toolbar allows you to see Class and ID Information, similar to a menu option on the Firefox toolbar.

FIGURE 12.17
The class and id information for each element appears in a tool tip when you hover over the indicator that says a class or id is present.

The DOM and Site Testing

You may have noticed the acronym DOM on some of the menus shown in the browser tools. (Fi fox has it in the Tools menu of the Web Developer toolbar.) DOM is the *Document Object Model*. T DOM is a way to manage XHTML document structure by treating elements on the page as obje that can be assigned behaviors, attributes, and content.

The W3C describes it at `www.w3.org/DOM` like this:

> "The Document Object Model is a platform- and language-neutral interface that will allo programs and scripts to dynamically access and update the content, structure, and style o documents. The document can be further processed and the results of that processing can incorporated back into the presented page."

Looking at the DOM tree gives you a tree outline of a document's structure, which may help y decipher questions of inheritance or document flow.

Figure 12.18 is a view of the DOM tree for `www.webteacher.ws`, using Safari's Debug menu Selecting a particular element from the tree structure on the left shows the code in that element the right.

When Netscape shows the DOM tree, the results are more informative; see Figure 12.19. In Netscape, you'll find the DOM inspector under Tools ➢ Web Development ➢ DOM Inspector. Y can see information in the right panel explaining the item highlighted in the left panel. The hig lighted item in the left panel says "LINK." The right panel shows that the link is to a style shee gives the href and type and other information.

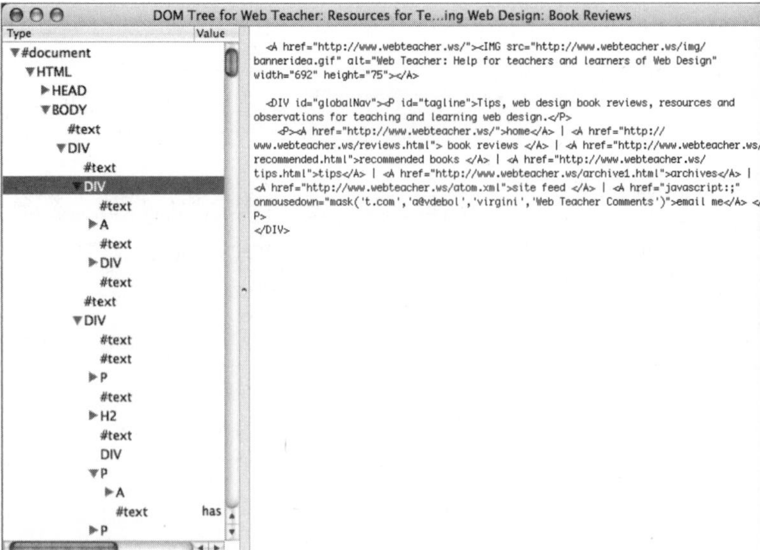

FIGURE 12.18
A Safari-generated DOM tree reveals the structure of a document.

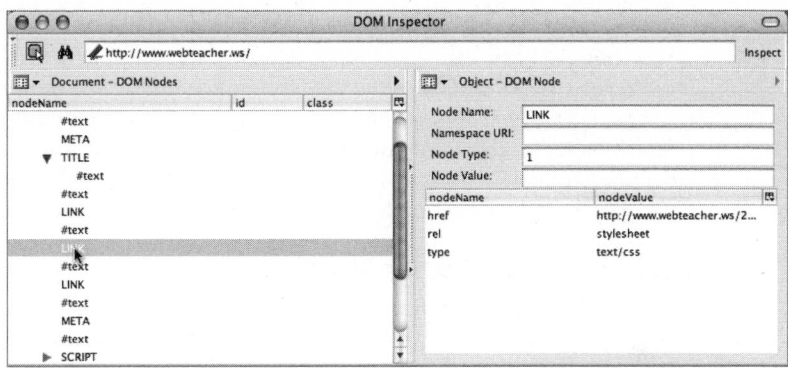

FIGURE 12.19
Netscape's DOM tree view gives different information about the page content.

With Firefox's DOM inspector open, there is a small drop-down menu at the upper left that allows you to select what you want to inspect: DOM Nodes, Stylesheets, or Javascript Object.

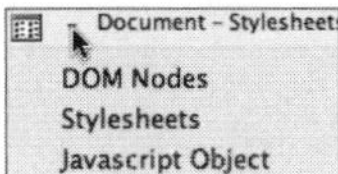

When you select Stylesheets from the drop-down menu, you can see computed styles that affect an element. You can also see what pixel dimensions the browser is giving to your relative measures such as ems. When you select DOM node from the drop-down menu, any DOM node you click is outlined in red on the web page so you can see where it's rendered.

Testing and Validation: a Summary

Figure 12.20 is a checklist you can use as a summary of the main items to check when testing a site. The last item, search-engine friendliness, is the subject of the next section.

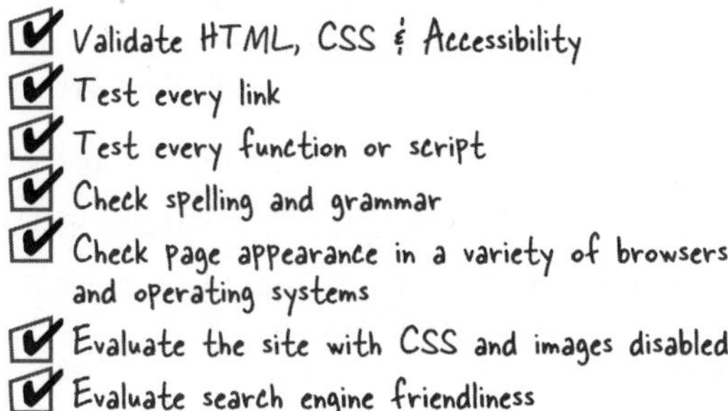

Site Testing Checklist
Validate HTML, CSS & Accessibility
Test every link
Test every function or script
Check spelling and grammar
Check page appearance in a variety of browsers and operating systems
Evaluate the site with CSS and images disabled
Evaluate search engine friendliness

FIGURE 12.20
Check every page in your site.

Telling the Search Engines You Are There

You want people to visit your site. You could e-mail your URL to every person on the planet, or yo could register the URL with the search engines. The second option is much more efficient.

Once the search engines have your URL, they index the contents of your site. When people search on topics that your content matches, your URL is returned to the searcher. This is not a overnight phenomena. It takes a while. Your placement in the search results will depend on ho well you've tailored your site for search engines, a process known as search engine optimizatio

Tailoring Your Site for Search Engines

Before you even think about going to the search engines and registering your site with them, you need to make your site search engine–friendly. I've mentioned a few tips for search engines previ ously, but here are some tips that will help make your pages show up fairly well in the search engin

- Have a good page title that gives information about content on the page.
- Have an `h1` element at the top of the page that contains words describing the contents the page.
- Use text with important keywords early in the page. If your site offers movie reviews, the "movie reviews" would be considered a keyword in your content.
- Use `alt` text for images.
- Use link text that describes what the link is about.
- Use description and keyword `meta` tags in the document head, for example:

```
<meta name="description" content="Write a sentence describing your site." />
<meta name="keywords" content="keyword, keyword phrase, keyword, keyword
phrase" />
```

- Use simple, easy-to-navigate, and valid code.

There are also some things you should not do if you want good search engine results:

- *Don't* use images in place of text or well-written content. Images provide no information your most important blind users: the search engines.
- *Don't* use Flash or other multimedia in place of well-written content.
- *Don't* use link text such as "Click Here" that provides no information about the link.

The search engines "index" your pages, which means they read the contents of the page and keep an index of what it is about. When a user does a search, the search engine looks through th indexed databanks of relevant content and returns sites that have content that match the search term. If a user searches for "movie reviews" and your page has content saying "movie reviews," th search engine will add your site to the search results the user sees. The keywords don't have to b an exact match. Your site might say, "We have hundreds of reviews of classic movies." The searc engines are smart enough to match that up to a search for "movie reviews."

Using keywords in your content does not mean you just "stuff" or list numerous keywords without any interesting context. The content must be interesting to readers, while still telling them (with well chosen terms) what your site is about and what services or information or products they can expect to find there. Content that is informative to a visitor is also informative to a search engine.

Publicizing Your Site

When you first launch a site, no one is linked to your site, so the search engines don't know you are available on the Web. If other sites are linked to your site, the search engines will generally find it simply by following links. Announce your site in various ways, promote it with news releases or other publicity so that you can garner incoming links from other sources.

You can go directly to the search engines and directories and register your site. This will let them know your URL exists. Once the search engines know you are there, your URL will come up in a search for your site name or URL. It may take longer before you see results when you search for your keywords—perhaps months—so you must be patient.

Many search engines use the Open Directory at `http://dmoz.org`. If you register there, you will be included in All the Web, AltaVista, Gigablast, Google USENET, Google, HotBot, Lycos, Teoma, WiseNut, Yahoo!, and many others. Registering in the Open Directory is free.

As soon as you open the main page at `dmoz.org` you see a "Suggest URL" link, but don't use it until you have drilled down in the directory structure and located the directory topic that most closely matches your content. This process can be somewhat inexact depending on your site's topic, but you should attempt to get in the right area before suggesting your URL.

For example, if you are registering a site containing movie reviews, you might select Arts ➢ Movies ➢ Reviews. There are even finer-grained options when you reach that point, or you might decide that this is the moment to click Suggest URL. If you click Suggest URL here, you will be adding your site to the Category: Arts: Movies: Reviews directory. You will be asked for your URL and your site description and to agree to some terms of use. Being in a certain category of the directory does not limit how you show up in the search engine results. Suppose you wrote about Cameron Diaz in a review of a movie. Someone who searched for "Cameron Diaz" in one of the search engines using Open Directory might see your site in the search results, even though they weren't searching for movie reviews.

There are more specialized search engines for some topics. If you are writing content on one of these topics, you probably know about the search engines on that particular topic. For example, there is a specialized chemistry search engine at `www.chemindustry.com`. If your site is about chemistry, you should register with both `dmoz.org` and `chemindustry.com`.

You can also go to each individual search engine and register the site. Be sure to read their information carefully and make sure you are meeting their guidelines and requirements. Most search engines offer free registration. Some charge a fee for priority service.

If your site is well planned using the preceding points and you are registered with the major search engines, there is no need to pay anyone who promises to register you with hundreds of search engines.

Paying for ad placement with the search engines themselves is a different matter. It is worthwhile to consider paid ads or keyword ads with some of the search engines if you are selling a product and want your site to appear in the advertising section when search results are displayed related to your keywords.

KEEPING SEARCH ENGINE ROBOTS OUT

Search engines create indexes by using machines called *robots* or search bots to index everything on your site. If you have something on your site that you don't want indexed or don't want to show up in search engine results, you can exclude the search engine robots from indexing certain directories.

There are all sorts of reasons why you might not want certain parts of your site indexed by search engines. Perhaps you have a directory called `test` on your server where you try out new designs before you are ready to make them live. Perhaps you have a directory called `temp` on your server where you put things temporarily, such as a screen shot you took for a friend or a photo of something you are selling on eBay. Perhaps you have a directory on your server called baby where you put photos of your kids so your grandmother in Tennessee can see them, but you don't want the general public to know they are there.

If you have a situation like that, you can use a robots exclusion file, which must be named `robots.txt`, to list directories that robots should not enter.

To exclude robots from the directories suggested in the previous examples, create a text file named `robots.txt` and include only this information:

```
User-agent: *
Disallow: /test
Disallow: /temp
Disallow: /baby
```

This exclusion uses a wildcard (*) to exclude all robots from visiting URLs starting with `test`, `temp`, and baby. Put that file in the top-level directory of your website, and no robots will index those sections of your site.

Understanding Your Audience

You need to know what people are looking for when they come to your site so you can make th information they seek easy to find. Once you understand what your users want, you must mak sure your site provides that information in an easy-to-find manner so you can entice your visit to return to the site again. For example, if you write a new movie review every week, returning v itors will want easy access to the new reviews as well as easy access to the older reviews that a still available. It helps you to know whether visitors are entering the site directly on a page with older review, or if they are heading for the page with the newest review.

You can get some basic information about traffic, links coming in, and other information at `www.alexa.com`. Google offers free analytical tools that (naturally) tie in nicely with Googl AdWords at `www.google.com/analytics`. You do not have to be using Google AdWords to make use of Google Analytics.

If your site uses internal search, you normally get reports about what search terms were used i internal searches. (This is not the same as search terms used in search engines that led visitors t your site.)

Most servers provide some sort of service that tracks and analyzes use. These statistical tool give you the number of times a page has been visited, the URL your visitors came from, the wor used in searches that led to your page, the browser your visitors use, and sometimes even the screen resolution of the visitor. Pay attention to the statistics for your site, because it helps you understand your visitors.

FIGURE 12.21
The Webalizer information provided by my hosting company shows referrers, among many statistics.

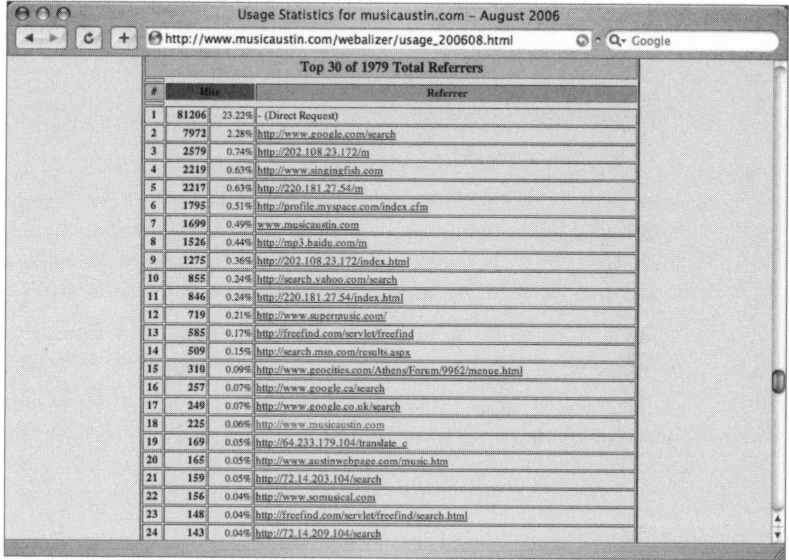

Top 30 of 1979 Total Referrers

#	Hits		Referrer
1	81206	23.22%	- (Direct Request)
2	7972	2.28%	http://www.google.com/search
3	2579	0.74%	http://202.108.23.172/m
4	2219	0.63%	http://www.singingfish.com
5	2217	0.63%	http://220.181.27.54/m
6	1795	0.51%	http://profile.myspace.com/index.cfm
7	1699	0.49%	www.musicaustin.com
8	1526	0.44%	http://mp3.baidu.com/m
9	1275	0.36%	http://202.108.23.172/index.html
10	855	0.24%	http://search.yahoo.com/search
11	846	0.24%	http://220.181.27.54/index.html
12	719	0.21%	http://www.supermusic.com/
13	585	0.17%	http://freefind.com/servlet/freefind
14	509	0.15%	http://search.msn.com/results.aspx
15	310	0.09%	http://www.geocities.com/Athens/Forum/9962/menue.html
16	257	0.07%	http://www.google.ca/search
17	249	0.07%	http://www.google.co.uk/search
18	225	0.06%	http://www.musicaustin.com
19	169	0.05%	http://64.233.179.104/translate_c
20	165	0.05%	http://www.austinwebpage.com/music.htm
21	159	0.05%	http://72.14.203.104/search
22	156	0.04%	http://www.somusical.com
23	148	0.04%	http://freefind.com/servlet/freefind/search.html
24	143	0.04%	http://72.14.209.104/search

One of the hosting companies I use provides a statistical analysis tool called Webalizer as part of the hosting package. Figure 12.21 shows a Webalizer chart of the top 30 total referrers that sent visitors my way.

You don't get any personal information from these statistical tools. You do get a good idea about what people are looking for when they visit and what equipment they are using to view your site. That knowledge about your audience can help you make decisions about site design and site content. For example, I don't see anyone visiting my site using Netscape 4.*x*, so it is probably safe for me to forget about making sure my styles work in Netscape 4 the next time I redesign.

If your hosting company does not provide you with enough information when you use the analysis tools that come with your hosting package, there are many such tools available on the Internet that you can install and use.

A HANDY SERVER CONTROL FILE

Many web hosting companies use Apache, a Linux-based open-source tool, for their servers. When you open an account with a web hosting company, you should be given information about the type of server the account will be using. Unless you have a need for Front Page extensions, it is my recommendation that you choose a Linux server running Apache rather than a Windows server. It's cheaper and often more secure than a Windows server.

You can use the form labeled "What's that site running?" at `uptime.netcraft.com` and find out the type of server being used on any site.

If your site uses an Apache server, there is a very handy file called `.htaccess` (the leading period must be included in the filename) that can control all sorts of things. The `.htaccess` file (or "distributed configuration file") provides a way to make configuration changes on a per-directory basis. The `.htacess` file, containing one or more directives, is placed in a particular document directory on the server, and the directives apply to that directory and all its subdirectories.

You can read the entire `.htaccess` tutorial from Apache here:

```
http://httpd.apache.org/docs/howto/htaccess.html
```

A more complete tutorial appears here:

```
http://wsabstract.com/howto/htaccess.shtml
```

You can do many things with `.htaccess` directives, but I only want to show you one. That directive relates to the file users see if they request a filename on your site that does not exist. This can happen because the user made a typo when entering the filename in the browser location bar or if you deleted something that was there for a while and the search engines picked it up and linked to it before you deleted it.

If you don't create a custom error document, the server provides one in the form of a 404 error page that basically says, "The file you are looking for does not exist on this server."

A custom error page—a custom 404 page, in this case—tells the user that the file does not exist on the server, but it can provide helpful links to the site menu or other ways for the user to find a way back into your site navigation or home page. To see an example of a custom 404 page, go to `www.amazon.com/oops.html`. This page doesn't exist, so you see the custom 404 page Amazon.com designed.

You create a custom 404 page and put it on your Apache server. For example, you might put it in a folder called `errors` with the filename `notfound.html`. Then the directive in the `.htaccess` file would read:

```
ErrorDocument 404 /errors/notfound.html
```

That is the entire content of the `.htaccess` file if you only have this one directive. Save it as text (but without any `.txt` file extension; it must be saved as `.htaccess` with no file extension) and put it in the top level directory on the site.

You can use `.htaccess` directives to password-protect certain directories on a site or to do many other useful chores.

Real-World Scenario

Passing muster with the online validators is not easy. It helps if you use standards through every ste of the site building and validate pages as you go along. Using valid XHTML and CSS will be a big he in ensuring that pages look as you want cross-browser, so it pays to validate your XHTML and CS throughout the design process.

MusicAustin

When a site uses advertising from outside sources, as MusicAustin at `www.musicaustin.com` doe it's very difficult to pass validation. The code generated by various advertising links is beyond yo control and creates many validation errors (see Figures 12.22 and 12.23).

If you run the validators on MusicAustin and look at the 34 errors mentioned at the top of th page in Figure 12.23, you see that all 34 come from code in the ads. So the creator of MusicAusti (me!) has done everything in her power to create valid code, but has decided that having advert ing on the page is more important than passing validation. Because the only errors are in the ad it's a safe assumption that the page is up to standards in every other way and should behave acro browsers. Even though the page fails, I know from this test that everything under my control is valid. If anything appeared in the error list that was *not* in an ad, I would fix it. It isn't perfect, but it's a choice I can live with.

A complication caused by using the W3C validators to check your code is that if the HTML won't validate, the CSS validators complain about it when you check your CSS. You have to scroll past the complaints to see the CSS test results.

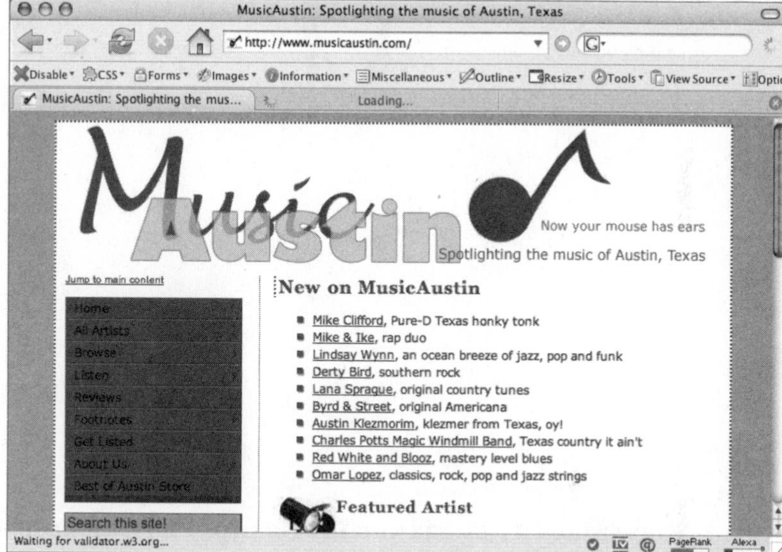

FIGURE 12.22
The MusicAustin home page. Farther down the page there are a couple of ads with ad code generated by the advertisers.

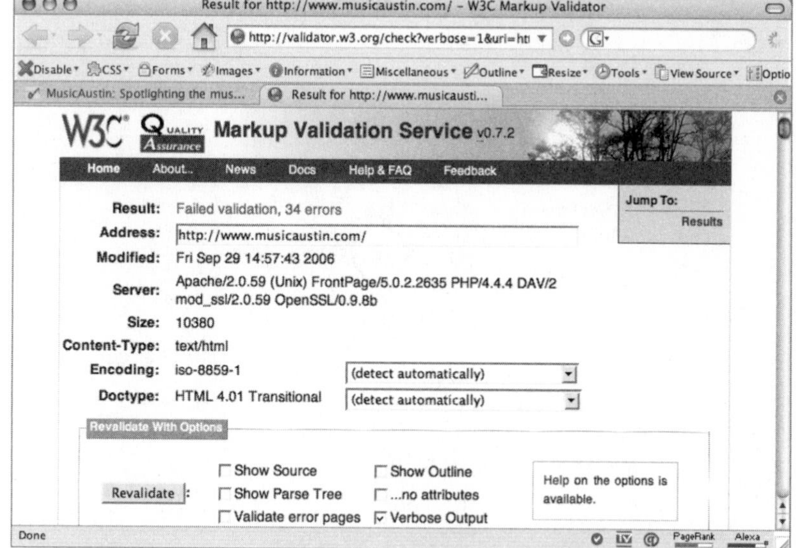

FIGURE 12.23
The W3C HTML Validator fails MusicAustin on a validation check, listing 34 errors.

Another good test, mentioned previously, is to test with no CSS. With CSS disabled, I am rea
sured that the site is still completely usable (see Figure 12.24).

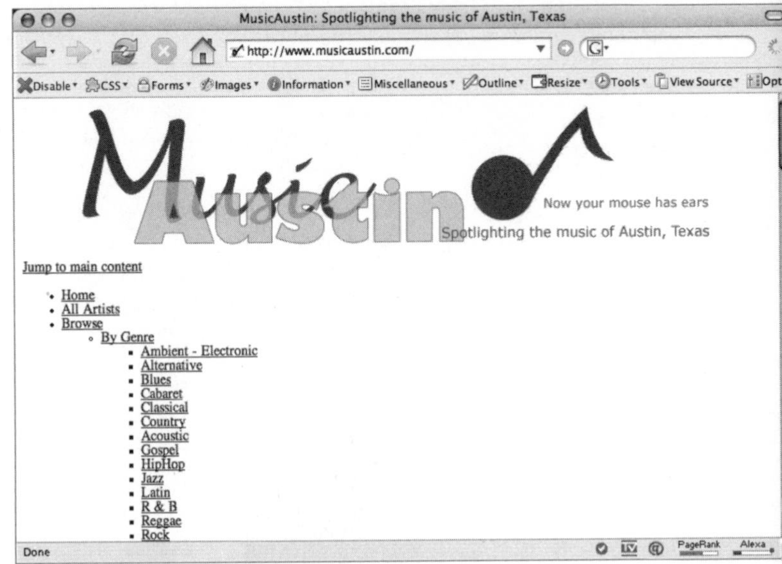

FIGURE 12.24 The MusicAustin site with CSS disabled is still easy to navigate and use, even if not as appealing visually.

New Mexico Association for Health, Physical Education, Recreation, and Dance

What a difference an ad can make. The New Mexico Association for Health, Physical Educatior
Recreation, and Dance (NMAHPERD) site at `www.nmahperd.org` uses no ads (see Figure 12.25)

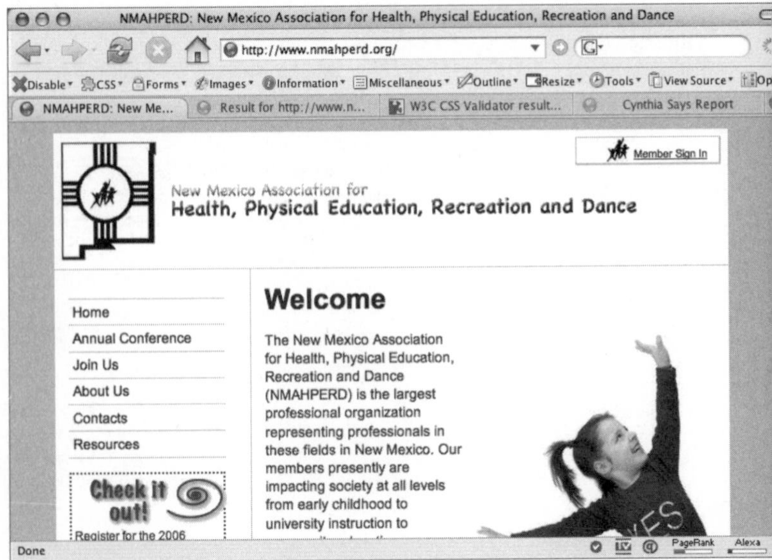

FIGURE 12.25 The home page of the New Mexico Association for Health, Physical Education, Recreation, and Dance

The same designer (me again) created this site with the intention of using standards and accessible design. As you see in Figures 12.26, 12.27, and 12.28, the site passed the HTML, CSS, and WAI validation tests successfully.

Running such validation tests is just the beginning of the testing process. There are other tests to run and lots of work to do clicking through the site to make sure everything is where it should be and working right.

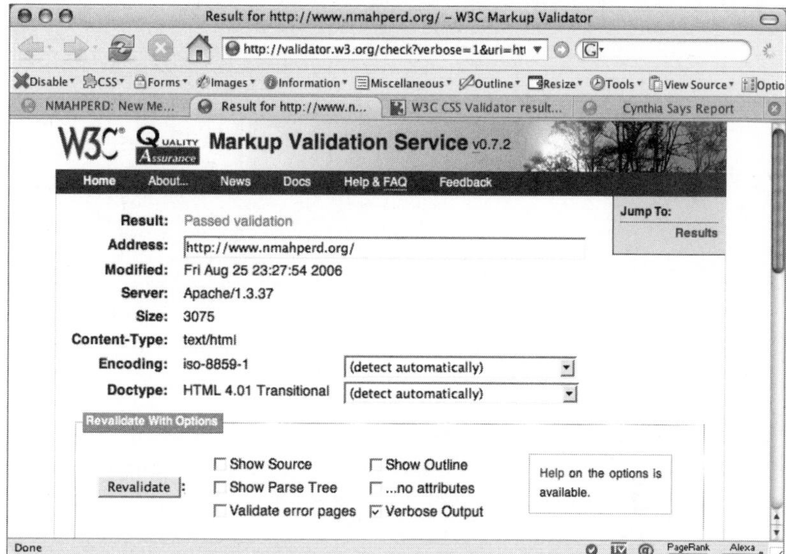

FIGURE 12.26 The NMAHPERD home page passes HTML validation.

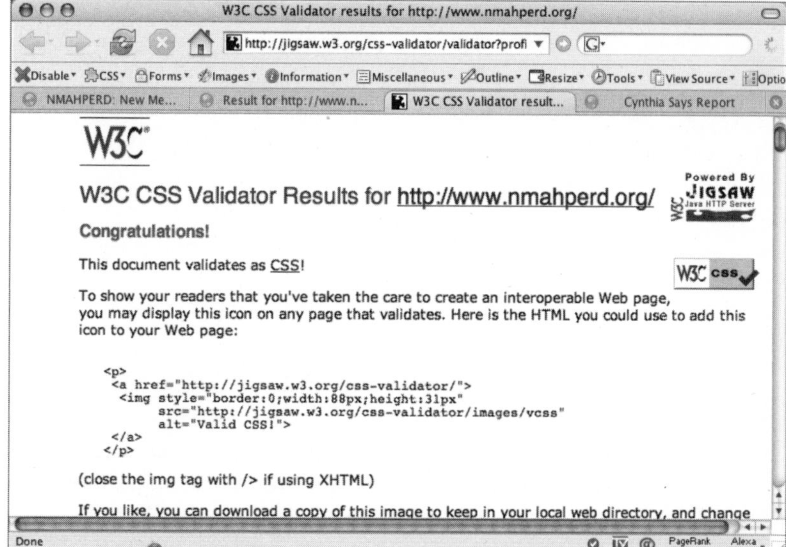

FIGURE 12.27 The NMAHPERD home page passes CSS validation.

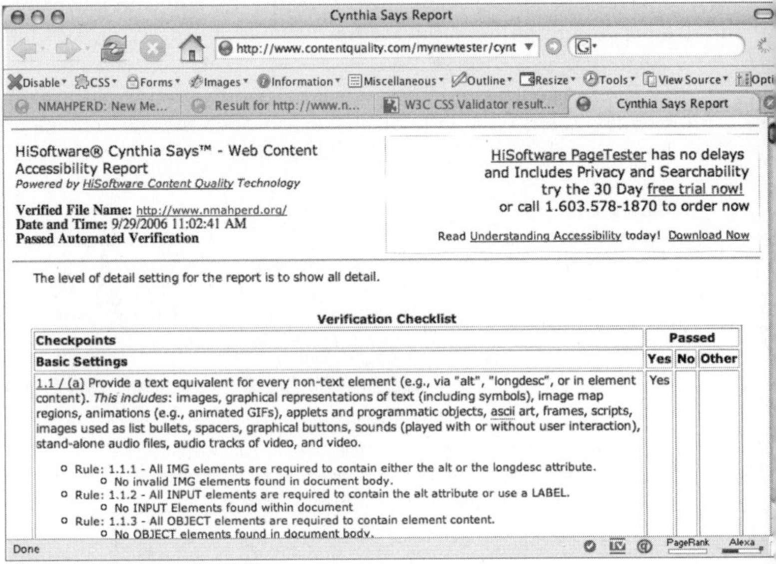

FIGURE 12.28 The NMAHPERD home page passes WAI validation.

The Bottom Line

It isn't enough to create a web page. You must also put it on a server so it's seen on the World Wi Web. That involves getting server space and testing the site once it's on the server.

Create a four- or five-page website of your own design. It can be about an organization, a perso a topic, or something else of interest. Use it to complete the following activities.

Use FTP to put files on a server. The most common way to put the files that make up you website on a server is with the File Transfer Protocol, or FTP.

Master It Use one of the FTP tools included on the CD, or an FTP tool of your own choosin to move your site to the server.

Get a domain name and server space. If you want your own domain name and server spac you will have to pay for it. It's also possible to find free hosting.

Master It Do some research online. Visit several free and for-fee hosting companies. Co pare costs, services, plans, and support guarantees. Decide whether to not to buy a doma name or use free hosting. Decide where to put your site. Be ready to explain your choice

Test your site. Once your files are on the server, find your URL in a browser and test ever thing about your site to be sure it is working properly.

Master It Test the site yourself with as many browsers and Internet devices are you pc sibly can. Validate your XHTML and CSS using the free tools provided by the W3C. Che your pages for accessibility. Be prepared to show your results in a browser.

Identify search engine submission tools. After your site is posted on the Web, you need t register with the search engines so that they know you are there and can send people your w

Master It At `yahoo.com`, find the "Suggest a Site" link in the page footer. Register your s for free. You must register with Yahoo! to do this.

Or, go to `dmoz.org` and submit your URL.

Chapter 13

CSS for Weblogs

Publishing your thoughts and information with a weblog, or *blog*, is increasingly popular. In the beginning, blogs were like online journals, with people spilling out thoughts that might have previously been written in some more private format such as a diary. But weblogs have come a long way since then and are now used for all sorts of purposes.

Blogs are different from the websites you've learned about thus far in several ways. Published material in a blog (a *post*) is stored (archived) in a database. Individual posts can be retrieved from that database by date, sometimes by topic, or through a search. The readers of a blog can subscribe to a blog. Each time a new post is published, a notification is sent to the subscriber. Blog readers can comment on blog posts. While a blog *is* a website, it has unique properties that make it both a good or a bad choice for web publishing, depending on your needs.

Your local newspaper sports writer might use a blog to provide information and reflections on local sports that didn't make it into the newspaper but are of interest to the paper's readers. Your favorite band may have a blog on their site to make it easy to add updated news about concerts and tours. Commercial sites that use blogging software to manage content are becoming more and more common.

If your cell phone takes pictures, it can e-mail photos directly to a *moblog* (for mobile weblog). These have been used for everything from documenting a person's life in photos to sending in photos and locations of potholes to a city road administration blog.

In this chapter you will learn to:

- Describe the advantage of blogs over traditional sites.
- Understand how to create a blog.
- Identify features of Blogger and WordPress blogs.
- Identify ways to configure and customize a blog.

Advantages of Blogging

It's not all roses. There are several disadvantages to using a weblog format to publish your content. With Blogger, the primary disadvantage is that the information tends to get disorganized over time. The main linking system is to archives of previous posts, which are organized in monthly or weekly increments by date. In other words, it doesn't provide well thought out main navigation categories that lead to subsections on specific topics. Other weblog software, including WordPress, allows you to categorize posts by topic, which is a good organizational aid. A disadvantage people find after starting a blog in a burst of enthusiasm is that a blog requires a time commitment. Once you finish a normal site and get it posted, you don't have to commit time to updating it frequently the way you do a blog.

However, the advantages of weblogs are what draw people into using them, so I'll detail a fe of the advantages for you:

Ease of use You can publish to a weblog using only a browser from any Internet-connectec device or, as I mentioned earlier, a cell phone with e-mail capability.

Preexisting designs Most blogging companies provide professionally designed templates t hold your content. This chapter will show you how to modify a template using your XHTMI and CSS skills.

If you are happy using one of the provided template designs, you don't need to know anythir about HTML or CSS to create an attractive blog.

Web practice and experience As a person interested in HTML and CSS, or if you intend to pursue employment with your XHTML and CSS skills, you may want to include a weblog ir your portfolio or resume. In that case, it's important to show a weblog that you successfully created or modified to fit your requirements.

Group participation A weblog can be under the control of a single individual, or many people ca be allowed to post to it. Some weblogs allow your users to comment on your posts, which can lea to some lively discussions or even a book, as with `www.simplebits.com`, where Dan Cederholm used comments from his weblog in the book *Web Standards Solutions: The Markup and Style Handbo*

Fresh and syndicated content Blogs are updated constantly, often daily. The flip side of the requirement to keep your content fresh is that if your content appeals to people, you will have steady stream of return visitors. The freshness of content on a website can help maintain gooc search engine rankings. (Sites that seldom get updated tend to recede from the search engine' radar over time.) Content is syndicated with "feeds" that automatically let people who subscril to your feed know when you've published something new.

Incoming links Blogs on a topic similar to yours link to you. Your friends with blogs link t you. People link to specific posts of particular interest. The number of incoming links you ca generate for a blog increases the blog's popularity and its search engine ranking.

Low cost A final important advantage is that some weblog companies provide free hostin

Where to Sign Up for a Blog

There are several blogging software sources with good reviews. WordPress (`www.wordpress.org`) free, with a focus on web standards and usability. In 2001, I signed up with Blogger (`www.blogger.co` and have been happy enough to stay with it since. Blogger has a free version and provides free ho ing for your blog on BlogSpot. I also have a couple of WordPress blogs. Because I have access and accounts with Blogger and WordPress, they will be our examples in the following pages. That do not imply that I endorse them over other blogging tools that might suit your needs.

There are other companies offering weblog services or software that have good reputations, including Movable Type (`www.movabletype.org`) and Greymatter (`www.noahgrey.com/greysoft` I've heard good things about Typepad (`www.typepad.com`), although it is not free.

Check out all of these options and make a choice that is best for what you are trying to accor plish with your weblog, as I'll describe next.

What to Look for in Blog Software

If you stick with the free hosting, for example at blogspot.com or at wordpress.com, you have only limited customization options.

But other services allow you to download and install the blog software on your own server. Doing this allows you maximum customization. If you plan to install a blog on your own server, you want flexibility. You must be able to make changes to both the XHTML and the CSS. You need access to the XHTML used in the template, and you need to be able to use XHTML in your posts. You need access to the style sheets, and you need the option of making them either external or embedded style sheets, or both.

Good help files and directions must be available. Read through the help files (they may be called something else, like Knowledge Base or FAQ) to see if they are clear and complete enough to get you going. It's also a good idea to be sure that you have a way to make e-mail contact for technical support questions.

Once those two requirements—customization and help—are satisfied, the other features will be based on your personal choice. Some things you might take into consideration are

- How much the service costs
- Whether you can add the weblog to an existing site or a new domain
- Whether you want to let users comment on your posts
- Whether you want to let other people besides yourself post to the blog
- Whether you can organize your posts into categories

Getting Started with Blogger

Before you can customize a weblog, you have to either get the software (if you are using a tool such as Movable Type), or sign up for an account with the weblog provider of choice (if you are using a blog hosting company like Blogger) and get the basic setup done.

I'll step you through some of the basics of starting and configuring a new Blogger blog to be published free on BlogSpot. Later in the chapter you'll see a similar process with a new WordPress blog to be published by `wordpress.com`. If you want to follow along with the steps, you can create a blog and then delete it later.

With Blogger, the process begins at `www.blogger.com`. If you don't already have an account, follow the onscreen directions to get one. After you sign in, you are offered the opportunity to create a blog (Figure 13.1).

Give the blog a name, and select a URL (Figure 13.2). The URLs hosted free on BlogSpot will always be `http://`*`somename`*`.blogspot.com`, where *`somename`* is the URL you make up.

Next, you select one of the templates (Figure 13.3). These are actually wonderful templates created by CSS gurus such as Dave Shea (`www.mezzoblue.com`) and Douglas Bowman (`www.stopdesign.com`). I love orange, so I picked one called Sand Dollar by Jason Sutter (Figure 13.4). However, it doesn't really matter which one you pick. That is all it takes to be ready to start posting (Figure 13.5).

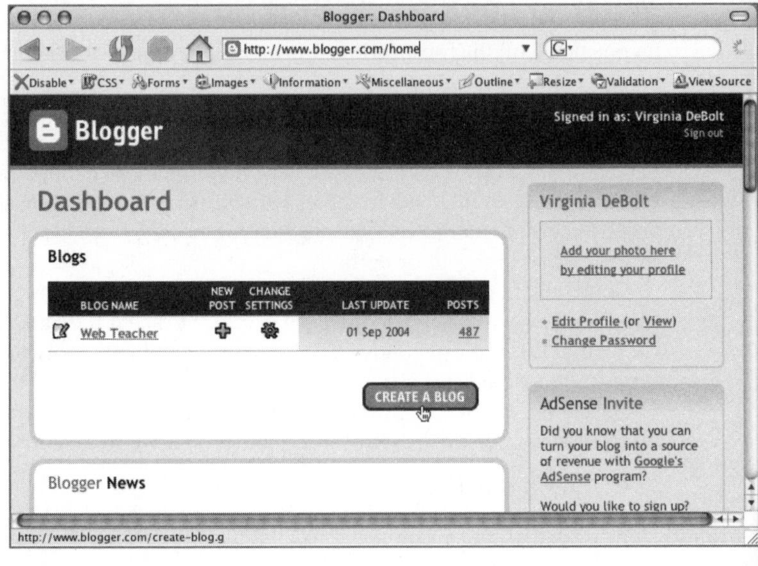

FIGURE 13.1 After signing in to your account at Blogger, select the Create a Blog option.

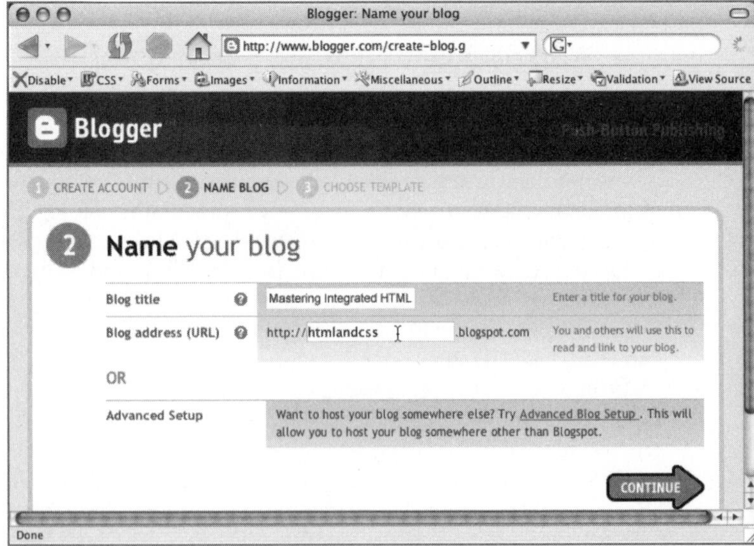

FIGURE 13.2 The new blog needs a name and a URL, which you create.

FIGURE 13.3 After naming the blog, you see a selection of templates for the blog.

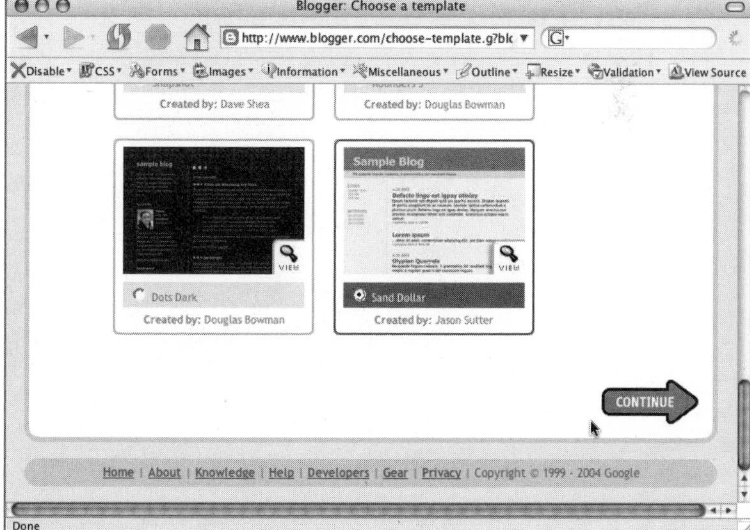

FIGURE 13.4 Scroll through the available templates to find something that catches your eye. This template is named Sand Dollar.

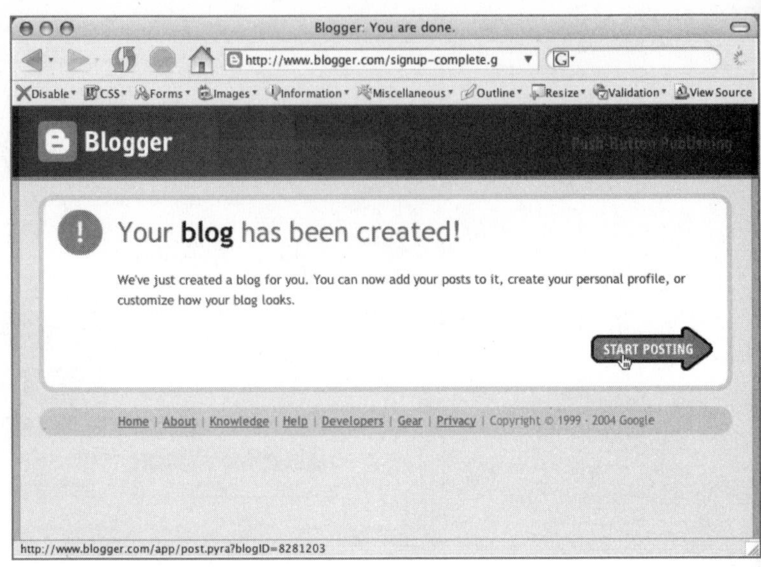

FIGURE 13.5
You can now start publishing posts on your new blog.

Configuring a BlogSpot Blog

The work space for the Blogger has four main menu items: Posting, Settings, Template, and Vie Blog. Each of these main items has several secondary level options, such as those you see under t Settings tab (Figures 13.6, 13.7, and 13.8).

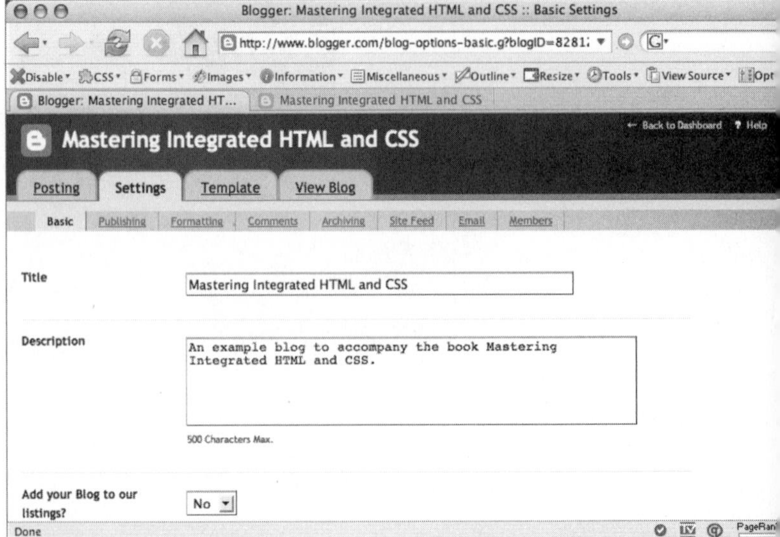

FIGURE 13.6
The Basic Settings ask for a blog description, which becomes part of every page of your weblog.

Site feeds are valuable. Blogger uses Atom (`www.atomenabled.org`). Blogger describes site feeds by saying, "When a regularly updated site such as a blog has a feed, people can subscribe to it using software for reading syndicated content called a 'newsreader.' People like using readers for blogs because it allows them to catch up on all their favorites at once. Like checking e-mail." Another very popular site feed tool is RSS (Really Simple Syndication). Many weblog companies use RSS. One of the chief advantages of writing a blog over a traditional web page is that each time you update, your subscribers are notified (Figure 13.9), so turn on the subscription features.

The rules specifying who can post to the blog are under the Members option. (Figure 13.10).

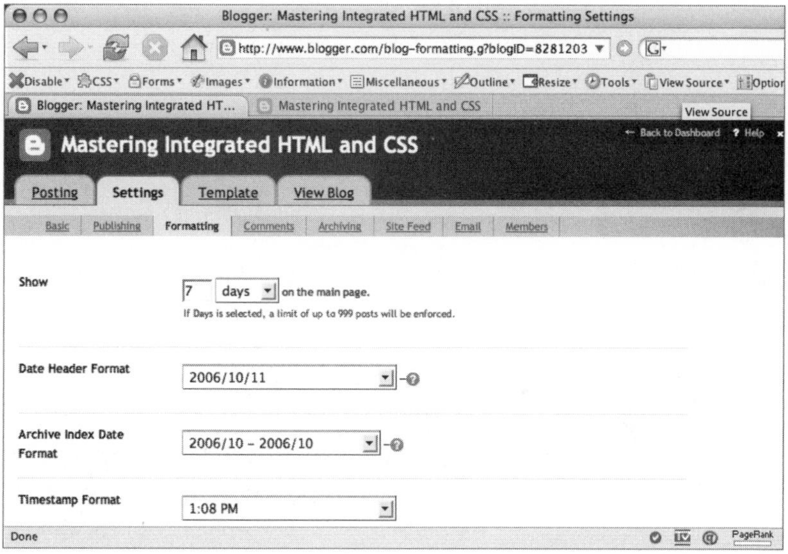

FIGURE 13.7
In the Formatting Settings, you set up how you want things such as dates to be formatted.

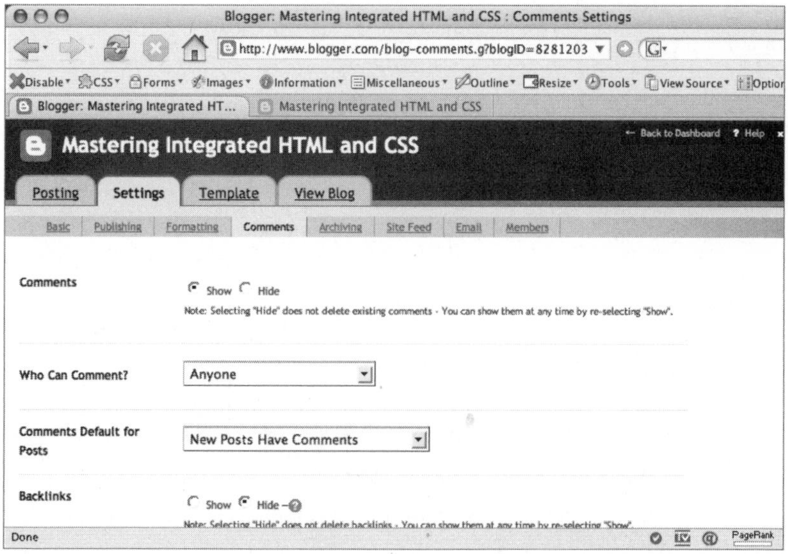

FIGURE 13.8
Decide whether you want to allow comments on your posts and set up the rules for that under the Comments Settings.

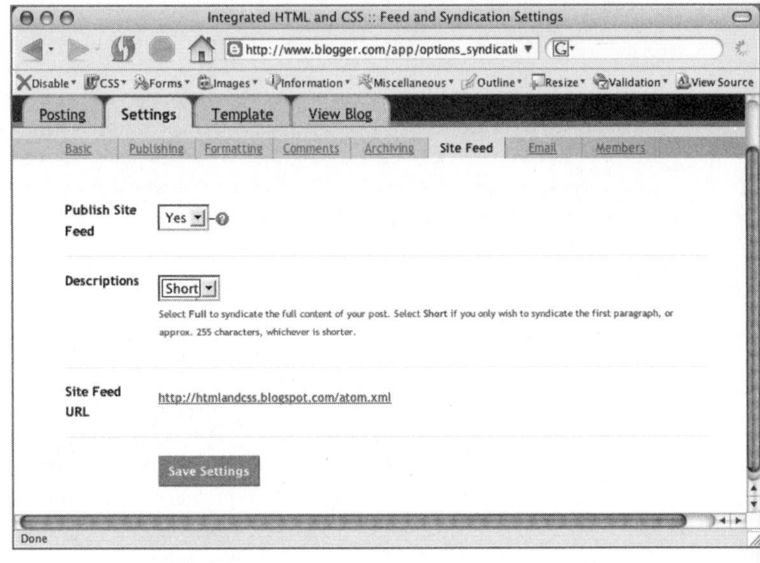

FIGURE 13.9 People who subscribe to your site feed get a notice in their newsreader each time you publish a new post.

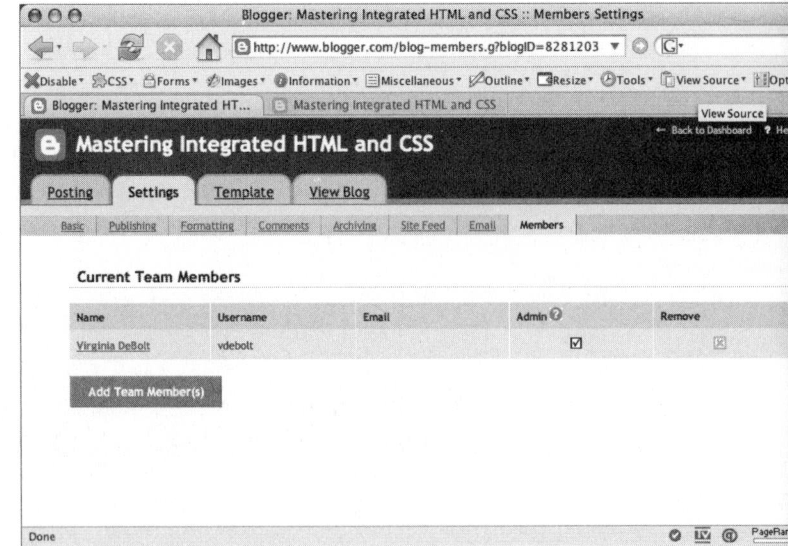

FIGURE 13.10 The only person allowed to write posts will be me, but I have allowed anyone to comment on my posts so users can still have a say.

RESOURCES

The International Standard for the representation of dates and times is ISO 8601. You can see W3C-suggested date and time formats at `www.w3.org/TR/NOTE-datetime`.

You can read more about RSS at `http://rss.userland.com`.

Some bloggers publish RSS feeds with Feedburner at `www.feedburner.com`. Feedburner also manages podcast feeds.

Publishing to Your Blogger Blog

Once you have all the settings to your liking, you can visit your URL—in this case `http://htmlandcss.blogspot.com`—and look at your post (Figure 13.11). If you see an error, you can go back to Blogger, edit your post, and republish (Figures 13.12 and 13.13).

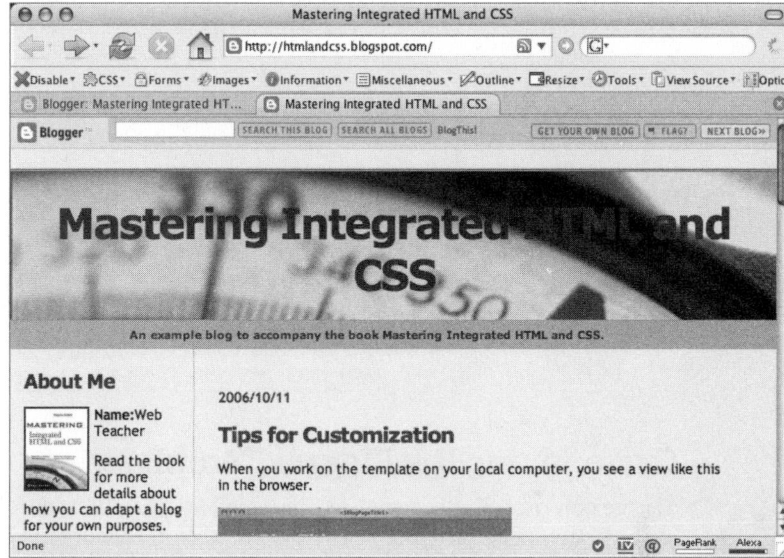

FIGURE 13.11 The latest post appears at the designated URL on BlogSpot just as planned. You will learn how the heading image was customized later.

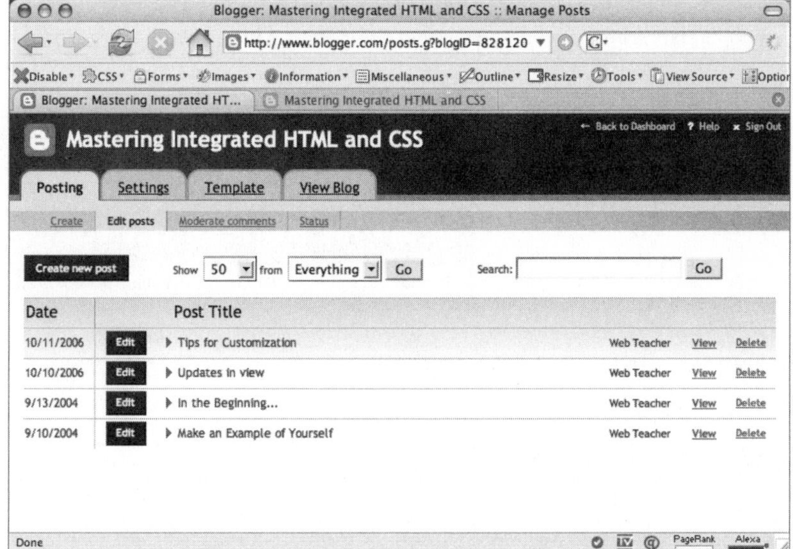

FIGURE 13.12 You can edit or delete posts any time after they have been published while signed in to your blog at blogger.com.

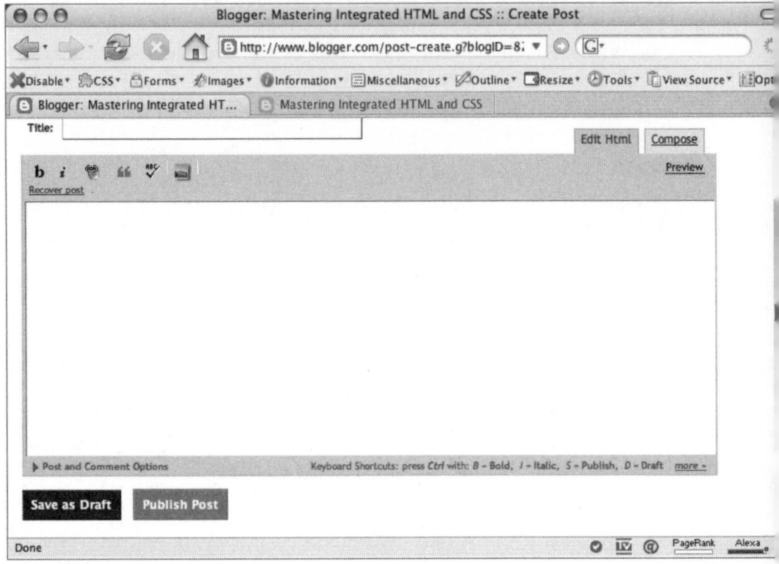

FIGURE 13.13 When creating or editing posts, you can preview your post, save it as a draft, or publish (or republish) it using the buttons at the bottom. Note the options for bold, italic, hyperlinks, block quotes, spell checking, and image insertion across the top of the post editing window.

Customizing the Blogger Template

You are now ready for the template. The template is in an editable form field that you are free to mo ify, save, and republish. Since you cannot see all of it in Figure 13.14, I have put a copy on the acco panying CD called `template_start.html`. Excerpts from the template are also shown in Listing 13 In the listing, highlighted items indicate special Blogger codes that can be moved around in the doc ment but must not be deleted; bracketed ellipses mark omissions. In particular, I left out the embedd style because I'll present that completely a little later in a more readable format than the template us

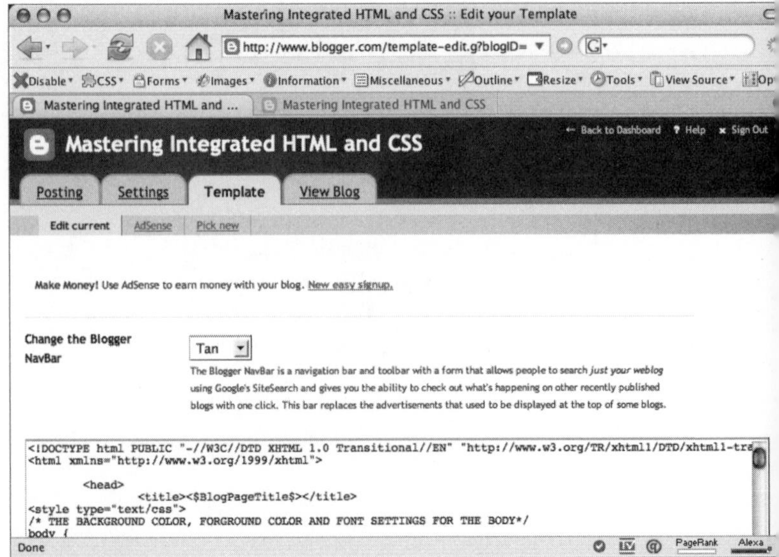

FIGURE 13.14 The template can be edited and saved under the Template menu.

LISTING 13.1: The Template for Blogger's Sand Dollar Design

```
<html>
<head>
   <title><$BlogPageTitle$></title>
   <style type="text/css">
      body{margin:0px;padding:0px;background:#f6f6f6;color:#000000;
           font-family:"Trebuchet MS",Trebuchet,Verdana,Sans-Serif;}
      [...]
   </style>
   <$BlogMetaData$>
</head>
<body>
<div id="header">
   <h1>
      <ItemPage><a href="<$BlogURL$>"></ItemPage>
      <$BlogTitle$>
      <ItemPage></a></ItemPage>
   </h1>
   <p id="description"><$BlogDescription$></p>
</div>

<!-- Main Column -->
<div id="mainClm">

   <!-- Blog Posts -->
   <Blogger>
      <BlogDateHeader>
         <h3><$BlogDateHeaderDate$></h3>
      </BlogDateHeader>
      <a name="<$BlogItemNumber$>"> </a>
      <BlogItemTitle><h2><BlogItemURL><a href="<$BlogItemURL$>"></BlogItemURL>
         <$BlogItemTitle$><BlogItemURL></a></BlogItemURL></h2></BlogItemTitle>
      <div class="blogPost">
         <$BlogItemBody$><br />
         <div class="byline">[...]</div>
      </div>
      <ItemPage>
      <div class="blogComments">
         <BlogItemCommentsEnabled><a name="comments"></a>Comments:
            <BlogItemComments>
            <div class="blogComment">
               <a name="<$BlogCommentNumber$>"></a>
               <$BlogCommentBody$><br />
               <div class="byline">[...]</div>
               <$BlogCommentDeleteIcon$>
            </div>
            </BlogItemComments>
            <$BlogItemCreate$>
```

```
            </BlogItemCommentsEnabled><br /> <br />
            <a href="<$BlogURL$>">&lt;&lt; Home</a>
        </div>
        </ItemPage>
    </Blogger>
<!-- In accordance to the Blogger terms of service, please leave this button
      somewhere on your blogger-powered page. Thanks! -->
        <p><a href="http://www.blogger.com"><img width="88" height="31"
            src="http://buttons.blogger.com/bloggerbutton1.gif" border="0"
            alt="This page is powered by Blogger. Isn't yours?" /></a></p>
</div>

<!-- Sidebar -->
<div id="sideBar">
    <$BlogMemberProfile$>
    [...]
    <h6>archives</h6>
    <ul>
        <BloggerArchives><li><a href='<$BlogArchiveURL$>'><$BlogArchiveName$></a><
li></BloggerArchives>
        <!-- Link to the front page, from your archives -->
        <script type="text/javascript">if (location.href.indexOf("archive")!=-1)
document.write("<li><strong><a href=\"<$BlogURL$>\">Current Posts</a></strong></
li>");</script>
    </ul>
</div>
</body>
</html>
```

Anything that begins and ends with $, such as <$BlogURL$> represents a macro variable—o of the placeholders that makes Blogger work and brings parts of your page out of a database ar puts it in the document as it is generated. You can change the locations of these things in the sour order, but you cannot delete them. Otherwise, everything in the embedded styles and the mark is fair game for your customization.

Working in the template-editing window (Figure 13.14) is rather difficult because there is no li wrapping. Although it adds a step, I find it much easier to select the entire template code, copy and paste it into a text editor. I make any changes I want in the text editor and paste them back in the template-editing window.

Changing the DOCTYPE Declaration

The first thing I noticed about the template was that it didn't have a DOCTYPE declaration. The are XHTML tags in the markup—for example,
—but without a proper DOCTYPE declaratic the XHTML syntax causes errors from the HTML validator. The validator goes into a tizzy and decid for itself to try HTML 4.01 Transitional as the DOCTYPE, which will not validate (Figure 13.15). You also don't want any DOCTYPE switching that will cause the document to render in quirks mode, so a proper XHTML Transitional DOCTYPE declaration is needed.

The first change to make to the template is to change `<html>` to

```
<!DOCTYPE html PUBLIC "-//W3C//DTD XHTML 1.0 Transitional//EN"
  "http://www.w3.org/TR/xhtml1/DTD/xhtml1-transitional.dtd">
<html xmlns="http://www.w3.org/1999/xhtml">
```

Open `template_start.html` document so you can work along. Immediately Save As by a new name so that the original document is still there just in case you make a mess of things and want to go back to the original. Save the working version as `template_finish.html`.

You can open either `template_start.html` or `template_finish.html` from your local computer in the browser. The Blogger tags will show up as text because the page isn't in the proper place to pull the info from the Blogger database. However, as you can see in Figure 13.16, the effects of the embedded styles on layout, colors, and fonts are apparent.

If you make a change in Blogger's template editing window, save the changes, and republish the blog, you can run the validator again. You may still get errors, but some you cannot change in your customization efforts because Blogger is responsible for them (Figure 13.17).

If you decide to publish a blog of your own, I urge you to keep working on the HTML until you manage to get it through the validator successfully. However, in the interests of getting to the CSS, I'm going to drop the discussion of it for now and move on. (Valid code may not be possible using the free hosting on BlogSpot, but if you go beyond this first step as a blogger, you need to strive for valid code.)

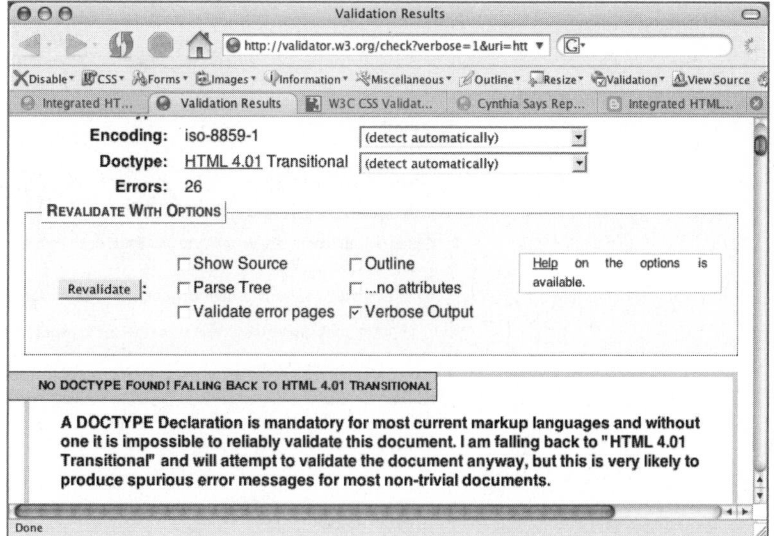

FIGURE 13.15 The W3C HTML validator points out immediately that the page has no DOCTYPE and that validation fails.

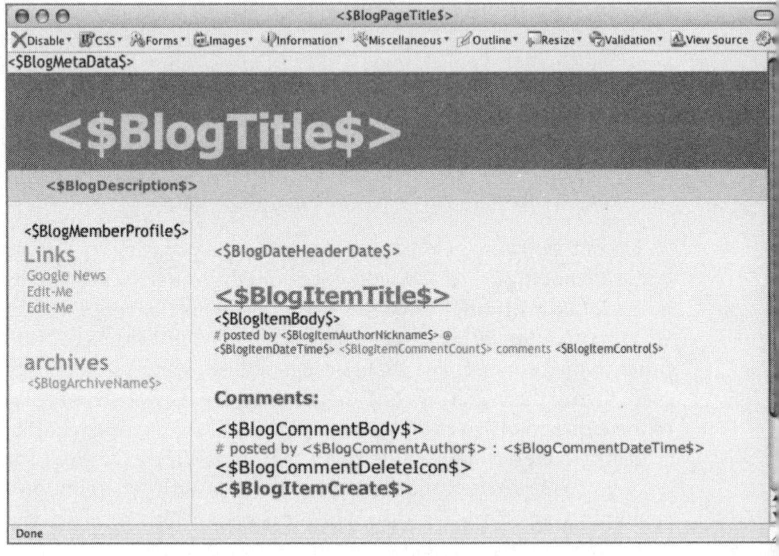

FIGURE 13.16 Working on the template on your local machine lets you see any changes to the CSS, but the Blogger tags are displayed as plain text.

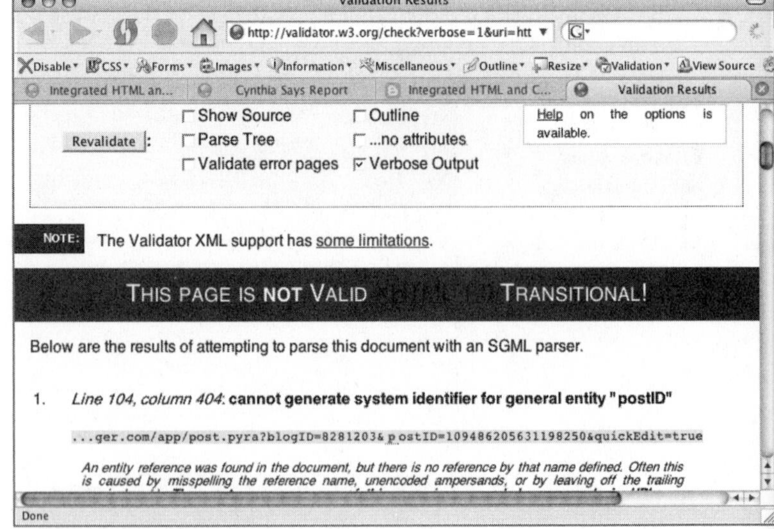

FIGURE 13.17 A valid DOCTYPE helps, but the document still does not pass the validation test.

Customize the Blogger CSS

Take a close look at the embedded styles in the template. In Listing 13.2, you see only the `style` e ment. The rules have been reformatted for easier reading, and comments have been inserted to he you identify what the styles are controlling. If you would like to insert this entire section of refo matted and commented styles into `template_finish.html` in place of the `style` element alreac there, it is provided for you on the accompanying CD in a file called `formatted_styles.txt`. I makes finding and changing specific CSS rules much easier.

I'll explain the specific details about how I customized this template so you can understand the steps needed to customize a template of your own choosing.

LISTING 13.2: Selected Blogger Template Styles, Reformatted and Commented

```
<style type="text/css">
/*  Settings for the body  */
body {
  margin:0px;
  padding:0px;
  background:#f6f6f6;
  color:#000000;
  font-family:"Trebuchet MS",Trebuchet,Verdana,Sans-Serif;
}
/*  Link colors  */
a {
  color:#DE7008;
}
a:hover {
  color:#E0AD12;
}
[...]
/*  This is the right column where the blog posts go.  */
div#mainClm {
  float:right;width:66%;
  padding:30px 7% 10px 3%;
  border-left:dotted 1px #E0AD12;
}
/*  This is the column on the left side where the profile, links,
    and archives go.  */
div#sideBar {
  margin:20px 0px 0px 1em;
  padding:0px;
  text-align:left;
}
/*  This is at the top where the blog title and blog description go.  */
#header {
  padding:0px 0px 0px 0px;
  margin:0px 0px 0px 0px;
  border-top:1px solid #eeeeee;
  border-bottom:dotted 1px #E0AD12;
  background:#F5E39E;
  color:white;
}
/*  A series of heading rules. Note the lack of a semicolon after the final
    rule declaration in some of the following. The semicolon is not required on
    the last declaration but is good practice and I suggest you add them.  */
h1,h2,h3,h4,h5,h6 {
  padding:0px;
```

```
  margin:0px;
}
h1 a:link {
  text-decoration:none;
  color:#F5DEB3
}
h1 a:visited {
  text-decoration:none;
  color:#F5DEB3
}
h1 {
  padding:25px 0px 10px 5%;
  border-top:double 3px #BF5C00;
  border-bottom:solid 1px #E89E47;
  color:#F5DEB3;
  background:#DE7008;
  font:bold 300% Verdana,Sans-Serif;
  letter-spacing:-2px;
}
h2 {
  color:#9E5205;
  font-weight:bold;
  font-family:Verdana,Sans-Serif;
  letter-spacing:-1px;
}
[...]
/*  The rules for the list in the sidebar  */
#sideBar ul {
  margin:0px 0px 33px 0px;
  padding:0px 0px 0px 0px;
  list-style-type:none;
  font-size:95%;
}
#sideBar li {
  margin:0px 0px 0px 0px;
  padding:0px 0px 0px 0px;
  list-style-type:none;
  font-size:95%;
}
/*  The rules for the description  */
#description {
  padding:0px;
  margin:7px 12% 7px 5%;
  color:#9E5205;
  background:transparent;
  font:bold 85% Verdana,Sans-Serif;
}
```

```
/*  Two rules for the appearance of the posts  */
.blogPost {
  margin:0px 0px 30px 0px;
  font-size:100%;
}
.blogPost strong {
  color:#000000;
  font-weight:bold;
 }
/* A series of rules for the anchor tags in the unordered list in the sidebar */
#sideBar ul a {
  padding:2px;
  margin:1px;
  width:100%;
  border:none;
  color:#999999;
  text-decoration:none;
}
#sideBar ul a:link {
  color:#999999;
}
#sideBar ul a:visited {
  color:#999999;
}
#sideBar ul a:active {
  color:#ff0000;
}
#sideBar ul a:hover {
  color:#DE7008;
  text-decoration:none;
}
[...]
```

You can change anything in that `style` element. You can change styles, add styles, remove styles. For the purposes of this example, it's enough to change the color scheme of the header with a two-column layout of elements. A few changes in color scheme will give you a basic understanding of how to customize the Blogger CSS.

Using Blogger on Your Own Server

With Blogger, you can completely start from scratch with a whole new layout the way I did with the layout on Web Teacher (`www.webteacher.ws`). Web Teacher has its own domain; it does not use BlogSpot free hosting. Even though the template is completely mine, the pages are published by Blogger and the Blogger tags must be retained. The links to the posts, the comments, the archives, and other Blogger activities are all carried on at Blogger, even though the blog publishes to my domain.

Blogger, unlike WordPress, does not give you the blogging software free to install a blog on your server. Even a Blogger blog on your own server is powered by Blogger.

Is having your own server important to the success of your blog? It's no doubt considered more professional. However there are some wildly popular blogs published on BlogSpot, for example PostSecret at `http://postsecret.blogspot.com`. PostSecret proved so popular that the creator of the site now has books, major art shows, and other highly successful outgrowths from the community participation and general interest in the blog. Kyle MacDonald at `http://oneredpaperclip.blogspot.com` traded his way from a single red paper clip to a house using a free blog at BlogSpot.

A New Color Scheme

The new colors for this blog are based on the cover of this book. Instead of a photo of my face, I fill out my Blogger profile with a photo of the book cover (Figure 13.18).

The process of customizing the template mainly involves figuring out which of the styles control the appearance of whatever you want to change. I've made several changes to the Sar Dollar appearance, which I'll explain. I bid a fond farewell to the orange and changed the `h1` element foreground `color` to a red from the book's cover, `#9A090E`, and the `background` to a image from the cover. I also centered the heading. (It wraps at the screen resolution in the scre captures. It may not wrap on your screen if you look at the actual site.) To allow more of the `background-image` to show, I increased the `padding-bottom` to 20px. And to work with the `text-align: center` change, I changed the `padding-right` to 0px.

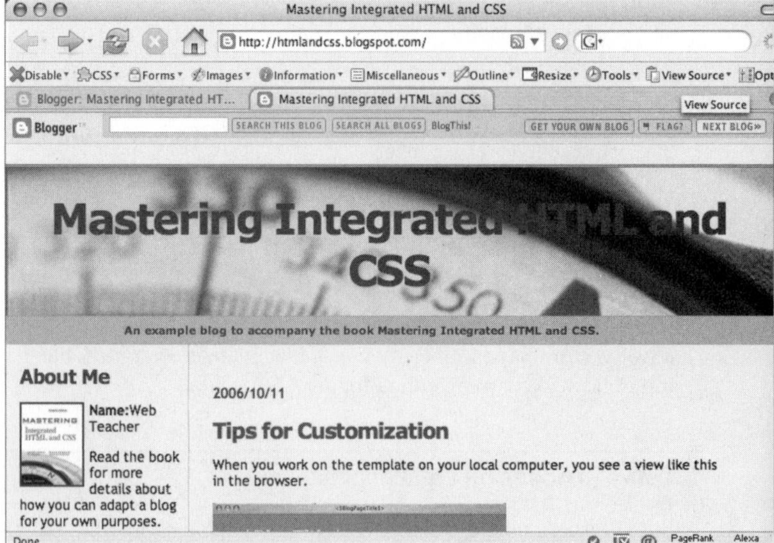

FIGURE 13.18
The book image shows up on BlogSpot as my profile.

To help you stay oriented to what's changing, I'll show you the entire style rule, with the changes highlighted, like this:

```
h1 {
  text-align: center;
  padding:25px 0px 20px 0px;
  border-top:double 3px #BF5C00;
  border-bottom:solid 1px #E89E47;
 color:#9A090E;
 background: url(http://www.webteacher.ws/img/blogspotbanner.jpg) no-repeat left
top;
  font: bold 300% Verdana, Sans-Serif;
  letter-spacing:-2px;
}
```

The next change is to a couple of colors in the `header div`. I change the `background-color` to #B6BEC1, the gray shade from the cover. I will remove the value for `color`, as it isn't needed.

```
#header {
  padding:0px 0px 0px 0px;
  margin:0px 0px 0px 0px;
  border-top:1px solid #eeeeee;
  border-bottom:dotted 1px #E0AD12;
  background:#B6BEC1;

}
```

The `color` in the `description` needs to change to #9A090E as well:

```
#description {
  padding:0px;
  margin:7px 12% 7px 5%;
  color:# 9A090E;
  background:transparent;
  font:bold 85% Verdana,Sans-Serif;
}
```

The `h2` element has a color set at `#9E5205`; however, the `h2` element rule in the `$BlogItemTitle$` is overridden by the color `#DE7008` set for the a elements. In order to change the color of the `$BlogItemTitle$`, I must change the a element color to #9A090E:

```
a {
  color:#9A090E;
}
```

The `blogComments` should be #9A090E as well:

```
.blogComments {
  padding:0px;
  color:# 9A090E;
  font-size:110%;
  font-weight:bold;
  font-family:Verdana,Sans-Serif;
}
```

The words "Links" and "archives" in the left column are `h6` element. They will be `color: #9A090E` also:

```
h6 {
  color:# 9A090E;
  font-size:140%;
}
```

The sidebar link colors also need to be changed. I'll stick with the red (#9A090E):

```
#sideBar ul a {
  padding:2px;
  margin:1px;
  width:100%;
  border:none;
  color:# 9A090E;
  text-decoration:none;
}
#sideBar ul a:link {
  color:#9A090E;
}
#sideBar ul a:visited {
  color:#9A090E;
}
#sideBar ul a:active {
  color:#9A090E;
}
#sideBar ul a:hover {
  color:#9A090E;
  text-decoration:none;
}
```

Make those changes and reload the page. Results should be similar to Figure 13.19.

The "View Source" Secret to Blogger Modifications

If you are working a Blogger template on your local computer, you see Blogger tags, as in Figures 13. or 13.19. When you are working this way, you sometimes cannot tell which CSS selectors are connected to specific things on the page that are rendered when the page is viewed. You have to do a of detective work.

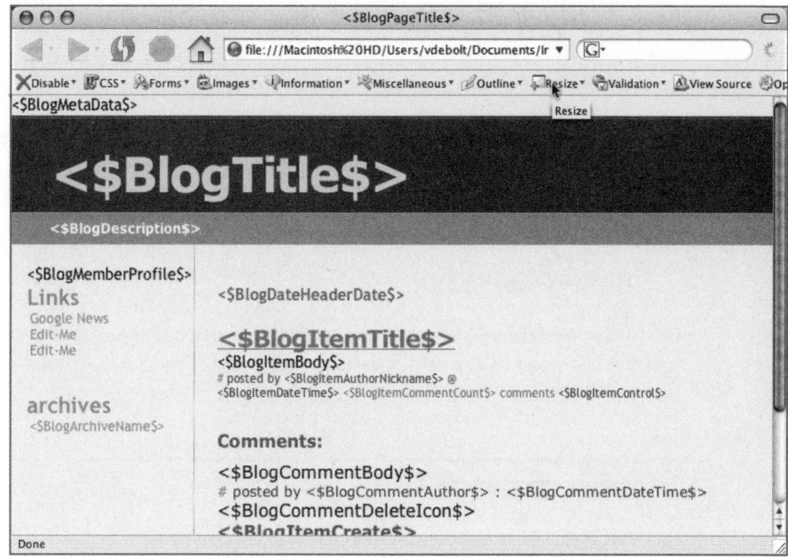

FIGURE 13.19
You should be able to see the new color rules in effect when looking at your changes in the browser.

The secret to figuring out what CSS rule is in use is to save the template (if you're editing on your hard drive, paste it into the Blogger template-editing window) and republish the blog (refer back to Figure 13.14). Then visit your blog on the Web and use View Source. With View Source, you don't see mysterious things like `$BlogDescription$`, you see the actual HTML that is rendered on the page in place of the Blogger macros in the template. If you are working directly in the Template editing window instead of on your hard drive, simply save and publish the page to view the source.

Using the browser's View Source command, I can see that the words "About Me" in the sidebar are `h2` elements assigned to the class `sidebar-title`. I would like these words to match the `h6` style for color and size of the other headings (Links, archives) in the sidebar, so I change the rule in the template to this:

```
h2.sidebar-title {
  color:#9A090E;
  margin:0px;
  padding:0px;
  font-size:140%;
}
```

Now the colors and size match, but the `font-weight` of the `h2` used for "About Me" is greater than that of the `h6` elements used for "Links" and "archives." Using View Source I see that the "About Me" is in the profile-container, which currently has no rule. It's in the section of empty rules in the style sheet. I add a selector and rule to make it blue like the other headings:

```
/*THESE CONTROL THE PROFILE. NOTE THAT SOME OF THE SELECTORS CURRENTLY HAVE NO
RULES*/
#profile-container { }
#profile-container h2 {color:#224968;}
```

I change XHTML in the Links and Archives headings from h6 to h2, giving my sidebar headin a uniform look. I also want a capital letter A on "archives":

```
<h2>Links</h2>
   <ul>
      <li><a href="http://www.webteacher.ws/">Web Teacher</a></li>
      <li><a href="http://www.vdebolt.com/">Virginia DeBolt</a></li>
      <li><a href="http://www.wiley.com/WileyCDA/WileyTitle/productCd-
047009754X.html">Wiley Publishing</a></li>
   </ul>
<h2>Archives</h2>
```

Of course, there are many more changes I could make in margin, padding, border, and othe properties used in the styles for this template. These examples should be sufficient to get you started with your own weblog modifications.

BLOGGING RESOURCES

Several books have been published that are solely devoted to the topic of blogging. These include:

- *The Power of Many* by Christian Crumlish (Sybex, 2003).
- *Blogging: Genius Strategies for Instant Web Content* by Biz Stone (New Riders, 2002).
- *Who Let the Blogs Out? A Hyperconnected Peek at the World of Weblogs* by Biz Stone (St. Martin's Griffin, 2004). Biz Stone works for Blogger, so this book may contain good tips for Blogger users.
- *The Weblog Handbook: Practical Advice on Creating and Maintaining Your Blog* by Rebecca Blood (Perseus Books Group, 2002).
- *Naked Conversations: How Blogs are Changing the Way Businesses Talk with Customers* by Robert Scoble and Shel Israel (Wiley, 2006).
- *Blog On: Building Online Communities with Web Logs* by Todd Stauffer (McGraw-Hill/Osborne Media).
- *Blogging for Dummies* by Brad Hill (For Dummies, 2006).

There are also books specific to certain weblog types, such as *Sams Teach Yourself Movable Type in 24 Hours* by Porter Glendenning and Molly Holzschlag (Sams, 2004). And there is a chapter about the styling of Eric Meyer's blog, "Thoughts from Eric," in *More Eric Meyer on CSS* by Eric Meyer (New Riders, 2004).

Websites that track blogs are numerous, with Technorati being a favorite at www.technorati.com. Technorati lets you find blogs by topic and by popularity. It's a good place to register your blog if you have one, because you have access to their statistics about incoming links and other information when you're registered there. Bloglines at www.bloglines.com manages your blog subscriptions, lets you search blogs, and offers to publish your blog.

WordPress Hosted Free

Sign up for a new blog with WordPress at http://wordpress.com/signup. You supply a user name and your e-mail. You can opt to have the username serve as the blog name or create the blog name later. Your URL will be http://*somename*.wordpress.com, where *somename* is a nar you create (see Figure 13.20).

You will receive an e-mail giving you a password and allowing you to activate the new blog. When you activate it, you are shown your URL—this example is `http://mastering.wordpress.com`—and asked to give your blog a title (see Figure 13.21).

Once the blog is established and the account is active, further sign-ins to the account take place at `http://`*`somename`*`.wordpress.com/wp-login.php`. When you are signed in to your blog account, a blue bar across the top of the blog provides access to a Dashboard and various controls for your blog. My Account ➤ Edit Profile lets you change your password and define your blog a bit. See Figure 13.22, where the blue bar is shown against the default WordPress blog theme.

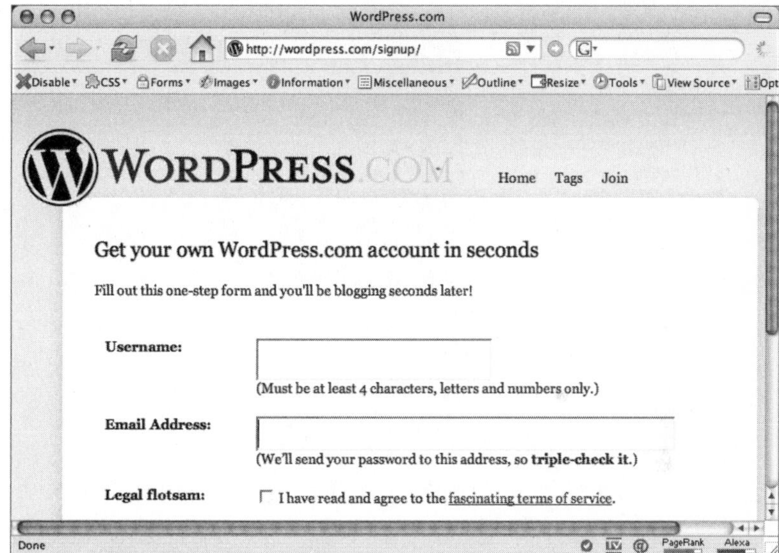

FIGURE 13.20 The signup is simple for a WordPress blog.

FIGURE 13.21 When you activate your WordPress blog, you give it a title and learn your URL.

To configure the blog, work your way through each of the options. You can perform tasks such as adding links to your blogroll, writing new posts, and setting up users (see Figure 13.23).

Blogs are one place where outgoing links are valuable. In WordPress, these go in the blogroll. You link to your favorite blogs, and you hope that other bloggers link to you. This increases your visibility and your traffic. One way to get noticed by other bloggers is to go their site and leave a comment. They may return the visit and add you to their outgoing links as a result.

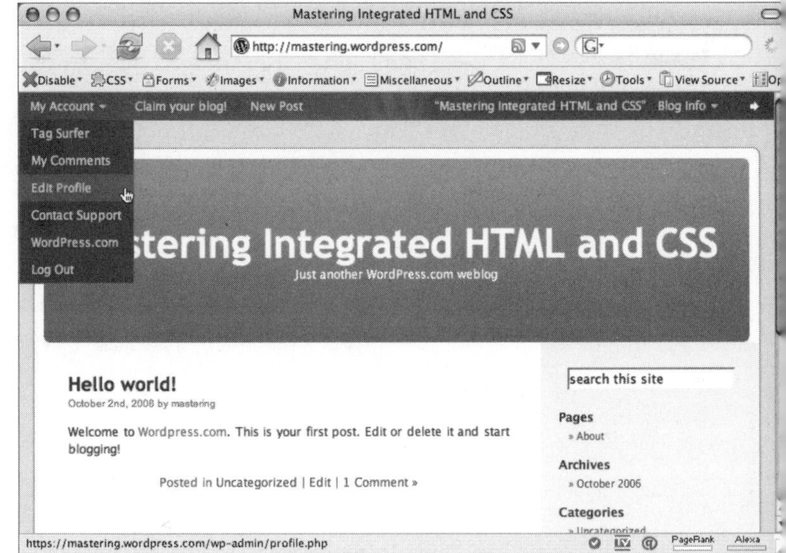

FIGURE 13.22
This is the default WordPress theme. When you are signed in to your blog, you have access to a number of menu options in a bar across the top of the screen.

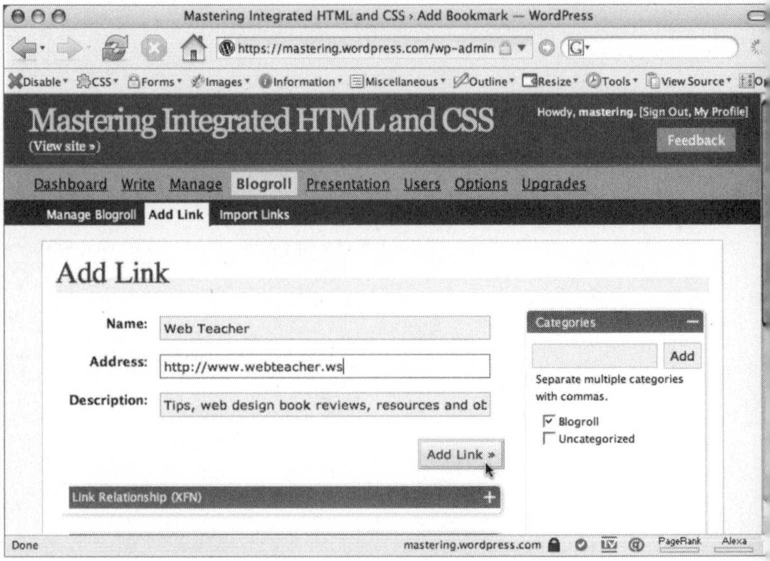

FIGURE 13.23
Adding links is simple, with no knowledge of HTML required.

You will probably spend some time as you first set up the blog on the option called Presentation. Here's where you choose the template—WordPress calls them "themes"—you like (see Figure 13.24).

Under the Presentation options for the theme I selected, I can choose my own header image (see Figure 13.25). There's an Edit CSS option under Presentation, too, but it is not free. You can pay for an upgrade and edit the CSS for the theme you've picked, as described earlier in the chapter.

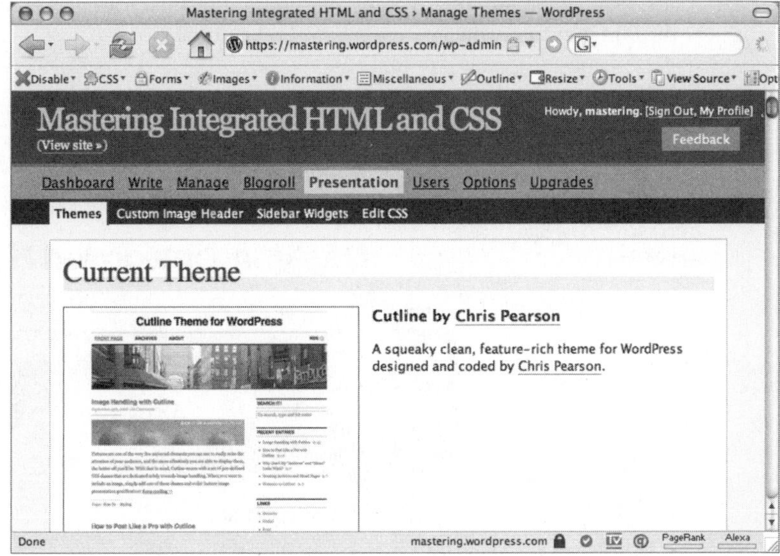

FIGURE 13.24
Under Presentation, you scroll down the page to find a theme you like. When clicked, it appears at the top of the page as your selected theme.

FIGURE 13.25
The theme I selected has an option to allow me to upload my own header image.

Choosing a new theme or uploading your own header image results in an instant change in t way the blog is rendered. You can see your progress in configuring the site at any time by clicki the View Site link. Figure 13.26 shows my site after I've clicked the View Site link.

An advantage of WordPress (and any other blog with the same functionality) is the ability to c ate categories for your posts. This creates very helpful menu items that link to all the posts you' written in a particular category. Categories give a blog some organization and are much more u ful than a mere archive. You invent your own categories and add the names under the Categor heading on the Write Post page (see Figure 13.27).

FIGURE 13.26 As you choose a theme or make changes, you can view the changes instantly by clicking View Site, as I've done here.

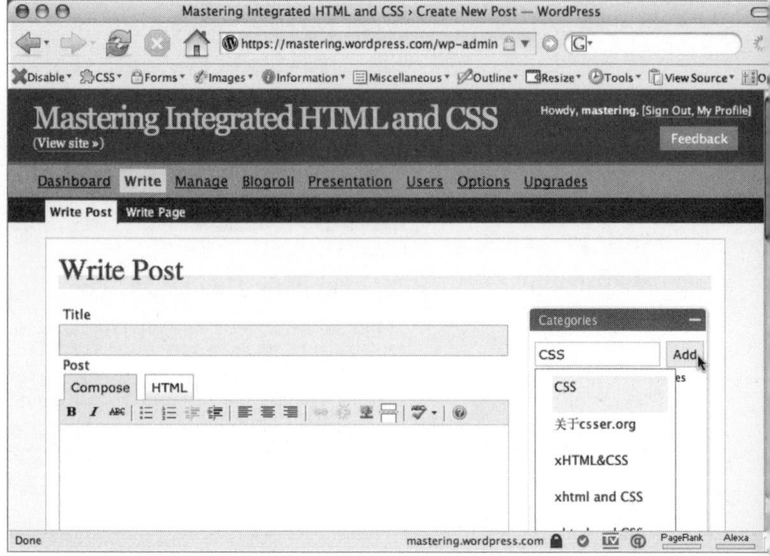

FIGURE 13.27 WordPress has a feature that categorizes posts, which is very helpful in organizing your site.

Another very nice feature at WordPress is the ability to create pages (see Figure 13.28).

New pages are static XHTML pages, not blog posts. The method for creating and editing them is the just the same as for posts, but they are not posts. They are for material on your site that you want everyone to have access to all the time, such as a FAQ about participating in a community blog. They are linked separately on the blog menu. The location of the link depends on the theme you pick—the theme in the example has a page called "About" in the menu at the top. Each new page uses the blog theme, so if you choose a different theme, all the pages change to match.

AN EXAMPLE

A WordPress-hosted blog that I keep up is First 50 Words (`http://first50.wordpress.com`). This blog is for creative writing practice. The subject matter may not interest you, but you can see a more fully developed set of categories, blogroll links, posts, and pages there.

FIGURE 13.28
On the Write menu you can choose to create a new post or a new page.

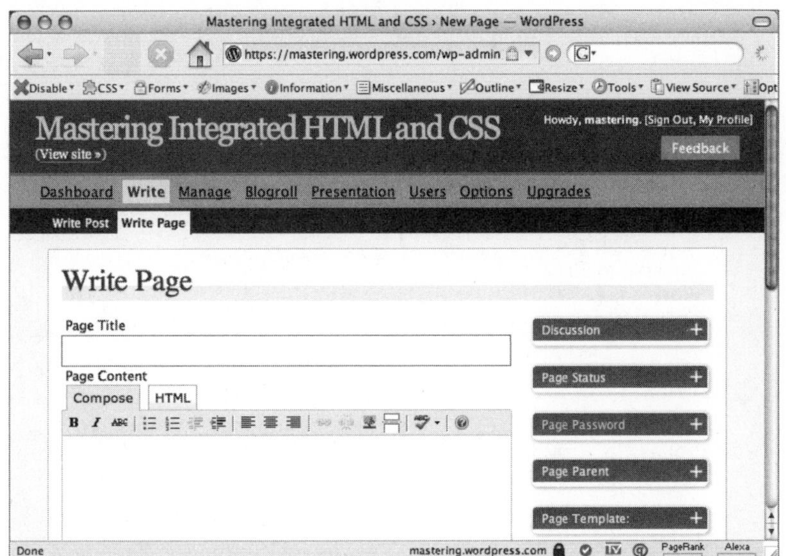

Publishing to Your WordPress Blog

WordPress provides a form where you enter your post, similar to the one you saw previously at blogger.com. Sign in to the blog and go to the Dashboard. Select Write ➤ Write Post. The post form opens (see Figure 13.29).

Some WordPress themes have an Edit option available to the signed-in blog owner on each post. This theme does not, but all WordPress posts are available for editing under Manage ➤ Posts (see Figure 13.30).

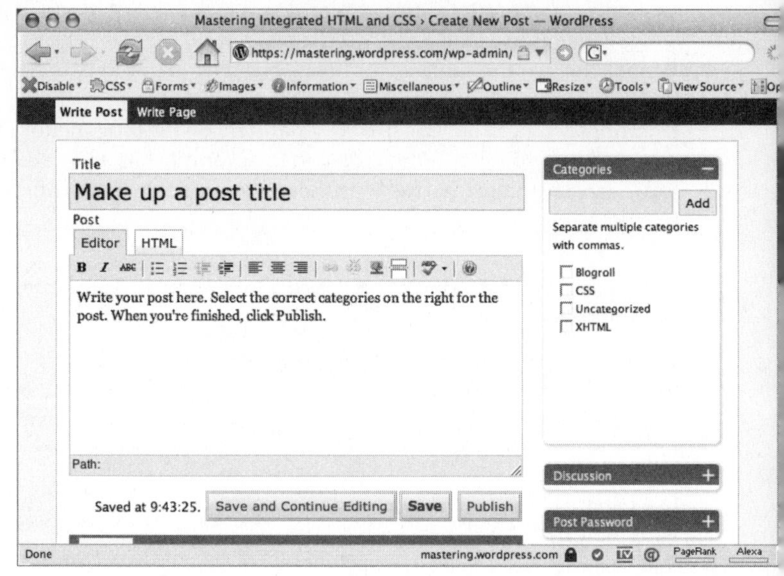

FIGURE 13.29
Write a title and your post in these form fields. Select the categories for the post on the right. You can Save, Save and Continue Editing, or Publish when you've finished. Scroll down the page and you find an upload image field that permits you to add images to a post.

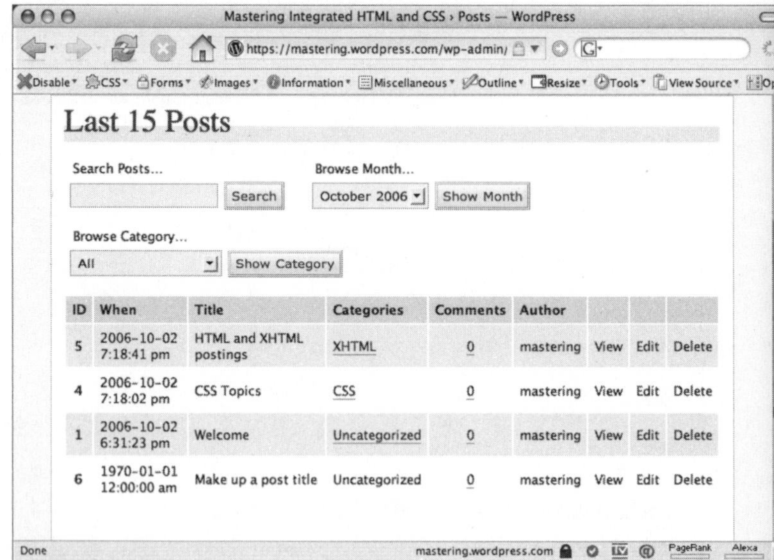

FIGURE 13.30
Any post can be viewed, edited, deleted, or recategorized from the Manage ➤ Posts menu.

WordPress on Your Server

If you want to download and install WordPress on your own server, start at `www.wordpress.org`. Note that the download packages are at `wordpress.org`, not `wordpress.com`. The server you're using must have PHP and MySQL. WordPress recommends Apache or Litespeed but says that any server with PHP and MySQL will do. The download is free from WordPress.

Unlike publishing a Blogger blog on your own server, with WordPress the software is on your server, and you are not tied in to any resource but your own server when you publish your blog.

You download a ZIP or TAR file, which you unzip onto your hard drive. WordPress has two sets of installation instructions: a five-minute install, which lists a few steps, or a detailed installation manual if you need it.

You must go to your server and set up a MySQL database, probably using the C-panel (described briefly in Chapter 12). Don't let the words "set up a MySQL database" worry you. You'll find it only involves a few steps in the C-panel, and your hosting company will have Help files if you need them.

When the database is ready and waiting, make some simple changes to a couple of the files in the WordPress package you unzipped. The WordPress instructions tell you exactly what to change. Then upload everything to the location you want the blog to have on your server. Open a browser to a particular file mentioned in the WordPress instructions, click a choice or two, and you have your own working blog on your own server.

Everything works like the examples from WordPress in the previous section, except now you have access to all the files, including the CSS. Here's how to find the style sheets. For example, suppose you put the WordPress package in a directory on your server called `blog`. Further, suppose that you are using the theme called `classic`. Follow this path to find the CSS file: `blog` ➤ `wp-content` ➤ `themes` ➤ `classic` ➤ `style.css`. You can do anything you want to the CSS.

The CSS is exactly like what you've learned about in this book. The rest of WordPress is written in PHP, which is beyond the scope of this book. If you want to completely create your own theme you need to learn enough about PHP to figure out how all the bits and pieces of PHP fit into the overall page creation. If you open any of the PHP files, you'll see some recognizable XHTML, so it isn't as daunting as it sounds.

WordPress Resources

WordPress 2: Visual Quickstart Guide by Maria Langer and Miraz Jordan (Peachpit Press, 2006) will help you with WordPress and getting around in the PHP. A book mentioned previously in this chapter, *Blogging for Dummies* by Brad Hill, also has WordPress information.

WordPress allows the use of plug-ins, which add functionality to a blog. With the right plug-ins, you can make a WordPress blog into a content management system. The WordPress Codex contains the complete guide to WordPress, including this information about plug-ins: `http://codex.wordpress.org/Plugins`.

Real-World Scenario

When you have a very popular blog, advertising dollars come pouring in your direction. Two of t most popular are Engadget and Boing Boing.

Engadget

Engadget is about products and gadgets (`www.engadget.com`); see Figure 13.31.

The site covers all sorts of products: phones, PDA, audio, GPS devices, computers, cameras, games, home entertainment, and much more. It allows comments, so consumers can add their ov thoughts about the products featured on Engadget. We live in an age where consumers love to compare notes on their toys and get in on the latest big thing. Engadget honed in on that and h a loyal readership and plenty of interested advertisers as a result. Thousands of people subscri to Engadget's feed, and there are thousands of incoming links.

FIGURE 13.31 Engadget features new products and gadgets.

Boing Boing

This site bills itself as "a directory of wonderful things" and is highly eclectic in its approach to wh might, in fact, be a wonderful thing (`www.boingboing.net`). It could be an event, a product, a ne item, a podcast, a VW bus with gull-wing doors, a snapshot of the way an eBay purchase was pack or a Photoshop contest. There's no predicting what will catch the interest of Boing Boing. Much o is irreverent and possibly even offensive—you've been warned (see Figure 13.32).

The site has a large following, with many comments on its posts. Like Engadget, thousands people subscribe to Boing Boing's feed, and there are thousands of incoming links.

These two sites, or any blog that brings in lots of traffic, can bring in lots of advertiser mone (You must customize the blog to place the ads in the template or theme in order for them to appea By their very nature, blogs are updated regularly with fresh content. If you hit on a formula th appeals to a high enough percentage of the population and keeps them coming back day after d for more, you may manage to make a living simply by blogging.

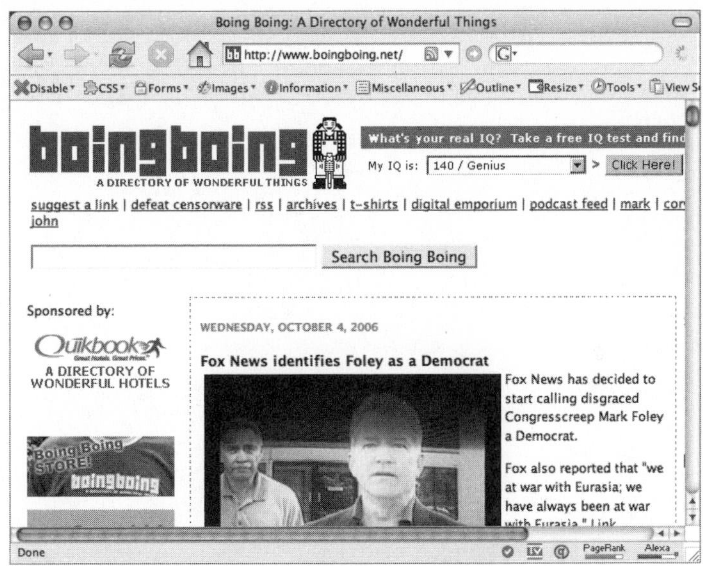

FIGURE 13.32
The unpredictably irreverent Boing Boing takes a look at the world's "wonderful things."

The Bottom Line

Weblogs are popular because they are easy and flexible. Sites sometimes include blogs as a part of the overall site plan. Sometimes a site is built completely as a blog.

Describe the advantage of blogs over traditional sites. A blog is a website, but it has certain characteristics that distinguish it from a traditional website.

Master It List at least three advantages of blogging over traditional websites.

Understand how to create a blog. Some blogs you must download and install. Others let you answer a few basic questions, give you free hosting, and you're publishing.

Master It You can delete a blog as instantly as you can create one. Create one of your own at either BlogSpot or WordPress.

Identify features of Blogger and WordPress blogs. Differences between Blogger and WordPress (or Movable Type, Typepad, or others) will determine which one is right for you.

Master It Complete the table in the file `blogs.html` from the accompanying CD. Fill in the missing columns with Yes or No to indicate the presence of a feature. You can use a qualified Yes or No answer if needed. As an option, add another column for any other blog software you are interested in researching.

Identify ways to configure and customize a blog. You can use what you know about XHTML and CSS to take the basic elements for a blog and add your own designs and modifications to make a unique and distinctive blog.

Master It Make changes to the blog you created in the preceding exercise. Be able to identify the places where you customized.

Chapter 14

Design Basics

Creating a web page is a form of visual communication. There are exceptions to this, of course, but most of the time website creators are concerned with appearance and how the visual elements work together to convey their message.

In this chapter you will explore a few of the basic design ideas that can make your web pages more successful. Design is a huge topic, so this chapter narrows things down significantly and focuses only on a few major concepts related to web page design.

To get the most out of this chapter, refer to the "Real-World Scenario" near the end of each chapter to reexamine those sites in terms of the design principles covered here; once you've done that, you may find yourself bringing a designer's perspective to almost every site you visit.

In this chapter you will:

- Understand the basics of creating a visual hierarchy.
- Examine the ways to create contrast.
- Examine the value of repetition in web design.
- Understand how alignment and proximity can affect a web page design.

Wireframes

Wireframes are like schematics or blueprints for websites. They help visualize the layout, the content, the navigation, header and footer, and so on.

A wireframe is a simple sketch that focuses on how a site works, rather than on an actual design. Wireframes can be created in any media: on paper, with graphing software, in HTML, or in Photoshop. Part of the purpose of wireframes is to remove the design so that it does not distract from the way the site will work. Some designers even recommend sticking to grayscale so there won't be any color to attract the eye or represent a design feature.

Elements that go into a comprehensive wireframe of a home page or a site template should include header, footer, navigation, content of various kinds, logos, labels, and image placeholders. But these elements should be conceived as placeholders (frames made of wire) and not designed elements. The design comes later. You simply want a basic schema for where the common web objects will be placed on a page.

In the following pages, wireframe-like page diagrams are used to make various points about page design. There are no exercise files on the accompanying CD for this chapter.

Layout

Web pages open at the top left of the page (for languages such as English). The height from the t and the width from the left within the user's view of the page depends entirely on the device bei used to display the page. Web page layouts are top heavy—the most important information nee to be at the top of the page. The term often used—borrowed from the newspaper world—is to p the main content "above the fold." In terms of a newspaper, the big stories must be at the top of t page so that they can be seen on the news stands before the page is unfolded. In terms of a web page, the concept of being above the fold refers to that part of the page the user sees before scrollir There's really no way to know how much of a page is revealed to an individual user, so the top loading of information is important for vital items.

The above-the-fold logic leads to page designs that start like Figure 14.1, where site identific tion and main navigation are clustered near the top left of the page.

A logo is an important orientation element. It helps the user understand where they are. Testi confirms that most users expect a logo to be in the top-left corner of the page and that they look there to find it.

The idea of putting the main design elements near the top of a design doesn't necessarily apply to other types of design such as art or advertising or textiles, but it is important in we page layout.

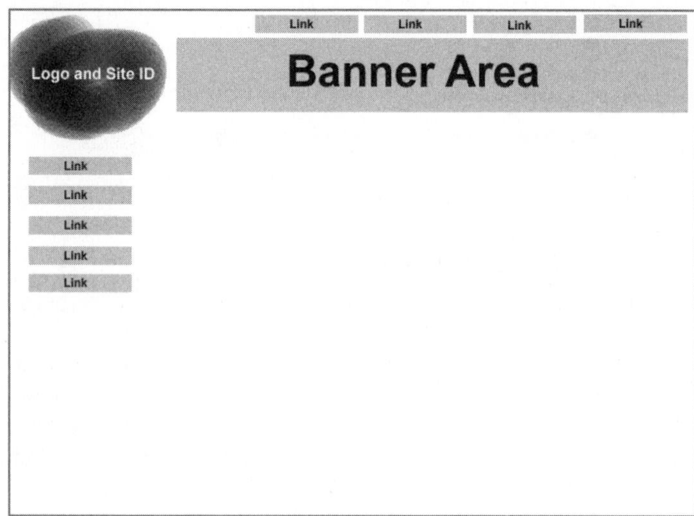

FIGURE 14.1 Important elements need to be seen at a glance with no scrolling, so they are often clustered near the top left of a page.

Visual Hierarchy

In order to communicate effectively, the design must establish a visual hierarchy for the viewer. It must let the viewer see at a glance what's the most important content on the page and how the various items are related to each other.

One way to establish hierarchy is to create a focal point. The focal point draws the viewer's attention by being strong in the sense that it dominates the page. It screams, "Look here! This is the most important thing on the page!" Focal points are created with contrast. It can be contrast in size, color, texture, balance, or form, as shown in Figure 14.2.

Headings are important in setting up a visual hierarchy. The six possible heading elements in XHTML are one way to create hierarchy. An `h1` is of more importance in the visual hierarchy than an `h2`.

The heading must lead the eye directly to the related content. Robin Williams, in her wonderful book *The Non-Designer's Design Book* (listed in the resources section at the end of the chapter), calls this idea "proximity." Items that are related must be in close proximity to one another. Without the help of proximity to lead the eye from one element to the element related to it, the visual hierarchy falls apart and any sense of what the page is about begins to get fuzzy. As you see in Figure 14.3, it appears that the heading is related to the element below it, when, in fact, it's meant to relate to the text quite some distance away. That's a proximity problem.

It isn't enough to merely put the heading above the related content. It must look related by proximity as well. For example, in Figure 14.4, the B heading looks as if it is related to the text right above it! Figure 14.5 shows an arrangement that is easier to understand.

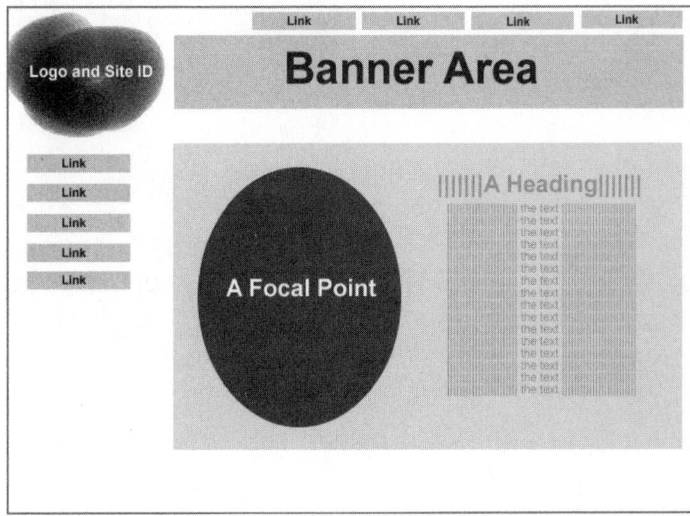

FIGURE 14.2
Several types of contrast create this focal point: light and dark, size and shape, variety, color, and alignment.

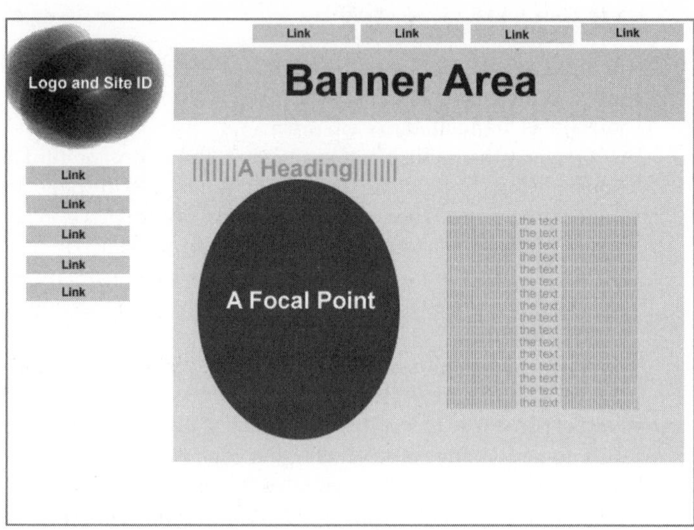

FIGURE 14.3
If the heading is not in close proximity to the text it heads, then the visual hierarchy of the page is muddled and the user can't make sense of your organization.

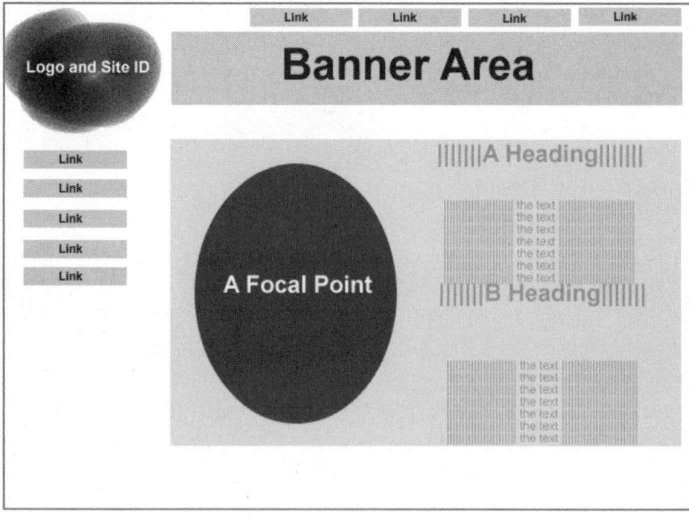

FIGURE 14.4
The B heading and the text it heads don't appear to be related by proximity in this arrangement.

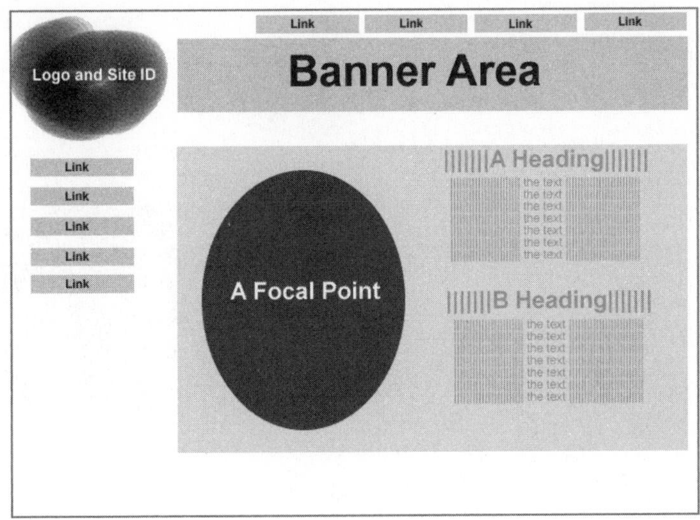

FIGURE 14.5 This layout creates a much more understandable visual hierarchy, with the headings in close proximity to the text they head.

More about Contrast

Contrast is used in web pages to create rollover effects and current page indicators (Figure 14.6). Current page indicators are an important aspect of the visual hierarchy of the page, because they help users stay oriented and let them know where they are and where they can go next.

Contrast can be created with form or variety as well—creating difference creates contrast. The simple addition of a different shape by one of the links (Figure 14.7) is enough contrast to create a current page indicator.

You need to consider contrast when you make your choices for the site's color scheme. It is particularly important that the contrast between the color in the background and the color of the foreground text be great enough to be distinguishable even by the color-blind or low-vision users of your site. When thinking about contrast, remember that the user may have different background and foreground color settings than your defaults. Setting background and foreground colors for major page elements is important in making sure your contrasting colors work.

If you use background images, the contrast between any colors, patterns, or textures in the background and colors in the foreground text must be sufficient or the text becomes difficult to see.

Headings, of course, are meant to contrast in size with the text they head, as well as different levels of headings. You can create contrast with typefaces or fonts, as well. In Figure 14.8, the playful nature of the font in A Heading is quite a contrast from the staid sans-serif of the remaining fonts on the page. A playful font also creates a contrasting emotional tone for the element.

Don't get carried away with typefaces and use eight or ten on a page, however. Remember the need for consistency in your pages, which is achieved through repetition.

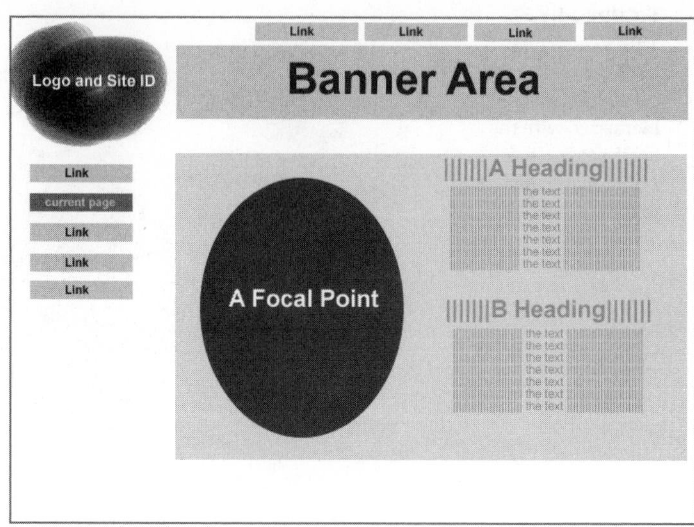

FIGURE 14.6
Contrast is used to create a current page indicator.

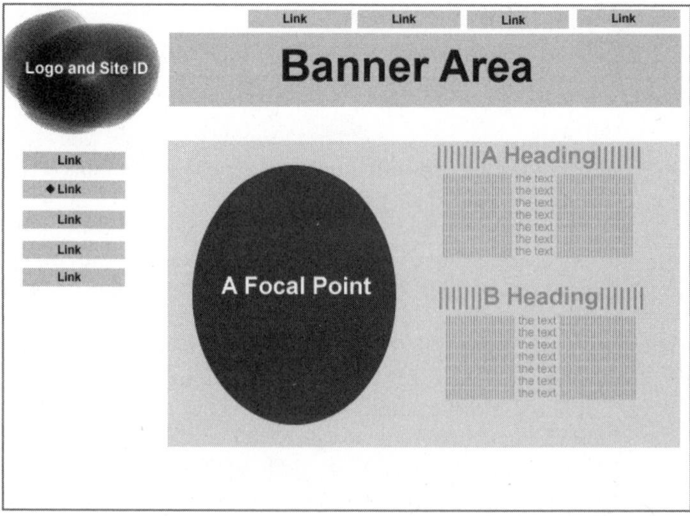

FIGURE 14.7
The diamond shape next to one link creates a contrasting element, distinguishing it from the other links.

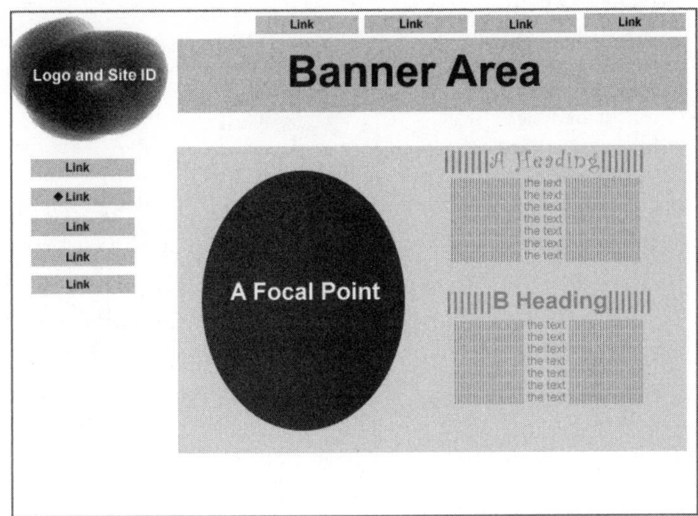

FIGURE 14.8
The use of typography and various fonts can create focal points and contrast and add to a sense of visual hierarchy and emphasis.

Consistency and Repetition

Pages in your site have to be consistently designed. The placement of elements on the page, the location of the navigation, the colors used, the fonts used—all these things must be consistent throughout the site. This consistency is achieved partly through repetition. Repetition ties things together that aren't connected by proximity. For example, in Figure 14.9, the repetition of the same font for several elements on the page such as logo, banner, and headings ties the page together in a consistent design.

You see repetition in Figure 14.9 in the size and shape of the links, both on the left main menu area and at the upper right where one presumes the site utilities would be.

You don't want the footer to be a focal point (Figure 14.10), so design it with minimal contrast elements: small sizes, lighter colors, and repeating use of the less showy font used on the page.

Adding the footer to the page in alignment with other page elements brings up another important design basic—alignment.

FANCY FONTS

An unusual font such as the fanciful one in Figure 14.9 probably has to be inserted on the page as an image. You should not assume that the average viewer of your page has such a specialized font installed on their computer.

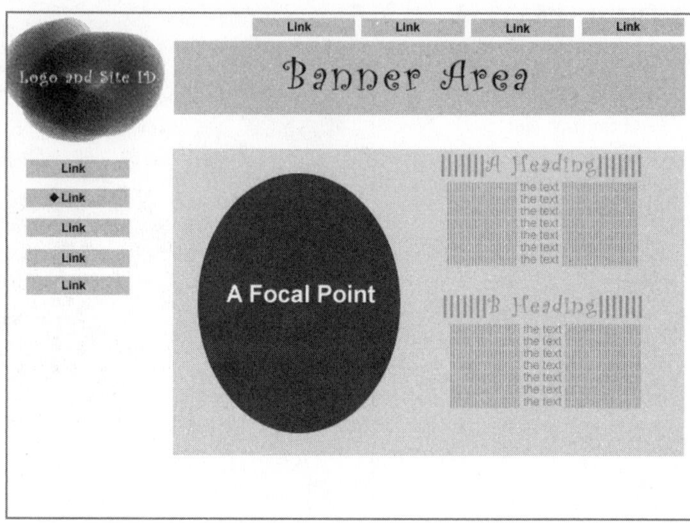

FIGURE 14.9
Use repetition in font, size, color, or placement to create a consistent design from page to page.

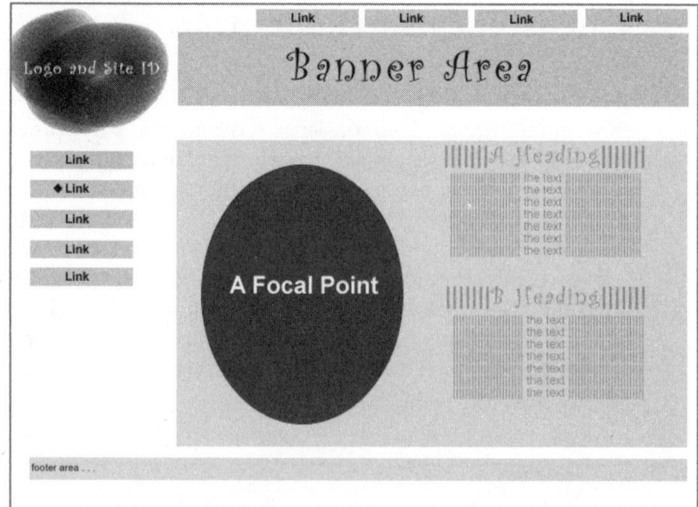

FIGURE 14.10
Repeat design elements such as fonts in the footer, but do so in ways that decrease the emphasis on that part of the design.

Alignment

Elements on a page can be aligned left, right, centered, and—for text—justified. In Figure 14.10, t paragraph areas called "the text" are justified. To make lines of text align on the right as well as t left, the software must adjust the spaces between letters and words. In the real world, using jus fied text on the web is chancy. Not all browsers implement it correctly, and it can lead to strang large gaps between words in some situations, making the text hard to read and odd looking.

For English and similar languages, left-aligned text (or ragged-right text, as it is also called), li that in Figure 14.11, is easier to read than either centered or right-aligned text.

If I change the layout so that the text in the paragraphs is centered (Figure 14.12), the footer is centered on the page, and the navigation on the upper right is centered within the right column. The design no longer seems to hang together or look unified, and things seem accidentally placed on the page.

I have seen sites where every single thing on the page was centered down the same center line. This is very difficult to read and makes establishing a visual hierarchy next to impossible. You can see what I mean in Figure 14.13, where a text-heavy page you are familiar with is centered.

Right alignment can be effective in small doses for contrast or variety—perhaps with headings or as in the navigation at the upper right, but most elements, especially paragraphs, would be hard to read, as in Figure 14.14.

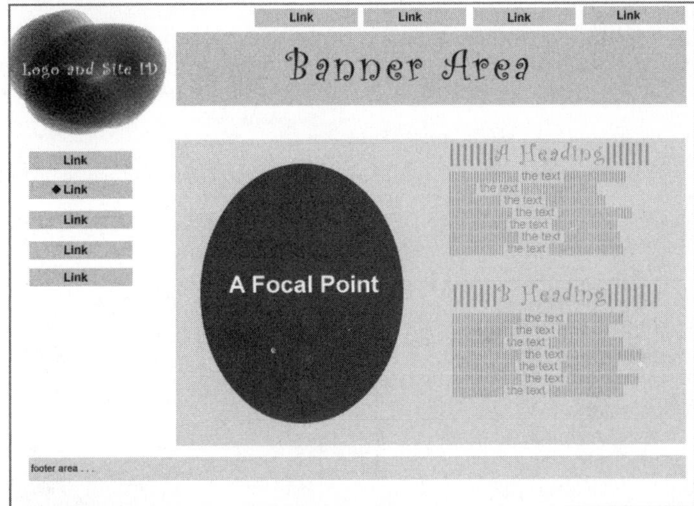

FIGURE 14.11 The paragraph text is left aligned, as is every other element on the page except the navigation at the upper right. The navigation in the upper right is aligned right.

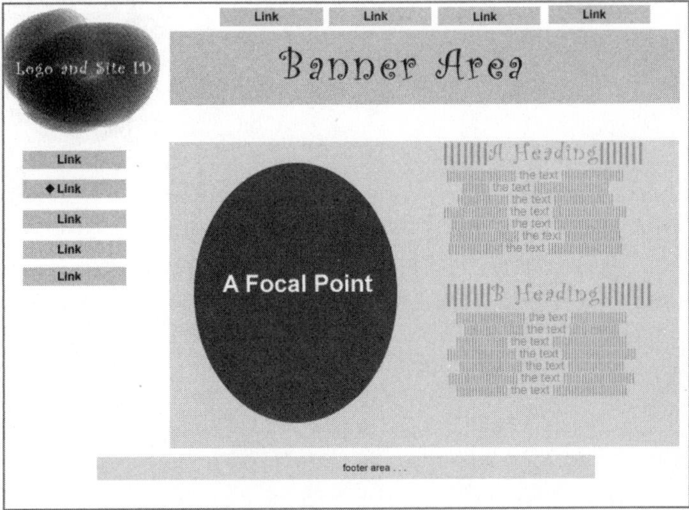

FIGURE 14.12 Centering the paragraph text, the footer, and the top navigation does not look good and makes the paragraph text very hard to read.

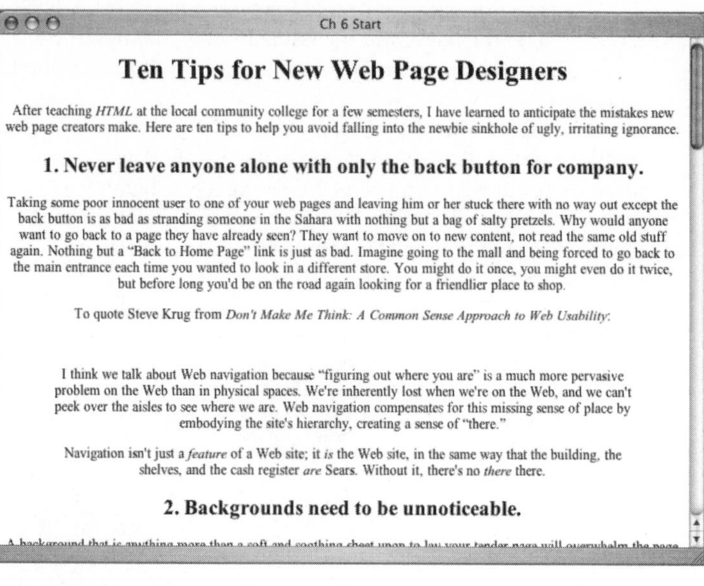

FIGURE 14.13
Centering elements should not be avoided in every situation, but for this page, centering is a very bad idea.

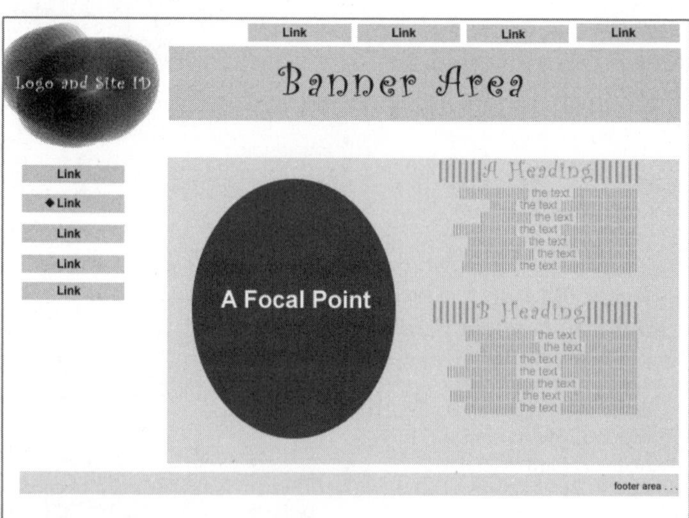

FIGURE 14.14
Making everything right aligned looks planned and organized, but the paragraphs are hard to read. Use right alignment in small doses.

For this example page, left alignment for everything but the top navigation works best. Note th left alignment does not mean that everything is lined up on the left side of the page. It simply mea that most of the elements on the page share left alignment, and further, the various elements are ting on shared imaginary alignment lines. The eye connects elements along these invisible line

I've added some lines to Figures 14.15 and 14.16 so you can see where elements repeatedly use the same lines to establish unity in the design.

To wind up the case for alignment, look at a page (Figure 14.17) that has no common alignment or shared lines of alignment. Eek, what a mess!

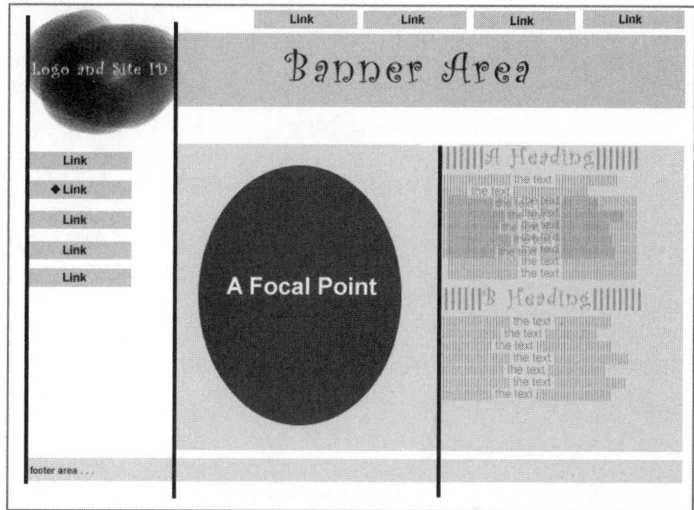

FIGURE 14.15
Heavy lines mark the places on the page where elements are visually connected to other elements by their shared left alignment.

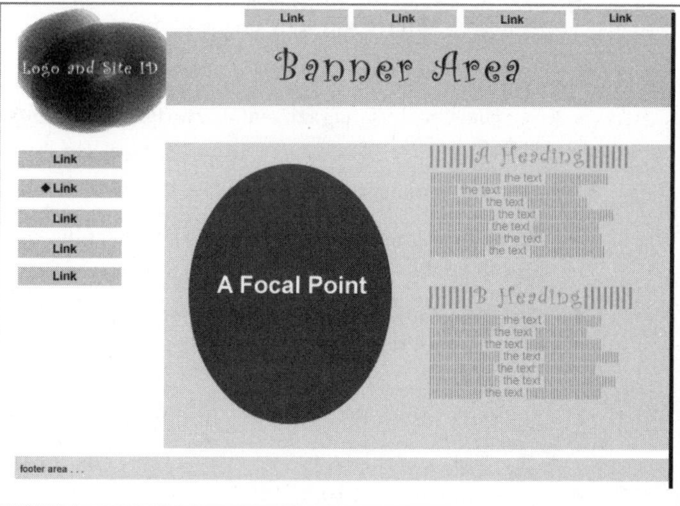

FIGURE 14.16
Several elements on the page are visually connected by the same line on the right.

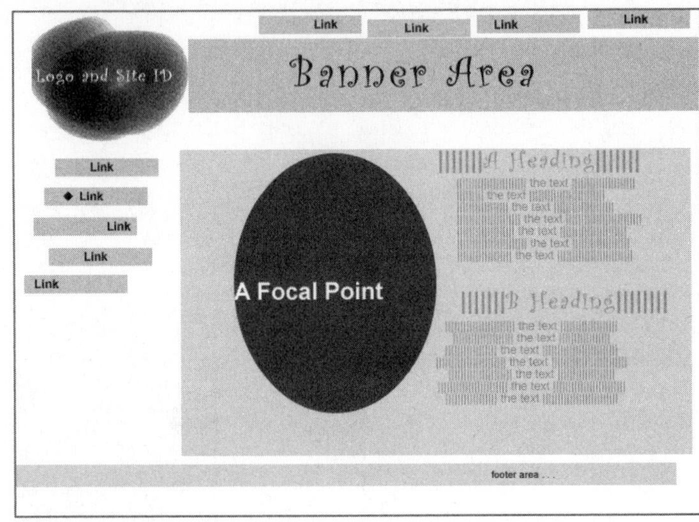

FIGURE 14.17
An alignment nightmare, which serves to show you what a difference a line makes, even an invisible line.

Resources

If you would like to extend your knowledge of design, here are some suggestions to get you start

General design resources include:

- *Dmitry's Design Lab* on WebReference.com at `www.webreference.com/dlab` contains artic written by Dmitry Kirsanov on the basics of design proper.
- Graphics.com at `www.graphics.com` has tips and resources for creative design.
- *Dynamic Graphics* magazine at www.dynamicgraphics.com has articles and tutorials on design.

Typography resources include:

- Planet Typography at `www.planet-typography.com` has typography information and downloadable fonts.
- Web Style Guide: Typography at `www.webstyleguide.com/type` discusses a number o factors about typography. This entire guide, not just the section on type, is a good over resource.

Resources for inspiration display award-winning or exceptionally designed sites. Some suc sites include:

- Inspiration King at `www.inspirationking.com`
- CSS Beauty at `www.cssbeauty.com`
- Net Diver at `www.netdiver.net`

- Style Gala at `www.stylegala.com`
- Web Standards Awards at `www.webstandardsawards.com`

Color resources offer help with finding a compatible color scheme to ensuring the contrast between colors works for all users. Such sites include:

- Web Whirlers at `www.webwhirlers.com/colors`
- HTML Basics: Choosing a Color at `www.devx.com/projectcool/Article/19817/page/1`
- Color Schemer Online at `www.colorschemer.com/online.html`
- VisCheck simulates color blindness at `www.vischeck.com`

Helpful books include:

- *The Non-Designer's Design Book* by Robin Williams (Peachpit Press, 2004). If you've never had any art or design training, this is the book for you.
- *The Non-Designer's Web Book* by Robin Williams and John Tollett (Peachpit Press, 3rd edition, 2005). The good design versus bad design comparisons are powerful design lessons.
- *Fresh Styles for Web Designers: Eye Candy from the Underground* by Curt Cloninger (New Riders, 2001). Inspirational idea book.
- *The Web Design WOW Book* by Jack Davis and Susan Merritt (Peachpit Press, 1998). Another inspirational idea book.

Real-World Scenario

The two examples for this chapter make heavy use of images. Also consider other sites with more text, perhaps the *New York Times* site you looked at in an earlier chapter, to understand more about the principles of design for sites with heavy use of text.

The Mirror Project

The Mirror Project at `www.mirrorproject.com` is a fascinating community site. Members send photos of themselves as reflections—not just reflections in mirrors, but in any reflective surface such as puddles, the side of a truck, a doll's eye, or an oven door. The site is all about the images, and the navigation is organized around browsing through the images in various ways (see Figures 14.18 and 14.19).

Inner pages repeat the color scheme of the home page. The colors are muted to make the images the focal point of each page. All inner pages are consistent in design and layout, keeping the focus on the photos.

The images on the home page are links to the latest contributions to the site and serve as navigation leading into the latest photos. The traditional navigation links are placed at the lower right of the page. For this site, breaking the above-the-fold guideline for traditional navigation placement works, because return visitors want quick access to the newest photos.

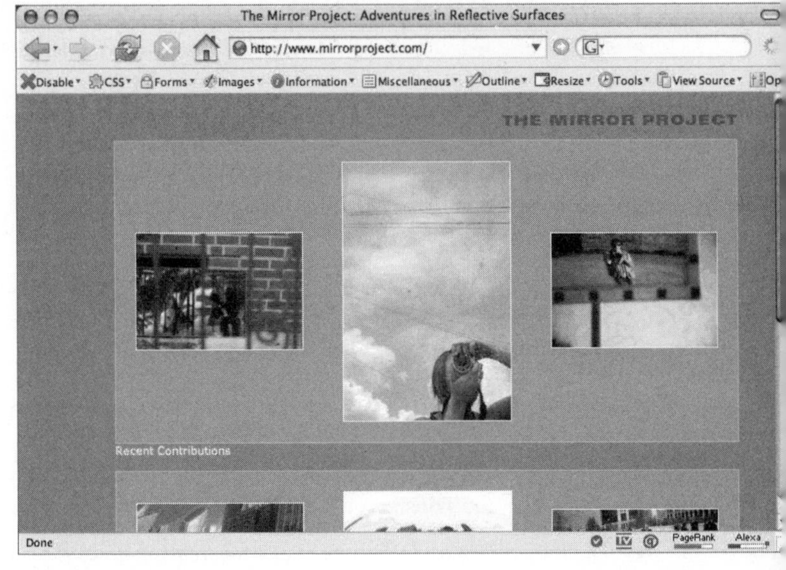

FIGURE 14.18
The home page of The Mirror Project shows attention to color, contrast, size, and alignment and emphasizes the images in the visual hierarchy of the page. Navigation is at the bottom of the page (not shown).

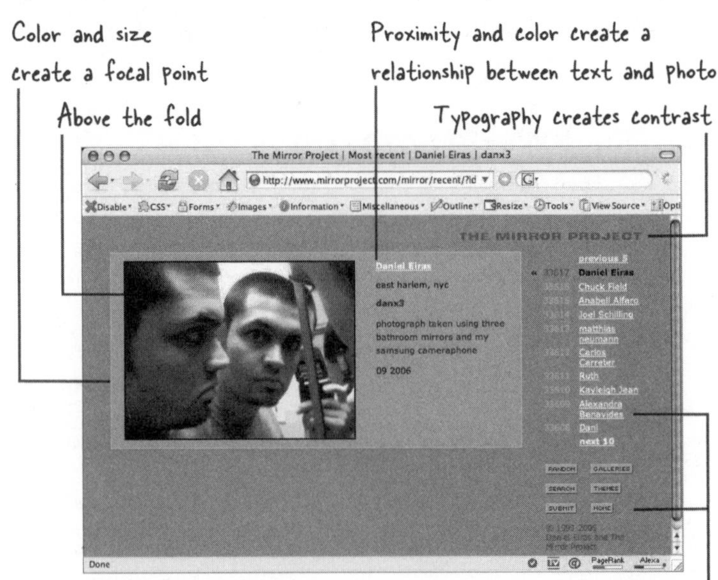

FIGURE 14.19
An inner page of The Mirror Project where the focal point is a particular photo sent in by a community member. Note the careful alignment of the menu items on the right.

Museum Victoria

Museum Victoria is the site of an Australian museum at `http://museum.vic.gov.au`. The home page shows careful attention to hierarchy, alignment, and contrast (see Figure 14.20).

In the Virtual Showcase at Museum Victoria, one of the collections is called "Caught and Coloured" (`www.museum.vic.gov.au/caughtandcoloured/Collection.aspx`). It shows a large collection of zoological illustrations from Colonial Victoria (see Figure 14.21). The images are laid out in divs, not in a table, with each one linking to a further collection of illustrations of that type.

On both of the Museum Victoria pages shown, the main navigation is at the top and left of the page or above the fold.

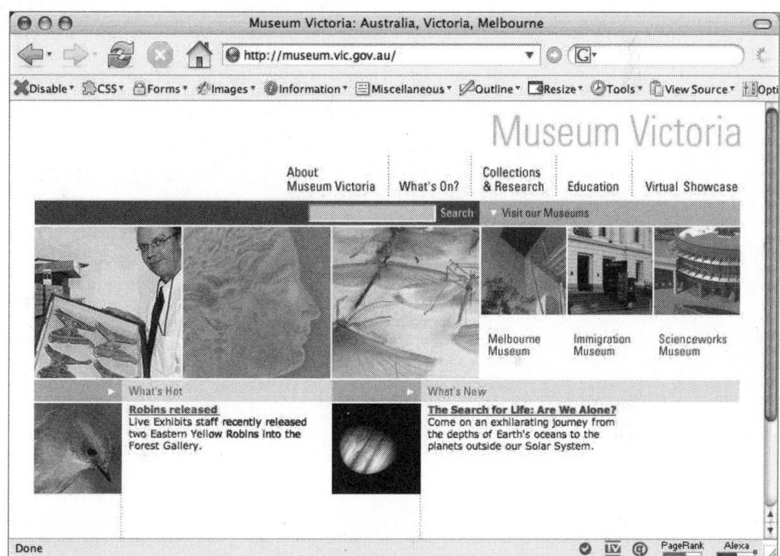

FIGURE 14.20 Everything is aligned perfectly on the Museum Victoria page, with text, images, colored bars, and other page elements above the fold. Focal points are created with rotating images in the larger image blocks.

CSS Properties

Every factor of visual design is achieved with CSS, but there were no new CSS properties discussed in this chapter.

The Bottom Line

In this chapter, you dipped a toe into the ocean of design by looking at some of the factors that are important in designing web pages. You discovered more about the importance of consistent design, or repetition in design. In addition, you learned about the importance of careful alignment of page elements to create unity in your designs.

Understand the basics of creating a visual hierarchy. Create visual hierarchy with above-the-fold layout, size, placement, contrast, and headings.

Master It Visit `www.oneida.com` and explain how this site creates a visual hierarchy.

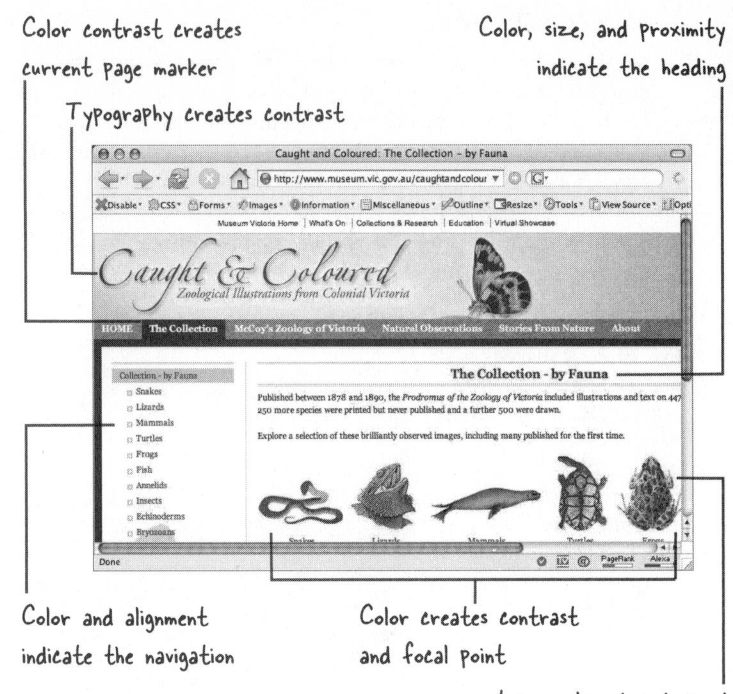

FIGURE 14.21
The "Caught and Coloured" showcase in the museum shows illustrations in a neatly aligned array of div elements.

Examine the ways to create contrast. Contrast can be achieved with size, color, typograph form, or placement.

Master It Visit `www.bethmeth.com` and explain how this site creates contrast.

Examine the value of repetition in web design. The placement of elements on the page, th location of the navigation, the colors used, the fonts used—all these things must be consister throughout the site. This consistency is achieved partly through repetition. Repetition ties things together that aren't connected by proximity.

Master It Explore the inner pages of the Oneida site. Explain how the site uses repetiti to create a consistent look on their inner pages.

Understand how alignment and proximity can affect a web page design. Alignment and proximity create unity and connection in a design; they create a relationship between the sep rate design elements.

Master It Visit `www.campaignmonitor.com` and explain how this site uses alignment ar proximity.

Chapter 15

XHTML and CSS for Handhelds

More and more people each day access the Internet with a small, handheld, mobile device such as a cell phone, BlackBerry, or PDA (Personal Digital Assistant) such as a Palm Pilot. These devices, because of their screen sizes and the various technologies they rely on, present significant challenges to the web author attempting to create a universally accessible, attractive site. As the numbers of potential users of such devices continues to grow, it becomes important to provide what usability and accessibility help you can to browsers visiting with handhelds. According to `www.mobiledesign.org`, there are 1.5 billion mobile devices in use. This is a much higher number than the number of computer users. This chapter will help you make your content more accessible to them.

I've stressed two basics throughout this book: clear semantic markup and separation of content from presentation. These basics are all-important in any discussion about content that works in every device. Without them, no style sheet can overcome the accessibility and usability problems your page may have. After you've nailed the basics, creating a style sheet for the `handheld` media type *may* provide help to *some* users of handheld devices.

In this chapter you will:

- Identify some of the obstacles to designing for handheld devices.
- Write styles for the `handheld` media type.
- Examine the available handheld resources and the tools for testing your handheld media styles.

Inherent Obstacles to Web Authoring for Handhelds

As you've seen throughout this book, an important goal of effective web design and authoring is to create sites that work for the widest possible range of users and computer platforms. But there are no standards or consistency in handheld devices capable of web browsing. It's a fractured market. Consider these facts:

- Some devices, especially phones, use only WAP (Wireless Application Protocol). Phones labeled WAP2 can use regular websites with XHTML and CSS.
- Some devices, such as the BlackBerry, offer users a choice between WAP and regular browsing.
- Some devices only support HTML 3.2. Some support HTML 4. Some support XHTML.

- Some devices support CSS. Some do not. Those that do support CSS understand `link` bett than `@import`.
- Some phones apply screen styles as well as handheld styles; others ignore both.
- Screen widths range from 100 pixels to 320 pixels for phones.
- Screen widths range from 320 pixels to 640 pixels for PDAs.
- Some devices have monochromatic screens. Some have color.
- Some software, such as AvantGo on either a phone or a PDA, offer users a choice as to whether they want images to display or not.
- Most devices can't handle tables, floats, frames, JavaScript, pop-ups, or dynamic menus. Some devices, however, will display simply formatted tables and JavaScript when there is a `meta` element declaring the document `HandheldFriendly`.

In light of all those variables, what's a poor designer to do? A solid foundation of semantic markup and separation of content from presentation helps. Beyond that, there are a few basic C rules that will help your handheld visitors who can use CSS.

> **MOBILE RESOURCES**
>
> The previously mentioned `www.mobiledesign.org` is a Yahoo discussion group on mobile design. They have an article giving ten reasons to design for mobile at `www.mobiledesign.org/articles/10_reasons_to_publish_to_mobile.php`.
>
> Mobile Monday at `www.mobilemonday.net/mm/` is a community of mobile industry professionals.
>
> A site to help designers for mobile devices is `www.littlespringsdesign.com`.
>
> *Designing the Mobile User Experience* by Barbara Ballard (Wiley, 2007) is an excellent new book on the topic.

A Solid Foundation

A page that uses the solid foundation of semantic XHTML and separation of content from p sentation, described throughout this book, will help you develop the CSS for a handheld sty sheet.

On the accompanying CD, there is a folder called `handheld` for Chapter 15. Copy the enti folder to your computer. Open the files `ch_15index.html` and `screen.css` in your text edit This is a familiar page (Figure 15.1) that was modified for this chapter. The last time you work with this page was in Chapter 5. See Figures 5.17 and 5.18 for a reminder of how the page looked then.

The revised XHTML in `ch15_index.html` is shown in Listing 15.1. Changes in the XHTML fr the version you used in Chapter 5 are highlighted in the listing.

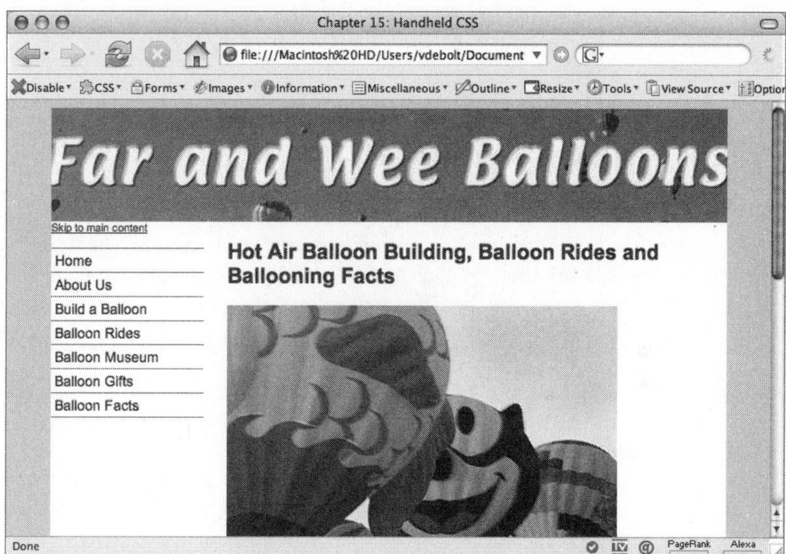

FIGURE 15.1 The modified Far and Wee Balloon page in a normal browser view

LISTING 15.1: The Revised Far and Wee Balloon Page

```
<!DOCTYPE html PUBLIC "-//W3C//DTD XHTML 1.0 Transitional//EN" "http://www.w3.org/
TR/xhtml1/DTD/xhtml1-transitional.dtd">
<html xmlns="http://www.w3.org/1999/xhtml">
<head>
<title>Chapter 15: Handheld CSS</title>
<link href="screen.css" rel="stylesheet" type="text/css" />
</head>
<body>
<div id="container">
  <div id="sitename">
    <h1><span></span>Far and Wee Balloons</h1>
    <!-- end of the sitename div -->
  </div>
  <div id="nav">
  <a href="#content" class="small">Skip to main content</a>
  <ul id="navlist">
  <li><a href="#">Home</a></li>
  <li><a href="#">About Us</a></li>
  <li><a href="#">Build a Balloon </a></li>
  <li><a href="#">Balloon Rides </a></li>
  <li><a href="#">Balloon Museum</a></li>
```

```
    <li><a href="#">Balloon Gifts</a> </li>
    <li><a href="#">Balloon Facts</a></li>
    </ul>
    <!-- end of the nav div -->
    </div>
    <div id="content">
      <h2>Hot Air Balloon Building, Balloon Rides and Ballooning Facts </h2>
      <img src="img/threeballoon.jpg" alt="Some of the styles of hot air balloons
  that our customers might design" width="400" height="300" />
    <p>Welcome to Far and Wee Balloons, where your dreams of floating on air can
  come true. We design and make hot air balloons for every use. Our balloons will
  give you a magical ride over country, mountains, and ocean.</p>
      <p>Come to our famous build-a-balloon design shop and you can enjoy a test
  flight in one of our many pre-made balloons. We organized birthday, anniversary,
  wedding, honeymoon and many other special occasion balloon flights for up to 100
  people!</p>
      <p>Inside these pages you can examine some of the many example balloon photo
  as seen at balloon races, fiestas and rallies all around the world. </p>
      <p>It's all fun at Far and Wee Balloons. Don't wait another minute to begin
  your fun by coming by our Balloon Museum or our famous build-a-balloon design
  shop. Both are located in Timbuktu on the Avon right off US Interstate Highway
  165.</p>
      <h3>The Balloon Museum</h3>
      <p>See balloons from history and do experiments with the science of air. Sta
  in the same gondola that went around the world in 90 days and never made history
  Thrill to the roar of the gas burners and the silence of the wind in our balloon
  flight simulator with surround sound and rock-a-billy motion enhancers. </p>
      <p>Our Balloon Museum computers will let you design your own patterns and
  shapes for the balloon in your future. So get here now! </p>
    <!-- end of the content div -->
    </div>
    <div id="footer">&copy; Far and Wee Balloons, 2007
      <!-- end of the footer div -->
    </div>
  <!-- end of the container div -->
  </div>
  </body>
  </html>
```

Note that the h1 heading contains an empty span element for image replacement. There is a styled #navlist on the page, but the links don't link to actual pages. There is a skip navigation li on the page, too.

The screen.css file sets up the layout and the image replacement rules. See Listing 15.2 for t complete file.

LISTING 15.2: The Screen Media Styles in *screen.css*

```
/*basic structure and organization*/
body {
   font: 100% Arial, Helvetica, sans-serif;
   background: #CCD7FF;
   color: #333333;
}
#container {
   width: 90%;
   background: #FFFFFF;
   margin: 0px auto;
}
#nav {
   width: 25%;
   float: left;
}
#content {
   margin-left: 26%;
}
#footer {
   font-size: 80%;
   clear: both;
   margin-top: 1em;
border-top: 1px solid #648EBA;
padding: 1em;
}
/*IR heading styles*/
#sitename h1 {
   font: 80% Georgia, "Times New Roman", Times, serif;
   margin: 0px;
   position: relative;
   height: 113px;
   width: 100%;
}
#sitename h1 span {
   background: url(img/h1bg.jpg) no-repeat center;
   position: absolute;
   height: 100%;
   width: 100%;
}
/* navigation */
#navlist {
   padding-left: 0;
   margin-left: 0;
```

```
      border-bottom: 1px solid #CCD7FF;
      width: 90%;
   }
   #navlist li {
      list-style: none;
      margin: 0;
      padding: 0.25em;
      border-top: 1px solid #CCD7FF;
   }
   #navlist li a {     text-decoration: none;
   }
   /* classes */
   .small {
      font-size: 80%;
   }
```

Note the percentage-based layout with the #nav using a `float: left` rule. In Chapter 4 yc used image replacement involving an exact pixel size. Because this revised Far and Wee Ballo layout uses a percentage, the `h1` width is set to 100 percent, rather than to the exact size of the replacement image as it was in Chapter 4. Otherwise the image replacement (IR) technique is t same as that in Chapter 4. Also changed is the styled navigation list, which is similar to what y learned in Chapter 9.

Testing Your Page

While it is best to test your pages with actual handheld devices, I don't have the capability to that. Opera offers two tools that I'll use instead. The first tool is found in the Opera browser under View ➤ Small Screen (Figure 15.2).

FIGURE 15.2 The Opera browser has a Small Screen option in the View menu.

Even with no handheld styles attached to `ch15_index.html` yet, it looks pretty good in the Opera small screen view (Figure 15.3).

Note that the Opera Small Screen view ignores the background image for the `h1 span` anc simply displays the text. Also note that it resizes the photo of the balloons to fit the available space. It also ignores the `float: left` on the `nav` and linearizes the content. With the content linearized, you see the usability value of the skip navigation link added before the `nav`:

```
<a href="#content" class="small">Skip to main content</a>
```

(See Chapter 7 for more about this feature.)

The semantic markup of the content has come through with shining colors, even before any handheld style rules have been added to the page. This test may come close to results you could expect from a device with a larger screen and XHTML capability such as a BlackBerry, but it might not be representative of how the page would display on a less capable device. Opera's Small Screen view is a helpful test, but you cannot depend on all handheld devices following this example, even though many come close.

Opera has a special browser for handheld devices called Opera Mini. It is available for download at `www.opera.com`. Opera also has an online simulation tool called the Opera Mini simulator at `www.opera.com/products/mobile/operamini/demo.dml`. (The page being tested must be on a server to use this simulator.) Figure 15.4 shows how the balloon page looks in the mini simulator.

You see very similar results with the simulator and the Small Screen view. In both, the image replacement rules are ignored and the `h1` is displayed as text. The image is shown but at a size that fits the screen. The `float` is ignored and the content is linearized. Again, you see proof that the solid foundation of semantic XHTML and separation of content from presentation has gone a long way toward making the page usable on the small screen. However, there is more you can do to make it usable by writing a handheld-specific style sheet for the page.

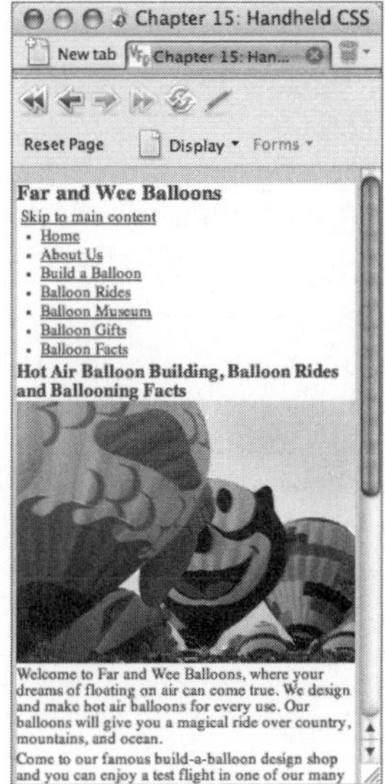

FIGURE 15.3
Using Opera Small Screen view, the page looks usable even without a handheld style sheet.

FIGURE 15.4
The page before a handheld style sheet is attached in the Opera Mini simulator.

Opera Mini™ simulator

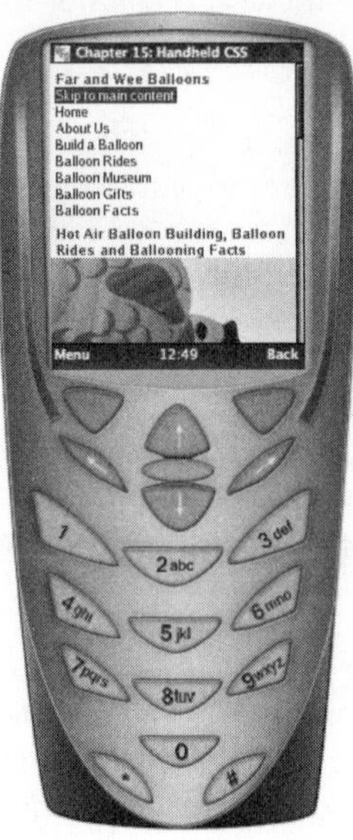

PASSING FANCY OR TRUE DIRECTION?

Many sites now create a special area for mobile users. Yahoo! Mobile is an example at `http://mobile.yahoo.com`. Google offers mobile users the opportunity to get their e-mail, Google maps, and more at `www.google.com/mobile`. It's an interesting trend to watch. Will the demand for more and more adaptations to sites for mobile devices increase, or will the mobile devices eventually develop to the point where specialized subsites are not needed?

Cameron Moll is one of the leaders in mobile design. His discussion about whether or not it's wise to create separate pages for mobile devices is, in part, at `www.cameronmoll.com/archives/000428.html`. Moll has a book about mobile web design in the works at the time of this writing. By the time you read this, it will be available and should be informative.

CSS: Keep it Simple

In this section, you'll write a style sheet of handheld rules for the `ch15_index.html` page. Ope a blank text document and save it with the filename `hh.css`. This will contain the rules for you handheld style sheet.

The link to a handheld style sheet goes in the `ch15_index.html` `head` after the other style sh link. It uses a `media="handheld"` attribute and is written like this:

```
<link href="hh.css" rel="stylesheet" type="text/css" media="handheld" />
```

Not all handheld devices support CSS. The devices that *do* support CSS don't all support the *sa* CSS. One device may understand a rule and the next will not. Keep things as simple as possible wh writing CSS for handhelds.

Remember that the handheld styles are in the cascade after the screen media styles, so you need rules only for things that should be different.

Start by reviewing the section of the style sheet that determines basic structure and layout. Black text on a white background for the `body` is a good practice. Use relative measures for everything (percentages or ems) instead of pixels. Make liberal use of `display: none` to eliminate anything from the handheld display that isn't absolutely essential. (Links to external sites, decorative images, and other items that don't add essential content can be eliminated with `display: none`.)

Remove the float rule on the `nav`, just in case a more sophisticated handheld recognizes it. With the float removed, the width and margins of the divs need a bit of adjusting. Remove the images in the content div from the display, too. (This choice is optional, since many devices let the user choose whether to view images. As you saw, the simulators show the images at reduced sizes, not a bad result.) Here are some suggested rules for the new `hh.css` style sheet.

```
body {
   background: #FFF;
   color: #000;
}
#nav {
   width: 50%;
   float: none;
}
#content {
   margin-left: 1%;
}
#content img {
   display: none;
}
```

FIGURE 15.5
A few simple rules regarding color and image display in a handheld style sheet create this change.

Opera Mini™ simulator

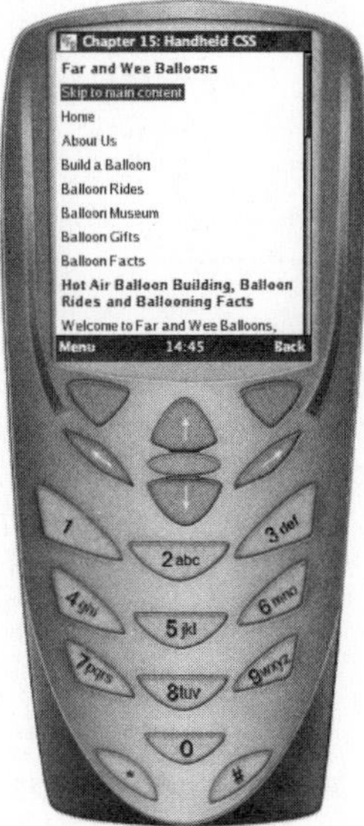

The Opera Mini simulator shows the results of those changes in Figure 15.5.

Looking at the page in Opera Small Screen view reveals something interesting (Figure 15.6).

For whatever reason, the presence of a handheld style sheet prompted Opera's Small Screen view to honor the image replacement rule. Other browsers may do this as well. One of the reaso for using image replacement on this page was so that the image could be eliminated for handhelc so try this addition to the `hh.css` rules:

```
#sitename h1 {
   position: static;
   font-size: 130%;
   height: 1em;
   width: auto;
}
#sitename h1 span {
   display: none;
}
```

These two rules overrule the `position: absolute` rule in `screen.css`, reset the size of the h and stop the `h1 span` from displaying; see Figure 15.7.

The new rules cause no change in the display on the Opera Mini simulator. It still appears as Figure 15.5.

Listing 15.3 gives the complete set of rules used in `hh.css`.

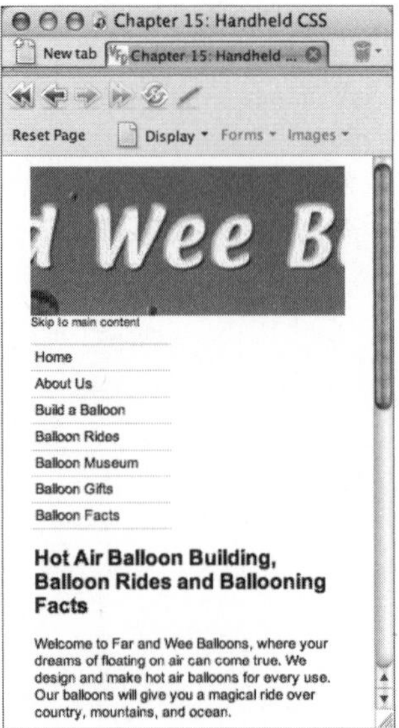

FIGURE 15.6
Now that the `hh.css` is attached to the page, Opera Small Screen view shows the background image in the h1 span.

FIGURE 15.7
With changes to the image replacement rules, Opera's Small Screen view removes the background image in the heading.

LISTING 15.3: The *hh.css* Rules

```
/*basic structure and organization*/
body {
   background: #FFF;
   color: #000;
}
#nav {
   width: 50%;
   float: none;
}
#content {
   margin-left: 1%;
}
#content img {
   display: none;
}
/*IR heading styles*/
#sitename h1 {
   position: static;
   font-size: 130%;
```

```
    height: 1em;
    width: auto;
}
#sitename h1 span {
    display: none;
}
```

Testing with the Handheld Style Sheet

BrowserCam (`www.browsercam.com`), mentioned previously for testing web pages, is expandin with a DeviceCam option. As of this writing, the only handheld OS DeviceCam test is for Windo Mobile 5, but the DeviceCam service may grow and become more helpful for testing pages in oth small devices in the future. DeviceCam test results are shown in Figures 15.8 and 15.9.

As you see in Figure 15.9, some devices may ignore your handheld style sheet completely. Ke in mind, however, that many mobile devices that are capable of rendering either screen or han held styles often ask the user which they prefer as a default choice. You cannot control what th user chooses, but you can provide presentation rules that will accommodate either choice.

MORE HELPFUL TOOLS

The Firefox Web Developer toolbar has an option to toggle which style sheet affects the page under CSS ➤ Display CSS by Media Type. If you select Handheld, you'll get a fair idea of how some devices will display your page.

For Dreamweaver 8 users, there's a Style Rendering toolbar (explained in Chapter 16) that allows you to look at your page in Design View as it would be rendered by whatever style sheet media type you select.

FIGURE 15.8 DeviceCam test results for Explorer 5 with Windows Mobile 5 show the handheld styles in use.

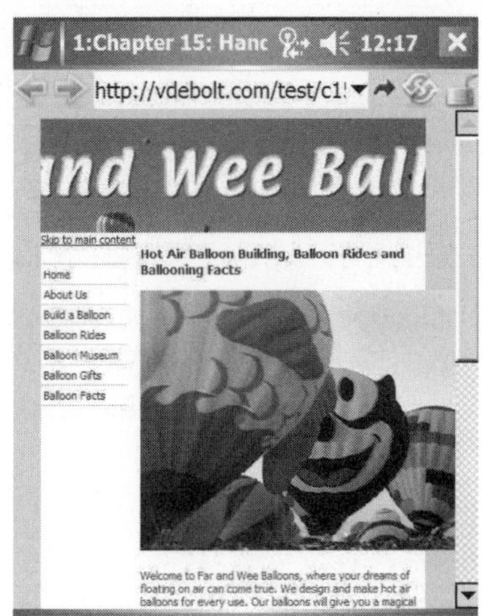

FIGURE 15.9
DeviceCam test results for Opera 8.6 on Windows Mobile 5 show that the handheld styles are ignored and the screen styles are used.

Developer Resources for Handhelds

Most individual handheld device and browser makers provide sites for developers. You can learn what HTML, XHTML, or CSS the device supports, if any. There may be tips for developers and helpful information about making web pages work in the particular device.

The two Opera testing tools and BrowserCam used in the previous section are valuable, but if you are targeting a particular device there is no substitute for testing on the real thing. Some resources are suggested in the next sections. If the device you need isn't mentioned, look for information on the manufacturer's or device OS maker's site.

BlackBerry

User choice rules over designer choice in the BlackBerry. The BlackBerry has different options for browsing, including using either WAP or a regular browser. If you select the regular browser, the BlackBerry gives you a choice of using style sheets or not. If you say yes, then you get a choice of whether to use handheld or screen media type. The user can decide whether to use WML (Wireless Markup Language), HTML or both, whether to allow cookies, tables, background and foreground color, embedded media, and JavaScript. The BlackBerry can handle large applications such as Lotus Notes for e-mail. A BlackBerry is a phone, too.

There is no online BlackBerry simulator, but you can download and install a BlackBerry simulator from: `www.blackberry.com/developers/downloads/simulators`.

The BlackBerry developer pages start at `www.blackberry.com/developers/started`.

The browser built into the BlackBerry is Mozilla 4. You can also download the Opera Mini to the BlackBerry at `www.opera.com/products/mobile/operamini`.

AvantGo

AvantGo calls itself a content service for PDAs and SmartPhones. It can be installed on Palm Treo, BlackBerry, Windows Mobile Pocket PC, Windows Mobile Smartphone, and several varieties of mobile phones.

WML AND WAP

Before devices using Wireless Application Protocol (WAP) were capable of using HTML and XHTML, there was the Wireless Markup Language (WML). WML is defined as an XML 1 application. It is similar to XHTML in many ways. Learning WML when you know XHTML isn't a big problem. WML may be phased out eventually as more devices continue to become capable of displaying HTML and XHTML. Of course, you would only use WML to build separate pages for mobile users.

WML pages are called "decks." The deck contains "cards" which display text, links, input fields, images, and other elements, often using the familiar markup of XHTML. Pages are saved with the file extension `.wml`.

The DTDs for WML are not at the W3C. One source of the WML DTD is `www.wapforum.org`. Here's an example of a WML page:

```
<?xml version="1.0"?>
<!DOCTYPE wml PUBLIC "-//WAPFORUM//DTD WML 2//EN"
"http://www.wapforum.org/DTD/wml2.dtd">
<wml>
<card id="home" title="Home">
<p>Welcome to my page</p>
</card>
<card id="c2" title="Card 2">
<p>This is card two.</p>
</card>
</wml>
```

W3 Schools has a WML formatting tutorial beginning at `www.w3schools.com/wap/wml_format.asp`. Opera supports WML, and there is a Mozilla Firefox WML browser at `http://wmlbrowser.mozdev.org`.

The AvantGo developer pages are at

```
http://corp.avantgo.com/avantgo/developer/channel_developer
```

AvantGo Version 5 supports some CSS, HTML 4.01, DOM, and JavaScript. The user has cont over choices such as whether or not to accept images. AvantGo is one of the systems that recogniz the `meta` element for pages that are specially formatted to be `HandheldFriendly`.

The code for the `meta` element is:

```
<meta name="HandheldFriendly" content="True">
```

To qualify as a handheld friendly page, the page author should write code that is semantic a formatted with the only basic HTML tags. There should be no DOCTYPE declaration, simply a opening `<html>` element.

Palm

Palm has a downloadable emulator at `www.palmos.com/dev/tools/emulator`. The Palm developer pages are at `www.palmsource.com/developers`. There is a Palm OS for Palm devices. Windows Mobile and AvantGo will also run on Palm devices, including the Palm Treo.

Windows

Microsoft has Windows Mobile and Pocket PC for PDAs and phones. The Windows Mobile pages begin at `www.microsoft.com/windowsmobile`. The Pocket PC subsection of the Windows Mobile information pages begin at `www.microsoft.com/windowsmobile/pocketpc`. Microsoft doesn't offer emulators, but it does provide online demos in the Help and How To section of the site that demonstrate how several mobile devices look with Windows OS installed. Links to demos are at `www.microsoft.com/windowsmobile/help/default.mspx`.

Phones

Phone manufacturers have information for developers on their sites that will provide some help when planning pages for handheld devices. Motorola has this site: `http://developer.motorola.com` and Sony Ericsson offers developer information at `http://developer.sonyericsson.com/site/global/home/p_home.jsp`. Sony Ericsson also has tutorials for formatting audio and video material for their phones.

READ ALL ABOUT IT

Naturally, the W3C has some ideas about mobile devices, including Mobile Web Best Practices at `www.w3.org/TR/mobile-bp`. The W3C CSS Mobile Profile candidate recommendation is at `www.w3.org/TR/css-mobile`.

A List Apart published an article called "Pocket-Sized Design: Taking Your Website to the Small Screen" at `www.alistapart.com/articles/pocket`.

Cameron Moll wrote a series of articles on Mobile Web Design. They begin at `www.cameronmoll.com/archives/000398.html`.

CSS Properties

You knew it all already. No new CSS properties were introduced in this chapter.

Real-World Scenario

Brainstorms and Raves, at `www.brainstormsandraves.com`, discusses web design, development, standards, typography, music, and more from the perspective of blogger Shirley Kaiser, who is the author of *Deliver First Class Web Sites: 101 Essential Checklists* (Sitepoint, 2006) and a member of the Web Standards Group. She decided to accommodate mobile users in two ways: by including a handheld style sheet for the main page, and by creating a special text-only version of the site fo mobile users, at www.brainstormsandraves.com/mobile.

In the Opera browser, the main page of Brainstorms and Raves appears as shown in Figure 15. A quick glance at View Source for the home page reveals the following style sheets in use:

```
<link rel="stylesheet" type="text/css" href="/mtcss2/simple.php" title="default
media="screen" />
<link rel="stylesheet" type="text/css" href="/mtcss2/screen.css" media="screen,
projection" />
<link rel="alternate stylesheet" href="/mtcss2/larger.php" type="text/css"
title="larger" media="screen" />
<link rel="alternate stylesheet" href="/mtcss2/contrast.php" type="text/css"
title="contrast" media="screen" />
<link rel="stylesheet" media="print" href="/mtcss2/print.php" type="text/css" /
<link rel="stylesheet" type="text/css" href="/mtcss2/hh.css" media="handheld" /
```

You see style sheets for screen, projection, larger type, higher contrast, print, and handheld. look at the site in the Opera Mini simulator confirms that the handheld styles are serving the p pose nicely. There are some links to get through at the top of the screen, but a Skip to Content li makes passing them easy (see Figure 15.11).

The site's banner image, with its distinctive font and styling, has been resized and optimized f the small screen instead of using the image replacement method demonstrated in the chapter. Th allows the mobile user to see the nicely designed title in a form meant for handhelds and helps t site retain some of its identity in the mobile device.

Brainstorms and Raves goes one step beyond that, however, and provides a special section the site for mobile users. There's a view of that in a normal computer monitor with the Opera browser in Figure 15.12.

FIGURE 15.10
A normal computer monitor view of Brainstorms and Raves

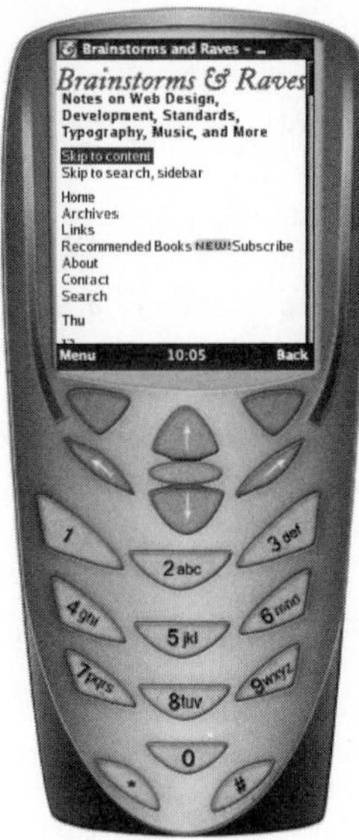

FIGURE 15.11
The regular main page has a handheld style sheet, which works well in this simulation.

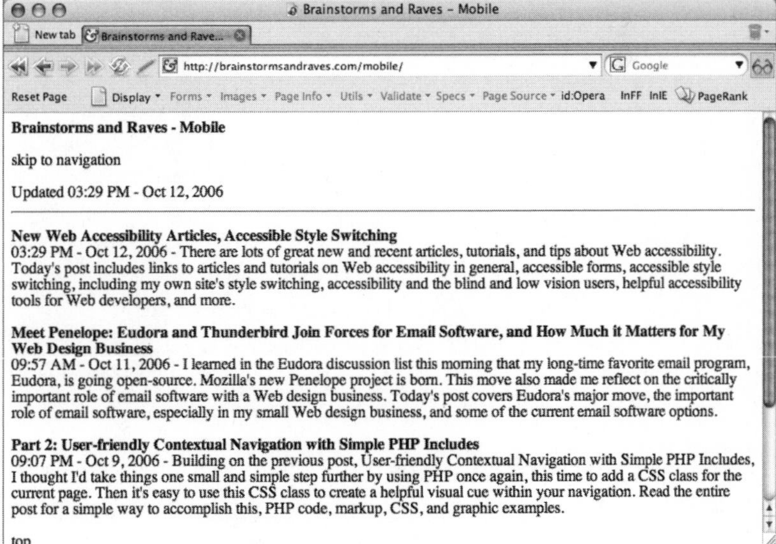

FIGURE 15.12
The `brainstorms-andraves.com/mobile` page looks like this in a computer monitor.

The mobile pages are very simple: minimally formatted text with few links. There are no sty sheets, not even a handheld one, but there is this `meta` element:

```
<meta name="HandheldFriendly" content="True">
```

This `meta` element tells the server for certain types of mobile devices that you optimized you page for viewing that type of a mobile device. Without it, tables, JavaScript, and certain image ta will be dropped when the page is downloaded.

Although it sounds like extra work to create the mobile-friendly page, this site uses Moveab Type blogging software. (See Chapter 13 for more about blogging software.) Kaiser created tem plates for Movable Type so that when she publishes a post, Movable Type publishes a copy of including mobile-friendly archives—all in mobile-friendly format via the template she created. I entirely automated, just like the rest of the site publishing.

In the Opera Mini simulator, you see an easy-to-use site consisting entirely of text (see F ure 15.13).

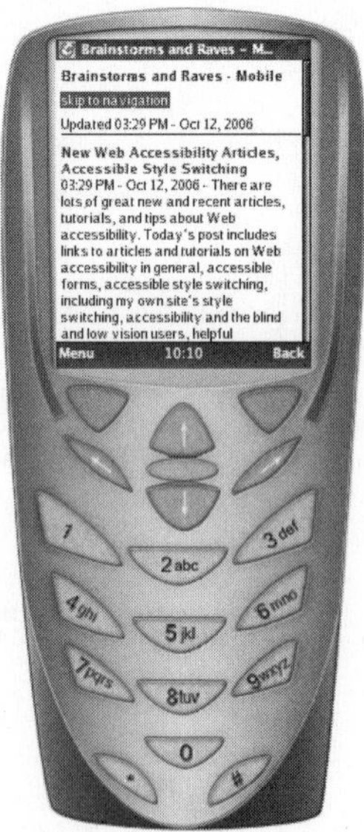

FIGURE 15.13
The mobile page of Brainstorms and Raves in the Opera Mini simulator is quick, easy to read, and easy to use.

The Bottom Line

Two basics: clear semantic markup and separation of content from presentation are all-important any discussion about content that works in every device. Without them, no style sheet can overco the accessibility and usability problems your page may have. If you have the basics, then creating style sheet for the media type handheld may provide help to some users of handheld devices.

Identify some of the obstacles to designing for handheld devices. There are no standard or consistency in handheld devices capable of web browsing. It's a fractured market.

Master It Discuss the problems involved in creating styles for handheld devices. Try to come up with some that were not mentioned in the list in the chapter section called "Inherent Obstacles to Web Authoring for Handhelds," but that you have understood from working in this chapter.

Write styles for the handheld media type. Handheld style sheets use a `media="handheld"` attribute. Not all handheld devices support CSS. The devices that *do* support CSS don't all support the *same* CSS.

Master It Take a page of XHTML from the `flowerpagesite` in Chapter 9 and write a handheld style sheet for it. Alternatively, write a handheld style sheet for an XHTML page of your own design. Test as best you can.

Examine the available handheld resources and testing tools. There are several available simulators that can be downloaded or used online to test handheld displays. Most companies that make handheld devices or software for handheld devices offer support to developers.

Master It Opera Small Screen view, Opera Mini simulator, and DeviceCam were explored in this chapter. Other possible testing devices were also mentioned. Explain which you think would be the most valuable to you. Give your reasons.

Chapter 16

Writing CSS with Dreamweaver 8

This chapter is for people who own Dreamweaver. Originally developed by Macromedia and now owned by Adobe, Dreamweaver is the web development environment that most professionals consider the best available if they choose to use such a tool as an adjunct to hand coding. More than just an HTML code editor, it's a WYSIWYG tool, which means *What You See Is What You Get*. In Dreamweaver, you write in a text document window and Dreamweaver translates that into HTML or XHTML in the background. But if you want, you can work directly in the XHTML.

The examples and exercises will show images from Dreamweaver 8, but older versions of Dreamweaver such as MX and MX 2004 behave in much the same way. You can learn about writing CSS with Dreamweaver even if you don't own the latest version.

With your advanced knowledge of sound XHTML structure and CSS, you can use Dreamweaver to write code as clean and standards-compliant as doing it by hand, because you can examine or work directly in the code with a single click.

One specific aspect of using Dreamweaver—writing CSS—is the topic of this chapter. I'm going to assume that you've used the software and understand the basic terminology related to the Dreamweaver workspace. This chapter is for people who know something about Dreamweaver but want to polish the skills needed to write CSS with Dreamweaver. If you're not getting the results you want or are confused about some of the basics of the Dreamweaver CSS interface, this chapter will help you. I'll just jump right into the middle of things with no preliminary Dreamweaver basics.

In this chapter you will:

- Identify Dreamweaver's CSS tools.
- Use Dreamweaver to create a style sheet.
- Use Dreamweaver to edit styles.
- Learn how to avoid possible Dreamweaver pitfalls.

Add Structure with Dreamweaver's Insert Div Tool

There's always more than one way to accomplish any task in Dreamweaver. The tools specifically meant to write CSS work in tandem with other aspects of the program and can often be used in more than one way.

On the accompanying CD, there is a Chapter 16 folder called `rocks`. Copy it to your computer. It contains `ch16_index.html` and a subfolder with a few images. Open `ch16_index.html` in Dreamweaver. (You can't use Dreamweaver's CSS tools if you don't have an open document.) The complete file is shown in Listing 16.1.

LISTING 16.1: The *ch16_index.html* Page

```
<!DOCTYPE html PUBLIC "-//W3C//DTD XHTML 1.0 Transitional//EN" "http://www.w3.or
TR/xhtml1/DTD/xhtml1-transitional.dtd">
<html xmlns="http://www.w3.org/1999/xhtml">
<head>
<meta http-equiv="Content-Type" content="text/html; charset=ISO-8859-1" />
<title>Chapter 16</title>
</head>
<body>
<h1>Kasha-Katuwe Tent Rocks National Monument</h1>
<p><img src="images/topofpark.jpg" alt="The view from Lookout Point" width="400"
height="300" /> </p>
<h2>Splendid Erosion Among the White Cliffs </h2>
<p>Kasha-Katuwe Tent Rocks National Monument, located between Santa Fe and
Albuquerque is on  the land of the Pueblo de Cochiti and managed by the Bureau c
Land Management. The cone-shaped tent rock formations are the products of volcan
eruptions that occurred 6 to 7 million years ago and left pumice, ash and tuff
deposits over 1,000 feet thick.  &ldquo;Kasha-Katuwe&rdquo; means &ldquo;white
cliffs&rdquo; in the traditional Keresan language of the Pueblo. </p>
<p>President Clinton declared the area a national monument in 2001. The monument
is open for day use, but may be closed by order of the Cochiti Pueblo Tribal
Governor. A 1.2 mile (1.9 km) recreation trail leads up through a slot canyon to
lookout point where the tent rocks may be viewed from above. The walk through th
slot canyon is very easy. There's a short but strenuous climb at the end to reac
Lookout Point. A 1.3 mile (2 km) loop trail leads past their base. The park is
located between 5700 and 6400 feet (1737-1951 m) above sea level.</p>
<p>The national monument is only a few minutes drive from either Santa Fe or
Albuquerque. The area to explore is small, with a rather short hike. It's a
perfect day trip, with time for a picnic lunch at one of the tables provided nea
the parking area at either the start or end your jaunt through the centuries of
erosion  you see in the slot canyon. </p>
<p>The only way to see the view in the photo above is to make the climb to the
Lookout Point. However patterns, colors, tent shaped rocks, and other beautiful
rock displays may be seen in the slot canyon.</p>
<p> Carry water. </p>
<h3>Hours</h3>
<ul>
  <li>Winter (November 1 to March 31)
    8:00 a.m. to 5:00 p.m.  </li>
  <li>Summer (April 1 to October 31)
    7:00 a.m. to 7:00 p.m.</li>
</ul>
<h3>Directions</h3>
```

```
<p><em>From Albuquerque</em>, take I-25 to Exit 259. Follow the signs on NM 22 to
Kasha-Katuwe Tent Rocks National Monument. Turn right off NM 22 at the pueblo
water tower painted like a drum (quite a ways off the road) onto Tribal Route 92,
which connects to Forest Service Road 266. Travel five miles on a rough gravel
road to the national monument.</p>
<p><em>From Santa Fe</em>, take  Exit 264 off I-25 onto NM 16. Turn right off NM
16 onto NM 22, and follow the signs to  the national monument on Route 92
described above. </p>
<h3>Fees</h3>
<ul>
  <li>Vehicle: $5.00</li>
  <li>Accredited Public &amp; Private Schools require a
    No Fee, Day-use permit  from BLM</li>
  <li>Commercial Tours, Adventure Tours, Destination Tours and Non-Profit
Organizations require
    special-use permit  from BLM </li>
  <li>Display Golden Eagle, Age or Access Passports on dashboard</li>
</ul>
<h3>Helpful Links</h3>
<ul>
  <li><a href="http://www.nm.blm.gov/recreation/albuquerque/kasha_katuwe_
maps.htm">BLM trail map </a></li>
  <li><a href="http://www.nm.blm.gov/recreation/albuquerque/kasha_katuwe.htm">BLM
Rio Puerco office</a> </li>
  <li><a href="http://www.newmexico.org/index2.php">NM Tourism Dept </a></li>
  <li><a href="http://www.recreation.gov/detail.cfm?ID=3118">Recreation.gov</a></
li>
  <li><a href="http://www.srh.noaa.gov/forecast/
MapClick.php?CityName=Albuquerque&amp;state=NM&amp;site=ABQ">Albuquerque weather</
a></li>
</ul>
<p>Photos by Virginia DeBolt</p>
</body>
</html>
```

There are no styles attached to this document. In Dreamweaver's Design view it looks like Figure 16.1.

As with other screen captures in this book, you'll notice a difference in what you see if you are a Windows user. Even though the Mac version of Dreamweaver looks a little different from the Windows version, you'll find that the options and functions are exactly the same.

I have a plan in mind for this content. The following divs need to be added to `ch16_index.html` to give the page structure: `container`, `masthead`, `content`, `side`, `footer`. A wireframe of that plan is shown in Figure 16.2.

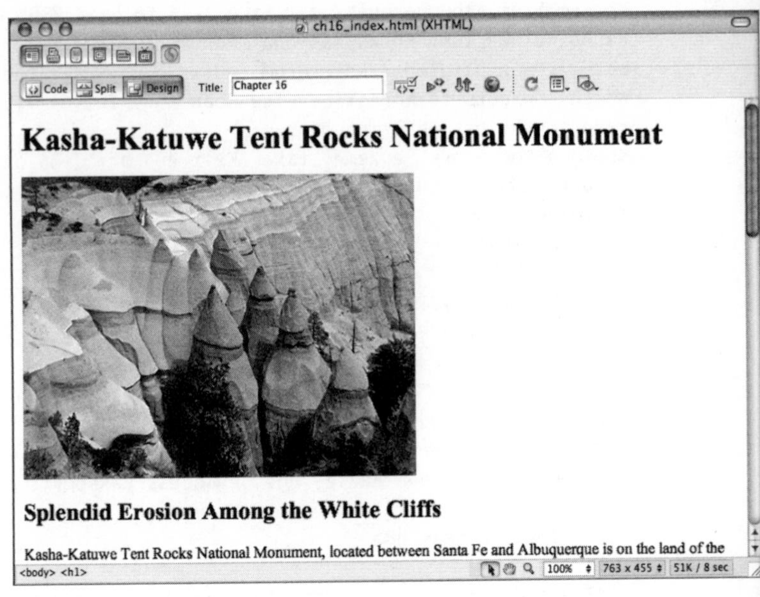

FIGURE 16.1
The ch16_index.html file in Dreamweaver's Design view before any styles are added

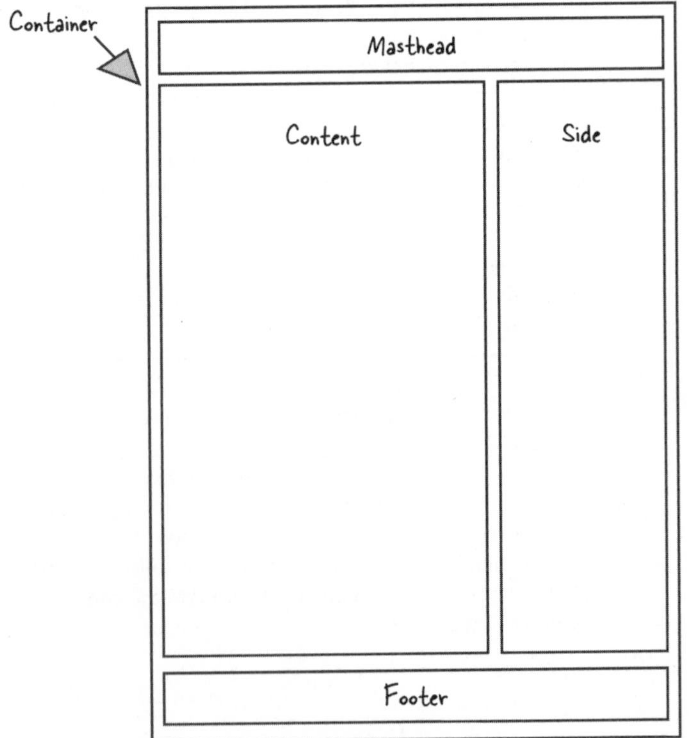

FIGURE 16.2
A wireframe sketch of the planned layout for ch16_index.html

You could go into Code view and quickly add these divs, but here's a way to let Dreamweaver do the insertion. The Dreamweaver tool for adding the `div` tag with an `id` to the content of the page is the Insert Div Tag button in the Layout category of the Insert Bar (see Figure 16.3).

FIGURE 16.3
The cursor is pointing at the Insert Div Tag button on the Layout category of the Insert bar.

The first `div` to add is `container`. In the document, choose Edit ➤ Select All. That selects everything in the body. With all the content highlighted, click the Insert Div Tag button. The Insert Div Tag dialog box opens. With something selected in the document, Dreamweaver assumes you want to wrap the `div` around the selection, which is indeed what you want to do. If you didn't have anything selected, Dreamweaver would offer to create a `div` at the point where your cursor was resting.

You can assign the `div` to a class or an id. Type **`container`** in the ID field (see Figure 16.4).

Notice that there's a button on the dialog box that allows you to create a New CSS Style for this element right away. Ignore that and continue to build structural divs into the document. The New CSS Style button can be handy, but right now you don't need it.

There are two ways to check to make sure you wrapped the `div` around exactly what you wanted. The `div` is shown with a dotted outline in Design view (see Figure 16.5).

You can also check what you did with the Insert Div tool by selecting Code view and seeing that the entire content of the body element is indeed enclosed in a `div` with the ID `container` (see Figure 16.6).

Highlight the `h1` and use the Insert Div Tag button to wrap it in a `div` with the id `masthead`. The `content div` will contain the image, the `h2`, and the paragraphs that follow the `h2` down to "Carry water" (see Figure 16.7).

AVOID THE DRAW LAYER TOOL

Next to the Insert Div Tag is a button for the Draw Layer tool. This also creates a `div`, but it uses absolute positioning and is not helpful for what you are going to accomplish with this layout. The Draw Layer tool is a holdover from the days before designers really understood how to make CSS layouts work. (The Insert Div Tag button is fairly new among the Dreamweaver tools: a very welcome addition.)

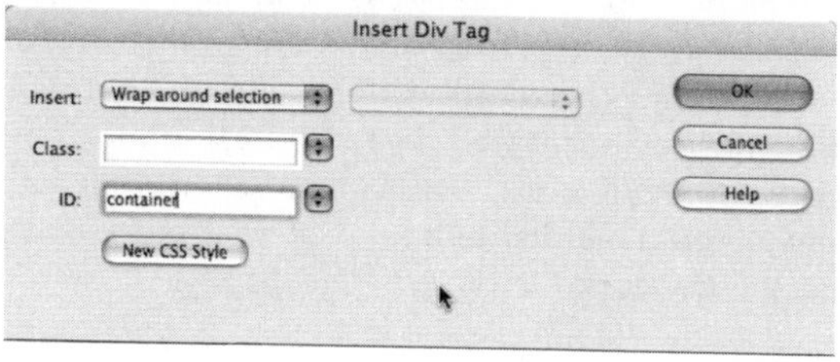

FIGURE 16.4
The material highlighted in the document will be wrapped in a `div` with the `id` container.

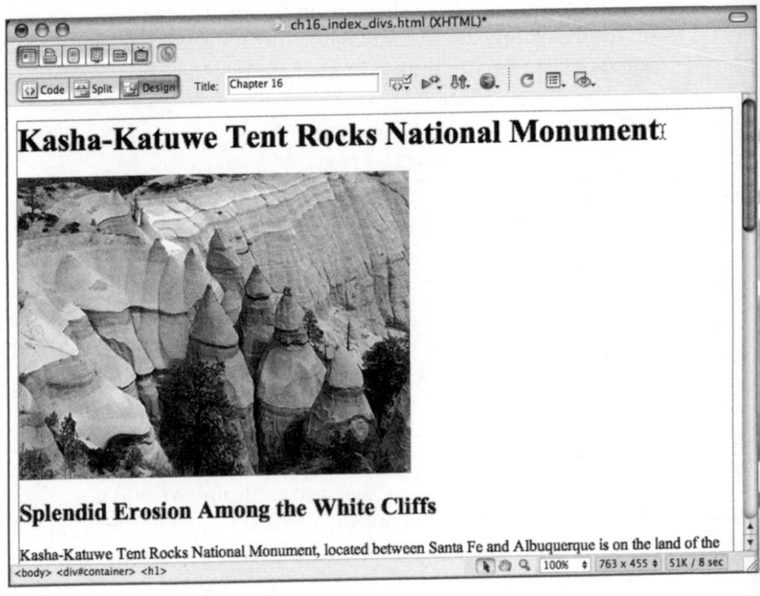

FIGURE 16.5
In Design view, the new container `div` is shown with a dotted outline.

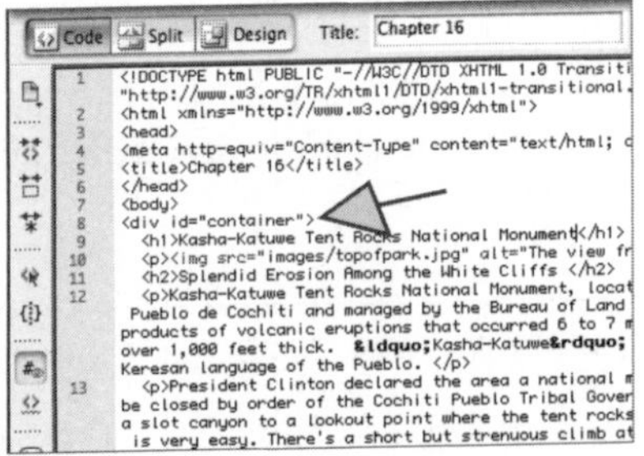

FIGURE 16.6
There's the new opening `div` tag with your `id` in Code view. Scroll down the page to find the closing tag to make sure that everything you wanted inside that `div` is actually there.

The material with the `h3` headings goes in the `side div`. Highlight *Hours, Directions, Fees,* ar *Helpful Links* with the accompanying material under them. Don't include the "Photo by Virgini DeBolt" since that will be the footer. (Sigh, you're stuck once again making a page based on phot to which I own the copyright.) See Figure 16.8.

Finally, highlight that last sentence and use Insert Div Tag to make the `footer`.

You can take text from anywhere and paste it into Dreamweaver. There you can make su the formatting (headings, lists, paragraphs, etc.) is semantically sound and use Insert Div Tag make the document CSS ready by adding the CSS structure and selector hooks you'll need t write your style rules. The changed `ch16_index.html` page is shown in Listing 16.2, with th new material highlighted. Look at your page in Code view and compare it with Listing 16.2 check your work.

FIGURE 16.7
Wrap the highlighted material in a `div` with the `id` content.

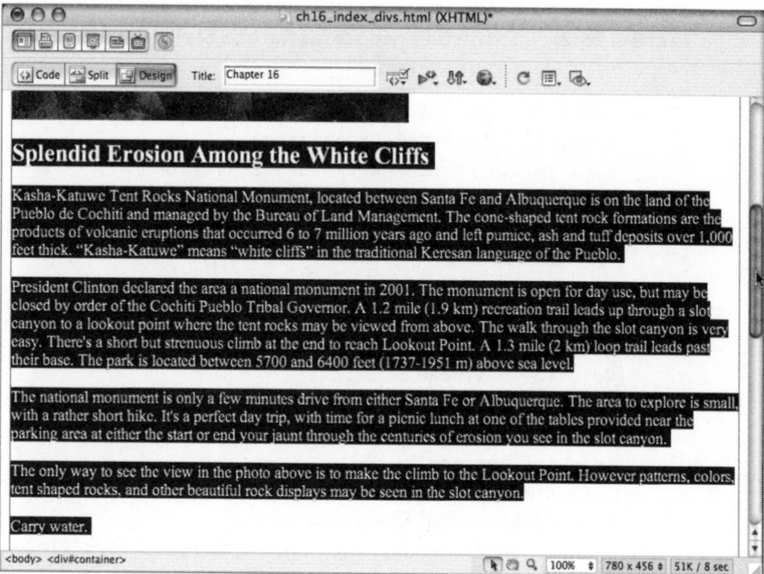

FIGURE 16.8
This material will be in the `div` with the ID side.

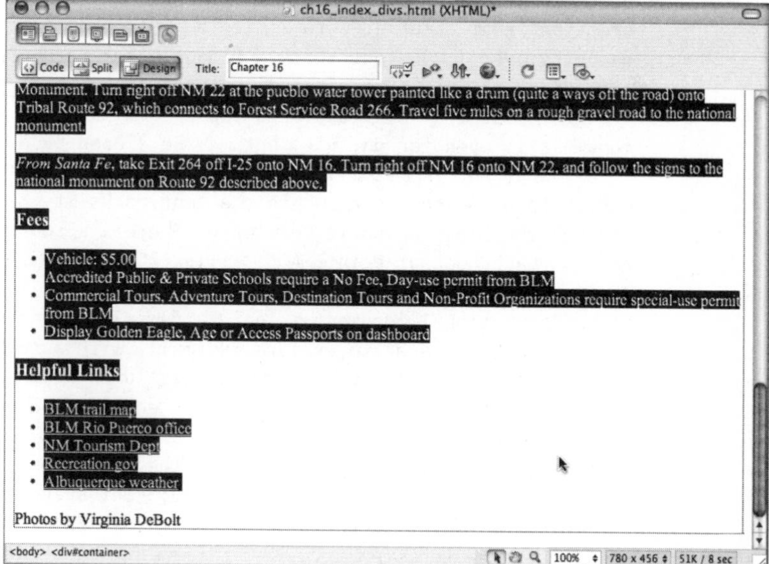

LISTING 16.2: Structural Hooks for the CSS Styles You'll Write Were Added with the Insert Div Tag Command

```
<!DOCTYPE html PUBLIC "-//W3C//DTD XHTML 1.0 Transitional//EN" "http://www.w3.or
TR/xhtml1/DTD/xhtml1-transitional.dtd">
<html xmlns="http://www.w3.org/1999/xhtml">
<head>
<meta http-equiv="Content-Type" content="text/html; charset=ISO-8859-1" />
<title>Chapter 16</title>
</head>
<body>
<div id="container">
 <div id="masthead">
   <h1>Kasha-Katuwe Tent Rocks National Monument</h1>
 </div>
 <div id="content">
   <p><img src="images/topofpark.jpg" alt="The view from Lookout Point"
width="400" height="300" /> </p>
   <h2>Splendid Erosion Among the White Cliffs </h2>
   <p>Kasha-Katuwe Tent Rocks National Monument, located between Santa Fe and
Albuquerque is on  the land of the Pueblo de Cochiti and managed by the Bureau
Land Management. The cone-shaped tent rock formations are the products of volcan
eruptions that occurred 6 to 7 million years ago and left pumice, ash and tuff
deposits over 1,000 feet thick.  &ldquo;Kasha-Katuwe&rdquo; means &ldquo;white
cliffs&rdquo; in the traditional Keresan language of the Pueblo. </p>
   <p>President Clinton declared the area a national monument in 2001. The
monument is open for day use, but may be closed by order of the Cochiti Pueblo
Tribal Governor. A 1.2 mile (1.9 km) recreation trail leads up through a slot
canyon to a lookout point where the tent rocks may be viewed from above. The wal
through the slot canyon is very easy. There's a short but strenuous climb at the
end to reach Lookout Point. A 1.3 mile (2 km) loop trail leads past their base.
The park is located between 5700 and 6400 feet (1737-1951 m) above sea level.</p
   <p>The national monument is only a few minutes drive from either Santa Fe or
Albuquerque. The area to explore is small, with a rather short hike. It's a
perfect day trip, with time for a picnic lunch at one of the tables provided nea
the parking area at either the start or end your jaunt through the centuries of
erosion  you see in the slot canyon.</p>
   <p>The only way to see the view in the photo above is to make the climb to t
Lookout Point. However patterns, colors, tent shaped rocks, and other beautiful
rock displays may be seen in the slot canyon.</p>
   <p> Carry water.</p>
 </div>
 <div id="side">
   <h3>Hours</h3>
```

```
    <ul>
      <li>Winter (November 1 to March 31)
        8:00 a.m. to 5:00 p.m.  </li>
       <li>Summer (April 1 to October 31)
         7:00 a.m. to 7:00 p.m.</li>
     </ul>
    <h3> Directions</h3>
    <p><em>From Albuquerque</em>, take I-25 to Exit 259. Follow the signs on NM 22
to  Kasha-Katuwe Tent Rocks National Monument. Turn right off NM 22 at the pueblo
water tower painted like a drum (quite a ways off the road) onto Tribal Route 92,
which connects to Forest Service Road 266. Travel five miles on a rough gravel
road to the national monument.</p>
    <p><em>From Santa Fe</em>, take  Exit 264 off I-25 onto NM 16. Turn right off
NM 16 onto NM 22, and follow the signs to  the national monument on Route 92
described above.</p>
    <h3>Fees</h3>
    <ul>
      <li>Vehicle: $5.00</li>
      <li>Accredited Public &amp; Private Schools require a
        No Fee, Day-use permit  from BLM</li>
      <li>Commercial Tours, Adventure Tours, Destination Tours and Non-Profit
Organizations require
        special-use permit  from BLM</li>
      <li>Display Golden Eagle, Age or Access Passports on dashboard</li>
      </ul>
    <h3>Helpful Links</h3>
    <ul id="nav">
      <li><a href="http://www.nm.blm.gov/recreation/albuquerque/kasha_katuwe_
maps.htm">BLM trail map </a></li>
       <li><a href="http://www.nm.blm.gov/recreation/albuquerque/kasha_
katuwe.htm">BLM Rio Puerco office</a></li>
       <li><a href="http://www.newmexico.org/index2.php">NM Tourism Dept</a></li>
       <li><a href="http://www.recreation.gov/detail.cfm?ID=3118">Recreation.gov</
a></li>
       <li><a href="http://www.srh.noaa.gov/forecast/
MapClick.php?CityName=Albuquerque&amp;state=NM&amp;site=ABQ">Albuquerque weather</
a></li>
    </ul>
  </div>
  <div id="footer">
      <p>Photos by Virginia DeBolt </p>
    </div>
</div>
</body>
</html>
```

DREAMWEAVER RESOURCES

The number of books about Dreamweaver is huge. I recommend *Macromedia Dreamweaver 8 for Windows and Macintosh* by Tom Negrino and Dori Smith (Peachpit Press, 2006). I'm a bit biased about that one, because I was a contributing writer. Also, *Dreamweaver MX 2004 Savvy* by Christian Crumlish and Lucinda Dykes (Sybex, 2004) ,though not about the latest version of Dreamweaver, is a good book.

The CSS Styles Panel

The Dreamweaver CSS Styles Panel is the chief workhorse of the tools for CSS. With no style she
and no styles, the panel sits waiting at the moment (see Figure 16.9).

Start right off by clicking the Attach Style Sheet button (it looks like a chain link), even thou
you don't have a style sheet yet. This part of the Dreamweaver tools always confuses people, b
that's really how it works.

The Attach External Style Sheet dialog box appears (Figure 16.10). In the File/URL box, type t
name you want for your style sheet. How about `dw.css`? Select the Link radio button and use t
drop-down menu to select the media type "screen." Click OK. Take a look at the document in Co
view. You should see a link to the style sheet in the document head like this one:

```
<link href="dw.css" rel="stylesheet" type="text/css" media="screen" />
```

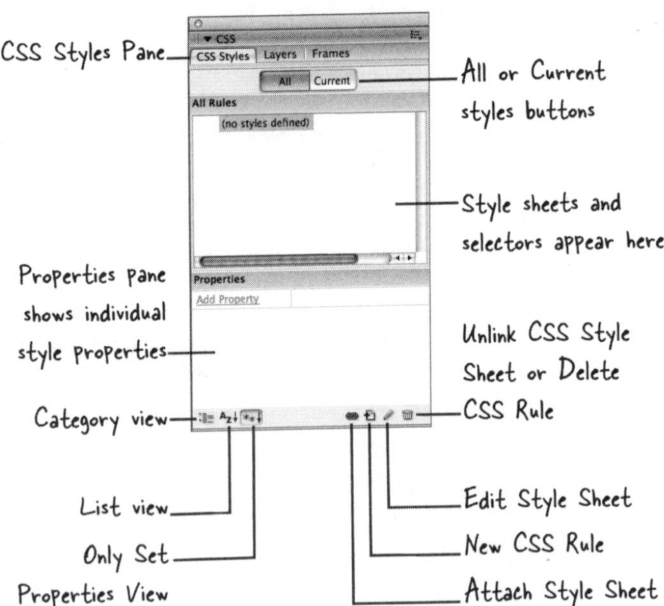

FIGURE 16.9
The Dreamweaver CSS Styles Panel. Below it is the Properties pane.

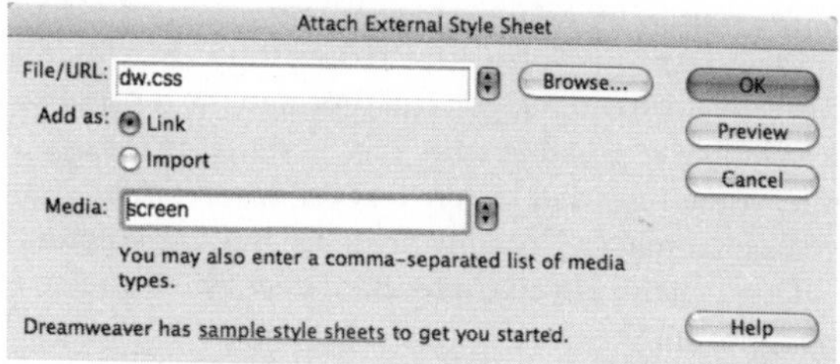

FIGURE 16.10
In the Attach External Style Sheet dialog, you browse to find an existing style sheet or type in the name of the style sheet you plan to create.

Click the New CSS Rule button (a plus sign) and the New CSS Rule dialog box opens (Figure 16.11). First notice the lower part of the dialog box. Dreamweaver knows you have a link to a style sheet called `dw.css` in the document. It assumes you want the new style in that style sheet. The style sheet doesn't exist, but just keep going, and all will become clear. (Also note the This Document Only radio button. That would insert an embedded style sheet in the document head.)

Dreamweaver categorizes CSS selectors as Class, Tag, or Advanced. Select Tag this time. You can use the pull-down menu to the right of Tag field to pick any HTML tag from the list, or you can just type the tag. Start with the basics and select or type **body**. Click OK.

At last, Dreamweaver acknowledges the mystery of the nonexistent style sheet. An alert box appears with the message, "File `dw.css` does not exist. Do you want to create it?" Click Yes.

The CSS Rule Definition dialog box opens. Here's where you write style rules. Dreamweaver has managed to put almost every possible style you will ever want to write into this dialog by using categories for the information. The first category is Type (see Figure 16.12).

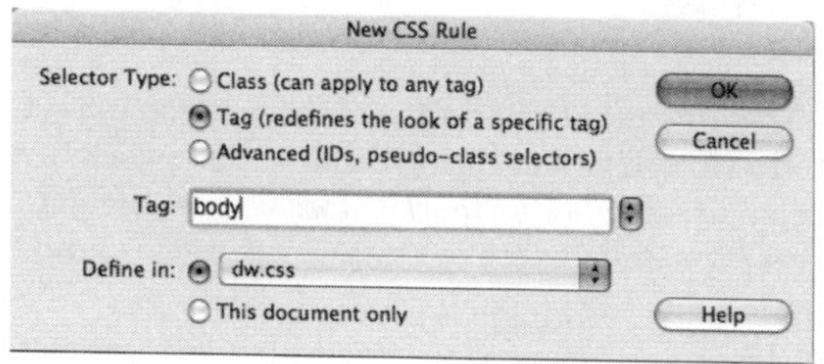

FIGURE 16.11
In the New CSS Rule dialog, decide on a selector and specify where you want the new style to be written.

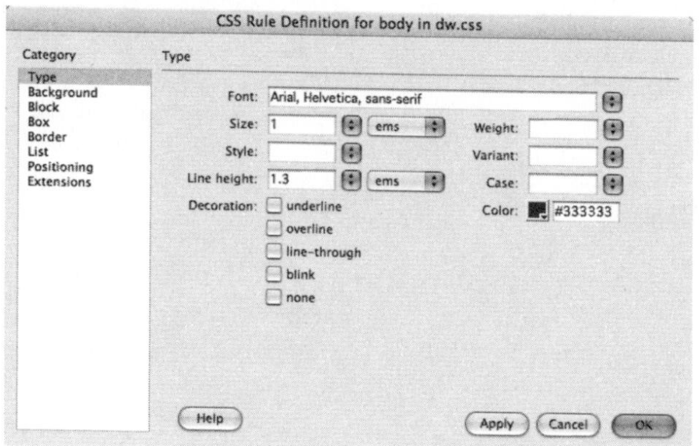

FIGURE 16.12
The options for style rules in the Type category in the CSS Rule Definition dialog

I selected a font (`font-family`), size (`font-size`), line-height, and color from this category. Yo can select various options from the drop-down menus. If you want something that you don't see the drop-down menu, you can type it in the form field, as I did in the size and line-height fields. Yo know what is possible with CSS, and that makes you smarter than Dreamweaver. If you want t enter something that Dreamweaver doesn't offer among its options, do it. That's why the fields a editable; it makes Dreamweaver as smart as you are, too.

Don't click OK yet. Go to the Category list and select Background to display the options show in Figure 16.13.

Every page needs a background color. I selected #FFFFFF (pure white) and immediately obscur it with a background image (`images/bodybg.jpg`) set to repeat. Although Dreamweaver does no use correct CSS property names in the CSS Rule Definition dialog, it isn't a problem to understan how the choices you make are translated into the CSS rules you're familiar with writing. For examp in the Background category, it's clear that you're writing rules for the properties `background-colo` `background-image`, `background-repeat`, and `background-position`.

Look through the rest of the Categories, just to get familiar with how Dreamweaver organiz the CSS properties. You're finished defining the body rule, so click OK after you've looked arou a little more.

If you look at the Files panel in Dreamweaver, you should see `dw.css` among your files. Doub click to open it in the document window and you will see your new rule:

```
body {
font: 1em/1.3em Arial, Helvetica, sans-serif;
color: #333333;
background: #FFFFFF url(images/bodybg.jpg) repeat;
}
```

This rule is in CSS shorthand, because on my setup, I selected that option in the Dreamweav Preferences. If you don't have that option selected in Preferences, you may see the body rules wr ten out in full, not shorthand. Since you are familiar with writing CSS in shorthand, you may wa to set your Preferences to write shorthand, as I did.

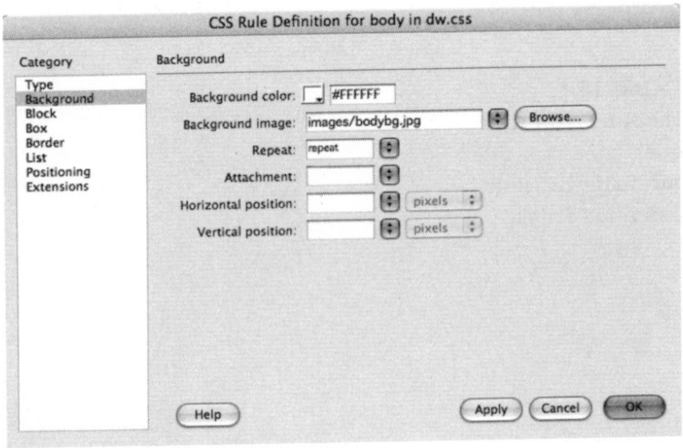

FIGURE 16.13
The options for style rules in the Background category include Background Image and Repeat.

Dreamweaver's Code view is exactly like your text editor. You can type directly in the document in Code view, just as if you were working on the file in a text editor. This is true for the CSS and for the XHTML. You can change styles, move styles around, copy styles, or delete styles right here in the `dw.css` file. You can also edit and delete styles using the CSS Styles panel tools. Code view has code highlighting, line collapsing (starting in Dreamweaver 8), and code hints that your ordinary text editor may not have.

Look at the `ch16_index.html` in Design view now, and you see the effect of the `body` style in setting a background and font rules (see Figure 16.14).

FIGURE 16.14
The styles you created for the body selector appear in Design view.

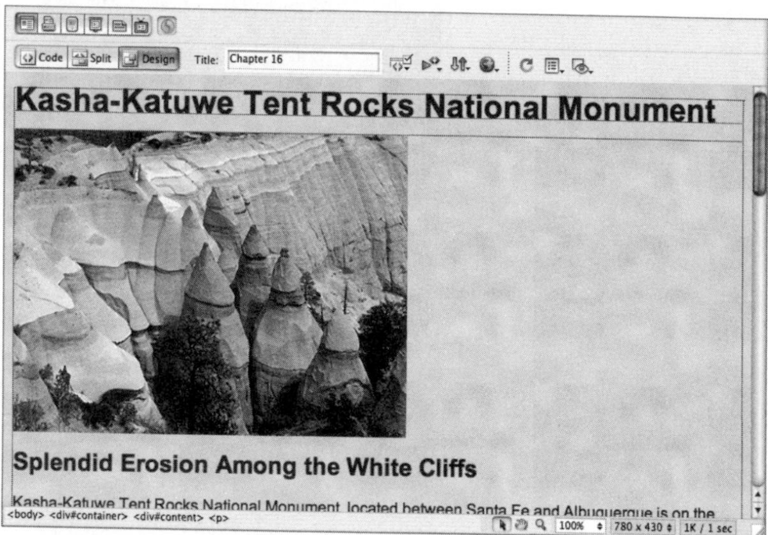

Defining Advanced Selectors

You inserted some divs and ids into the XHTML, which will be used to achieve the layout shown in Figure 16.2. Dreamweaver lumps IDs, descendant selectors, and pseudo class selectors into the Advanced category on the New CSS Rule dialog.

When something exists in the HTML, you can select it with the Tag selector at the bottom of the document window. Select `div#container` (see Figure 16.15).

With that tag selected, click the plus sign to add a New CSS Rule (see Figure 16.16).

Dreamweaver makes suggestions in the New CSS Rule dialog when you have something selected. (This can amount to overkill, as you'll see in a bit. It's both a help and a pitfall.) It already has the radio button for Advanced selected and has filled in the form field with what it thinks you want to create a rule for: the selector `#container`. Since this is exactly what you want to create, click OK and move on the to CSS Rule Definition for #container dialog box. Add rules for a `background-color` (`#C6BAB2`) in the Background category (see Figure 16.17).

In the Box category (as in box model) give the `div` a width of 90 percent and right and left margins of 5 percent (see Figure 16.18).

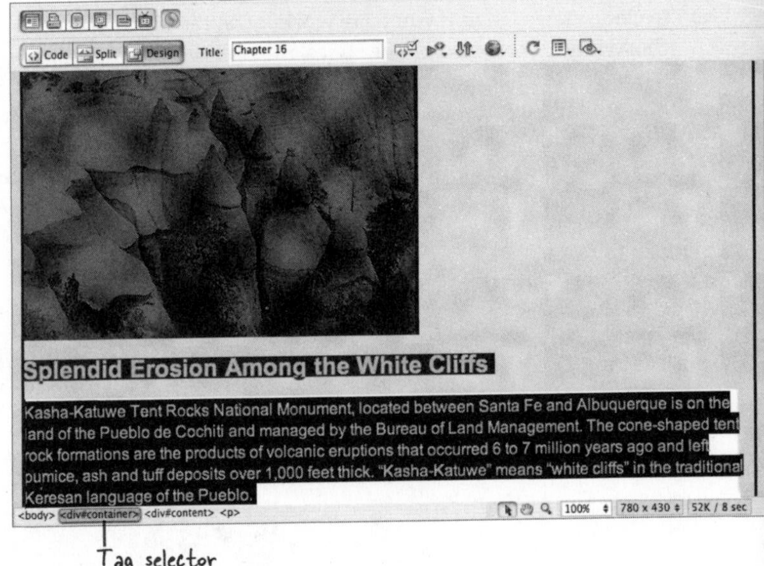

FIGURE 16.15 When the Tag selector is used to select `div#container` at the lower left of the document window, the container `div` is selected in the document as well.

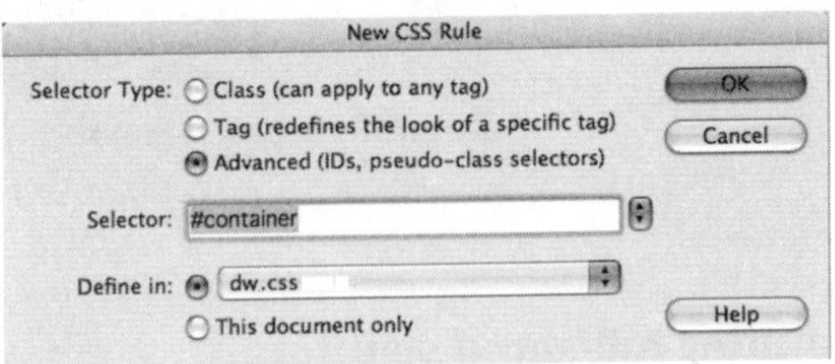

FIGURE 16.16 Dreamweaver suggests options in the New CSS Rule dialog based on what you have selected in the document window.

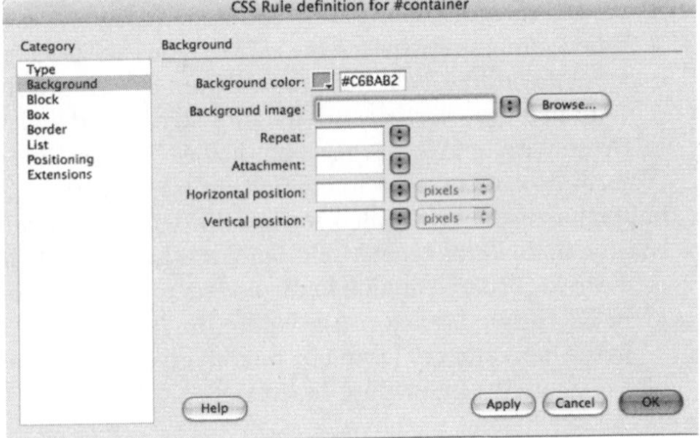

FIGURE 16.17 Add a background-color rule for the container.

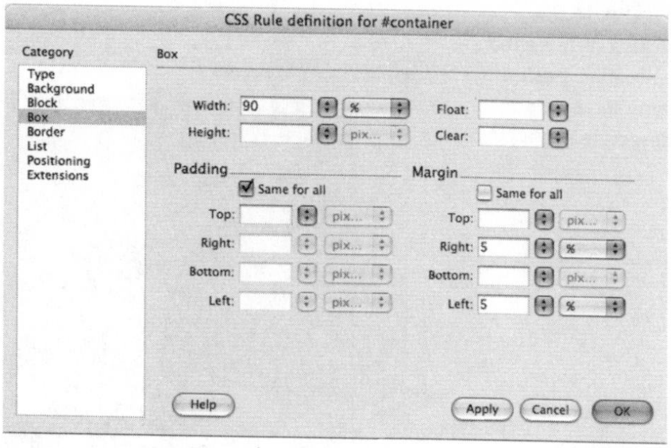

FIGURE 16.18
The rules for element width, padding, and margin are in the category Box.

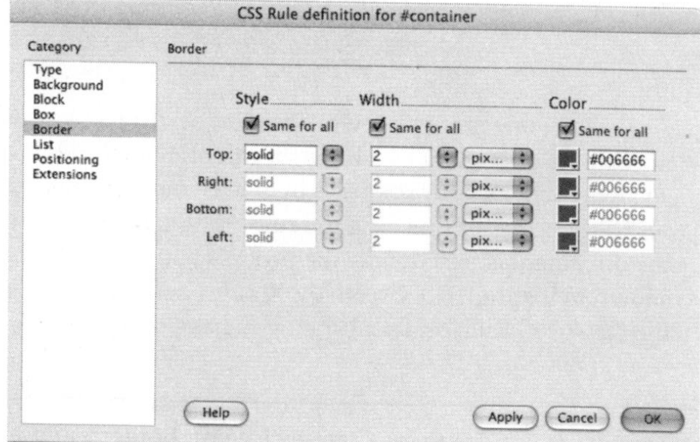

FIGURE 16.19
The Border category lets you specify each border style, width, and color separately or the same for all.

Use the Border category to assign a solid, 2-pixel-wide border of dark green (#006666) to the `div` (see Figure 16.19).

In Design view, you see the effect of the new rule in a display similar to that of a browser view (see Figure 16.20).

LINE-HEIGHT AND UNITS

Line-height rules can be written with no unit (ems, pixels, percent) expressed. You can read more about this at `www.meyerweb.com/eric/thoughts/2006/02/08/unitless-line-heights`.

Since the body rule uses a line-height of 1.3em, rather than simply 1.3, you can see the effect of that in Figure 16.20, where the heading text is squished together. Dreamweaver won't let you create a line-height rule in the CSS Rule Definition dialog without a unit of measure such as ems or pixels, but you can easily edit the style sheet by hand to take it out.

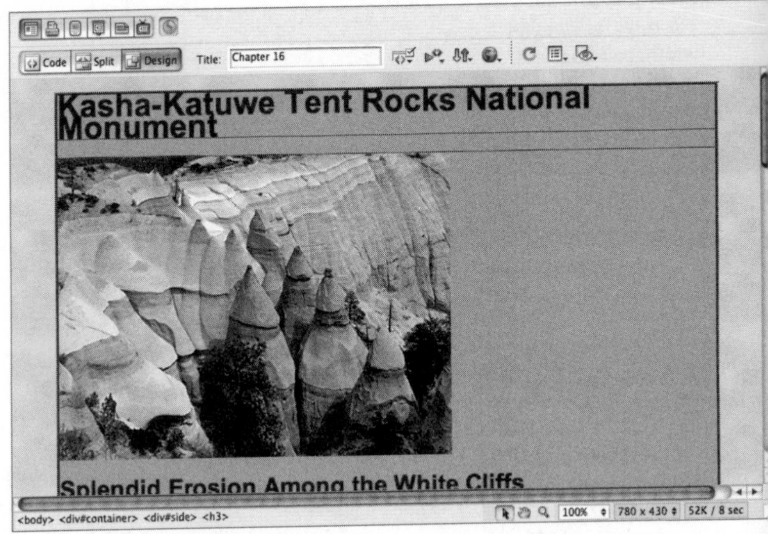

FIGURE 16.20
With a style for the container, Design view shows the new style.

Design view is not a browser, and it doesn't act like one. It merely attempts to render the appe ance of the document as a browser might. Sometimes it does very well and sometimes it doesn so always check your progress in at least one browser as you work.

The process for finishing the rules for the layout using the other structural divs you inserted the document is exactly like the process you used with `container`. The rules I suggest for this a shown in Listing 16.3. Create these rules in `dw.css` using the Dreamweaver CSS Styles Panel a the New CSS Rule button. When you have that finished, you'll explore more Advanced selecto

LISTING 16.3: The Rules Creating Layout, Borders, and Alignment

```
#masthead {
   width: 100%;
   border-bottom: 2px solid #AA9588;
}
#content {
   float: left;
   width: 70%;
   margin-top: 0px;
   padding-top: 0px;
   padding-left: 1em;
}
#side {
   width: 24%;
   margin-top: 0px;
   margin-left: 75%;
   padding: 0px 5px 0px 2px;
   border-left: 2px solid #AA9588;
```

```
    }
    #footer {
        text-align: center;
        clear: both;
        width: 100%;
        border-top: 2px solid #AA9588;
        font-size: 0.7em;
    }
```

With these rules in place, the Design view of the document changes to what you see in Figure 16.21.

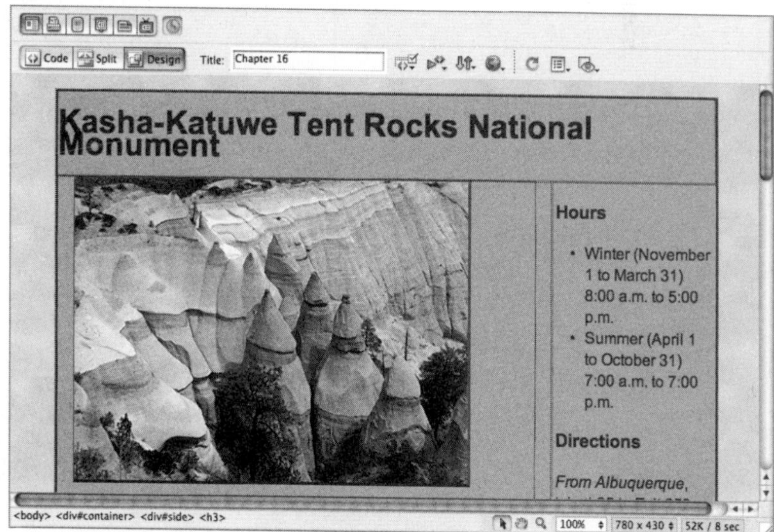

FIGURE 16.21 The styles in Listing 16.3 change the Design view to reflect layout, borders, padding, and other rules.

Defining Grouped Selectors

You know about grouped selectors, but Dreamweaver doesn't offer up that choice in its New CSS Rule dialog. It falls under the category of Advanced Selectors. Select the radio button for Advanced, then type the selector you want in the field. Try it with the `h1, h2, h3` selector as in Figure 16.22.

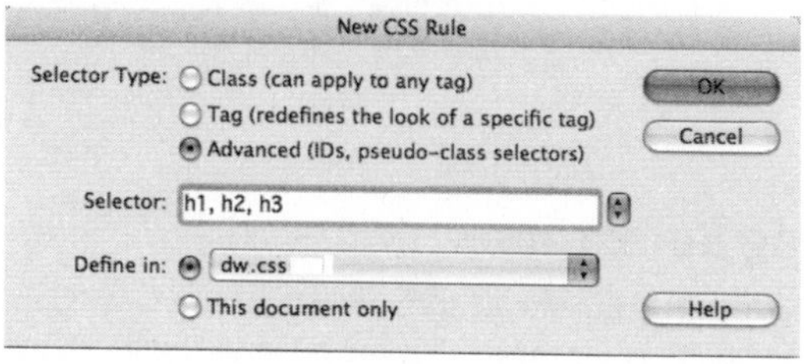

FIGURE 16.22 Grouped selectors must be typed in Dreamweaver's selector field by the user.

New CSS Rule
Selector Type: Class (can apply to any tag)
Tag (redefines the look of a specific tag)
Advanced (IDs, pseudo-class selectors)
Selector: h1, h2, h3
Define in: dw.css
This document only
OK
Cancel
Help

In the Type Category, assign the color #006600 and the `font-family: Georgia, "Times N` `Roman", Times, serif` to this group of headings and click OK.

The `font-size` in the `side div` could be smaller. The group selector `#side li, #side p` wou select both the lists and the paragraphs. Type the group selector in the New CSS Rule dialog, a define the `font-size` to 0.9 ems and the `line-height` to 1.3 ems (see Figure 16.23).

These two rules for grouped selectors are reflected in Design view; Figure 16.24 shows the res

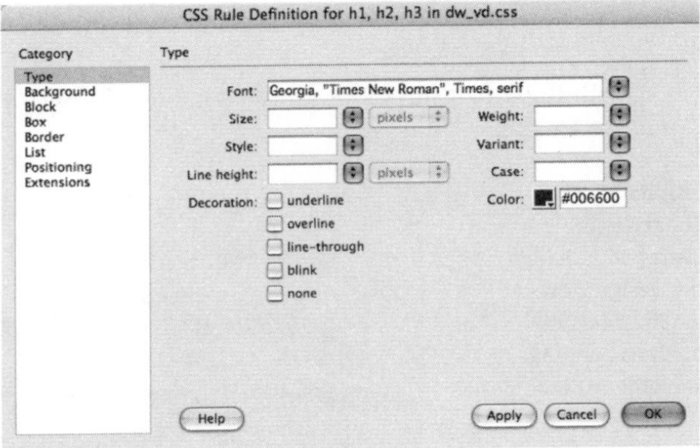

FIGURE 16.23 The CSS Rule definition for `h1, h2, h3` writes a rule for a group selector.

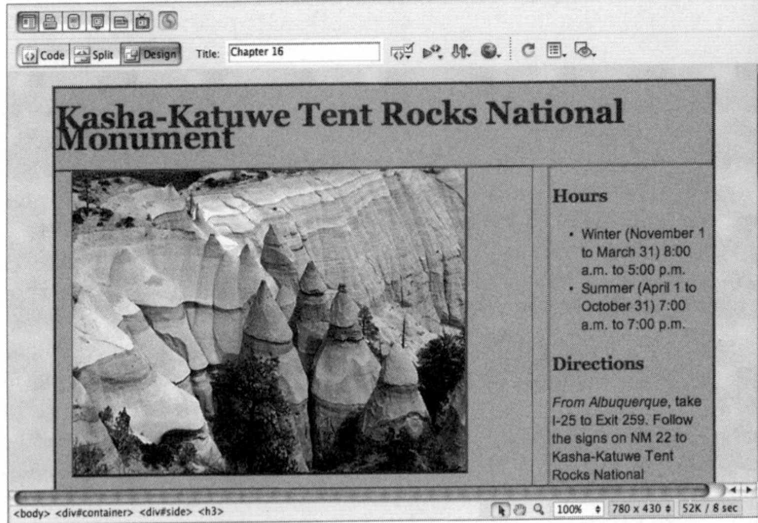

FIGURE 16.24 Design view shows the two grouped selector rules.

Tag Selectors

The heading tags need some work. In the New CSS Rule dialog, select the Tag radio button an then create rules for the `h1`, the `h2`, and the `h3` elements individually. There's an image to use a background with the `h3` elements and several other suggestions in Listing 16.4. Use the CSS R Definition dialog to enter the rules.

LISTING 16.4: Several Individual Rules for the Heading Elements

```
h1 {
   font: bold 1.3em/1.6em;
   letter-spacing: 1px;
   text-align: center;
}
h2 {
   font: bold 1.3em;
}
h3 {
   font-size: 1.1em;
   line-height: 1.2em;
   font-weight: bold;
   background: url(images/headingsline.jpg) no-repeat center bottom;
   width: 98%;
   font-variant: small-caps;
   border-right: thin solid #AA9588;
   border-bottom: 2px solid #AA9588;
}
```

As you enter each rule in the style sheet, you see it take effect in Design view. When all three are finished, you see something like Figure 16.25.

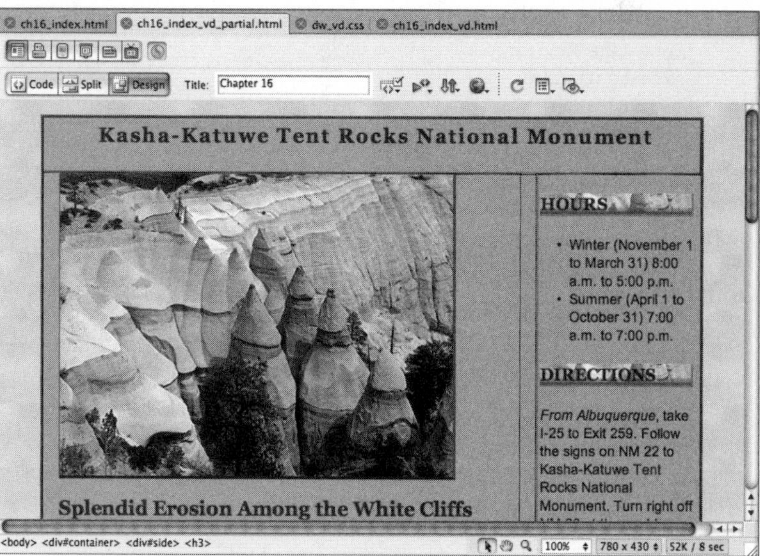

FIGURE 16.25
Three new heading rules are reflected in Design view.

More Advanced Selectors

A few elements left to style include the lists and the links on the side. I think a border around t image would be attractive, as well.

Begin by giving the `ul` with the links an `id`. Add it by hand in the code. If you click on the lin in the document window and then look at Code view or Split view (see Figure 16.26), your curs is near where you want it in the code. Type **`id="nav"`** in the opening `ul` tag.

Previously I mentioned that Dreamweaver's helpfulness with regard to Advanced Selectors could be a bit of overkill. Select ul#nav from the Tag selector at the bottom of the document windo (see Figure 16.27).

Click the plus sign to create a New CSS Rule based on this selection and Dreamweaver gives y far more than you need as an advanced selector. It goes through the whole document tree (see F ure 16.28).

You don't need `#container #side #nav` as a selector. Overkill. An `id` is unique, there's or one element named `nav`, and the context Dreamweaver suggested as a descendant selector is n needed to style this element. In the same way that you can type in the selector field, you can al delete. So delete everything but `#nav` and define a `margin-left: 0` and `padding-left: 0` ru for the `nav` (see Figure 16.29).

Styles I suggest for the navigation are shown in Listing 16.5. They all fall into Dreamweave Advanced category, but you will be required to type in the selectors `#nav li`, `#nav li a`, ar `#nav li a:hover` by hand. You'll find the `list-style-type` rule in the List category (see F ure 16.30).

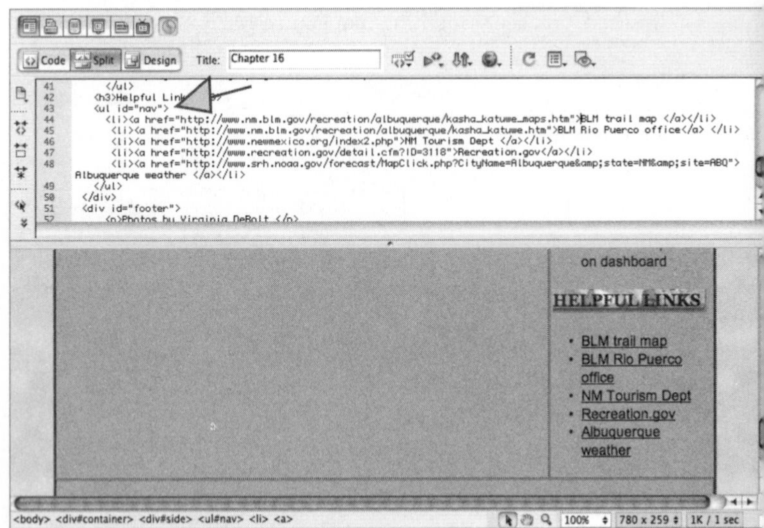

FIGURE 16.26
In Split view, you can type changes in the code and see Design view at the same time. Note the `id` added to the `ul` where the arrow indicates.

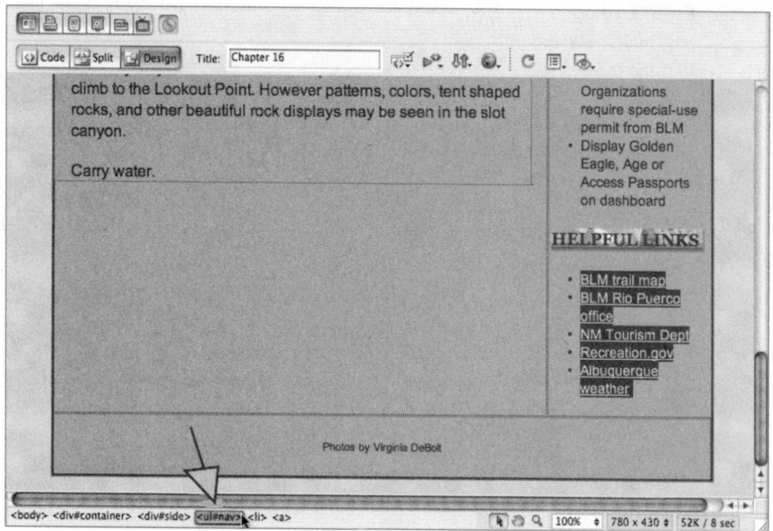

FIGURE 16.27
The Tag selector used to select ul#nav

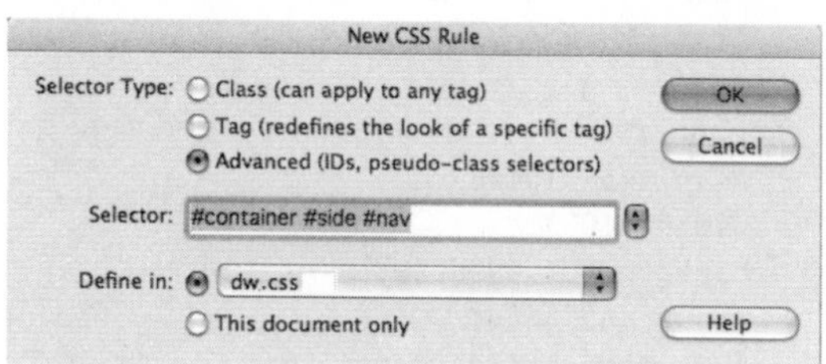

FIGURE 16.28
Dreamweaver gives you the whole hierarchy leading up to #nav. Since an id is a unique element, all you need is #nav as a selector.

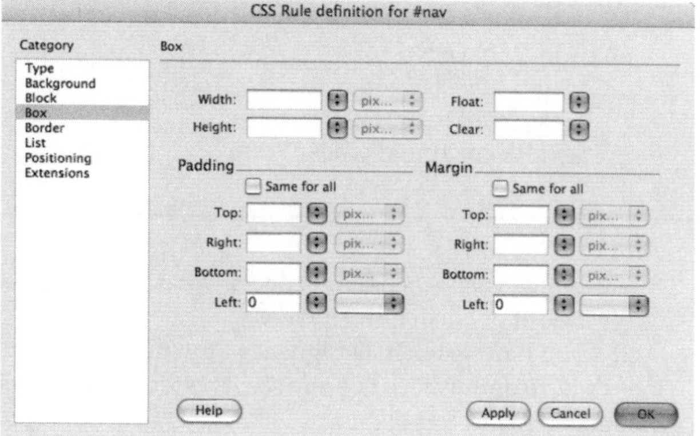

FIGURE 16.29
Remove the margin and padding from the left of the nav element.

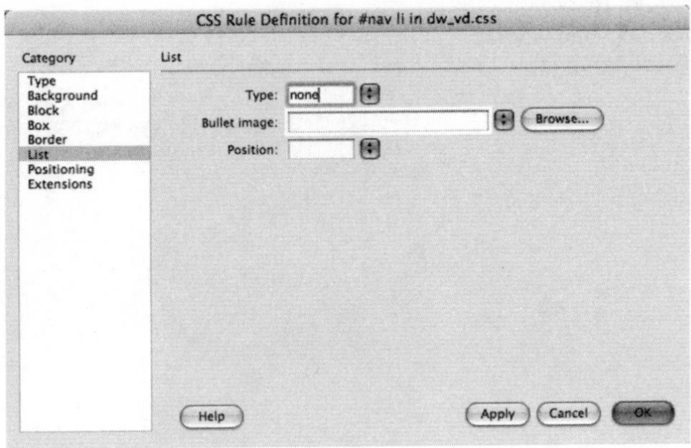

FIGURE 16.30
Set the list-style-type to none in the List category.

LISTING 16.5: Use Dreamweaver's Style Tools to Add These Rules

```
#nav li {
   padding-left: 0px;
   list-style: none;
}
#nav li a {
   display: block;
   width: 100%;
   background: #99CC99;
   color: #006666;
   text-decoration: none;
   line-height: 1.5em;
   border-bottom: 1px solid #006666;
}
#nav li a:hover{
   color: #FFFFFF;
   background: #003300;
   text-decoration: underline;
}
```

Design view shows a semblance of what you've styled (Figure 16.31). You can't click the lin or see the rollovers in Design view.

It's a bit hard to tell in Design view, but the top link in the list doesn't have an upper border a looks a little unfinished. You can see it better in a browser (Figure 16.32). You'll add that in the n section.

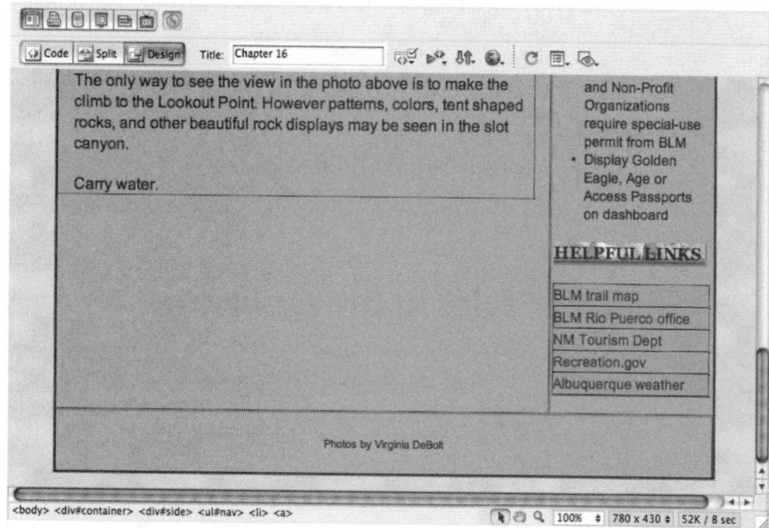

FIGURE 16.31
You get an idea of how the links look in Design view, but the rollovers won't work unless you preview the page in a browser.

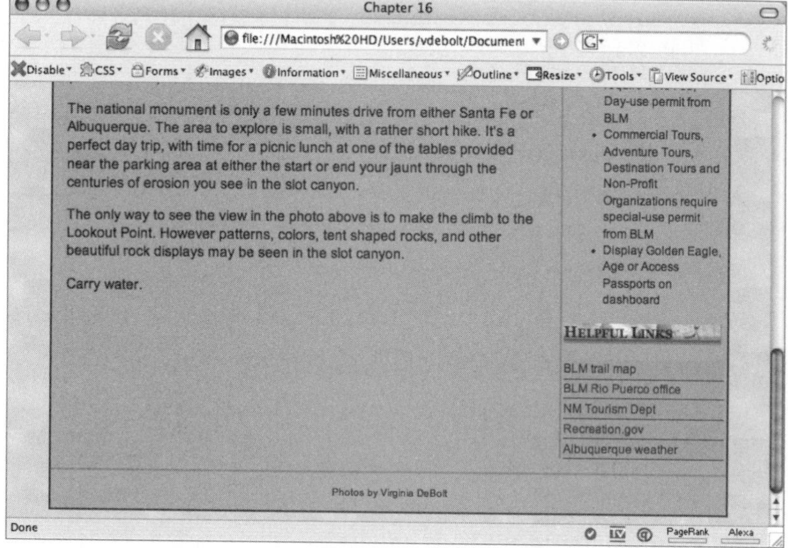

FIGURE 16.32
In Firefox, you can get a better view of the navigation. A border at the top would make the appearance more finished.

A final Advanced rule would put borders around the image. Try adding this new rule with Dreamweaver:

```
#content img {
    border-right: 3px solid #666666;
    border-bottom: 3px solid #333333;
    border-top: 1px solid #666666;
    border-left: 1px solid #666666;
}
```

Editing Styles in Dreamweaver

In the example you can add a top border to the nav element by editing the existing style for nav Styles can be edited in Dreamweaver using the CSS Styles panel with the Edit Style button (it loo like a pencil). You can also add or edit rules in the Properties pane. The All and Current button offer useful information about any existing rule in your style sheet. Figures 16.33 and 16.34 sho their respective displays.

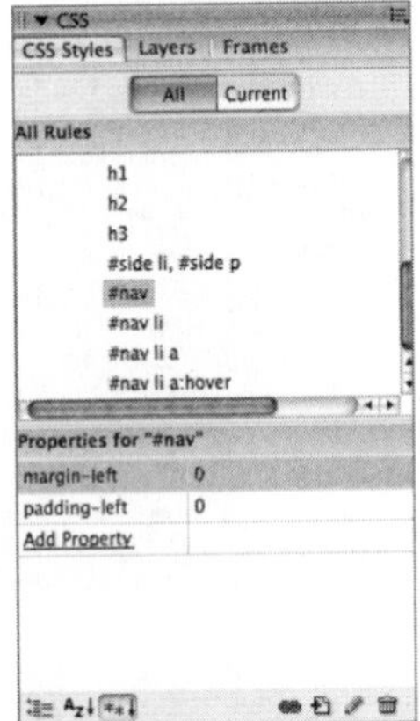

FIGURE 16.33 The CSS Style panel with All selected allows you to select #nav from the existing styles and see its properties in the Properties pane. You can edit the style by clicking the pencil icon or by changing or adding properties in the Properties pane.

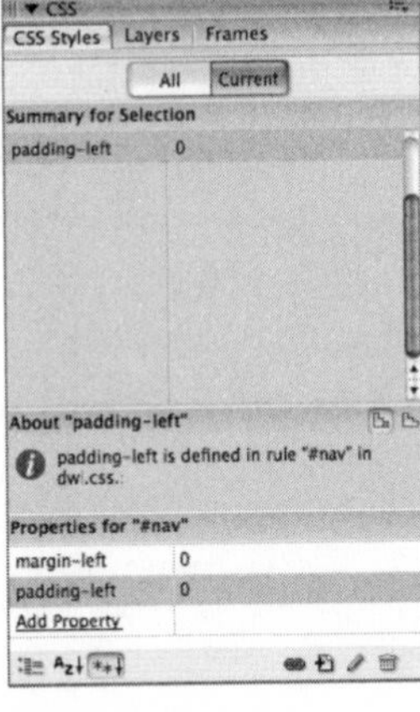

FIGURE 16.34 The CSS Style panel with Current selected gives you a summary of the current selection. Under it is the Information pane, which tells more about the property selected in the Properties pane. You can edit the style by clicking the pencil icon or by changing or adding properties in the Properties pane.

Why not try it both ways? Let's edit with the Edit Style button and then try the same thing in the Properties pane. You will add the following rule to the #nav selector: `border-top: 1px solid #006666`.

Select `#nav` in the CSS Styles panel and click the Edit CSS button. The same CSS Rule definition dialog you are familiar with opens (see Figure 16.35).

Go to the Border category and enter the rule. You can add to or change any rule this way. You could also use the Edit Style button to remove everything you just did, but don't do it that way.

Here's a different way to remove the property you just added. With the `#nav` selector highlighted, highlight the `border-top` rule in the Properties pane (Figure 16.36). Then click the Trashcan icon to delete that property. It doesn't delete the whole `#nav` rule, just the highlighted property. Be brave. Do it.

Now create the same rule again, using a different method. In the Properties pane there's an Add Property link. Click it and form field opens up. The property can be typed in or selected from a drop-down menu (see Figure 16.37).

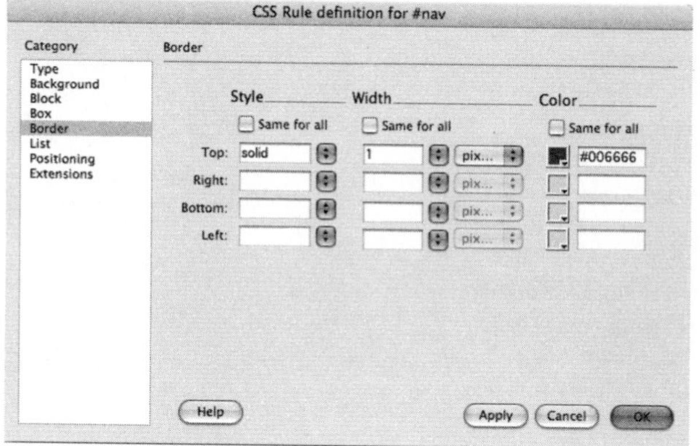

FIGURE 16.35
When you highlight a selector in the CSS Styles panel and click the Edit Style button, you see the familiar CSS Rule Definition dialog.

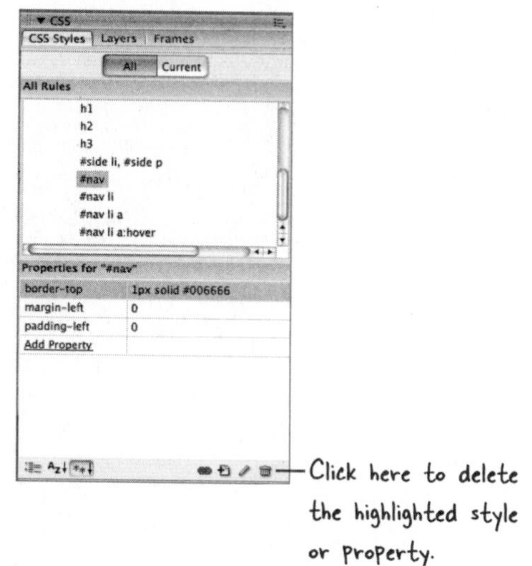

FIGURE 16.36
Click the trashcan, and the highlighted property will be gone.

When you have the property, click to the right of it and another empty field opens up. Type th values you want in it. It accepts shorthand, so you can type **1px solid #006666** if you want (see Fi ure 16.38).

Leave the new rule this time, and check in the browser to see the `border-top` on the nav bar (s Figure 16.39).

Which way to edit CSS is best or easiest? You decide which one you like, or use them both as th mood suits you. If you strongly prefer one method, you can set the Dreamweaver Preferences t edit that way when you double-click a selector in the CSS Styles Panel.

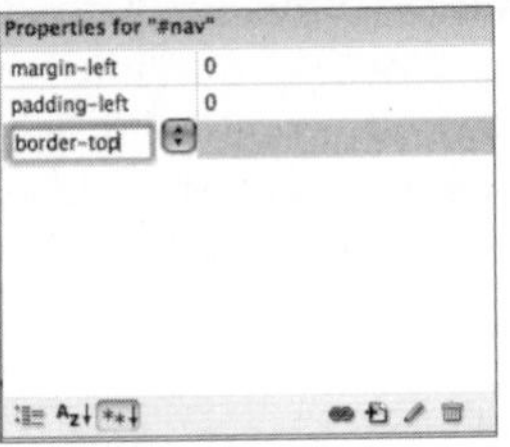

FIGURE 16.37 New properties can be added in the Properties pane. If you're not sure about the exact name, use the drop-down menu to pick any property you need.

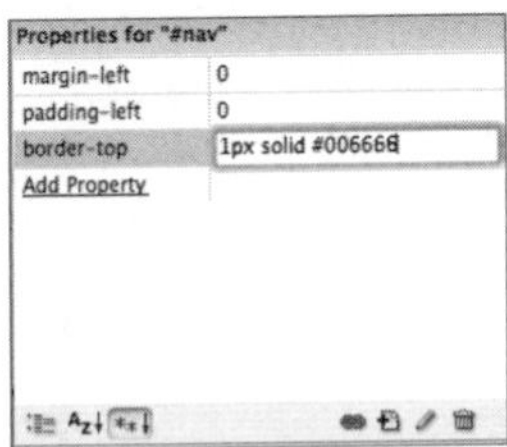

FIGURE 16.38 Type the values you want directly in the form field. Depending on the property and value you are working with, there may be drop-down menu options to assist you when adding values.

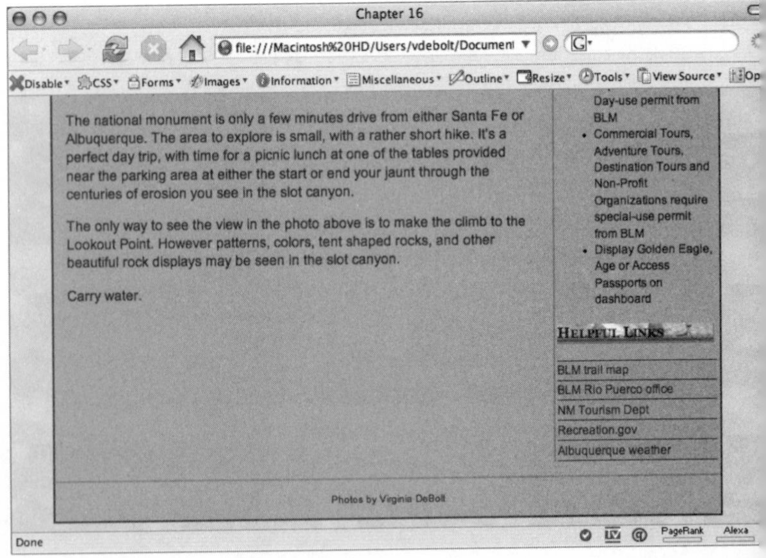

FIGURE 16.39 It's easier to see the border-top on the nav element in the browser than in the Design view.

INFO PANE

All sorts of information may show up in the Info pane, depending on the selector or property you select. You can look in the Info pane if you have a cascade problem or are not sure what rule a property was inherited from. It was only mentioned briefly here, but it is a helpful CSS tool in Dreamweaver 8.

Classes and the Property Inspector

To make optimal use of Dreamweaver when writing styles, stay away from the Property Inspector. The Property Inspector *will* add styles to your page. People who complain that Dreamweaver shouldn't be used because it adds bloat and unnecessary code to a page probably stumbled into the pitfall of using the Property Inspector to create new styles. When you add a style from the Property Inspector, a `span` and a `class` are added to the document (bloat), and the `class` is given a generic and unhelpful name like "style1." The style rule may be embedded in the `head` rather than added to an external style sheet, which also leads to confusion.

All is not lost where the Property Inspector is concerned, however. When you have a `class` defined in your external style sheet and you want to assign that `class` to an element on your document page, the Property Inspector is the perfect tool to use.

For example, the lists in `side` could be moved to the left a bit, in my opinion (Figure 16.40).

The styled `nav` is a list, and I don't want to move it around. But the other two lists in `side` could be shifted to the left. If I create a `class` and assign it to the two lists I want to move, the list in `nav` will be unaffected.

When you assign the `class`, you will assign it to the opening `ul` for each list you want to shift to the left. But when you write the selector, you'll include the `li` element, so that what you actually move to the left is the list item.

Click the plus sign to write a New Style. Choose the Class radio button and then type a class name in the box. You need to include the leading period, for example, `.moveleft li` (see Figure 16.41).

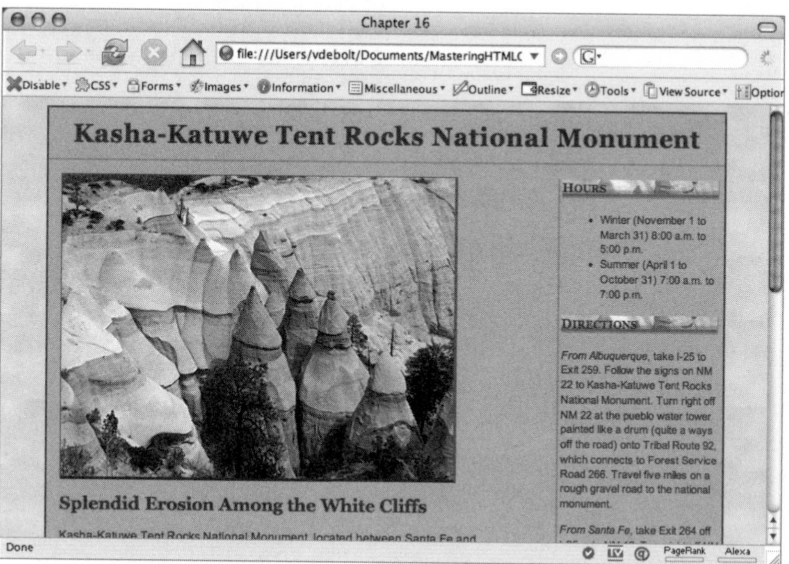

FIGURE 16.40
The bulleted list would look better moved to the left a bit.

Assign a `margin-left:-15px` rule. Now that the `class` is in the style sheet, the easiest way t assign it to an element in the document is with the Property Inspector. It is a two-step process. Fir select the element you want to style with the Tag Selector (the `ul`). Then find the class you want i the drop-down Style menu on the Property Inspector. Among the options on the drop-down Sty menu, you'll find the name of the new class. Select it (see Figure 16.42).

Assign the class to the lists under the headings Hours and Fees. Note that when either list is selected in the document window, the Tag selector reflects the assigned class, as does the Style menu in the Property Inspector (see Figure 16.43).

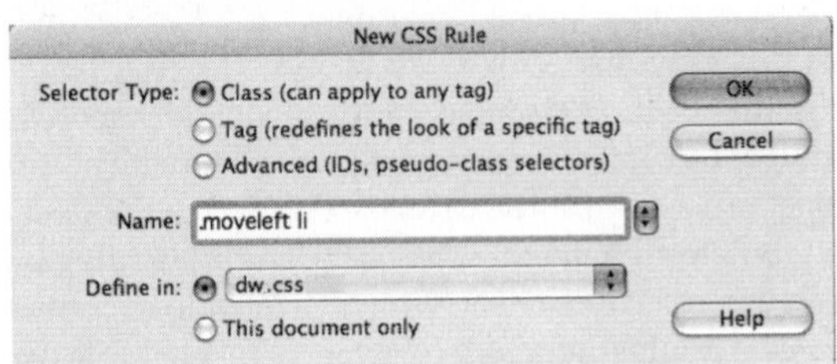

FIGURE 16.41
Type the leading period in the field with the class name.

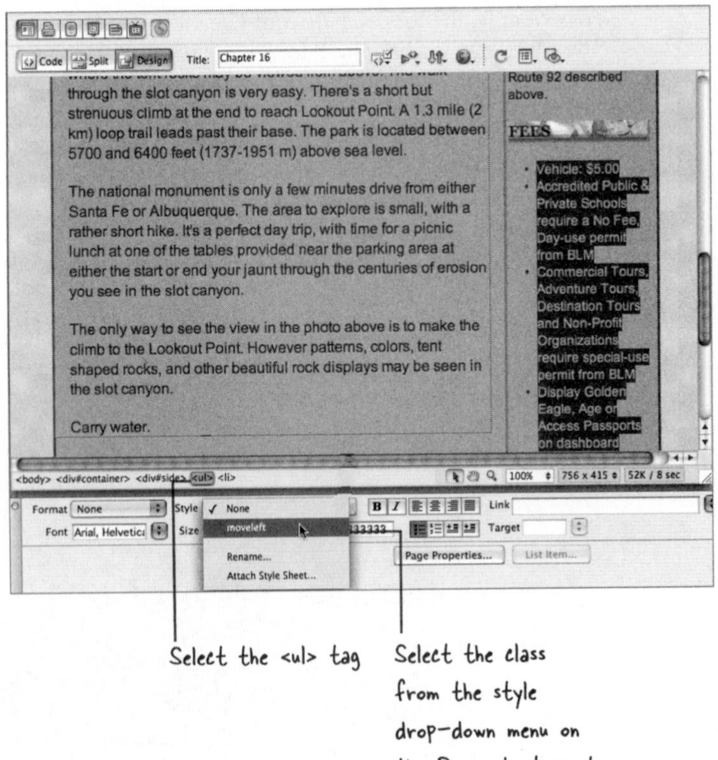

FIGURE 16.42
Assigning a class to an element is easy with the Property Inspector. First select the element with the Tag selector. Then find the class in the drop-down style menu on the Property Inspector and select it.

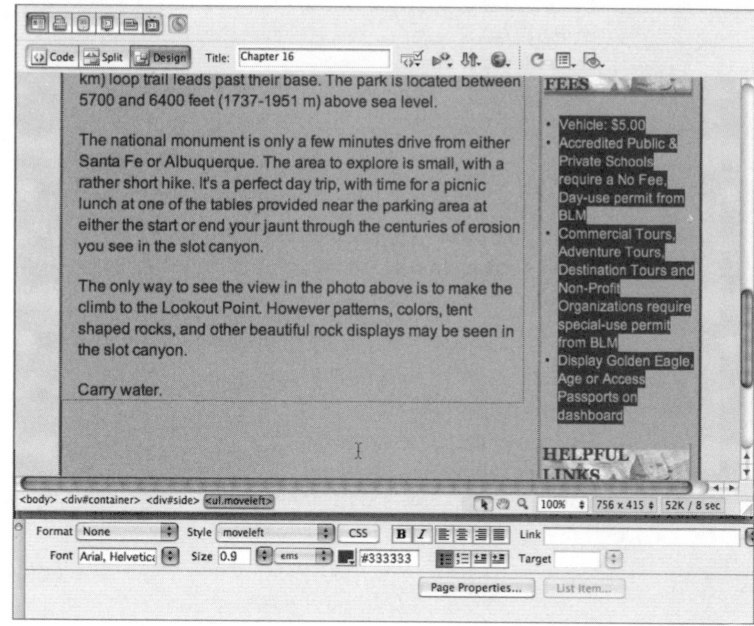

FIGURE 16.43 A glance at either the Tag selector or the Property Inspector tells you when an element has a class assigned.

The completed `dw.css` is shown in Listing 16.6. Your styles may not be in the same order as these, but that doesn't matter in this case.

LISTING 16.6: The Finished `dw.css` Page

```
body {
   font: 1em/1.3em Arial, Helvetica, sans-serif;
   color: #333333;
   background: #FFFFFF url(images/bodybg.jpg) repeat;
}
#container {
   background: #C6BAB2;
   width: 90%;
   margin-right: 5%;
   margin-left: 5%;
   border: 2px solid #006666;
}
#masthead {
   width: 100%;
   border-bottom: 2px solid #AA9588;
}
#content {
```

```
   float: left;
   width: 70%;
   margin-top: 0px;
   padding-top: 0px;
   padding-left: 1em;
}
#content img {
   border-right: 3px solid #666666;
   border-bottom: 3px solid #333333;
   border-top: 1px solid #666666;
   border-left: 1px solid #666666;
}
#side {
   width: 24%;
   margin-top: 0px;
   margin-left: 75%;
   padding: 0px 5px 0px 2px;
   border-left: 2px solid #AA9588;
}
#footer {
   text-align: center;
   clear: both;
   width: 100%;
   border-top: 2px solid #AA9588;
   font-size: 0.7em;
}
h1, h2, h3 {
   color: #006600;
   font-family: Georgia, "Times New Roman", Times, serif;
}
h1 {
   font: bold 1.3em/1.6em;
   letter-spacing: 1px;
   text-align: center;
}
h2 {
   font: bold 1.3em;
}
h3 {
   font-size: 1.1em;
   line-height: 1.2em;
   font-weight: bold;
```

```
    background: url(images/headingsline.jpg) no-repeat center bottom;
    width: 98%;
    font-variant: small-caps;
    border-right: thin solid #AA9588;
    border-bottom: 2px solid #AA9588;
}
#side li, #side p {
    font-size: 0.9em;
    line-height: 1.3em;
}
.moveleft li{
    margin-left:-15px;
}
#nav {
    margin-left: 0;
    padding-left: 0px;
    border-top: 1px solid #006666;
}
#nav li {
    padding-left: 0px;
    list-style: none;
}
#nav li a {
    display: block;
    width: 100%;
    background: #99CC99;
    color: #006666;
    text-decoration: none;
    line-height: 1.5em;
    border-bottom: 1px solid #006666;
}
#nav li a:hover{
    color: #FFFFFF;
    background: #003300;
    text-decoration: underline;
}
```

When you add a new style using the Dreamweaver tools, they put it at the end of the style sheet. This can cause your style sheet to become disorganized and may affect the cascade. The only way to add CSS comments to a Dreamweaver style sheet is by hand. The styles can be rearranged, commented, and organized as you need them to be by editing directly in the style sheet, just as you would organize styles and insert comments using any other text editor.

The Style Rendering Toolbar

A helpful CSS tool in Dreamweaver 8 (not present in earlier versions) is the Style Rendering toolb (Figure 16.44). Find it under View ➤ Toolbars ➤ Style Rendering.

With this toolbar, you can toggle all the styles completely off in Design view. You can see th page rendered in Design view according to any attached style rules you have for the various med types. Handy!

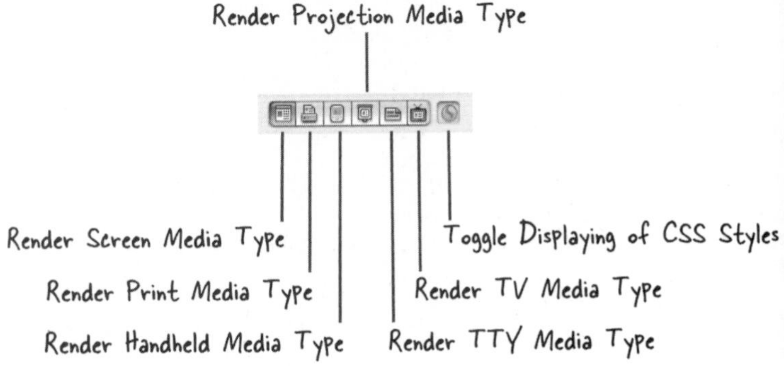

FIGURE 16.44
The Style Rendering toolbar

CSS Properties

No new CSS properties were discussed in this chapter. That's because you're smarter than Dreamweaver.

Real-World Scenario

A site meant especially for Dreamweaver (and other web development topics and products) is Community MX at `www.communitymx.com`, shown in Figure 16.45. The site provides tutorials Macromedia product extensions, downloadable page designs, and articles by certified experts Dreamweaver and other topics. Some of the content is free, but some of it requires registration a a nominal fee.

One of the CSS experts who writes regularly for Community MX is Zoe Gillenwater, whose name you recognize as the technical editor of this book. In Figure 16.46 you see an inner page a Community MX featuring one of Zoe's articles, "Full Height CSS Layouts with Footers."

You find reliable information at Community MX. There is a concern for good coding practic and standards, as well as accessibility. It's a good source of information if you want to improve your web development skills.

FIGURE 16.45 The main page of Community MX with links to articles, tutorials, and extensions for a range of products, including Dreamweaver

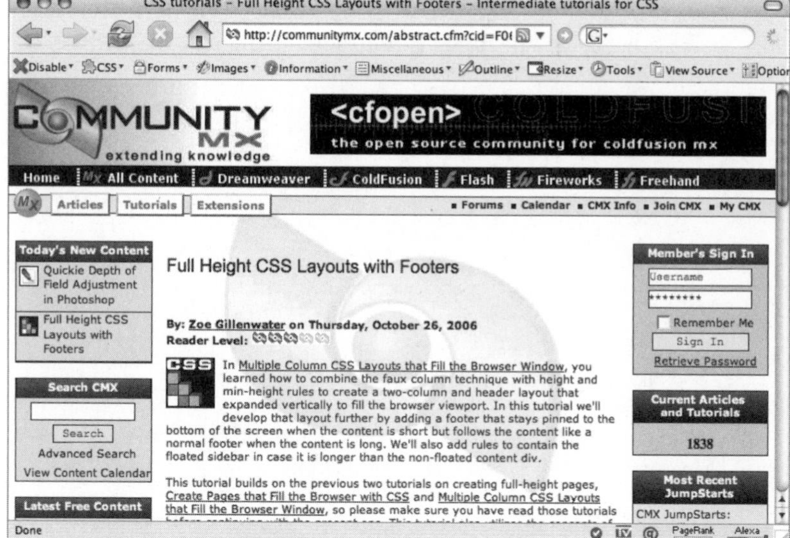

FIGURE 16.46 An inner page at Community MX with an article about using CSS to create a page layout

The Bottom Line

Dreamweaver can write clean XHTML and almost any style rule when you learn the ins and ou of using it effectively.

Identify Dreamweaver's CSS tools. The major tools are the CSS Styles panel, the Property Inspector, and the Style Rendering toolbar.

Master It Summarize the uses for the CSS Styles panel, the Property Inspector, and the Style Rendering toolbar.

Use Dreamweaver to create a style sheet. Dreamweaver can add links to style sheets and crea new rules for the attached style sheet.

Master It Use the `ch16_index.html` page, but start from scratch to make your own la out and styles for it. Demonstrate your results in a browser. Combine this exercise with t following one.

Use Dreamweaver to edit styles. Styles can be edited using the CSS Rule Definition dialog in the Properties pane of the CSS Styles panel.

Master It Combine this with the preceding exercise. The process of creating your own layo and design for the exercise page will lead to many opportunities to edit styles as you creat them. If you have a preferred way of editing styles, explain what it is and why.

Learn how to avoid possible Dreamweaver pitfalls. Dreamweaver offers multiple ways t perform some tasks. Some may create pitfalls. CSS may not be written in the optimal way.

Master It What specific pitfalls were mentioned?

Appendix

The Bottom Line

Each of The Bottom Line sections in the chapters suggest exercises to deepen skills and understanding. Sometimes there is only one possible solution, but often you are encouraged to use your skills and creativity to create something that builds on what you know and lets you explore one of many possible solutions.

Chapter 1: How to Write XHTML and CSS

Identify what constitutes a website. Websites are built with many interconnected technologies and applications. You should be familiar with how XHTML and CSS fit into that puzzle.

Master It Describe the purpose of XHTML and CSS in building a web page.

Master It Solution XHTML is used to mark up text into meaningful content blocks or elements such as headings, lists, paragraphs, tables, and quotes.

CSS is used to create a presentation for the content in the XHTML. That presentation can determine placement, color, font, background, and many other factors.

Identify what XHTML and HTML are. XHTML and HTML are markup languages. XHTML is an extension of HTML based on XML, itself a markup language.

Master It What do the acronyms HTML and XHTML mean?

Master It Solution HTML stands for Hypertext Markup Language. XHTML stands for Extensible Hypertext Markup Language.

Explain similarities and differences in XHTML and HTML. Since XHTML is based on HTML, there are many similarities between the two. The important differences arise from the distinction that XHTML uses XML syntax, while HTML is not required to follow XML syntax rules.

Master It List XML syntax rules that XHTML must follow. Make note of any that do not apply to HTML.

Master It Solution All tags must be closed. Empty elements are closed with a forward slash at the end of the tag. The empty element terminator rule does not apply to HTML.

Specific DOCTYPE declarations are required. HTML can use DOCTYPEs, but it isn't required.

All elements, attributes, and values must be in lowercase. HTML can use either upper- or lowercase tags, attributes, and values.

All values must be enclosed in quotation marks. Every attribute must be given an explic value. HTML can do this, but it isn't required.

Comments are not valid within a tag.

Comments may not contain two hyphens in a row, other than at the beginning and end the comment.

Describe what CSS is. CSS stands for Cascading Style Sheets, a specification that sets out properties and values that may be applied to the presentation of HTML or XHTML element

Master It Explain how CSS rules are applied to a web page.

Master It Solution Style rules are embedded in the web page itself, or linked or import into a web page.

Write XHTML syntax. Meaningful elements in the content of a web page are marked up wi XHTML tags, which may or may not have attributes and values giving more information abo the element.

Master It To demonstrate XHTML syntax, write two complete XHTML elements dem strating the difference between an element with attributes and values and one without.

Master It Solutions An example suggested in the chapter for an element with no attribu and value is `<p>A paragraph element</p>`.

An example suggested in the chapter for an element with an attribute and value is `<img src="animage.gif" />`.

Other solutions may also be correct.

Write CSS syntax. Style rules are written with *selectors* and *declarations*. The most basic sel tor is the element selector. Other types of selectors include adjacent-sibling selectors, attribu selectors, child selectors, class selectors, ID selectors, descendant selectors, pseudo class sele tors, pseudo element selectors, the universal selector, and group selectors.

For each selector, the declarations of properties and values for that selector govern how the e ment will display. Together the selector and declarations make up a style rule or, more simp a style.

Master It Write a style rule for the selector `h1` that sets the `font-family` to `Arial, Helvetica, sans-serif` and sets the `font-size` to `1.5em`. Write the rule in full and then write it again in shorthand.

Master It Solution In full:

```
h1 {
font-family: Arial, Helvetica, sans-serif;
font-size: 1.5em;
}
```

In shorthand:

```
h1 {
font: 1.5em Arial, Helvetica, sans-serif;
}
```

Chapter 2: Location, Location: Where to Put a Style

Understand and use the cascade to resolve style conflicts. When the browser reads your XHTML page, it reads (or cascades) from top to bottom and external to internal. Assuming there is no user style sheet to consider, the browser first reads the style rules in linked external files. Next, it reads the rules in the embedded `style` element in the document head. Finally, it reads any inline style rules.

Master It Explain what the conflict is in these two styles, and describe how the rules of the cascade would resolve the conflict.

```
body {
    font: 1em Verdana, Arial, Helvetica;
}
h1 {
    font-size: 1.8em;
}
```

Master It Solution The `h1` `font-size` is inherited from the `body` style. Because the `h1` rule comes later in the cascade, the `h1` will display with a `font-size` of 1.8em.

Understand where styles can be located and how that affects the cascade. Styles cascade from the user agent (such as a browser), the user, and a web author. CSS can be integrated with `link` elements, by `@import` directives, and by styles embedded in the XHTML page itself. If the same element can be selected by two or more rules, then the cascade determines which style will be displayed.

Master It Explain how an external style sheet would be affected by the presence of an embedded style.

Master It Solution The embedded style is further down in the cascade, or in closer proximity to the affected element. Embedded styles prevail over external styles.

Use *link* or *@import* to link to an external style sheet.

Master It Write XHTML links to one style sheet called `main.css` and to a style sheet called `forms.css`. Use `link` for one and `@import` for the other.

Master It Solution

```
<link href="main.css" rel="stylesheet" type="text/css" />
<style type="text/css">
@import url(forms.css);
</style>
```

Other solutions may also be correct.

Understand inheritance and know when it applies to a style. XHTML documents are constructed in a hierarchical relationship where elements are descended from antecedent elements. Many properties of the parent element are inherited by the child elements.

Master It Create an outline of a document tree demonstrating the hierarchical relationship of the following elements. An `html` element, containing a `body` element, containing a `div` element, containing an `h1` element.

Master It Solution

```
<html>
    <body>
        <div>
            <h1>
            </h1>
        </div>
    </body>
</html>
```

Understand specificity and use it to your advantage when creating selectors. The W3C h a set of mathematical formulas to determine the weight (or importance) of any particular sty rule. Selectors with higher specificity or more weight override styles with less weight.

Master It Calculate the specificity of the following selectors:

h1

h2.feature

div h2

#content

Master It Solution

0, 0, 1

0, 1, 1

0, 0, 2

1, 0, 0

Four-digit solutions (for example, 0, 0, 0, 1) are also correct. Solutions explained in terminolo about `id` and `class` specificity or using the *a, b, c* model are also correct.

Chapter 3: Page Basics: DOCTYPE, Head, Body, and Body Styles

Understand the DOCTYPE or DTD. A Document Type Definition (DTD) is the set of rules f the particular type of HTML or XHTML your page uses. Its inserted in the XHTML as the DO TYPE declaration. Its placed first in the document, before the opening html tag and head eleme

Master It Write the three XHTML DOCTYPEs and the three HTML 4.01 DOCTYPEs. Th write a brief explanation of the difference between strict, transitional, and frameset.

Master It Solution The XHTML DOCTYPES:

```
<!DOCTYPE html PUBLIC "-//W3C//DTD XHTML 1.0 Strict//EN"
   "http://www.w3.org/TR/xhtml1/DTD/ xhtml1-strict.dtd">
<!DOCTYPE html PUBLIC "-//W3C//DTD XHTML 1.0 Transitional//EN"
   "http://www.w3.org/TR/xhtml1/DTD/xhtml1-transitional.dtd">
<!DOCTYPE html PUBLIC "-//W3C//DTD XHTML 1.0 Frameset//EN"
   "http://www.w3.org/TR/xhtml1/DTD/xhtml1-frameset.dtd">
```

The HTML DOCTYPES:

```
<!DOCTYPE HTML PUBLIC "-//W3C//DTD HTML 4.01//EN"
        "http://www.w3.org/TR/html4/strict.dtd">
<!DOCTYPE HTML PUBLIC "-//W3C//DTD HTML 4.01 Transitional//EN"
        "http://www.w3.org/TR/html4/loose.dtd">
<!DOCTYPE HTML PUBLIC "-//W3C//DTD HTML 4.01 Frameset//EN"
        "http://www.w3.org/TR/html4/frameset.dtd">
```

Written descriptions of the differences will vary but should point out that no presentational or deprecated attributes are allowed in the HTML or XHTML with a strict DOCTYPE.

Use an appropriate DOCTYPE on your page. Either a strict HTML 4.01 or XHTML DOCTYPE that is validated will produce good results if the goal is pure separation of content from presentation. Transitional DOCTYPES allow for the use of *some* presentational material mixed into the content or XHTML. Valid transitional documents are also a good choice.

Master It Explain what DOCTYPE you would use for a new business site for the neighborhood bowling lanes.

Master It Solution Answers will vary. Any convincingly justified decision for either transitional or strict HTML or XHTML is acceptable.

Write elements in the document head. The `head` contains the page title, links to style sheets, and `meta` elements and can also contain other material such as JavaScripts. Information in the document head does not appear on the browser page; therefore `head` elements cannot be styled for presentation. The `head` must include a `title` element.

Master It Here is a small section from the head of the home page of the Real-World Scenario site *Vitamin*. Explain what each element is.

```
<head>
<meta http-equiv="Content-type" content="text/html; charset=utf-8" />
<title>Vitamin - A resource for web developers, designers and entrepreneurs</
title>
<link type="text/css" media="all" rel="stylesheet" href="/css/main.css" />
<link type="text/css" media="all" rel="stylesheet" href="/css/home.css" />
<script src="/scripts/global20060504.js" type="text/javascript"></script>
</head>
```

Master It Solution The elements are as follows:

`<head>` The opening head tag.

`<meta>` A meta element setting the character set to UTF-8.

`<title>...</title>` The title element giving the title of the page.

`<link>` A link to the `main.css` style sheet.

`<link>` A link to the `home.css` style sheet.

`<script>` A link to a JavaScript.

`</head>` The closing head tag.

Other descriptions of these elements may also be correct.

Write CSS for the body of your document. The body element contains everything that appe in the browser window. The body is the basic container for everything on your page and can b styled with CSS presentation rules.

The style for the body of your document can determine (among other things) background col background image, and margins.

Master It Do at least three of the following exercises using the CSS style sheet you creat in Chapter 3. Demonstrate your results in a browser.

1. Change the background color to #93C or to #0D520F.
2. In an image editing program, resize `ch3bg_sm.gif` so that it is 100×100 pixels in size a save it with the filename `ch3bg100.gif`. Then change the name of the image in the u value to the new name.
3. Use the new 100×100 pixel GIF with the `background-repeat` set to `repeat-y`. Then t it set to `no-repeat`.
4. Make or find a different background image and use it instead of `ch3bg_sm.gif`. Try with at least three repeat or position rules.
5. Change the `margin-top` and `margin-left` measurements to 5 percent.
6. Change every `margin` to `0` in one shorthand declaration.

Master It Solution Results will vary, but you should be able to demonstrate your work a browser and be able to pinpoint which of the exercises you did.

Chapter 4: Headings and Heading Styles

Use CSS rules for color, font, background, and border to create distinctive headings. It i an effective visual help to give headings a distinctive look. It makes a page easier to scan fo particular block of information or content.

Master It Add an `h4` element to the `ch4_stretchy.html` page and write a style rule for Change the `h1` in `ch4_stretchy.css` to be centered and a different color. Demonstrate t results in a browser.

Master It Solution Solutions will vary. The heading should be centered using `text-alig center`.

Use a *class* selector to style headings. Unlike `id` elements, which must be unique on the page, a `class` can be used more than once.

Master It Assign the class `feature` to the exercise page with `h2` headings. Use the sam class for both headings. Then rewrite the rule for the class to completely change the appe ance of the headings to a style of your own design. Demonstrate the results in a browse

Master It Solution Answers will vary; however, both the `h2` elements must have the sa appearance.

Use image replacement to create headings. Many more fonts are available as graphics th can be displayed as text. When decorative fonts are required, designers replace or hide the te in various ways and use images instead.

Master It Use the file `floatingonair.jpg` from the accompanying CD and one of the image replacement techniques described in the chapter to replace the heading *Floating on Air* in the XHMTL page. Be ready to explain the pros and cons of the method you selected and to demonstrate the results in a browser.

Master It Solution Results will vary depending on the method of image replacement chosen. You should demonstrate awareness of the pros and cons of the method and demonstrate the results in a browser.

Understand and use the visual formatting model (or box model) that determines how XHTML elements respond to CSS rules. The box model determines the interaction of content, padding, border, and margin in all its various combinations. A box should have content. Padding, border, and margin are optional and can be used in numerous ways.

Master It Create a page of example headings that demonstrate the following box model uses:

1. Content with no padding, border, or margin
2. Content with padding and a border
3. Content with a margin but no border and no padding
4. Content with a lot of top and bottom padding
5. Content with borders and a lot of left and right margin

Master It Solution Results will vary. When demonstrating the page in a browser, you should be able to identify individual examples of padding, border, and margin.

Chapter 5: Page Divisions: *div* for Structure and Layout

Use *div* and *id* to create structure for styling. XHTML elements such as headings, paragraphs, lists, and block quotes create structure in a document. That basic semantic information can be grouped into content blocks that share a common purpose in a `div` element. With an `id` creating a unique identifier for the content block, CSS can be used to present the content block in numerous ways.

Master It On `ch5_threecol.html` and `ch5_threecol.css` make modifications to do the following:

1. Create a "navbar" `div` and a "news" `div` within this element on the page:

```
<div id="left">
      <p>Navigation</p>
      <ul>
        <li>link one</li>
        <li>link two</li>
        <li>link three</li>
        <li>link four</li>
        <li>link five</li>
      </ul>
      <h3>News Items</h3>
      <p>All the latest flower news and blurbs about specials and stuff and
nonsense goes here.</p>
    </div>
```

2. Create CSS rules for the two new divs. The two new structural elements should hav different appearances. Be ready to demonstrate your results in a browser.
3. Make changes to `ch5_threecol.css` to improve the padding, headings, and other features of the presentation. Be prepared to demonstrate your work in a browser.

Master It Solution

1. The two new divs should be inserted thus:

```
<div id="left">
  <div id="navbar">
  <p>Navigation</p>
      <ul>
        <li>link one</li>
        <li>link two</li>
        <li>link three</li>
        <li>link four</li>
        <li>link five</li>
      </ul>
   </div>
   <div id="news">
      <h3>News Items</h3>
      <p>All the latest flower news and blurbs about specials and stuff and
nonsense goes here.</p>
   </div>
</div>
```

2. The CSS created to style the new elements will vary. Demonstrate your results in a browser.
3. CSS will vary. The widths of the columns may need to be reduced a bit if padding o margin is added. Demonstrate your results in a browser.

Create layouts with *absolute* and *relative* positioning. Absolute positioning removes an element from the document flow and positions it with regard to its nearest positioned ancest Relative positioning maintains the element's orientation to the document flow but offsets it position within its container relative to its spot if it were in the flow.

Master It

1. On `ch5_start.css`, use `position: absolute` to place the `div id="content"` eleme in a precise location along with an absolutely positioned nav element. Then enlarge t text several times using the browser menu. What happens?
2. On `ch5_threecol.css`, use `position: relative` to shift the new navbar you creat a few pixels to the left or right. Demonstrate your results in a browser.

Master It Solution

1. After enough enlargements, the text will overlap and be unreadable.

2. You may quickly move the navbar a few pixels to the right using `left` and `top` values. Remember that negative left values or positive right values can be used.

Create layouts based on *float, margin,* and *z-index*. Text wraps around a floated element. To create the appearance of columns, an element next to a `float` can be given a margin value that will prevent it from wrapping around the floated element. `Z-index` deals with the fact that more than one element can occupy the same position on a page. The elements can be stacked in a particular order using `z-index`.

Master It

1. Using Figure 5.21 as your guide, create the *all floats with negative margin–fixed width* layout. Alternatively, create your own version of a two- or three-column design using `float`. Demonstrate your results in a browser. (Feel free to use content and images from the Far and Wee Balloon page or from The Flower Page to fill in some content. Or provide your own content and images.)
2. On `ch5_z-index.css`, change the `z-index` value of the selector `#two` to a higher value such as 10. What happens? Now change the `z-index` value of the selector `#two` to `-2`. What happens? Demonstrate your results in a browser.

Master It Solution

1. Answers will vary. The results should be demonstrable in a browser.
2. With a `z-index` of `10`, `#two` pops to the top of the stacking order. With a `z-index` of `-2`, `#two` moves to the bottom of the stacking order.

Understand *float* for images and other floated elements. The purpose of the `float` property is to move an element to either the right or left side of its parent element. Elements such as `images`, `callouts`, `pullquotes`, and other page layout features are often used with float. The text next to the floated element wraps around it, unless it is cleared. If it is cleared, it appears beneath the float.

Master It There are three small images in the `right` element on the page `ch5_threecol.html`. Apply a CSS `float` property to them and add any other rules need to make the images display nicely. Demonstrate your results.

Master It Solution Use the selector `#right img` to add the new rules for these images. Answers will vary. Check results in a browser.

Use *clear* with floated elements. The `clear` property forces an element to move below any float on the left or right sides, or both.

Master It Use `ch5_threecol.css` to float the image in the `content` div. Then force the paragraph text that follows it the clear the floated element.

Master It Solution Add the selector `#content img` to the CSS and create a rule floating it either left or right.

There are several ways to make the following paragraph clear the float. Based on what you know now, you may create a `class` with the `clear` property to apply to the paragraph. Or you may create a selector such as `#content p` that applies a `clear` rule to every paragraph in the content box. The second solution is a bit of overkill. Use of a `class` would be the best option at this point in your learning.

Chapter 6: Paragraph and Text Styles

Identify helpful XHTML elements for formatting text, including `em`, `strong`, `acronym`, `abb` `cite`, `q`, `blockquote`, `big`, `small`, `sub`, `sup`, `code`, `var`, and others. Long strings of letters a words must be formatted in ways that help readers understand organization, content, and p pose. Adding to the heading and paragraph elements from past chapters, this chapter provid a number of other helpful text formatting elements.

Master It Find the document `mark_me_up.html` on the accompanying CD. Use all the things you have learned up to this point to format and style the document.

Master It Solution Solutions will vary. At a minimum, there should be XHTML page bui ing elements such as `DOCTYPE`, `title`, `html`, `body`, and so on. Logical formatting of headin and paragraphs is needed. The angle brackets in the snippet of XHTML and the copyright symbol at the end should be expressed with character entities. There are also opportunities use `acronym`, `abbr`, `em`, `sup`, `sub`, `code`, `text-indent`, and `cite`. Minimal CSS rules should style body, headings, paragraphs, and `blockquote` and any other elements used.

Understand and use CSS selectors including child selectors, adjacent selectors, and attribu selectors.

Master It Make the following changes to `mark_me_up.html and its accompanying style sheet:`

1. Add an `em` element to one of the headings. Then write a CSS child selector rule that w style only that `em` element and no other `em` elements on the page.
2. Assign the first paragraph a `class` or `id` of "intro" and use an attribute selector to cre a style for the first paragraph.

Master It Solution Solutions will vary. Here are some likely approaches you may take

1. One logical place for this is `What Do <em>You</em> Remember?` You may have form ted this as an `h2` or `h3`, in which case, the child selector would be `h2 > em {`*`some rul`* or `h3 > em {`*`some rule`*`}`. Other implementations are also acceptable.
2. In the XHTML, you should add either `<p id="intro">` or `<p class="intro">` to t formatting. The CSS rule would then be either `p[class=intro] {` *`some rule`* `}` or `p[id=intro] {` *`some rule`* `}`.

Create generated content. Although not widely used, its possible to generate content from t CSS rather than the XHTML. The `:before` and `:after` pseudo-elements are examples of ge erated content.

Master It Include this in the work on `mark_me_up.html`. Add generated content to eith the all media or print styles.

Master It Solution Generated content can be placed in either the screen (all media) sty sheet or in the print style sheet. You will most likely use the `:before` or `:after` pseudo e ments, since this is the only type of generated content described in detail in the chapter. Y will most likely choose the URL (`stabenow.com`) in the text for this. It is acceptable to ha it only in the print style sheet.

Create codes for special characters such as copyright symbols. Literally hundreds of spec characters have unique codes for display in XHTML.

Master It Include special characters in mark_me_up.html by using character codes where appropriate.

Master It Solution The copyright symbol can be either © or ©. The less than angle bracket is either < or <. The greater than angle bracket is either > or >.

Write a print style sheet. Reading large blocks of text online is difficult. Designers must take special care to ensure that their content is readable and that various elements on a page are easy to distinguish. Reading in print is less demanding on the reader in terms of eye tracking from line to line and line length. Material from the online world can be formatted to more closely resemble print from magazines and books when styling text for print.

Master It Make a print style sheet for mark_me_up.html.

Master It Solution Solutions will vary. Minimal acceptable CSS rules include changing margins to inches and font-size to points. You may choose a serif font for the print page. There is an opportunity to use :after for a URL.

Chapter 7: Links and Link Styles

Write relative and absolute hyperlinks. Relative links are used only within your own site. Any link to pages outside your site needs an absolute URL.

Master It Assume that the flowerpagesite has a subfolder in the cactus folder. The subfolder is named pricklypear. Write a link from the document pricklypearjam.html in that subfolder to the home page.

Also write a link from the pricklypearjam.html page to this Prickly Pear Sweets and Treats Page:

```
http://www.desertusa.com/magoct97/oct_pear.html
```

Master It Solution The links would look like this:

```
<a href="../../ch7index.html">Home</a>
<a href="http://www.desertusa.com/magoct97/oct_pear.html">Prickly Pear Sweets
and Treats</a>
```

Write hyperlinks for e-mail and to MP3 and PDF files. E-mail uses the mailto protocol. An e-mail link is an a element with the mailto protocol in the href attribute. An a element with an href attribute is all that is needed to link to files in the MP3 and PDF formats.

Master It Create a new line in the footer of ch7index.html and create an e-mail link to yourself there.

Master It Solution Addresses will vary, but the link should be like this:

```
<a href="mailto:someone@somewhere.com">Email Me</a>
```

Master It Write a link to this music clip on the Internet:

```
http://madykaye.com/girlsjustgotta.mp3
```

Master It Solution An absolute link is needed:

```
<a href=" http://madykaye.com/girlsjustgotta.mp3">Girls Just Gotta Swing</a>
```

Use images to create hyperlinks. An img element is enclosed in an a element to create a cli able image.

Master It In the right column of ch7index.html there are three images. Link them to t appropriate site subpages.

Master It Solution The complete right div:

```
<div id="right">
    <h3>Flower Highlights</h3>
    <p><a href="cactus/ch7cactus.html"><img src="img/orangecactus_sm.jpg"
alt="Orange Cactus" width="150" height="113" /></a></p>
    <p>The cactus blooms in spring. Heres how to encourage your cactus to
bloom: water it.</p>
    <p><a href="cactus/ch7cactus.html"><img src="img/redcactus_sm.jpg"
alt="Red Cactus" width="150" height="113" /></a></p>
    <p>A cactus in your garden can brighten up the scene in early spring. Th
rest of the year feel free to ignore it.</p>
    <p><a href="groundcover/ch7groundcover.html"><img src="img/groundcover_
sm.jpg" alt="White flowers" width="150" height="113" /></a></p>
    <p>Masses of flowers make good ground cover.</p>
  </div>
```

Use CSS to style hyperlinks. The a element can be styled with any CSS property you hav learned thus far, including color, margin, padding, border, background-color, and backgrour image. Its different states can be targeted with pseudo class elements.

Master It Create a completely different presentation for the links in flowerpagesite fro the styles used in the exercises. Create rules for the different pseudo class selectors and f the current page indicator. Be prepared to demonstrate your results in a browser. Create backup copy of your current style sheet before you begin making changes.

Master It Solution Presentations will vary but should address issues involving link sta and the current page indicator.

Use CSS to create pop-up text. By nesting a span element in an a element, you can cause te to pop up in various locations on the page when the a element is in the hover state.

Master It Remove the margin-top from the #news selector. Then add a z-index rule to t #mainnav a:hover span selector to keep it on top even if it overlaps other text. When wou you consider this a good use of a pop-up? Demonstrate in the browser.

Master It Solution You may comment out or completely remove the #news rule from t style sheet, or you may change the value on the margin-top.

Any z-index value above 1 can be used, since nothing else on the page is assigned a z-ind value.

You may have various ideas about when this might be useful, particularly with other typ of layouts or for other types of links, perhaps inline links. Although it obscures the text beneath it, as soon as the cursor moves away from the hyperlink, the text is visible again, you may be able to devise creative ideas for a presentation such as this.

Chapter 8: Multimedia, Images, and Image Styles

Understand basic functions of graphics software. Image skills essential for web pages including cropping, sizing, changing resolution, and understanding transparency.

Master It If you have a way to create a new background graphic or to crop the 1200-pixel file provided on the CD, try using a background graphic of about 600px for the background image of the banner (see Figure 8.38). Instead of using `no-repeat`, have it repeat on the horizontal axis only. Compare the results with what you did for Figure 8.38.

Master It Solution If you crop the `banner_bg.jpg` provided to 600px and have it repeat, you will quickly see that it creates a glaring pattern mismatch in the background when it repeats. The results you get with an image of your own will vary. If you're learning XHTML and CSS in a group, try comparing notes with your classmates about the qualities that make a good repeating background image.

Place images on web pages. The `img` element requires two attributes: `src` and `alt`. Other attributes may include `width`, `height`, `title`, and `longdesc`.

Master It Go to a site like `www.freeimages.co.uk` and download some images. Create an XHTML page and some CSS styles to use one or more images. Be ready to demonstrate your work in a browser.

Master It Solution Results will vary. All images should appear in the browser and have appropriate `alt` text. Layouts and presentation will vary.

Build horizontal and vertical navigation bars with images. Images used as hyperlinks are common practice on the Internet. Images in a navigation bar are often called buttons and may change for various link states such as `:hover` and `:visited`, depending on the CSS rules used.

Master It Find or create a few button images to use as navigation on the page you created in the previous exercise. Since you only have one page to work with, you can link the buttons to other pages you have in Chapter 8 or to external sites like `yahoo.com`. Be prepared to demonstrate your results in a browser.

Master It Solution Results will vary. The number of buttons used will vary, as will the layout and how they are linked. Check each in a browser.

Use images to create a photo gallery. Photo galleries come in a multitude of formats but generally employ a series of small or thumbnail images as links to larger images.

Master It On the `Ch8_smallimage.html` page, reverse the position of the photo and the text. Put the text on the left and the image on the right in each `div`.

Instead of centering the body of `Ch_smallimage.html` using a fixed width, try centering with a `body` width set to a percentage value to create a more accessible `body` size.

Master It Solution The image positions are determined with `float`.

Give the `body` a percentage value and `margin-left` and `margin-right` percentage values that add up to 98 percent. (Staying just slightly short of the 100 percent marks avoids box model issues.)

Understand how to add multimedia objects to web pages. Because of varying browser support and legal restrictions placed on Microsoft, three redundant types of code are needed to add multimedia to a web page.

Master It Set the Flash file to `value="true"` for the loop `param` and see what happens. T other changes. Demonstrate your results in a browser.

Master It Solution The change to the loop values (all three will need changing) will resu in the movie playing over and over. Other changes will vary.

Chapter 9: Lists and List Styles

Lists are the workhorses of the Web. They are easy to read, make finding information go quickl help you set up ordered steps or processes, and accommodate a myriad of marker types and nu bering schemes. This versatility makes lists popular for many different situations.

Write every type of list. There are three types of lists in use on the Web: ordered, unordere and definition. Ordered and unordered lists are constructed of a simple series of list items. D inition lists contain terms and their accompanying definitions.

Master It Make a list with information about your friends, family, CD collection, produ warranties, pets, or some other type of information you are interested in. Nest the list to least two levels, more if it makes sense with your topic.

When you have the list built, write some CSS rules for it. Be as creative as you can in yo presentation. Be prepared to demonstrate your list in a browser.

Master It Solution Answers will vary. This can be done as either an unordered list or definition list. An ordered list wouldn't be semantically sensible unless you can supply compelling justification for ordering the information, such as siblings in birth order. Be su that the nested list is within the `li` tags of the parent list item. Try to show creative use c color, border, background, positioning, and other properties in styling the list.

Use CSS to control the presentation of lists. Any CSS property can be applied to the pres tation of lists.

Master It Instead of making the `star.gif` apply to every marker on your page of unor dered lists, see what happens if you do this: `ul ul {list-style: url(star.gif);}`. Whe does the star first appear in the list? When is it inherited? What happens if the `ul ul` rule h the star as a background image rather than a `list-style-type`? Is the star inherited?

Master It Solution When the star is inserted in the second-level list using `list-style` it will be inherited in the third-level list as well. When it is a background image it will n be inherited. Further, the `list-style: none` rule must be used to remove a marker so t image in the background shows through as a marker.

Use lists as vertical, horizontal, and CSS pop-up navigation elements. A list can contain any textual element, including links. Because navigation menus on web pages are often a lis of links, lists are often used to create menus and nav bars. Using `display: block` or `displa inline` or `floats`, lists can be styled with CSS rules that make them appear in a button-lik vertical or horizontal display.

Master It Pick either the horizontal or the vertical list exercise and try using backgrour images instead of background colors to create the rollover effect. Use `hoverbg.jpg`, `linkbg.j` or `visitedbg.jpg` from the accompanying CD if you need images for this (or make you own). You did something like this in Chapter 7 with `background-image`, but the knowled you gained from Chapter 9 makes it a much more attractive option for a menu. Demonstr your results in a browser.

Master It Solution Answers will vary. You may decide to use only two images for this, although three are offered as suggestions. Be prepared to show your results in a browser.

Chapter 10: Tables and Table Styles

Write the XHTML for a table. The `table` element is composed of a number of horizontal table rows (`tr`) that are filled with cells of table data (`td`). As rows are added to the table, the cells in each row create a vertical column. Both rows and columns in a table can contain table header elements (`th`) as row or column labels.

Master It Make a new table with your own information, perhaps something like the names, ages, birthplaces, and favorite movies of people you know. Use this table for all the exercises that follow.

Master It Solution Solutions will vary. The table should have `th` elements at the very least, with other elements as needed such as caption. If planning ahead to the accessibility elements in the next exercise, other elements may be present.

Use elements and attributes to make a table accessible. A caption element, a summary attribute, scope attributes, or `id`s for header elements add to a table's accessibility.

Master It Add a caption element, a summary attribute, scope attributes, or `id`s for headers attributes to ensure your table's accessibility.

Master It Solution Solutions will vary. All tables should have a caption and summary. Some will have scope attributes while others will have headers attributes.

Write CSS to control the presentation of a table. Tables can be styled with possible selectors such as `table`, `th`, `td`, `thead`, `tbody`, `caption`, and any classes or `id`s you create.

Master It Use styles to give your table an attractive appearance.

Master It Solution Solutions will vary. Consideration should be given to font choice, table width and padding, the use of borders and color, alignment, or any other properties that affect appearance.

Chapter 11: Forms and Form Styles

Forms allow interaction with visitors. They are used to take orders, gather information, solicit feedback, collect votes, search, and interact with web applications or databases.

The three Master It exercises for this chapter are to be completed together as a single assignment.

Write XHTML for form elements. The essential attributes of the `form` element include `method` and `action`. Individual `form` elements you learned to create include `fieldset`, `legend`, `input`, `textarea`, `select`, `radio button`, `checkbox`, and the `Submit button`.

Master It Create a form of your own design. You can work it into the Far and Wee Balloon or the Flower Page designs, or you can create something completely original. Use all of the form elements you learned about.

Master It Solution Solutions will vary. Each form must include opening and closing form tags, an action attribute on the opening form tag, some number of input elements (each with type and name attributes), and a Submit button (input element with type="submit" and a value attribute). Demonstrate the form in a browser.

Create style rules for forms. Any CSS rules you have learned up to this point for `font`, `background`, `color`, `border`, `padding`, `alignment`, `position`, and `width` can be used to writ styles for forms. However, certain things about the appearance and function of `form` elemen remain in the control of the browser as a means of ensuring accessibility and usability in forr

Master It Write styles for the form you created in the previous exercise.

Master It Solution Answers will vary. At a minimum there should be CSS rules for pa colors and fonts. Form elements that may be addressed by CSS include `form`, `fieldset`, `legend`, `label`, and others.

Use XHTML elements to ensure accessible forms. `Form` elements need a `label`. The `labe` `for` markup should be used for clarity and usability.

Master It. Use `label` elements with `for` attributes and input elements with `id` attributes your form.

Master It Solution Solutions will vary. The `for` attribute of the label element must mat the `id` attribute of the input element that it is labeling exactly. (Neither has to match the na attribute of the input elements.) Each `id` can only be used once per page.

Chapter 12: Publishing and Testing Your Pages

It isn't enough to create a web page. You must also put it on a server so it's seen on the World Wi Web. That involves getting server space and testing the site once it's on the server.

Create a four- or five-page website of your own design. It can be about an organization, a pers a topic, or something else of interest. Use it to complete the following activities.

Use FTP to put files on a server. The most common way to put the files that make up you website on a server is with the File Transfer Protocol, or FTP.

Master It Use one of the FTP tools included on the CD, or an FTP tool of your own cho ing, to move your site to the server.

Master It Solution Finding the URL for the server in a browser and actually seeing th files on the WWW will be proof of success with FTP.

Get a domain name and server space. If you want your own domain name and server spa you will have to pay for it. Its also possible to find free hosting.

Master It Do some research online. Visit several free and for-fee hosting companies. Co pare costs, services, plans, and support guarantees. Decide whether to not to buy a doma name or use free hosting. Decide where to put your site. Be ready to explain your choice

Master It Solution Each person will make an individual choice based on a number of f tors such as finances, readiness to have a professional space on the Internet, and hosting plans. Be ready to explain why you chose the server space you decide to use.

Test your site. Once your files are on the server, find your URL in a browser and test ever thing about your site to be sure it is working properly.

Master It Test the site yourself with as many browsers and Internet devices as you pos bly can. Validate your XHTML and CSS using the free tools provided by the W3C. Chec your pages for accessibility. Be prepared to show your results in a browser.

Master It Solution Fix any problems that you find. Retest and revalidate.

Identify search engine submission tools. After your site is posted on the Web, you need to register with the search engines so that they know you are there and can send people your way.

Master It At `yahoo.com`, find the "Suggest a Site" link in the page footer. Register your site for free. You must register with Yahoo! to do this.

Or, go to `dmoz.org` and submit your URL.

Master It Solution At Yahoo!, they encourage you every step of the way to pay for a listing. You must be careful and hunt for the free option to succeed in getting a free listing.

At DMOZ, you must make sure you have found the proper category for your site before you suggest your URL.

Chapter 13: CSS for Weblogs

Weblogs are popular because they are easy and flexible. Sites sometimes include blogs as a part of the overall site plan. Sometimes a site is built completely as a blog.

Describe the advantage of blogs over traditional sites. A blog is a website, but it has certain characteristics that distinguish it from a traditional website.

Master It List at least three advantages of blogging over traditional websites.

Master It Solution Choices will vary. Possibilities include ease of use, that few technical skills are required, ease of updating, low cost, community interaction, or others.

Understand how to create a blog. Some blogs you must download and install. Others let you answer a few basic questions, give you free hosting, and you're publishing.

Master It You can delete a blog as instantly as you can create one. Create one of your own at either BlogSpot or WordPress.

Master It Solution Be prepared to give your URL and show your blog in a browser. You'll use it again in the last Master It exercise. If you don't want to maintain it after demonstrating that you were able to create it, feel free to delete it.

Identify features of Blogger and WordPress blogs. Differences between Blogger, WordPress (or Movable Type, Typepad, or others) will determine which one is right for you.

Master It Complete the table in the file `blogs.html` from the accompanying CD. Fill in the missing columns with Yes or No to indicate the presence of a feature. You can use a qualified Yes or No answer if needed. As an option, add another column for any other blog software you are interested in researching.

Master It Solution

TABLE A.1: Features of Blogger and WordPress Blogs

FEATURE	BLOGGER	WORDPRESS
Well-designed templates	Yes	Yes
Comment options	Yes	Yes
Customizable	Yes	Limited on wordpress.com

TABLE A.1: Features of Blogger and WordPress Blogs *(CONTINUED)*

FEATURE	BLOGGER	WORDPRESS
Can be used on your own server	Yes	Yes
Free	Yes	Yes
Categories allowed	No	Yes
Pages allowed	No	Yes
Syndication allowed	Yes	Yes
Good help and support info	Yes	Yes

Identify ways to configure and customize a blog. You can use what you know about XHTM and CSS to take the basic elements for a blog and add your own designs and modifications to ma a unique and distinctive blog.

Master It Make changes to the blog you created in the preceding exercise. Be able to id tify the places where you customized.

Master It Solution Solutions will vary. If the blog is on BlogSpot, you can change both t template and the CSS. On WordPress with free hosting, your choices are limited to simp modification of the theme such as adding links or choosing categories, since you aren't allowed access to the XHTML and CSS.

Chapter 14: Design Basics

In this chapter, you dipped a toe into the ocean of design by looking at some of the factors th are important in designing web pages. You discovered more about the importance of consiste design, or repetition in design. In addition, you learned about the importance of careful aligr ment of page elements to create unity in your designs.

Understand the basics of creating a visual hierarchy. Create visual hierarchy with above the-fold layout, size, placement, contrast, and headings.

Master It Visit `www.oneida.com` and explain how this site creates a visual hierarchy.

Master It Solution Answers will vary. One possible answer: Oneida uses above-the-fo design with a large image as a focal point. A menu made with contrasting colors and smal sized type tops the large image. Under the focal point image are related items in matchi colors, but they are made distinct in the hierarchy by the use of dividing lines, typograpl and color. Material under the fold is in alignment with the more important material at th top of the page.

Note: The suggested solutions for the web pages in these exercises are based on their appe ance on a particular day. Since websites change often, the suggested solutions may not ap to the site's appearance on the day of your visit.

Examine the ways to create contrast. Contrast can be achieved with size, color, typography, form, or placement.

Master It Visit `www.bethmeth.com` and explain how this site creates contrast.

Master It Solution Answers will vary. One possible answer: Bethlehem Methodist uses primarily size and color. Contrast is also created with typography of different sizes, cases, and colors. Once again, material under the fold is in alignment with the more important material at the top of the page.

Examine the value of repetition in web design. The placement of elements on the page, the location of the navigation, the colors used, the fonts used—all these things must be consistent throughout the site. This consistency is achieved partly through repetition. Repetition ties things together that aren't connected by proximity.

Master It Explore the inner pages of the Oneida site. Explain how the site uses repetition to create a consistent look on their inner pages.

Master It Solution Answers will vary. One possible answer: the same layout and global nav is repeated on each inner page. The subnavigation is always on the left with photos of individual products shown in aligned arrays on the lower right of the page. Even though the products change from page to page, the appearance is very consistent.

Understand how alignment and proximity can affect a web page design. Alignment and proximity create unity and connection in a design; they create a relationship between the separate design elements.

Master It Visit `www.campaignmonitor.com` and explain how this site uses alignment and proximity.

Master It Solution Answers will vary. One possible answer: this site is interesting because it deliberately places certain items out of alignment to create contrast and a focal point. Every other element on the page is carefully aligned with three columns below the fold. In the two columns to the left, headings are immediately under the image they as associated with, in a contrasting color. Text follows in close proximity, creating an association between the image, heading, and text in the eye of the visitor. The column on the right uses dividing lines to create contrast and separate items into visual proximity.

Chapter 15: XHTML and CSS for Handhelds

Two basics: clear semantic markup and separation of content from presentation are all-important in any discussion about content that works in every device. Without them, no style sheet can overcome the accessibility and usability problems your page may have. If you have the basics, then creating a style sheet for the media type handheld may provide help to some users of handheld devices.

Identify some of the obstacles to designing for handheld devices. There are no standards or consistency in handheld devices capable of web browsing. Its a fractured market.

Master It Discuss the problems involved in creating styles for handheld devices. Try to come up with some that were not mentioned in the list in the chapter section called "Inherent Obstacles to Web Authoring for Handhelds," but that you have understood from working in this chapter.

Master It Solution Possible additions to the "Inherent Obstacles" list might include di culty in testing on the targeted device, lack of simulators, lack of centrally located docum tation about handheld devices and what each supports in terms of HTML and CSS, and other suggestions.

Write styles for the handheld media type. Handheld style sheets use a `media="handheld` attribute. Not all handheld devices support CSS. The devices that *do* support CSS don't all support the *same* CSS.

Master It Take a page of XHTML from the `flowerpagesite` in Chapter 9 and write a handheld style sheet for it. Alternatively, write a handheld style sheet for an XHTML pa of your own design. Test as best you can.

Master It Solution Basic decisions about background color and foreground color contra floats, navigation aids, and images would be needed for either the Chapter 9 page or a pa of your own page. Test with one of the Opera choices, unless you have a subscription to BrowserCam.

Examine the available handheld resources and testing tools. There are several available simulators that can be downloaded or used online to test handheld displays. Most compani that make handheld devices or software for handheld devices offer support to developers.

Master It Opera Small Screen view, Opera Mini simulator, and DeviceCam were explor in this chapter. Other possible testing devices were also mentioned. Explain which you thi would be the most valuable to you. Give your reasons.

Master It Solution Answers will vary. Someone who works for a company where eve employee is given a device with Windows Mobile 5 might find DeviceCam the perfect choice. Others may favor the Opera Mini simulator for its more accurate portrayal of sty for phones. Others might suggest that installing the BlackBerry simulator is the best optic There is no single correct answer, as long as you can give good reasons for your choice. An it bears repeating, there is no substitute for testing with the real device, if possible.

Chapter 16: Writing CSS with Dreamweaver 8

Dreamweaver can write clean XHTML and almost any style rule when you learn the ins and ou of using it effectively.

Identify Dreamweavers CSS tools. The major tools are the CSS Styles panel, the Property Inspector, and the Style Rendering toolbar.

Master It Summarize the uses for the CSS Styles panel, the Property Inspector, and the Style Rendering toolbar.

Master It Solution A possible answer: The CSS Styles panel is used to add, edit, delete, examine style rules. The Property Inspector is most useful when picking existing classes assign to selected elements. The Style Rendering toolbar allows you to see different style sheets rendered in Design view.

Use Dreamweaver to create a style sheet. Dreamweaver can add links to style sheets and create new rules for the attached style sheet.

Master It Use the `ch16_index.html` page, but start from scratch to make your own layo and styles for it. Demonstrate your results in a browser. Combine this exercise with the f lowing one.

Master It Solution Solutions will vary. Basic elements that should be included are background colors, good color contrast, attractive and readable font and font size choices, and a layout that flows sensibly.

Use Dreamweaver to edit styles. Styles can be edited using the CSS Rule Definition dialog or in the Properties pane of the CSS Styles panel.

Master It Combine this with the preceding exercise. The process of creating your own layout and design for the exercise page will lead to many opportunities to edit styles as you create them. If you have a preferred way of editing styles, explain what it is and why.

Master It Solution Answers will vary. Some will have a preference for the CSS Rule Definition dialog box or for the Properties pane for editing styles. As long as you have a reason for preferring one over the other it doesn't matter which you use. Nor does it matter if you use both.

Learn how to avoid possible Dreamweaver pitfalls. Dreamweaver offers multiple ways to perform some tasks. Some may create pitfalls. CSS may not be written in the optimal way.

Master It What specific pitfalls were mentioned?

Master It Solution Specifically mentioned were improper use of the Property Inspector and relying on Dreamweaver's suggestions for Advanced selectors in every circumstance. Possible disorganization and cascade issues may arise if the user doesn't arrange the Dreamweaver style sheet by hand. Other pitfalls may be suggested from the experience of having tried to use Dreamweaver prior to reading this chapter. For example, many users don't realize they can type Advanced selectors of their own choosing in the selector field and draw the erroneous conclusion that Dreamweaver can't do what they want to do.

ilossary

mbols

TTLIST

erm used in a DTD to mean the list of attributes an ment may have.

attrs

term used in a DTD to indicate the list of either quired or implied attributes an element has.

mport

directive contained in the head of an HTML or ITML page to the browser to use a particular style eet to format that page.

nportant

directive added onto the end of a CSS declaration at gives it precedence over all other declarations, cept those in user style sheets also marked with `nportant`.

solute link

nks in a website can be *relative* or absolute. Abso- e links list the complete *URL* for a document and lude a protocol, a server, and a filename. `http://` `w.wiley.com/` is an absolute link.

solute measure

size set with a fixed *value*, such as in pixels, that does t automatically adapt to the user's preferences.

solute positioning

method of removing an element from the *document w* and positioning it with regard to its *containing ck.*

jacent sibling selector

CSS selector specifying rules that match elements sed on a sibling relationship. The syntax is

```
ement1 + Element2
```

where `Element2` is the subject of the selector. The selector matches if `Element1` and `Element2` share the same parent in the document tree and `Element1` immediately precedes `Element2`.

alpha channel transparency

A variable type of transparency possible in *PNG* images that allows up to 254 levels of partial transparency in an image.

ancestor

An element one level above the element it contains. The contained elements are known as *descendant elements*.

Active Server Pages (ASP)

A programming language used to create dynamic and interactive web pages.

attribute

Optional part of an HTML or XHTML *element*, assigned as part of the element's *opening tag*. The attribute must have a *value* assigned. Attributes assign certain *properties* to the element.

attribute selector

A CSS selector that specifies rules that match elements based on their attributes as defined in the source document. The syntax is

```
element[attribute] {rule;}
```

B

block-level element

An element that automatically begins on a new line, is followed by an automatic line break, and fills its parent element horizontally.

blog

A contraction of *weblog*. A weblog is a website that is easily updated on a daily basis with dated posts. Reader feedback is often encouraged in the form of comments. Links to other blogs are another common feature of blogs.

bookmarklet

A link that behaves like a normal bookmark (or favorite) but also has a brief script to produce a particular action when the link is clicked.

box model

Every element on a page generates a rectangular box. The box model is a visual model that browsers use to interpret visual directives. The box includes its content as well as optional padding, border, and margin. The box model is a standard specification; however, some browsers misinterpret the specifications with regard to the model.

browser

A software program used for finding and displaying various kinds of Internet resources, including web pages.

C

cache

A folder on your computer where the browser stores downloaded style sheets, images, and web pages that have already been viewed. Once a *CSS* file is stored in cache, it does not have to be downloaded again the next time it is needed.

cascade

The application hierarchy underlying the rules of CSS—determining the order in which style sheets and style rules will be applied to a given page.

Cascading Style Sheets (CSS)

The system of style rules that define the visual appearance of a structured HTML or XHTML page by specifying the positioning, color, and other characteristics of the structural elements. Styles can be located either on the page or stored in a separate (`.css`) file. The cascade determines the order of precedence of style rules based on their location.

character entity

In XHTML, any symbol, mark, or other character used in writing that must be entered on a web pa with a special code. Also known as *special charact*

child element

Within the hierarchy of an HTML or XHTML pag an element that is nested exactly one level within another. The two elements have a parent-child relationship.

child selector

A CSS *selector* that uses the syntax

`Element1 > Element 2`

The child selector matches `Element 2` when it is t child of `Element 1`.

class

1. An HTML or XHTML *attribute* used to apply a C class name to an element. The same class value c be assigned to multiple elements.
2. A CSS *selector* for which style rules can be writt

closing tag

HTML and XHTML syntax that terminates an element. It consists of a forward slash and the elemen name. Elements are contained within *opening tags* a closing tags. In *empty elements*, there are no closing tags. Instead, the terminating forward slash is contained within the element tag.

color code

A series of letters and numbers that signifies a speci color for a web page that can be assigned to an element in the HTML, XHTML, or CSS. *RGB* colors c be expressed as hexadecimal codes (for example, #FF0000), with decimal codes (for example, `255,0,` or percentage codes (for example, 100%, 0%, 0%). There are 17 colors that can be identified by name (for example, `red`). A *web-safe color*, which consists of matched pairs of hexadecimal numbers or letter such as #FF0000, can be expressed in shorthand. Fo example, the matched pairs of #FF0000 expressed i shorthand are #F00.

mments

mments are used to provide information, identify rticular areas of a document, or annotate a docu- ent in various ways. Comments can be used in TML, XHTML, and CSS and are a way of telling e browser, "Don't display this." The syntax of an HTML comment is:

```
!-- comment here -->
```

e syntax of a CSS comment is

```
 comment here */
```

ntaining block

block-level element that contains the element in estion. A contained element is wrapped or nested another element. It can be another element within e XHTML or the initial containing block, which is ways the `html` element.

ntextual selector

CSS selector used to create rules for an *element* sed on its relationship to the ancestor from which s descended. Also known as *descendant selector*. e syntax is

```
lector selector
```

th a space between the selectors.

S

e *Cascading Style Sheets.*

claration

mponent of a CSS rule, consisting of a *property* d a property *value*. A complete rule contains a *ector* and a declaration block, which contains one more declarations.

fault

e browser's built-in interpretation of how an TML or XHTML element should be displayed. u can change the default display with element ributes and *values* or with *CSS* rules.

deprecated element

An HTML or XHTML element that has been dropped from the current *DTD* but was available in previous DTDs is considered deprecated. Deprecated elements can be used with transitional DOCTYPEs, but not with *strict* DOCTYPEs.

descendant element

An HTML or XHTML element contained within another element. For example, an `h1` element on a web page might be a descendant of the body element.

descendant selector

See *contextual selectors.*

DNS

See *Domain Name Server.*

***DOCTYPE* declaration**

A declaration placed at the beginning of an HTML or XHTML page stating the markup language and language version of the document. The DOCTYPE declaration may include the *URI* to the particular *DTD* in use on the page.

***DOCTYPE* switching**

Some browsers may change from *standards mode* to *quirks mode* depending on the document's *DOCTYPE declaration*. If the *URI* to a specific *DTD* is not included in the DOCTYPE declaration, certain browsers switch to rendering in quirks mode.

Document Object Model (DOM)

The programming interface that allows browsers to treat elements on a web page as objects that can be manipulated with CSS or scripts.

Document Type Definition (DTD)

The specification that sets out the elements and attributes allowed in a particular version of HTML or XHTML. There are three DTDs for HTML and XHTML: *transitional, strict,* or *frameset.*

DOM

See *Document Object Model.*

Domain Name Server (DNS)

Maps a domain name to a server on the Internet where that domain's files are hosted in order to find a specific website.

dots per inch (dpi)

DPI expresses the number of dots a printer can print per inch. A better measure for online resolution is *pixels per inch (ppi)*.

dpi

See *dots per inch.*

DTD

See *Document Type Definition.*

document flow

The direction in which elements in an HTML or XHTML lay out when positioned with the default value of static. Normally, a document in English flows from top to bottom and from left to right.

E

elastic design

A design created with relative measures such as ems that will change according to the user's font size.

element

A semantic structure in HTML or XHTML markup that is used to structure content within a document. For example, the `p` element identifies text marked up as a paragraph. A nonempty element includes an *opening tag*, the content of the element such as text or other elements, and a *closing tag*. An *empty element* has no closing tag or content but is simply made up of a single tag. In XHTML, it includes a forward slash before the final bracket of the tag.

embedded style

A style rule contained in the head element of a particular HTML or XHTML document. Also called an *internal style.*

empty element

An HTML or XHTML *element* that contains no text. In empty elements, there is no *closing tag*. In XHTML, closure is required, so the terminating forward sla is contained within the element tag.

Extensible Hypertext Markup Language (XHTM

HTML is the coded format language used for creating hypertext documents on the World Wide We XHTML is an extensible version of HTML written *XML* specifications. XHTML is interoperable wit future document types and modules that will rep duce, subset, and extend HTML

Extensible Markup Language (XML)

The W3C's set of rules for interchange of structur data on the World Wide Web, which defines how XHTML is written.

external style sheet

A text document containing CSS rules. It is attach to an HTML or XHTML page using the `link` eleme or @import directive to control the presentation c the page.

F

File Transfer Protocol (FTP)

An Internet *protocol* that allows users to transfer fi to or from another computer or server.

fixed positioning

A method of positioning an HTML or XHTML el ment in a fixed position in the viewport using the CSS declaration `position: fixed`.

fluid design

See *liquid design.*

frameset

One of three *DTDs* for HTML and XHTML. Used only when the website is constructed with frame that is, when two or more HTML or XHTML pag are loaded into a single browser window, each ir separate frame. The frameset is a single documer that sets up the arrangement of the windows to c play the various HTML or XHTML pages in a sit

FTP

See *File Transfer Protocol.*

nerated content

ntent generated from CSS rules rather than the ntent of the document. CSS may create content fore or after elements, insert endnotes or foot-tes, add markers or counters or move elements other locations in a document.

F

e *Graphic Interchange Format.*

aphic Interchange Format (GIF)

e of the image formats displayed by web browsers. GIF contains a limited number of colors and may be npressed and saved with a specific subset of those ors. GIF images may use index transparency. They useful as logos, buttons, and other images with ver colors.

up selector

comma separated list of CSS selectors, all using same declaration block. The syntax is

```
lector, selector, selector {rule;}
```

aders

HTML and XHTML attribute used with `td` ele-nts to aid accessibility by associating the data th a particular table header (`th`) element.

ver

mouseover.

ML

Hypertext Markup Language.

TP

Hypertext Transfer Protocol.

pertext

xt that contains links to other documents.

pertext Markup Language (HTML)

narkup language used to create web pages. It ntifies the structural *elements* of a page so that browser software can display it, using either the software's own *defaults* or CSS rules.

Hypertext Preprocessor (PHP)

A scripting language whose primary purpose is to generate HTML content.

Hypertext Transfer Protocol (HTTP)

A web protocol used to transfer *hypertext* documents from one computer to another.

I

id

A unique name assigned to an *element*. An `id` name must be unique on a page and cannot be assigned to more than one element per page. 1. A name assigned as a specific HTML or XHTML attribute to apply a name to an element. 2. A CSS selector for which style rules can be written. 3. A JavaScript trigger or identifier which may be used programmatically.

image optimization

A range of techniques used to reduce the file size of an image so that it downloads quickly.

image replacement

A CSS technique to hide text from view so that a graphically designed element can be used in place of the text.

inheritance

A CSS concept based on the fact that *elements* in an HTML or XHTML document are nested within one another in a *parent/child* or *ancestor/descendant* relationship. Child elements inherit the rules of their parents, except for those CSS properties that are never inherited.

inline element

Any elements contained in the flow of a line of text, such as `em`, `img`, or `span`. There is no line break following an inline element.

inline style

A CSS rule written in the style *attribute* of a particular *element* on a page to style that element only.

internal style

See *embedded style*.

Internet

The international collection of connected computer networks. The World Wide Web (WWW) is part of the Internet but is not the Internet itself. The Internet includes many parts besides the WWW, such as e-mail.

Internet Service Provider (ISP)

The company providing Internet connection service to a home or business.

ISP

See *Internet Service Provider*.

J

Joint Photographers Expert Group (JPEG)

One of the image formats displayed by web browsers. A JPEG image may contain millions of colors and is suitable for photographs and other images with nuanced color. A JPEG cannot display any type of transparency.

JPEG

See *Joint Photographers Expert Group*.

K

keyword

Some CSS properties allow particular keywords as values. Keywords may be used as values for font-size and color. Keywords are used in HTML or XHTML meta elements.

L

liquid design

A flexible type of page design using percentages as a measure that resizes when the user changes the browser width.

M

markup

Markup is added to the content of a document using characters and tags such as <h1>, <p>, or <blockquote> to describe the text.

media attribute

A method of specifying the media where the styl are to be rendered (e.g., graphical displays, televisi screens, handheld devices, speech-based browser Braille-based tactile devices, etc.). Assigning a med attribute to a CSS style sheet assigns its rules to o a specific medium such as print.

mouseover

A special effect on a web page created when the mouse is passed over or held over an element. A mouseover effect can be used to change a color o a graphic, for example.

O

opening tag

HTML and XHTML syntax that identifies the *elem* it precedes. Opening tags may contain *attributes* a *values* that define the element. See also *closing tag*

P

page

An individual HTML or XHTML document. We sites are constructed of related web pages.

parent element

Within the hierarchy of an HTML or XHTML pa an *element* that contains another element, nested exactly one level within the containing element. T containing element is the parent of the nested (o *child*) element.

permissions

Rules set on a server for files and folders that spec who has permission to read, write, or execute fil

P

: *Hypertext Preprocessor.*

el

e smallest element of a graphics display. One el makes one dot on a computer monitor.

els per inch (ppi)

it of measure that expresses the resolution of a ital image or a computer monitor or other dis- y device.

rtable Network Graphic (PNG)

e of the image formats displayed by web browsers. e the *JPEG*, a PNG may display millions of ors. Like the *GIF*, a PNG may use transparency. 'NG may display index transparency but may o display alpha transparency. With alpha trans- ency, more than one color may have more than level of transparency within the selected image.

G

Portable Network Graphic.

int

neasure of font size used in print.

i

pixels per inch.

log

t of an XHTML document that precedes the head ment. The prolog includes an optional XML dec- tion as well as the *DOCTYPE declaration* for the ument.

perty

SS *declaration* consists of a property and a *value*. perty is a characteristic of the element. The prop- y and its value describe the effect you want the ted *selector* to have.

tocol

etailed specification of the scheme being used to hange information between two connected com- ers. Some of the protocols used with websites are TP, FTP, and mailto.

pseudo class

Fictional class. A pseudo class is not part of the content of the document. Rather it depends of the state of an element at a given moment, perhaps a moment in active state or hover state. The CSS rule is applied only for so long as the element remains in the given state. The following pseudo classes can be CSS selectors: `:first-child`, `:link`, `:visited`, `:hover`, `:active`, `:focus`, and `:lang`.

pseudo element

Fictional *element*. Certain things that don't exist in a document, such as an element creating the first letter of a line, or the first line of a paragraph, can be created with pseudo elements. The syntax is

```
selector:first-line
```

or

```
selector:first-letter
```

The before and after pseudo elements are used together with the generated content features of CSS to insert content either before or after an element. The syntax is

```
selector:before
```

or

```
selector:after
```

Q

quirks mode

When a browser interprets a web page using its own particular set of old rules (as opposed to *standards mode*), it is referred to as quirks mode.

R

red, green, and blue (RGB)

The system of additive colors used on a computer screen. All colors are created by combining different levels of red, green, and blue.

RGB

See *red, green, and blue.*

relative link

Within an HTML or XHTML page, a link that is written as a pathway from the link's location to the page where the linked document is located. Links within a website can be relative or *absolute*.

relative measure

A measurement that is set according to the user's preferences and can be reduced or enlarged by the user as needed.

relative positioning

In CSS, the placement of an element offset by the amount specified from its position in the normal *document flow*.

robot

Software used to canvas everything found on the Internet and add it to a search engine database.

rollover

See *mouseover*.

rule

A CSS rule consists of a selector and a declaration. The syntax is

```
selector {declaration}
```

S

selector

A CSS *rule* consists of a selector and a *declaration*. In CSS, pattern matching rules determine which style rules apply to elements in the document tree. These patterns are called selectors. If all conditions in the pattern are true for a certain element, the selector matches the element and the attributes and values specified in the declaration block are applied to the element.

semantic markup

HTML or XHTML markup that uses elements logically to structure the document according to the semantic meta-content (that is, the type of content) represented by the text, such as headings semantically tagged as heading elements or lists tagged as list elements.

server

A computer that provides access to web pages, fil and programs.

site

See *website*.

special characters

See *character entities*.

specificity

A means of conflict resolution in CSS that allows style rules to have relative importance based on standardized algorithm. A more specific rule has more importance than a less specific rule and wo therefore be applied over the less specific rule.

stacking order

In a layered document, the stacking order of a given layer may be defined in the stacking cont using *z-index*.

standards mode

When a browser interprets a web page using sta dards mode, it follows the W3C standards that it implemented and supports rather than using old rendering methods present in *quirks mode*.

strict

A *DTD* that allows the use of a limited set of eleme and attributes that does not include deprecated el ments and attributes.

structure

In HTML and XTHML, semantic markup applied content such as headings, lists, paragraphs, table block quotes, and links. Text can also be structur with *class* and *id* attributes.

style

A CSS rule determining the presentation of a par ular *element* on a web *page*.

style sheet

A text document containing one or more CSS rules style sheet may be linked or imported into any number of HTML or XHTML documents.

ıtax

e formal rules determining how code such as (TML, CSS, or any markup, scripting or program-ng language will be written.

;

. HTML and XHTML markup command. A tag code used to give an *element* its name. Most ments require an opening and closing tag, delin-ing where a certain type of content begins and ls. See *empty element*.

nsitional

. HTML and XHTML *DTD* that allows elements ınd in the strict DTD but also allows deprecated ments from previous versions of a DTD that are longer included in the strict DTD.

iform Resource Indicator (URI)

ints out the location of a resource. URI is an brella term including *URLs* and other types resource indicators.

iform Resource Locator (URL)

ints out the location of a resource.

iversal selector

CSS selector that matches the name of any element e. The syntax is *.

ɾI

Uniform Resource Indicator.

L

Uniform Resource Locator.

lid

scribes markup that follows the specifications of a rticular *DTD*.

validate

To check the syntax of a document against the standard specifications. Tools used for this purpose are called validators.

value

The specific option selected for a CSS property or HTML/XHTML attribute. A CSS *declaration* consists of *properties* and values. HTML and XHTML elements can be assigned *attributes* and *values*. The value for the property `color`, for example, might be a hexadecimal *color code* such as #3366FF. In CSS, a value must be followed by a semicolon (;). In XHTML, all values must be enclosed in quotation marks.

viewport

The visible area of the browser window in which the page is displayed.

visual formatting model

In the visual formatting model, each element in the document tree generates zero or more boxes according to the *box model*. The layout of these boxes is governed by box dimensions and type (*block* or *inline*), positioning scheme (normal flow, float, and absolute), relationships between elements in the document tree, and external information (for example, *viewport* size, intrinsic dimensions of images, and so on).

W

W3C

See *Worldwide Web Consortium*.

weblog

A web based publication with periodically updated articles. Readers of a weblog may comment on articles and may subscribe to the weblog.

web-safe color

One of a limited set of colors that should display uniformly across all platforms.

website

A collection of various related files such as HTML, images, scripts, and other resources found at a particular *URL* on the World Wide Web.

whitespace

That part of a page that contains no characters or images.

whois

A searchable database of domain name registrations.

wireframe

A sketch or schematic of the major features of a web page as an outline or form. No actual design details are included.

Wireless Application Protocol (WAP)

A protocol used by handheld devices such as phones.

Worldwide Web Consortium (W3C)

A group of experts who work to develop specifications and guidelines for web technologies.

X

XHTML

See *Extensible Hypertext Markup Language.*

XML

See *Extensible Markup Language.*

XML declaration

An *XML* declaration tells a browser the version c XML that is used on a web page.

Z

z-index

The front-to-back dimension on a web page is represented by a z-axis, which is used when obje are layered or overlap each other. An element h the same *stacking context* as its parent unless it is assigned to a different stack level with the z-ind property. An element with a higher z-index value in front of, or closer to the viewer, than an eleme with a lower z-index value.

ndex

)te to the Reader: Throughout this index **boldfaced** page numbers indicate primary discus-
)ns of a topic. *Italicized* page numbers indicate illustrations.

B

E

F

G

H

M

N

O

P

S

T

U

V

W

X

Y

Z